T0380297

ODE OYO

ODE OYO

Oladipupo Omo Aresa

iUniverse

ODE OYO

iUniverse books may be ordered through booksellers or by contacting:

iUniverse
1663 Liberty Drive
Bloomington, IN 47403
www.iuniverse.com
1-800-Authors (1-800-288-4677)

Because of the dynamic nature of the Internet, any web addresses or links contained in this book may have changed since publication and may no longer be valid. The views expressed in this work are solely those of the author and do not necessarily reflect the views of the publisher, and the publisher hereby disclaims any responsibility for them.

Any people depicted in stock imagery provided by Getty Images are models, and such images are being used for illustrative purposes only.
Certain stock imagery © Getty Images.

ISBN: 978-1-5320-6302-2 (sc)
ISBN: 978-1-5320-6303-9 (e)

Print information available on the last page.

iUniverse rev. date: 01/17/2019

PROLOGUE

Alaafin Oyo, as head of Yoruba nation and the African peoples of the world, this is specially dedicated to you. The innocent question of a primary school pupil (Title) became a subject of research. It started in early 1960s.

Many things were revealed in the course of the research

1. English and Yoruba (also known as King's Yoruba, standard Yoruba, Pure Yoruba or Oyo Language) are two sides of a coin.
2. The two languages are expressed in similar pattern.
3. In this part of the world, from Congo through south Sudan, down to Senegal, we speak one language and its dialects
4. The language of each nation of the world could be likened to the ripples generated in concentric circles when a lump of gold is dropped into still waters.
5. In this country, we do not have tribes nor ethnic groups, we have Yoruba people, Yoruba language and its dialects
6. These dialects came about as a result of migrations and lack of reference materials.
7. The research also revealed that the major languages of the world could be linked to one source.
8. A good grasp and knowledge of Oyo language would give one insight into several international languages as French, German, Spanish, Italian, Portuguese, Greek and Latin.

As example if we are to trace a line from the center of aforementioned concentric circles (among many) and assume A B C D E F G H I J K and M. Group B migrates from group A. Group C migrates from B Group D migrates from group C and so on.

Where there is no insurmountable barrier in its path, such as ocean, the line continues ad infinitum and dialects would continue to be created.

As this continues, the main language continues to change. In the process of time, the alteration gets to minority M. The dialect becomes completely different from language A.

However, the analysis of dialect M will reveal elements of A. Some distance after M may not reveal elements of similarity.

Examples:

i.   Igbomina West, Igala, Igbomina East (Popularlly called Igbo) Ikwere etc
ii. Ikale, Ilaje, Ijaw, Ogoni, Kalabari etc
iii. Nupe, Bassa, Basa Kwomu, Bassa nge etc

The Bible, Ifa and Quran testify that Yoruba language was there in the beginning. They also testify that Africa is the source of creation. These prove that the garden of Eden was in Africa. Yoruba was the means of communication in the garden of Eden.

Oyo language or pure Yoruba or kings Yoruba or standard Yoruba or simply Yoruba has the following alphabets.

A	B	D	E	E	F	G	GB	I	H
J	K	L	M	N	O	O	P	R	S
T	U	W	Y						

Yoruba language has a single normal S. We do not have SH sound.

When explorers came to this part of African continent they could not speak our language properly. In the process they created many shackled sounds as shi, she shu, sho, sha, yen and the like.

Their notorious markets also helped to spread these sounds. Their successors also wrote books using them.

For example: Travels and Explorations in Yorubaland (1854-1858) By W. H. Clarke.

In Nigeria today, although there are some far flung migrations, the rest peoples are Yorubas. All the minorities are Yoruba people. We are all the same people. From Borno to Bakassi, Kano to Zuru Kaduna to Port Harcourt, Gobir to Benin, Koto Kolofin to Lokeoja, Kafanchan to Onisha, Jos to Ijebu, Mokokowa, Ibiyidaa, Akano, Mina etc.

The border line runs from sudan to Senegal along the southern borders of sahara desert.

In addition, Yorubas also constitute a large portion of the following countries:

Argentina

Mexico

America

Jamaica

Cuba

Dominican

Paraguay

Equador

Guiana

Colombia

Haiti

Brazil

Chile

Uruguay

Trinidad and Tobego

Bolivia

Venezuela

Leeward and Windward Islands

etc.

DEDICATION

1. Heads of towns and villages
2. Priests of Ifa
3. Pastors and Imams
4. Early researchers: Olubikin, Osanyinbikin, Olayika, Obaranikosi, Agbonmiregun and Ewalu

To God be All Glory

Oladipupo is a tool for development and progress. Each part is about five times its size – depending on how good an individual is at signs and punctuation. The materials used so far (from A to Z) add up to a minor percentage of Yoruba language but whoever masters these should be able to cope in our villages.

Other products include:

1. Dictionary (Complete in Yoruba)
2. Pronunciation CD
3. Computer soft and Hard Copies
4. Thesaurus
5. Others

- Double letters are avoided
- Where two or more words are brought together, they do not necessarily follow the English way.

Some simple words

Abajo, Akololo, Alabajo, Sunkun, Kugu, Du, Dun, Iru, Aduru, Alawusa Ogbifo, Ajagbila, Gbajare, Ibogi, Ajoji, Atipo, Oru, Aajin, Oganjo, Tagiri, Elegbe Kese, Kiji, Opelope, Gogo

Please before you apply that pen or microphone, get Yoruba language properly. We have to avoid shackles and curses

SOME YORUBA NAMES

ADEBOBOLA	ADEBUKOYE	ADEDUNMOLA
ADEAGBO	ADEBUNMI	ADEDUNMOYE
ADEBADEWA	ADEBUSAYO	ADEDUNTAN
ADEBAMIDELE	ADEBUSIYI	ADEDUNUNKE
ADEBAMIJI	ADEBUSOLA	ADEDUNUNNI
ADEBAMIJI	ADEBUSOYE	ADEEKANYE
ADEBAMIJI	ADEDAMADE	ADEEKO
ADEBAMIRO	ADEDAMOLA	ADEEYO
ADEBANBO	ADEDAMOYE	ADEFARATI
ADEBANJO	ADEDAPO	ADEFEMI
ADEBANKE	ADEDAYO	ADEFENWA
ADEBARE	ADEDEJI	ADEFEYINTI
ADEBAYO	ADEDEJO	ADEFI
ADEBIMPE	ADEDEJO	ADEFIKOYO
ADEBISI	ADEDEWE	ADEFILA
ADEBISOLA	ADEDIBU	ADEFINHAN
ADEBISOYE	ADEDIGBA	ADEFIOLA
ADEBIYI	ADEDIJI	ADEFIOLA
ADEBO	ADEDIPUPO	ADEFISAYO
ADEBO	ADEDIRAN	ADEFISOYE
ADEBOBAJO	ADEDIRIN	ADEFOLAJUWONLO
ADEBOBOYE	ADEDIYIN	ADEFOLAKEMI
ADEBOJE	ADEDOJA	ADEFOLAMI
ADEBOLA ADEBOLU	ADEDOKUN	ADEFOLARIN
ADEBORI	ADEDOLAPO	ADEFOLAWE
ADEBOSIPO	ADEDOTUN	ADEFOLAWIYO
ADEBOWALE	ADEDOYIN	ADEFOLAYAN
ADEBOYE	ADEDOYIN	ADEFOWOKAN
ADEBOYE	ADEDUNMADE	ADEFOWOWE
ADEBUKOLA	ADEDUNMI	ADEFUNBI

ADEFUNKE	ADEJINMI	ADELAJA
ADEFUNMI	ADEJOBI	ADELAKIN
ADEFUNPE	ADEJOKE	ADELAKUN
ADEGBAMI	ADEJOYE	ADELANA
ADEGBAYI	ADEJULOYE	ADELANI
ADEGBEMI	ADEJUMO	ADELAYEADELAYO
ADEGBEMILEKE	ADEJUMOBI	ADELEGAN
ADEGBEMISOLA	ADEJUWON	ADELEKAN
ADEGBEMISOYE	ADEKAITAN	ADELEKE
ADEGBENGA	ADEKALE	ADELERU
ADEGBENJO	ADEKANMI	ADELEYE
ADEGBENLE	ADEKANNBI	ADELODUN
ADEGBENRO	ADEKANOLA	ADELOJU
ADEGBESAN	ADEKEHIN	ADELOLA
ADEGBILE	ADEKEMI	ADELOWO
ADEGBITE	ADEKEYE	ADELOWOTAN
ADEGBOLA	ADEKIITAN	ADELOYE
ADEGBOYE	ADEKILE	ADELU
ADEGBOYEGA	ADEKOJO	ADELUDE
ADEGEYE	ADEKOLA	ADELUSAYO
ADEGOKE	ADEKOLUEJO	ADELUSI
ADEGOROYE	ADEKOMI	ADELUSOLA
ADEGUN	ADEKOYA	ADELUSOYE
ADEGUNLOLA	ADEKOYEJO	ADELUYI
ADEGUNWA	ADEKUNBI	ADEMABO
ADEHANLOYE	ADEKUNKE	ADEMADEGUN
ADEIBUKUN	ADEKUNLE	ADEMADEWA
ADEIFE	ADEKUNMI	ADEMAYOKUN
ADEINOYE	ADELABI	ADEMAYOMI
ADEITAN	ADELABU	ADEMAYOWA
ADEJARE	ADELAGAN	ADEMESO
ADEJENROLA	ADELAGUN	ADEMOLA

ADEMOYEGUN	ADERIBIGBE	ADESOSIN
ADEMOYEJE	ADERIIKE	ADESOYE
ADEMULEGAN	ADERINKOMI	ADESUBOMI
ADEMUYIWA	ADERINOLA	ADESUNKANMI
ADENIJI	ADERINTO	ADESUNNBO
ADENIKE	ADERINWALE	ADESUPO
ADENINHUN	ADEROBA	ADESUYI
ADENIRAN	ADEROGBA	ADETAYO
ADENITAN	ADEROJU	ADETIEHIN
ADENIYI	ADERONKE	ADETOKUN
ADENRELE	ADERONMU	ADETOKUNBO
ADEOBA	ADEROPO	ADETOLA
ADEOGUN	ADERUIGBA	ADETOMIWA
ADEOJO	ADESAKIN	ADETONA
ADEOLA	ADESANMI	ADETOOBERU
ADEOLU	ADESANYA	ADETOOFARATI
ADEOMI	ADESEEKE	ADETORO
ADEONIYE	ADESESAN	ADETOSOO
ADEOSUN	ADESEUN	ADETOUN
ADEOTI	ADESEWA	ADETOYE
ADEOYE	ADESEYE	ADETOYINBO
ADEPATE	ADESIDA	ADETUBERU
ADEPEGBA	ADESIKE	ADETULA
ADEPEJU	ADESILE	ADETUNDE
ADEPELE	ADESINA	ADETUNJI
ADEPEMO	ADESIPE	ADETUNMIBI
ADEPITAN	ADESIPO	ADETUNMIKE
ADEPOJU	ADESIYAN	ADETUNMISE
ADEPONLE	ADESOJI	ADETUNMOBI
ADEPOSI	ADESOKAN	ADETUNWASE
ADERANTI	ADESOLA	ADETUTU
ADEREMI	ADESOPE	ADETUYI

ADEWALE	ABISOLA	AJAMU
ADEWANWA	ABISOYE	AJIBI
ADEWEMIMO	ABORISADE	AJALA
ADEWOLA	ABEGUNDE	AJADI
ADEWOLE	ABIDEMI	AJIBEWA
ADEWOLU	ABODERIN	AJILADE
ADEWOYE	ADAMU	AJAO
ADEWUMI	AIBINOMO	AJAYI
ADEWUNI	ABIDOYE	AJANI
ADEWUSI	ABODUNRIN	AJEIGBE
ADEWUYI	ADUBI	AJOKE
ADEYANJU	ADUFE	AJOGBE
ADEYEFA	ADUKE	AJUWON
ADEYEGA	ADUNOLA	AKANO
ADEYEMI	ADIGUN	AKANDE
ADEYEMO	ADIKA	AKANBI
ADEYEYE	AADIBI	AKANKE
ADEYI	AFON	AKANMU
ADEYINKA	AFOLABI	AKANJI
ADEYONBO	AFOLAYAN	AKERELE
ADEYOOLA	AGBOADE	AKINFENWA
ADEYOOYE	AGBOOLA	AKINLOYE
ADEYOSADE	AGBEKE	AKINJIDE
ADEYOSOLA	AINA	AKINYODE
ADEYOSORE	AJIBADE	AKINYOOLA
AASA	AJIBOWU	AKINADE
ABEKE	AJIBOYE	AKANMU
ABEO	AJIBOLA	AKINLABI
ABIKE	AJIBIKE	AKINPELU
ABIOYE	AKALA	AKINKUNMI
ABOLADE	AJIBESIN	AKINGBADE
ABIADE	AJAGBE	AKINRINADE

AKINTONDE	ASAKE	BANKOLE
AKINTONWA	ASANDE	BANKEFA
ALABA	ASANI	BABAJIDE
ALIBI	ATANDA	BALOGUN
ALADE	ATOLE	BAMIGBADE
ALAO	ATINUKE	BAMIGBOYE
ALAKE	ATILADE	BAMIGBOLA
ALANI	ATOYEBI	BAMIDELE
ALARI	ATEERE	BAMIGBOSE
ALAMU	ATOKE	DURODELA
ALAASOKO	AWENI	DUROORIKEE
ALALADE	AWELE	DUROSAKIN
AMOO	AWOLOLA	DUROSAWO
AMOLE	AWONIKE	DIEKOLA
AMOPE	AWOSORO	DIEKADE
AMOKE	AYOOLA	DIEKIYI
AMOKE	AYOADE	EESUOLA
AMUSAN	AYONI	ENIADE
APEKE	AYINDE	ENIITAN
APINKE	AYANGADE	ENIOLA
AREO	AYINLA	EYINADE
AREMU	AYEGBOYIN	EYINOYE
ARAMIDE	BABALOLA	FABUNMI
ARALOYIN	BABARINDE	FADELE
ARAOYE	BABATUNDE	FALABI
ARIBASOYE	BABARIMISA	FALEKE
AARINADE	BOLARINWA	FALADE
AARINOLA	BABATOLA	FALADE
AARINOYE	BOLATITO	FAWOLE
ARINLADE	BOLADALE	FAJOYE
ASAMU	BOLAJOKOO	FAYOKE
ASABI	BIBITAYO	FASOLA

FAKEYE

FATAYO

FATOKI

FARAMADE

FARAMOLA

FARAYOOLA

FAKOREDE

FAHINTOLA

FOLAWIYO

FOLASADE

FOLAHAN

FOLARIN

FADEKE

GBADERO

GBADAMOSI

GBADEGESIN

GBENJO

GBADEBO

GBADEYAN

You can substitute Ade for Ogun, Omo, Sango, Oye, Omi, Ode, Aye, Ola, Iyi, Oyin, Owo, Olu, So, Oosa, Ibi, Opa ile, Agbala, Iyun, Segi, Ibu, Osun, Okun, Ifa, Odu, Oke, Ayan, Are, Baba, Iya, Iji, Eji, Agbe, Aro, Ilu, Ewe, Awo, Oke, Akin, Aje, Efun, Omo, Oba, etc.

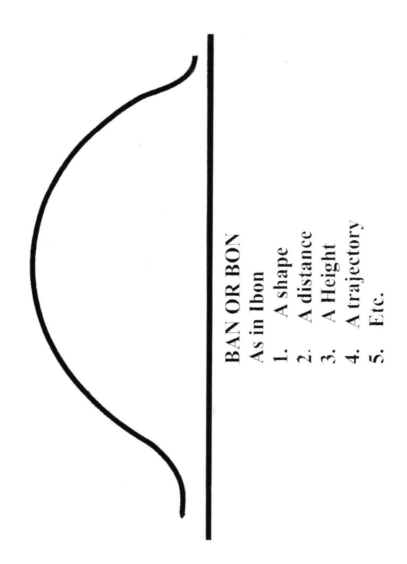

BAN OR BON

As in Ibon

1. A shape
2. A distance
3. A Height
4. A trajectory
5. Etc.

WORD (x)	EQUIVALENT (y)	WORD (x)	EQUIVALENT (y)
Aal	aajo	Abbess	bababo
Aar	aran	Abbey	babase
Aardvark	aranjnwanka	Abbot	babaeto
Aardwolf	aranjnwojifa	Abbreviate	aberonwnyo
Aaron	aranse	Abbreviation	aberonyoon
Aaronic	aranseko	Abc	abe
Aasvogel	asawngunje	Abcoulomb	abekilembe
Ab	abe	Abdicate	abejnkoyo
Aba	abo	Abdomen	abejnmo
Abaca	aboka	Abduce	abedise
Abaciscus	abokasesi	Abduct	abediki
Abacist	abokasi	Abdul	abederu
Abacus	abokasi	Abeam	abemo
Abaddon	abojain	Abecedarian	abeknjorain
Abaft	abofia	Abed	abeje
Abalone	abolohun	Abednego	abejainlo
Abampere	abompnran	Abel	abejo
Abandonee	abonjoinse	Abelard	abejogba
Abandoned	abonjoinde	Abele	abejon
Abase	abooso	Abelia	abejain
Abasid	aboosojo	Abelmosk	abejomosia
Abashed	abosunde	Abedare	abejnran
Abate	abote	Aberdeen angus	abegbain anigun
Abates	abotesi	Aberance	aberaisi
Abator	aboteran	Aberdonian	abegbainhn
Abattoir	abotterai	Aberethy	aberante
Abaxial	abosojo	Aberrant	aberrantn
Abaya	aboyan	Aberration	aberraiyoon
Abb	aboe	Abet	abeti
Abba	baba	Abettor	abetiran
Abbacy	babasan	Abeyance	abeyinse
Abbassid	babasoojo	Abfarad	abefanjn
Abbatial	babatejo	Abhenry	abeherai
Abbe	bababe	Abhensive	abehesiwin

1

WORD (x)	EQUIVALENT (y)	WORD (x)	EQUIVALENT (y)
Abhor	abehira	Abnormal	abeniranjo
Abhorrence	abehirrasi	Abnormality	abeniranjotn
Abhorrent	abehirratn	Abo	abo
Abib	ababo	Aboard	aboogba
Abidance	abajinsi	Abode 1	abogbe
Abide	abajin	Abode 2	abogbe
Abiding	abajingnni	Abolish	aboojnse
Abidjan	abajingan	Abolition	aboojnyoon
Abiel	abanjo	Abolitionary	aboojnyoonrai
Abiet	abati	Abolitionist	aboojnyoonsi
Abigail	abagbile	Abolla	aboojnra
Ability	aberontn	Aboma	aboomo
Abiogenesis	abakognhunso	Abominable	aboomohebe
Abiosis	abakoso	Abominate	aboomoheyo
Abiotrophy	abakotnraphe	Abondroit	abongbnte
Abiurritant	aberraitn	Aboon	aboosi
Abirritate	aberraituyo	Aboral	agberaijo
Abject	abejnkn	Aborigin	agberaigin
Abjure	abejoran	Aboriginal	agberaiginijo
Abla	aban	Aborigine	agberaigini
Ablate	abanyo	Abort	abooseyo
Ablate	abanyo	Abortion	abooseyoon
Ablation	abanyoon	Abortive	abooseyowin
Ablative	abanyowin	Abound	abonunjo
Ablaut	abanyi	About	abonunta
Ablaze	abansun	Above	aboowin
Able	aberon	Above-board	aboowin-bugba
Ablegate	aberongiyo	Abracadabra	abankodiban
Abluent	abeluyo	Abrade	abanjin
Ablution	abeluyoon	Abraham	abanhe
Ably	aberonse	Abrahan	abanhun
Abnegate	abehungiyo	Abram	abanmo
Abnegation	abehungiyoon	Abrasion	abansa
Abney	abehunse	Abrasive	abansawin

WORD (x)	EQUIVALENT (y)	WORD (x)	EQUIVALENT (y)
Abreact	abesiaknti	Abstergent	abesetanto
Abreaction	abesiakntiyon	Abstinence	abesatinsi
Abreast	abesinmi	Abstract	abesekyo
Abridge	abangbon	Abstracted	abesekyode
Abroad	abongbi	Abstraction	abesekyoon
Abrogate	abongiyo	Abstruse	abesetnran
Abrupt	aberanpi	Abulia	abujan
Abscess	abesiknso	Absurd	abesurajn
Abscond	abesikn	Abundance	abejoinsi
Absciss	abesikiso	Abundant	abejointn
Abscissa	abesikisoo	Abuse	abusia
Abscission	abesikisoosi	Abusive	abusiawin
Abscond	abesikiji	Aburbe condita	aburagbe kindita
Abseil	absejn	Abutment	abutemutto
Absence	abesnsi	Abutilon	abutejnsi
Absent	abesita	Buttal	abuttnjo
Absent reo	abesita rekn	Abuzz	abusu
Absentee	abesitase	Aby	abeya
Absenteeism	abesitasemosi	Abysm	abesnmo
Absinthe	abesoosin	Abysmal	abesnmojn
Absolute	abesinleyo	Abyss	abesn
Absolute	abesinletn	Abyssal	abesnlo
Absolutely	abesinletnlo	Acacia	akosia
Absolution	abesinleyoon	Academia	akojinmosi
Absolutism	abesinletnmosi	Academic	akojinmuka
Absolve	abesinlewin	Academician	akojinmukasi
Absorb	abesinra	Academy	akojinmo
Absorbent	abesinratn	Acadia	akogbisi
Absorber	abesinrasi	Acadian	akogbihn
Absorption	abesinrapnyoon	Acajou	akojoin
Abstain	abesatelu	Acaleph	akojophn
Absetemious	abesitnmosi	Acalephan	akojophnni
Abstention	abesitnmosi	Acanthe	akokise
Absterge	abesetan	Acanthocephalon	akokiseknphijn

WORD (x)	EQUIVALENT (y)	WORD (x)	EQUIVALENT (y)
Acanthus	akokisesi	Accommodating	akkimmodiyognni
A cappella	akopnjnra	Accommodation	akkimmodiyoon
Accede	akknjin	Accompaniment	akkimpansemutto
Accedence	akknjinsi	Accompany	akkimpanse
Accelerando	akkjnrainde	Accomplice	akkimpansi
Accelerate	akknjnraiyo	Accomplish	akkimpanse
Acceleration	akknjnraiyoon	Accomplished	akkimpansede
Accelerative	akknjnraiyoran	Accomplishment	akkimpansemutto
Acceleragraphy	akknjnranganphe	Accord	akkigba
Accelerometer	akknjnramuto	Accordance	akkigbese
Accent	akknto	According	akkigbagnnilo
Accentuate	akkntoyo	Accordion	akkigbaasun
Accept	akknpnti	Accost	akkisi
Acceptable	akknpntibe	Account	akkaleyo
Acceptance	akknpntisi	Accountable	akkaleyobe
Access	akknso	Accountancy	akkaleyosn
Accessible	akknsobe	Accountant	akkaleyone
Accession	akknsoon	Accouter	akkileyosi
Accessory	akknsoorai	Accouterments	akkileyosimuttosi
Access road	akknso ronjn	Accredit	akknrangbi
Access time	akknso tinmo	Accredited	akknrangbide
Accidence	akkijindasi	Accretion	akknrangbisi
Accident	akkijindate	Accroach	akknrakho
Accidental	akkijindatotejo	Accrue	akkirai
Accidentalism	akkijindatejomosi	Accubation	akkuobeyoon
Accidentally	akkijindatejin	Acculturation	akkunjiaranyoon
Accident-prone	akkijindate	Acculturation	akkunjiranyoon
Accipiter	akkiponsi	Accumbent	akkuobeyo
Acciptrine	akkipontain	Accumulate	akkunmoleyo
Acclaim	akkanmo	Accumulation	akkunmoleyoon
Acclamation	akkanmoyoon	Accumulator	akkunmoleyoran
Acclimatize	akkiunmuyose	Accuracy	akkunraisn
Accolade	akkijojin	Accurate	akkunraiyo
Accommodate	akkimmodiyo	Accursed	akuosede

WORD (x)	EQUIVALENT (y)	WORD (x)	EQUIVALENT (y)
Accusation	akkunseyoon	Acetic	akitiko
Accusative	akkunseyowin	Acetic acid	akijo akitiko
Accusation	akkunseyoon	Acetify	akitife
Accusatorial	akkunseyoraijo.	Aceto	akiti
Accusatory	akkunseyorai	Acetometer	akitimuto
Accuse	akkunse	Acetone	akitihun
Accused	akkunsede	Acetous	akitisi
Accustom	akkunseto	Acetous	akitisi
Accustomed	akkunsetode	Acetophenon	akitiphini
Accustomize	akkunroin	Acetum	akitima
Ace	ase	Acetyl	akitilo
Acea	asesi	Acetylate	akitiloyo
Aceae	asesise	Acetylene	akitilohun
Acedia	akndasi	Acetylide	akitiloji
Aceidama	aknjnma	Acetylocholine	akitilokhilehun
Acellular	aknjjnra	Acetylocholineteras	akitilokhilehuntnran
Acentric	akntiraiko	Acetylsalicytic	akitilosajosnko
-aceous	asuwa	Acetyldeucy	akitilojinwasn
Acephalous	aknphijosi	Achaen	akhoin
Acequia	aknkun	Achaean	akhoinhn
Acerate	aknrayo	Achaemanid	akhoinminijo
Acerbate	aknrabuyo	Achates	akhinyosi
Acerbic	aknrabuko	Ache	akhie
Acerbity	aknrabutn	Achelous	akhnjosi
Aceric	aknrako	Achene	akhnun
Acerose	aknrase	Achemar	akhnmura
Acervate	aknraweyo	Acheron	akhnrun
Acescent	aknseknti	Acheulian	akhnleyan
Acetabulum	akitibejnma	Acheval	akhnwajo
Acetal	akitijo	Achieve	akhiwinmutto
Acetaldehyde	akitijojinhoji	Achilles heel	akhijjinsi helo
Acetamide	akitimuji	Achilles tendon	tinjoin akhijjnsi
Acetanilide	akitihnloji	Achitophel	akhitophilo
Acetate	akitiyo	Achlamydeous	akhilemunjinsi

WORD (x)	EQUIVALENT (y)	WORD (x)	EQUIVALENT (y)
Achlorhydria	akhilorhaigbain	Ack-ack	akikaki
Achonodroplasia	akhilegbnpabsia	Acknowledge	aknknmojngbon
Achroma	akhironmo	Acknowledgement	aknknmojngbonmutto
Achromatic	akhironmuko	Acline	akiunko
Achromatin	akhironmutin	Acme	akemo
Achromatin	akhironmotie	Acne	akehun
Achromatise	akhironmuse	Acnode	akenijain
Achromatopsia	akhironmutopnsia	Acock	akiko
Achromatous	akhironmusi	Acoelomate	akilomuyo
Achromic	akhironmuko	Acol	akijin
Achydi	akhojn	Acolyte	akijinte
Acicula	akikuo	Acompte	akimpnto
Acicular	akikuoran	Aconite	akinnute
Aciculate	akikuoyo	Acom	akinra
Aciculum	akikuoma	Acoustic	akisitako
Acid	akijo	Acoustics	akisitakosi
Acidic	akijoko	Acouvert	akiwinto
Acidometer	akijoknmuto	Acpetinium	akipntinima
Acidometry	akijoknmutorai	Acquaint	akikuntan
Acidophil	akijoknphero	Acquaintance	akikuntansi
Acidophile	akijoknpheron	Acquiesce	akikunsekn
Acidophilus	akijoknpheronsi	Acquiescence	akikunseknsi
Acidosis	akijoknso	Acquest	akikunyo
Acidulate	akijoleyo	Acquire	akikunra
Acidulous	akijolesi	Acquirement	akikunramutto
Acidity	akijotn	Acquisition	akikunseyoon
Acierate	akiraiyo	Acquisitive	akikunseyowin
Aciform	akifonmo	Acquit	akikunto
Acinaciform	akihunsefonmo	Acquittal	akikuntojo
Aciniform	akihunfonmo	Acquitance	akikuntosi
Acinous	akihunsi	Acrasia	akirasia
Acinus	akihunsi	Acre	akiran
Acious	akisi	Acreage	akirangun
Acity	akitn	Acrid	akirajo

WORD (x)	EQUIVALENT (y)	WORD (x)	EQUIVALENT (y)
Acridine	akirajoin	Actinide	akntieji
Acridity	akirajotn	Actinism	akntiemosi
Acrilan	akirajin	actinium	akntiema
Acrimony	akirameni	action	akntieko
Acrimonious	akiramenisi	actinochem	akntiekokhnmo
Acrobat	aknrabota	actinograph	akntiekoganpha
Acrobatics	aknrabotakosi	actinoid	akntiekojo
Acrocarpous	aknrakopansi	actinolite	akntiekoleyo
Acrodont	aknradeyo	actinology	akntiekomuto
Acrodrome	aknragbnmo	actinomorphic	akntiekomophanko
Acrogen	aknragin	actinomycete	kntiekomunknto
Acrogenic	aknraginko	actinomuycosis	akntiekomunkiso
Acrolein	aknraroin	action	akntiesi
Acrolith	aknralisi	actinopod	akntiekopindie
Acromegaly	aknramuganlo	actinotherapy	akntiekosinranpo
Acromion	aknramusi	actinozoan	akntiekosinhn
Acronym	aknramosi	action	akntiyon
Acropetal	aknrapntijo	actionable	akntiyonbe
Acrophobia	aknraphobua	activate	akntiweyo
Acropolis	aknrapnjinsi	active	akntiwin
Acrosome	aknrasoomo	active service	serawnsi akntiwin
Acrospire	aknraseporai	activism	akntiwinmosi
Across	akonso	activity	akntiwinto
Acrostis	akonsiso	actomyosin	akntomunsie
Acroter	akontnra	acton	akntin
Acrylic	akoraileko	actor	akntiran
Acrylic acid	akijo akoraileko	actress	akntibo
Act	aknti	actual	akntijo
Acta	aknte	actualize	akntijose
Actin	akntie	actuality	akntijotn
Actinal	akntiejo	actually	akntijjn
Acting	akntignni	actuary	akntirai
Actinia	akntieni	actuate	akntiyo
Actinic	akntieko	actuator	akntiyoran

WORD (x)	EQUIVALENT (y)	WORD (x)	EQUIVALENT (y)
aculeate	akunjnyo	Addendum	addijinma
acuity	akuntn	Adder	addisi
acumen	akunmini	Addict	addikn
acuminate	akunminayo	Addicted	addiknde
acuminous	akunminasi	Addictive	addiknwin
acupressure	akunpesisorai	Additament	additemutto
acupuncture	akunpukyoran	Addition	addiyoon
acuse	akuose	Additional	addiyoonjo
acute	akuntn	Additive	addiyowin
-acy	sn	Addle	adduo
Acyclic	asnkiunko	Address	adigbiso
Acyclovir	asnkonwirai	Addressee	adigbisose
Ad	adi	Addressograph	adigbisoganpha
Adacyylin	adikoijan	Adduce	addisi
Adage	Adigun	Adducent	addiknti
Adagio	adigio	Adduct	addiki
Adam	adamo	Adductive	addikiwin
Adamant	adamotn	Ademption	akinmpnyoon
Adamantean	adamntnhn	Ade	ajin
Adamantine	adamotnhun	Adeem	adimo
Adamic	adamoko	Adela	adijn
Adamite	adamote	Adelaide	adijnjoin
Adams	adamosi	Adeline	adijnhun
Adamsite	adamosootn	Adelphous	adijnphnsi
Adapt	adapnti	Aden	adikun
Adaptable	adapntibe	Adenectomy	adikunkntemo
Adaptation	adapntiyoon	Adenine	adikunhun
Adapter	adapntisi	Adenitis	adikunso
Adaptive	adapntiwin	Adeno	adikn
Adaptor	adapntiran	Adenocarcinoma	adiknkosikiknmo
Adaxial	adaasojo	Adenohypophysis	adiknhopinpheso
Add	addi	Adenoids	adiknjosi
Addax	addisn	Adenoma	adiknmo
Addend	addijn	Adenosine	adiknso

WORD (x)	EQUIVALENT (y)	WORD (x)	EQUIVALENT (y)
Adept	adipnti	Admeasure	adimuwanran
Adequate	adikunto	Admin	adimini
Adhere	adiheran	Adminicle	adiminikuo
Adherent	adiheranto	Adminiculate	adiminikunyo
Adhesion	adihesoon	Administer	adiminiseto
Adhesive	adihesowin	Administrate	adiminisetoyo
Adhibit	adihigbeyo	Administration	adiminisetoyoon
Adhibition	adihigbeyoon	Administrative	adiminisetoyowin
Ad hoc	adikia	Administrator	adiminisetoran
Adiabatic	adibotako	Admirable	adimuranbe
Adiaphorous	adiphirainsi	Admiral	adimurajn
Adiathermancy	adisinronmoosn	Admiralty	adimurajntn
Adieu	adilolu	Admiration	adimuranyoon
Ad infinitum	adi inifinitnma	Admire	adimuran
Adios	adipose	Admissible	adimusinbe
Adit	adiyo	Admission	adimusinse
Adjacent	adijaknti	Admit	adimutn
Adjective	adijnknwin	Admittance	adimuttnsi
Adjoin	adijinto	Admittedly	adimuttndelo
Adjoum	adijinran	Admixture	adimuluran
Adjudge	adijugbon	Admonish	adimenise
Adjudicate	adijugbonkoyo	Admonition	adimenitosi
Adjunct	adijokn	Admonitor	adimenitoran
Adjure	adijuran	Admonitory	adimenitorai
Adjuration	adijuranyoon	Adnate	adihunyo
Adjuratory	adijuranrai	Ad nauseam	adi helesemo
Adjust	adijuse	Adnexa	adihunsi
Adjustment	adijusemutto	Adnoun	adiknun
Adjutant	adijutotn	Ado	ade
Adjuvant	adijuwate	Adobe	adebn
Ad lib	adi liba	Adobo	adeboo
Ad libitum	adi libayoma	Adolescence	adejnseknsi
Ad litem	adi lito	Adolescent	adejnseknti
Adiman	adimaye	Adonai	adebua

WORD (x)	EQUIVALENT (y)	WORD (x)	EQUIVALENT (y)
Adonic	adebuko	Adulthood	adejiahinjo
Adonis	adebusi	Adultrant	adejiarantn
Adopt	adepnte	Adulterant	adejiarantn
Adoption	adepntesi	Adulterate	adejiaranyo
Adoptionist	adepntesi	Adulterer	adejiaransi
Adoptive	adepntewin	Adulterine	adejiarain
Adorable	aderanbe	Adulterous	adejiaransi
Adoration	aderanyoon	Adultery	adejiarai
Adore	aderan	Adumbrant	adembute
Adom	aderai	Adumbrate	adembuyo
Ad patres	adi pantosn	Adumbration	adembuyoon
Adrastus	agbansetosi	Adumbrative	adembuyowin
Adrenal	agbainjo	Adust	adisia
Adrenalin	agbainjan	Advance	adiwainsi
Adrenergic	agbainrailokn	Advanced level	adiwainside jnwin
Adrenocortical	agbainkisitekojo	Advancement	adiwainsimutto
Adrenocortcotropic	agbainkisitekitnrapnko	Advantage	adiwaintegun
Adrian	agbain	Advantageous	adiwaintegunsi
Adriano	agbainkn	Advection	adiwinkyoon
Adriatic	agbainko	Adventist	adiwintisi
Adrift	agbanfia	Adventious	adiwintisi
Adroit	agbointe	Adventure	adiwintirai
Adroite	agbointo	Adventurer	adiwintiraise
Adscititious	adisekititosi	Adventurous	adiwintiraisi
Adscript	adisekoraipn	Adverb	adiwinbe
Adsorb	adisorabe	Adversary	adiwinserai
Adsorbate	adisorabeyo	Adverse	adiwinse
Adsorbtion	adisorabeyoon	Adversity	adiwinsetn
Adsuki	adisuki	Advert	adiwinte
Adularia	adejnran	Advertisement	adiwintesimutto
Adularescence	adejnranseknsi	Advertising	adiwintesignni
Adulate	adejnyo	Advice	adiwokn
Adulation	adejnyoon	Advisable	adiwosebe
Adult	adejia	Advise	adiwose

WORD (x)	EQUIVALENT (y)	WORD (x)	EQUIVALENT (y)
Advisedly	adiwosedelo	Aero-	anroin
Adviser	adiwosesi	Aeroballistics	anroinrobosukosi
Advisory	adiwoserai	Aerobe	anroinbu
Advocaat	adiwnkote	Aerobatics	anroinbotakosi
Advocate	adiwnkotn	Aerobation	anroinbukosi
Adynamia	adaineemua	Aerobiology	anroinbakologbon
Adytum	adaintoma	Aerocartography	anroinkositeganphe
Adze	adise	Aerocycle	anroinsnkuo
Aecial	ankejo	Aerodonetics	anroindehunkosi
Aedes	anjinsi	Aerodrome	anroingbnmo
Aedile	anjnle	Aerodynamics	anroindainsemuko
Aeetes	antosi	Aerodyne	anroindainhun
Aegean	angina	Aerofoil	anroinfonjio
Aegeus	angnsi	Aerogel	anroinginlo
Aegis	angnso	Aerogen	anroingin
Aegrtat	anganteyo	Aerogenics	anroinginkosi
Aegypt	angnpnti	Aerogrmme	anroinganmmo
Aemia	anmua	Aerograph	anroinganpha
Aeneid	anhunjo	Aerography	anroinganphe
Aeneous	anhunsi	Aerohydroplane	anroinhogbnpany
Aeolian harp	hapan anjinhn	Aerology	anroinlogbon
Aecolic	ankijinko	Aeromancy	anroinmoyesn
Aeolotropic	anjintnrapnko	Aerometer	anroinmuto
Aeon	anle	Aerometry	anroinmutorai
Aequian	ankunhn	Aeronautics	anroinheyokosi
Aerasthema	anransuwnma	Aerophobe	anroinphobe
Aerate	anraiyo	Aerophobia	anroinphobua
Aerator	anrairan	Aerophore	anroinphiran
Aerial	anraijo	Aeroplane	anroinpanyum
Aeric	anraiko	Aerosol	anroinsinle
Aeriferous	anraifirosi	Aerospace	anroinsipase
Aerification	anraifikoyoon	Aerosphere	anroinsephirai
Aeriform	anraifoonmo	Aerotaxis	anrointesanso
Aerify	anraife	Aerotropism	anrointnrapnmosi

11

WORD (x)	EQUIVALENT (y)	WORD (x)	EQUIVALENT (y)
Aesthete	ansuwato	Affusion	afunsoon
Aesthetics	ansuwako	Aficionado	afisoonde
Aetiology	anyologbon	Afield	afisajo
Afar	afan	Aflame	afanmuna
Affable	afanbe	Afflatus	afanyosi
Affair	afanrai	Afloat	afonlefo
Affect	afnkoi	Aflux	afolusi
Affectation	afnkoiyoon	Afoot	afontn
Affected	afnkoide	Afore	afonrai
Affecter	afnkoisi	Afraid	afanjo
Affection	afnkoiyoon	Affranchise	afankhnse
Affectional	afnkoiyoonjo	Afresh	afesnsn
Affectionate	afnkoiyoonyo	Africa	afanko
Affective	afnkoiyowin	African	afankohn
Affectivity	afnkoiwintn	Afrikaner	afankaran
Affenpinscher	afnpohasekhnsi	Afro	afon
Afferent	afiroyo	Afro-caribbean	afon-kosibehn
Affetuoso	afntisi	Aft	afitn
Affiance	afihnsi	After	afitn
Affidavit	afidaawiti	Afterbirth	afitnbirosi
Affiliate	afijnyo	Afterlife	afitnlifin
Affiliation	afijnyoon	Aftermath	afitnmosi
Affiliation order	orojnra afijnyoon	Afterwards	afitnwegba
Affinity	afinitn	Again	agini
Affirm	afiroin	Against	aginisi
Affirmative	afiroinyowin	Agal	agijo
Affix	afisn	Agalactia	agilekesi
Afflict	afankn	Agallock	agillokin
Affiliction	afanknyoon	Agalmatolite	agijomutoleyo
Affluent	afoluyo	Agama	agimo
Affray	afanse	Agamete	agimutn
Affricate	afankoyo	Agamic	agimuko
Affront	afontn	Aganche	agikhn
Affuse	afunsi	Agar	agira

WORD (x)	EQUIVALENT (y)	WORD (x)	EQUIVALENT (y)
Agaric	agiraiko	Agro	agbiro
Agaricic	agiraikiko	Aghast	aghasi
Agata	agito	Agile	agile
Agate	agiyo	Agility	agiletn
Agatha	agisan	Aging	agbagnni
Agathodemon	agisijinmoha	Agitate	agitoyo
Agave	agiwin	Agio	agio
Agaze	agiso	Agiotage	agiotegun
Age	agba	Agist	agbito
Age	agun	Agitate	agitoyo
Aged	agbade	Agitation	agitoyoon
Agee	agbasi	Agitator	agitoyoran
Ageism	agbamosi	Agitato	agitotoo
Agelong	agbalogun	Agitprop	agiteponpo
Agency	aginsn	Agley	agnroin
Agenda	aginjin	Aglossa	agonsoo
Agendum	aginjinma	Aglow	agonyo
Agenesis	agnhunso	Agnail	agihelo
Agent	aginite	Agnate	agihelo
Agent procateur	aginte ponwnkotirai	Agnes	aginise
Age of consent	agba ofa kinsesita	Agni	agini
Aggeratum	agunsetoma	Agnomen	aginimue
Agglomerate	agbilomuraiyo	Agnosia	aginisia
Agglutinate	agbiletinyoon	Agnostic	aginisuko
Agglutinative	agbiletinyowin	Agnostician	aginisukohn
Agglutinin	agbiletingin	Ago	alo
Aggrandize	agbiranjnse	Agog	agonko
Aggravation	agbiranweyoon	Agogee	agonkose
Aggregate	agbiraigiyo	Agon	agon
Aggregation	agbiraigiyoon	Agonic	agonko
Aggression	agbiraisoon	Agonist	agonsi
Aggressive	agbiraisoowin	Agonistic	agonsiko
Aggressor	agbiraisooran	Agonize	agonse
Aggrieved	agbirawude	Agony	agonse

WORD (x)	EQUIVALENT (y)	WORD (x)	EQUIVALENT (y)
Agora	agonro	Aiguillette	aagunjntin
Agoraphobia	agonrophobua	Aikido	aakide
Agouti	agonte	Ail	aalo
Agraffe	agirofe	Ailanthus	aalotnsi
Agranulocyte	agiroinlosnyo	Aileron	aaloroin
Agranulocytosis	agiroinlosntoso	Ailing	aalognni
Agrapha	agirophn	Ailment	aalomutto
Agraphia	agirophia	Aimless	alemolabo
Agrarian	agirorain	Air	arie
Agree	agiran	Airbase	ariebooso
Agreeable	agiranbee	Air-bed	arie beje
Agreement	agiranmutto	Airbome	arieboroin
Agric	agiraiko	Air-brick	arie-banki
Agriculture	agiraikunjiaran	Airbus	arie busa
Agrimony	agiraimeni	Aircraft	ariekanfia
Agrobiology	agirobakologbon	Airedale	ariedajn
Agrology	agirologbon	Airer	ariesi
Agronomy	agiroknmo	Airifield	ariefisajo
Agrostology	agirosetologbon	Air force	arie foonse
Agrotechny	agirotokhnse	Airgun	arie gunta
Aground	agonjoin	Airhead	ariehegbi
Aguardiente	agungbainyo	Air hostess	arie hinsibo
Aguscalientes	agunsekojointosi	Airless	arielabo
Ague	aganse	Airlift	arielifia
Aguish	agansi	Airline	arielehun
Ahead	ahegbi	Airliner	arielehunsi
Ahem	ahemo	Airspace	ariesipase
Ahimsa	ahimose	Airy	ariese
Ahistorical	ahisetoraikojo	Aisle	asajn
Ahoy	ahise	Aisne	asahun
Ahriman	ahiraimoye	Aitch	aatokha
Aid	aajo	Aitchbone	aatokhaboun
Aide	aajosi	Ajar	ajarai
Aiguilles	aagunjjn	Ajax	ajasi

WORD (x)	EQUIVALENT (y)	WORD (x)	EQUIVALENT (y)
Ajee	ajnse	Alasaka	ajnsekuo
Aka	tms	Alaska	ajnsekun
Akela	aknlo	Alastor	ajnsiran
Akimbo	akinboo	Alatau	ajntele
Akin	akisi	Alate	aleyo
Akinesis	akihunso	Alation	aleyoon
Akinteto	akihunto	Alb	ajnbo
Al	ajo	Alba	ajnbe
-al	jo	Albacore	ajnbekiran
A la	ajo	Albania	ajnbehun
Alabaster	ajoboseto	Albany	ajnbeyun
Ala carte	a jo kositn	Albata	ajnbeto
Alacha	ajokhoi	Albatross	ajnbetnraso
Alack	ajokin	Albedo	ajnbede
Alacrity	ajoknratn	Albeit	ajnbeyo
A laddin	ajojnto	Alberca	ajnbesnko
Ala fin	ajofini	Alberich	ajnberaikhi
Ala king	ajo kinga	Albert	ajnbeta
Alafia	ajojan	Alberta	ajnbetan
Alameda	ajomujn	Albertite	ajnbetayo
Alamo	ajomo	Albescent	ajnbeseknti
Alamode	ajomodie	Albigenses	ajnboginsesi
Alamort	ajomorate	Albigension	ajnboginsoon
Alanine	ajonihe	Albinism	ajnboknmosi
Alan	ajoin	Albino	ajnbokn
Alannah	ajoinhan	Albite	ajnboyo
Alap	alepn	Alborak	ajnbokun
Alar	ajnra	Album	ajnboma
Alam	ajnron	Albumen	ajnbomi
Alaming	ajnrongnni	Albumenize	ajnbomise
Alarmist	ajnronsi	Albumin	ajnbomisi
Alarum	ajnronma	Albuminate	ajnbomiyo
Alary	ajnrai	Albuminoid	ajnbomijo
Alas	ajnse	Albuminuus	ajnbomisi

WORD (x)	EQUIVALENT (y)	WORD (x)	EQUIVALENT (y)
Albuminuria	ajnbomiran	Aldrin	ajnderan
Albumose	ajnbomase	Ale	amikan
Alcaeus	ajnkoinsi	ale	ajon
Alcaic	ajnkoiko	aleatoric	ajontoraiko
Alcalde	ajnkojojin	aleatory	ajontorai
Alcatraz	ajnkotnrasi	alec	ajonkn
Alchemize	ajnhnmose	alecithal	ajonkisejo
Alchemy	ajnkhnmo	aleck	ajonki
Alcibiades	ajnkibajinsi	alecto	ajonkito
Alcidine	ajnkijoin	alee	ajonse
Alcinotis	ajnkiknso	alegar	ajongira
Alcman	ajnkimoye	alehouse	ajonhinlese
Alcohol	ajnkiun	alemanic	ajonmayeko
Alcoholate	ajnkiunyo	alembic	ajnmbeko
Alcoholic	ajnkiunko	alembicate	ajnmbekoyo
Alcoholism	ajnkiunmosi	alenconlac	ajnkinlesi
Alcoholise	ajnkiunse	alert	ajnrato
Acoholometer	ajnkiunmuto	a level	ajnwinlo
Alcoholysis	ajnkiunjinso	alevin	ajnwini
Alcoran	ajnkiran	alewife	ajnwofin
Alcosol	ajnkisoojn	Alexander	ajnsejnra
Alcove	ajnkiwo	Alexandria	ajnsejnran
Alcuim	ajnkun	Alexandraian	ajnsejnraihn
Alcyone	ajnsnhun	Alexandrine	ajnsejnrain
Aldan	ajijn	Alexandrite	ajnsejnraiyo
Aldebaran	ajijinhoji	Alexia	ajnsia
Al dente	ajn jinate	Alexipharm	ajnsiaphisan
Alder	ajijnra	Alfalfa	ajnfanfe
Alderman	ajijnramaye	Alfresco	ajnfesnki
Aldine	ajnjoin	Alga	ajngi
Aldol	ajndejo	Algae	ajngie
Aldose	ajndesun	Algarroba	ajngnban
Aldosterone	ajndesetnroin	Algebraic	ajngnbanko
Aldosteronism	ajndesetnroinmosi	Algebraist	ajngnbansi

WORD (x)	EQUIVALENT (y)	WORD (x)	EQUIVALENT (y)
Algedonic	ajngndunko	Alienation	ajnseyoon
Algedonics	ajngndunkosi	Alienie	ajnsesi
Algeria	ajngnran	Alienism	ajnsemosi
Algerine	ajngnroin	Alienist	ajnsesi
Algemon	ajngnmeni	Alienor	ajnseran
Algesia	ajngnsia	Alforja	ajnfonja
Algetic	ajngnko	Alferia	ajofijnran
Algid	ajngijo	Alight2	alighe
Algin	ajngan	Align	ajogn
Alginate	ajnganyo	Alignment	ajognmutto
Algicide	ajngikeku	Alike	alikn
Algoid	ajngijo	Aliment	ajemutto
Algol	ajngonjo	Alimentary	ajemuttoria
Algolagnia	ajngongognni	Alimentation	ajemuttoyoon
Algology	ajngielogbon	Alimentative	ajemuttoyown
Algometer	ajngonmuto	Alimony	ajemeni
Algonikian	ajngonknhn	Aline	alehun
Algonquian	ajngonkunhn	Aliped	alipode
Algonquin	ajngonkun	Aliphatic	aliphanko
Algophobia	ajngonphobua	Aliquant	alikunte
Algor	ajngira	Aliquot	alikuinto
Algorism	ajngiramosi	Alist	alisi
Algorithm	ajngiraisiro	Alite	aliyo
Algous	ajngisi	Alive	aliwa
Alias	ajosa	Alizarin	ajosurain
Alibi	ajogbu	Alkahest	ajokanhesi
Alibility	ajogbeserontn	Alkalema	ajokaunma
Alible	ajobe	Alkalescence	ajokaunseknsi
Alice	ajosua	Alkalescent	ajokaunseknti
Alidade	ajojnde	Alkali	ajokaun
Alien	ajnse	Alkali	ajokaun
Alienable	ajnseron	Alkalic	ajokaunko
Alienage	ajnsegun	Akalify	ajokaunfe
Alienate	ajnseyo	Alkalimeter	ajokaunmuto

WORD (x)	EQUIVALENT (y)	WORD (x)	EQUIVALENT (y)
Alkalimetry	ajokaunmutorai	Allen	key
Alkalinity	ajokawntn	Allergen	ajjoraigin
Alkalize	ajokaunse	Allergic	ajjorailosi
Alkalosis	ajokaunso	Allergy	ajjorailo
Alkaloid	ajokaunjo	Allethrin	ajjosuran
Alkanse	ajokaunn	Alleviate	ajjowanyo
Alkene	ajokyun	Alleviation	ajjowanyoon
Alkulate	ajokyunyo	Alleviative	ajjowanyowin
Alkylation	ajokyunyoon	Alley	ajjosun
Alkyne	ajokyun	Alleyed	ajjosunde
All	ajjo	Alliance	ajjose
Allah	oluwa, olodumare	Allied	ajjode
Allan	ajjoin	Allegation	ajjogirase
Allantoid	ajjointejo	Alligator	ajjogirasi
Allantoidal	ajjointejosi	All-in	ajjo-ninu
Allantion	ajjointeni	Allusion	ajjosoon
Allantois	ajjointeso	Alliterate	ajjoteraiyo
Allay	ajjosn	Alliteration	ajjoteraiyoon
All comers	ajjo-kiawasi	Allo	allo
Allecret	ajjokna	Allocate	alloknyo
Allegation	ajjognyoon	Allocation	alloknyoon
Allege	ajjogn	Allocator	alloknyorai
Allegedly	ajjogndelo	Allochthonous	allokhisinsesi
Allegiance	ajjoginisi	Allocution	allokunyoon
Allegiant	ajjoginite	Allodia	allodasi
Allegoric	ajjognraiko	Allodium	allodasima
Allegorise	ajjognraise	Allogamy	allogimo
Allegorist	ajjognraisi	Allogenic	alloginko
Allegory	ajjognrai	Allograft	alloganfia
Allegretto	ajjogitaito	Allometry	allomutorai
Allegro	ajjogiran	Allons	allosi
Allelomorph	ajjojinmophan	Allonym	allosimo
Alleluia	ajjojnhan	Allopatric	allopanraiko
Allemande	ajjomujo	Allophone	allophohun

WORD (x)	EQUIVALENT (y)	WORD (x)	EQUIVALENT (y)
Allophone	allophohun	Alpha	ajophn
Allot	alloti	Alphabet	ajophnbe
Allotment	allotimutto	Alphanumeric	ajphnyunmoraiko
Allotrope	allotianpon	Alpine	ajopohun
Allotropy	allotnrape	Already	ajoregboin
Allow	allowe	Alright	ajoraigbe
Allowance	allowesi	Alsace	ajosesi
Alloy	allose	Alsatia	ajosesin
Allude	allujin	Alsatian	ajosesinhn
Allure	alluran	Also	ajosoo
Allusion	allusoon	Also-ran	ajosoo-rain
Alluvial	alluwojo	Alt	ajoto
Alluvium	alluwoma	Altair	ajotnro
Ally	allojo	Altarpiece	ajotnropansi
Ally1	allojin	Alter	ajotnra
Alma mater	ajnmo muto	Alteration	ajotnrayoon
Almanav	ajnmokin	Altercate	ajotnrakoyo
Almighty	ajomugbitn	Alter ego	ajotnra egbn
Almond	ajnmenijo	Alternate	ajotnranyo
Almon	ajnmeni	Alternative	ajotnranyowin
Almoner	ajnmenisi	Alternator	ajotnranyoran
Almoravides	ajnmoraiwojinsi	Althea	ajosnni
Almost	ajnmosua	Alti	ajnte
Alms	ajnmosi	Altigraph	ajnteganpha
Aloe	ajnsi	Altimeter	ajntemuto
Aloft	alofia	Altiphano	ajntepankn
Alone	alohun	Altisonant	ajntesoseto
Along	alogun	Altitude	ajntetujin
Alongside	alogunsoopo	Altitudinal	ajntetujinjo
Aloof	alofon	Alto	ajnto
Aloud	aloodun	Altogether	ajntognsira
Alopecia	alopnkuo	Altona	ajntohun
Alp	ajopn	Altorelievo	ajntorejownni
Alpaca	ajopnki	Altostratus	ajntosetnresi

WORD (x)	EQUIVALENT (y)	WORD (x)	EQUIVALENT (y)
Altricial	ajntaraisejo	Amalthea	amujosin
Altruism	ajntnramosi	Amanda	amujina
Altruist	ajntnrasi	Amanita	amuhunto
Altruistic	ajntnrasuko	Amanuensis	amuhunsiso
Aludel	ajojnlo	Amaranth	amurainsi
Alula	ajojn	Amaranthine	amurainsua
Alum	ajoma	Amarelle	amuranjjo
Alumina	ajomina	Amaryllius	amuraijjosi
Aluminate	ajominayo	Amass	amosso
Aluminiferous	ajominafirosi	Amateur	amoterai
Aluminium	ajominase	Amateurish	amoteraise
Aluminum	ajominima	Amati	amuto
Alumna	ajomani	Amative	amutowin
Alumni	ajomeni	Amativeness	amutowinisi
Alumnus	ajomenisi	Amatol	amutojin
Alunite	ajoheyo	Amatory	amutorai
Alutaceous	ajotesuwa	Amaurosis	amuriranso
Alveolar	ajowinjinran	Amaze	amusia
Alveolate	ajowinjinwo	Amazon	amusia
Alveolus	ajowinjinsi	Amazon	amusiasi
Alveopalata	ajowinpanjnte	Amazonite	amusiasiyo
Alvin	ajowin	Ambary	amberai
Alvine	ajowini	Ambasaador	ambesoojnran
Always	ajowelosi	Ambassadress	ambesoojnbo
Alyssum	ajosunma	Ambage	ambegbun
Alzhemer	ajohesimo	Amber	ambena
Am	ami	Ambergris	ambenagan
Amabel	amubejn	Ambi	amba
Amability	amuberontn	Ambiance	ambainsi
Amadavat	amujnweto	Ambidexter	ambajinsetnra
Amadou	amujona	Ambidexterity	ambajinsetnraito
Amalgam	amujogan	Ambidextrous	ambajinsetnraito
Amalgamate	amujoganyo	Ambience	ambansi
Amalgamation	amujoganyoon	Ambient	ambanto

WORD (x)	EQUIVALENT (y)	WORD (x)	EQUIVALENT (y)
Ambiguity	ambagbitn	Amelia	amujia
Ambiguous	ambagbisi	Ameliorate	amujnrayo
Ambit	ambatin	Ameloblast	amujnbansia
Ambitendency	ambatinjosn	Amen	amuse
Ambition	ambatinsi	Amen sa st tho ro	amuse se sti sinro
Ambitious	ambatinse	Amenable	amuseron
Ambivalence	ambawajnso	Amend	amudan
Ambivalent	ambawajnto	Amende	amudanse
Anbiversion	ambawinsoon	Amendment	amudanmutto
Ambivert	ambawinte	Amends	amudansi
Amble	ambejn	Amenity	amuyetn
Ambler	ambejnra	Amenorrhea	aminirrhoin
Amblygonite	ambajingonyo	Ament	aminito
Amblyopia	ambajinpa	Amentaceous	aminitosuwa
Ambo	amboo	Amentia	aminitie
Amboceptor	ambooknpnran	Amentiferous	amnitofirosi
Ambrosia	ambesuase	Amerce	amuraisi
Ambrosiaceous	ambesuasesi	America	amuraiko
Ambrosial	ambesuasejo	American	amuraikohun
Ambrosian	ambesuasehn	Amerikanize	amuraikohunse
Ambry	amberai	Americium	amuraikima
Ambsace	ambeseri	Amerind	amuraijn
Ambucycle	ambesnkuo	Amethyst	amusiosuhun
Ambucyde	ambesnjin	Ametropia	amutnrapan
Ambulacral	ambejnknrajo	Amharic	amheranko
Ambulacrum	ambejnknrama	Ami	ami
Ambulance	ambejnsi	Amiability	amisiberontn
Ambulant	ambejnte	Amiable	amisibe
Ambulate	ambejnyo	Amicable	amisikobe
Ambulatory	ambejnyorai	Amid	amida
Ambuscade	ambusakojin	Amide	amiji
Ambush	ambuso	Amidin	amidate
Amelcom	amujnkinran	Amido	amide
Amere	amurai	Amidogen	amidegin

WORD (x)	EQUIVALENT (y)	WORD (x)	EQUIVALENT (y)
Amidol	amidejin	Amok	amoka
Amigo	amigon	Amole	amolose
Amidships	amidasunpnsi	Among	amogn
Amidst	amidasi	Amoral	amoranjo
Amine	amini	Amorettol	amoranto
Amino acid	akijo aminiko	Amorino	amorain
Aminipyrine	aminikoperoin	Amorist	amoransi
Amir	amuran	Amorous	amoransi
Amiss	amusin	Amorphous	amophansi
Armistice	amusikn	Amort	amorate
Amitosis	amutinso	Amortization	amorateseyoon
Amity	amuntn	Amortize	amoratese
Ammeter	ammuto	Amortizement	amoratesemutto
Ammo	ammo	Amos	amoosa
Ammocete	ammoknyo	Amount	amounte
Ammonal	ammohejo	Amour	amoranse
Ammonia	ammohesi	Amour proper	amoran ponpesi
Ammoniac	ammohesiko	Amove	amosun
Ammoniate	ammohesiyo	Amp1	ampn
Ammonite	ammohetn	Amp2	ampn
Ammonium	ammohema	Ampelopsis	ampnlopnso
Ammunition	ammuheyoon	Amperage	ampnragun
Amnesia	amihunsia	Ampere	ampnran
Amnesty	amisintn	Ampersand	ampnrasejn
Amniocentesis	aminihnknteso	Amphetamine	amphntemini
Amnion	aminihn	Amphi	amphi
Amniote	aminihnto	Amphiarthrosis	amphiransiraso
Amniotic	aminihnko	Amphiaster	amphiseto
Amobarbital	amoboosnbajo	Amphibian	amphibehn
Amock	amokoi	Amphibilogy	amphibelogbon
Amodiaquin	amodasikun	Amphibiotic	amphibekiko
Amoeba	amoba	Amphibious	amphibesi
Amoebiasis	amobaso	Amphiblastula	amphibansiajn
Amoeboid	amobajo	Amphibole	amphibejoin

WORD (x)	EQUIVALENT (y)	WORD (x)	EQUIVALENT (y)
Amphibolic	amphigboloko	Amplexcaul	amporonsikojn
Amphibology	amphigbologbon	Ampliative	amporonyowin
Amphiboly	amphigbolo	Amplication	amporonkoyoon
Amphibrach	amphibakho	Amplicative	amporonkoyowin
Amphicarpous	amphikopansi	Amplicatory	amporonkoyorain
Amphicoelous	amphikijnsi	Amplifier	amporonfisi
Amphichroic	amphikhiranko	Amplify	amporonfe
Amphictyon	amphikotnsi	Amplitude	amporontujin
Amphictyonic	amphikotnsiko	Ampoule	ampinle
Amphicyrtic	amphisnrako	Ampilla	amponjnra
Amphidilpoid	amphidiponjo	Ampullaceous	ampnjnrasuwa
Amphigean	amphignhn	Amputate	ampnteyo
Amphigastrium	amphigisiraima	Ampulation	ampnteyoon
Amphigenesis	amphignhunso	Amputator	ampnteran
Amphigenous	amphiginisi	Amputee	ampnteyun
Amphigory	amphilorai	Amrita	amraito
Amphilogism	amphilognmosi	Amstel	amsetn
Amphimacer	amphimusosi	Amster	amseto
Amphimixis	amphimulusi	Amuck	amukiti
Amphineuran	amphihunran	Amulet	amujntn
Amphion	amphinko	Amuse	amusie
Amphioxus	amphisinsi	Amusement	amusiemutto
Amphipod	amphipindie	Amusement arcade	araikojin amusiemutto
Amphiprostyle	amphiponsetnron	Amusiwe	amusiewin
Amphisbaena	amphisebnhun	Amusema	amusiemo
Amphitheatre	amphisinseto	Amy	amun
Amphithecium	amphisinkima	Amygdala	amungbile
Amphitrichous	amphitnraikhosi	Amygdalaceous	amungbilesuwa
Amphitropolus	amphitnrapinjnsi	Amygdalate	amungbileyo
Amphitryon	amphiterain	Amygdale	amungbijn
Amphora	amphiran	Amygdalic	amungbijnko
Amphoric	amphirankin	Amygdalin	amungbijain
Ampicillin	ampokijnra	Amygdaline	amungbilehun
Ample	amporon	Amygdaloid	amungbilejo

WORD (x)	EQUIVALENT (y)	WORD (x)	EQUIVALENT (y)
Amygdule	amungbijan	Anabranch	ahebanyasi
Amyl	amunle	Anacardiaceous	ahekogbainsuwa
Amylase	amunlese	Anacatharsis	ahekosnraso
Amylene	amunlehun	Anachorism	ahekhiraimosi
Amylic	amunleko	Anachronism	ahekhironmosi
Amylo	amunla	Anaclasis	ahekanso
Amylodetrin	amunlajinsetnran	Anaclastic	ahekansuko
Amylogen	amunlagin	Anaclinal	ahekonjo
Amylogenic	amunlaginko	Anaclisis	ahekonso
Amyloid	amunlajo	Anaclitic	ahekonko
Amyloidosis	amunlajoso	Anacoluthia	ahekijosan
Amylitic	amunlako	Anacolution	ahekijoyoon
Amylopectin	amunlapansia	Anaconda	ahekinjn
Amyloplastide	amunlapansiaji	Anacoustic	ahekisitako
Amylopsin	amunlapnsie	Anacreon	aheknroin
Amylose	amunlase	Anacreonic	aheknroinko
Amylum	amunlama	Anacrusis	ahekiranso
Amyotonia	amuntohan	Anacrustic	ahekiransuko
Amyotrophy	amuntnraphe	Anadem	ahejinmo
Amytal	amuntejo	Anadiplosis	ahediponso
An	ani/ni	Anadromous	ahegbnmosi
Ana-	ahe	Anaemia	ahemua
Ane	ahun	Anaerobe	aheraibu
Anabaena	ahebinhe	Anaerobic	aheraibuko
Anabantid	ahebintejo	Anaesthesia	ahesunwnsia
Anabaptist	ahebopitisi	Anaesthetic	ahesunwnko
Anabas	aheboosi	Anaesthetist	ahesunwnsi
Anabasis	ahebooso	Anaesthetize	ahesunwnse
Anabatic	ahebotako	Anaglyph	ahegilopha
Anabiotic	ahebako	Anaglyphic	ahegilophako
Anableps	ahebepnsi	Anaglypia	ahegilopan
Anaboli stroid	aheboojinko suraijo	Anagoge	ahegonko
Anabolism	aheboojinmosi	Anagogic	ahegonkokn
Anabolite	aheboojinyo	Anagram	aheganmo

WORD (x)	EQUIVALENT (y)	WORD (x)	EQUIVALENT (y)
Anal	ahejn	Anaphrodisia	ahephonjnsia
Analcite	ahejnkiyo	Anaphrodisiac	ahephonjnsiako
Analects	ahejnkisi	Anaphylactoid	ahephelekejo
Analemma	ahejnmmo	Anaphylaxis	ahephelosiso
Analeptic	ahejnpnko	Anaplasia	ahepansia
Analfin	ahejnfin	Anaplastic	ahepansuiko
Analgesia	ahejngisia	Anaptotic	ahepntiseso
Analgesic	ahejngisiko	Anaputna	aheputa
Analog	ahejogin	Anarchism	ahekhnramosi
Analogist	ahejoginsi	Anarchist	ahekhnrasi
Analogize	ahejoginse	Anarchy	ahekjnra
Analogous	ahejoginsi	Anarthria	ahesoraran
Analogue	ahejogbiso	Anarthrous	ahesorasi
Analogy	ahejogbon	Anasarca	aheseraiko
Analphabetic	ahejophnbeko	Anastasia	ahesetnsia
Analysand	ahejinsangbn	Anastigmatic	ahesetnguokn
Analyse	ahejinse	Anastomose	ahesetomuse
Analysis	ahejinso	Anastomosis	ahestomuso
Analyst	ahejinsi	Anastrophe	ahesetnraphe
Analytical	ahejinkojo	Anatase	ahetose
Analyze	ahejinse	Anathema	ahesinmi
Anamnesis	ahemumosi	Anathematize	ahesinmise
Anamnestic	ahemumosiko	Anatolia	ahetojia
Anamporphism	ahemophansi	Anatomical	ahetemukojo
Anamorphoscope	ahemophansokipon	Anatomist	ahetemosi
Ananda	ahejina	Anatomize	ahetemose
Anandrous	ahejnrasi	Anatropous	ahetnrapnsi
Ananias	ahesise	Anatto	aheyato
Ananthous	ahetnsesi	Anaxagoras	ahesegonransi
Ananym	ahemeyn	Anaximander	ahesemudainsi
Anapeptotic	ahepnpotiko	Ancaeus	ahunkoisi
Anapest	ahepnsia	Ance	anikn anisi/se/si
Anaphase	ahephanse	Ancestor	aniknsiran
Anaphora	ahephoran	Ancestral	aniknsiraijo

WORD (x)	EQUIVALENT (y)	WORD (x)	EQUIVALENT (y)
Ancestry	aniknsirai	Androcephalous	agboinknphijnsi
Anchor	anikhiran	Androcles	agboinkuosi
Anchorage	anikhirangun	Androclinium	agboinkiunma
Anchorite	anikhiranyo	Androecium	agboinknma
Anchorman	anikhiranmoye	Androgen	agboingin
Anchovy	anikhinwn	Androgenous	agboinginsi
Ancient regime	regbimo anisun	Androgyne	agboinloyun
Ancient	anikinra	Androgynous	agboinloyunsi
Ancient	anikinra	Android	agboinjo
Ancillary	anikunrai	Andrology	agboinlogbon
Ancipital	anikipntejo	Andromache	agboinmokhn
Anchusa	anikhunsa	Andromed	agboinmujn
Anchusin	anikhinsiu	Andromeda	agboinmujina
Ancon	anikin	Andromorphous	agboinmophansi
Ancona	anikihun	Andros	agboinse
Ancy	ansan sn	Androsphinx	agboinsphisia
Ancylostomiasis	ansnlosetomuso	Androspore	agboinseporai
And	ati/anjn	Androsterone	agboinsetnroin
Andabata	anjinbato	Androus	agboinsi
Andalusia	anjnlesia	Andry	agboini
Andalusite	anjnlesuyo	Andvari	anjwaro
Andaman	anjnmoye	Andy	anijnse
Andante	anjnletn	Ane	ahun
Andantino	anjnlete	Anear	ahunra
Anderson	anjnrasin	Anecdote	ahunkndeto
Andersine	anjnrasun	Anechoic	ahnukhinko
Andersite	anjnrasuyo	Anele	ahunjn
Andes	anjnsi	Anemia	ahunmua
Andiron	anjnrran	Anemic	ahunmuako
Andradite	anigbanjnto	Anemo	ahunmin
Andrew	agbainwa	Anemochore	ahunminkhinran
Andria	agbain	Anemograph	ahunminganpha
Andro	agboin	Anemology	ahunminlogbon
Androcentrism	agbainkntiraimosi	Anemometer	ahunminmuto

WORD (x)	EQUIVALENT (y)	WORD (x)	EQUIVALENT (y)
Anemometrograph	ahunminmitnraganpha	Angiotensin	anigiotinsie
Anemometry	ahunminmutorai	Angiotomy	anigiotemo
Anemone	ahunmini	Angle	anigun
Anemophillous	ahunminphewesi	Angle1	anigun
Anemophily	ahunminpheroin	Angle2	anigun
Anemoscope	ahunminsokipon	Angler	anigunran
Anemotropism	ahunmintnrapnmosi	Anglican	anggileko
Anencephalic	ahunknphijnko	Anglicism	angbilekomosi
Anent	ahunyo	Anglicist	angbilekosi
Anergy	ahunrailo	Anglicize	angbilekose
Aneroid	ahunraijo	Anglo-	angbilo
Anesthesia	ahunsunwnsialogbon	Anglomania	angbilomoyisi
Anesthetic	ahunsunwnko	Anglophile	angbilopheron
Anesthetize	ahunsunwnse	Anglo-saxon	angbilo-sanson
Anestrus	ahunsetnrai	Angora	angonran
Anethole	ahunsijoin	Angostura	angbilosiran
Aneuploid	ahunponjo	Angry	angbnrai
Aneurysm	ahunraimo	Angst	angbnsi
Anew	ahunwa	Angstrom	anignsetnron
Anfractuous	anifanknsi	Anguiform	angbunfon
Angel	anigbanja	Anguilla	angbunran
Angel cake	koki anigbanja	Anguine	angbunhun
Angelic	anigbanjako	Anguish	angbunsi
Angelica	anigbanjaki	Angular	anigunran
Angelolatry	anigbanjaterai	Angularity	anigwnrantn
Angelology	anigbanjalogbon	Angulate	anigunleyo
Angelus	anigbanjasi	Angulation	anigunleyoon
Anger	anignra	Angustate	anigunseyo
Angina	anigihun	Angwantibo	anigiuntebo
Angio	anigio	Anhelation	aniheleyoon
Angiography	anigioganphe	Anhidrosis	anihigbnso
Angiology	anigiologbon	Anhinga	anihigini
Angioma	anigiomo	Anhydrate	anihogbanyo
Angiosperm	anigiosepnron	Anhydride	anihogbanji

WORD (x)	EQUIVALENT (y)	WORD (x)	EQUIVALENT (y)
Anhydrite	anihogbante	Anisole	anisiajn
Anhydrous	anihogbansi	Anisomeric	anisiamuraiko
Anigh	anighan	Anisomerous	
Anil	aniro	Anisometric	anisiamutoraiko
Anile	aniron	Anisometropi	anisiamutnrapan
Aniline	anilehun	Anisophyllou	anisiaphewesi
Animadvert	animadiwinte	Anisophylly	anisiaphewese
Animal	animojn	Anisospore	anisiaseporai
Animal	animojn	Anisotropic	anisiatnrapnko
Animalcula	animojnkuosi	Anisotropy	anisiatnrapo
Animalculae	animojnkuose	Anita	anito
Animalcule	animojnkuo	Anker	aniknra
Animalculisn	animojnkuomosi	Ankerite	aniknraiyo
Animalculum	animojnkuoma	Ankh	anikho
Animalism	animojnmosi	Ankle	anikoi
Animality	animojntn	Anklet	anikoito
Animalize	animojnse	Ankus	anikiso
Animate	animuyo	Ankylose	anikoilose
Animated	animuyode	Ankylosis	anikoiloso
Animation	animuyoon	Ankylostomia	anikoilosetomuso
Animator	animuyoran	Anlace	anilesi
Anime	animo	Anlage	anilegn
Animist	animusin	Ann	anihn
Animism	animumosi	Anna	anihun
Animosity	animosetn	Annalist	anihunjosi
Animus	animusa	Annals	anihunjosi
Anion	anisi	Annam	anihunma
Anise	anise	Annapolis	anihunpnjnsi
Aniseed	anisegbn	Annatto	anihunto
Aniseikonia	anisekoinri	Anne	anihun
Aniseikonic	anisekoinkn	Anneal	anihunle
Anisette	anisetin	Annectent	anihunkiti
Aniso	anisia	Annelid	anihunjo
Anisogamy	anisiagimo	Annex	anihunsii

WORD (x)	EQUIVALENT (y)	WORD (x)	EQUIVALENT (y)
Annexation	anihunsiiyoon	Anopheles	aniphijnsi
Annexe	anihunsin	Anorak	anikira
Annihilate	annihuleyo	Anorectic	anirasiatiko
Annihilation	annihuleyoon	Anorexia	anirasia
Annihilationism	annihuleyoonmosi	Anorexic	anirasiako
Anniversary	anniwinserai	Another	anisiran
Annodomini	annkodemini	Anorthic	anirosiko
Annotate	annkoteyo	Anorthite	anirosiyo
Annotation	annkoteyoon	Anorthoscope	anirosisokipon
Announce	annkonso	Anorthosite	anirosisuyo
Announcement	annkonsomutto	Anoxemia	aniosimua
Announcer	annkonsosi	Anoxia	anisia
Annoy	anknsia	Ansa	aniso
Annual	anknlujo	Ansate	anisoto
Annualized	anknlujosede	Anser	aniserai
Annity	anknluto	Anserine	aniserain
Annul	anknjn	Answer	anifesi
Annular	anknjnra	Answerable	anifesibe
Annulate	anknjnyo	Answering machine	makhihunanifes
Annulet	anknjntn	Answerphone	anifesiphohun
Annulose	anknjnse	Ant	ante
Annlus	anknjnsi	Antcow	ante kiwo
Annunciation	anknhunsoyoon	Anta	antn
Annus mirabilis	anise muraibej	Antacid	antnkijo
Anode	anijoin	Antagonism	antegonmosi
Anode	anijoin	Antagonist	antegonsi
Anodize	anijoinse	Antagonize	anegonse
Anodyne	anidaini	Antarctic	antnknrako
Anoint	anitoni	Antarctica	antnknraki
Anomalous	animujisi	Ante	ante
Anomaly	animujise	Ante-	antin
Anomie	animise	Antea	anteni
Anon	anini	Anteater	antejesi
Anonymous	aninimosi	Antebelum	antinbejnma

WORD (x)	EQUIVALENT (y)	WORD (x)	EQUIVALENT (y)
Antebrachium	antinbankhima	Anthony	ansisase
Antecede	antinknjin	Anthophore	ansisaphiran
Antecedence	antinknjinsi	Anthophorous	ansisaphiransi
Antecedent	antinknjinto	Anthotaxy	ansisatesan
Antecamber	antinkhombo	Anthozoan	ansisasinhn
Antedate	antindayo	Anthozoid	ansisasinjo
Antediluvian	antinjnluwin	Anthracene	ansnreknsa
Antelope	antinlopn	Anthracite	ansnrekiyo
Antemeridian	antinmuraijoin	Anthracnose	ansnreknse
Antemeridiem	antinmuraijnma	Anthracoid	ansnrekijo
Antemortem	antinmositnse	Anthraquinone	ansnrekunleni
Antenatal	antinheyojo	Anthrax	ansnresi
Antenna	antinhun	Anthropo	ansnrapo
Antennule	antinhunjn	Anthropocentric	ansnrapokntiraiko
Antepenultimate	antinpnyajntemuyo	Anthropoid	ansnrapojo
Ante-post	antin/pinseto	Anthropology	ansnrapologbon
Anterior	antinrairan	Anthropomorphism	ansnrapomophanmosi
Antero	antinran	Anthropomorphous	ansnrapomophansi
Ante-room	antin roomo	Anthroponomy	ansnrapoknmo
Anthem	ansinmo	Anthropopathism	ansnrapopanisionmosi
Anthemion	ansinmosi	Anthropopathy	ansnrapopanisio
Anther	ansinra	Anthropophagi	ansnrapophije
Antheridiophore	ansinraijophiran	Anthropophagic	ansnrapophijeko
Antherozoid	ansinraisinjo	Anthropophagite	ansnrapophijeyo
Anthesis	ansinso	Anthropophagy	ansbrapophijese
Anthesteria	ansinsuaran	Anthurium	ansunraima
Anthill	antehijjn	Anti	antn
Antho	ansisa	Anti-abortion	antn-abooseyoon
Authocephalous	ansisaknphijnsi	Anti-aircraft	antn-araikanfe
Anthoceros	ansisaknrasi	Antibiosis	antnbakoso
Anthocyanin	ansisasnknsi	Antibiotic	antnbako
Anthodium	ansisajoma	Antibody	anitnbojain
Anthologize	ansisaloghonse	Antic	antnko
Anthology	anisalogbon	Anticatalyst	antnkotijoinsi

WORD (x)	EQUIVALENT (y)	WORD (x)	EQUIVALENT (y)
Antichrist	antnkhiraisi	Antilogy	antnlogbise
Anticipant	antnkipnte	Antimacassar	antnmaknsooran
Anticipate	antnkipanyo	Antimask	antnmosia
Anticipation	antnkipanyoon	Antimere	antnmura
Anticipative	antnkipanyowin	Antimolecule	antnmojnkun
Anticipatory	antnkipanyorai	Antimonial	antnmenijo
Anticlastic	antnkansuko	Antimonic	antnmeniko
Anticlimax	antnkiunmolu	Antimonous	antnmenisi
Anticilinal	antnkihunjo	Antimony	antnmeni
Anticilinoriun	antnkihunraima	Anmonyl	antnmenilo
Anticlockwise	antnkonkowogbon	Antimotagen	antnmotegin
Anticoherer	antnkiheraisi	Antiunion	antnnini
Anticyclone	antnsnkonhun	Antinode	antnnijain
Antidepressant	antnjinpesisote	Antinomian	antnnimoin
Antidote	antndeyo	Antinomy	antnnimo
Antidromic	antngbnmuko	Antinous	antnnisi
Antienergistic	antnenrailosiko	Antinovel	antnnkowinjo
Antietam	antntoma	Antioch	antnkho
Antifreeze	antnfesiasn	Antiochian	antnkhohn
Antigen	antngin	Antiochus	antnkhosi
Antigone	antnlohun	Antiope	antnpon
Antigua	antngun	Antiparticle	antnpantekuo
Antihistamine	antnhisetnmini	Antipasto	antnpanseto
Anticer	antnknra	Antipater	antnpanto
Antiketogenesis	antnkntognhunso	Antipathetic	antnpansioko
Antiknock	antnknkon	Antipathy	antnpansio
Antilegalist	antnjngnjosi	Antiperiodic	antnpnraijoko
Antilipoid	antnlepojo	Antiperspirant	antnpnraseporaite
Antilithic	antnlesiko	Antiphologistic	antnphelogbiko
Antilles	antnjnrasi	Antiphon	antnpho
Anti-lock	antn-lokn	Antiphonal	antnphohunjo
Antilog	antnlogbi	Antiphony	antnphohun
Antilogarithm	antnlogbiraimosi	Antiphrasis	antnpojinjo
Antilogous	antnlogbisi	Antipodal	antnpojinjo

WORD (x)	EQUIVALENT (y)	WORD (x)	EQUIVALENT (y)
Antipode	antnpojin	Antoine	antohun
Antipodes	antnpojinsi	Antoinette	antohuntn
Antipope	antnpopon	Antonia	antonisi
Antipyic	antnpeko	Antonio	antonikn
Antipyretic	antnperanko	Antony	antonise
Antipyrine	antnperain	Antonym	antosimo
Antiquarian	antnkunrain	Antre	antnran
Antiquary	antnkuerai	Antrorse	antnrase
Antiquated	antnkuetode	Antrum	antnranma
Antique	antnkue	Antrustion	antnranseyoon
Antiquity	antnkuetn	Anuria	anrau
Antirrhinum	antnrrhanma	Anu	anu
Antiscians	antnsekinsi	Anubis	anubosi
Anti-semite	antn-semito	Anuran	anuniru
Antisepsis	antnsepnso	Anuresis	anuremiso
Antiseptic	antnsepitiko	Anury	anuremi
Antiserum	antnserama	Anus	ansu
Antisocial	antnsookojo	Anvil	anworo
Anti-tank	antn-tejnkn	Anxiety	ansiatn
Antitetanic	antntntehako	Anxious	ansiasi
Antitetanus	antntntehasi	Any	anni
Antitheism	antnsinmosi	Anybody	annibojain
Antithesis	antnsinso	Anyhow	annihinwo
Antithetical	antnsinkojo	Anyone	annileni
Antitoxin	antntoosia	Anything	annisingn
Antitrades	antntnrejinsi	Anyway	anniwelo
Antitragus	antntnregbosi	Anywhere	anniwhnran
Antivenin	antnwininu	Aorta	aranto
Antiviral	antnwarunjo	Aosta	asooto
Antivirotic	antnwarunko	Apace	apase
Antivirus	antnwarun	Apache	apankhn
Antler	antejnra	Apgoge	apangonko
Antilia	antejnsi	Apalachee	apanlekhun
Antilion	antelesia	Apanage	apangun

WORD (x)	EQUIVALENT (y)	WORD (x)	EQUIVALENT (y)
Aparejo	apanraijon	Apium	apoma
Aparri	apanrrai	Apivorous	aporawinrumsi
Apart	apante	Aplanatic	apanhunko
Apartheid	apntejo	Aplasia	apansia
Apartment	apantemutto	Aplastic	apansiako
Apastia	apansetie	Aplomb	aponbon
Apastron	apansetnron	Apnoea	apokomi
Apathetic	apansioko	apocalypse	apinkojinpnse
Apathy	apansio	apocalyptic	apinkojinpnko
Apatite	apantiyo	aphis	aphisi
Ape	apini	aphlogistic	aphilogbiko
Apeak	apnke	aphonia	aphoha
Apeman	apinimoye	aphonic	aphohako
Apepsia	apnposia	aphorism	aphiraimosi
Apercu	apnrakuo	aphorist	aphiraisi
Aperients	apnraito	aphorize	aphiraise
Aperiodic	apnraijoko	Aphotic	aphooko
Aperitif	apnraitefe	aphrodisiae	aphonjnsiako
Aperture	apnrairan	Aphrodite	aphonjnto
Apery	apinirai	Aphrodite	aphonjnto
Apex	apnsi	Aphtha	aphiha
Aphaeresis	aphiraiso	Aphthoid	aphihajo
Aphagia	aphijesi	aphthosis	aphihaso
Aphakia	aphikoi	aphyllous	aphewesi
Aphanisis	aphiniso	aphylly	aphewese
Aphanite	aphinito	apiarn	aporasi
Aphasia	aphisia	apiarian	aporahn
Aphelion	aphejnsi	apiarist	aporaraisi
Aphemia	aphemua	apiary	aporarai
Aphengoscope	aphenagnsekipon	apical	apnkojo
Apheresis	apheraiso	apices	apnkosi
Aphesis	apheso	apiculate	apnkoleyo
Aphid	aphije	apiculture	apokunjiaran
Apish	apinise	apiculus	apnkolesi

WORD (x)	EQUIVALENT (y)	WORD (x)	EQUIVALENT (y)
apiece	aponsi	Apology	apilekobe
apiology	aporalogbon	Apologetic	apilekobesn
apis	aposin	Apologist	apilekobesi
apish	apinise	Apologize	apilekobese
apium	apoma	Apology	apilekobe
apivorous	aporawinrunsi	Apomixis	apinmosesi
aplanatic	apanhunko	Apomorphine	apinmophini
aplasia	apansia	Aponeurosis	apinhunranso
aplastic	apansiako	Apopemptic	apinpnmpeko
aplomb	aponbon	Apopetalous	apinpntijowa
apnoea	apoknmi	Apophasis	apinphiso
apocalypse	apokojinpnse	Apophyge	apinphegn
apocalyptic	apokojinpnko	Apophyllite	apinpheweyo
apocopate	apokiponyo	Apophyllous	apinphewesi
apocope	apokipon	Apophysis	apinpheso
apocrustic	apoknraiko	Apoplectic	apinpnraknko
apocrypha	apinkoraiphn	Apoplexy	apinpnrase
apocryphal	apinkoraiphnjo	Aport	apinta
apocynaceous	apinsnsesuwa	Aposepalous	aposepanjosi
apocynin	apinsnsesi	Aposiopesis	aposeponso
apocynum	apinsnsema	Apospory	aposepnrai
apod	apidie	Apostasy	aponsetnsn
apodal	apidiejo	Apostate	apinsetnyo
apodictic	apindiknko	Apostatize	aponsetnyose
apodosis	apidieso	Apostem	apinsetoma
apogamy	apigimo	Aposteriori	apinsetoranrai
apogee	apogonse	Apostle	aponsetoron
apogeal	apogonjo	Apostolate	apinsetojinyo
apogeotropism	apogonletnrapnmosi	Apostolic	apoinsetojinko
apolitical	apinjnkojo	Apostolici	apnsetojinsi
Apollo	apilleko	Apostrophe	apinsetnraphe
Apollonius	apillekohnsi	Apostrophize	apinsetnraphese
Apollos	apillekosi	Apothecary	apinsinkorai
Apollon	apillesi	Apothecium	apinsinkima

WORD (x)	EQUIVALENT (y)	WORD (x)	EQUIVALENT (y)
Apothegm	apinsingnmo	Apparatus	apanraito
Apothem	apinsinmo	Apparel	apanralo
Apotheosis	apinsinsooso	Apparent	apanrato
Apotheosize	apinsinsoose	Apparition	apanraiuyoon
Apotropaism	apintnrapanmosi	appeal	apanle
Appal	apnle	Appear	apanro
Appellation	apanlleyoon	Appearance	apanrosi
Appellative	apanlleyowin	Appease	apansnse
Append	apnjon	Appellant	apanlletn
Appendage	apnjongun	Appellate	apanlleyo
Appendecton	apnjontemo	Apoplexy	apinpnrase
Appendicitis	apnjonkiso	Aport	apinta
Appendicle	apnjonkuo	Aposepalous	aposepanjosi
Appendicular	apnjonkuoran	Aposiopesis	aposeponso
Appendiculat	apnjonkunleyo	Apospory	aposepnrai
Appendix	apnjonsi	Apostasy	apinsetnsn
Appertain	apntelu	Apostate	pinsetnyo
Appetite	apntite	Apostatize	apinsetnyose
Appetizer	apntisesi	Apostem	apinsetoma
Appetizing	apntisegnni	Aposteriori	apinsetoranrai
Applaud	apanlejn	Apostle	apinsetoron
Applause	apanlese	Apostolate	apinsetojinyo
Apple	aporon	Apostolic	apinsetojinko
Appliance	apanlosi	Apostolic	apinsetojinsi
Applicable	apanloknbe	Apostrophe	aponsetnraphe
Apothem	apinsinmo	Apostrophize	apinsetnraphese
Apotheosis	apinsinso	Apothecary	apinsinkorai
Apotheosize	apinsinsoose	Apothecium	apinsinkima
Apotropaism	apintnrapanmosi	Apothegm	apinsingnmo
Appal	apnle	Apollos	apillekosi
Appalachian	apnlekhihn	Apollyon	apillesi
Appalling	apnllegnni	Apology	apilekobe
Appaloosa	apnloose	Apologia	apilekobesi
Apanage	apangini	Apologist	apilekobesi

WORD (x)	EQUIVALENT (y)	WORD (x)	EQUIVALENT (y)
Apologize	apilekobese	Apices	apnkosi
Apology	apilekobe	Apiculate	apnkoleyo
Apomixes	apinmosei	Apiculture	apokunjiaran
Apomorphine	apinmophini	Apiculus	apnkolesi
Aponeurosis	apinhunranso	Apiece	aponsi
Apopemptic	apinpnmpeko	Apiology	aporalogbon
Apopetalous	apinpntijowa	Apis	aposin
Apophasis	apinphiso	Appalachian	apnlekkihm
Apophyge	apinpheg	Appalling	apnllegnni
Apophyllite	apinpheweyo	Appaloosa	apnloose
Apophyllous	apinphewesi	Apanage	apangini
Apophysis	apinpheso	Apparatus	apanraito
Apoplectic	apinpnrknko	Apparel	apanralo
Apocopate	apoknponyo	Apparent	apanrato
Apocope	apoknpon	Apparition	apanraiyoon
Apocrustic	apoknraiko	Appeal	apanle
Apocrypha	apinkoraiphn	Appear	apanro
Apocryphal	apinsnsesuwa	Appearance	apanrosi
Apocynin	apinsnsesi	Appease	apansnse
Apocynum	apinsnsema	Appellant	apanlletn
Apod	apidie	Appellate	apanlleyo
Apodal	apidiejo	Appellation	apanlleyoon
Podictic	apindiknko	Appellative	apanlleyowin
Apodosis	apidieso	Append	apnjon
Apogamy	apigimo	Appendage	apnjongun
Apogee	apogonse	Appendectomy	apnjontemo
Apogee	apogonse	Appendicitis	apnjonkiso
Apogeal	apogonjo	Appendicle	apnjonkuo
Apogeotropis	apogonletnrapnm	Appedicular	apnjonkuoran
Apolitical	apinjnkojo	Appendiculate	apnjonkunleyo
Apollo	apilleko	Appendix	apnjonsi
Apollonius	apillekohnsi	Appertain	apntelu
Apiary	aporarai	Appetite	apntite
Apical	apnkojo	Appetizer	apntisesi

WORD (x)	EQUIVALENT (y)	WORD (x)	EQUIVALENT (y)
Appetizing	apntisegnni	Appro	apon
Applaud	apanlejn	Approach	aponkho
Applause	apanlese	Approachable	aponkhoberon
Apple	aporon	Approbation	aponbeyoon
Appliance	apanlosi	Appropriate	aponpanyo
Applicable	apanloknbe	Approval	aponwinjo
Applicant	apanlokntn	Approve	aponwin
Application	apanloknyoon	Approx	aponse
Applicator	apanloknran	Approximal	aponsemujo
Applied	apanlode	Approximate	aponsemuyo
Appliqué	apanlokun	Approximation	aponsemuyoon
Apply	aponlo	Appurtenance	apuratinsi
Appoint	apintoni	Appurtenant	apuratinte
Appointment	apintonimutto	Appulse	apujnso
Appollo	apinllo	Appulsion	apujnsoon
Apportion	apintasi	Apraxia	apansia
Apportionment	apintasimutto	Apricot	apankiti
Appose	apinse	April	apanlo
Apposite	apinseyo	Apriori	a panrai
Apposition	apinseyoon	Apron	aponsi
Appraisal	apansajo	Apropos	aponpinsi
Appraise	apansa	Apse	apese
Appreciable	apesikibe	Apsis	apeso
Appreciate	apesikiyo	Apt	apnti
Appeciator	apesikiyoran	Apteral	apntnrajo
Appreciative	apesikiyowin	Apterous	apntnrasi
Appreciation	apesikiyoon	Aptitude	apntitujin
Apprehend	apesihejin	Apyretic	aperanko
Apprehension	apesihesoon	Aqua	akun
Apprehensive	apesihesowin	Aquaba	akunbe
Apprentice	apesintnsi	Aqualung	akunlugn
Appressed	apesisode	Aquamarine	akunmurami
Appressor	apesisoran	Aquaplane	akunpanyun
Apprise	apanse	Aqua regia	akun regisi

WORD (x)	EQUIVALENT (y)	WORD (x)	EQUIVALENT (y)
Aquarelle	akunraijjo	Arachne	arankhini
Aquarium	akunraima	Arachnid	arankhinijn
Aquarius	akunraisi	Arachnoid	arankhinijo
Aquarus	akunronsi	Arachnology	arankhinilogbon
Aquatic	akunko	Arad	aranjn
Aquaint	akuntoni	Arafura	aranfirai
Acquaintance	akuntonisi	Aragon	arangon
Aquatint	akunteyo	Argonese	arangonse
Aqua vitae	akun woteni	Aragonite	arangonyo
Aqueduct	akundikiti	Araguala	arngunsi
Aqueous	akunsi	Arak	aranki
Aquifer	akunfiro	Arakan	arankin
Aqueferous	akunfirosi	Araliaceous	aranjnsuwa
Aqueform	akunfon	Araldite	aranjoyo
Aquifuge	akunfungbi	Aram	aranmo
Aquila	akunjn	Aramaic	aranmuko
Aquilegia	akunjngan	Aramean	aranmuhn
Aquiline	akunlehun	Aran	aranjn
Aquilo	akunlo	Aranda	aranjina
Aquinas	akunhesi	Aranha	aranha
Aquitaine	akuntohun	Araneac	arainka
Aquose	akunse	Aranese	arainse
Aquosity	akunsetn	Araneous	arainsi
Ar	aran	Aransas	aransun
Ar	aran	Arany	arainse
Arab	aranbo	Arapaho	aranpnho
Araesque	aranbokun	Arapalma	aranpnma
Arabella	aranbojjn	Ararat	aranrae
Arabia	aranbosi	Araroba	aranrobe
Arabian	aranbohn	Aras	aransa
Arabic	aranboko	Araucan	araunkojn
Arabist	aranbose	Araucania	arankojina
Arable	aranbejn	Araucaria	arankoran
Araceous	aransuwa	Arawak	aranwki

WORD (x)	EQUIVALENT (y)	WORD (x)	EQUIVALENT (y)
Arawakan	aranwakin	Arc	aka
Arbalest	aranbounsi	Arcade	akajin
Arbela	aranbejn	Arcadia	akajina
Arbiter	arangbotn	Arcadian	akajinasi
Arbitrable	arangbotnbe	Arcadic	akajnko
Arbitrage	arangbotnran	Arcady	akajnse
Arbitral	arangbotnjo	Arcana	akahun
Arbitrament	arangbotnmutto	Arcane	akajn
Arbitrary	arangbotnrai	Arcanum	akajnma
Arbitrate	arangbotnyo	Arcature	akatnran
Arbitration	arangbotnyoon	Archoutant	akabonnte
Arbitrator	arangbotnran	Arch1	akhnra
Arbitress	arangbotnbo	Arch2	akhnra
Arbitrix	arangbotnse	Arch-	akhnra
Arbly	aranbanse	Archaean	akhnrain
Arboloco	aranbooloki	Archaeo	akhranko
Arborl	aranbosi	Archaeology	akhnrankologbon
Arbor	aranbos	Archaeopteryx	akhnrankopntiraifo
Arboreal	aranbosinjo	Archaeomix	akhnrankoransi
Arboreous	aranbosinsi	Archaic	akhnrako
Arborescent	aranbosinseknti	Archaical	akhnrakojo
Arboretum	aranbosintema	Archaise	khnrase
Arbori	aranbosia	Archaism	akhnramosi
Arboriculture	aranbosiakunjiaran	Archaist	akhnrasi
Arboriform	aranbosiafon	Archaistic	akhnrasiko
Arborization	aranbosiaseyoon	Archangel	akhnranigbanja
Arbor vitae	aranbosi wintnse	Archbishop	akhnrabasupo
Arborous	aranbosiasi	Archbishopric	akhnrabasupanko
Arbour	aranborai	Archdeacon	akhnrajinkoni
Arbuscle	aranbosikuo	Archdeaconry	akhnrajinkonirai
Arbuscule	aranbosekuo	Archdiocese	khnradioknse
Arbute	aranbuyo	Archducal	akhnradiknjo
Arbuthnot	aranbusiton	Archduchess	akhnradikhnbo
Arbutus	aranbotnsi	Archduchy	akhnradikhnse

WORD (x)	EQUIVALENT (y)	WORD (x)	EQUIVALENT (y)
Archduke	akhnradikn	Architect	akhiratoknti
Archean	akhnrain	Architectonic	akhiratokntiko
Archeao	akhnrako	Architecture	akhiratokntiran
Arched	akhnrade	Architrave	akhiratnrewin
Archegoniophore	akhnragonhunphiran	Archive	akhirawin
Archegonium	akhnragonhunma	Archivist	akhirawinsi
Archelaus	akhnralesi	Archivology	akhirawnlogbon
Archenteron	akhnratnrain	Archivolt	akhirawnjia
Archeology	akhrakologbon	Archon	akhnrasi
Archaeopteryx	akhnrakopntiraifo	Archway	akhnrawelo
Archaeomis	akhnrakoransi	Archy	akhnrase
Archaeozonic	akhnrakosinko	Arc lamp	aka lepon
Archaic	akhnrako	Arcograph	akapganpha
Archaism	akhnramosi	Arctalpine	akatnjopohun
Archer	akhnraran	Arctic	akatnko
Archery	akhnrarai	Arctic circle	akatnko kiratuo
Arches	akhnrasi	Arcturus	akatnraisi
Archespore	akhnraseporai	Arcuate	akato
Archetype	akhnratnpon	Arcus	akasi
Archi	akira	Arad	agbaa
Archibold	akhirabojon	Ardeb	aranjn
Archicarp	akhirakopan	Arden	aranjnsi
Archidiaconal	akhirajnkonijo	Ardency	arandaisn
Archidiaconate	akhirajnkonitn	Ardent	arandainje
Archilochian	akiralokhihn	Ardor	aranjnra
Archilochus	akhiralokhisi	Ardour	aranjnrai
Archimandrite	akhiramogbainto	Arduous	arandisi
Archimedes	akhiramojinsi	Are1	arai
Archimime	akhiramimi	Are2	arai
Archine	akhirahun	Area	araisi
Arching	akhiragnni	Areca	araikn
Archipelago	akhirapnlogon	Areic	araikn
Archiphoneme	akhiraphohunmo	Arena	araihun
Archiplasm	akhirapanson	Arene	aroin

WORD (x)	EQUIVALENT (y)	WORD (x)	EQUIVALENT (y)
Aren't	araiti	Argillous	araigeresi
Areo	araiko	Arginine	araiginihun
Areola	araikojn	Arginusae	araiginhunsin
Areolar	araikojnra	Argive	araigiwin
Areolate	araikojnyo	Argle	araigiron
Areology	araikologbon	Argo	aralo
Aerometer	araikomuto	Argol	arailojn
Areopagite	araikopngunyo	Argolis	arailojnsi
Areopagus	araikopngunsi	Argon	arailo
Ares	araise	Argonaut	arailotu
Arête	araitn	Argonne	arailohun
Arethusa	araisunsi	Argos	arailosn
Arezzo	araisse	Argosy	arailose
Argal	araigijo	Argot	arailoto
Argala	araigijn	Argue	araigbiso
Argali	araigija	Argufy	araigbifo
Argand	araigidan	Argument	araigbimutto
Argent	araigiton	Argumentation	araigbimuttoyoon
Argantan	araigitonsi	Argumentative	araigbimuttoyowin
Argantage	araigitonyo	Argun	araigun
Argantation	araigitonyoon	Argute	araigunte
Argenteuli	araigitonleargentic	Argy-bargy	arailo-bosilo
Argentferous	araigitonfirosi	Argyle	arailoron
Argent	araigiton	Argyll	arailorron
Argentina	araigitonhun	Argyll	arailorron
Argentine	araigitonhun	Argyrodite	arailorajnyo
Argentite	araigitonyo	Argyrols	arailorajn
Argentol	araigitonjin	Aria	aran
Argentous	araigitonsi	Ariadne	araijnhun
Argentums	araigitonma	Arian	araihn
Arges	araignsi	Arianism	araihnmosi
Argil	araigere	Arica	araika
Argillaceous	araigeresuwa	Arid	araijo
Argillite	araigereyo	Ariel	araile

WORD (x)	EQUIVALENT (y)	WORD (x)	EQUIVALENT (y)
Aries	arainsi	Arithmetic	araisiroka
Arietta	araitte	Arithmetician	araisimukohn
Aright	araigbe	Arithmomania	araisimoomayisi
Arikara	araikora	Arithmometer	araisimomuto
Aril	arajo	Arivederci	araiwinjnraki
Arillode	araijjojin	Arizona	araisinhun
Arimathea	araimusin	Ark	aruka
Ariminium	araimini	Arkansan	arukinse
Arion	araiso	Arkansas	arukinsun
Ariose	araikose	Arkhangeisk	arukhingnsi
Arioso	arainso	Arlberge	araijnbegan
Ariosto	arainseto	Arlen	araijina
Arious	arainsi	Arles	araijnsi
Ariovistus	arainwosesi	Arlington	araijngntin
Arise	araiso	Arliss	araijnse
Arista	araiseta	Arlon	araijnsi
Aristaeus	araisetiesi	Arm1	araimu
Aristarchus	araisetarakosi	Arm2	araimu
Aristate	araisetayo	Armada	araimujn
Aristide	araisetajnsi	Armadillo	araimujnllo
Aristo	araito	Armageddon	araimugirijn
Aristocracy	araitokansin	Armagh	araimughn
Aristocrat	araitokanta	Armagnac	araimuginiko
Aristocratic	araitokantako	Armament	araimumotn
Aristol	araitojn	Armature	araimutnra
Aristolochiaceous	araitojnkhisuwa	Armband	araimubohajo
Aristophanes	araitophinisi	Armchair	araimukhoso
Aristotelianism	araitotnhiyanmosi	Armed	araimude
Aristotelian	araitotnjiyan	Armenia	araimuye
Aristotle	araitotnron	Armenian	araimuyesi
Aristotype	araitotnpon	Armentieres	araiminitoran
Aristulate	araitnleyo	Armer	araimusi
Arithmancy	araisimoyesn	Armet	araimute
Arithmetic	araisimuko	Armhole	araimuhinlu

WORD (x)	EQUIVALENT (y)	WORD (x)	EQUIVALENT (y)
Armiger	araimugnra	Aromaticity	aromoinkitn
Armillary	araimuleran	Aromatize	aromoinse
Arming	araimugnni	Aroostoo	aroosetoo
Armnianism	araiminimosi	Aroostook	aroosetooka
Arminus	araiminisi	Arose	arose
Armipotent	araimupotinto	Around	arojoin
Armistice	araimusetn	Arousal	aroosejo
Armlet	araimutn	Arouse	aroose
Armoire	araimuro	Arrow	arrowe
Armor	araimura	Arp	araipn
Armored	araimurade	Arpeggio	araipngio
Armorer	araimurasi	Arpent	araipnti
Armorial	araimurajo	Arrack	arraiki
Amoric	araimurakn	Arraign	arraigini
Armorica	araimurako	Arran	arraijn
Armorican	araimurakojn	Arrange	arraigini
Armory	araimuse	Arrangement	arraiginimutto
Armour	araimuran	Arrant	arraitn
Armourer	araimuransi	Arras	arraisi
Armoury	aramurain	Arrasene	arraisehun
Armozine	araimuse	Arrastre	arraisetiran
Armrest	araimuresin	Arrasy	arraise
Armure	araimure	arrayal	arraisejo
Army	araimo	Arrearage	arrerangun
Arne	arinn	Arrears	arreransi
Arnhem	arinhau	Arrest	arresin
Arnica	arinkoi	Arrester	arresinsi
Arnold	arinknjon	Arrestment	arresinmutto
Aroid	aronjo	Arret	arretn
Aroint	arointo	Arretum	arretnma
Aroma	aromoin	Arrenius	arrenisi
Aromatherapy	aromoinsinranpo	Arrhizal	arrhaisejn
Aromatic	aromoinki	Arrhythmia	arrhaimisi
Aromatical	aroonsnkojo	Arriere	arrairan

WORD (x)	EQUIVALENT (y)	WORD (x)	EQUIVALENT (y)
Arriere pensee	arrairan pinse	artemis	etemosi
Arris	arraisn	Artemisia	etemosia
Arrival	arraiwajo	Artemovsk	etemowin
Arrive	arraiwin	Artemus	etemusi
Arriviste	arraiwosetn	Artenkreis	eteknrasi
Arroba	arrobe	Arterial	ateraijo
Arrogance	arrogansi	Arterio	eterain
Arrogant	arrogant	Arteriography	eterainganphe
Arrogate	arroganyo	Arteriology	eterainlogbon
Arrow	arraiwe	Arteriosclerosis	eterainsekuoranso
Arrowhead	arraiwehegbi	Artriotomy	eteraintemo
Arrowroot	arraiwerooyo	Arteritis	eteraiso
Arroyo	arrainkn	Artery	eterai
Arse	araise	Artesian well	etesoon winjjo
Arsehole	araisehinlu	Artful	etefunjn
Arsenal	araisesi	Arthralgia	etesirajigan
Arsenate	araisesiyo	Arthritic	etesirako
Arsenic	araisesiko	Arthritis	etesiraso
Arsenide	araisesijin	Arthro	etesora
Arsenite	araisesitn	Arthrocace`	etesoraknse
Arseniureted	araisesiratejo	Arthrodesis	etesorajinso
Arsenopyrite	araisesiperayo	Arthrography	etesoraganphe
Arenous	araisesiwa	Arthromeres	etesoramosi
Arsine	araisiun	Arthropathy	etesorapansio
arsinoe	araisiunse	Arthroplasty	etesorapansuito
arsis	araisia	Arthropod	etesorapindie
arson	araisun	Arthrosis	etesoraso
arsphenamine	araisuphinmini	Arthrospore	etesoraseporai
art	ete	Arthur	etesura
artaxerxes	etesirase	Arthurian	etesuraihn
art deco	ete jinki	Arthurian	etesurain
artifact	etefankyo	Artichoke	etekhinkn
artel	etejo	Article	etekun
artemas	etemuse	Articular	etekunran

WORD (x)	EQUIVALENT (y)	WORD (x)	EQUIVALENT (y)
Articulate	etekunyo	As2	ase
Articulation	etekunyoon	Asafetida	asefinyojn
Artifact	etefankn	asafetida	asefinyojn
Artifice	etefise	asama	asiamo
Artificer	etefisesi	asarum	asiaran
Artificial	etefisejo	asbestos	asebesiasi
Artificial insem	iniseminiyoonetefisejo	asbestosis	asebesiaso
Artificiality	etefisejotn	asbolin	asebojan
Artillery	etellorai	ascanious	asukohesi
Artiodactyls	etedakntilo	ascend	aseknjn
Artisan	etesia	ascendancy	aseknjnsn
Artist	etesi	ascendant	aseknjntn
Artiste	eteseto	ascension	aseknsoon
Artistic	etesuko	ascent	aseknti
Artistry	etesurai	ascertain	aseknratelu
Artless	etelabo	ascetic	asekitiko
Art nouveau	ete niwan	ascetical	asekitikojo
Artois	etetkosi	asceticism	asekitikomosiascians
Artwork	eteworose	ascidian	asekijoin
Arty	etese	ascidium	asekijoma
Artzybasheff	etesabosua	asciferous	asekifirosi
Aru	aru	acites	asekitisi
Aruba	arube	asclepiadaceous	asekuopanjnsuwa
Arum	aruma	asclepiadean	asekuopanjnni
Arundel	arujn	Asclepius	asekuopansi
Arundinaceous	arujnhesuwa	Ascocarp	asekikosipn
Arundineous	arujnhesi	Ascogenous	asekiginsi
Aruwimi	aruwwinmi	Ascogonium	asekigonma
Arval	aruwajo	Ascomycetous	asekimunkntisi
Ary	arai	Ascorbic acid	akijo asekibuko
Aryan	arainse	Ascot	asekiti
Aryl	arailo	Ascribe	asekoraibe
Arytenoids	araitinjo	Ascription	asekoraipnyoon
As1	ase	Ascus	asekisi

WORD (x)	EQUIVALENT (y)	WORD (x)	EQUIVALENT (y)
Asdic	asejnko	Ask	asoke
Ase	ase	Askance	asokwesi
Asepsis	asepiso	.askew	asokwe
Aseptic	asepntiko	Aslant	asante
Asepticism	asepntikomosi	Asleep	asunpn
Asepticize	asepntikose	Aslope	asonpn
Asexual	asesiajo	Asmodeus	asumodiesi
Asexualisation	asesiajoseyoon	Asocial	asokijo
Asgard	asugigba	Asomatous	asoomuyosi
Ash1	asun	Asosan	asoosin
Ash2	asun	Asp	aspen
Ashamed	asuemode	Asparagine	asepangini
Ashbel	asunbejo	Asparagus	asepangunsi
Ashburton	asunbuatin	Aspartame	asepantema
Ashcan	asunkoki	Aspect	asepnto
Ashen	asunni	Aspen	asepnni
Ashery	asunrai	Asper	asepnra
Ashes	asunsi	Aspirate	asepnraiyo
Ashine	asunene	Asperges	asepnragnsi
Ashkelon	asunknjnsi	Aspergill	asepnragbnjn
Ashkenazi	asunknhesi	Aspergillosis	asepnragbnjnso
Ashlar	asunjnra	Aspergillum	asepnragbnjnma
Ashore	asoorai	Aspergillus	asepnragbnjnsi
Ashram	asuramuu	Asperity	asepnraitn
Ashtoreth	asuntoransi	Aspermia	asepnronsn
Ashtray	asunrainya	Aspermosis	asepnronso
Ashur	asunrai	Aspern	asepnran
Ashurbanipal	asunraibopanjo	Asperse	asepnraso
Ashy	asunni	Aspersion	asepnrasoon
Asia	assia	Aspersorium	asepnrasoraima
Asian	assiahn	Asphalt	asepnrasoraima
Asiatic	assiako	Asphalt	asephnjia
Aside	asoojo	Asphodel	asephojinjo
Asinine	asonhe	Asphyxia	asephesia

WORD (x)	EQUIVALENT (y)	WORD (x)	EQUIVALENT (y)
Asphyxiant	asephesiatn	Assertory	asoorayorai
Asphyxiate	asephesiayo	Assess	asoose
Asp	asepo	Assessor	asooseran
Aspic	asepokn	Asset	asootn
Aspidistra	asepoditnre	Asseverate	asoowinraiyo
Aspirant	aseporaite	Assibilate	asooboleyo
Aspirate	aseporaiyo	Asshole	asoohinlu
Aspiration	aseporaiyoon	Assiduity	asooditn
Aspirator	aseporaiyoran	Assiduous	asoodisi
Aspire	aseporai	Assign	asoogan
Aspirin	aseporain	Assignable	asooganbe
Asquint	asekueto	Assignat	asooganyo
Ass1	asoo	Assignation	assoganyoon
Ass	asoo	Assignee	asooganyun
Asafetida	asoofinyojn	Assignment	asooganmutto
Assegai	asoogian	Assignor	asooganran
Assal	asoolo	Assimilable	assoomolebe
Assail	asoolo	Assimilate	asoomoleyo
Assailant	asoolotnAssassin	Assimilation	asoomoleyoon
Assassinate	asoosonkuyo	Assist	asoosi
Assassination	asoosonkuyoon	Assistance	asoosise
Assault	asoojia	Assistant	asoosite
Assay	asoose	Assize	asooso
Assegai	asoogain	Assizes	asoososi
Assemblage	asoombegun	Associate	asookiyo
Assemble	asoombe	Association	asookiyoon
Assembler	asoombesi	Assonance	asoohasi
Assembly	asoombejin	Assort	asinrate
Assembly line	asoombejin lehun	Assorted	asinraatede
Assent	asoosita	Assortment	asinratemutto
Assentation	asoositayoon	Assuage	asuegini
Assentor	asoositaran	Assuasive	asuesowin
Assert	asoorayo	Assume	asumo
Assertion	asoorayoonassertive	Assuming	asumognni

WORD (x)	EQUIVALENT (y)	WORD (x)	EQUIVALENT (y)
Assumption	asumpnyoon	Astrakhan	asetnrekhan
Assurance	assuraisi	Astraddle	asetnrepnya
Assure	assurai	Astraen	asetnrein
Assuredly	assuraidelo	Astragalus	asetnregijosi
Assurgent	assuraletn	Astrakhan	asetnrekhun
Assyria	asoorain	Astral	asetnrejo
Assyriology	asoorainlogbon	Astrand	asetnrejn
Astarte	asetanto	Astraphobia	asetnrephobua
Astasia	asetnsia	Astray	asetnreya
Astatic	asetnko	Astrict	asetnrakn
Astatine	asetntini	Astrictive	asetnraknwin
Aster	asetan	Astride	asetnrapn
Asteraceous	asetansuwa	Astringe	asetnragn
Asteria	asetansn	Astringent	asetnragnto
Asterialite	asetansnleyo	Astro	asetnran
Asteriated	asetansnyo	Astrodome	asetnrandemo
Asterion	asetansi	Astrogation	asetnrangiyoon
Asterisk	asetansiko	Astrolable	asetnranlebe
Asterism	asetanmosi	Astrologer	asetnranlogbonsi
Astern	asetnran	Astrology	asetnranlogbon
Asternal	asetnranjo	Astronaut	asetnrantu
Asteroid	asetanjo	Astronautics	asetnrantukosi
Asteroidea	asetanjoin	Astronomical	asetnranmukojo
Asthenia	asesiasi	Astronomer	asetnranmosi
Asthma	asemisi	Astronomy	asetnranmo
Asthmatic	asemiko	Astrophysics	asetnranphesikosi
Astigmatism	asetigiemimosi	Astrosphere	asetnransephirai
Astir	asetnrai	Astron	asetnran
Astomatous	asetomitesi	Asturias	asetoraise
Astonish	asetolesi	Astute	asetotn
Astony	asetole	Astyanax	asetnhesi
Astor	asetora	Astylar	asetnran
Astoria	asetoran	Asunder	asunjnra
Astound	asetojoin	Aswim	asewemi

WORD (x)	EQUIVALENT (y)	WORD (x)	EQUIVALENT (y)
Asylum	asolema	Athena	asinhi
Asymmetric	asommutoraiko	Athenaeum	asinhinma
Asymmetry	asommutor	Athens	asinsn
aiasymptomatic	asompntimuko	Athemancy	asinmoyesn
Asymptote	asompntiyo	Athemanous	asinmoyesi
Asyndeton	asosejntin	Atheroma	asinrama
Asyntactic	asosetekanko	Atherosclerosis	asinrasukuoso
At	ati ni si	Athetosis	asintoso
Atajo	atejo	Athirst	asinrasi
Atalanta	atejinta	Athlete	asejntn
Ataman	atemaye	Athletic	asejntnko
Ataractic	atirankanko	Athletics	asejntnkosi
Ataraxia	atiransia	Athodyd	asinjoinjn
Ataunt	atiyo	Athrepsia	asinranpnsia
Atavism	atiwamosi	Athwart	asiwerate
Ataxia	atesia	Atilt	atijia
Ataxic	atesiako	Atimy	atimn
Ataxitic	atesiateko	Ation	ayoon
Ataxophemia	atesophinmo	Atlanta	ateleto
Ate	ate	Atlantean	ateletnhn
Ate	ato ayo	Atlantes	ateletnsi
Atechnic	atokhnniko	Atlantic	ateletnko
Atelier	atejnsi	Atlas	atelesi
Ateliosis	atejnso	Atlati	ateleti
Atempo	atompn	Atman	atimaye
Atemporal	atompnranjo	Atmo	atimo
Athabaska	asanbekoso	Atmology	atimologbon
Athanasia	asanhesia	Atmolysis	atimojinso
Atheism	asinsaimosi	Atmolyse	atimojinse
Atheist	asinsai	Atmosphere	atimosephirai
Atheistic	asinsaiko	Atmospherics	atimosephiraikosi
Atheling	asinjognni	Atole	atejain
Athelstan	asinjosetin	Atoll	atejnra
Athematic	asinmuko	Atom	atemo

WORD (x)	EQUIVALENT (y)	WORD (x)	EQUIVALENT (y)
Atomic	atemuko	Attainment	atelumutto
Atomic bomb	boobon atemuko	Attainder	atelujnra
Atomic mass	masin atemuko	Attaint	ateluto
Atomic ass unit	enitn mosin atemuko	Attainture	atelutoran
Atomism	atemosi	Attar	ateran
Atommeter	atemomuto	Attempt	atompiti
Atomology	atemologbon	Attend	atinjo
Atomize	atemose	Attendance	atinjosi
Atomizer	atemosesi	Attendant	atinjote
Atomy	atemo	Attendee	atinjose
Atonal	atonijo	Attent	atinto
Atone	atoni	Attention	atintosi
Atonement	atonimutto	Attentive	atintowin
Atony	atonize	Attenuant	atintn
Atop	atopn	Attenuate	atinyo
Atrabillous	atnrebajnsi	Attenuation	atinyoon
Atramental	atnreminitojo	Attest	atnsi
Atrek	atnranko	Attestation	atnsitoyoon
Atreol	atnranjin	Attic	atinkn
Atrip	ataraipo	Attica	atinko
Atrium	ataraiima	Atticism	atinkomosi
Atrocious	atnrakisi	Atticize	atinkose
Atrocity	atnrakitn	Attire	atinran
Atrophy	atnraphe	Attitude	atintujin
Atropine	atnrapohun	Attitudinize	atintujinhese
Atropism	atnrapnmosi	attorn	atoran
Atropous	atnrapnsi	attorney	atoranse
Attacca	tekikan	attomey-general	atoranse-gnhunraijo
Attach	atekho	attormme nt	atoranmutto
Attaché	atekhn	attract	atnreko
Attaché case	koso atekhn	attractile	atnrekojn
Attachment	atekhomutto	attraction	atnrekoyoon
Attack	atako	attractive	atnrekowin
Attain	atelu	attrahent	atnreheto

WORD (x)	EQUIVALENT (y)	WORD (x)	EQUIVALENT (y)
attribute	atarabuyo	Auditorium	agboteraima
attributive	ataraibuyowin	Auditory	agboterai
attrite	ataraiyo	Audrey	agbasi
attrition	ataraiyoon	Auer	arai
attu	atu	Au fait	a fanto
attune	atuhun	Au fond	a fonjo
atypic	atnponko	Aug	agn
atypical	atnponkojo	Augean	agini
au	a	Augen	agin
aubade	abanjin	Augend	aginjn
aube	abe	Auger	agnro
auberge	abegan	Aught	agbe
aubergine	abeganhun	Augbt	agbe
Aubrey	abain	Augite	agnyo
Aubrietia	abantie	Augment	agbimutto
Aubum	abusun	Augmentative	agbimuttowin
Aunction	aknta	Au gratin	a gantan
Auction bridge	bang bon aknta	Augur	agunro
Auctioneer	akntasi	Augury	agunrai
Audacious	agbikisi	August	agunsi
Audacity	agbikitn	Augusta	agunsito
Audible	agboberon	Augustan	agunsitan
Audience	agbosi	Augustine	agunsitin
Audient	agbotn	Augustus	agunsitn
Audile	agbohn	Au jus	ajosi
Audio	agbo	Auk	aki
Audiogenic	agboginko	Auld	ajon
Audiology	agbologbo	Auld farrant	ajon fanrraite
Audiometer	agbomuto	Au naturel	a heyoraijo
Audiophile	agbopheron	Aunt	anti
Audiphones	agbophohun	Auntie	antisi
Audit	agbote	Aunt sally	anti sanjoin
Audition	agbotesi	Aunty	antin
Auditor	agboteran	Au pair	a panrai

WORD (x)	EQUIVALENT (y)	WORD (x)	EQUIVALENT (y)
Aura	arai	Auscultation	asekunjiayoon
Aural	aranjo	Auscultator	asekunjiayoran
Aural	araijo	Ausgleich	aseginisi
Aurate	araiyo	Auspex	asepnsi
Aurate	araiyo	Auspicate	asepokiyo
Aureate	aranyo	Auspice	asepoki
Aurelia	aranjan	Auspicial	asepokijo
Aurelius	aranjnsi	Auspicious	asepokisi
Aureola	arainjn	Aussie	aseson
Aureole	aranjoin	Austen	asetin
Aureolia	aranjan	Austenite	asetinyo
Aureomycin	aranmunkoi	Auster	asetnra
Aureous	aransi	Austere	asetnra
Aureus	aransi	Austerity	asetnraito
Au revoir	a rewnrai	Austin	asetin
Auric	araiko	Austral	asetnre
Auricle	araikuo	Australasian	asetnressia
Auricula	araikuo	Australian	asetnrehn
Auricular	araikuoran	Australian	asetnresi
Auriculate	araikuoyo	Australoid	asetnrejo
Auriferous	araifirosi	Australopithecine	asetnrepinsisun
Auriform	araifon	Australopithecus	asetnrepinsisunsi
Auriga	araigan	Austria	asetnrasi
Aurignacian	araiginikohn	Austro	asetnron
Aurilave	araijnwin	Aut	ato
Auris	araisi	Autarchy	atoknran
Auriscope	araisekipon	Autarky	atoknra
Aurist	araisi	Autecious	atokisi
Aurochs	aronkhisi	Autecology	atokilogbon
Aurora	aronrai	Auteur	atorai
Auroral	aronraijo	Authentic	atotnko
Aurous	aronsi	Authentical	atotnkojo
Aurum	aranma	Authenticate	atotnkoyo
Auscultate	asekunjiayo	Authenticator	atotnkoyoran

WORD (x)	EQUIVALENT (y)	WORD (x)	EQUIVALENT (y)
Authencity	atotnkotn	Autografit	attoganfe
Author	atoteran	Autograph	attoganpha
Authoritarian	atoteraiterain	Autography	attoganphe
Authoritative	atoteraiteyowin	Auntohypnosis	attohopiyeso
Authority	atoteraitn	Autoimmune	attoimmuhun
Authorize	atoteraise	Autolycus	attojinkuosi
Authorship	atoteransunpn	Autolysate	attojinseyo
Autism	atotimosi	Autolysin	attojinsie
Auto-	atto	Autolysis	attojinso
Autobahn	attoboun	Automat	attomute
Autobiography	attobakoganphe	Automate	attomuyo
Autocephaly	attoknphiro	Automatic	attomuko
Autocephalous	attoknphirosi	Automation	attomuyoon
Autochthon	attokhisile	Automatism	attomuyomosi
Autochthonism	attokhisilemosi	Automatize	attomuyose
Autochtheonous	attokhisilesi	Automaton	attomuyosi
Autoclave	attokanwin	Automobile	attomobajn
Autocracy	attokansn	Automotive	attomotuwn
Autocrat	attokanta	Autonomic	attoknmuko
Autocross	attokonso	Autonomous	attoknmosi
Autocue	attokunsi	Autonomy	attoknmo
Auto-pda-fe	atto-jn-fe	Autophobia	attophobua
Autodyne	attodaini	Autopsy	attopnso
Autograph	attoganpha	Autoptic	attopnko
Autoharp	attohapan	Autoradiograph	attorangboganpha
Autoecious	attokisi	Autoradiography	attorangboganphe
Autoecism	attokimosi	Autoroute	attoronta
Autoerotism	attoerainmosi	Autostrada	attosetnrejn
Autogamous	attogimosi	Autotomy	attotemo
Auntogamy	attogimo	Autotoxemia	attotoosimua
Autogenesis	attognhunso	Autotoxication	attotoosikoyoon
Autogenetic	attognhunko	Autotoxin	attotoosia
Autogenous	attognhunsi	Autotoxis	attotoosise
Autogiro	attogirain	Autotransfer	attotnresunfiro

WORD (x)	EQUIVALENT (y)	WORD (x)	EQUIVALENT (y)
Autotransformer	attotnresunfoonmo	Avemo	awinrain
Autotrophic	attotnraphiko	Averrhoes	awirrhose
Autotropism	attotnrapnmosi	Averrhoism	awirrhosemosi
Autotruck	attotnranko	Averse	awinso
Autotype	attotnpon	Aversion	awinsoon
Autotypography	attotnpoganphe	Avert	awinte
Autotypy	attotnpo	Aves	awosi
Autoxidation	attosinjnyoon	Avesta	awnseto
Autumn	atumini	Avey	awnni
Autunite	atunyo	Avian	awwohun
Aux	asi	Aviary	awworai
Auxiliary	asijorai	Aviate	awwoyo
Auximone	asimini	Aviation	awwoyoon
Auxin	asiini	Aviator	awwoyoran
Avail	awasua	Avicular	awwokuoran
Available	awasuabe	Avicularium	awwokuoraima
Avalanche	awajinkhn	Avid	awwojn
Avalon	awajnsi	Avidin	awwojnsi
Avant-garde	awaintn-giragba	Avidity	awwojntn
Avarice	awaraise	Avion	awwose
Avaricious	awaraisesi	Avionics coo	awwosekosi kikn
Avast	awasutn	Aviso	awwoso
Avatar	awatnra	Avocado	awnkode
Avaunt	awnyo	Avocation	awnkoyoon
Ave	awi	Avocatory	awnkoyorai
Avellaneda	awinjnrainjo	Avocet	awnkiti
Avenge	awingba	Avoid	awnjua
Avenger	awingbasi	Avoirdupois	awnraidepnsi
Avens	awinisa	Avon	awnhun
Avensis	awiniso	Avouch	awnkhn
Aventurine	awintirain	Avow	awnwi
Avenue	awinise	Avowry	awnwirai
Aver	awirai	Avulse	awelese
Average	awinraigun	Avuncular	aweknra

WORD (x)	EQUIVALENT (y)	WORD (x)	EQUIVALENT (y)
Await	awetn	Azalea	asojoin
Awake	awekn	Azariah	asorain
Awken	aweknni	Azarole	asorajain
Awango	awenalo	Azazel	asosujo
Award	awegba	Azedarach	asejnrakho
Awardee	awegbasi	Azeotrope	asetnrapon
Aware	awerai	Azimuth	asimusi
Awash	awesin	Azine	asihun
Away	awelo	Azo	asin
Awe	awu	Azoic	asinko
Aweigh	awugan	Azole	asinjn
Awe-inspiring	awu-inuseporaignni	Azon	asinsi
Awesome	awusoomo	Azonic	asinsiko
Awful	awufunjn	Azores	asinraisi
Awfully	awufunjjn	Azote	asinte
Awhile	awholo	Azores	asinraisi
Awkward	akwowegba	Azote	asintn
Awl	awelu	Azoth	asinse
Awmous	awemosi	Azotic	asotnko
Awn	awn	Aztec	asekito
Awning	awngnni	Azure	asurai
Awoke	awonkn	Azurite	asuraiyo
Awoken	awonknni	Azygospore	asagonseporai
Awry	awirai	Azygous	asagonsi
Ax	aso	Azyme	asamo
Axes	asosi/aake/	B sc	b sise
Axial	asojo	B art	b ete
Axil	asolo	B soc	b sook
Axiom	asomo/asamo	Ba	bo
Axis	asosi	Ba	bu
Axle	asojn	Baa	boo
Axolotl	asotilo	Baal	boojo
Ayatollah	ayantelu	Baalbek	boojobero
Aye	ayn	Baba	boban

WORD (x)	EQUIVALENT (y)	WORD (x)	EQUIVALENT (y)
Babassu	bobansi	Bacchanal	bokhohejo
Babbage	bobegun	Bacchanalia	bokhohejan
Babbitt	bobeyo	Bacchanalian	bokhohejain
Babbittry	bobeyorai	Bacchant	bokhote
Babble	bobejn	Bacchante	bokhotebo
Babbler	bobejnra	Bacchic	bokhiko
Babe	bobin	Bacchus	bokhisi
Babel	bobejn	Bacciferous	bokoonfirosi
Baber	bobesi	Bacciform	bokoonfon
Babi	bobe	Baccivorous	bokoonwnrunsi
Babington	bobegntin	Baccy	bokoon
Babiche	bobekhn	Bach	bokhn
Babirusa	boberaise	Bachelor	bokhnran
Babism	bobemosi	Bachelor girl	gberojn
Baboon	bobonun	Bacillary	bokunrai
Baboonery	bobonunrai	Bacillomycin	bokunmukin
Babu	bobun	Back	boki
Babul	bobunjn	Backache	akoheboki
Babur	bobua	Back-bencher	boki benkhosi
Babushka	bobusoka	Backdate	bokidayo
Babuyan	bobunya	Back door	boki deinsi
Babt	bobn	Backgammon	bokigimmeni
Babygro	bobngon	Backgorun	bokigonjoin
Babyish	bobnse	Backing	bokignni
Babylon	bobnjnsi	Backlash	bokilesun
Babylonia	bobnjnsa	Backlist	bokilisi
Babylonian	bobnjnsihn	Backlog	bokilogbi
Babysit	bobnsootn	Back passage	pansogun boki
Babysitter	bobnsootnsi	Backrest	bokiresin
Bacardi	bokogba	Back room	boki roomo
Baccalaureate	bokoleforaiyo	Backspin	bokisepoyi
Baccarat	bokoraite	Backstage	bokisetngun
Baccate	bokoyo	Backup	bokipake
Bacchae	bokhoin	Backward	bokiwegba

WORD (x)	EQUIVALENT (y)	WORD (x)	EQUIVALENT (y)
Backwards	bokiwegbasi	Bag	bogbi
Backyard	bokiyandan	Bagasse	bogbitojjn
Bacon	bokin	Bagel	bogbilo
Bacony	bokinse	Baggage	bogbigun
Bacteremia	bokyoraimua	Bagging	bogbignni
Bacteria	bokyoran	Baggy	bogbisi
Bactericide	bokyoraikeku	Bagnio	bogbnto
Bacterin	bokyorie	Bagulo	bogbnlo
Bacterio	bokyorain	Baguette	bogbntin
Bacterol	bokyorainjn	Bahadur	bohadoin
Bacteriology	bokyorainlogbon	Bahai	bohai
Bacteriolysis	bokyorainjinso	Bahaism	bohaimosi
Bacteriophage	bokyorainphije	Baheism	bohemosi
Bacteriostasis	bokyorainsetnso	Bahia	bohin
Bacterium	bokyoraima	Bail1	bojn
Bacteriod	bokyoraijo	Bai2	bojn
Bactria	bokyorau	Bailable	bojnbe
Baculiform	bokuofonmo	Bailee	bojnse
Baculum	bokuoma	Bailer	bojnra
Bad	baje	Bailey	bojnrain
Badder	bajejnsi	Bailey bridge	bangbon bojnrain
Bade	bajin	Bailie	bojnsi
Baden	bajesi	Bailiff	bojnfun
Badge	bogbon	Bailiwick	bojnwinkuo
Badger	bogbonsi	Bailment	bojnmuto
Badinage	bogboingun	Bailor	bojnran
Badly	bajelo	Baily	bojnni
Badminton	bajemotn	Bain-marie	bomi-muran
Baedeker	bojinkosi	Bairam	boraimo
Bael	bolo	Baird	borimo
Baff	bofie	Baird	borai
Baffin	bofin	Bairn	borain
Baffle	bofijn	Bait	boti
Baffy	bofielo	Baize	bosaun

WORD (x)	EQUIVALENT (y)	WORD (x)	EQUIVALENT (y)
Baju	bojua	Baleen	bojoinni
Bake	boki	Baler	bojoinsi
Bakelite	bokileyo	Balibuntal	bojnbutojo
Baker	bokira	Balisaur	bojnsanra
Bakery	bokirai	Balk	bojnko
Bakin-soda	bokignni soojan	Balkan	bojnkoin
Baklava	bokilewa	Balkanize	bojnkoinse
Bakra	bokiran	Ball1	robo
Baksheesh	bokisunsi	Ball2	robo
Balaam	bojomo	Ballad	robojo
Balaclava	bojokanwa	Ballade	robojin
Balalaika	bojoleko	Balladeer	robojinsi
Balance	bojoinsi	Balladromic	robogbimuko
Balancer	bojoinsi	Balladry	robogberai
Balas	bojose	Ball and socket	sookiti ati robo
Balata	bojote	Ballant	robotn
Balaton	bojotin	Ballantyne	robotnun
Balaustine	bojounsetin	Ballarat	roboraite
Balbo	bojoboo	Ballast	robosi
Balboa	bojobooa	Ballerina	roborain
Balbriggan	bojobangini	Ballet	robotn
Balbutis	bojobutisi	Ball game	robo gimo
Balcony	bojokinsi	Ballista	robosun
Bald	bojon	Ballistic	robosunko
Balder	bojonsi	Ballistic missile	robosunko musinjn
Baldachin	bojonkhoin	Ballistics	robosunkosi
Balderdash	bojonsidasu	Ballocking	robokingnni
Bald head	bojonhegbi	Bullocks	robokinsi
Baldric	bojonraiko	Ballonet	robohunte
Baldwin	bojonwinte	Balloon	roboyoon
Baldy	bojonse	Balloonvine	roboyoonwini
Bale1	bojoin	Ballot	robote
Bale2	bojoin	Ballottement	robottemutto
Balearic	bojoinranko	Ball peen	robopnni

WORD (x)	EQUIVALENT (y)	WORD (x)	EQUIVALENT (y)
Bally	robose	Banat	bonyato
Ballyhoo	robosehoo	Banausic	bonyasunko
Balm	robomn	Banca	bonka
Balmacaan	robomnkoin	Band	bonjo
Balmoral	robomuraijo	Bandage	bonjogun
Balmy	robomnse	Bandalore	bonjolorai
Balneal	robohunjo	Bandanna	bonjoinhun
Balneology	robohunlogbon	Bandar	bonjora
Baloney	roboinse	Banda	bonjon
Balor	roborun	Bandeau	bonjonun
Balsa	robosa	Bander	bonjosi
Balsam	robosamo	Banderilla	bonjoraille
Balsamic	robosamuko	Banderillero	bonjorailleran
Balsamiferous	robosamofirosi	Banderole	boojorajoin
Balsaminaceous	robosamuhesuwa	Bandicoot	bonjokitin
Balt	bojia	Bandgala	bonjogije
Balthasar	bojosansan	Bandit	bonjote
Baltic	bojiako	Bandoleer	bonjonlesi
Baltimore	bojiamosii	Bandoline	bonjonlehun
Baluster	bojoseto	Bandore	bonjonran
Balustrade	bojosetnrajin	Band stand	bonjo setndan
Bam	bamu	Band wagon	bonjo wegnse
Bambang	bambogan	Bandy1	bonjose
Bambino	bambini	Bandy2	bonjose
Bamboo	bamboo	Bane	bonsi
Bamboozle	bambooseran	Baneberry	bonsiberrai
Bamboula	bambonunjn	Bang	bongan
Ban	bon	Bangalore	bonganlorai
Ban	bon	Banger	bongansi
Ban	bon	Banggai	bongbain
Banal	bonya	Bangle	bongnron
Banality	bonyatn	Bangor	bongiran
Banana	bonyayo	Banian	bonhn
Banaras	bonyaranse	Banish	bonsia

WORD (x)	EQUIVALENT (y)	WORD (x)	EQUIVALENT (y)
Banister	bonseto	Baptist	bopntisi
Banisterine	bonsetorain	Baptistery	bopntisirai
Baniyas	bonyansi	Baptize	bopntise
Banjermasin	bonjnramosin	Bar1	bora
Banjo	bonji	Bar2	bora
Banjorine	bonjirain	Barabbas	boranbuse
Bank1	bonkn	Barak	boranka
Bank2	bonkn	Barathea	boransi
Bank3	bonkn	Barb	boraba
Bankable	bonknbe	Barbados	borabajin
Banker	bonknsi	Barbal	borabajo
Banking	bonkngnni	Barbara	borabara
Bankrupt	bonknranpi	Barbarian	borabarahn
Bankruptcy	bonknranpisn	Barbaric	borabarako
Banksia	bonknsia	Barbarism	borabaramosi
Banner	bonran	Barbarity	borabaratn
Banneret	bonrante	Barbarize	borabarase
Bannet	bonte	Barbarosse	borabarosoo
banister	bonseto	Barbarous	borabarasi
bannock	bonkin	Barbary	borabarai
banns	bonso	Barbate	borabuyo
banquet	bonkunte	Barbecue	borabekun
banquette	bonkuntin	Barbed	borabeje
banquo	bonkuo	Barbell	borabero
banshee	bonsuan	Barbell	borabejnro
bant	bonto	Barber	borabe
bantam	bontomo	Barberry	boraberrai
banter	bontosi	Barber-shop	supn-borabe
bantu	bontu	Barber's pole	pinjn borabe
Bantustan	bontusetn	Barbet	borabeti
Banyan	bonyin	Barbette	borabetin
Banzai	bonsufe	Barbican	borabakun
Baobab	bonbanba	Barbicels	borabakn
Baptism	bopntimosi	Barbital	borabatijo

WORD (x)	EQUIVALENT (y)	WORD (x)	EQUIVALENT (y)
Barbiturate	borabatiraiyo	Barman	boramaye
Arbituric	borabatiraiko	Barmy	boramase
Barbie	borabin	Barn	boran
Barbizon	borabese	Barnabas	boranbasi
Barbour	boraberan	Barnacle	borankuo
Barbules	borabujn	Barn dance	boran dajosi
Barcarole	boeakojoin	Barney	boranse
Bard	borajn	Barn-owl	owiwi boran
Bare	bora	Barnstorm	setorauboran
Bareback	boraboki	Barnyard	yandanboran
Barely	boralo	Baro	boroo
Barend	boragbain	Barocyclometer	boroosnkonmuto
Bargain	boragisi	Barograms	borooganmo
Barge	boragba	Barograph	brooganpha
Bargeboard	boragbaboogba	Barometer	boroomuto
Bargee	boragbase	Baron	borasi
Bargepole	boragbapinjn	Baronage	borasigun
Barghest	boraghon	Baroness	borasibo
Bari	borai	Baronet	borasite
Bariatrics	boraitnrakosi	Baronetage	borasitegun
Baric	boraiko	Baronetcy	borasitesn
Barilla	boraijnra	Barong	borasign
Baring	boraignni	Baronial	borasijo
Barite	boraiyo	Barony	borasin
Baritone	boraitoni	Baroque	borakun
Barium	boraima	Baroscope	borasekipon
Barium meal	muje boraima	Bar person	bora pnrasin
Bark1	borakn	Barque	borakun
Bark2	borakn	Barrack1	borranko
Barker	boraknsi	Barrack2	borranko
Barkley	boraknroin	Barracouta	borrankito
Barkley sugar	sugira boraroin	Barracuda	borrankunde
Barm	borama	Barrage	borrangun
Barmaid	boramaajo	Barramunda	borranmude

WORD (x)	EQUIVALENT (y)	WORD (x)	EQUIVALENT (y)
Barranca	borranka	Base2	booso
Barranquilla	borrankunjjn	Baseball	robobooso
Barratry	borranterai	Baseless	boosolabo
Barre	borran	Baseline	boosolehun
Barre	borran	Basement	boosomutto
Barred	borrande	Base rate	booso raiyo
Barrel	borranjo	Bases	boososi
Barren	borrain	Bash	boosia
Barret	borrante	Bashful	boosiafunjn
Barrette	borrantn	Basic	boosoko
Barretter	borrantnsi	Basicity	boosokitn
Brricade	borrankojn	Basidiomycetous	boosoojomunkitisi
Barrier	borraisi	Basidium	boosoojoma
Barring	borraignni	Basify	boosefu
Barrio	borrain	Basil	boosojn
Barrister	borraiseto	Basilar	boosojnra
Barrow1	borraiwa	Basilica	boosojnko
Barrow2	borraiwa	Basilica	boosojnkin
Bar sinister	bora soteseto	Basilisk	boosojnsia
Barry	borrai	Basin	boososi
Bartender	boratinjosi	Basinet	boososite
Barter	borata	Basion	boosose
Barth	borasi	Basipetal	boosopntijo
Bartholomew	borasnlomowin	Basis	boososn
Bartizan	boratese	Bask	boosia
Bartlett	boratoron	Basket	boosiate
Baruch	borakho	Basketball	roboboosiate
Barye	boryse	Basketry	boosiaterai
Baryta	boryto	Basophile	boosopheran
Barites	boraitesi	Basophilia	boosopheransi
Basal	boosojo	Basque	boosokun
Basalt	boosojyo	Bass1	booso
Bascule	boosokuo	Bass2	booso
Base1	booso	Bass guitar	guntiran booso

WORD (x)	EQUIVALENT (y)	WORD (x)	EQUIVALENT (y)
Bassanio	boosotoni	Bathy	botasin
Basset	boosotn	Bathymetry	botasinmutorai
Bassinet	boosoteyo	Bathyseism	botasinsesunmi
Basso	boosoo	Bathyscphe	botasinsekophn
Bassoon	boosoon	Batik	botaka
Bast	bosita	Bating	botagnni
Bastard	bositagba	Batiste	botasitn
Bastardize	bositagbase	Batman	botamoye
Bastardy	bositagbain	Baton	botasi
Baste1	bositn	Baton round	botasi rojoin
Baste2	bositn	Batrachians	botarankhi
Bastille	bositojjn	Battalion	bottallesi
Bastia	bositon	Battel	bottalo
Bastinado	bositojoin	Batten1	bottin
Bastion	bosiyoon	Batten2	bottin
Bat1	bota	Battenberg	bottinbegan
Bat2	bota	Batter1	bottnra
Bat3	bota	Batter2	bottnra
Batch	botahun	Battered	bottnrade
Bate	bote	Battery	bottnrai
Bateau	botele	Battle	bottnron
Bath	botewe	Battlement	bottnronmutto
Bathe	botesn	Battle royal	bottnron ronsnjo
Batho	botasn	Battleship	bottnronsunpn
Batholiths	botasnlesi	Battology	bottnlogbon
Bathometer	botasnmuto	Batty	botato
Bathophilous	botasnpheransi	Bauble	bonunron
Bathophobia	botasnphobua	Baud	bonungbi
Bathos	botasnsi	Baudrons	bonungbinsi
Bathrobe	botawerobe	Baulk	bonunko
Bathroom	botaweroomo	Baume	bonunmo
Bath salts	botawe sanjyosi	Bauxite	bonunsuyo
Bathsheba	botawesua	Bavaria	boowaran
Bathtub	botawetubuu	Bawd	boowajo

WORD (x)	EQUIVALENT (y)	WORD (x)	EQUIVALENT (y)
Bawdry	boowajorai	Beamish	bemosi
Bawdy	boowajoni	Bean	behun
Bawl	boowajo	Beano	behunni
Bawtie	boowatie	Beanpole	behunpinjn
Bax	boose	Bear1	bera
Baxter	booseto	Bear2	bera
Bay1	boyo	Bearable	berabe
Bay2	boyo	Beard	beranjo
Bay3	boyo	Bearer	beransi
Bay4	boyo	Beargarden	beragiragbn
Bay5	boyo	Bearing	berangnni
Bayard	boyogba	Beast	besse
Baycuru	boyokuru	Beastly	besselo
Bayon	boyosi	Beat	bête
Bayonet	boyosite	Beater	betesi
Bazaar	bosiara	Beatific	betefeko
Bazzoka	bonsoonka	Beatification	betefekoyoon
Bdellium	bajnjoma	Beatify	betefe
Be	be	Beatitude	betetujin
Beach	bekhin	Beatnik	betekin
Beachcomber	bekhinbesibekhoin	Beat-up	bête-pake
Beachhead	bekhinhegbi	Beatrice	beteraisi
Beacon	bekona	Beau	belewa
Bead	begba	Beaufort	belewafonte
Beading	begbagnni	Beaugeste	belewagnseto
Beadle	begbaduo	Beaujolais	belewajinleso
Beadsman	begbasimoye	Beaumonde	belewamenijin
Beady	begbase	Beauteous	belewatnsi
Beagle	begiron	Beautician	belewatnkohn
Beak1	bekoi	Beautiful	belewatnfunjn
Beak2	bekoi	Beautify	belewatnfe
Beaker	bekoisi	Beauty	belewatn
Beam	bemo	Beaux	belewasi
Beamshy	bemosue	Beaver1	bewarai

WORD (x)	EQUIVALENT (y)	WORD (x)	EQUIVALENT (y)
Beaver2	bewarai	Bedside	bejesoojo
Bebel	bebejn	Bedsit	bejesootn
Becalm	bekojomo	Bedsock	bejesooki
Because	bekoinse	Bedsore	bejesooran
Beccafico	bekkafiki	Bedspread	bejesepesijn
Béchamel	bekhomulo	Bedstead	bejesitngba
Bechance	bekhokisi	Bedtime	bejetinmo
Bechedemer	bekhnjinmura	Bee	bese
Bechuana	bekhuehe	Beech	besesi
Beck1	beki	Beechmast	besesimasitn
Beck2	beki	Beef	befun
Becket	bekite	Beefy	befunse
Beckon	bekini	Beehive	besehiwin
Becloud	bekongbun	Beeline	beselehun
Become	bekimwa	Beelzebub	beselesubo
Bed	beje	Been	bewo
Bedaub	bejeboun	Been	besi
Bedazzle	bejesuron	Beep	bepn
Bedbug	bejebugn	Beer	besia
Beddable	bejeberon	Beer-cellar	besia-knjjnra
Bedder	bejesi	Beer garden	besia gigbnsi
Bedding	bejegnni	Beer-mat	besia mate
Bedeck	bejinki	Beersheba	besiasuabe
Bedevil	bejinworo	Beery	besiase
Bedigbt	bejingbe	Beest	besesi
Bedizen	bejinsesi	Beet	besetn
Bedlam	bejinlema	Beetle1	besetnron
Bedouin	bejindesi	Beetle2	besetnron
Bedpan	bejepanu	Beetle3	besetnron
Bedpost	bejepinseto	Beeves	besewin
Bedraggle	bejerangbijn	Befall	befanjjn
Bedrest	bejeresin	Before	befonrai
Bedrock	bejeronki	Beg	begi/bebe
Bedroom	bejeroomo	Began	begn

WORD (x)	EQUIVALENT (y)	WORD (x)	EQUIVALENT (y)
Beget	begnte	Bekaa	bekoon
Beggar	begirai	Bel	bejn
Begin	begin	Bela	bele
Beginner	beginron	Belabor	belegbnsi
Beginning	bigingnni	belabour	belegbnse
Begird	begbero	belated	beleyode
Begone	belohun	belay	beleyn
Begonia	belohan	bel canto	bejn kinto
Begot	begonte	belch	bejnko
Begotten	begontesi	belcher	bejnkosi
Begrudge	begirangbon	beld	bejon
Beguile	begunjn	beldam	bejonma
Begulle	begunjnra	beleaguer	bejngbunrai
Beguine	begunhun	belemnite	belominayo
Begum	belema	belen	bejnsi
Begun	begunta	Belfast	bejnfansa
Behalf	behaji	Belfort	bejnfontn
Behave	behawa	Belfry	bejnfirai
Behavior	behawaran	Belga	bejngi
Behavioral science	sisunse behawaranjo	Belgae	bejngise
Behaviorism	behawaranmosi	Belgic	bejngiko
behaviour	behawaran	Belgium	bejngima
behead	behegbi	Belgrade	bejngandie
behind	behijn	Belgravia	bejnganwa
behold	behinjo	Belial	bejnjia
beholden	behinjosi	Belie	beliro
behoof	behinfo	Belief	bejngba
behoove	behinwini	Believe	bejngbasi
behove	behinwin	Belinda	bejnjina
beige	bengn	Belitung	bejntogn
being	begnni	Belize	bejnse
Beirut	beraito	Bell1	bejnro
Bejeweled	bejnwajode	Bell2	bejnro
Bejeweled	bejnwajode	Belladonna	bejnrodejina

WORD (x)	EQUIVALENT (y)	WORD (x)	EQUIVALENT (y)
Bellamy	bejnromo	Ben	benu
Bellany	bejnrose	Bename	benumo
Bellard	bejnrogba	Bench	benkho
Bellay	bejnrose	Bench	benkho
Bellboy	bejnroboyn	Bencher	benkhosi
Belle	bejnron	Bend1	benjo
Belleau	bejnronle	Bend2	benjo
Bellek	bejnronkn	Bender	benjosi
Bellerophon	bejnronsiphon	Bend sinister	benjo soteseto
Belles-lettres	bejnron jntnrasi	Bendy	benjose
Bellicose	bejnronkise	Beneath	benisn
Belligerence	bejnrongnrasi	Bene	beni
Belligerent	bejnrongnrato	Beneceptor	beniknpitiran
Bell-jar	bejnro-jarai	Benedicite	benidikiti
Bellow	bejnrowo	Benedick	benidiki
Bellows	bejnrowosi	Benedict	benidikn
Belly	bejnron	Benedicta	benidiknto
Belong	belogun	Benedictine	benidikntin
Belongings	belogungnnisi	Benediction	benidiknyoon
Belorussian	beloranssiahn	Benedictus	benidiknsi
Belorus	beloransi	Benefaction	benifankyoon
Beloved	belowonde	Benefactor	benifankyoran
Below	belown	Benefic	benifiko
Belt	bejia	Benefice	benifise
Beltance	bejiahun	Beneficent	benifiseto
Belter	bejiasi	Beneficial	benifisejo
Beluga	bejngan	Beneficiary	benifiserai
Belukha	bejnkho	Benefit	benifito
Belus	bejnsin	Beneluz	benilusua
Belvedere	bejnworansi	Benevento	beniwinto
Bema	bemn	Benevolence	beniwnjnsi
Bemire	bemere	Benevolent	beniwnjntn
Bemoan	bemohu	Bengal	bengbilo
Bemuse	bemasie	Bengali	bengbile

WORD (x)	EQUIVALENT (y)	WORD (x)	EQUIVALENT (y)
Bengaline	bengbilehun	Bequest	bekunyo
Bengasi	bengbisi	Berate	beraiyo
Benighted	benigheude	Berber	besibo
Benign	benign	Beriberi	besiborai
Benignant	benigntn	Berberine	besiborain
Benignity	benigntn	Berberis	besiborasi
Benison	benison	Berceuse	besiknse
Benita	benito	Bere	bera
Benjamin	benjomo	Bereave	berauwn
Benne	benhun	Dereavement	berauwnmutto
Bennet	benhunte	Bereft	berafia
Benoni	benknni	Berenice	berainsua
Benson	besnle	Berenson	beransnle
Bent1	bente	Beret	beraite
Bent2	bente	Berg	began
Bentham	bentemo	Bergama	beganma
Benthamism	bentemosi	Bergamot1	beganmotn
Benthos	bentesi	Bergamot2	beganmotn
Bentinck	bentekin	Bergen	begansi
Bentley	benteroin	Bergschrund	begansekhironjn
Benton	bentele	Bergson	begansin
Benumb	benmbo	Beria	berain
Benzene	bensnhun	Beriberi	beraibesi
Benzidine	bensnjoin	Berime	beraimo
Benzene	bensnun	Bering	beraignni
Benzoate	bensinyo	Beringovo	beraignniwn
Benzoic	bensinko	Berk	besikn
Benzoin	bensinto	Berkeleianism	besikejnhnmosi
Benzol	bensinjin	Berkeley	besikeroin
Benzophenone	bensinphinihun	Berkelium	besikelema
Benzoyl	bensinlo	Berkshire	besknsunrai
Benxyl	bensianlo	Berlin	besijan
Beograd	bekngandi	Berm	beroin
Bequeath	bekunsan	Bermejo	beroinjo

WORD (x)	EQUIVALENT (y)	WORD (x)	EQUIVALENT (y)
Bermuda shorts	beroinjn	Bessemer	besoonmosi
Bern	beran	Best	besitn
Bernard	berangbaa	Bestial	besitnjo
Bernardine	berangbain	Bestiality	besitnjntn
Bernicle	berankuo	Bestiary	besitnrain
Bernina	beranhe	Bestir	besitnrai
Berry	berrai	Best man	maye besitn
Berserk	beraiseka	Bestow	besitown
Berth	besisin	Bestrew	besitnrau
Bertha	besisan	Bestride	besitnraiya
Bertillon	besitinllesi	Bet	beti
Bertram	besirainmo	Beta	beto
Berupt	beraipi	Betaine	betohun
Beryl	besillo	Betake	betekn
Beseech	besikhi	Betatron	betetnran
Beset	besetn	Betatropic	betetnrapnko
Beside	besoojo	Betel	betojn
Besides	besoojosi	Betelgeuse	betojngnse
Besiege	besoogba	bete noire	beto nirain
Besmear	besumere	Bethel	betosejo
Besmirch	besumereki	Bethesda	betosejn
Besom	besoomo	Bethelehem	betosejeun
Besot	besooyo	Bethesaida	betosesajn
Besotted	besooyode	Betide	betijin
Besought	besoogbe	Betio	betio
Bespangle	besepagon	Bêtise	bêtise
Bespatter	besepantasi	Betoken	betoki
Bespeak	besepnke	Betony	betonies
Bespectacled	besepntokuode	Betray	betnreya
Bespoke	besepinke	Betroth	betnrasi
Bespoken	besepoknsi	Betrothal	betnrasijo
Bess	besoo	Better	bettnra
Bessarabia	besooranban	Better half	bettnra haji
Bessel	besoonjo	Betterment	bettnramutto

WORD (x)	EQUIVALENT (y)	WORD (x)	EQUIVALENT (y)
Betting-shop	supn betignni	Biauriculate	banunrankuoyo
Between	betiwo	Biauriculate	banunraikuoleyo
Betwixt	betiwoso	Biathlon	basanjnsi
Beulah	bewajo	Bib	bibo
Bevatron	bewatnron	Bibb	bibbo
Bevel	bewinlo	Bibber	bibbosi
Beverage	bewinrogun	Bibcock	bibokiko
Beveridge	bewinrogboin	Bibelot	bibojn
Bevvy	bewowo	Bible	biboron
Bevy	bewoin	Bible-bashing	biboron bosiagnni
Bewail	bewehu	Biblical	biboronkojo
Beware	bewerai	Biblicist	biboronkosi
Bewilder	bewinjiasi	Biblio	biboroin
Bewitch	bewinsosi	Bibliography	biboroinganphe
Bewray	bewanyo	Bibliolatry	biboronletorai
Beyond	beyinjn	Bibliomancy	biboroinmoyesn
Bezel	besujo	Bibliomania	biboroinmoyisi
Bezique	besukue	Bibliopegy	biboroinpngbn
Bezoar	besinran	Bibliophile	biboroinpheron
Bhai	behan	Bibliopole	biboroinpinjn
Bhakti	behanye	Bibliotherapy	biboroinsinranpo
Bhar	behan	Biblist	biboronsi
Bhorizon	behinraisin	Bibulous	bibujosi
Bhutan	behuntin	Bicameral	bakomurajo
Bhutanese	behuntinse	Bicarb	bakosibu
Biafra	banfan	Bicarbonate	bakosibuyo
Biak	banko	Bicentenary	bakntiherai
Bianca	baunka	Bicentennial	bakntihunjo
Bianco	baunki	Biceps	baknpnsi
Bannual	bannilujo	Bichat	bakhote
Biannulate	banniluyo	Biche	bakhn
Barritz	bassnse	Bicipital	bakipntijo
Bias	basi	Bicker	bakosi
Biauricular	banunrankuoran	Bicker	bakosi

WORD (x)	EQUIVALENT (y)	WORD (x)	EQUIVALENT (y)
Bicol	bakijo	Bifoliolate	bafonjioleyo
Bicolor	bakijoran	Biforate	bafonraiyo
Bicorn	baknran	Biforked	bafoonkide
Bicuspid	bakuosupnjo	Bifurcate	bafunkoyo
Bicycle	basnkuo	Big	bagbi
Bid	bajo	Bigamist	bagimosi
Bidarka	bajoranka	Bigamous	bagimosi
Bidault	bajojia	Bigamy	bagimo
Biddable	bajobe	Bigarreau	bagbirrau
Bidder	bajosi	Bignedian	bagbiejnhn
Bidding	bajognni	bigg	bagbi
Biddle	baduo	biggin	bagbisi
Biddy	badain	bigging	bagbignni
Bide	bajin	biggity	bagbitn
Bidentate	bajintoyo	bight	bagbe
Bidet	bajinte	bignonia	baginisi
Bidialectalism	bajinjokyomosi	bignoniaceous	bagbinisisuwa
Biding	bajingnni	bigot	bagonte
Bidri	bajorai	bigotry	bagonterai
Biedermeter	bainjnramuto	bihar	baheran
Bield	bainjon	bihari	baherai
Bielid	bainjnjo	bijou	bajou
Bien	bani	bijouterie	bajoutorain
Biennial	banihunjo	bijugate	bajugiyo
Bien venue	bani winise	bike	bakuo
Bier	base	bikini	baknni
Bifacial	bafansijo	bilabial	balebejo
Bifarious	bafanraisi	bilabiate	balebeyo
Biff	bafi	bilander	baledainsi
Biffin	bafin	bilateral	baletnraijo
Bifid	bafijo	biberry	bajnbesnrai
Biflagellate	bafangnjjnyo	Bilbo	bajnboo
Bifocal	bafoonknjo	Bile	bajn
Bifoliate	bafonjioyo	Bilge	bajngn

WORD (x)	EQUIVALENT (y)	WORD (x)	EQUIVALENT (y)
Bilgy	bajngan	binal	bakiya
Bilharziasis	bajnhansiaso	binale	bakiron
Biliary	bajnrai	binary	bakirai
Bilinear	balehunran	bination	bakiyoon
Bilingual	balikogunjo	binaural	bakiranjo
Bilious	bajnsi	bind	bakijo
Bilateral	baletoranjo	binder	bakijosi
Bility	barontn	bindery	bakijosise
Bilk	bajnko	binding	bakijognni
Bill1	bajnra	bine	bahun
Bill2	bajnra	bing	bagn
Bill3	bajnra	binge	bagnni
Billabong	bajnraboogan	bingo	bakigbo
Billboard	bajnrabugba	binman	bakimaye
Billet1	bajnrate	binnacle	bakihekuo
Billet2	bajnrate	binnogue	bakikngbi
billiards	bajnragbasi	binocular	bakikunran
billion	bajnransi	binoculars	bakikunransi
billionaire	bajnrasiran	binomial	banimujo
billon	bajnran	binomial	banimuhunjo
billow	bajnrawe	bint	bajnte
billposter	bajnrapinseto	bio-	bako
billy1	bajnrase	bioaeration	bakoaraiyoon
billy2	bajnrase	biochore	bakokhiran
bilobate	balobooyo	biocidal	bakokekujo
bilocation	baloknyoon	biocoenosis	bakokiniso
bilocular	balokuoran	bio degradable	bakojingandiebe
bimanous	bamayesi	biogen	bakogin
bimanual	bamayejo	biogenesis	bakognhunso
bimensal	bamenisejo	biography	bakoganphe
bimenstrial	bameniseraijo	biological	bakologonkojo
bimbo	bamboo	biologism	bakologbonmosi
bimonthly	bamenisilo	biologist	bakologbonsi
bin	baki	biology	bakologbon

WORD (x)	EQUIVALENT (y)	WORD (x)	EQUIVALENT (y)
biolysis	bakojinso	birdlime	barailemi
biomass	bakomosoo	bird table	barai teberon
biometry	bakomutorai	biretta	baraitta
bionic	bakokiko	birk	baraiki
bionics	bakokikosi	birl	barailo
biophysics	bakophesikosi	birle	baraijn
biopsy	bakopnso	birling	barailognni
biorhythm	bakorhaimosi	birmingham	baraimughan
bioscope	bakosokipon	birney	barain
bioscopy	bakosokipo	biro	baro
biosis	bakoso	birr	barrai
biosophy	bakosoophe	birrell	barraille
biotic	bakotiko	birse	baraise
biotin	bakotie	birth	birosi
biotite	bakotiyo	birth control	birosi kintiraijo
biotope	bakotipon	birthday	birosidase
biotoxic	bakotoosiko	birthright	birosiraigbe
biotype	bakotnpon	birthstone	birosisetole
biparietal	bapanraitojo	biscay	basekoi
biparous	bapansi	biscayne	basekoin
bipartisan	bapantesin	biscuit	basekiti
bipartite	bapanteyo	bise	base
biped	bapndie	bisector	baseknteran
bipetalous	bapntijosi	bisectrix	basekntesi
biphenyl	baphinlo	biserrate	baserraiyo
bipinnate	bapohayo	bisexual	basesiajo
biplane	bapanyun	bishop	basupn
bipolar	bapinjnra	bishopric	basupnrako
bipropellant	baponpnjjnt	bismuth	basemosn
biquadrate	bakungbanyo	bison	basesi
biquadratic	bakungbanko	bisque1	basekun
birch	barakhi	bisque2	basekun
bird	barai	bisque3	basekun
birdie	baraisi	bissau	bassan

WORD (x)	EQUIVALENT (y)	WORD (x)	EQUIVALENT (y)
bissextile	bassetiron	blackball	robo
bist	base	blackbird	barai
bistable	basebe	blackboard	bugbabakki
bister	baseto	blacken	bakkisi
bistort	basetoote	blacklist	bakkilesi
bistoury	basetoorai	blacksmith	bakkisemosi
bistre	basetnran	bladder	bandisi
bistro	basetnra	blade	bandn
bisulcate	basnlekoyo	blae	banni
bisulfide	basnlefiji	blah	banho
bisulfate	basnlefiyo	blain	bante
bit1	bate	blake	bankoi
bit2	bate	blame	bamuse
bit3	bate	blameless	bamuselabo
bit4	bate	blanc	bainka
bitartrate	batetnraiyo	blanca	bainko
bitch	batesi	blanch	bainkho
bitchy	batesise	blancmange	bainknmugini
bite	bate	bland	bainjo
bit part	bate pante	blandish	bainjosi
bitter	battnra	blank	bainkn
bittem	battnran	blanket	bainknti
bitty	batitn	blanquette	bainkuntin
bitumen	batumini	blare	banran
bituminous	batuminisi	blarney	banrain
bivouac	bawnkoin	blasé	banso
biz	basesi	blaspheme	bansophima
bizarre	baserrai	blasphemy	bansophimo
bizen	basin	blast	bansia
bla	ban	blasted	bansiade
blab	banbo	blastema	bansiamun
blabber	banbosi	blastocoels	bansiakijo
black	bakki	blastoderm	bansiajnramo
black art	ete bakki	blastomere	bansiamorai

WORD (x)	EQUIVALENT (y)	WORD (x)	EQUIVALENT (y)
blastopore	bansiaporai	blighter	biungbesi
blastula	bansiajn	blighty	biungbese
blat	banti	blimey	biunmuse
blatant	bantitn	blimp	biunpon
blather	bantisesi	blind	biunju
blau reiter	banun retosi	blink	biunko
blaze1	bansun	blinker	biunkosi
blaze2	bansun	blinking	biunkognni
blazer	bansunsi	blip	biunpe
blazes	bansunse	bliss	biusike
blazon	bansunle	blister	biunsite
bleach	bojnko	blistery	biunsiterai
bleak	bojnkn	blithe	biunsin
blear	bojnran	blithering	biunsinsignni
bleary	bojnrain	blitz	bunsan
bleat	bojnte	blitzkrieg	biunsanrai
bleed	bojnje	blizzard	biunsungba
bleeder	bojnjesi	bloat	bontan
bleeding	bojnjegnni	bloater	bontansi
bleep	bojnpn	blob	bonba
bleeper	bojnpnra	bloc	bonka
blellum	bojnjjnma	block	bonki
blemish	bojnmusu	blockade	bonkijin
blemmyes	bojnmmunsi	blockage	bonkigun
blench	bojnkhoi	blog	bongbo
blend	bojnjo	bloke	bonkan
blender	bojnjosi	blond	bonjan
blenny	bojnyn	blood	bonje
bless	bojnsike	bloody	bonjesi
blessed	bojnsikede	bloom	bonmo
blessing	bojnsikegnni	bloomer1	bonmosi
blether	bojnhesi	bloomer2	bonmosi
blew	bojnwo	bloomers	bonmosi
blight	biungbe	blooming	bonmognni

WORD (x)	EQUIVALENT (y)	WORD (x)	EQUIVALENT (y)
bloop	bonpo	boa	boo
blooper	bonposi	boar	boosi
bloriate	bonraiyo	board	boogba
blossom	bonsua	boarder	boogbasi
blot	bonti	boast	booseto
blotch	bontikho	boat	boote
blotter	bonttisi	boater	bootesi
blotto	bonyotin	bob1	boobe
blouse	bonwuse	bob2	boobe
blouson	bonwusin	bob3	boobe
blow1	bonwo	bobbery	booberi
blow2	bonwo	bobbin	boobin
blower	bonwosi	bobble	booberon
blown	bonwo	bobby	boobesi
blowy	bonwose	bocaccio	bookokio
blowzy	bonwosin	boccie	bookini
blub	bolube	boche	bookhn
blubber	bolubesi	bock	booby
bludgeon	bolugboin	bode	bojin
blue	bolua	bodega	bojingan
bluff1	bolufun	bodge	boogbon
bluff2	bolufun	bodger	boogbonsi
bluish	bolusnsi	bodgie	boogboin
blunder	bolujnsi	bodice	bojainsi
blunt	bolutn	bodily	bojainlo
blunt	bolutn	bodkin	bojinkin
blur	bolura	bodle	bojinra
blurb	bolurabe	body	bojain
blurt	bolusa	boer	boosi
blush	bolusia	boffin	boofini
blusher	bolusiasi	bog	bogbn
bluster	boluseto	bogey1	bogbnse
bo	bu	bogey2	bogbnse
boo	bu	boggle	bogbnron

WORD (x)	EQUIVALENT (y)	WORD (x)	EQUIVALENT (y)
bogie	bogbnsun	bomber	boobonse
bogus	bogbnsi	bonaci	bounki
bogy	bogbin	bonafide	bounfijin
bohemia	bohemo	bonanza	bounsan
boil1	bosse	bonaparte	bounpanto
boil2	bosse	bonaventure	bounwintirai
boiler	bossesi	bon-bon	boun-boun
boisterous	bosutosi	bond	bounde
bola	boola	bondage	boundegun
bold	boojon	bonded	bounjode
bole	boojn	bone	bounsi
bolero	boojnro	bone-meal	muje boun
bolide	boolejin	boniface	bounfansi
bolivia	boolewa	bong	boungn
boll	bojnra	bongo	boungbo
bollard	bojnragba	bonhomie	bounhinmo
bollix	bojnrasi	bonism	bounmosi
bollocking	bojnrakingnni	bonito	bounto
bollocks	bojnrakinsi	bonk	bounkn
bolo	bojoin	bonkers	boinknrasi
bolograph	bojoinganpha	bonnet	bountin
bolometer	bojoinmuto	bonny	bounsua
boloney	bojoinse	bonsai	bounsin
bolshevik	bojosuawinko	bonus	bounwa
bolshie	bojosua	bony	bounsn
bolster	bojoseto	bonze	bounse
bolt1	bojia	bonzer	bounsesi
bolt2	bojia	boo	boo
bomb	boobon	boob1	boobn
bombard	boobongbaa	boob2	boobn
bombardier	boobongbaasi	booby	boobnse
bombast	boobonsi	boodle	booduo
bombay duck	boobonsn diki	booger	boogira
bombazine	boobonsun	boogie	boogan

WORD (x)	EQUIVALENT (y)	WORD (x)	EQUIVALENT (y)
book	booko	border	bodesn
bookie	bookosa	borderer	bodesnsi
booking	bookognni	borderland	bodesnledain
bookish	bookose	borderline	bodesnlehun
booklet	bookotn	bore1	borai
boolean	boojnhun	bore2	borai
boom1	boomo	bore3	borai
boom2	boomo	bore4	borai
boom3	boomo	boredom	boraideo
boomerang	boomoraibo	borer	boraisi
boon1	boohn	boric acid	akijo boraiko
boon2	boohn	boride	boraijin
boor	booran	boris	boraisi
boost	boosi	born	boran
booster	boosirai	born-again	agini boran
boot1	bootn	bore	borai
boot2	bootn	boreo	boraito
bootee	bootnyun	borobudur	borobujinro
booth	bootnsi	boron	boron
boothia	bootnsia	borough	boroungba
booty	bootnlo	borrow	borraiwa
booze	boose	borscht	borasikho
boozer	boosesi	borstal	borasujo
booze-up	boose pake	bort	booseyo
bop1	boopn	boryl	boorailo
bop2	boopn	borzoi	booraisin
bora	booran	boscage	bosikogn
boracic	booranko	bosh	bosue
borage	boorangun	bosk	bosia
boraginaceous	boorangansuwa	bosket	bosiate
borate	booraiyo	bosom	bosinmi
borax	booraisi	boss1	bosin
borazon	booraisin	boss2	bosin
bordeaux	bodelesi	bossy	bosinse

WORD (x)	EQUIVALENT (y)	WORD (x)	EQUIVALENT (y)
boston	bosinle	bound4	bounjn
bosun	bosun	boundary	bounjnrai
bot	boote	bounder	bounjnra
bota	boota	boundless	bounjnlabo
botanize	bootehunse	bounteous	bountosi
botany	bootehun	bounty	bountn
botch	bootesi	bouquet	bounkunto
bote	botn	boubon	bounbale
both	boosi	bourgeois	boungansi
bother	boosira	bourgeoisie	boungansia
botheration	boosiraiyoon	boum	bounran
bottle	boottnron	bournvita	bounranwiti
bottle bank	bohakn boottnron	bourse	bounsan
bottleneck	hunko boottnron	bout	bounta
bottom	boottnmo	boutique	bountakun
bottom line	lehun boottnmo	bouzouki	bounsunki
botulism	boottnjemosi	bovine	bownhun
bouchee	bounkhn	bowl	bowo
boucle	bounkuo	bow2	bowo
boudoir	bounderai	bow3	bowo
bouffant	bounfetn	bowel	bowolo
bougainvillaea	bounginyownjjn	bowen	bowose
bough	boungha	bower	bowosi
bought	boungbe	bowie	bowoni
bouillon	bounjnrasi	bowl1	bowojn
boulder	bounjojn	bowl2	bowojn
boule	bounjo	bowler1	bowojnra
boulevard	bounjowegba	bowler2	bowojnra
bounce	bounso	bowline	bowojnhun
bouncer	bounsosi	bowling	bowojngnni
bouncing	bounsognni	bowman	bowomoye
bound1	bounjn	box1	bosi
bound2	bounjn	box2	bosi
bound3	bounjn	box3	bosi

WORD (x)	EQUIVALENT (y)	WORD (x)	EQUIVALENT (y)
boxer	bosirai	bracken	bankoin
boy	boyn	bracket	bankoto
boycott	boynkiti	brackish	bankosu
boyle	boynjn	bract	bankyo
boyo	boyi	bracteate	bankyoto
bozo	bosin	bracteole	bankyojoin
bra	bon	brad	banda
bra	bansi	bradawl	bandawojo
brabanco griffon	banbonkin ganfole	brady	bandain
brabanconne	banbonkini	bradycardia	bandainkogbasi
brabant	banbote	brae	banni
brabble	banboron	brag	banga
braccate	bankoyo	braga	bangan
brace	banso	braganca	bangbainko
bracelet	bansotn	braggadocio	bangadeka
bracer	bansosi	braggart	bangate
bracero	bansora	bragget	bangato
brach	bankho	bragi	bangi
brachial	bankhojo	brahma	banhemo
brachiate	bankhoyo	brahman	banhemoye
brachio	bankhoi	brahmin	banhemuye
brachiotomy	bankhoitemo	braid	bandi
brachiopod	bankhoipindie	brail	bansa
brachiosaurus	bankhoisanrasi	braille	bangbn
brachistochrone	bankhosetokhnroin	brain	bansi
brachium	bankhoma	brainy	bansise
brachy	bankhoin	brain pan	bansi panu
brachycephalic	bankhoinknphejoko	brainstem	bansisutoma
brackycranic	bankhoinkarainko	braise	bansun
brachydromic	bankhoingbnmuko	braser	bansunsi
brachylogy	bankhoinlogbon	braize	bansan
banchypterous	bankhoinpitnransi	brake1	bankn
brachyuran	bankhoinrain	brake2	bankn
bracing	bansognni	brake3	bankn

WORD (x)	EQUIVALENT (y)	WORD (x)	EQUIVALENT (y)
brake4	bankn	brattice	banttnsi
brake lining	lehungnni bankn	brattle	banttnron
bramante	banmoyato	braun	banun
bramble	banmbejo	bravado	banwainde
brambling	banmbejognni	brave	banwain
bran	bain	bravery	banwainrai
branch	bainkho	bravissimo	banwasoomo
branchia	bainkhoi	bravo	banwain
branchiate	bainkhoiyo	bravura	banwarain
branchio	bainkhoin	braw	banwe
branchiopod	bainkhoinpindie	brawl	banwejo
brancusi	bainkunsi	brawn	banwn
brand	bainjo	brawny	banwnni
brandel	bainjolo	braxy	bansai
brandenburg	bainjoinbuganbrander	bray	banyan
brandes	bainjosi	brayer	banyansi
brandied	bainjode	braza	bansa
brandish	bainjosun	braze	bansu
brandy	bainjose	brazen	bansuai
branle	bainji	brazier1	bansura
branny	bainyn	brazier2	bansura
brant	bainte	brazil	bansujo
braque	bankun	breach	besikho
brash	bansia	bread	besigba
brasier	bansosi	breadline	besigbalehun
brass	bansoo	breadth	besigbaade
brassage	bansoogun	break	besikn
brassard	bansoogba	breakable	besiknron
brasserie	bansooran	breakage	besikngun
brassica	bansooko	breaker	besiknsi
brassicaceous	bansookosuwa	breakneck	besiknhunko
brassiere	bansoorai	bream	besimo
brassy	bansoose	breast	besinmi
brat	bantn	breast	besinmi

WORD (x)	EQUIVALENT (y)	WORD (x)	EQUIVALENT (y)
breath	besise	brewery	besiwerai
breathalyzer	besisejnsnra	brewster	besiweseto
breathe	besise	brian	banye
breather	besisesi	briar1	banre
breathless	besiselabo	briar2	banre
breccias	besikikan	briaraeus	banreinsi
brecham	besikhom	briard	bangba
breck	besiki	bribe	banbe
bred	besijo	bribery	banberai
brede	besiwe	brick	banko
bree	besin	brickbat	bankobota
breech	besikhoi	brickle	bankojn
breeches	besikhoisi	brickler	bankojnra
breed	besinjo	bricole	bankuo
breeder	besinjosi	bridal	banjinjo
breeding	besinjognni	bride	banjin
breeze1	besisun	bridegroom	banjingonmo
breeze2	besisun	bridesmaid	banjinmaajo
breezy	besisunse	bridge1	bangbon
bregma	besigan	bridge2	bangbon
breloque	besilokun	bridgehead	bangbonhegbi
bren	besini	bridget	bangbonte
brent	besinyo	bridle	banjinron
brest	besnsi	bridoon	banjinun
brethren	besisinrin	brie	bansu
breton	besitin	brief	banfun
bretton	besittin	briefless	banfunlabo
breve	besiwin	brier1	banso
brevet	besiwnti	brier2	banso
breviary	besiwnrai	brieux	banwasi
brevity	besiwntn	brig	bangi
brew	besiwe	brig1	bangi
brew	besiwe	brig2	bangi
brewage	besiwegun	brigade	bangidie

WORD (x)	EQUIVALENT (y)	WORD (x)	EQUIVALENT (y)
brigadier	bangidiesi	brisling	bansiagnni
brigalow	bangijowa	bristle	bansiaron
brigand	banganjo	Bristol	bansiajin
brigandine	banganjoin	bristow	bansiawa
brigantine	bangantin	brit	bante
briggs	bangbisi	britain	bantelu
bright	banghon	britannia	bantehun
brighten	banghons	britannic	bantehunko
brill1	banjnra	briticism	bantekimosi
brill2	banjnra	british	bantesua
brilliance	banjnransi	briton	bantesi
brilliant	banjrante	britany	bantese
brilliantine	banjnrantin	brittle	banteron
brim	banmu	britzska	bantesaka
brimmer	banmmuran	broach	bonkho
brimstone	banmusetole	broad	bongbaa
brin	ban	broaden	bongbaasi
brinded	bandide	broca	bonko
brindled	banduode	brocade	bonkodie
brine	banmi	brocatelle	bonkotojjjn
bring	bangn	broccoli	bonkile
bringing	bangngnni	broch	bonkhi
brink	bankn	broche	bonkhn
brinkmanship	banknmoyesunpn	brochette	bonkhntin
briny	banse	brochure	bonkhunran
briquette	bankuntin	brock	bonko
brio	banni	brocken	bonkoin
brioche	bannikhn	brocket	bonkoto
briolette	bannijntin	Brockton	bonkotin
briquet	bankuntn	brod	bonde
brisance	banhansi	broddle	bondeduo
brisbane	banbaun	broderie anglaise	anigbilese bonderan
brisk	bansia	brogan	bongin
brisket	bansia	broggerite	bonginraiyo

WORD (x)	EQUIVALENT (y)	WORD (x)	EQUIVALENT (y)
brogue1	bongbiso	brood	boinjn
brogue2	bongbiso	broody	boinjnse
broil	bonse	brook1	boinkun
broil	bonse	brook2	boinkun
broiler	bonsesi	broom	boinmo
broke	bonkan	broose	boinse
broken	bonkanse	brose	boson
broker	bonkansi	bros	bonsi
brokerage	bonkansigun	broth	bonsi
brolly	bonjnrase	brothel	bonsijo
broma	bonmu	brother	bonsira
bromal	bonmulu	brought	bonungbe
bromate	bonmuyo	brouhaha	bonunhanhan
bromatology	bonmuyologbon	brow	bonwo
bromatotherapy	bonmuyosinranpo	brown	bonwon
brome	bonma	brownie	bonwonni
bromeliaceous	bonmajansuwa	browning	bonwongnni
bromide	bonmiji	browse	bonwose
brominate	bonminiyo	brucellosis	buruknjjnso
bromine	bonmini	brucine	burukihun
bromism	bonmimosi	brucite	burukiyo
bromo	bonmo	bruges	burugnsi
bronchial	bonunkhijo	bruin	buruni
bronchitis	bonunkhiso	bruise	burusun
bronchocele	bonunkhiknjin	bruiser	burusunsi
bronchotomy	bonunkhitemo	bruit	buruto
bronchus	bonunkhiwa	brumaier	burumurai
bronco	bonunka	brumal	burumujn
bronk	bonunkn	brumby	burumbe
brontide	bonuntijin	brume	burumi
brontosaurus	bonuntosanra	brummagem	burummagio
bronx	bounsn	brummie	burumini
bronze	bounse	Brummell	burumujjn
brooch	boinkhi	brunch	burukhn

WORD (x)	EQUIVALENT (y)	WORD (x)	EQUIVALENT (y)
brunet	burute	buccaneer	bukoknsi
brunette	burutn	buccinator	bukiheyoran
brunhild	buruhnhijon	bucentaur	bukntirai
brunnehilde	buruhnhijn	bucephalus	buknphejosi
Bruno	buruko	bucer	buknra
brunswick	burusuwoki	Buchenwald	bukhinwejon
brunt	buruta	buck1	buki
brush	burusue	buck2	buki
brusk	burusia	buck3	buki
brusquerie	burukunran	buckeen	bukin
brussel	burusoolo	bucket	bukite
brutal	burutnjo	buckle	bukiron
brutal	burutnjo	buckler	bukironsi
brutality	burutnjotb	bucko	bukiko
brutalize	burutnjose	buckra	bukiran
brute	burutn	buckram	bukiranmu
brutify	burutnfe	buckshee	bukisua
brutish	burutnsi	bucolic	bukijinko
bruxism	burusemosi	bud	bugbn
bryology	boroinlogbon	budapest	bugbnpnsia
bryony	boroinse	buddha	bugboin
bryozoan	boroinsinhn	buddhism	bugboinmosi
brython	boraisnle	buddle	bugbnduo
bt	biti	buddleia	bugbnduosi
bub	bube	buddy	bugbnse
bubal	bubejo	budge	bugban
bubaline	bubejohun	budgerigar	bugbanraigan
bubble	buberon	budget	bugbate
bubler	buberonsi	budgie	bugbanse
bubbly	buberoin	buff	bufan
bubo	bubo	buffalo	bufanlo
bubonic	bubounko	buffer1	bufiro
bubonocele	bubounknjn	buffer2	bufiro
buccal	bukojo	buffert1	bufite

WORD (x)	EQUIVALENT (y)	WORD (x)	EQUIVALENT (y)
buffet2	bufite	bulldozer	bujnradesesi
buffle	bufijn	bulla	bujnran
buffo	bufo	bullarium	bujnranraima
buffoon	bufoosi	bullate	bujnrayo
bufo	bufo	bullers	bujnrasesi
buffy	bufanni	bullet	bujnranta
bug	bugi	bulletin	bujnrante
bugger	bugira	bullion	bujnransi
buggery	bugirai	bullish	bujnransia
buggy	bugini	bully1	bujnrase
bugle	bugiron	bully2	bujnrase
bugloss	bugonsoo	bully3	bujnrase
buhach	buhakho	bulwark	bujnwako
build	bukojn	bum1	bumo
builder	bukojnsi	bum2	bumo
building	bukojngnni	bumble	bumberon
built	bukojia	bumming	bummognni
buirdly	burailo	bump	bumpn
buka	buka	bumpiness	bumpnnisi
bulb	bujnbe	bumper	bumpnsi
bulbar	bujnberan	bumpkin	bumpnkin
bulbiferous	bujnbefirosi	bumptious	bumpntisi
bulbil	bujnbelo	bumpy	bumpnse
bulbous	bujnbesi	bun	buha
bulbul	bujnbujn	buna	buhe
bulgar	bujngan	bunch	bukhun
bulge	bujngn	bunco	bukin
bulimia	bujnma	buncombe	bukinmbo
bulk	bujnko	bund	budi
bulky	bujnkon	bunderat	budiranyo
bull1	bujnra	bundle	buduo
bull2	bujnra	bung	bugan
bull3	bujnra	bungalow	buganlewa
bulldoze	bujnradese	bungee	buganse

WORD (x)	EQUIVALENT (y)	WORD (x)	EQUIVALENT (y)
bungle	buganron	burg	bugan
bunguran	buganrain	burgage	bugangun
bunlon	bujnsi	burgas	bugansi
bunion	buhasi	burgee	buganse
bunk1	bukn	burgeon	bugansi
bunk2	bukn	burger	buganran
bunk3	bukn	burgess	bugansin
bunker	buknra	burgh	bugbe
bunkum	buknkuo	burgher	bugbesi
bunny	buhnyn	burglar	bugbejnra
Bunsen burner	busesi busunsi	burglarize	bugbejnrase
Bunt	butan	burglary	bugbejnrai
buntal	butanjo	burgle	bugbejn
bunting1	butangnni	burgo	bugbo
bunting2	butangnni	burgonet	bugbotin
bunya	buyan	burgoo	bugboo
buoy	bonunwa	burgos	bugbose
buoyage	bonungun	burgoyne	bugboin
buoyancy	bonunsn	burgrave	buganwo
buoyant	bonuntn	burgundy	bugundain
buprestid	bupesisujo	burial	busnjo
bur	bugi	burier	busnsi
buran	bugan	burin	busate
burble	bugibe	burka	bukwe
burbot	bugibeyo	burke	bukwo
burden	bugbisi	burl	busujo
burden	bugbisi	burlap	busujnpan
burdock	bugbiko	burlesque	busujnkunsi
bureau	burain	burley	busujoin
bureaucracy	burainkansn	burly	busujo
bureaucrat	burainkanta	burma	busumo
bureau de change	burain de khojngba	burmarigold	busumuraigondon
buret	buraitn	burmese	busumose
burette	buraitin	burn1	busun

WORD (x)	EQUIVALENT (y)	WORD (x)	EQUIVALENT (y)
burn2	busun	bus	busa
burne	busuhun	bushar	busaboosn
burner	busunsi	busby	busabeya
burnet	busunte	busera	busaran
burnham	busunhan	bush1	buso
burning	busungnni	bush2	buso
burnish	busuase	bushed	busode
burnisher	busuasesi	bushel	busojo
burnley	busunroin	bushido	busode
burnoose	busunso	bushing	busognni
burne	busunsi	bushtit	busota
burnt	busuntn	bushveid	busowinjo
buroo	busuko	bushwhack	busowhakin
burp	busupn	bushwhacker	busowhakinra
burr	busai	bushy	bnsose
burred	busaide	business	busianisi
bureo	busaiko	busk	buseko
burrow	busawo	busk	buseko
burry	busasn	busker	busekosi
bursa	bussan	buskin	busekin
bursal	bussanjo	buskit	busekiti
bursar	bussansi	bus lane	busa letu
bursary	bussanrai	buss	busoo
burse	busse	bust1	busetn
burseraceous	busseraisuwa	bust2	busetn
bursiform	bussefon	bustard	busetngbaa
bursitis	bussanso	buster	busetnsi
burst	bussia	bustic	busetnko
burster	bussiasi	bustier	busetnra
burton	butin	bustle1	busetnron
buru	busu	bustle2	busetnron
burundi	busujo	busy	busia
bury	busnse	busy lizzie	busia lesunse
bury	busnse	busyness	busianisi

WORD (x)	EQUIVALENT (y)	WORD (x)	EQUIVALENT (y)
but	bute	butyrin	buterain
butadiene	butejini	busom	businmo
butane	butena	buy	bura
butanethiol	butenasinjin	buyer	burasi
butanoic	butenako	buzz	busu
butanol	butenajin	buzzard	busugba
butanone	butenahun	buzzer	bususi
butch	butekhn	by	beya
butcher	butekhnra	bye1	beyin
butchery	butekhnrai	bye2	beyin
bute	bute	byelorussian	beyinlorussiahn
butene	butehun	bygone	beyalohun
butane dioic	butena jinko	by-law	beya leofin
buteo	buteko	byline	beyalehun
butler	butejnra	bypass	beyapanso
butlery	butejnrai	byplay	beyapansie
buttl	butta	byre	beyara
butt2	butta	byrl	beyarajo
butt3	butta	byrnes	beyaransi
butt4	butta	byroad	beyaronjn
butte	buttn	byron	beyaron
butter	buttnra	byssinosis	beyasooknso
butterfly	buttnrafolo	byssus	beyasoowa
butterine	buttnrain	bystander	beyasetndansi
buttery1	buttnra	byte	beyatn
butter2	buttnra	byzantine	beyasehuntin
buttock	buttoki	ca	ko
button	buttnsi	cab	kobn
buttress	buttnso	cabal	kobnjo
butty	buttnse	cabala	kobnjn
butyl	butelo	cabalist	kobnjnsi
butylene	butelohun	cabalistic	kobnjnsuko
butyraceous	buteraisuwa	caballada	kobnjjnde
butyrate	buteraiyo	caballero	kobnjjnro

WORD (x)	EQUIVALENT (y)	WORD (x)	EQUIVALENT (y)
caballine	kobnjjnhun	cachectic	kokhnkyoko
cabana	kobnhe	cachet	kokhnti
cabane	kobnhun	cachexia	kokhnsia
cabaret	koboosnto	cachinnate	kokhinhunyo
cabas	kobnsi	cacholong	kokhilogun
cabasset	cobnsoote	cachou	kokhiun
cabbage	kobngun	cachucha	cokhuhe
cabell	kobejjn	cacique	kokikun
caber	kobesn	caciqueism	kokikunmosi
cabeza	kobesa	cackle	kokiron
cabby	kobeo	caco	koki
caber	kobesn	cacodemon	kokijinmoha
cabin	kobnsi	cacodyl	kokidilo
cabin-boy	boyn-kobnsi	cacoepy	kokinpo
cabinet	kobnte	cacoethes	kokinsesi
cabinet-maker	maknsi-kobnte	cacoethes	loquendi
cable	koberon	cacogenics	kokiginkosi
cablegram	koberonganmo	cacography	kokiganphe
cabman	kobnmaye	cacology	kokilogbon
cabochon	kobookhoin	cacomistle	kokimusitnron
cabojubi	koboojobn	cacophonous	kokiphohunsi
caboodle	kobooduo	cacophony	kokiphohun
caboose	koboose	cactaceous	kokitisuwa
cabotage	kobntogun	cactus	kokitisi
cabresta	kobnsisua	cacumen	kokunmosi
cabrilla	kobanjjn	cacuminal	kokunmohejo
cabriole	kobanjoin	cacus	kokunsi
cabriolet	kobanjointn	cad	kojn
cacanny	kokohnyn	cad	kogbi
cacao	kokoin	cadaster	kogbiseto
cacciatore	kokoontoran	cadaver	kogbiwnra
caceres	koknransi	cadaverine	kogbiwnrahun
cachalot	kokhijotin	cadaverous	kogbiwnrasi
cache	kokhn	caddie	kogbisi

WORD (x)	EQUIVALENT (y)	WORD (x)	EQUIVALENT (y)
caddis	kogbiso	caernarvon	koinseranwin
caddo	kogbin	caesalphiniaceous	koinsejophinisuwa
caddy1	kogbise	caesar	koinsiran
caddy2	kogbise	caesarean	koinsirain
cade	kode	caesarism	koinsiranmosi
cadelle	kodejjn	caesium	koinsooma
cadence	kodesi	caesura	koinsuran
cadency	kodesn	caetano	kointekn
cadent	kodeyo	café	kofin
cadenza	kodesa	cafeteria	kofinteran
cadet	kodiete	cafetiere	kofinterai
cadette	kodietin	caffeine	kofiehun
cadge	kogbgn	caffelatte	koffinletin
cadgy	kogbignse	caftan	kofitin
cadi	kogbe	cag	kogi
cadillac	kogbejnkn	cage	kogn
cadiz	kogbisi	cagey	kognse
cadmean	kogbimuhn	cagliari	kogiunrai
cadmium	kogbmuma	cagoule	kogonjn
cadmus	kogbimusi	cagoulard	kogonjngba
cadre	kogbiran	cahier	kohisi
caduceus	kogbiwesi	cahoots	kohintusi
caducity	kogbikitn	caiaphas	koiphnsn
caduceus	kogbikisi	caiman	koimoye
caecillius	koinkunsi	cain	koise
caecum	koinkuo	cainca	koikin
caelian	koinleyan	caine	koihun
caelum	koinlema	cainite	koiseto
caen	coini	cainozoic	koiknsinko
caenogenesis	koinkngnhunso	caique	koikun
caenozoic	koinknsinko	caira	koirin
caeoma	koinknma	caird	koirejn
caerimoniarius	koinsemeniransi	cairene	koiranni
caerleon	koinsejnle	cairn	koiran

WORD (x)	EQUIVALENT (y)	WORD (x)	EQUIVALENT (y)
cairngorm	koirangnsun	calaverite	kojowinraiyo
cairo	koiran	calayan	kojoyan
caisson	koisoon	calcaneum	kojokohunma
caithnessshire	koisnnisisurain	calcar	kojokora
caitiff	koitefe	calcarate	kojokoraiyo
caius	koiwa	calcareous	kojokoransi
cajeput	kojnpo	calcariferous	kojokoraifirosi
cajole	kojinre	calceate	kojoknyo
cajolery	kojinrerai	calceolaria	kojoknjinrain
cajon	kojnle	calceolate	kojoknjinyo
cajun	kojon	calces	kojoknsi
cajuput	kojopn	calchas	kojokhise
cake	koki	calci	kojoki
cal	kojo	calcic	kojokiki
calabash	kojoboo	calcicolous	kojokikijinsi
calabazilla	kojobosujjn	calcicosis	kojokikiso
calaboose	kojoboose	calciferol	kojokifirojin
calabrese	kojobesue	calciferous	kojokifirosi
caladium	kojojnma	calcification	kojokifikoyoon
calamanco	kojomoyeki	calcifugous	kojokifungbisi
calamander	kojomujnra	calcify	kojokife
calamary	kojomurai	calcimine	kojokimini
calambak	kojomubo	calcinatory	kojokintoran
calamine	kojomini	calcine	kojokin
calamint	kojomuhnyo	calciphilous	kojokipheransi
calamite	kojomuyo	calcipholous	kojokiphijinsi
calamitous	kojomutnsi	calcite	kojokiyo
calamity	kojomutn	calcitration	kojokitiraiyoon
calamondin	kojomodan	calcium	kojokima
calamus	kojomusi	calcography	kojokiganphe
calando	kojodinto	calcsinter	kojokisotnra
calandria	kojodinran	calspar	kojosaupan
calash	kojosun	calctuff	kojokiofan
calathus	kojosesi	calculable	kojoknlebe

WORD (x)	EQUIVALENT (y)	WORD (x)	EQUIVALENT (y)
calculate	kojoknleyo	caliginous	kojnginsi
calculated	kojoknleyode	caligula	kojngbila
calculating	kojoknleyognni	calamanco	kojnmoyeki
calculation	kojoknleyoon	calipee	kojnpnse
calculator	kojoknleyoran	caliper	kojnpnra
calculus	kojoknlesi	caliph	kojnphan
caldarium	kojojnraima	caliphate	kojnphantn
caldecott	kojojinkitti	caliphate	kojnphantn
caldera	kojojinra	calisaya	kojnsanya
caldron	kojojnron	calisthenics	kojnsunwnkosi
caledonia	kojngbile	calix	kojnsi
caledonian	kojngbilehn	calk	kojnki
calefacient	kojnfanseto	call	kepe
calefactory	kojnfanknyorai	call	kojnra
calendal	kojoinjnjo	callant	kojnrae
calendar	kojoinjnran	caller	kojnrasi
calender	kojoinjnra	call-girl	kojnra girin
calends	kojoinjnsi	calligraphy	kojnranganphe
calendula	kojoinjnle	calling	kojnragnni
calenture	kojointoran	calliope	kojnrapon
calesa	kojnsa	callipygian	kojnrapogan
calescence	kojnsisun	calliper	kojnrapnra
calf1	kojnfe	callisthenics	kojnrasunwnkosi
calf2	kojnfe	callisto	kojnranseto
calgary	kojngirai	callistratus	kojnransetnretosi
calboun	kojnboun	callosity	kojnrasetn
caliber	kojnbesi	callous	kojnrasi
calibrate	kojnbeyo	callow	kojnrawe
calibre	kojnberan	callus	kojnrase
caliche	kojnkhn	calm	kojomu
calicle	kojnkuo	calmative	kojomuyowin
calico	kojnki	calmy	kojomuse
california	kojnfonhan	calomel	kojoinmulo
californium	kojnfonhunma	calomondiu	kojoinmojnle

WORD (x)	EQUIVALENT (y)	WORD (x)	EQUIVALENT (y)
caloocan	kojokoon	calyptra	kojinpntiran
caloosahatchee	kojosoohekhunyo	calyptrate	kojinpntiraito
calorescence	kojoraiseknsi	calyx	kojinsi
caloric	kojoraiko	cam	komu
caloricity	kojoraikitn	camail	komulo
calorie	kojorain	camaraderie	komurajinran
calorific	kojoraifiko	camarilla	komuraijjo
calorification	kojoraifikoyoon	camas	momusu
calorifics	kojoraifikosi	camber	kombesn
clorimeter	kojoraimuto	cambist	kombesi
calotte	kojointin	cambium	kombama
caloyer	kojoinyesi	cambodia	komboojn
calpac	kojopanka	camboose	komboose
calque	kojokun	cambria	komberai
caltrop	kojotnrapn	cambrian	komberain
calumet	kojomuto	cambric	komberaika
calumniate	kojomuhayo	cambridge blue	komberaigbon
calumny	kojomuha	cmbyses	kombesosi
calutron	kojotnran	camcorder	komkigbasi
calvados	kojowadesi	came	komwa
calvaria	kojowarain	camel	komujn
calvary	kojowarai	cameleer	komujnrai
calve	kojowin	camellia	komujnrain
calves	kojowinsi	camelopard	momujnpogbaa
calvin	kojowini	camelopardalis	komujnpogbaajosi
calvinism	kojowinimosi	camelot	komujnto
calvinistic	kojowinisiko	camembert	kommubete
calvities	kojowitisi	camenae	komihin
calx	kojosi	cameo	komukn
calyces	kojinknsi	camera	komura
calycine	kojinkin	cameral	komurajo
calycle	kojinkuo	cameralistics	komurajosekosi
calydon	kojindeha	camera lucida	komura lusoojn
calypso	kojinpnsoo	cameraman	komuramoye

WORD (x)	EQUIVALENT (y)	WORD (x)	EQUIVALENT (y)
camerlingo	komurailetosi	campsite	kompnsoote
cameronian	komurainyan	campus	kompnro
cameroon	komurainsi	campylotropal	kompelotnrapnjo
camilla	komujjn	camry	komurai
camion	komule	can1	koki
camisa	komusan	can2	koki
camisado	komusande	cana	koki
camise	komuse	canaan	kokinhun
camisole	komusoole	canaanite	kokinhunte
camlet	komutn	canada	kokingba
camomile	kommojn	canadian	kokingbahn
cammorra	kommurra	canadianism	kokingbahnmosi
camou	komini	canaille	kokijnran
camouflage	kominifangun	canal	kokijo
camp1	kompn	canalage	kokijogun
camp2	kompn	canaler	kokijosi
campaign	kompangn	canaletto	kokijotto
campaigner	kompangnsi	caniculate	kokijokunyo
campanero	kompanhunro	caniculus	kokijokunsi
campania	kompansi	canalize	kokijose
campanile	kompanjn	cananga	kokingan
campanology	kompanknlogbon	canapé	kokinpan
campanula	kompanjn	canard	kokigbaa
campanulate	kompanjnyo	canary	kokirai
campeche	kompnkhn	canasta	kokiseta
camper	kompnsi	canaster	kokiseto
campestral	kompnsetnrajo	canberra	kokibesse
camphene	komphini	cancan	koknhn
camphogen	komphigen	cancel	koknse
camphol	komphijin	canceler	koknsesi
camphor	komphirun	cancell	koknjjn
camphorate	komphirunyo	cancellate	koknjjnyo
campion	kompnsi	cancellation	koknjjnyoon
campo	kompin	cancelli	koknjjnra

WORD (x)	EQUIVALENT (y)	WORD (x)	EQUIVALENT (y)
cancer	koknra	cankered	kokirunde
cancerate	koknrayo	cankerous	kokirunwa
cancerous	koknrasi	cankery	kokirunsi
canceroid	koknrajo	canna	kokina
candela	kokijojn	cannabin	kokinabue
candelabrum	kokijojnberan	cannabinol	kokinabuejin
candent	kokijotn	cannabis	kokinabu
candescence	kokijosesunsi	cannae	kokinani
candia	kokijosi	canned	kokide
candid	kokijo	cannel	kokilo
candida	kokijon	cannelon	kokilosi
candidate	kokijoyo	cannelloni	koklloun
candidacy	kokijosn	cannellure	kokillorai
candide	kokijodan	canner	kokisi
candido	kokijode	cannery	kokirai
candied	kokijodun	cannes	kokisn
candle	kokiduo	cannibal	kokibuje
candor	kokijoran	cannibalism	kokibujemosi
candour	kokijorai	cannibalize	kokibujese
candy	kokidun	cannikin	kokikin
cane	kokiu	cannon	kokinina
canella	kokiujnra	cannonade	kokininajin
canephorus	kokiuphiransi	cannoneer	kokininasi
canescence	kokiuseknsi	cannon-ball	robo kokinina
canescent	kohuseknti	cannonry	kokininarai
canes	kokiusi	cannot	kokiniti
caney	kokise	cannula	kokinujn
cangue	kokigan	cannulate	kokinujnyo
canicular	kokikuoran	canny	kokise
canine	kokihe	canoe	kokisa
canions	kokoonsi	canon	kokisn
canis	kokiso	canonical	kokisnkojo
canister	kokiseto	canonist	kokisnsi
canker	kokirun	canonize	kokisnse

WORD (x)	EQUIVALENT (y)	WORD (x)	EQUIVALENT (y)
canon law	leewo kokisn	cantor	kokitiran
canonry	kokisnrai	cantrip	kokitaraipo
canoodle	kokijoduo	cantus	kokitisi
canopus	kokiponsi	cantrip	kokitaraipo
canopy	kokipon	cantus	kokitisi
canorous	kokiransi	canty	kokitise
canossa	kokisoo	canuck	kokiki
canso	kokiso	canvas	kokiwoso
canst	kokisi	canvass	kokiwanso
cant1	kokiti	cany	kokisn
cant2	kokiti	canyon	kokisnsi
cantab	kokitiba	canzone	kokisinhun
cantabile	kokitibajn	canzonet	kokisinhunte
cantabridgian	kokitibangbahn	cap	kopn
cantala	kokitojn	capability	kopnberontn
cantaloup	kokitolopo	capable	kopnbe
cantankerous	kokitoknrasi	capacious	kopnkisi
cantata	kokitoto	capacitance	kopnkitisi
cantate	kokitoyo	capacitor	kopnkitiran
cantatrice	kokitotnraisi	capcity	kopnkitn
canteen	kokitoon	capapie	kopnpon
canter	kokitn	caparison	kopnraisn
canterbury	kokitnburai	cape1	kopin
cantharides	kokisanraijinsi	cape2	kopin
cantharidin	kokisanraijie	caperl	kopinjn
cantharis	kokisanraisi	capelin	kopinjan
canthus	kokisanwa	capella	kopinjjn
canticle	kokitekuo	caper	kopnra
cantilever	kokitejnwinsi	capercaillie	kopnrakojnran
cantina	kokitehe	Capernaum	kopinrainma
cantle	kokitoron	capias	kopnso
canto	kokito	capillaceous	kopnjnransuwa
canton	kokiti	capillarity	kopnjnranraitn
cantonment	kokitimutto	capillary	kopnjnranrai

WORD (x)	EQUIVALENT (y)	WORD (x)	EQUIVALENT (y)
capital	kopntejo	capriole	kopnraijoin
capital gain	ginte kopntejo	capripants	kopnraipata
capitalism	kopntejomosi	caprock	kopnraki
capitalist	kopntejosi	caproic acid	akijo kopnraki
capitalize	kopntejose	capsaicin	kopnsankin
capitates	kopnteyo	capsian	kopnsoohn
capitation	kopnteyoon	capsicum	kopnsookuo
capitol	kopntejin	capsize	kopnsoose
capitular	kopntira	capstan	kopnsihun
capitulary	kopntirarai	capsulate	kopnsnleyo
capitulate	kopntirayo	capsule	kopnsnle
capitulum	kopntima	capsulize	kopnsnlese
capo	kopnni	capt	kopnte
capon	kopnyo	captain	kopntelu
caporal	kopnranjo	caption	kopntesi
caporetto	kopnrantto	captious	kopntisi
capot	kopntin	captivate	kopntiwinyo
capote	kopnto	captive	kopntiwin
cappadocia	kopandekia	captivity	kopntiwintn
capparidaceous	kopanraidesuwa	captor	kopntira
capper	kopnsi	capture	kopntiran
cappuccino	kopnpoki	capuchen	kopnkhn
capreolate	kopnrejinyo	capuchin	kopnkhoin
capri	kopnrai	caput	kopntin
capric	kopnrai	capybara	kopoborai
capriccio	kopnraikio	car	kosi
capriccioso	kopnraikioso	carabao	kosebaun
caprice	kopnraisn	carabid	kosebajo
capricious	kopnraisnsi	carabin	kosebn
capricom	kopnriki	carabineer	kosebnsi
capricornus	kopnraikiransi	carabiniere	kosebnran
caprification	kopnraifikoyoon	caracal	kosekojo
caprifig	kopnraifigi	caracalla	kosekojjn
caprine	kopnrain	caracara	kosekorain

WORD (x)	EQUIVALENT (y)	WORD (x)	EQUIVALENT (y)
carack	koseki	carbonari	kosiburai
caracole	kosekijoin	carbonate	kosibuyo
caractacus	kosekitikunse	carbonic	kosibuko
caracul	kosekuo	carbonize	kosibuse
carafe	kosefin	carbonizer	kosibusesi
carageen	kosegini	carbonyl	kosibulo
caramel	kosemujo	carbora	kosibura
caramelize	kosemujose	carborundum	kosiburaunjoma
carangold	kosengondon	carboxylase	kosibusinlose
carapace	kosepase	carboy	kosiboyn
carat	kosete	carbuncle	kosibukuo
caravan	kosewain	carburet	kosiburantn
caravansary	kosewainsirai	carburettor	kosiburanttnra
caravel	kosewinlo	carburizer	kosiburaisesi
caraway	kosewelo	carbylamine	kosibujnmini
carb	kosiboo	carcajou	kosikojin
carbamate	kosiboomuyo	carcanet	kosikointo
carbamic	kosiboomuko	carcass	kosikuso
carbamide	kosiboomujin	carcassonne	kosikusohun
carbazoic	kosiboosinko	carcel	kosiknjo
carbene	kosibini	carcharias	kosikhoraise
carbide	kosibajo	carcinogen	kosikikngin
carbine	kosibanun	carcinoma	kosikiknmo
carbineer	kosibanunsi	card1	kogba
carbinol	kosibanunjin	card2	kogba
carbo	kosiboo	cardamom	kogbamumo
carbohydrate	kosiboohogbnyo	caardboard	kogbabugba
carbolate	kosiboojinyo	cardcase	kogbakoso
carbolated	kosiboojinyode	cardenas	kogbasan
carboliec	kosiboojinko	cardia	kogbain
carbolize	kosiboojinse	cardiac	kogbainki
carbon	kosibu	cardialgia	kogbainjogan
carbonaceous	kosibusuwa	cardigan	kogbaingan
carbonado	kosibude	cardinal	kogbainle

WORD (x)	EQUIVALENT (y)	WORD (x)	EQUIVALENT (y)
cardinalate	kogbainleyo	carious	kosiasi
cardinality	kogbainletn	cark	kosiki
cardio	kogbako	carl	kosile
cardiogram	kogbakoganmo	carline	kosilehun
cardiograph	kogbakoganpha	carliing	kosilegnni
cardioid	kogbakojo	carmagnole	kosimognjoin
cardiology	kogbakologbon	carmelite	kosimuleyo
cardiotomy	kogbakotemo	carminative	kosiminiyowin
carditis	kogbakoso	carmine	kosimini
cardoon	kogbaun	carnage	kosngun
cardphone	kogbaphohun	carnal	kosnle
care	kosn	carnallite	kosnleyo
careen	kosnsi	carnassial	kosnsoojo
careenage	kosnsigun	carnation	kosnyoon
career	kosnrai	carnauba	kosnbaun
careerist	kosnraisi	carnegie	kosngini
careless	kosnlabo	carnellan	kosnjosi
caress	kosnsoo	carnet	kosnte
caret	kosnto	carnify	kosnfe
cargador	kosigndera	carnival	kosnwajo
cargo	kosilo	carnivore	kosnwnrun
carib	kosiabe	carnivore	kosnwnrun
caribbean	kosiabehn	camivore	kosnwnrun
caribou	kosiabonun	camivorous	kosnwnrunsi
caricature	kosiakntoran	camosity	kosnsetn
caries	kosiasi	camot	kosihnte
carillon	kosiajjoin	camotite	kosihnteyo
carina	kosiahe	carob	kosiboo
carinate	kosiaheyo	caroche	kosikhn
caring	kosngnni	carol	kosijin
carinthia	kosiatosi	carolean	kosijoin
carioca	kosiaka	carolina	kosijinhe
cariogenic	kosiaginko	caroline	kosijinhun
cariole	kosiajn	carolingian	kosijingnhn

WORD (x)	EQUIVALENT (y)	WORD (x)	EQUIVALENT (y)
carolus	kosijinwa	carrion	kosirain
carom	mosimo	carromata	kosiramuta
carotene	kositinun	carrot	kosirate
carotid	kositinjo	carrotin	kosiratie
carotte	kosittn	carroty	kosiratin
carousal	kosnlesejo	carry	kosirai
carouse	kosnlese	carse	kosise
carousel	kosnleseje	carsick	kosisokoi
carp1	kopan	cart	kosite
carp2	kopan	cartage	kositegba
carpal	kopanjo	carte	kositn
carpale	kopanle	cartel	kositnjo
carpediem	kopanjomu	carter	kositnra
carpel	kopanle	cartesian	kositnsihn
capellate	kopanlleyo	cart-horse	kosite-hiso
carpenter	kopantosi	carthusian	kositunsehn
carpentry	kopantorai	cartilage	kositnrangn
carpet	kopati	cartilaginous	kositnranginisi
carpeting	kopatignni	cartogram	kositoganmo
carphology	kophanlogbon	cartography	kositoganphe
carpo	kopon	cartomancy	kositomoyesn
carpogenous	koponginsi	carton	kositele
carpogonium	kopongonma	cartoon	kositelo
carpology	koponlogbon	cartophily	kositophiroin
carpophagous	koponphijewa	cartouche	kositokhn
carpophore	koponphiran	cartridge	kositeraigbon
carport	kosipinta	cartwheel	kositewhinlo
carpus	kopansi	cart-wright	kosite wangbe
carracel	kosisnsujo	cartulary	kositelorai
carrageen	kosisngini	carub	kosibn
carrel	kosirajo	caruca	kosunka
carrel	kosirajjo	carucage	kosikogn
carriage	kosiraigun	carucate	kosikayo
carrier	kosiraisi	caruncle	kosikuo

WORD (x)	EQUIVALENT (y)	WORD (x)	EQUIVALENT (y)
carvacrol	kosiwakuojn	casino	kosookn
carve	kosiwn	cask	kosia
carvel	kosiwnlo	casket	kosiato
carven	kosiwnni	casper	kosipnra
carver	kosiwnra	casque	kosikun
carvery	kosiwnrai	casquette	kosikuntin
carving	kosiwngnni	cassaba	kosoobe
caryatid	kosiyatojo	cassareep	kosooranpn
caryophyllaceous	kosiyinphewesuwa	cassata	kosooto
caryopsis	kosiyinpnso	cassation	kosooyoon
casaba	kosaboo	cassava	kosoowa
Casanova	kosaknwa	casse	kosoo
cascabel	kosabujo	casserole	kosoosejoin
cascade	kosajin	cassette	kosootin
cascara	kosara	cassia	kosooe
cascarilla	kosarajjn	cassimere	kosoomura
case1	koso	cassiopela	kosoonpnjn
case2	koso	cassis	kosooso
casein	kososi	cassiterite	kosootnraiyo
case-law	kosoleofin	cassock	kosooki
casemate	mosomote	cassone	kosooahun
casement	kosomutto	cassoulet	kosooleyo
casera	kosoran	cassowary	kosoowarai
casework	kosowinsise	cast	kosoto
cash	koson	castalia	kosotojan
cash and carry	koson ati kosirai	castanet	kosotote
cash-book	booko koson	caste	kosotn
cashew	kosonwin	casteism	kosotnmosi
cashier1	kosonrai	castellan	kosotnlloye
cashier2	kosonrai	castellated	kosotolloyode
cashmere	kosonmura	castelry	kosotnlorai
cashpoint	kosonpintoni	caster	kosotosi
cash register	koson regiseto	castigate	kosotogiyo
casin	kosoo	castile	kosotojn

WORD (x)	EQUIVALENT (y)	WORD (x)	EQUIVALENT (y)
casting	kosotognni	catalyze	kotajinse
castle	kosotoron	catamaran	kotamurain
castlery	kosotorai	catamenia	kotamuhan
castor	kosotnra	catamite	kotamuyo
castrate	kosotnreyo	catamnesis	kotaminiso
castrato	kosotnreto	catamount	kotamonunte
castro	kosotnra	catamountain	kotamonuntelu
casual	kosuejo	cataphonic	kotaphohunko
casualty	kosuejotn	cataphonics	kotaphohunkosi
casuist	kosusi	cataphoresis	kotaphiranso
casuistry	kosusirai	cataphyll	kotaphewe
cat	koti	cataplasia	kotapansia
cata-	kota	cataplasm	kotapanson
catabasis	kotaboso	cataplexy	kotapojnse
catabolism	kotaboojinmosi	catapult	kotapnjia
catabolite	kotaboojinyo	cataract	kotirankyo
catachresis	kotakhoso	catarrh	kotirha
cataclinal	kotakihunjo	catastasis	kotasetnso
cataclysm	kotakinsun	catastrophe	kotasetnraphe
catacomb	kotakimbe	catastrophism	kotasetnraphemosi
catadromous	kotagbnmosi	catatonia	kotatohan
catafalque	kotafanjokun	catch	kotikhi
catalan	kotajnhn	catching	kotikhignni
catalase	kotajnse	catchline	kotikhilehun
catalepsy	kotajnpnsn	catchment	kotikhimutto
catalina	kotajnhe	catchy	kotikhise
catalo	kotalo	cate	kotn
catalog	kotalogn	catechesis	kotnkhnso
catalogue	kotalogbiso	catechetic	kotnkhnko
catalpa	kotajnpan	catechin	kotnkhie
catalyse	kotajinse	catechism	kognkhamosi
catalysis	kotajinso	catechist	kotnkhasi
catalyst	kotajinsi	catechize	kotnkhase
catalytic	kotajinko	catechol	kotnkhijin

103

WORD (x)	EQUIVALENT (y)	WORD (x)	EQUIVALENT (y)
catecholamine	kotnchijinmini	catnap	kotipan
catechumen	kotnkhunmuye	catnip	kotipin
categorematic	kotngonranmuko	catoptrics	kotipotnrakosi
categorical	kotngonraikojo	cattell	kottijjo
categorize	kotngonraise	cattery	kottirai
category	kotngonrai	cattle	kottiron
catena	kotnhe	catty	kottn
catenary	kotnherai	caucsian	koinkosehn
catenate	kotnheyo	caucasoid	koinkosejo
catenoid	kotnhejo	caucus	koinkoso
catenulate	kotnheleyo	cauda	koindi
cater	kotnra	caudad	koindijn
caterer	kotnrasi	caudal	koindijo
caterpillar	kotnrapojnran	caudata	koindito
caterwaul	kotnrawejn	caudate	koindiyo
cathari	kosinrain	caudex	koindisn
catharsis	kosinraso	caudle	koinduo
cathartic	kosinrako	caught	koingbe
cathay	kosinse	cauk	koinki
cathedral	kosingbanle	caul	koinjo
cathepsin	kosinpnsin	cauldron	koinjngboin
cather	kosinro	caulescent	koinjnsiknto
catherine	kosinroin	caulicle	koinjnkuo
catheter	kosintnra	cauline	koinjnhun
catheterize	kosintnraise	caulis	koinjnsi
cathexia	kosinsia	caulk	koinjnko
cathode	kosinjoin	caulome	koinloma
catholic	kosinjinke	caup	koinpn
catholicism	kosinjinkemosi	causal	koinsejn
catholicize	kosinjinkese	causalgia	koinsejngan
catholicon	kosinjinkin	causality	koinsejotn
catholyte	kosinjoinyo	causation	koinseyoon
cation	kotiun	causative	koinseyowin
catkin	kotikin	cause	koinse

WORD (x)	EQUIVALENT (y)	WORD (x)	EQUIVALENT (y)
causerie	koinseran	cavy	kowoin
causey	koinsesi	caw	kowi
caustic	koinsuko	caxton	kosnyole
causticity	koinsukitn	cay	koyin
cauterant	kointnrate	cayenne	koyinhun
cauterize	kointnraise	cayman	koyinmaye
cautery	kointnrai	cayuga	koyungi
caution	koinyoon	cayuse	koyunse
cautionary	koinyoonrai	ce	kn/se/si/so
cautious	koinyowa	cease	knsise
cavalcade	ckowajokojin	ceaseless	knsiselabo
caval	kowajn	ceboid	knboojo
cavalier	kowajnsi	cebu	knbu
cavalry	kowajnrai	cechy	knkho
cavan	kowain	cecil	knkun
cavatina	kowatie	cecilia	knkunsi
cave	kowo	cecropia	knknrapan
caveat	kowotn	cecum	knkuo
caveator	kowotnran	cedar	knjnra
cavein	kowonu	cedam	knjnran
caveman	kowomoye	cede	knjin
cavendish	kowodainsi	cedilla	knjinjan
cavern	kowosn	cedric	knjnrako
cavernicolous	kowosnkijnsi	cedula	knjinjoin
cavemous	kowosnsi	ceiba	knban
cavesson	kowosoole	ceil	knle
cavetto	kowotito	ceilidh	knlejnha
caviar	kowora	ceiling	knlegnni
caviar	koworain	ceilometer	knlemuto
cavil	kowora	ceja	knja
caving	kowognni	celadon	knjojnsi
cavitation	kowoteyoon	celandine	knjojoin
cavity	kowotn	celation	knjoyoon
cavort	kownta	cele	knjn

WORD (x)	EQUIVALENT (y)	WORD (x)	EQUIVALENT (y)
celebes	knjnbesi	celt	knjia
celebrant	knjnbetn	celtic	knjiako
celebrate	knjnbeyo	celticism	knjiakomosi
celebration	knjnbeyoon	celtist	knjiasi
celebrity	knjnbetn	cement	knmutto
celeriac	knjnraiko	cementation	knmuttoyoon
celerity	knjnraitn	cementite	knmuttoyo
celery	knjnrai	cemetery	knmutoraicementum
celsta	knjnsito	cenacle	knkuo
celeste	knjnsuto	cenci	knki
celestial	knjnsutojo	cene	knsa
celestine	knjnsutin	cenesthesia	knsasunwnsia
celestite	knjnsutinyo	ceno	knkn
celia	knjnsi	cenobite	knknbayo
celiac	knjnko	cenobium	knknboma
celebacy	knjnbesn	cenogenesis	knkngnhunso
celibate	knjnbeyo	cenogonal	knkngunjo
cell	knjjn	cenotaph	knkntephe
cella	knjjna	canote	knknto
cellar	knjjnra	cenozoic	knknsinko
cellarage	knjjnragun	cense	knkisun
cellarer	knjjnrasi	censer	knkisesi
cellaret	knjjnrato	censor	knkiseran
cello	knjjoin	censorious	knkiseraisi
cellophane	knjoinphehun	censurable	knkisuranbe
cellphone	knjjnphohun	censure	knkisuran
cellular	knjjnleran	census	knkisusi
cellulite	knjjnleyo	cent	knti
celluloid	knjjnlejo	cental	kntijo
cellulose	knjjnlese	centare	kntoran
celo	knjnto	centare	kntoran
celotex	knjntosn	centaur	kntorai
celsius	knjosunsi	centaurus	kntoraisi
celsus	knjosunsi	centaury	kntorai

WORD (x)	EQUIVALENT (y)	WORD (x)	EQUIVALENT (y)
centavo	kntown	centro	kntira
centenarian	kntihunraihn	centrobaric	kntiraboosnko
centenary	kntihunrai	centroid	kntirajo
centennial	kntihunjo	centromere	kntiranmuran
centennium	kntihunma	centrosphere	kntirasephirai
center	kntisi	centrosome	kntirasoomo
centerboard	bugbakntisi	centrum	kntirama
centering	kntisignni	centum	kntima
centesimal	kntisoomujn	centumvir	kntimawi
centesimo	kntisoomo	centumvirate	kntimawiraiyo
centi-	knte	centuple	kntiporon
centigrade	kntegandie	centuplicate	kntiporonkoyo
centigram	knteganmo	centurial	kntiraijo
centiliter	kntelitn	centuried	kntiraide
centiliter	kntelitnran	centurion	kntirain
centillion	kntejnrasi	century	kntirai
centimanus	kntemuhnsi	ceori	knnirai
centime	kntemo	ceos	knnisi
centimeter	kntemuto	cephaeline	knphnjohun
centimo	kntema	cephalad	knphijnjo
centipede	kntepndie	cephalalgia	knphijnlegan
centner	knteran	cephalic	knphijnko
cento	kntiko	cephalin	knphijan
central	kntiraijo	cephalization	knphijnseyoon
centralism	kntiraijomosi	cephalo	knphijoin
centralize	kntiraijose	cephalocaudal	knphijoinkoindijo
centre	kntiran	cephalochordate	knphijoinkigbayo
centerboard	bugbakntiran	cephalometer	knphijoinmuto
centric	kntiraiko	cephalonia	knphijoinhan
centrifugal	kntiraifungbajo	cephalopod	knphijoinpindie
centrifuge	kntiraifungbi	cephalothorax	knphijoinsinrasi
centriole	kntiraijoin	cephalous	knphijoinsi
centripetal	kntiraipntijo	cephas	knphisi
centrist	kntiraisi	cepheid	knphinjo

WORD (x)	EQUIVALENT (y)	WORD (x)	EQUIVALENT (y)
cepheus	knphinsi	ceria	knrain
ceraceous	knrasuwa	ceric	knraiko
ceram	knramo	cerifirous	knrafirosi
ceramal	knramujn	cerigo	knrailo
ceramic	knramuko	ceriph	knraiphe
ceramics	knramukosi	cerise	knraise
cerargyrite	knraganraiyo	cerite	knraiyo
cerastes	knraseto	cerium	knraima
cerate	knrayo	cermet	knramuto
cerated	knrayode	cemrnuous	knrahunwa
cerato	knrato	cero	knraa
ceratodus	knratojnsi	cerography	knraaganphe
ceratoid	knratojo	ceroon	knraasi
Cerberus	knraburaisi	cerotic	knraako
cercaria	knrakosia	cerotype	knraatnpon
cercopithecoid	knrakiposinkijo	cerous	knraasi
cercus	knrakuo	certain	knratelu
cere	knran	certainly	knratelulo
cereal	knranjo	certainty	knratelutn
cerebellum	knranbejjnma	certes	knratesi
cerebral	knranbajo	certifiable	knratefebe
cerebrate	knranbayo	certificate	knratefekoyo
cerebration	knranbayoon	certified cheque	khnkun knratefede
cerebrain	knranbansi	certify	knratefe
cerebrospinal	knranbonsupohunjo	certiorari	knrateranrai
cerebrum	knranbanma	certitude	knratetujin
cerement	knranmuto	cerulean	knrjoin
ceremonial	knranmenijo	cerumen	knramuye
ceremonious	knranmenisi	ceruse	knrase
ceremony	knranmeni	cerussite	knrasooyo
cerenkov	knranknwn	cervantes	knrawaintosi
ceres	knransi	cervical	knrawokijo
ceresin	knransie	cervico	knrawoki
cereus	knranwa	cervicofacial	knrawokifansejo

WORD (x)	EQUIVALENT (y)	WORD (x)	EQUIVALENT (y)
cervin	knrawoni	chacome	khokimo
corvine	knrawohun	chad	khogbe
cervix	knrawosi	chaeta	khointe
cervoid	knrawojo	chaeto	khointo
cesar	knsiran	chaetodon	khointojain
cesarean	knsirain	chaetognath	khointognhesi
cesious	knsoowa	chaetopod	khointopindie
cesium	knsooma	chafe	khofi
cespitose	knsopntose	chafer	khofiro
cess	knsin	chaff	khofon
cessastion	knsinseyoon	chaffer	khofonsi
cession	knsinsi	chaffinch	khofansi
cessionary	k nsinsirai	chaffy	khofonlo
cesspit	knsinpo	chaft	khofia
cest	knsa	chagas	khogisun
cesta	knsato	chagres	khogira
cestode	knsatojin	chagrin	khogiran
cestus	knsatosi	chain	kholo
cetacea	kntekoi	chair	khoso
cetacean	kntecoin	chair-lift	khoso lefia
cetane	kntehun	chairman	khosomoye
ceteris paribus	kntiraisi panraibe	chairperson	khosopnrasin
cetology	kntologbon	chaise	khosun
cetus	kntisi	chaise longue	khosun logunso
Cevennes	knwinhnsi	chalaza	kholesun
ceuta	knunto	chalcedon	kholesndain
ceylon	knyojnsi	chalcedony	kholesndainse
ceyx	knyosi	chalcedonyx	kholesndainsesi
chabazite	khobooseyo	chalcid	kholesnjn
chablis	khobiunsi	chalco	kholeki
chabouk	khobounka	chalcocite	kholekisuyo
chace	khose	chalcography	kholekiganphe
cha-cha	kho kho	chalcolithic	kholekilesiko
chaco	khoki	chalder	kholejnra

WORD (x)	EQUIVALENT (y)	WORD (x)	EQUIVALENT (y)
chaldron	kholejnran	championship	khompnsisunpn
chalet	kholete	champlain	khompanto
chalice	kholesi	champlevé	khomporonwin
chalk	kholiki	chance	khokisi
chalkitis	kholikiso	chancel	khokisijn
challenge	khojnrangbe	chancellery	khokisijnrai
challis	khojnrase	chancellor	khokisijnran
chalumean	khojnmuhn	chancery	khokisirai
chalybean	khojoinbehun	chancify	khokisife
chalybeate	khojoinbeyo	chancre	khokiknran
cham	khomu	chancroid	khokiknrajo
chamade	khomujin	chancy	khokisn
chamber	khombo	chandelier	khokiduojnra
chamberlain	khomboleto	chandelle	khokiduojn
chambermaid	khombomaajo	chandler	khokiduosi
chambray	khombain	chandlery	khokiduorai
chameleon	khomujosi	change	khokign
chamfer	khomfesi	changeable	khokignbe
chamfrain	khomfanlu	changeling	khokigngnni
chaminade	khominijin	change-over	ownra khokign
chamois	khomuso	channel	khohun
chammy	khommun	channelise	khohunse
chamomile	khomomujn	channing	khohungnni
chamonix	khomenisi	chant	khote
champ1	khompn	chantage	khotegun
champ2	khompn	chanter	khotesi
champacol	khompankijin	chanterelle	khoteranjjn
champagne	khompangini	chanteuse	khotebo
champaign	khompangun	chantey	khotese
champak	khompanki	chanticleer	khotekuosi
chapers	khompnrasi	chantry	khoterai
champerty	khompnratn	chaos	khosia
champignon	khompngnsi	chaotic	khosiaka
champion	khompnsi	chap1	khope

WORD (x)	EQUIVALENT (y)	WORD (x)	EQUIVALENT (y)
chap2	khope	chariot	khoraitin
chaparajos	khoperanjosi	charioteer	khoraitinsi
chaparral	khoperrajo	charisma	khoraisin
chapatti	khopanye	charitable	khoraitobe
chape	khope	charity	khoraito
chapel	khopejo	charivari	khoraiwerai
chaperon	khoperon	chark	khoranki
chaplain	khopanto	charkha	khoranka
chaplet	khopetn	charlady	khoranledie
chapman	khopemaye	charlatan	khoranletue
chaps	khopesi	charles	khoranjosi
chappie	khopon	charleston	khoranjositin
chapter	khopnti	charlotte	khoranjotin
chaqueta	khokunta	charm	khoron
char1	khoran	charming	khorongnni
char2	khoran	charm	khorau
char3	khoran	charnel	khoraulo
char4	khoran	charon	khoransi
charabanc	khoranbekn	charpoy	khoranpon
characin	khorankin	charqued	khorankuode
character	khorankitn	charqui	khorankuo
characteristic	khorankitnko	charry	khoranse
characterize	khorankitnse	chart	khorantn
charactery	khorankitnrai	charta	khoranto
charactonymy	khorankitoma	charter	khorantnra
charade	khoranjo	charterage	khorantnragun
charbon	khoranboun	chartered	khorantnrade
charcoal	khorankijo	chartism	khorantnmosi
chard	khoranjn	chartist	khorantnsi
chardin	khoranjnsi	chartography	khorantoganphe
charge	khorangn	chartreuse	khorantnrinse
charger	khorangnsi	charwoman	khoranwinmoye
charily	khorailo	chary	khoransi
chariness	khorainisi	charybdis	khoransiijosi

WORD (x)	EQUIVALENT (y)	WORD (x)	EQUIVALENT (y)
chase1	khoonsi	chauvinism	khowonmosi
chase2	khoonsi	chauvinist	khowonsi
chaser	khoonsise	cheap	khnpan
chasm	khoonsin	cheapen	khnpansi
chasse	khosoo	cheat	khnte
chasseur	khosoorai	check	khnkn
chassis	khosooso	checked	khnknde
chaste	khositn	checker1	khnknsi
chasten	khositnsi	checker2	khnknsi
chastise	khositnse	check-in	khnkn-nu
chastity	khositn	checkmate	khnknmote
chasuble	khosube	checkout	khnknnita
chat	khoti	checkpoint	khnknpintoni
chateau	khotiele	check-up	khnkn pake
chattelain	khotielesi	cheddar	khnjjnra
chatelaine	khotieleni	cheddite	khnjjnyo
chatline	khotielehun	cheechako	khnkhoinko
chatel	khotijo	cheek	khnkun
chater	khotisi	cheeky	khnkunse
chatillon	khotijnrain	cheep	khnpe
chatoyant	khotonte	cheer	khnro
chattahoochee	khotehoonchn	cheerio	khnroin
Chattanooga	khottingoon	cheerless	khnrolabor
chattel	khottilo	cheery	khnrose
chatter	khottirai	cheese	khnsun
chatty	khottise	cheesed	khnsunde
chaucer	khoknra	cheesy	khnsunse
chaucerian	khoknrain	cheetah	khntusi
chaucey	khoknse	chef	khnfn
chauffer	khofiran	cheka	khnka
chauffeur	khofirai	chela	khnle
chaulmoogra	khojnmoogan	chelate	khnleyo
chausses	khosoosi	chelicera	khnleknra
chautanqua	khotaku	chelicerate	khnleknrayo

WORD (x)	EQUIVALENT (y)	WORD (x)	EQUIVALENT (y)
chellean	khnlejnhun	cherubini	khnrabnsi
chelonia	khnlohun	chervil	khnraworo
chelonian	khnlohunsi	cherronets	khnrrantesi
chelp	khnlope	cheshire	khnsurain
chelsea	khnlosa	chess	khnso
chemical	khnmukojo	chessboard	bugbakhnso
chemin	khnmun	chessel	khnsojo
chemise	khnmuse	chessman	khnsomaye
chemisette	khnmusetin	chest	khnta
chemist	khnmusi	chests	khntasi
chemistry	khnmusorain	chester	khntayunti
chemoceptor	khnmoknpitairan	chesty	khntase
chemoprophylaxis	khnmoponpheleso	cheval de fries	khnwajn di fanse
chemosmosis	khnmosunmiso	chevalet	khnwajnte
chemostat	khnmosetnti	chevalier	khnwajnsi
chemotaxis	khnmotesanso	chevals	khnwajnsi
chemotherapeutant	khnmosinranpntn	chevelure	khnwinjnran
chemotherapy	khnmosinranpo	cheviot	khnwuto
chemotropism	khnmotnrapnmosi	chevon	khnwusi
chemurgy	khnmorailo	chevron	khnwuron
chenille	khnhnjjn	chhevrotain	khnwurontelu
chenille	khnhnjjn	chevy	khnwuse
cheope	khnnipn	chew	khnwe
cheque	khnkun	chewy	khnwese
chequer	khnkunsi	Cheyenne	khnynhun
cherio	khnrain	chez	khnse
cherish	khnrasua	chi	khi
chemobyl	khnmoboolo	chia	khini
chemozem	khnmosinmo	chian	khihn
cherokee	khnraikoon	chianti	khihnyo
cheroot	khnrooyo	chiapas	khinipnsi
cherry	khnrorai	chiaroscuro	khinirosekiron
chert	khnrayo	chiasma	khisemo
cherub	khnrabn	chiasmatypy	khisemotnpo

WORD (x)	EQUIVALENT (y)	WORD (x)	EQUIVALENT (y)
chiasmus	khisemosi	chignon	khignni
chiastolite	khisetoleyo	chigoe	khigie
chibcha	khibukho	chihuahua	khihonhon
chibouk	khibounko	chilblain	khilobaun
chic	khiko	child	khijnn
chicago	khikogon	childe	khijnn
chicalote	khikolote	childerman	khijnnramoye
chicane	khikoin	childhood	khijnnbinjo
chicanery	khikoinrai	childing	khijnngnni
chicano	khikokn	childish	khijnnse
chichi	khi khi	children	khijnnrin
chick	khikn	child's play	khijnn si pansie
chickabiddy	khiknbadie	chile	khijn
chickadee	khikndudu	chili	khijn
chickaree	khiknrun	chiliad	khijnjo
chickasaw	khiknsawo	chiliarch	khijnkhnra
chicken	khiknni	chiliasm	khijnsemo
chickester	khikntosi	chill	khijnra
chick-pea	khikn pon	chilli	khijnran
chicle	khikuo	chillon	khijnrain
chicory	khikirai	chilly	khijnrase
chicote	khikite	chilo	khile
chide	khijon	chilopod	khilepindie
chided	khijonde	chilopodology	khilepindielogbon
chief	khifin	chiltem	khijntnran
chiefly	khifinlo	chime	khimu
chieftain	khifintelu	chimera	khimuran
chiel	khilo	chimere	khimurain
chiffchaff	khifokhofo	chimerical	khimuraikojo
chiffon	khifon	chimla	khimojn
chiffonire	khifonran	chimney	khimunyo
chifforobe	khifirobe	chimp	khimpn
chigetai	khignyon	chimpanzee	khimpnnisu
chigger	khignsi	chin	khini

WORD (x)	EQUIVALENT (y)	WORD (x)	EQUIVALENT (y)
china	khihe	chiromancy	khiromayesn
chinaman	khihemaye	chiron	khiroin
chinch	khikhn	chiropody	khiropindiesi
chinchilla	khinkhijjn	chiropractic	khiropankyoko
chine	khihun	chiropter	khiropnti
chinese	khinase	chirp	khiropn
chink	khinko	chirr	khirore
chink1	khinko	chipy	khiropo
chink2	khinko	chirrup	khirorepo
chinless	khihnlabo	chisel	khisajn
chino	khihn	chiseled	khisajnde
chinoiserie	khihnsunran	chit1	khito
chinook	khinhnko	chit2	khito
chinos	khiniso	chit	khite
chinquepin	khikunpoha	chital	khitojo
chintz	khinisue	chitarrone	khitorrain
chintzy	khinisuesi	chit chat	khito khoti
chip	khipn	chitin	khitose
chipboard	bugbakhipn	chiton	khitosi
chipmunk	khipnmuki	chitral	khitnrajo
chipolata	khipnjnte	chitter	khittorai
chippendale	khipnjinron	chitterling	khittoraignni
chipper	khipnra	chivalrous	khiwajnrasi
chippewa	khipnwa	chivalry	khiwajnrai
chippy	khipnni	chivaree	khiwarai
chirality	khirajotn	chive	khiwin
chirico	khiraiki	chivy	khiwoin
chirimen	khiraimuye	chivvy	khiwowo
chirk	khirako	chlamydate	kholemundayo
chirm	khiramo	chlamydeous	kholemundesi
chiro	khiro	chlamydospore	kholemundeseporai
chirognomy	khiroginimo	chlamys	kholemunsi
chirognostic	khiroginisuko	chloanthite	khonsinyo
chirograph	khiroganpha	chlodwig	khonjnwogbi

WORD (x)	EQUIVALENT (y)	WORD (x)	EQUIVALENT (y)
chloe	khonre	chocaholic	khoknjinko
chlor	khonra	chock	khoki
chloracetophenon	khonrakitiphini	chocolate	khokileyo
chloracne	khonrakohun	choctaw	khoknwe
chloral	khonrajo	choice	khisisa
chloramine	khonramini	choir	khorai
chlorambucil	khonrambukun	choirboy	khoraiboyn
chloramphenicol	khonramphinkijin	choiseul	khoisejn
chloranthy	khonrainso	choke	khokn
chlorate	khonraiyo	choker	khoknra
chlordane	khonranjain	choking	khokngnni
chlorella	khonranjjn	choky	khoknse
chlorenchyma	khonrainkhoma	cholagog	khojngonko
chloric	khonraiko	cholangiotomy	khojntogiotemo
chloride	khonraijin	chole	khojn
chlorinate	khonrainyo	cholecyste	khojnsnsi
chlorine	khonrain	choledochoplasty	khojndakhipanswitn
chlorinity	khonraintn	choler	khojnra
chlorite	khonraiyo	cholera	khojnrau
chloro	khonrin	choleric	khojnrakn
chloroform	khonrinfoon	cholesterol	khojnsetora
chlorohydrin	khonrinhogbain	choli	khole
chloromycetin	khonrinmunkitie	choline	kholehun
chlorophane	khonrinphehun	cholinergic	kholehunganko
chlorophyll	khonrinphewe	cholla	kholle
chloroplast	khonrinpansia	chondrify	khogboinfe
chloroprene	khonrinpesihun	chondriosome	khogboinsoomo
chloroquine	khonrinkunhun	chondrite	khogboinyo
chlorosis	khonrinso	chondro	khogboin
chlorous	khonrinsi	chondroid	khogboinjo
chlorpicrin	khonrapokan	chondroma	khogboinmo
chlorpromazine	khonraponmusin	chondrostei	khogbointnsi
chlortetracycline	khonratnrasnkiun	chondrotomy	khogbointemo
choancocyte	khohunsnyo	chondrule	khogboinrun

WORD (x)	EQUIVALENT (y)	WORD (x)	EQUIVALENT (y)
chomp	khompn	chorizon	khoraisnle
choose	khinisa	chorography	khoroinganphe
choosy	khisisase	choroid	khoroinjo
chop1	khoje	choroscript	khoroinsekoraipn
chop2	khoje	chortle	khorate
chop3	khoje	chorus	khoraisi
cho pin	khojosi	chorzow	khorawnsi
chopine	khojoin	chose	khinsa
chop logic	khoje logbiko	chose ju gee	khinsa jogun
chopper	khojesi	chosen	khinsase
choppy	khojepo	chota	khinto
chopusey	khojesuese	choux	khonsi
choragus	khoragunsi	chough	khonfo
choral	khorajo	chouse	khosue
chorale	khorajn	chow	khiwa
chorasmia	khoramosi	chowder	khiwajnra
chord1	khorajo	chow mein	khiwamute
chord2	khorajo	chowry	khiwarai
chordata	khorajote	chrematicity	khiranmutekitn
chordate	khorajotn	chrematistic	khiranmutesuko
chore	khoran	chresard	khiransegba
chorea	khorain	chrestomathy	khiransetomuhn
choreograph	khorangnpha	chris	khiraise
choreography	khoranganphe	chrism	khiraison
choreology	khoranlogbon	chrismatory	khiraisontorai
choreomania	khoranmayisi	chrisom	khiraisnmi
choriamb	khoraimbo	christ	khiraisi
choric	khoraikn	christen	khiraisin
chorise	khoraise	christendom	khiraisindemo
chorion	khoraisi	christian	khiraisihn
choripetalous	khoraipntijosi	Christian era	oore khiraisihn
chorist	khoraise	christiana	khiraisihun
chorister	khoraiseto	christianity	khiraisihntn
chorizo	khoraisin	christmas	khiraisimusn

117

WORD (x)	EQUIVALENT (y)	WORD (x)	EQUIVALENT (y)
christology	khiraisilogbon	chronogram	khironkoganmo
chroma	khironmu	chronograph	khironkoganpha
chromate	khironmuyo	chronological	khironkologbikojo
chromatic	khironmuko	chronology	khironkologbon
chromaticity	khironmukitn	chronometer	khironkomuto
chromatics	khironmukosi	chronometry	khironkomutorai
chromatid	khironmujo	chrys	khoraisi
chromatin	khironmutie	chrysalid	khoraisanjojn
chromatism	khironmumosi	chrysalis	khoraisanjosi
chromato	khironmuto	chrysaniline	khoraisanlehun
chromatogram	khironmutoganmo	chrysanthemum	khoraisantehemo
chromatography	khironmutoganphe	chrysarobin	khoraisanrobin
chromatology	khironmutologbon	chryseis	khoraiseso
chromatolysis	khironmutojinso	chrysene	khoraisehun
chromatophore	khironmutophiran	chryso	khoraisoo
chrome	khironma	chrysoberyl	khoraisoobelo
chromic	khironmako	chrysolite	khoraisooleyo
chrominance	khironmahunsi	chrysoprase	khoraisoopanse
chromite	khironmayo	chrysotile	khoraisootijn
chromium	khironmuma	chthonian	khosinhehn
chromo	khironmo	chub	khunbe
chromogen	khironmogin	chubasco	khunbekise
chromogenesis	khironmoginiso	chubb	khunbo
chromogenic	khironmoginko	chubby	khunbobe
chromolithography	khironmolesiganphe	chuck1	khunki
chromomere	khironmomure	chuch2	khunki
chromophore	khironmophiran	chuckle	khunkiron
chromophotograph	khironmophotinganph	chucky	khunkise
chromosome	khironmosoomo	chudder	khunjnra
chromotype	khironmotnpon	chufa	khunfan
chronaxy	khironsian	chuff	khunfun
chronic	khironko	chuffed	khunfunde
chronicle	khironkojn	chuffy	khunfun
chrono	khironko	chug	khungbi

WORD (x)	EQUIVALENT (y)	WORD (x)	EQUIVALENT (y)
chukker	khunknra	ciborium	kiboraima
chum	khunmo	cicada	kikoji
chummy	khunmmo	cicala	kikojn
chump	khunmpn	cicatrice	kikotnraiso
chunder	khunjnsi	cicatricule	kikotnraikuo
chunk	khunkn	cicatrix	kikotnraisi
chkunker	khunkasi	cicatrize	kikotnraise
chunky	khunkan	cicely	kiknlo
chunnel	khunhun	cicero	kiknro
chunter	khuntosi	cicerone	kiknroin
chupatty	khunpanto	cichilid	kikhilejo
church	khunsin	cichoriaceous	kikhinraisuwa
churchgoer	khunsinlosi	cicisbeo	kikisoobe
churchy	khunsinse	-cide	keku
churl	khunsijo	cider	kijnra
churlish	khunsijose	cidevant	kijnwatn
chum	khunsun	cig	kigi
churr	khunssn	cigar	kigiran
chute1	khunyo	cigarette	kigirantin
chute2	khunyo	cigarillo	kigiraijoin
chutney	khunteyin	cilia	kijia
chuttle	khuntoron	ciliate	kijiayo
chutzpah	khunsopa	cilice	kijiasi
chvash	khunwesi	ciliolate	kijiatoleyo
chuzen ji	khunjnsun	cilium	kijiama
chyle	khojn	cimarron	kimurarin
chyme	khomi	cimex	kimusi
chymiferous	khomifirosi	cimmerian	kimmuraihn
chymosin	khomosie	cimon	kimeni
chymotrypsin	khomoteraipnsie	cinch	kikhn
chymotrypsinogen	khomoteraipnsiegin	cinchona	kikhnsia
ci	ki	cinchonidine	kikhnsiajoin
cibber	kibesn	cinchonine	kikhnsiahun
cibol	kibejin	cinchonism	kikhnsiamosi

WORD (x)	EQUIVALENT (y)	WORD (x)	EQUIVALENT (y)
cinchonize	kikhnsiase	cipher	kiphira
cincinnati	kikinhunye	cipolin	kipinjan
cincture	kikntorai	circa	kirako
cinder	kijnran	circadian	kirakojain
cinderella	kijnrainllo	circassia	kirakosooa
cine-	kisun	circassian	kirakosoohn
cineaste	kisunseto	circe	kirase
cinecamera	kisunkomura	circean	kirasehn
cine	kisun	circinate	kirakinto'
cinema	kisunmo	circinus	kirakinsi
cinematic	kisunmuko	circle	kirakuo
cinematography	kisunmutoganphe	circlet	kirakuote
cinematome	kisunmotemu	circuit	kirakuota
cinemaverite	kisunmownraito	circuitous	kirakuotasi
cineograph	kisunganpha	circuitry	kirakuotarai
cineole	kisunjoin	circuity	kirakuotn
cinerama	kisunranmo	circular	kirakuoran
cineraria	kisunranrai	circularize	kirakuoraise
cinerarium	kisunranraima	circulate	kirakuoyo
cinerator	kisunraiyosi	circulation	kirakuoyoon
cinereous	kisunransi	circulatory	kirakuoyorai
cinerin	kisunrie	circum-	kirakuo
cineritious	kisunraitesi	circumcise	kirakuoknse
cingulum	kingunlema	circumcision	kirakuoknsoon
cinnabar	kinheboosn	circumference	kirakuofirosi
cinnamic	kinhemuko	circumflex	kirakuofolosn
cinnamon	kinhemeni	circumfluent	kirakuofoluyo
cinnamyl	kinhemulo	circumfuse	kirakuofunse
cinquain	kinkunto	circumgyrate	kirakuoloraiyo
cinque	kinkun	circumlocution	kirakuolokunyoon
cinquecentist	kinkunkntisi	circummure	kirakuomuran
cinquecento	kinkunkinto	circumnutate	kirakuoyunteyo
cinquefoil	kinkunfonjio	circumpose	kirakuopose
cinquepace	kinkunpasecion	circumrotate	kirakuoroteyo

WORD (x)	EQUIVALENT (y)	WORD (x)	EQUIVALENT (y)
circumscissile	kirakuosekisoojn	citation	kitoyoon
circumspect	kirakuosepnto	cite	kito
circumstance	kirakuosetnsi	citheron	kitiserain
circumvallate	kirakuowajnrayo	cithara	kitiseran
circumvent	kirakuowinta	cither	kitisesi
circumvolution	kirakuownjnyoon	cithem	kitisemo
circus	kirakunsi	citify	kitife
cire	kiran	citizen	kitisin
cire per due	kiran pnra disi	citizenry	kitisinrai
cirencester	kirainknseto	citra	kitiran
cirque	kirakun	citral	kitiranjo
cirrate	kirraiyo	citrate	kitiraiyo
cirrhosis	kirrhanso	citreous	kitiransi
cirri	kirrai	citric	kitiraiko
cirriped	kirraipnjn	citrine	kitirain
cirro	kirro	citroen	kitiroin
cirrocumulus	kirrokuojnsi	citron	kitiron
cirrose	kirrose	citronella	kitiroinjjn
cirrostratus	kirrosuraintiwa	citronellal	kitrioinjjno
cirrous	kirrosi	citrus	kitiraisi
cirrus	kirronsi	city	kitn
cis	kise	civ	kiwn
cisalpine	kisejnpohun	civet	kiwnti
cisco	kiseki	civic	kiwako
cislunar	kiselujnran	civics	kiwakosi
cismontane	kisemenitelu	civil	kiworo
cissold	kisnsoojon	civilian	kiworohn
cist	kisn	civility	kiworotn
cistaceous	kisntosuwa	civilization	kiworoseyoon
cistercian	kisntnrahn	civilize	kiworose
cistem	kisntnran	civism	kiwomosi
cistron	kisntnron	civvy	kiwowo
cistus	kisntosi	civvies	kiwowosi
citadel	kitogbile	claas	kanse

WORD (x)	EQUIVALENT (y)	WORD (x)	EQUIVALENT (y)
claber	kanbesn	clapped out	kanpade nita
clack	kanko	clapper	kanpasi
clactonian	kankyoleyan	clapperboard	bugbakanpasi
clad	kangba	claque	kankun
cladding	kangbagnni	clara	kanran
cladoceran	kangbaknrain	clarabella	kanranbejjn
cladode	kangbade	clarain	kanranto
cladophyll	kangbabphewe	clare	kanrai
claim	kanlemo	clarence	kanraisi
claimant	kanlemotn	clarendon	kanraijnle
clairvoyance	kanraiwinisi	claret	kanraitn
clam	kanma	clarify	kanraife
clamant	kanmatn	clarionet	kanraifon
clamatorial	kanmateraijo	clarino	kanraiho
clambake	kanmbokn	clarion	kanraiso
clamber	kanmbesi	clarissa	kanraisoo
clammy	kanmmse	clarity	kanraito
clamor	manmaran	clark	kanrake
clamour	kanmarai	claro	kanron
clamp1	kanmpo	clarty	kanratn
clamp2	kanmpo	clary	kanrai
clamp down	kanmpo juan	clase	kanse
clamper	kanmposi	clash	kansia
clan	kanbi/iyekan	clasp	kansupo
clandestine	kanjinsuhun	class	kansoo
clang	kanke	classic	kansooko
clanger	kankesi	classical	kansookojo
clangor	kankeran	classicalism	kansookojomosi
clangour	kankerai	classicality	kansookojotn
clank	kanko	classicism	kansookomosi
clannish	kanhun	classicist	kansookosi
clansman	kanmoye	classics	kansookosi
clap1	kanpa	classification	kansoofikoyoon
clap2	kanpa	classified	kansoofide

WORD (x)	EQUIVALENT (y)	WORD (x)	EQUIVALENT (y)
classify	kansoofe	cleaner	kojnmosi
classis	kansooso	cleanly1	kojnmolo
classless	kansoolabo	cleanly2	kojnmolo
classmate	kansoomate	cleanse	kohnmose
classroom	kansooroomo	clear	kojnra
classy	kansoose	clearance	kojnrasi
clastic	kansuko	cleat	kojnte
clathrate	kansureyo	cleavage	kojnwinigun
clatter	kanttosi	cleave1	kojnwini
claude	kanwnjin	cleave2	kojnwini
claudel	kanwnjinjo	cleaver	kojnwinisi
claudius	kanwnjnsi	cleavers	kojnwinise
clause	kanwnse	cleck	kojnki
claustrophobia	kanwnsetnraphobua	cleed	kojnjo
classless	kansoolabo	cleek	kojnkn
classmate	kansoomate	clef	kojnfa
classroom	kansooroomo	cleft1	kojnfia
classy	kansoose	cleft2	kojnfia
clastic	kansuko	cleisto	kojnseto
clathrate	kansureyo	cleistogamous	kojnsetogimosi
clatter	kanttosi	clematis	kojnmuso
claude	kanwnjin	clement	kojnmuto
claudel	kanwnjinjo	clemency	kojnmusn
claudius	kanwnjnsi	clementine	konjnmutin
clause	kanwnse	clench	kojnkhn
claustrophobia	kanwnsetnraphobua	cleobulus	kojnbujn
clavichord	kanwokhiranjo	cleome	kojnmoin
clavicle	kanwokuo	cleomenes	kojnmoinhun
clavicom	kanwokisn	cleon	kojnsi
clavier	kanwosi	cleopatra	kojnpanrain
clavius	kanwose	clepe	kojnpe
claw	kanwo	clepsydra	kojnpnsogban
clay	kanyin	cleptomania	kojipntimayisi
clean	kojnmo	clerestory	kojnransetorai

WORD (x)	EQUIVALENT (y)	WORD (x)	EQUIVALENT (y)
clergy	kojnsin	clincher	kiukhisi
clergyman	kojnsinmoye	cline	kihun
cleric	kojnraise	cling	kiugan
clerical	kojnraisejo	clinic	kiunko
clericalism	kojnraisejomosi	clinical	kiunkojo
clericals	kojnraisejosi	clinician	kiunkohn
clerid	kojnraijo	clink1	kiunke
clerihew	kojnraihe	clink2	kiunke
clerisy	kojnraiso	clinker	kiunkesi
clerk	kojnrai	clinker	kiunkesi
clever	kojnwa	clino	kiuhun
cleves	kojnwnsi	clinometer	kiuhunmuto
clevis	kojnwaso	clinostat	kiuhunsetnti
clew	kojnwe	clinquant	kiunkunyo
clian	kiunhn	clinton	kiunto
cliché	kiunkn	clitonia	kuntosi
click	kiunko	clio	kiunko
clicker	kiunkosi	cliometric	kiunkomutoraikosi
client	kiuntan	clip1	kiunpa
clientele	kiuntanjo	clip2	kiunpa
cliff	kiunfn	clipboard	bugbakiunpa
cliffy	kiunfnse	clipper	kiunpasi
climacteric	kiumokntaku	clipple	kunpajn
climagram	kiumoganmo	clipping	kiunpagnni
climate	kiumota	clique	kiunkun
climato	kiumotin	cliquish	kiunkunso
climatology	kiumotinlogbon	clisere	kiunsura
climax	kiumolu	clishmaclaver	kiunsomukanwnsi
climb	kiumbe	clistase	kiunsetosi
climber	kiumbesi	clisthenes	kiunsusinhun
clime	kiumo	clitellum	kiuntojjnma
clinandrium	kiunhngbanma	clithrophobia	kiunsnraphobua
clinanthium	kiunhnsinma	clitic	kiunko
clinch	kiukhi	clitoris	kiunranso

WORD (x)	EQUIVALENT (y)	WORD (x)	EQUIVALENT (y)
clive	kiunwn	clothes-line	lehn-konsonsi
cloaca	konkoin	clothier	konsonrai
cloak	kokoin	clothing	konsongnni
cloakroom	kokoinroomo	cloud	kongbun
clobber1	konbosi	cloudy	kongbunsi
clobber2	konbosi	clouet	kontio
cloche	konkhn	clough	kongha
clock	konko	clour	konrai
clockwise	konkowogbon	clout	konta
clod	konjo	clouterly	kontasilo
cloddish	konjosi	clove1	konwin
clodpate	konjopnyo	clove2	konwin
clog	kongbi	clove3	konwin
cloisonné	konsoleyo	cloven	konwnni
cloister	konsoto	cloven hoof	hinfo kownni
cloistered	konsotode	clover	konwnsi
cloistress	konsotobo	clovis	konwaso
cloistral	konsotorijo	clown	known
clomb	konmbe	cloy	konyn
clomp	konmpn	club	koluba
clone	konhun	clubby	kolubasi
clonus	konhunsi	clubbable	kolubaron
clonk	konke	clubland	ledainkoluba
close1	konsu	cluck	koluki
close2	konsu	clue	koluse
closet	konsutn	clueless	koluselabo
close-up	konsu pake	clump	kolumpn
clostridium	konsutaraijoma	clumsy	kolumsia
closure	konsurai	clung	kolugan
cloot	kontie	clunk	kolukn
clot	konsa	cluny	koluyn
cloth	konsso	clupeid	kolupnjn
clothe	konson	clupeoid	kolupnjo
clothes	konsonsi	cluster	kolutosi

WORD (x)	EQUIVALENT (y)	WORD (x)	EQUIVALENT (y)
clutch1	koluki	coarctation	kirankioyoon
clutch2	koluki	coaptation	kipatoyoon
clutter	koluttnra	coarse	kisiase
clyde	kojinde	coarsen	kisiasi
clydesdale	kojindejnle	coast	kisunse
clype	kojinpn	coastal	kisunsejo
clypeate	kojinpnyo	coaster	kisunsesi
clypus	kojinpnsi	coastguard	kisunsegungba
clyster	kojinseto	coastline	kisunselehun
co	ki	coat	kitn
coacervate	kiaknraweyo	coated	kitnde
coacervation	kiaknraweyoon	coatee	kitnse
coach	kikho	coati	kitnsi
coachload	kikhologbn	coating	kitngnni
coachman	kikhomoye	coat of arms	araimusi kitn
coaction	kiakntiyon	coat tail	kitn tele
coadjutant	kiadijote	coax	kiso
coadjutor	kiadijoteran	coaxer	kisosi
coadunate	kiadiheyo	coaxial	kisosijo
coagulant	kiaganlete	cob	kiboo
coagulase	kiaganlese	cobalt	kiboojia
coagulate	kiaganleyo	cobaltic	kiboojiako
coagulum	kiaganlema	cobaltite	kiboojiayo
coahulla	kiahunjjn	cobaltious	kiboojiasi
coak	kiaki	cobber	kiboosi
coal	kijo	cobble1	kibooron
coaler	kijosi	cobble2	kibooron
coalesce	kijosesi	cobbler	kibooronsi
coalition	kijoyoon	cobblers	kibooronse
coalman	kijomaye	cobbles	kibooronso
coalmine	kijomihun	cobelligerent	kibejjognranto
coaltar	kijotan	cobia	kibua
coaming	kimugnni	coble	kibejn
coarctate	kirankioyo	cobra	kibaun

WORD (x)	EQUIVALENT (y)	WORD (x)	EQUIVALENT (y)
cobweb	kiboowinbe	cocker	kikkoran
coca	kiko	cockerel	kikkoranjo
coca cola	kiko kile	cockiness	kikkonisi
cocaine	kikoin	cockish	kikkose
cocainism	kikoinmosi	cockle	kikkojn
cocainise	kikoinse	cockney	kikkoinse
cocarboxylase	kikosibosinlose	cockpit	kikkopon
cocarcinogen	kikosikikngin	cockroach	kikkoronkho
coccid	kikkijo	cocksure	kikkosurai
coccidioidomycosis	kikkijoinjomunkiso	cocktail	kikkotele
coccidiosis	kikkijoinso	cock-up	kikko pake
cocciferous	kikkifirosi	cocky	kikkose
coccoid	kikkijo	coco	kiki
coccolith	kikkilisi	cocoa	kikin
coccus	kikkuosi	coconut	kikiyunte
coccyx	kikkinsi	cocoon	kikoon
cochin	kikhini	cocotte	kikittn
cochineal	kikhihunjo	coction	kikntiyon
cocina	kikona	cod	kidi
cochlea	kikharai	cod1	kidi
cochleate	kikharaiyo	cod2	kidi
cocinera	kikihunse	cod3	kidi
cock1	kikko	codder	kidijnra
cock2	kikko	coddle	kididuo
cockade	kikkojin	code	kidie
cock a doodle	kikko dainduo	codeine	kidiehun
cockahoop	kikkohinpin	codex	kidiesi
cockaign	kikkogini	codger	kidiegisi
cockalorum	kikkojoranma	codices	kidieknsi
cockatiel	kikkotiejo	codicil	kidiekun
cockatoo	kikkotoo	codicology	kidiekologbon
cockatrice	kikkotasi	codification	kidiefikoyoon
cockayne	kikkoin	codify	kidiefe
cockchafer	kikkokhaforo	codling1	kidiejognni

WORD (x)	EQUIVALENT (y)	WORD (x)	EQUIVALENT (y)
codling2	kidiejognni	coggle	kigiron
codon	kidisi	cogitate	kigiteyo
codpiece	kidipansi	cogitoergosum	kigitorailosumo
codress	kigbaisoo	cognac	kiginiko
coel	kinjn	cognate	kiginiyo
coelacanth	kinjnkosi	cognition	kiginiyoon
coelenterate	kinjntnraiyo	cognizable	kiginiseron
coelenteron	kinjntnrain	cognizance	kiginisesi
coelica	kinjnko	cognizant	kiginisetn
coelo	kinjin	cognize	kiginise
coelom	kinjinmo	cognomen	kiginimuye
coelostat	kinjinsetnti	cognoscente	kiginiseknto
coeno	kinkn	cog-wheel	kigi-whinlo
coenocytes	kinknsnto	cohabit	kihabesi
coenure	kinknran	cohabitation	kihabesiyoon
coenurus	kinknransi	cohere	kiheran
coenzym	kiensaimo	coherence	kiheransi
coequal	kiekunjo	coherent	kiheranto
coerce	kiraiso	coherer	kiheransi
coercion	kiraisoon	cohesion	kihesoon
coercive	kiraisowin	cohesive	kihesowin
coercivity	kiraisewintn	coho	kihin
coetaneous	kitehunsi	cohobate	kihinbooyo
coeval	kiwajn	cohoes	kihinisi
coexist	kiesnse	cohonk	kihinko
coexistence	kiesnsesi	cohort	kihinseto
coffee	kifini	cohosh	kihinsu
coffer	kifiro	cohune	kihun
coffin	kifitn	coif	kinfi
coffle	kifijn	coiff	kinfin
coft	kifia	coiffeur	kinfinraicoiffure
cog	kigi	coil	kinwe
cogent	kiginto	coil	kinlo
cogger	kigirai	coimbatore	kinmbooto

WORD (x)	EQUIVALENT (y)	WORD (x)	EQUIVALENT (y)
coin	kinse	colette	kijntn
coinage	kinsegun	colewort	kijnwoole
coincide	kinsekijo	colic	kijnko
coincidence	kinsekijosi	coligny	kijngini
coincident	kinsekijointn	colima	kijnmo
coincidental	kinsekijointnjo	colin	kijnhn
cointreau	kinsetorau	coliseum	kijnsuma
coir	kiracoistrill	colitis	kijnso
coit	kita	collaborate	kijjoberaiyo
coition	kitayoon	collage	kijjogun
coitus	kitasi	collagen	kijjogin
coke1	kikn	collapse	kijjopise
coke2	kikn	collar	kijjoran
col.	Kijo	collard	kijjogba
cola	kilecolander	collaret	kijjorantn
colatitudes	kijokoyele	collasiri	kijjosoorai
colchester	kijokhntasi	collate	kijjoto
colchicine	kijokhikihun	collateral	kijjotora
colchicum	kijokhikuo	collation	kijjoyoon
colchis	kijokhisi	collator	kijjotoran
colcothar	kijokitihan	colleague	kijjolegbe
cold	kijnn	collect1	kijjokn
cole	kijn	collect2	kijjokn
colectomy	kijnkntemo	collectable	kijjoknberon
colemanite	kijnminiyo	collection	kijjoknyoon
coleoptera	kijoinpntiran	collective	kijjoknwin
coleoptile	kijoinpntiron	collectivism	kijjoknwinmosi
coleorhiza	kijoinrhaisa	collectivize	kijjoknwinse
coleslaw	kijnsanwe	collector	kijjoknran
colessee	kijnsoose	colleen	kijjoni
colessor	kijnsoora	college	kijjogn
colette	kijntin	collegial	kijjognjo
coleus	kijnsi	collegian	kijjognsi
coley	kijnse	collegiate	kijjognyo

WORD (x)	EQUIVALENT (y)	WORD (x)	EQUIVALENT (y)
collegium	kijjognma	collyrium	kijoseraima
collembola	kijjomboojn	collywobbles	kijosewinberon
collenchyma	kijjoinkhoma	colo	kijoin kijoko
collet	kijjotn	colocynth	kijoinsnsi
collide	kijjoso	cologarithm	kijoingbisiro
collie	kijjose	cologarithm	kijoingbiraimosi
collied	kijjodu	cologne	kijoingini
collier	kijjoran	colombes	kijoinbesi
colliery	kijjorai	colombia	kijoinban
colligate	kijjogiyo	colombo	kijoinboo
colligative	kijjogiyowin	colon1	kijoinsi
collimate	kijjomote	colon2	kijoinsi
collimator	kijjomoteran	colonel	kijoinsilo
collinear	kijjohunran	colonial	kijoinsijo
collins	kijjoinsi	colonialism	kijoinsijomosi
collinsia	kijjoinsia	colonies	kijoinsi
collision	kijjoinsoon	colonist	kijoinsi
collocate	kijjoinknyo	colonitis	kijoinsiso
collocation	kijjoinknyoon	colonize	kijoinsise
collocutor	kijjoinkunran	colonization	kijoinsiseyoon
collodion	kijjoindisi	colonnade	kijoinhunjin
collogue	kijjoingbiso	colonnette	kijoinhuntin
colloid	kijjoinjo	colony	kijoinse
collop	kijjoinpn	colophon	kijoinpho
colloquial	kijjoinkunjo	colophony	kijoinphohun
colloquialism	kijjoinkunjomosi	color	kijoran
colloquium	kijjoinkunma	colorado	kijorande
colloquy	kijjoinkunse	coloration	kojoranyoon
collotype	kijjointnpon	coloratura	kijorantorai
collude	kijjojin	colorific	kijoraifiko
collusion	kijjososi	colorimeter	kijoraimuto
collusive	kijjosowin	colored	kijorande
colluvium	kijjowoma	coloring	kijorangini
colly	kijose	colorless	kijoranlabo

WORD (x)	EQUIVALENT (y)	WORD (x)	EQUIVALENT (y)
colossae	kijoinsoo	colure	kijorain
colossal	kijoinsoojo	coly	kijoi
colosseum	kijoinsooma	colyone	kijoihun
colossus	kijoinsoosi	colza	kijosa
colostomy	kijoinsetomi	com-	kim
colostrums	kijoinsetnroma	coma	kimun
colostomy	kijointemo	coma berenices	kimun berainkosi
colour	kijoran	comanchean	kimayekhnhn
colouration	kijorranyoon	comate	kimate
colous	kijoinsi	comatose	kimuntose
colpitis	kijopnso	comatula	kimuntojn
colpo	kijopin	comatulid	kimuntojnjo
colportage	kijopintagun	comb	kimbo
colporteur	kijopintarai	combat	kimbota
colposcopy	kijopinsokipo	combatant	kimbotatn
colt	kijia	combative	kimbotawin
colter	kijiasi	combe	kimbe
coltish	kijiasu	comber	kimbesi
colubrid	kijoberaijn	combi	kimba
colubrine	kijoberain	combination	kimbahunyoon
columba	kijomba	combinative	imbahunyowin
columbae	kijombai	combine	kimbahun
columban	kijombaun	combings	kimbognnisi
columbarium	kijomberaima	combo	kimboo
columbia	kijomban	combust	kimbuna
columbiad	kijombanjn	combustible	kimbunabe
columbine	kijombahun	combustion	kimbunayoon
columbite	kijombayo	come	kimwa
columbus	kijombusa	comedo	kimwade
columella	kijomujjn	comeat	kimwate
column	kijommo	comeatable	kimwateberon
columnar	kijommora	comeback	kimwaboki
columnation	kijommoyoon	comeby	kimwabeo
columnist	kijommosi	comecon	kimwakin

WORD (x)	EQUIVALENT (y)	WORD (x)	EQUIVALENT (y)
comedian	kimwadunsi	commandment	kimadainmutto
comedienne	kimwadunbo	commando	kimmadainko
comedown	kimwajuan	commediadell	kimmudunjnjjo
comedy	kimwadun	commemorate	kimmumoraiyo
comely	kimwalo	commemoration	kimmumoraiyoon
come-on	kimwa-hin	commence	kimmuse
comer	kimwasi	commencement	kimmusemutto
comestibles	kimwajeraisi	commend	kimmudan
comet	kimwatu	commendam	kiamudanmo
comether	kimwatura	commendable	kimmudanbe
cometo	kimwato	commendate	kimmudanyo
comeuppance	kimwapansi	commendation	kimmudanyoon
comfit	kimfito	commendatory	kimmudanyorai
comfort	kimfonto	commensal	kimmusujo
comfortable	kimfontobe	commensurable	kimmusuraibe
comforter	kimfontosi	commensurate	kimmusuraiyo
comfortless	kimfontolabo	comment	kimmutto
comfrey	kimfesin	commentary	kimmuttorai
comfy	kimfe	commentate	kimmuttoyo
comic	kimuko	commentator	kimmuttoyoran
comical	kimukojo	commerce	kimmurasi
comines	kiminisi	commercial	kimmurasijo
coming	kimwagnni	commercialism	kimmurasijomosi
comitatus	kimutntos	commercialize	kimmurasijose
comitia	kimutnsi	commere	kimmure
comity	kimutn	commie	kimmun
comma	kimma	commination	kimmoheyoon
command	kimmadain	comminatory	kimmoheyorai
commandant	kimmadaintn	commingle	kimmunigiron
commandeer	kimmadainse	comminute	kimminiyo
commander	kimmdainsi	comminution	kimminiyoon
commander-in-chief	khifin ni kimmadainsi	commis	kimmusi
commandery	kimmadainrai	commiserate	kimmuseraiyo
commanding	kimmadaingnni	commiseration	kimmuseraiyoon

WORD (x)	EQUIVALENT (y)	WORD (x)	EQUIVALENT (y)
commissar	kimmusinran	communion	kimmuhunsi
commissariat	kimmusinraite	communiqué	kimmuhunkun
commissary	kimmusinrai	communism	mimmuhunmosi
commission	kimmusinse	communist	kimmuhunsi
commission-agent	aginte kimmusinse	communist party	pantesi kimmuhunsi
commissionaire	kimmusinseran	community	kimmuhunto
commissioner	kimmusinsesi	communise	kimmuhunse
commissure	kimmusinrai	commutable	kimmutinbe
commit	kimmutn	commutation	kimmutinyoon
commitment	kimmutnmutto	commutative	kimmutinyowin
committal	kimmuttnjo	commutator	kimmutinyoran
committee	kimmuttnse	commute	kimmutin
commode	kimmodie	commuter	kimmutinsi
commodious	kimmodiesi	commutual	kimmutinjo
commodity	kimmodietn	como	kimo
commodore	kimmodieran	comoro	kimoro
common	kimmeni	comose	kimose
commonality	kimmenijotn	comp	kimpn
commonalty	kimmenijotn	compact1	kimpanko
commoner	kimmenisi	compact2	kimpanko
common ground	kimmeni gonjoin	compadre	kimpangbain
common law	kimmeni leewo	companion	kimpansesi
commonly	kimmenilo	companionable	kimpansebe
common or garden	kimmeni abi giragbn	companionship	kimpansesunpn
commons	kimmenise	company	kimpanse
commotion	kimmotusi	comparable	kimpanrabe
communal	kimmuhunjo	comparative	kimpanrayowin
commune1	kimmuhun	compare	kimpanra
commune2	kimmuhun	comparison	kimpanrasi
communicable	kimmuhunkobe	compart	kimpante
communicant	kimmuhunkotn	compartible	kimpantebe
communicate	kimmuhunkoyo	compartment	kimpantemutto
communication	kimmuhunkoyoon	compartmental	kimpantemuttojo
communicative	kimmuhunkoyowin	compartmentalize	kimpantemuttojose

WORD (x)	EQUIVALENT (y)	WORD (x)	EQUIVALENT (y)
compass	kimpanso	complete	kimpontn
compassion	kimpanson	complex	kimporon
compassionate	kimpansonyo	complexion	kimporonse
compatible	kimpantobe	complexity	kimporontn
compatriot	kimpantnrato	complexus	kimporonsi
compeer	kimpnrai	compliance	kimpanse
compel	kimpnlo	compliant	kimpantan
compellation	kimpnlloyoon	complicacy	kimpansiasn
compendious	kiapnjonsi	complicate	kimpansiayo
compendium	kimpnjonma	complication	kimpansiayoon
compensable	kimpnsanbe	complice	kimpansi
compensate	kimpnsanyo	complicity	kimpankitn
compensation	kimpnsanyoon	compliment	kimpanmutto
compensatory	kimpnsanyorai	complimentary	kimpanmuttorai
compere	kimpnran	compline	kimpanlale
compete	kimpnti	compluvium	kimpoluwoma
competence	kimpntisi	comply	kimpnlo
competent	kimpntito	compo	kimpin
competition	kimpntiyoon	component	kimpinseto
competitive	kimpntiyowin	compony	kimpinse
competitor	kimpntiyoran	comport	kimpinta
compilation	kimpojnyoon	compose	kimpinse
compile	kimpojn	composer	kimpinsesi
compiler	kimpojnra	composite	kimpinsite
complacency	kimpanknsn	composition	kimpinsiyoon
complacent	kimpanknti	compositor	kimpinsitoran
complain	kimpanto	compos mentis	kimpinso muttosi
complainant	kimpantotn	compost	kimpinseto
complaint	kimpantosi	composure	kimpinsurai
complaisant	kimpansotn	compote	kimpote
complanate	kimpannayo	compound1	kimpojoin
complect	kimponkiti	compound2	kimpojoin
complement	kimponmutto	comprador	kimpanjnra
complementary	kimponmuttorai	compreg	kimpesign

WORD (x)	EQUIVALENT (y)	WORD (x)	EQUIVALENT (y)
comprehend	kimpesihejo	con-	kin
comprehensible	kimpesihesnbe	conakry	kinkorai
comprehension	kimpesihesnse	conamore	kinmoinran
comprehensive	kimpesihesnwin	conant	kinte
compress	kimpesiso	conation	kinyoon
compression	kimpesisoon	conative	kinyowin
compressor	kimpesisoran	conatus	kinyosi
compris	kimpansi	conbrio	kinbain
compromise	kimponmuse	concatenation	kinkotinyoon
compt	kimpnti	concave	kinkowo
compte rendu	kimpnto raindi	concavity	kinkowotn
comptibel	kimpntiron	concavoconcave	kinkownkinkowo
comptometer	kimpntimuto	concavoconvex	kinkownkinwinsn
compton	kimpntisi	conceal	kinknjo
comptroller	kimpntnronjjosi	concede	kinknjin
compulsion	kimpnlese	conceit	kinknyo
compulsive	kimpnlesewin	conceited	kinknyode
compulsory	kimpnleserai	conceivable	kinknwinberon
compunction	kimpnkunyoon	conceive	kinknwin
compurgation	kimpnragiyoon	concent	kinknti
compuragator	kimpnragiyoran	concenter	kinkntiran
computation	kimpnteyoon	concentrate	kinkntiraiyo
compute	kimpnte	concentration	kinkntiraiyoon
computer	kimpntesi	concentration camp	kompn kinkntiraiyoon
computerize	kimpntesise	concentric	kinkntiraiko
comrade	kimurajin	concept	kinknpnti
comradery	kimurajinrai	conception	kinknpntiyoon
comstockery	kimsetokirai	conceptual	kinknpntijo
comtism	kimtnmosi	conceptualize	kinknpntijose
comus	kimusi	concem	kinknran
con1	kin	concemed	kinknrande
con2	kin	concerning	kinknrangnni
con3	kin	concert	kinknrate
con4	kihe	concerted	kinknratede

135

WORD (x)	EQUIVALENT (y)	WORD (x)	EQUIVALENT (y)
concertante	kinknrateto	concoction	kinkikyoon
concertina	kinknratehe	concolorous	kinkijoransi
concertino	kinknrateko	cconcomitant	kinkimutn
concertmaster	kinknratemasitn	concord	kinkigba
concerto	kinknrato	concordance	kinkigbasi
concession	kinknsoon	concordant	kinkigbatn
concessionary	kinknsoonrai	concordat	kinkigbato
concessive	kinknsoowin	concorde	kinkigbain
conch	kinkhi	concourse	kinkiraise
concha	kinkho	conceremation	kinknranmoyoon
conchie	kinkhin	concrescence	kinknranseknsi
conchiferous	kinkhifirosi	concrete	kinknrantn
conchiolin	kinkhinijan	concretion	kinknranyoon
conchobar	kinkhiboosn	concretize	kinknranyose
conchoid	kinkhijo	concubine	kinkunbahun
conchoidal	kinkhijojo	concubitant	kinkunbatotn
conchology	kinkhilogbon	concupiscence	kinkunposeknsi
conchoscope	kinkhisekipon	concur	kinkunra
conchy	kinkhise	concurrence	kinkunrraisi
concierge	kinkirign	concurrent	kinkunrraito
conciliar	kinkunran	concuss	kinkunso
conciliate	kinkunyo	concussion	kinkunsoon
conciliation	kinkunyoon	condemn	kindaamu
conciliatory	kinkunyorai	condemnation	kindaamuyoon
concise	kinkise	condensation	kindikunseyoon
concision	kinkisoon	condensate	kindikunseyo
conclamant	kinkanmotn	condense	kindikunse
conclamation	kinkanmoyoon	condenser	kindikunsi
conclave	kinkanwin	condescend	kindnseknjn
conclavist	kinkanwinsi	condescendence	kindnseknjnsi
conclude	kinkiranjin	condescension	kindnseknsoon
conclusion	kinkiransoon	condign	kindigan
conclusive	kinkiransowin	condiment	kindimutto
concoct	kinkikyo	condition	kindiyoon

WORD (x)	EQUIVALENT (y)	WORD (x)	EQUIVALENT (y)
conditional	kindiyoonjo	confederation	kinfnjnraiyoon
conditioner	kindiyoonsi	confer	kinfiro
condo	kinde	conference	kinfirosi
condole	kindejoin	conferment	kinfiromutto
condolence	kindejoinsi	confess	kinfnse
condom	kindemo	confessedly	kinfnsedelo
condominium	kindemohema	confession	kinfnsesi
condone	kindehun	confessional	kinfnsesijo
condor	kinderan	confessor	kinfnseran
condortiere	kinderantosi	confetti	kinfntto
conduce	kindisi	confidant	kinfidatn
conducive	kindisiwin	confide	kinfida
conduct	kindiki	confidence	kinfidasi
conductance	kindikisi	confident	kinfidato
conduction	kindikiyoon	confidential	kinfidatojo
conductive	kindikiwin	configurate	kinfigiraiyo
conductor	kindikiran	configuration	kinfigiraiyoon
conduit	kindite	configure	kinfigirai
condyle	kindainjn	confine	kinfinni
condyloid	kindainjnjo	confined	kinfinnide
condyloma	kindainjnmo	confinement	kinfinnimutto
cone	kinnu	confirm	kinfiroin
coneirad	kinnuraijo	confirmation	kinfiroinyoon
conepate	kinnupantn	confirmed	kinfiroinde
conpati	kinnupanti	confirmee	kinfiroinse
conestoga	kinnusetogi	confiscate	kinfisekoyo
coney	kinnuse	confiteor	kinfitorai
confab	kinfanbo	confiture	kinfitoran
confabulate	kinfanboleyo	conflagrant	kinfangantn
confection	kinfnkoiyoon	conflagration	kinfanganyoon
confectioner	kinfnkoiyoonsi	conflate	kinfanyo
confectionery	kinfnkoyoonrai	conflict	kinfanknti
confederacy	kinfnjnraisn	confluence	kinfolusi
confederate	kinfnjnraiyo	confluent	kinfoluto

WORD (x)	EQUIVALENT (y)	WORD (x)	EQUIVALENT (y)
conform	kinfoonmo	conglobation	kingonbuyoon
conformable	kinfoonmobe	conglomerate	kingonmuraiyo
conformation	kinfoonmoyoon	conglomeration	kingonmuraiyoon
conformist	kinfoonmosi	conglutinant	kingbiletiete
conformity	kinfoonmotn	conglutinate	kingbiletinyo
confound	kinfonjoin	conglutination	kingbiletinyoon
confounded	kinfonjoinde	conglutinous	kingbiletinsi
confraternity	kinfentiratn	congo	kignta
confrere	kinfesire	congou	kigntu
confront	kinfontn	congratulate	kingantoleyo
confrontation	kinfontnyoon	congratulation	kingantoleyoon
confucian	kinfunsehn	congregate	kingirangiyo
Confucius	kinfunsesi	congregation	kingirangiyoon
confuse	kinfunsia	congregational	kingirangiyoonjo
confusion	kinfunsiase	congregationalism	kingirangiyoonjomosi
confutation	kinfunteyoon	congress	kingiranso
confute	kinfunte	congressional	kingiraisoojo
conga	kingi	congressman	kingiransomoye
congaree	kingirain	congreve	kingiranwin
conge	kingn	congruence	kingirainsi
congeal	kingnjo	congruent	kingirainto
congee	kingnse	congruity	kingiraintn
congelation	kingnleyoon	congruous	kingirainsi
congener	kingnhunra	conic	kinnuko
congeneric	kingnhunraiko	conical	kinnukojo
congenetic	kingnhunko	conidiferous	kinunjofirosi
congenial	kingnhunjo	conidiophore	kinunjokophiran
congenital	kingnhuntojo	conidium	kinnujoma
conger	kingnra	conifer	kinnufiro
congeries	kingnraisi	coniferin	kinnufirote
congest	kingnse	coniferous	kinnufirosi
congestion	kingnseyoon	conine	kinnuhun
congius	kingisi	coniology	kinnulogbon
conglobate	kingonbuyo	conium	kinnuma

WORD (x)	EQUIVALENT (y)	WORD (x)	EQUIVALENT (y)
conjectural	kinjnknranjo	connivent	kinhunwinti
conjecture	kinjnknran	connoisseur	kinknsoorai
conjoin	kinjosi	connotation	kinkntoyoon
conjoint	kinjosito	connote	kinknto
conjugal	kinjogijo	connubial	kinknbajo
conjugate	kinjogiyo	cono	kinkn
conjugation	kinjogiyoon	conodont	kinkndeyo
conjunct	kinjokn	conoid	kinknjo
conjunction	kinjoknyoon	conquer	kinkoin
conjunctiva	kinjuknwa	conqueror	kinkoinran
conjunctival	kinjuknwajo	conquest	kinkoinsi
conjunctive	kinjuknwin	conquistador	kinkuntodera
conjunctivitis	kinjuknwinso	conrado	kinrade
conjuration	kinjuranyoon	cons	kins
conjure	kinjuran	consanguineous	kinsangunhunsi
conjurer	kinjuransi	consanguinity	kinsangunhuntn
conjuror	kinjuraran	conscience	kinsisunse
conjury	kinjurai	conscientious	kinsisuntosi
conk1	kinkn	conscious	kinsisesi
conk2	kinkn	consciousness	kinsisesisn
conker	kinknra	conscript	kinsekoraipn
con man	kinmaye	consecrate	kinseknrayo
conn	kin	consecution	kinsekuntesi
connate	kinheyo	consecutive	kinsekuntewin
connatural	kinheyoranjo	consensual	kinsesisujo
connect	kinhunkn	consensus	kinsesi
connection	kinhunkyo	consent	kinsesita
connective	kinhunkyoon	consentaneous	kinsesitelusi
connector	kinhunkiyoan	consentience	kinsesitansi
conner	kinhunsi	consequence	kinsekunrasi
conning tower	kinhungnni	consequent	kinsekunra
conniption	kinhunpntisi	consequential	kinsekunrajo
connivance	kinhunwinsi	consequently	kinsekunralo
connive	kinhunwin	conservancy	kinserawinsn

WORD (x)	EQUIVALENT (y)	WORD (x)	EQUIVALENT (y)
conservation	kinserawinyoon	conspicuous	kinsepokunsi
conservationist	kinserawinyoonsi	conspiracy	kinseporaisn
conservation of	kinserawinyoon	conspirator	kinseporairan
conservative	kinserawinyosi	conspire	kinseporai
conservative part	pante kinserawinyown	constable	kinsetnbe
conservatoire	kinserawinyoran	constabulary	kinsetnberai
conservatory	kinserawinyorai	constancy	kinsetnsn
conserve	kinserawin	constant	kinsetntn
consider	kinsoojora	constantine	kinsetntehun
considerable	kinsoojorabe	constellation	kinsetojjnyoon
considerate	kinsoojoraiyo	consternation	kinsetnranyoon
consideration	kinsoojoraiyoon	constipate	kinsetipanyo
considering	kinsoojoraignni	constipation	kinsetipanyoon
consign	kinsoogan	constituency	kinsetintusn
consignatory	kinsooganyorai	constituent	kinsetintutn
consignment	kinsooganmutto	constitute	kinsetintuyo
consist	kisoosi	constitution	kinsetintuyoon
consistency	kinsoosisn	constitutional	kinsetntuyoonjo
consistent	kinsoosito	constitutive	kinsetintuyowin
consistory	kinsoosirai	constrain	kinsetnkiun
consociate	kinsookiyo	constraint	kinsetnknun
consocies	kinsookisi	constrict	kinsetnkyo
consolation	kinsinleyoon	constriction	kinsetnkyoon
console1	kinsinle	constrictor	kinsetnkyosi
console2	kinsinle	constringe	kinsetnringin
consolidate	kinsinlejoyo	constringent	kinsetnrainginte
consolidation	kinsinlejoyoon	construct	kinsetnrako
consols	kinsinlasi	construction	kinsetnrakoyoon
consommé	kinsoommo	constructive	kinsetnrakowin
consonance	kinsosesi	construe	kinsetnrase
consonant	kinsoseto	consubstantial	kinsnbesetntejo
consort1	kinsorate	consubstantiation	kinsnbesetnteyoon
consort2	kinsorate	consuetude	kinsuetujin
consortium	kinsoratema	consul	kinsnle

WORD (x)	EQUIVALENT (y)	WORD (x)	EQUIVALENT (y)
consular	kinsnleran	content1	kintito
consulate	kinsnleyo	content2	kintito
consult	kinsnleto	contented	kintitode
consultancy	kinsnletosn	contention	kintitoyoon
consultant	kinsnletote	contentious	kintitosi
consultation	kinsnletoyoon	contentment	kintitomini
consultive	kinsnletowin	conterminate	kintironheyo
consume	kinsumo	contermination	kintironheyoon
consumer	kinsumora	conterminous	kintironhesi
consumerism	kinsumoraimosi	contest	kintinsi
consummate	kinsummoyo	contestant	kintinsitn
consumption	kinsumpnyoon	context	kintiso
consumptive	kinsumpnyowin	contexture	kintisoran
cont.	kinte	contiguous	kintigansi
contact	kintekan	contiguity	kintigantn
contact lens	kintekan jnhnsi	continence	kintihunsi
contact print	kintekan pante	continent1	kintihuntn
contagion	kintegbun	continet2	kintihunto
contagious	kintegbunsi	continental	kintihuntojo
contagium	kintegbunma	contingency	kintiginsn
contain	kintelu	contingent	kintiginte
container	kinteluran	continual	kintihunjo
containerize	kinteluraise	continuance	kintihunhesi
containment	kintelumutto	continuation	kintihunyoon
contaminate	kintelumuyo	continue	kintihunsi
contango	kintehalo	continuity	kintihuntn
contemplate	kintompanyo	continuo	kintihunko
contemplative	kintompanyowin	continuous	kintihunse
contemporaneous	kintompnrainsi	continuum	kintihunma
contemporary	kintompnranrai	conto	kinto
contempt	kintompnti	contort	kintorai
contemptible	kintompntibe	contortionist	kintoraiyoonsi
contemptuous	kintompntisi	contour	kintoorai
contend	kintijn	contra	kintire

WORD (x)	EQUIVALENT (y)	WORD (x)	EQUIVALENT (y)
contra-	kintire	contrivance	kintiraiwinsi
contraband	kintirebonjo	contrive	kintiraiwin
contraception	kintireknpntisi	contrived	kintiraiwinde
contraceptive	kintireknpntiwin	control	kintiraijo
contract	kintireko	controller	kintiraijjosi
contractable	kintirekobe	controversial	kintiraiwinsojn
contract bridge	bangbon kintireko	controversy	kintiraiwinso
contractible	kintirekobe	controvert	kintiraiwinte
contractile	kintirekoran	contumacious	kintumosnsi
contraction	kintirekoyoon	contumacy	kintumosn
contractor	kintirekosi	contumely	kintumojn
contractual	kintirekojo	contuse	kintuse
contradict	kintiredikn	contusion	kintusesi
contradiction	kintirediknsi	conundrum	kinnugbiro
contradictory	kintirediknrai	conurbation	kinraibeyoon
contradistinction	kintiredisitinknyoon	convalesce	kinwajosesi
contrail	kintirelo	convalescent	kinwajoseknti
contralto	kintirejnto	convallaria	kinwajjoran
contraption	kintirepntisi	convection	kinwinkntisi
contrapuntal	kintirepntojo	convector	kinwinknti
contrariety	kintireraitn	convene	kinwini
contrary	kintirerai	convener	kinwinise
contrast	kintiresi	convenience	kinwinisi
contravallation	kintirewajjnyoon	convenient	kinwinito
contravene	kintirewini	convent	kinwinti
contrayerva	kintireyarawa	conventicle	kinwintikuo
contrectation	kintirankyoyoon	convention	kinwintiyoon
contredanse	kintirandajo	conventional	kinwintiyoonjo
contretemps	kintirantomposi	conventual	kinwintijo
contribute	kintiraibuyo	converge	kinwingan
contribution	kintiraibuyoon	conversant	kinwinsoote
contributory	kintiraibuyorai	conversation	kinwinsoyoon
contrite	kintiraiyo	conversational	kinwinsoyoonjo
contrition	kintiraiyoon	conversationalist	kinwinsoyoonjosi

WORD (x)	EQUIVALENT (y)	WORD (x)	EQUIVALENT (y)
conversazione	kinwinsosoon	cooky	kikonase
converse1	kinwinso	cool	kijain
converse2	kinwinso	coolant	kijainte
conversion	kinwinsoon	cooler	kijainsi
convert	kinwinte	coolidge	kijaingbon
converter	kinwintesi	coolie	kijainse
convertible	kinwintebe	coomb	kimboo
convertite	kinwinteyo	coon	kikoon
convex	kinwinsn	coontie	kikoontie
convey	kinwinlo	coop	kipon
conveyance	kinwinlosi	co-op	kipon
conveyor	kinwinloran	cooper	kiponra
conveyor belt	bejia kinwinloran	cooperage	kiponraigun
convict	kinwokn	cooperate	kiponraiyo
conviction	kinwoknyoon	cooperation	kiponraiyoon
convince	kinwosi	cooperative	kiponraiyowin
convivial	kinwowojo	coopery	kiponrai
convocation	kinwnkoyoon	co-opt	ki-opnti
convoke	kinwnko	coordinate	ki orojnhunyo
convoluted	kinwnjnyode	coost	kisooto
convolution	kinwnjnyoon	coot	kitin
convolvulus	kinwnjnwelesi	cooter	kitinra
convoy	kinwnse	cootie	kitinsi
convulse	kinwelese	cootle	kitinron
convulsion	kinwelesoon	cop	kipn
cony	kinse	copaiba	kipnbaun
coo	kikun	copal	kipnjo
cooch	kikhoon	coparcenary	kipanknrai
cooee	kikunse	coparcener	kipanknra
cook	kikona	copartner	kipantesi
cookbook	bookokikona	cope1	kipon
cooker	kikonasi	cope2	kipon
cookery	kikonarai	copeck	kiponko
cookie	kikonani	copemicus	kipnrankosi

WORD (x)	EQUIVALENT (y)	WORD (x)	EQUIVALENT (y)
copasetic	kipnseko	coquito	kikunte
copier	kipesi	cora	kirai
coping	kipngnni	coracle	kirakuo
copiopia	kipnpan	coral	kirajo
copious	kipesi	coralli	kirajjo
copolymerization	kiposemuraiseyoon	coralline	kirajjohun
cop-out	kipn nita	corallite	kirajjotn
copper1	kipipon	coralloid	kirajjojo
copper2	kipipon	corallum	kirajjoma
coppice	kipiposi	coram populo	kiramo popnlo
copple	kiporon	corantyn	kirateyn
copra	kipnran	corban	kirabon
copremia	kipesimua	corbel	kirabejn
coprology	kipirologbon	corble	kirabe
coprophagous	kipirophijesi	cord	kigba
coprophilia	kipiropheron	cordage	kigbagun
coprophilious	kipiropheronsi	cordate	kigbato
copse	kipise	corded	kigbade
copt	kipiti	cordelia	kigbajan
coptic	kipitiko	cordelier	kigbajnran
copula	kipele	cordial	kigbajo
copulate	kipeleyo	cordierite	kigbaraiyo
copulation	kipeleyoon	cordiform	kigbafoonmo
copy	kipe	cordillera	kigbajjoran
copybook	bookokipe	cordite	kigbayo
copyist	kipesi	cordless	kigbalabo
copyright	kiperaigbe	cordoba	kigbaboo
coq au vin	win le kikun	cordon	kigbain
coquelico	kikunleki	cordonbieu	kigbainbo
coquet	kikuntn	cordonnet	kigbainte
coquette	kikuntin	cordovan	kigbawain
coquilla	kikunjjn	cords	kigbasi
coquille	kikunjjo	corduroy	kigbaraise
coquina	kikunna	cordy	kigbase

WORD (x)	EQUIVALENT (y)	WORD (x)	EQUIVALENT (y)
core	kiran	comelian	kimujohn
coregonus	kirangonsi	comelia	kimujan
corella	kiranjjn	comelius	kimujosi
corelli	kisijjo	comella	kimujjn
coreosis	kiranso	comer	kimusi
corer	kiransi	comerstone	kimurasetole
correspondent	kirresepojnto	comet	kimuto
corf	kirafan	cometcy	kimutosn
corgi	kiragi	comflake	kimfankuo
coriaceous	kiraisuwa	comflour	kimfonrai
coriander	kiraijnra	comflower	kimfonwara
corinthian	kiraisinhn	comice	kimusi
coriolanus	kiraijinhn	comish	kimuse
coriolis	kiraijnso	como	kimko
corisco	kiraisuki	comu	kimu
corium	kiraima	comucopia	kimukipan
cork	kirakn	comus	kimusi
corkage	kirakngun	comute	kimute
corked	kiraknde	comy	kimse
corked	kiraknde	corody	kirasindie
corker	kiraknsi	corolla	kirasinjjn
corky	kiraknse	corollary	kirasinjjnrai
corm	kiramo	coromandel	kirasinmudainjo
cormel	kiramojn	corona	kirasin
cormophyta	kiramopheto	coronach	kirasinkho
cormorant	kiramorantn	coronal	kirasinjo
com1	kim	coronary	kirasinrai
com2	kia	coronation	kirasinyoon
comaceous	kimsuwa	coroner	kirasinsi
com-cob	kim-kibo	coroniform	kirasinfoonmo
comcrake	kimkankn	coronet	kirasinte
comea	kimusi	corpora	kirapinran
comed	kimude	corpora11	kirapinranjo
comeille	kimujjo	corpora12	kirapinranjo

145

WORD (x)	EQUIVALENT (y)	WORD (x)	EQUIVALENT (y)
corporate	kirapinraiyo	corrigible	kirraignberon
corporation	kirapinraiyoon	corro borant	kirraberaitn
corporative	kirapinraiyowin	corroborate	kirraberaiyo
corporator	kirapinrairan	corroboree	kirraberaise
corporeal	kirapinrejo	corrode	kirrada
corposant	kirapinsetan	corrodentia	kirradatosi
corps	kirapnsi	corrosion	kirrasoon
corpse	kirapnse	corrosive	kirrasowin
corpulent	kirapnjnto	corrogant	kirragitn
corpus	kirapnse	corrugate	kirraigiyo
corpuscle	kirapnsekuo	corrupt	kirraipiyo
corrade	kirraijn	corruption	kirraipiyoon
corradate	kirraijnyo	corruptionist	kirraipiyoonsi
corral	kirraijo	corruptive	kirraipiyowin
corrasion	kirraisoon	corsac	kiraseka
correct	kirreto	corsage	kirasegn
correction	kirretoyoon	corsair	kiraserie
correctitude	kirretotujin	corse	kirase
corrective	kirretowin	corselette	kirasetn
correggio	kirregio	corset	kiraseto
corregidor	kirregijnran	corsetiere	kirasetoron
correlate	kirrejoyo	corsetry	kirasetorai
correlation	kirrejoyoon	corsican	kirasokoin
correlative	kirrejoyowin	cortege	kiratogin
correption	kirrepnyoon	cortes	kiratosi
correspond	kirresepojn	cortex	kiratose
correspondence	kirresepojnsi	corti	kirate
correspondent	kirresepojnto	cortical	kiratekojo
corrida	kirraijo	corticate	kiratekoyo
corridor	kirraijora	cortico	kirateki
corrie	kirraise	corticose	kiratekise
corriedale	kirraisejnle	corticosterone	kiratekisetorain
corrientes	kirraisetosi	corticotropin	kiratekitnrapan
corrigendum	kirraignjoma	cortin	kiratie

WORD (x)	EQUIVALENT (y)	WORD (x)	EQUIVALENT (y)
cortisone	kiratisoo	cosmo	kiseto
corufia	kiranfia	cosmodrome	kisetogbnmo
corundum	kiranjoinma	cosmogony	kisetogonse
coruscate	kiransekoyo	cosmography	kisetoganphe
corvee	kirawnse	cosmoline	kisetolehun
corvine	kirawohun	cosmology	kisetologbon
corvus	kirawosi	cosmon	kisetosi
corybant	kiraibotn	cosmonaut	kisetoheyo
corydalis	kiraijnlosi	cosmopolitan	kisetopinjntan
corydalus	kiraijnlowa	cosmopolite	kisetopinjnyo
corydon	kiraijnsi	cosmorama	kisetoranmo
corymb	kiraimbe	cosmos	kisetosi
coryphée	kiraiphnse	cosmotron	kisetoroin
corypheus	kiraiphnsi	coson	kisesi
corysa	kiraisa	coss	kisoo
cos1	kise	cossack	kisooko
cos2	kise	cosset	kisooti
cos3	kise	cost	kisi
cosec	kiseko	costa	kisito
cosecant	kisekoki	co star	ki setan
cosech	kisekhn	costard	kisigbaa
coseismal	kisesunmijo	costate	kisiyo
cosh1	kison	coster	kisise
cosh2	kison	costemonger	kisitnmoginisi
cosher	kisonsi	costing	kisignni
cosinage	kisohungun	costive	kisiwin
cosine	kisohun	costly	kisijn
cosmecology	kisetokilogbon	costomary	kisimorai
cosmetic	kisetoniko	costo	kisito
cosmetician	kisetonikohn	costotomy	kisitotemo
cosmetology	kisetonilogbon	costume	kisitamo
cosmic	kisetoka	costumer	kisitamora
cosmism	kisetomosi	costumier	kisitamoran
cosmium	kisetoma	cosy	kissn

WORD (x)	EQUIVALENT (y)	WORD (x)	EQUIVALENT (y)
cot	kiti	cough	kigbe
cot	kiti	cough	kihuko
cot	kiti	could	kalejn
cote	kitie	couldn't	kalejnti
coteau	kitiele	coulee	kalejnse
cotelette	kitietin	couleur	kalejnran
cotenant	kitinte	coulisse	kalejnsoo
cotentin	kitintan	couloir	kalelorai
coterie	kitieran	coulomb	kalelombe
coterminous	kitiraminisi	coulometer	kalelomuto
coth	kitihe	coulter	kalejiasi
cothumus	kitiheransi	coumarin	kalemurain
cotillion	kitijnransi	council	kalekun
cotoneaster	kitileniseto	councillor	kalekunran
cotopaxi	kitipinsia	counsel	kalesojn
cotquean	kitikunhn	counsellor	kalesojjnran
cottage	kittigun	counselor	kalesojnran
cottager	kittigunsi	count1	kaleyo
cotter	kittira	count2	kaleyo
cottier	kittiran	countable	kaleyoberon
cottise	kittise	countdown	kaleyodewn
cotton	kittisi	countenance	kaleyotinsi
cottony	kittisise	counter1	kaleyosi
cotyledon	kitilojnsi	counter2	kaleyosi
cotyloid	kitilojo	counter-	kaleyosi
couch1	kalekho	counteract	kaleyosiako
couch2	kalekho	counterfeit	kaleyosifite
couchant	kalekhote	countess	kaleyotnbo
couchette	kalekhntin	cuntless	kaleyolabo
couching	kalekhognni	countrified	kaleyoraifide
cou cou	kale kale	country	kaleyorai
coude	kalejin	countryside	kaleyoraisoojo
coueism	kalesamosi	country-wide	kaleyoraiwinjin
cougar	kilegira	county	kaleyose

WORD (x)	EQUIVALENT (y)	WORD (x)	EQUIVALENT (y)
coup	kilepn	cove1	kiwo
coup de tat	kilepn jin teyo	cove2	kiwo
coupe	kilepn	coven	kiwosi
coupe	kilepn	covenant	kiwositn
couple	kilepo	coventry	kiwositerai
couplet	kilepotn	cover	kiwera
coupling	kilepognni	coverage	kiweragun
coupon	kileposi	coverall	kiwerajjo
courage	kiraigun	cover girl	kiwera gberojn
courageous	kiraigunsi	coverlet	kiweratn
courante	kirainto	covert	kiwerate
courgette	kiraigntin	cover-up	kiwera pake
courier	kiraisi	covet	kiweti
courlan	kiraileni	covetous	kiwetisi
course	kiraise	covey	kiweyo
courser	kiraisesi	cov in	kiwo nu
court	kiraito	cow1	kiwo
courteous	kiraitosi	cow2	kiwo
courtesan	kiraitosie	coward	kiwogbaa
courtesy	kiraitosn	cowardice	kiwogbaasi
courtier	kiraitose	cowardly	kiwogbaalo
courtly	kiraitolo	cowbell	kiwobejnro
courtship	kiraitosunpn	cowboy	kiwoboyn
couscous	kiwakisi	cower	kiwora
cousin	kiwasin	cowl	kiwojn
couteau	kiwatiele	cowling	kiwojngnni
couth	kiwato	cow pea	kiwo pnni
couthle	kiwatojo	cowper	kiwopnra
couture	kiwatoran	cowrie	kiworan
couturier	kiwatoraisi	cowrin	kiworie
covalency	kiwajosn	cowry	kiworai
covalent	kiwajoto	cox	kisa
covalent	kiwajotn	coxi	kisaso
covalence	kiwajosi	coxsigia	kisasogan

WORD (x)	EQUIVALENT (y)	WORD (x)	EQUIVALENT (y)
coxswain	kisasewain	craigie	knragbnse
coy	kiyn	crake	knrake
coyote	kiyinto	cram	knramo
coypu	kiynpo	crambo	knrambo
coz	kisn	crammer	knrammosi
cozen	kisnsi	cramosisy	knramosin
cozzle	kisnron	cramp	knrapon
cozy	kisnle	cramped	knraponde
crab1	knrabe	crampon	knraponsi
crab2	knrabe	crampoon	knraponun
crab3	knrabe	cran	knra
crabbed	knrabede	cranach	knrako
crabby	knrabesi	cranberry	knraberrai
crack	knrabesi	cranbome	knrabonrain
crack	knrako	crandall	knrajnjo
cracker	knrakose	crane	knrahun
crackers	knrakosesi	cranesbill	knrahunbajnra
cracking	knrakognni	cranial	knrahejo
crackle	knrakon	craniate	knraheto
crackling	knrakongnni	cranio	knraheko
cracknel	knrakonlo	craniology	knrahekologbon
crackpot	knrakopote	cranniometer	knrahekomuto
cracky	knrakosi	craniosacral	knrahekosakaranjo
cracodenne	knrakidihun	craniotomy	knrahekotemo
cracow	knrakiwo	cranium	knrahema
cracy	kansn	crank	knrakan
cradle	kansn	crankle	knrakanjn
cradle	knraduo	crankous	knrakansi
craft	knrafia	crankpin	knrakanpoha
craftsman	knrafiamoye	cranky	knrakanse
crafty	knrafiase	cranmer	knrahamo
crag	knragba	crannog	knrahungon
craggy	knragbase	cranny	knrahasi
craig	knragbn	crants	knrato

WORD (x)	EQUIVALENT (y)	WORD (x)	EQUIVALENT (y)
crap	knrapn	craze	knrase
crapaud	knrapnjn	crazed	knrasede
crape	knrapon	crazy	knrasia
craps	knrapnsi	creak	knranke
crapple	knraporon	creaky	knrankese
crappy	knrapnpo	cream	knranmn
crapulence	knrapojnsi	creamer	knranmnse
crapulent	knrapojnto	creamery	knranmnrai
craquelure	knrakunleran	creamy	knranmnse
crash1	knrase	crease	knranse
crash2	knrase	create	knranyo
crashing	knrasegnni	creatine	knranyohun
crasis	knraseso	creatinine	knranyonhun
craspedomorphology	knrasepndiemophan-	creation	knranyoon
	logbon	creationism	knranyoonmosi
crass	knrasi	creative	knranyowin
crassamentum	knrasimutnma	creator	knranyosi
crassulaceous	knrasilesuwa	creature	knranyorai
-crat	kanta	crèche	knransun
cratch	kantakhi	credence	knrangbisi
crate	knrate	credendum	knrangbijnma
crater	knratesi	credent	knrangbito
-cratic	kantako	credential	knrangbitojo
cratomania	kantamohan	credibility	knrangbiberontn
cravat	knrawiti	credible	knrangbibe
crave	knrawn	credit	knrangbi
craven	knrawnni	creditable	knrangbibe
craving	knrawingnni	creditor	knrangbise
craw	knrawe	credo	knrangbe
crawl	knrawejn	credulity	knrangbatn
crawler	knrawejnra	credulous	knrangbasi
crawly	knrawelo	cree	knranso
cray	knraya	creed	knrangba
crayon	knrayasi	creek	knranka

WORD (x)	EQUIVALENT (y)	WORD (x)	EQUIVALENT (y)
creel	knranlo	crepuscule	knranpnsekuo
creep	knranpe	cres.	Knranse
creeper	knranpesi	cresc.	Knransekn
creepie	knranpese	crescendo	knranseknde
creepie peepie	knranpese pnpnse	crescent	knranseknti
creepy	knranpesn	crescive	knransekiwn
cremate	knranmana	cresol	knransoole
cremator	knranmanase	cress	knransoo
crematorium	knranmanama	cresset	knransooto
crème	knranmo	cressida	knransoojn
crème brulee	knranmo boroyun	crest	knransi
crème de la crème	knranmo jinle knranmo	cresyl	knransule
		cresylate	knransuleyo
crème de menthe	knranmo jn muttosi	cretaceous	knrantesuwa
cremona	knranmohe	crete	knrante
crenate	knranheyo	cretic	knranteko
crenature	knranheyorai	cretin	knrantie
crenation	knranheyoon	cretinism	knrantiemosi
crenel	knrainle	cretonne	knrantinhun
crenelate	knrainleyo	creusa	knransua
crenellate	knrainlleyo	creuse	knransun
crenulate	knrainleyo	crevasse	knranwesoo
crenulation	knrainleyoon	crevice	knranwo
creole	knranjoin	crew1	knranwa
creolin	knranjoinsi	crew2	knranwa
creolize	knranjoinse	crewe	knranwn
creophagous	knranphijesi	crewel	knranwnjo
creosol	knransoole	crib	koraibe
creosote	nransooto	cribbage	koraibegun
crepe	knranpn	cribbite	koraibeyo
crepitate	knranpitiyo	cribble	koraiberonc
crepitus	knranpitisi	cribriform	koraibanfoonmo
crept	knranpnti	crick	koraiki
crepuscular	knranpnsekuoran	cricket1	koraikite

WORD (x)	EQUIVALENT (y)	WORD (x)	EQUIVALENT (y)
cricket2	koraikite	criss-cross	koraisun-konso
cricketer	koraikitesi	crissal	koraisunjo
cricoid	koraikijo	crissum	koraisunma
cri de coeur	korai jin kiwara	cristate	koraisutote
cried	koraide	criterion	koraitnrasi
crier	koraisi	critic	koraitako
crikey	koraiknsi	critical	koraitakojo
crim	koram	criticaster	koraitakosotn
crime	korami	criticism	koraitakomosi
criminal	koramijo	criticize	koritakose
criminality	koramijotn	critique	koraitaku
criminate	koramiyo	critter	koraittnra
criminology	koramilogbon	crizzling	koraisunjognni
crimp	koraipon	croak	konke
crimplene	koraiponhun	croaker	konkesi
crimson	koraimpupa	croat	konte
cringe	koraign	crocein	konknte
cringle	koraignron	croaky	konkese
crinite	korainte	crochet	konkhnt
crinkle	koraikun	crocidolite	konkijoleyo
crinkum	koraikwo	crocin	konkin
crinoid	korainjo	crocine	konkinhun
crinoidea	korainjoin	crock	koko
crinoline	korainlehun	crock1	koko
crinum	korainma	crock2	koko
cripple	koraipiron	crockery	kokorai
crippler	koraipironsi	crocket	kokoto
crisis	koraiso	crocodile	konkijoron
crisp	koraisepn	crocodilian	konkijoronhn
crispate	koraisepnyo	crocoites	konkyo
crispation	koraisepnyoon	crocus	konkunsi
crisper	koraisepnsi	croesus	konseso
crispin	koraisepnse	croft	konfia
crispy	koraisepe	crofter	konfiasi

WORD (x)	EQUIVALENT (y)	WORD (x)	EQUIVALENT (y)
croissant	koinsoote	crotchety	kontekhotosi
croix de guerre	koinsi jin gbiran	croton	kontele
cro mag non	kon mogbile	crotonic	konteleko
crombec	konmboki	crouch	konlokha
cromlech	konmjnkho	croup1	konlopo
cromoma	konmurain	croup2	konlopo
cromwell	konmwinjjo	croupier	konloposi
crone	konni	crouse	konlose
cronk	konki	crouton	konlotele
crony	konnise	crow1	konwo
croo	koon	crow2	konwo
croodle	koonduo	crowd	konwode
crook	koonkoi	crowdle	konwoduo
crooked	koonkoide	crown	konwu
croon	koonhn	croze	konsu
crop	konpo	crozier	konsuran
cropper	konposi	crozzle	konsunron
croquet	konkunta	cru	koran
croquette	konkuntin	cruces	koransesi
croquignole	konkungnjoin	crucial	koransejo
croquis	konkunse	crucible	koranseron
crore	konroin	crucifer	koransefiro
crosier	konsoran	cruciferous	koransefirosi
cross	konso	crucifix	koransefisn
crossbar	konsoboosn	crucifixion	koransefiso
crosse	konsooe	crucify	koransefe
crossfire	konsofinna	cruck	koranki
crossing	konsognni	crud	korandi
crossopterygian	konsopintiraigan	crude	koranjn
crossover	konsownra	cruden	koranjnsi
crossroad	konsoronjn	crudity	koranjntn
crotalus	kontejnsi	cruel	koranlo
crotch	kontekho	cruelty	koranlotn
crotchet	kontekhoto	cruet	korante

WORD (x)	EQUIVALENT (y)	WORD (x)	EQUIVALENT (y)
cruik	korankun	cry	korai
cruise	koransun	cryer	koraisi
cruiser	koransunsi	crying	koraignni
cruller	koranllesi	cryo	korain
crumb	koranmbo	cryohydrate	korainhogbnyo
crumble	koranmbose	cryogen	koraingin
crumbly	koranmbolo	cryogenics	korainginkosi
crumbs	koranmbosi	cryolite	korainleyo
crumby	koranmbn	cryometer	korainmuto
crummy	koranmmo	cryonics	korainkosi
crump	koranmpn	cryophilic	korainpheronko
crumpet	koranmpnti	cryophorus	korainphiransi
crumple	koranmpnjo	cryoscopy	korainsekipo
crunch	korankhn	ryostat	korainsetnti
crunchy	korankhnse	cryotron	koraintnron
crunode	koranjoin	crypt	koraipnti
cruor	koranran	cryptesthesia	koraipntisunwnsia
crupper	koranpnra	cryptic	koraipntiko
crura	koranm	crypto	koraipnto
crural	koranmjo	cryptoclastic	koraipntokansiko
crus	koransa	cryptogam	koraipntogimo
crusade	koransejn	cryptogenic	koraipntoginko
crusade	koransejn	cryptogram	koraipntoganmo
cruse	koranse	cryptography	koraipntogranphe
crush	koransue	cryptology	koraipntologbon
crusoe	koransose	cryptomnesia	koraipntominisia
crust	koransi	cryptonym	koraipntomin
crustacean	koransekun	cryptopsychics	koraipntoposiakhosi
cruster	koransesi	cryptozoic	koraipntosinko
crusty	korantn	crystal	koraitnjo
crutch	koranta	crystalliferous	koraitnjjofirosi
crux	koranso	crystalligerous	koraitnjjogiransi
cruzado	koransude	crystalline	koraitnjjohun
cruzeiro	koranserain	crystallite	koraitnjjoto

WORD (x)	EQUIVALENT (y)	WORD (x)	EQUIVALENT (y)
crystallitis	koraitnjjoso	cuculiform	kunkuofoonmo
crystallize	koraitnjjose	cuculate	kunkuoyo
crystallo	koraitnjjoin	cucumber	kunkumbe
crystallography	koraitnjjoinganphe	cucumiform	kunkumfoonmo
crystalloid	koraitnjjoinjo	cucurbit	kunkunbeto
crystallomancy	koraitnjjoinmoyesn	cud	kundi
crystallon	koraitnjjoinsi	cudahy	kundiho
crystallose	koraitnjjoinse	cuddie	kundan
ct	keti kiti	cuddle	kunduo
cte	keti	cuddy	kundain
ctenidium	ketinjoma	cuddly	kunduose
ctenoid	ketinjo	cudgel	kungbilo
ctenophore	ketinphiran	cue1	kunse
cuanza	kunhnsa	cue2	kunse
cuarenta	kunrainta	cue-ball	kunse-robo
cub	kunba	cuenca	kunkoin
cuba	kunbo	cuesta	kunsita
cuban	kunbohn	cuff1	kunfi
cube	kunbe	cuff2	kunfi
cubeb	kunbebo	cuff-link	kunfi-lehako
cube root	kunbe rooyo	cui bono	kun iboohin
cubic	kunbeko	cufic	kunfeko
cubical	kunbekojo	cuirass	kunraiso
cubicule	kunbekuo	cuirassier	kunraisosi
cubicular	kunbekuoran	cuirbouilli	kunraibonunjjo
cubiculum	kunbekuoma	cuish	kunseha
cubism	kunbemosi	cuisine	kunsehun
cubit	kunbeto	culch	kuokhn
cubital	kunbetojo	cul-de-sac	kuo-jin-saaki
cubitus	kunbetosi	cul dee	kuo jiun
cuboid	kunbejo	-cule	kuo
cuchulain	kunkhijain	culet	kuote
cuckold	kunkijo	culex	kuosi
cuckoo	kunkiun	culgee	kuogun

WORD (x)	EQUIVALENT (y)	WORD (x)	EQUIVALENT (y)
culicide	kuokeku	cumaean	kuonihn
culinary	kuohunrai	cumber	kuobesn
cull	kunjnra	cumbersome	kuobesnsoomo
cullet	kunjnrate	cumbrance	kuobesnsi
cullion	kunjnrasi	cumbrous	kuobesnwa
cullis	kunjnraso	cumin	kuote
cully	kunjnrase	cumlaude	kuoleunjin
culm	kunjnma	cummerbund	kuomuraibejn
culmen	kunjnmuye	cumquat	kuokunyo
culmiferous	kunjnmofirosi	cumshaw	kuosuwe
culminant	kunjnmohetn	cumulate	kunmleyo
culminate	kunjnmoheyo	cumulative	kunmleyowin
culmination	kunjnmoheyoon	cumulet	kunmletn
culottes	kunjnitin	cumuliform	kunmlefoonmo
culpa	kunjnpan	cumulo	kunmlo
culpable	kunjnpanbe	cumulonimbus	kunmlohembesi
culprit	kunjnpante	cumulus	kunmlesi
cult	kunjia	cunaxa	kunhesia
cultch	kunjiakhn	cunctation	kunknteyoon
cultigens	kunjiagin	cunctator	kunknteran
cultivable	kunjiawnbe	cundum	kundimi
cultivar	kunjiawe	cuneal	kunhajo
cultivate	kunjiaweyo	cuneate	kunhayo
cultivation	kunjiaweyoon	cuneiform	kunhafoonmo
cultivator	kunjiaweran	cuniculus	kunkuosi
cultural	kunjiaranjo	cunner	kunran
culture	kunjiaran	cunnilingus	kuojnjognniwa
cultured	kunjiarane	cunning	kuojngnni
cultus	kunjiasi	cunt	kuntue
culver	kuowin	cup	kunpn
culverin	kuowini	cupar	kunpnra
culvert	kuowinte	cupel	kunpnjn
cum	kuo	cupellation	kunpnjjnyoon
cumae	kuoni	cupboard	bugbakunpn

WORD (x)	EQUIVALENT (y)	WORD (x)	EQUIVALENT (y)
cupid	kunpnjo	curcuma	kunrakunmo
cupidity	kunpnjotn	curcumin	kunrakunmu
cupola	kunpnjain	curd	kunradi
cuppa	kunpan	curdle	kunraduo
cupper	kunpnra	cure	kunrai
cuppy	kunpnpo	cure	kunrai
cupram	kunpanmo	cure-all	ajo-kunrai
cuprammonia	kunpanmmohan	curette	kunraite
cupreous	kunpansuwa	curettage	kunraitegun
cupric	kunpanko	curfew	kuofnwe
cupriferous	kunpanfirosi	curia	kunrain
cuprite	kunpanyo	curialism	kunraijomosi
cupro	kunpon	curie	kunrai
cupro-nickel	kunpon-hekijn	curing	kunraignni
cuprous	kunponsi	curio	kunrain
cuprum	kunponma	curiosity	kunraisetn
cup tie	kunpn tase	curious	kunrainsi
cupule	kunpuo	curitiba	kunraitobe
cur	kunra	curium	kunraima
curable	kunrabe	curl	kunralo
curacao	kunrakoin	curler	kunralosi
curacy	kunrasn	curlew	kunralowin
curacy	kunrasn	curlicue	kunrlokunse
curare	kunraran	curling	kunralognni
curarine	kunrarain	curly	kunralosi
curarize	kunraraise	curmudgeon	kunramogboin
curate	kunrate	currant	kunrraite
curate's egg	egbn kunratesi	currency	kunrraisn
curative	kunratewin	current	kunrraito
curator	kunratesi	current account	akaleyo kunrraito
curb	kunrabe	currently	kunrraitolo
curch	kunrakhn	curricle	kunrraikuo
curchie	kunrakhnni	curriculum	kunrraikolema
curculio	kunrakunjo	curriculum vitae	wintnsi kunrraikolema

WORD (x)	EQUIVALENT (y)	WORD (x)	EQUIVALENT (y)
currier	kunrransi	cusec	kunseka
curriery	kunrranrai	cush	kunsu
currish	kunrraisu	cushat	kunsuto
curry1	kunrrai	cushion	kunsuesi
curry2	kunrrai	cushitic	kunsuko
curse	kuose	cushy	kunsue
cursed	kuosede	cusp	kunsopn
cursive	kuosewin	cuspate	kunsopnyo
cursor	kuoseran	cuspid	kunsopnde
cursoriness	kuoserainisi	cuspidate	kunsopndeyo
cursory	kuoserai	cuspidation	kunsopndeyoon
curt	kuote	cuspidor	kunsopndera
curtail	kuotele	cuss	kunso
curtain	kuotelu	cussed	kunsode
curtal	kuotejo	custalorum	kunsetnjiama
curtate	kuoteyo	custard	kunsetngba
cartilage	kuotirangun	custer	kunseta
curtin	kuotie	custock	kunsetoki
curtis	kuotisi	custodian	kunsetodain
curtiss	kuotisoo	custody	kunsetodan
curtius	kuotiwa	custom	kunseto
curtsy	kuotisn	customary	kunsetorai
curule	kuoranjn	custom-built	kunseto-bulojia
curvaceous	kuowesuwa	customer	kunsetora
curvate	kuoweyo	customize	kunsetosi
curvature	kuoweran	custos	kunsetosn
curve	kuowin	custumal	kunsetojo
curvet	kuowinti	cut	kunte
curvi	kuowe	cutaneous	kuntehunwa
curvilinear	kuowelehun	cutaway	kuntewelo
curvity	kuowetn	cutch	kuntekhi
curvy	kuowese	cute	kuntin
cuzon	kuosnle	cuticle	kuntekuo
cuscus	kunsnka	cuticula	kuntekuosi

WORD (x)	EQUIVALENT (y)	WORD (x)	EQUIVALENT (y)
cutie	kuntesi	cyanopia	snknkopan
cutify	kuntefe	cyanosis	snknkoso
cutin	kuntie	cyanotype	snknkotnpon
cutinization	kuntieseyoon	cyanuric	snknraiko
cutinize	kuntiese	cybele	snberan
cutis	kunteso	cyber	snberai
cutlass	kuntelesi	cybernate	snberainyo
cutler	kuntejnra	cybemetics	snberainkosi
cutlery	kuntejnrai	cyberpunk	snberaipukn
cutlet	kuntetn	cybotaxis	snbotesanso
cut-off	kunte-ofan	cycad	snkojn
cut-out	kunte-nita	cyclades	snkanjnsi
cutter	kuntesi	cyclamate	snkanmuyo
cutting	kuntegnni	cyclamen	snkanmuye
cuttlefish	kunteronfisun	cyclas	snkansi
cutty	kuntese	cycle	snkuo
cuvee	kunwnun	cyclic	snkuoko
-cy	sn	cyclist	snkuosi
cyan	snkn	cyclo-	snkoi
cyanamide	snknmujin	cycloalkane	snkoijokehun
cyanate	snknyo	cyclocross	snkoikonso
cyanic acid	snknko	cyclogenesis	snkoignhunso
cyanide	snknjin	cyclogiro	snkoigirain
cyanin	snknha	cyclograph	snkoiganpha
cyanine	snknhun	cyclohexane	snkoihesohun
cyanite	snknyo	cycloid	snkoijo
cyano	snknko	cyclometer	snkoimuto
cyanocobalamin	snknkokibojomue	cyclometry	snkoimutorai
cyanogen	snknkogin	cyclone	snkoihun
cyanogenesis	snknkognhunso	cyclonite	snkoihunyo
cyanohydrin	snknkohogbnsi	cyclonoscope	snkoihunsekipon
cyanometer	snknkomuto	cycloparaffin	snkoipanrafin
cyanopathy	snknkopansio	cyclopean	snkoipnhn
cyanophilous	snknkopheron	cyclopedia	snkoipnjina

WORD (x)	EQUIVALENT (y)	WORD (x)	EQUIVALENT (y)
cyclopedic	snkoipnjnko	cymograph	snweganpha
cyclopentane	snkoipntelu	cymoid	snwejo
cyclophon	snkoiphin	cymometer	snwemuto
cycloplegia	snkoipogan	cymophane	snwephehun
cyclopropane	snkoiponpnhun	cymose	snwesn
cyclops	snkoipnsi	cymric	snweraiko
cyclorama	snkoiranma	cymry	snwerai
cyclosis	snkoiso	cynic	snseko
cyclosporine	snkoiseporain	cynical	snsekojo
cyclostome	snkoisetomu	cynism	snsemosi
cyclostrophic	snkoisetnraphiko	cynophobia	snsophobua
cyclostyle	snkoisetnron	cynosure	snsosurai
cyclothymia	snkoisiomua	cynthia	snsesia
cyclotron	snkoitnran	cynthus	snsesiasi
cyder	snjnra	cyperaceous	snpnrasuwa
cydonia	snjnsia	cypher	snphiro
cyesis	snseso	cypres	snpesise
cygnet	sngnyo	cypress	snpesiso
clinder	snlejnra	cyprian	snpanyan
cylindrical	snlejnraikojo	cyprinid	snpanjan
cylindroid	snlejnraijo	cyprino	snpankn
cyllene	snllehun	cyprinodont	snpankndeyo
cyma	snmu	cyprinoid	snpanknjo
cymar	snmura	cypriot	snpantin
cymarecta	snmuransita	cypripedium	snpanpnjnma
cymareverse	snmuranwinso	cyprus	snpansi
cymatium	snmutema	cypsela	snposujn
cymbal	snmbejo	cyrenaic	snranheko
cymbalo	snmbejoin	cyril	snraijn
cyme	snmo	cyrillic	snraijjnko
cymene	snmona	cyrus	snraisi
cymlin	snmojan	cyst	snsu
cymo	snwe	cystectomy	snsutntemo
cymogene	snwegini	cysteine	snsutnhun

WORD (x)	EQUIVALENT (y)	WORD (x)	EQUIVALENT (y)
cystic	snsuko	cytosine	sntosun
cysticercold	snsuknrasikijon	czar	siseran
cysticercus	snsuknrakisi	czarina	siseraini
cystic fibrosis	snsuko fibonso	czech	siseko
cystidium	snsujnma	czechoslovak	sisekosonwero
cystine	snsuhun	dab1	dabe
cystitis	snsuso	dab2	dabe
cystitome	snsutemu	dabble	daberon
cysto	snseto	dabster	dabeseto
cystocarp	snsetokopan	dacapo	dakopin
cystocele	snsetoknjn	dace	dakn
cystoid	snsetojo	dacey	daknse
cystolith	snsetolisi	dacha	dakho
cystoscope	snsetosekipon	dabchich	dabekhiki
cystostomy	snsetositemo	dachshund	dakhosihunjn
cystotomy	snsetotemo	dacia	dakin
cytase	sntese	dacite	dakiyo
cytaster	snteseto	dacker	dakira
-cyte	snte	dacoit	dakite
cytdine	sntejohun	dacolt	dakijia
cytherea	sntoherain	dacolty	dakijiase
cyto	snto	dacron	dakiron
cytodiagnosis	sntodasignso	dacryogenic	dakorainginko
cytogenesis	sntognhunso	dacryon	dakorain
cytogenetics	sntognhunkosi	dactyl	dakitile
cytology	sntologbon	dactylate	dakitileyo
cytolysin	sntojinsi	dactylic	dakitileko
cytolysis	sntojinso	datyliography	dakitiletoganphe
cytometer	sntomuto	dactylion	dakitilesi
cytomitome	sntomatemu	dactylo	dakitilo
cytophagy	sntophije	dactylogram	dakitiloganmo
cytopharynx	sntophisosi	dactylography	dakitilogranphe
cytoplasm	sntopanson	dactylology	dakitilologbon
cytoplast	sntopansia	dactyloscopy	dakitilosokipo

WORD (x)	EQUIVALENT (y)	WORD (x)	EQUIVALENT (y)
dad	dagba	daimen	dasemuye
dada	dagban	daimio	dasemini
daddle	dagbaduo	daimon	dasemoha
daddy	dagbase	dainty	daseto
dado	dadein	daiquiri	dasekunrai
daedal	daindejo	dairen	daserain
daedalus	daindejosi	dair	daseran
daemon	dainmoha	dairy	daserai
daff	dafi	dairying	daseraignni
daffing	dafignni	dairymaid	daseraimaajo
daffodil	dafinjnle	dairyman	daseraimoye
daffy	dafilo	dais	dasesi
daft	dafia	daisy	daseso
dag	dagn	dak	daki
dagan	dagbnsi	dakar	dakira
dagger	dagbnra	daker	daknra
daggle	dagbnron	dakin	dakin
daghestan	daghnseto	dakota	dkite
daglock	dagnlokn	dalai	dajain
dago	dagun	dalai lama	dajain lemo
dagoba	dagunbe	dale	dajn
dagoes	dagunsi	dall	dajnra
dagon	dagunse	dallas	dajnrasi
daguerrean	dagbiranrain	dalles	dajnraso
daguerreotype	dagbiraraintnpon	dalliance	dajnrasi
dah	daha	dally	dajnrase
dahlia	dahunjia	dalmatin	dajnmutn
dahabeah	dahunbeha	dalmatian	dajnmutnhn
dahana	dahunna	damatic	dajnmutnko
dahlia	dahijn	dalrymple	dajnraimpo
dahomey	dahinmosi	dal segno	dajn sugnni
dahoon	dahoon	dalton	dajntin
dail	dasejo	daltonian	dajntinhn
daily	daselo	datonism	dajntinmosi

WORD (x)	EQUIVALENT (y)	WORD (x)	EQUIVALENT (y)
daly	dalo	danaide	dajojainsi
dam1	damo	danaus	dajoinsi
dam2	damo	dance	dajo
damage	damogbun	d and c	jinleyoon ati kunsitagn
daman	damohn	dancette	dajotin
damanhur	damohnrai	dandelion	dajnduole
damao	damoin	dander	dajnra
damara	damorai	dandify	dajndanfe
damascene	damaseknsa	dandiprat	dajndanpante
damascus	damasekunsi	dandle	dajnduo
damask	damasia	dandruff	dajnraife
dambonite	dambuyo	dandy	dajndan
dame	damo	dane	dain
damiana	daminihun	dane ged	dain gnjon
damietta	daminito	dang	dagn
dammar	dammura	danger	dagnra
damn	daamu	danger list	lisi dagnra
damnabe	daamuberon	dangerous	dagnrasi
damnation	daamuyoon	dangle	dagnron
damnatory	daamuyorai	danish	dainso
damned	daamude	daniel	dainlo
damndest	daamudesi	danite	dainto
damnify	daamufe	dank	daknmi
damocles	damikunsi	dannebrog	dainnibongbi
damodar	damijnra	danny	dainse
damosel	damisujo	danse	dajosn
damp	damipn	danseuse	dajosesun
dampen	damipnsi	dantesque	daintesikun
damper	damipnra	dantist	daintesi
damsel	damase	danton	daintin
damson	damasin	danu	dajnun
dan	dajo	Danube	dajnunbe
danae	dajoni	danzig	dajnsegbi
danaid	dajojain	dap	dapn

WORD (x)	EQUIVALENT (y)	WORD (x)	EQUIVALENT (y)
daphine	daphini	darrow	darrowe
daphnis	daphinisi	darogha	darogan
dapper	dapepnra	dart	daraitn
dapple	dapepnron	dartboard	bugbadaraitn
daraf	daraife	darter	daraitnsi
darbles	daraibesi	darwin	darawin
darby and joan	daraibe ati jinhn	dawinian	darawinhn
dardanelles	daraijijjnsi	dash	dasun
dardanus	daraijnsi	dashboard	bugbadasun
dare	darai	dasheen	dasuani
daredevil	daraijinworo	dashiki	dasunki
darg	daragan	dashing	dasungnni
daric	darako	dastard	dasiagbaa
darrien	daraini	dastardly	dasiagbaalo
daring	daraignni	dasyure	dasnran
dario	darain	data	date
dariole	darainjin	datable	datebe
darius	daraisi	data capture	date kopnra
dark	dakun	data processing	date ponknsognni
darken	dakunsi	datary	daterai
dark horse	hiso dakun	date1	dayo
darkie	dakunse	date2	dayo
darkle	dakunjn	date-ine	lehun dayo
darkling	dakungnni	dative	datowin
darky	dakunse	datolite	dateleyo
darkness	daknnisi	datto	datto
darling	darajngnni	datum	datema
darlington	darajngnnitin	datura	dateran
dam1	damo	daub	danunba
dam2	damo	daube	danunbe
damed	damode	daubery	danunbera
damel	damosi	daugheter	danungbe
damer	damosi	daughter-in-law	danungbe leofin
daming	damognni	daunt	danuntn

165

WORD (x)	EQUIVALENT (y)	WORD (x)	EQUIVALENT (y)
dauntless	danuntnlabo	deal1	jinle
dauphin	danunphin	deal2	jinle
dauphine	danunphini	dealer	jinlesi
dauphiness	danunphinbo	dealings	jinlegnnisi
daur	darai	dealt	jinleyo
dauma	daraiha	deaminate	jinmuhunyo
daut	danunti	dean1	jinhun
dautie	danuntie	dean2	jinhnn
dave	dawin	deanery	jinhunrai
davenport	dawinpinta	dear	jinran
david	dawinjn	dearie	jinranni
davis	dawinsi	dearth	jinransi
davit	dawinte	death	dilesi
daviva	dawinwa	deb	jinbo
davos	dawnse	debacle	jinbokuo
davout	dawnnita	debark	jinborakn
davy	dawose	debag	dabogbi
daw	dawn	debar	daboosn
dawdle	dawnduo	debase	dabooso
dawn	dawnse	debatable	jinbotebe
day	dase	debate	jinbote
daylight	daseleghe	debauch	jinbonunkhn
daze	dasia	debauchee	jinbonunkhnse
dazzle	dasiaron	debaucher	jinbonunkhnsi
de-	da di din de jin	debauchery	dnbonunkhnrai
deacon	jinkoni	debenture	jinbetorai
deactivate	dakntiweyo	debilitate	dnberontnyo
dead	dilejn	debility	dnberontn
deaden	dilejnsi	debit	jigbese
deadline	dilejnlehun	debonair	jinbinrai
deadly	dilejnlo	debonne	jinbinhun
deaf	difan	deborah	jinberain
deaf-aid	aajo-difan	debouch	jinbonunkho
deafen	difansi	debridement	dnbanjnmutto

WORD (x)	EQUIVALENT (y)	WORD (x)	EQUIVALENT (y)
debrief	dnbanfin	decapolis	jinkopinjinsi
debris	jinberaisi	decapsulation	jinkopnsuoyoon
debt	jigbese	decarbonize	jinkosibuse
debtor	jigbesesi	decare	jinknran
debug	jinbugi	decastere	jinknsetnran
debunk	jinbukn	decastyle	jinknsetnron
debut	jinbute	decasyllable	jinknsollebe
debutante	jinbuteto	decathlon	jinknsajnsi
dec.	jinka	decating	jinkntignni
deca-	jinkn	decay	jinkoin
decade	jinknjan	decease	jinknsise
decadence	jinknjansi	deceased	jinknsisede
decadent	jinknjanto	decedent	jinkndato
decaffeinated	dinkofiniyode	deceit	jinknte
decagon	jinkngn	deceive	jinknwin
decagram	jinknganmo	decelerate	dinknjnraiyo
decahedron	jinknhegboin	december	jinknmbe
decal	jinknjo	decemvir	jinknmwirai
decalage	jinknjogun	decency	jinknsn
decalcification	jinknjokifikoyoon	decennary	jinknhunrai
decalcify	jinknjokife	decennial	jinknhunjo
decalcomania	jinknjokimohan	decennium	jinknhunma
decalescence	jinknjoseknsi	decent	daaknti
decaliter	jinknlitnra	decenter	dakntisi
decalitre	jinknlitnsi	decentralize	dakntiraijose
dacalogue	jinknjogbiso	eception	jinknposi
decameron	jinknmorain	deceptive	jinknpowin
decamp	dakompn	decem	jinknran
decanal	dakohunjo	deci-	dikn
decant	dakote	deciare	diknran
decanter	dakotesi	decibel	diknbele
decapitate	dakopnteyo	decide	diknjo
decapod	jinknpindie	decided	diknjode
decapodiform	jinknpindiefon	decidedly	diknjodelo

WORD (x)	EQUIVALENT (y)	WORD (x)	EQUIVALENT (y)
decider	diknjosi	decoct	dakikyo
decidua	diknjain	decoction	dakikyoon
deciduous	diknjainsi	decode	dakidie
decigram	diknganmo	decoke	dakikan
decile	diknjjo	decongestant	dakingnseyote
decillion	diknjjosi	decoherer	dakiheransi
decigram	diknganmo	decollate	dakijjoyo
deciliter	diknlitnra	décolletage	dakijjoteyogun
decilitre	diknlitnran	décolleté	dakijjote
decimal	diknmojn	decolorize	dakijoranse
decimalize	diknmojnse	decommission	dakimmusinse
decimate	diknmote	decompose	dakimpose
decimeter	diknmuto	decomposition	dakimposeyoon
decimetre	diknmutoran	decompression	dakimpesisoon
decipher	diknphira	decontaminate	dakintemuheyo
decision	diknsesi	décor	deknrn
decisive	diknsewin	decorate	deknranyo
decistere	diknsetnran	decoration	deknranyoon
deck	deki	decorative	deknranyowin
deck-chair	deki-khoso	decorator	deknranse
-decker	dekisi	decorous	deknransi
deckle	dekiron	decorticate	deknratnkoyo
declaim	dikanlemo	decorum	deknranma
declamation	dikanlemoyoon	decoupage	deknpangun
declaration	dikanraiyoon	decoy	dekoyn
declare	dikanrai	decrease	dnknrase
déclassé	dakansoo	decree	jinknrase
declassify	dakansoofe	decree nisi	jinknrase heso
declension	dakoroinsoon	decrement	dnknramutto
declination	dakihunyoon	decremeter	dnknramuto
decline	dakihun	decrepit	dnknrapnti
declinometer	dakihunmuto	decrepitate	dnknrapntiyo
decliitous	dakiunwotn	decrescendo	dnknraseknde
declivity	dakiunwoto	decrescent	dnknraseknti

WORD (x)	EQUIVALENT (y)	WORD (x)	EQUIVALENT (y)
dectetal	dnknratojo	deep	jnpon
decretist	dnknratosi	deepen	jnponsi
decretory	dnknratorai	deeply	jnponlo
decriminalize	dakoraminijose	deer	jinrain
decrudescence	dnkordieseknsi	deerlet	jinraintn
decry	jinkorai	def	dnfa
decryptograph	jinkoraipntoganpha	deface	dnfansi
decubation	jinkuobeyoon	de facto	dn fanknto
decuman	jinknmoye	defalcate	dnfanjoyo
decumbence	jinknmbesi	defalcation	dnfanjoyoon
decumbent	jnknmbeto	defame	dnfanmo
decuple	jnknporon	defamation	dnfanmoyoon
decuplicate	jnknpankoyo	default	dnfanjia
decurion	jnknrain	defeasance	dafnsesi
decurrent	dnkunrraito	defeasible	dafnsebe
decursive	dnkuosewin	defeat	dafntn
decurve	dnkuowin	defeatism	dafntnmosi
decury	jinkunrai	defecate	dafnkoyo
decussate	dakunsose	defect	dafnkoi
dedalous	jijinjosi	defective	dafnkoiwin
dedans	jijinhunsi	defenestration	defnnisetnreyoon
dedicate	jijinkiyo	defence	defnkosi
dedication	jijinkiyoon	defend	defnkojn
deduce	dndisi	defendant	defnkojntn
deduct	dndiki	defense	defnkose
deductible	dndikibe	defensible	defnkosebe
deduction	dndikiyoon	defensive	defnkosewin
deductive	dndikiwin	defensor	defnkoseran
dee	dise	defer1	dafiro
deed	didi	defer2	dafiro
deeded	didide	deferent	dafirointn
deek	kikin	deference	dafiroinsi
deem	dimu	deferential	dafirointojo
deemster	dimuseto	deterred payment	panyiomutto dafirrode

WORD (x)	EQUIVALENT (y)	WORD (x)	EQUIVALENT (y)
defervescence	dafirowinseknsi	deft	defia
defiance	dafiasi	defunct	dafunkn
defiant	dafiatn	defuse	dafunsi
deficiency	dnfisesn	defy	dafe
deficient	dnfiseto	degage	dagigun
deficit	dnfikiti	degenerate	dagnhunraiyo
defide	dnfijo	degeneration	dagnhunraiyoon
defilade	dnfijanjo	deglutinate	dagbiletinyo
defile1	dnfijan	degrade	dagandie
defile2	dnfijan	degree	dagirai
define	define	degression	dagiraisoon
definite	dafinitn	degust	dagnte
definite article	etekun dafinitn	dehisce	dahisekn
definition	dafiniyoon	dehom	dahuran
definitive	dafiniyowin	dehumanize	dahunmoyese
deflagration	defanganyoon	dehumidify	dahunmijnfe
deflate	defanyo	dehydrate	dahogbanyo
deflation	defanyoon	dehydrogenate	dahogbnginyo
deflect	defonjnko	dehypnotize	dahopiyese
deflexed	defonjnside	deicide	jinbokeku
deflocculate	defonkuoyo	deictic	jinboknko
deflorate	defonraiyo	deific	jinbofiko
defloration	defonraiyoon	deify	jinbofe
deflower	defonwara	deign	jinbogba
defluxion	dafolusoon	deinstitutionalize	jinisetintuyoonjose
defoliate	dafonjiayo	deil	jinbolo
deforest	dafonsnsi	deira	jinboran
defom	dafonmo	deism	jinbomosi
deformed	dadonmode	deist	jinbosi
deformity	dnfoonmotn	deity	jinbotn
defraud	dafande	déjà vu	jinjo wa
defray	dafanse	deject	dnjnkn
defrock	dafonki	de jeunner	jin jeunran
defrost	dafonsi	de jure	jin joran

WORD (x)	EQUIVALENT (y)	WORD (x)	EQUIVALENT (y)
deka	dekn	delict	jinlikyo
dekagram	deknganmo	delight	jinlighe
dekaliter	deknlitnra	delimit	jinlimutn
dekameter	deknmuto	delineate	jinlehunyo
dekare	deknran	delinquent	jinlihakunra
dekastere	deknsetoran	deliquesce	jinlikunsekn
dekko	dekio	deliration	jinliraiyoon
delaminate	jinlemiheyo	delirious	jinliraisi
delate	jijinto	delirium	jinliraima
delaminate	jijinmoheyo	delitescence	jinlitoseknsi
delaware	jijinwerai	deliver	jinliwaran
delay	jijinse	deliverance	jinliwaransi
delcredere agent	aginte jijinknrajinre	delivery	jinliwarai
dele	jijn	dell	jinjnra
delectable	jijnkitoberon	della cruscan	jinjnran koraseko
delectation	jijnkitoyoon	delocalize	jinloknjose
deleerit	jijnrate	delouse	jinlolese
delegant	jijngite	delphic	jinlephinko
delegate	jijngiyo	delphinine	jinlephinihun
delegation	jijngiyoon	delphinium	jinlephinima
delete	jijnyo	delta	jinleta
deleterious	jijnyoraisi	deltiology	jinletalogbon
deletion	jijnyoon	deltoid	jinletajo
delft	jijnfia	delude	jinlude
dell	jijnro	deluge	jinlugbn
della	jijnron	delusion	jinlusoon
deli	jinle	de luxe	jinlusan
deliberate	jinleberaiyo	delve	jinlwing
deliberation	jinleberaiyoon	demagnetize	jinmaginitese
deliberative	jinleberaiyowin	demagog	jinmugonko
delicacy	jinleknsn	demagogue	jinmugongbo
delicate	jinleknyo	demand	damadain
delicatessen	jinleknyosoon	demand feeding	damadain finjegnni
delicious	jinlesuwa	demarcate	damurakoyo

WORD (x)	EQUIVALENT (y)	WORD (x)	EQUIVALENT (y)
demarcation	damurakoyoon	democracy	jumokansn
dematerialize	damuteraijose	democrat	jumokanta
demarch	damurakhi	democratic	jumokansnko
demarche	damurakhn	democratize	jumokansnse
deme	jinmu	democritus	jumoknraisi
demean	damuhn	démodé	damodie
demeanor	damuhnran	demodulate	damodieleyo
demeanour	damuhnran	demodule	damodiele
dement	damnnite	demogorgon	jumogungbile
demented	damnnitede	demography	jumoganphe
dementia	damnnitie	demolselle	jinmolosujjn
dementia praecox	damnnitie pankinsi	demolish	damolesi
demerara	damuranran	demon	jinmosi
demerger	damuraigbi	demoniac	jinmosikoi
demerit	damuraite	demonic	jinmosiko
demersal	jinmuraisnjo	demonism	jinmosimosi
demesne	jinmusihun	demonolatry	jinmosiletorai
demeter	damuto	demonology	jinmosilogbon
demetrious	damutorainsi	demonstrable	jumosirainbe
demi-	dnmo	demonstrate	jumosirinyo
demigod	dnmogodi	demonstration	jumosirainyoon
demijohn	dnmojinhun	demonstrative	jumosirainyowin
demi-monde	dnmo-menide	demonstrator	jumosirainyoran
demiquaver	dnmokunwinro	demoralize	damoranjose
demise	dnmose	demote	dinmotn
demisemiquaver	dnmosemukunwinro	demotic	dinmotnko
demission	damosoon	demotivate	dinmotnweyo
demit	dnmotn	demur	jinmura
demitasse	dnmotnsoo	demure	jinmuran
demiurge	dnmoraigbi	demurrage	jinmurraigun
demivierge	dnmuworaign	demurral	jinmurraijo
demo	jumo	demurrer	jinmurraisi
demob	damobu	demy	jinmun
demobilize	damobajnse	demythologize	jinmunsnlogbonse

WORD (x)	EQUIVALENT (y)	WORD (x)	EQUIVALENT (y)
den	jinha	de novo	di nkown
denarius	jinharaisi	dencotee	dikunkitise
denary	jinharai	dense	dikunse
denationalize	jinhetnsejose	densimeter	dikunsemuto
denature	jinhetnran	densitometer	dikunsetomuto
dendriform	jinhagbnfoon	density	dikunsetn
dendrite	jinhagbnyo	dent	dato
dendritic	jinhagbnko	dental	datojo
dendro	jinhagbn	dental floss	datojo fonso
dendrochore	jinhagbn	dental surgeon	datojo suralesi
dendrochore	jinhagbnkhiran	dentalium	datojoma
dendrochronlogy	jinhagbnkiroinlogbon	dentate	datoyo
dendroid	jinhagbnjo	dentation	datoyoon
dendrolite	jinhagbnleyo	dentex	datosi
dendrology	jinhagbnlogbon	denti	datu
dendron	jinhagbnsi	denticle	datukuo
dene	jinhun	denticulate	datukunleyo
deneb	jinhunbe	dentification	datufikoyoon
denegate	jinhungiyo	dentiform	datufon
denegation	jinhungiyoon	dentifrice	datufansi
dengue	jingini	dentil	datule
deniable	jiyanberon	dentilingual	datulikognjo
denial	jiyanjo	dentine	datuhun
denier	jinyansi	dentist	datusi
denigrate	jiyanganyo	dentistry	datusirai
denim	dikunmo	dentition	datuyoon
denizen	dikunsin	dento	dato
denmark	dikunmurokn	dentoid	datojo
denominate	dinimoheyo	denture	datorai
denomination	dinimoheyoon	denty	datose
denominator	dinimoheran	denuclearize	dayunkojnraise
denote	dinkote	denude	dayunhoho
denouement	dnnknsemutto	denunciation	dankonsoyoon
denounce	dinkonso	deny	jiyan

WORD (x)	EQUIVALENT (y)	WORD (x)	EQUIVALENT (y)
deo	jinbo	deplore	diponrai
deodand	jinbodidan	deploy	jinponse
deodar	jinbodira	depoliticize	jinpinjntoknse
deodorant	jinbodirun	depone	dipinse
deodorize	jinbojnrunse	deponent	diponseto
deo favente	jino fanwato	depopulate	dapopnleyo
deogratias	jinboganyosi	deport	jinpinta
deo juvante	jinbo jowinte	deportation	jinpintayoon
deotic	jinbotnko	deportee	jinpintase
deontology	jinbosetologbon	deportment	jinpintamuto
deoxidize	jinbosinjise	deposal	dipinsijo
deoxygenate	jinbosinseginyo	depose	dipinsi
deoxyribo	jinbosinseraibn	deposit	dipinsito
dep.	dipa	deposit account	akaleyo dipinsito
depart	dipante	depositary	dipinsitorai
departed	dipante	deposition	dipinsitosi
departed	dipantede	depositor	dipinisitoran
department	dipantemutto	depository	dipinsitorai
departmental	dipantemuttojo	depot	dipote
department store	setoran dipantemutto	deprave	dnpanwin
departure	dipanterai	depravity	dnpanwintn
depauperate	dipanpnrayo	deprecate	dnpesikoyo
depegram	dipnganmo	depreciate	dnpesiknyo
depend	dipnjon	depreciation	dnpesiknyoon
dependable	dipnjonbe	depredate	dnpesidayo
dependant	dipnjointn	depredation	dnpesidayoon
dependence	dipnjonsi	depress	dnpesiso
dependency	dipnjonsn	depressant	dnpesisote
dependent	dipnjonto	depressed area	aria dnpesisode
depict	diponkiti	depression	dnpesisoon
depilate	diponleyo	depressive	dnpesisowin
depilatory	diponleyorai	depressor	dnpesisoran
deplete	dnponyo	deprivation	dapanwinyoon
deplorable	diponraibe	deprive	dapanwin

WORD (x)	EQUIVALENT (y)	WORD (x)	EQUIVALENT (y)
deprogram	daponganmo	dermatoglyphics	jnramotngilophekosi
depropriomotu	daponpanmuto	dermatoid	jnramotnjo
dept.	dapnte	dermatology	jnramotnlogbon
depth	dnpnsi	dermatome	jnramotemu
deputation	dipntoyoon	dermatophyte	jnramotnpheyo
depute	dipnto	dermatophytosis	jnramotnpheyoso
deputize	dipntose	dermatosis	jnramotnso
deputy	dipntosi	dermis	jnramoso
der	daran	dermo	jnramo
deracinate	darankoinyo	dermoid	jnramojo
deraign	darangbain	dermophytosis	jnramopheyoso
derail	darailo	dernier	jnrainsi
derange	daraigini	dero	jnro
derby	jnrabe	derogate	jnrogiyo
derecognize	darekiginise	derogation	jnrogiyoon
deregulate	daregileyo	derogatory	jnrogiyorai
dereism	dnremosi	derrick	jnrraiki
derelict	dnrejokyo	derrid	jnrraijo
dereliction	dnrejokyoon	derriere	jnrrairan
deride	dnraijin	derring-do	jnrraign-de
de rigueur	jin raigbiran	derringer	jnrraignsi
derisible	dnraisobe	derris	jnrraisi
derision	dnraisoon	derry	jinrrai
derisive	dnraisowin	derv	jnrawa
derisory	dnraisorai	dervish	jnrawnso
derivation	dnraiwinyoon	desalinate	jinsanjyo
derivative	dnraiwinyowin	descant	jinseknte
derive	dnraiwin	descartes	jinseknrasi
derm	jnramo	descend	dnseknjn
dermal	jnramojn	descendant	dnseknjnte
dermapterous	jnramopitnrasi	descendent	dnseknjnto
dermatitis	jnramoteso	descent	dnseknti
dermato	jnramotn	describe	jinsekorai
dermatogen	jnramotngin	description	jinsekoraipnyoon

WORD (x)	EQUIVALENT (y)	WORD (x)	EQUIVALENT (y)
descriptive	jinsekoraipnyowin	desman	jinsimaye
descry	dasekorai	desmid	jinsimuda
desecrate	dasekanyo	desmoid	jinsimujo
desegregate	dasegiragiyo	desmotropism	jinsimotnrapnmosi
deselect	dasejnsa	desna	jinsihun
desensitize	dasesnsntose	desolate	dasinleyo
desert1	daseratn	desolation	dasinleyoon
desert2	daseratn	desorption	jinsinrapnyoon
desert3	daseratn	despair	jinsepanrai
deserter	daseratnsi	desperado	jinsepnrade
desertification	daseratnfikoyoon	desperate	jinsepnrayo
desertion	daseratnsi	desperation	jinsepnrayoon
deserve	jinserawin	despicable	jinsipokobe
deserving	jinserawingnni	despise	jinsipose
dishabille	jinsuebajjn	despite	jinsipnti
desiccate	jinsookoyo	despoil	jinsipojia
desideratum	jinsoojoratima	despoliation	jinsipojiayoon
design	jinsoogan	despond	jinsiponjn
design	jinsoogan	desponent	jinsipohuntn
designate	jinsooganyo	despose	desipnse
designation	jinsooganyoon	despot	jinsipote
designedly	jinsoogandelo	despotism	jinsipotemosi
designee	jinsoganse	despumate	jinsipnmuyo
designer	jinsoogansi	desquamate	jinsikunmuyo
designing	jinsoogangnni	dessaline	jinssinlehun
desinence	jinsootesi	dessert	jinssetnra
desipience	jinsooposi	dessertspoon	jinssetnraseosi
desipient	jinsoopotan	dessiatine	jinssiatin
desirable	jinsooraibe	destabilize	dasetngbise
desire	jinsoorai	destination	jinsitinyoon
desirous	jinsooraisi	destine	jinsitin
desist	jinsoosi	destiny	jinsitinse
desk	jinsia	destitute	dnsitintuyo
desktop	jinsiatopn	destitution	dnsitintuyoon

WORD (x)	EQUIVALENT (y)	WORD (x)	EQUIVALENT (y)
destroy	dnsitnra	determinism	datnronhemosi
destroyer	dnsitnrase	deterrent	datnrroto
destruct	dasetnran	detersion	datnrosoon
destructible	dasetnranbe	detersive	datnrosowin
destruction	dasetnranyoon	detest	datnsi
destructionist	dasetnranyoonsi	detestable	datnsiberon
destructive	dasetnranwin	dethrone	dasinran
destructor	dasetnranran	detinue	datinse
desuetude	jinsuetujin	detonate	datohunyo
desultory	dasnjiarai	detonation	datohunyoon
detach	datekho	detonator	datohunran
detachment	datekhomutto	detour	datoorai
detail	datele	detoxify	datoosife
detain	datelu	detract	datnrekiti
detainee	dateluse	detractor	datnrekitisi
detect	datoknti	detrain	datnreto
detectaphone	datokntiphohun	detribalise	dataraibijose
detection	datokntisi	detriment	dataraimutto
detective	datokntiwin	detrimental	dataraimuttojo
detector	datokntiran	detrition	dataraiyoon
detent	datinto	detritus	dataraitesi
détente	datinyo	de trop	da tnrapn
detention	datinyoon	detrude	datoraijin
deter	datn	detruncate	datoraiknyo
deterge	datngi	dettingen	dattegini
detergency	datnginsn	detumescence	ditumoseknsi
detergent	datnginte	deucalion	diwakojoin
deteriorate	datnraiyo	deuce1	diwasi
determ	datnron	deuce2	diwasi
determinant	datnronhetn	deuce ace	diwa akn
determinate	datnronheyo	deus	diwa
determination	datnronheyoon	deuteragonist	diwatnragunsesi
determine	datnronhe	deuteranope	diwatnrainpn
determined	datnronhede	deuteranopia	diwatnrainpan

WORD (x)	EQUIVALENT (y)	WORD (x)	EQUIVALENT (y)
deuteric	diwatnrako	devoid	dawnjua
deuteride	diwatnraijin	devoirs	dawnraisi
deuterium	diwatnraima	devolution	dawnjnyoon
deutero	diwatnro	devolve	dawnjnwa
deuterogamy	diwatnroganmo	devonian	jinwnjnwa
deuteron	diwatnroin	devonian	jinwnhn
deuteronomy	diwatnroinmo	devoted	jinwntode
deutoplasm	diwatopanson	devotee	jinwntose
deutzia	diwatosia	devotion	jinwnyoon
deva	dnwa	devour	jinwnrun
devalue	dnwajoin	devout	jinwnta
devaluate	dnwajoinyo	dew	jinwn
devanagari	dawainganrai	dewar	jiwnran
devastate	jinwasetn	dewlap	jiwnlepn
devastating	jinwasetngnni	dewy	jiwnse
deve	jinwn	dexter	jinseto
devel	jinwnlo	dexterity	jinsetoraitn
develop	jinwnlopo	dexterous	jinsetoraisi
developer	jinwnloposi	dextral	jinsetnrejo
development	jinwnlopomutto	dextran	jinsetnrein
deviant	jinwontn	dextrin	jinsetnrain
deviate	jinwonyo	dextro	jinsetnran
device	jinwokn	dextrogyrate	jinsetnranloraiyo
devil	jinworo	dextrorse	jinsetnranrase
devilish	jinworosi	dextrose	jinsetnranse
devilment	jinworomutto	dey	jinye
devilry	jinwororai	dezincificatioin	jinsotikofikoyoon
devious	jinworosi	dhak	dhaki
devise	jinwose	dharma	dhamo
devisee	jinwosesi	dhama	dhama
devisor	jinwoseran	dhole	dhajoin
devitalise	dawintnjose	dhoti	dhatie
devitrify	dawintnraife	dhow	dhawain
devoice	dawnnso	dhu	dhudu

WORD (x)	EQUIVALENT (y)	WORD (x)	EQUIVALENT (y)
di-1	di	diagoras	dasigbase
di-2	di	diagram	dasiganmo
di-3	di eji pipo	diagraph	dasiganpha
dia.	dasi	diaheliotropism	dasihejotnrapnmosi
dia	dasi	dial	dijo
diabase	dasibooso	dialect	dijokyo
diabetes	dasigbe	dialectal	dijokyojo
diabetes insipidus	dasigbe isnpojnsi	dialectic	dijokyoko
diabetes mellitus	dasigbe mujnraisi	dialectical	dijokyokojo
diabetic	dasigbeko	dialectician	dijokyokohn
diablerie	dasiboojnran	dialectics	dijokyokosi
diabolical	dasibookojo	dialectology	dijokyologbon
diabolism	dasiboomosi	diallage	dijjogun
diabolise	dasiboose	dialing tone	toni dijognni
diabolo	dasiboolo	dialog	dilogn
diacaustic	dasikoinsuko	dalogism	dilogbimosi
diacetylmorphine	dasikntilomophini	dialogist	dilogbisosi
diachronic	dasikhironko	dialogue	dilogbiso
diachylon	dasikhojnsi	dialyse	dijojinso
diaconal	dasikinjo	dialyser	dijojinsosi
diaconate	dasikinyo	dialysis	dijojinso
diacritic	dasikoraitako	diamagnet	dasimogante
diacritical	dasikoraitakojo	diamagnetic	dasimaganteko
diactinic	dasikyoko	diamagnetism	dasimagantemosi
diadlphous	dasijophisi	diamante	dasimayetn
diadem	dasimegba	diameter	dasimuto
diadromous	dasigbnmosi	diametrical	dasimutoraikojo
diaeresis	dasireraso	diamine	dasimihun
diageotropism	dasigbiletnrapnmosi	diamond	dasimodan
diagnose	dasignse	diana	dasihe
diagnosis	dasignso	diandrous	digboinsi
diagnostic	dasignsuko	dianetics	dasihunkosi
diagnostics	dasignsukosi	dianoetic	dasiknko
diagonal	dasigunjo	dianoia	dasiknsi

WORD (x)	EQUIVALENT (y)	WORD (x)	EQUIVALENT (y)
dianthus	dasisinsi	diathermy	dasisinron
diapason	dasipansin	diathesis	dasisinso
diapedesis	dasipnjinso	diatom	dasitemo
diapente	dasipnyato	diatomic	dasitemuko
diaper	dasipnra	diatonic	dasitoniko
diaphanous	dasiphinisi	diatribe	dasitaraibi
diaphone	dasiphohun	diatropism	dasitnrapnmosi
diaphony	dasiphohunse	diazine	dasisun
diaphoresis	dasiphiranso	diazo	dasisin
diaphoretic	dasiphiranko	diazole	dasisinron
diaphragm	dasiphangon	diazonium	dasisinhnma
diaphysis	dasipheso	diazotise	dasisinse
diapir	dasipanra	diazepam	dasisepoun
diapophysis	dasipopheso	dibasic	dibooso
diapositive	dasiposeyowin	dibble	dibube
diarch	diknra	dibranchiate	dibainkhiyo
diarchy	diknran	dibromide	dibonmujin
diarist	dasiraisi	dicast	dikosoto
diarrhea	dasirhain	dice	disiun
diarrhoea	dasirhoin	dicentra	dikntire
diary	dasirai	dicephalous	diknphijnsi
diascope	dasisekipon	dicerous	diknrasi
diaspora	dasisepnra	dicey	diknse
diaspore	dasiseporai	dichasium	dikhosoma
diastalsis	dasisetnjnso	dichlamydeous	dikhanmunjinsi
diastase	dasisetnse	dichloramine	dikhonramini
diastasis	dasisetnso	dichloride	dikhonraiji
diastema	dasisutnma	dicho	dikho
diaster	dasiseto	dichogamy	dikhogimo
diastole	dasisetojn	dichotomy	dikhotemo
diastrophism	dasisetnraphimosi	dichroism	dikhironmosi
diastyle	dasisetnron	dichromatic	dikhoronmuko
diatessaron	dasitosooron	dick1	dikn
diathermancy	dasisinronsn	dick2	dikn

WORD (x)	EQUIVALENT (y)	WORD (x)	EQUIVALENT (y)
dickcissel	diknkisoolo	didynamous	didainsemosi
dickens	diknsi	die1	dile
dickensian	diknsian	die2	dile
dicker	diknsi	dieback	dileboki
dickey	diknse	die down	dile juan
dichlinous	dikhihunsi	diego	dilelo
dicliny	dikhihunse	diehard	dilehagba
dicotyledon	dikitilojnsi	dieldrin	dilogbain
dicrotic	diknrako	diencephalon	dienknphijnsi
dicta	diknto	diene	dilehun
dictaphone	dikntophohun	die off	dile ofan
dictate	dikntoyo	dieresis	direranso
dictation	dikntoyoon	diesel	dilesun
dictator	dikntotn	diesis	dileso
dictatorial	dikntotnraijo	diesnon	dilesn
diction	diknyoon	diestock	dilesetoki
dictionary	diknyoonrai	diet1	dilete
dictograph	dikntoganpha	diet2	dilete
dictum	dikntoma	dietary	dileterai
dictynid	dikntonjo	dietetic	dileteko
dicumarol	dikuoranjin	dietetics	diletekosi
dicynodont	disnkndeyo	diethylene	diletelohun
did	dide	diethylstilbestrol	diletelosetnraberoinjin
didache	didekhn	dietitian	diletehn
didactic	didekiko	dieu avecnous	diwa awinknsi
diddle	dideduo	dif-	difi
diddums	didedemasi	differ	difiro
didgeridoo	didegnraidein	difference	difiroinsi
didicoy	didekoin	different	difirointo
dido	didein	differentia	difirointosi
didrachma	digbankhnma	differential	difirointojo
didy	didain	differentiate	difirointoyo
didymium	didainmoma	difficult	difikunjia
didymous	didainmosi	difficulty	difikunjiase

181

WORD (x)	EQUIVALENT (y)	WORD (x)	EQUIVALENT (y)
diffidence	difidasi	digraph	diganpha
diffident	difidato	digress	digiraiso
diffract	difankyo	digression	digiraisosi
diffraction	difankyoon	digs	digisi
diffuse	difunse	digul	digunlo
diffuser	difunsesi	dihedral	dihejnrajo
diffusion	difunsoon	dihedron	dihejnran
diffusive	difunsewin	dihybrid	dihobajo
diffusivity	difwnsewintn	dihydromorphinone	dihogbnmophinihun
dig	digbe	dik dik	dika dika
digamma	digbemmo	dike1	dikn
digamy	digimo	dike2	dikn
digastrics	digisutnrako	diktat	diknte
digest	dignse	dilacerate	dileknrayo
digestion	dignseyoon	dilapidate	dilepndayo
digestive	dignsewin	dilapidated	dilepndayode
digger	digbesi	dilapidation	dilepndayoon
dight	digbe	dilatant	dileyotn
digit	digito	dilatation	dileyoyoon
digital	digitojo	dilate	dileyo
digitalin	digitojon	dilatometer	dileyomuto
digitalis	digitojosi	dilatory	dileyorai
digitalism	digitojomosi	dildo	dilede
digitate	digitoyo	dilemma	dilemmo
digitation	digitoyoon	dilettante	diletinto
digiti	digite	diligence	dileginsi
digitigrade	digitegandie	diligent	dileginte
digitize	digitese	dill	dijnra
digitoxin	digitoosia	dilly-dally	dijnrase dajnrase
diglot	digileto	diluent	diluto
dignified	diginifide	dilute	diluyo
dignify	diginife	dilution	diluyoon
dignitary	diginitorai	diluvial	diluwinjo
dignity	diginitn	diluvium	diluwinma

182

WORD (x)	EQUIVALENT (y)	WORD (x)	EQUIVALENT (y)
dim	dimi	dining-car	ditejegnni-kosi
dime	dimu	dinitro	dinitnra
dimension	dimusunse	dink	dikn
dimer	dimira	dinkum	diknma
dimercaprol	dimirakoponjo	dinkey	diknsi
dimerous	dimirasi	dinky	diknse
dimeter	dimuto	dinner	ditejerai
dimetric	dimutoraiko	dino	dikn
dimidiate	dimudayo	dinoceras	diknknrase
diminish	diminise	dinoflagellate	diknfangijjnyo
diminuendo	diminidinto	dinosaur	diknsanra
diminution	diminiyoon	dinothere	diknsinran
diminutive	diminiyowin	dint	ditn
dimissory	dimusinrai	diocesan	dioknsin
dimity	dimitn	diocese	dioknse
dimmer	dimmisi	diode	diojin
dimorphism	dimophansi	dioecious	diosekisi
dimple	dimporon	dioestrum	diosetnrama
dim-wit	dimi-winso	dioestrus	diosetnrasi
din	dite	diogenes	dioginisi
dinar	diteran	diol	dijin
dindle	diteduo	diomede	diomujn
dine	diteje	dionaea	diohunni
diner	ditejesi	dione	diohun
dinero	diterain	dionism	diohunmosi
dinette	ditejetin	dionysia	diosesia
ding	ditegn	dionysian	diosesiahn
dingbat	ditegnbota	dionysius	diosesiasi
ding-dong	ditegn-degn	diopside	diopnsoojo
dinghy	ditegnho	dioptase	diopntise
dingle	ditegnron	diopter	diopntirai
dingo	ditegnlo	dioptometer	diopntimuto
dingus	ditegnsi	dioptre	diopntiran
dingy	ditegnse	dioptre	diopntiran

WORD (x)	EQUIVALENT (y)	WORD (x)	EQUIVALENT (y)
dioptrics	diopntiraikosi	diplopod	diponpindie
diorama	dioranma	diplosis	diponso
dior	diora	diplosome	diponsoomo
diorite	dioraiyo	dipole	diponjn
dioscuri	diosekunrai	dipper	dipnra
dioxan	diosin	dippy	dipnpo
dioxide	diosinji	dipsas	dipnsesi
dioxin	diosinte	dipsey	dipnsn
dip	dipn	dipso	dipnsoo
diphase	diphanse	dipsomania	dipnsoonmnu
diphenylamine	diphinlomini	dipsomaniak	dipnsoomnuko
diphenylcyanarsine	diphinlosnrainsun	dipstick	dipnsetieko
diphonia	diphohan	dipteral	dipntiraijo
diphosgene	diphisegini	dipteran	dipntirain
diphtheria	diphisinran	dipterous	dipntiraisi
diphtheritic	diphisinraiko	diptych	dinpntnkho
diphthong	diphisogn	dire	dirai
diphyllous	diphewesi	direct	direto
diphyodont	diphedeyo	direction	diretosi
diplegia	dipojngan	directional	diretosijo
diplex	diporonsi	directive	diretowin
diplo	dipon	directly	diretolo
diplocardia	diponkogbasi	director	diretoran
diplococcus	diponkikunsi	directorate	diretoraiyo
diplodocidae	dipondekijoin	directory	diretorai
diplodocus	dipondekunsi	directress	diretobo
diploe	diponsi	dirge	dirogn
diploid	diponjo	dirham	dirohan
diploma	diponma	dirigation	diraigiyoon
diplomacy	diponmasn	dirigible	diraigibe
diplomat	diponmu	dirigo	dirailo
diplomatic	diponlemuko	diriment	diraimutto
diplomatist	diponlemusi	dirk	dirukn
diplopia	diponpan	dirl	diraijo

WORD (x)	EQUIVALENT (y)	WORD (x)	EQUIVALENT (y)
dimdl	dirunjo	discharge	disikhorangn
dirt	dirutn	disciple	disikiporon
dirty	dirutnsi	disciplinarian	disikipanrain
dis	disn	disciplinary	disikipanrai
dis-	disi pron dis	discipline	disikipanse
disability	disiaberontn	disclaim	disikanmo
disable	disiaberon	disclaimer	disikanmosi
disabuse	disiabuse	disclose	disikonsn
disadvantage	disiadiwaintegba	disco	disiki
disadvantaged	disiadiwaintegbade	discolor	disikijoran
disaffected	disiafnkoide	discolour	disikijoran
disagree	disiagirai	discomfit	disikimfito
disallow	disiajjowin	discomfort	disikimfonto
disappear	disiapnran	discompose	disikimpose
disappoint	disiapintoni	disconcert	disikinknrate
disappointment	disiapintonimutto	disconnect	disikinhunki
disapprobation	disiaponbeyoon	disconnected	disikinhunkide
disapprove	disiaponwin	disconsolate	disikinsnleyo
disarm	disiaromu	discontent	disikintito
disarmament	disiaromutto	discontinue	disikintihun
disarrange	disiarrangini	discontinuous	disikintihunsi
disarray	disiarranse	discord	disikigba
disassociate	disiassookiyo	discordant	disikigbatn
disaster	disiaseto	discotheque	disikitihekun
disastrous	disiasetose	discount	disikaleyo
disavow	disiawnwi	discountenance	dsikaletinsi
disband	disibonjo	discourage	disikiraigun
disbar	disiboonsn	discourse	disikiraise
disbelieve	disibejngbasi	discriminate	disikoramiyo
disburse	disibugisan	discursive	disikuosewin
disc	disiko	discus	disikunsi
discard	disikogba	discuss	disikunso
discern	disiknran	disease	disiase
discerning	disiknrangnni	disengage	disiengigun

WORD (x)	EQUIVALENT (y)	WORD (x)	EQUIVALENT (y)
disentangle	disientehagon	dispenser	disipnsansi
disestablish	disiesetnbesi	disperse	disipnrase
disfavor	disifanware	dispersion	disipnrasoon
disfavour	disifanwaire	dispirit	disipoora
disfigure	disifigiran	displace	disipankn
disgorge	disigbagun	displacement	disipanknmutto
disgrace	disiganson	display	disipansie
disguise	disigunse	disport	disipinta
disgust	disigunsi	disposable	disipinsibe
dish	disun	disposal	disipinsijo
dishable	disunbe	dispose	disipinsi
disk	disika	disposition	disipinsiyoon
diskette	disikntin	dispossess	disipinseso
dislike	disilikn	disproof	disiponfin
dislocate	disiloknyo	disproportion	disiponpinyoon
dislodge	disilogbn	disproportionate	disiponpinyoonyo
disloyal	disilosnjo	disprove	disiponwin
dismal	disimaji	disputable	disipntibe
dismantle	disimatnron	disputant	disipntitn
dismay	disimayn	disputation	disipntiyoon
dismiss	disimusin	disputatious	disipntiyosi
dismissive	disimusinwin	dispute	disipnti
dismount	disimounte	disqualify	disikunjofe
disown	disiowin	disquiet	disikuitn
disparage	disipanragun	disquietude	disikuitnjin
disparate	disipanrayo	disquisition	disikuiseyoon
disparity	disipanraitn	disregard	disiregigba
dispassionate	disipansonyo	disrepair	disirepanrai
dispatch	disipankhn	disreputable	disireputobe
dispel	disipnlo	disrepute	disireputo
dispensable	disipnsanbe	disrespect	disiresepnto
dispensary	disipnsanrai	disrobe	disirogbn
dispensation	disipnsanyoon	disrupt	disiraipi
dispense	disipnsan	dissatisfy	dissatnsefe

WORD (x)	EQUIVALENT (y)	WORD (x)	EQUIVALENT (y)
dissect	disseknte	distil	disitiele
disseise	dissesun	distill	disitielle
diseisin	dissesunte	distillate	disitielleyo
dissemble	dissembe	distillation	disitilelleyoon
disseminate	disseminayo	distiller	disitielleran
dissension	dissesisoon	distillery	disitiellerai
dissent	dissesita	distinct	disitinkyo
dissenter	dissesitasi	distinction	disitinkyoon
dissentient	dissesitatn	distinctive	disitinkyowin
dissepiment	dissepomutto	distingue	disitingan
dissertation	disseratoyoon	distinguish	disitingbise
disservice	disserawnsi	distinguished	disitingbisede
dissident	dissoodato	distract	disitnreyo
dissimilar	dissoomojnra	distraction	disitnreyoon
dissimulate	dissoomoleyo	distrain	disitnrain
dissipate	dissoopnyo	distraint	disitnran
dissipation	dissoopnyoon	distrait	disitnraite
dissociate	dissookiyo	distraught	disitnregbe
dissoluble	dissnlebe	distress	disitnraso
dissolute	dissnleyo	distressed	disitnrasode
dissolution	disnleyoon	distribute	disitaraibeyo
dissolve	dissnlewin	distribution	disitaraibeyoon
dissonant	dissosetn	distributive	disitaraibeyowin
dissuade	dissuejin	distributor	disitaraiberan
dissyllable	dissojnranbe	district	disitaraiko
distaff	disitnfin	distrust	disitnranse
distain	disitelu	disturb	disituba
distance	disitase	disturbance	disitubasi
distant	disitatn	disunion	disienise
distaste	disitesitn	disunite	disienito
distemper1	disitompnra	disuse	disilese
distemper2	disitompnra	disyllable	disojnranbe
distend	disitinjn	dit	date
distich	disitinhun	ditch	datekho

WORD (x)	EQUIVALENT (y)	WORD (x)	EQUIVALENT (y)
ditheism	dasinmosi	divestiture	dawinsntoran
dither	dasirai	divide	dawajin
dithionite	dasinleyo	dividend	dawajindan
dithionous	dasinlesi	divider	dawajinsi
dithyramb	dasiraimbo	dividual	dawajinjo
dithyrambic	dasiraimboko	divination	dawahunyoon
dittander	datedainsi	divine	dawahun
dittany	datese	diving bell	dawognni bejnro
ditto	dito	diviner	dawahunsi
dittography	ditoganphe	divinity	dawahuntn
ditty	ditose	divisible	dawasunbe
diu	dare	division	dawasun
diuresis	daremiso	divisive	dawasuwin
diuretic	daremiko	divisor	dawaseran
diurnal	darehunjo	divorce	dawnrasi
diva	dawan	divorcee	dawnrase
divalent	dawajotn	divot	dawnte
divan	dawain	divulge	dawelegn
divaricate	dawaraikoyo	divvy	dawowo
dive	dawo	dixie	disnsi
diver	dawosi	dixieland	disnsiledain
diverge	dawingun	dixit	disnto
divers	dawinse	dixon	disnse
diverse	dawinso	dizzy	disesia
diversify	dawinsofe	djibouti	dijobonunte
diversion	dawinsoon	do1	de
diversity	dawinsetn	do2	de
divert	dawinte	do.	de
diverticulitis	dawintekuoso	doab	debe
diverticulosis	dawintekuoso	doable	deberon
diverticulum	dawintekuoma	dobber-in	debesi ni
divertimento	dawintemutin	dobin	debain
divertissement	dawintesoomutto	dobby	debn
divest	dawinsn	dobie	deban

WORD (x)	EQUIVALENT (y)	WORD (x)	EQUIVALENT (y)
dobla	debejn	dodecagon	dejinkngun
doblon	debejnsi	dodecahedron	dejinknhejnran
dobra	deberai	dodecaphonic	dejinknphohunko
dobson	debusin	dodge	degbon
doc	dekn	dodgem	degboun
docent	deknto	dodger	degbonsi
dochandoris	dekhijnraisi	dodgy	degbonse
dochter	dekhitnra	dodo	dede
docile	dekale	dodown	dedewn
docility	dekaletn	doe	dese
dock1	dekin	doek	dekoi
dock2	dekin	doer	derai
dock3	dekin	does	desi
dock4	dekin	doff	defo
dockage	dekingun	dog	degbi
docker	dekinsi	dogcart	degbikosite
docket	dekinto	doge	degbn
dockland	dekinledain	dogged	degbide
dockmachie	dekinmokhisi	dogger	degbira
dockwalloper	dekinbwejnranra	doggerel	degbirajo
dockyard	dekinyandan	doggery	degbirai
doctor	dekntiran	doggish	degbisu
doctoral	dekntiranjo	doggo	degbilo
doctorate	dekntiraiyo	dogie	degbisi
doctrinaire	dekntirainse	doggy	degbise
doctrine	dekntirain	dogma	degbima
docudrama	dekngbanma	dogmatic	degbimuko
document	deknmutto	dogmatism	degbimumosi
documentalist	deknmuttojosi	dogmatize	degbimuse
documentary	deknmuttorai	do gooder	de gonjosi
documentation	deknmuttoyoon	dogtrot	degbitnratn
dodder1	dejijnra	dogy	degbise
dodder2	dejijnra	doha	dehan
doddle	dejiduo	doily	dejesi

WORD (x)	EQUIVALENT (y)	WORD (x)	EQUIVALENT (y)
doing	degnni	domesticate	demusinkoyo
do it	de ite	domesticity	demusinkitn
do-it-yourself	de ite lenikan	domicile	demukale
dolled	dejnrade	domiciliary	demukalerai
dolly	dejnrase	dominance	deminasi
dolabriform	dejnberaifoon	dominant	deminatn
dolby	dejnbe	dominate	deminayo
dolce	dejnsi	domination	deminayoon
doldrums	dejngbirosi	domineer	deminaran
dole	dejn	dominican	deminakn
dolerite	dejnraiyo	dominica	deminako
dolichocephallic	dejnkhiknphijjnko	dominical	deminakojo
dolichousaurus	dejnkhisanrasi	dominie	deminase
doline	dejnhun	dominion	deminasi
doll	dejnra	dominique	deminakun
dollar	dejnran	deminium	deminama
dollop	dejnrapn	domino	demina
dolly	dejnrase	dominus	deminase
dolman	dejnmaye	don1	debu
dolmen	dejnmuye	don2	debu
dolomite	dejnmuyo	dona	debun
dolorimetry	dejnraimutorai	donar	debusi
dolor	dejnran	donate	debuyo
dolour	dejnran	donation	debuyoon
dolorous	dejnraisi	donatist	debuyosi
doloroso	dejnraiso	donative	debuyowin
dolphin	dejnphin	done	debuse
dolphinarium	dejnphinraima	donee	debusesi
dolt	dejia	donegal	debusegnjo
dom	deo	donets	debutesi
-dom	demo	dong	debugn
domain	demorai	donga	debugan
dome	demu	dongola	debugonjn
domestic	demusinko	donizetti	debuseto

WORD (x)	EQUIVALENT (y)	WORD (x)	EQUIVALENT (y)
donjon	debujon	dorado	derade
donkey	debukn	doradus	derajns
donna	debuhun	dorcas	deraknse
donnan	debuhunsi	dorchaster	derakhntasi
donnish	debuhunse	dordogne	deradegini
donnee	debuhunse	dore	derai
donnerd	debuhungbe	doria	deran
donnert	debuhunto	dorian	derain
donor	deburan	doric	deraiko
donsie	debusie	doricism	deraikomosi
donut	debuto	doris	deraisi
donzel	debusujo	dormant	deramotn
doodad	deindagba	dormer	deramosi
doodle	deinduo	dormie	deramose
dook	deinki	dormitory	deramutorai
dool	deinjn	dormobile	deramobajn
doom	deinmo	dormouse	deramosio
doomsday	deinmodase	dormy	deramun
doomster	deinmoseto	dornick	derankin
doon	deinun	doronicum	derainkuo
door	deinsi	dorothy	derainsi
doorbell	deinsibejnro	dorsad	derasnjn
doorknob	deinsiknboo	dorsal	derasnjo
doorman	deinsimaye	dorsi	derasn
doormat	deinsimate	dorsiferous	derasnfirosi
doom	deinsin	dorsigrade	derasngandie
doorpost	deinsipinseto	dorsiventral	derasnwintnrajo
doorstep	deinsisutopn	dorso	derasoo
doorway	deinsiwelo	dorsum	derasuma
dope	depn	dorus	deraisi
dopester	depnseto	dory	derai
dopey	depnse	dosage	desungun
doppelganger	depnlogigansi	dose	desun
dor	dera	do-se-do	de se de

WORD (x)	EQUIVALENT (y)	WORD (x)	EQUIVALENT (y)
dosh	desu	doughty	deungbotn
dosimeter	desumuto	doughy	deungbose
dosimetry	desumutorai	douglas	deungansi
doss	desoon	doukhobors	deunkhoberan
dossal	desoonjo	douma	deunmo
dosser	desoonsi	doumpalm	deunmpanjomo
dossier	desoonse	dour	deunra
dossil	desoole	doura	deunran
dost	desa	douricouli	deunraikile
dot	detn	dourine	deunrain
dotage	detngun	douro	deunran
dotard	detngba	douse	deunsn
dotation	detnyoon	dove	dewin
dot com	detn kia	dovecot	dewinkiti
dote	dete	dovekie	dewinkin
doth	detnsi	dovetail	dewintele
dotted	detnde	dovish	dewintele
dotter	detnra	dovish	dewinse
dotterel	detnralo	dowager	dewngunsi
dottle	detnron	dowcet	dewnkiti
dotty	detotn	dowdy	dewndie
doual	deunjo	dowel	dewnjn
double	deunji	dowelling	dewnjngnni
double act	aknti deunji	dower	dewnsi
double agent	aginte deunji	dowery	dewnrai
double-book	booko deunji	dowf	dewnfe
doublet	deunjitn	dowie	dewnse
doubloon	deunjiroin	dowitcher	dewntekosi
doubly	deunjise	dowl	dewnjo
doubt	deungbu	down1	dewn
doubtless	deungbulabo	down2	dewn
douche	deunkhn	down3	dewn
dough	deungbo	downs	dewnse
doughnut	deungboyunti	downer	dewnsi

WORD (x)	EQUIVALENT (y)	WORD (x)	EQUIVALENT (y)
downy	dewnun	dragoman	gangimaye
dowry	dewnrai	dragon	gbangon
dowsabel	dewnsnbejo	dragonade	gbangonjin
dowse1	dewnsn	dragonet	gbangonte
dowse2	dewnsn	dragoon	gbangoon
doxastic	desinsuko	drag queen	kuneni gbangi
doxographer	desinganphasi	dragster	gbangiseto
doxology	desinlogbon	drain	gbanyo
doxy	desian	drainage	gbanyogun
doyen	desesi	draining-board	bugba-gbanyognni
doyley	deseroin	drainpipe	popongbanyo
doz.	desi	drake	gbanke
doze	desun	drakensberg	gbanknsibegan
dozen	desuan	dralon	gbanjnsi
dozy	desuse	dram	gbanmo
drab	gbanbu	drama	gbanma
drabble	gbanburon	dramatic	gbanmako
dracaena	gbankoinhun	dramatics	gbanmakosi
drachm	gbankhimi	dramatist	gbanmasi
drachma	gbankhnmo	dramatization	gbanmaseyoon
draco	gbanki	dramatize	gbanmase
dracone	gbankiun	drank	gbankn
draconian	gbankinhn	drant	gbantn
draconic	gbankinko	drape	gbanpon
draft	gbanfia	draper	gbanponra
draftee	gbanfiase	drapery	gbanponrai
draftsman	gbanfiamaye	drastic	gbansuko
drafty	gbanfiase	drat	gbanta
drag	gbangi	draught	gbangbe
dragee	gbagise	draughtboard	bugbagbangbe
draggle	gbagiron	draughtsman	gbangbemoye
drag-net	gbagi-hunte	draughty	gbangbesi
draggy	gbangise	dravidian	gbanwnjian
draghound	gbagihinjoin	draw	gbanwe

WORD (x)	EQUIVALENT (y)	WORD (x)	EQUIVALENT (y)
drawback	gbanweboki	dribble	gbebe
drawbridge	bangbongbanwe	driblet	gbebetn
drawee	gbanwese	dribs and drabs	gbebesi ati gbanbe
drawer	gbanwesi	dried	gbede
drawing	gbanwegnni	drier1	gbesi
drawl	gbonwelo	drier2	gbesi
drawn	gbanwn	driest	gbesii
dray	gbanyn	drift	gbefia
dread	gbaigbn	drifter	gbefiasi
dreadlocks	gbaigbnloknsi	drill1	gbejnra
dream	gbaimo	drill2	gbejnra
dreamy	gbaimose	drill3	gbejnra
drear	gbairan	drill4	gbejnra
dreary	gbairai	drily	gbelo
dredge1	gbaigbon	drin	gbesi
dredge2	gbaigbon	drink	gbekn
dredger1	gbaigbonsi	drip	gbepn
dredger2	gbaigbonsi	dripping	gbepngnni
dree	gbaise	drippy	gbepnse
dreel	gbailo	drive	gbewa
dreg	gbaigi	drive-in	gbewa-nu
dreggy	gbaigise	drivel	gbewalo
dregs	gbaigisi	driven	gbewasi
drei-bund	gbai-bujn	drive-on	gbewa-lo
dreich	gbaihe	driver	gbewasi
drench	gbainmi	drizzle	gbesun
dress	gbaiso	droger	gbngira
dressage	gbaisogun	drogue	gbngise
dresser1	gbaisosi	droit	gbnte
dresser2	gbaisosi	drolt	gbnjia
dressing	gbaisognni	drolt du sei gneur	gbnjia de sun gnran
dressy	gbaisose	droll	gbnjjo
drew	gbaiwo	drollery	gbnjjorai
drey	gbaise	drome	gbnmo

WORD (x)	EQUIVALENT (y)	WORD (x)	EQUIVALENT (y)
dromedary	gbnmojinrai	drupe	gbipon
drone	gbnhun	druse	gbise
drongo	gbnhungon	dry	gberai
drool	gbnjo	dryad	gberaijo
droop	gbnpon	dryer	gberaisi
drop	gbnpn	dry land	ledain gberai
dropper	gbnpnsi	dryly	gberailo
dropsy	gbnpnso	duad	diji
dropwort	gbnpnwoote	dual	dijo
droshky	gbnsuko	dualism	dijomosi
drosophila	gbnsoophijn	dualist	dijosi
dross	gbnso	dualistic	dijosuko
drought	gbngbe	duality	dijotn
drougbty	gbngbesi	dub1	digbe
drouk	gbnmi	dub2	digbe
droukit	gbnmitn	dubbing	digbegnni
drove1	gbnwa	dub he	digbe he
drove2	gbnwa	dubiety	digbetn
drover	gbnwasi	dubious	digbesi
drown	gbnwn	dubitable	digbetebe
drowse	gbnwesn	dubitate	digbeteyo
drowsy	gbnwesun	dubitative	digbeteyowin
drub	gbiba	dublin	digbesi
drudge	gbigbon	dubno	digbeko
drugery	gbigirai	du bois	di boosi
drug	gbigi	dubonnet	dibounte
drugget	gbigite	dubuque	dibukun
druggist	gbigisi	ducal	disejo
druid	gbijo	ducat	diseyo
drum	gbiro	duce	dise
drummer	gbiromosi	duchess	dikhnbo
drunk	gbikun	duchy	dikhnse
drunkard	gbikungbaa	duck1	dika
drunken	gbikunsi	duck2	dika

WORD (x)	EQUIVALENT (y)	WORD (x)	EQUIVALENT (y)
duckboard	bugbadika	dukedom	dikndemo
ducker	dikasi	dukhobors	dikhobosi
ducking	dikagnni	dulawan	dijnwin
duckling	dikajngnni	dulcet	dijnkiti
ducky	dikase	dulciana	dijnkinhe
duct	diki	dulcify	dijnkife
ductile	dikiron	dulcimer	dijnkimosi
dud1	digbu	dulcinea	dijnkinsi
dud2	digbu	dulheggia	dijnhegio
diddle	digbiduo	dulia	dijnsi
dude	digbi	dulkaada	dijnkinjo
dudeen	digbisi	dull	dijnra
dudgeon	digbusi	dullard	dijnragba
dudgeon	digbusi	dulles	dijnrasi
dudley	digburoin	dullsville	dijnrawoole
due	disan	dulong and petit	dilogun ati pntite
duel	dija	dulosis	diloso
dueling	dijagnni	dulse	dilose
duenna	dinihe	duluth	dilosi
dues	disi	duly	disanse
duet	diseto	duma	dima
duff1	difun	dumas	dimasn
duff2	difun	dumb	dimbe
duffel	difunlo	dumbague	dimbegan
duffer	difunsi	dumbarton	dimboositin
duffle	difunjn	dumbbell	dimbejnro
dufy	dife	dumdum	dimdima
dug1	digbe	dumfries	dimfansi
dug2	digbe	dummy	dimmo
dugong	digbegon	dumortierite	dimorateraiyo
dugout	digounta	dump	dimpn
duikerbok	diknraboo	dump	dimpn
dukas	dikosi	dumpish	dimpnse
duke	dikn	dumpling	dimpnjngnni

WORD (x)	EQUIVALENT (y)	WORD (x)	EQUIVALENT (y)
dumps	dimpnsi	dunsinane	dihnsohun
dumpy	dimpnse	dunt	dihn
dun	diha	duo	diko
dun	diha	duodecimal	dikojinkimajn
duna	dihe	duodecimo	dikojinkimo
dunajec	dihejn	duodecuple	dikojinkunpon
dunant	dihetn	duodecuplicate	dikojinkunpankojo
dunarea	diherain	duodenary	dikojinhunrai
dunbar	dihabe	duodenitis	dikojinheso
duncan	dihakin	duodeno	dikojinhe
dunce	dihasi	duodenum	dikojinhema
dunch	dihakho	duogravure	dikoganworan
dunciad	dihakijo	duolog	dikologn
dundee	dihajnse	duologue	dikologbiso
dunder	dihajnra	duotone	dikotoni
dune	dihun	dup	dipe
dung	digbe	dupata	dipanto
dungaree	digbnrain	dupe	dipn
dungeon	digbnsi	dupery	dipnrai
duniewassal	dihunwesojo	dupion	dipnse
dunite	dihayo	duple	dipo
dunk	dikun	duplet	dipotn
dunker	dikunsi	duplex	diporon
dunkirk	dikunknra	duplicate	dipankoyo
dunlin	dihnjan	duplicator	dipankoyoran
dunlop	dihnlopo	duplicature	dipankoyorai
dunnage	dihngun	duplicity	dipankitn
dunnakin	dihnkin	dupondius	diponjnsi
dunne	dihnhun	du pont	di ponte
dunnite	dihnhunyo	duppy	dipapo
dunno	dihnko	duquesne	dikunsin
dunnock	dihnkoki	dura	dirai
dunny	dihnse	dura	dirai
dunsany	dihnsanse	durability	diraiberontn

WORD (x)	EQUIVALENT (y)	WORD (x)	EQUIVALENT (y)
durable	diraibe	dut	ditto
durain	dirain	dutch	ditosi
dural	diraijo	duteous	ditnsi
duralumin	diraijomini	dutiable	ditnbe
duramater	diraimatn	duty	ditn
duramen	diraimini	duumvir	dimowirai
durameter	diraimuto	duumvrate	dimowiraiyo
durance	diraisi	duveen	diwnsi
durango	diraigon	duvetny	diwntise
durante	dirainyo	dux	disun
duration	diraiyoon	dvandva	dwinjnwa
durative	diraiyowin	dwarf	dwofe
durazzo	diraiseto	dwell	dwojjn
durban	dirabe	dwelling	dwojjngnni
durbar	dirabesi	dwindle	dwinduo
dure	dirai	dwine	dwini
durer	diraise	dy	dain
duress	diraiso	dyad	daindi
durex	diraisn	dyadic	daindiko
durham	diraihun	dyak	dainko
durian	deraihn	dyarchy	dainknran
during	diraignni	dybbuk	dainburo
durion	diraisi	dye	dainro
durmast	diraimasi	dyeing	dainrognni
duro	diron	dyer	dainrorai
durra	dirran	dying	dilegnni
durum	dirunma	dyke1	dainkn
dusk	disuki	dyke2	dainkn
dusky	disukise	dyna	dainse
dust	disia	dynameter	dainsemuto
dustbin	disiabojn	dynamic	dainsemuko
dust bowl	disia bowojn	dynamics	dainsemukosi
duster	disiasi	dynamism	dainsemumosi
dusty	disiase	dynamite	dainsemutn

WORD (x)	EQUIVALENT (y)	WORD (x)	EQUIVALENT (y)
dynamiter	dainsemutnsi	dysuria	dainsiran
dynamo	dainsemo	dytiscid	daintesnkijo
dynamogeny	dainsemognse	dyvour	dainwnrai
dynamometer	dainsemomuto	each	eni
dynast	dainsesi	eager	ejnra
dynasty	dainsetn	eagle	ejnron
dynatron	dainsetnran	eaglet	ejntn
dyne	dainsun	eager	ejnsi
dynode	dainsejoin	eaker	eknra
dys-	dainsi	ean	ehn
dyscrasia	dainsikansia	earl	eran
dysentery	dainsitnrai	ear2	eran
dysfunction	dainsifunknyoon	earl	eranjo
dysgenic	dainsiginko	early	eranlo
dysgeogenous	dainsigbileginwa	earn	eranhun
dyslexia	dainsironsia	earnest	eranhunsi
dyslogistic	dainsilogbisuko	earnings	eranhngnnisi
dysmenorrhoea	dainsiminikorhain	earphone	eranphohn
dyspeptic	dainsipnpoko	earth	eransin
dyspepsia	dainsipnposia	earthen	eransinsi
dysphagia	dainsiphije	earthling	eransingnni
dysphasia	dainsiphisia	earthly	eransinlo
dysphemism	dainsiphimumosi	earthquake	eransinkunko
dysphonia	dainsiphohan	earthy	eransinhn
dysphoria	dainsiphorain	ease	esie
dysphotic	dainsiphooko	easel	esiejo
dysplasia	dainsipansia	easement	esiemutto
dyspnoea	dainsipohnmi	easily	esielo
dysprosium	dainsiponsoma	easiness	esienisi
dyselology	dainsitojnlogbon	east	esesi
dysthymia	dainsisiomua	eastbound	esesibounjn
dystopia	dainsitopn	easter	esesitn
dystrophy	dainsitnraphe	easterly	esesitnlo
dystropy	dainsitnrapo	eastern	esesitnran

WORD (x)	EQUIVALENT (y)	WORD (x)	EQUIVALENT (y)
eastward	esesiwegba	eccrine	ekiknrain
easy	esesn	eccrinology	ekiknrainlogbon
eat	enje	ecdemic	ekijinmuko
eatable	enjebe	ecdemomania	ekijinmumohan
eater	enjesi	ecdysiast	ekidainsise
eau-de-cologne	enle-jin-kijoingn	ecdysis	ekidainso
eaves	enwnyo	ecdysone	ekidainsihun
ebb	ebn	ecesis	ekisuso
ebenezer	ebunsesi	echard	ekihagba
ebola	eboojn	echelon	ekihejnsi
ebonite	ebooynto	echeveria	ekihewinran
ebonize	ebooynse	echidna	ekhijohun
ebony	ebooyn	echinacea	ekhihunkoin
ebracteate	ebankyoto	echinate	ekhihunyo
ebullient	ebujnranto	schini	echini
ebullioscopy	ebujnransokipo	echino	ekhikn
ebullition	ebujnranyoon	echinoderm	ekhiknjnramo
eburnation	eburanyoon	echinoid	ekhiknjo
ec	eki	echinus	ekhiknsi
ecad	ekide	echo	ekihu
ecarto	ekiranto	echoic	ekihuko
ecbolic	ekiboojnko	echoism	ekihumosi
eccentric	akikntiraiko	echolalia	ekihujnjan
eccentricity	ekikntiraikitn	echolocation	ekihuloknyoon
ecchymosis	ekikhomuso	echo-sounder	soojoinsi-ekihu
eccles cake	ekikunsi koki	echt	ekiyo
ecclesiarch	ekikunsinknra	eck	ekiro
ecclesiastes	ekiknsinsesi	eckanka	ekirokan
ecclesiastic	ekikunsinseko	éclair	ekijnra
ecclesiastical	ekiknsinsekojo	eclampsia	ekijnmpnsia
ecclesiasticism	ekikunsinsekomosi	éclat	ekijnte
ecclesiasticus	ekikunsinseknsi	eclectic	ekijnkitiko
ecclesiolatry	ekikunsinletorai	eclipse	ekijipnse
ecclesiology	ekikunsinlogbon	eclipsis	ekijipnso

WORD (x)	EQUIVALENT (y)	WORD (x)	EQUIVALENT (y)
ecliptic	ekijipntiko	ectoproct	ekitaponkn
eclogite	ekilogbiyo	ectosark	ekitasanko
eclogue	ekilogbiso	ectype	ekitnpon
eco-	eki	ecu	ekun
ecocide	ekikeku	ecumenical	ekunminikojo
ecology	ekilogbon	ecumenicalism	ekunminikojomosi
econometrics	ekinknmutoraikosi	eczema	ekisema
economic	ekinknmuko	ed.	de
economical	ekinknmukojo	-ed1	de
economically	ekinknmukojjn	-ed2	ejn
economics	ekinknmukosi	edacious	ejnkisi
economist	ekinknmosi	edacity	ejnkitn
economize	ekinknmose	edam	ejnmo
economy	ekinknmo	edaphic	ejnphiko
ecorche	ekirakhn	eddy	ejndein
ecosphere	ekisephirai	edelweiss	ejnjowinso
ecossaise	ekisoonse	edema	ejnmi
ecosystem	ekisositnma	eden	ejnko
ecraseur	eknraserai	edentate	ejnkoteyo
ecru	eknrai	edentulous	ejnkotelosi
ecstasy	ekisetn	edestin	ejnsetin
ecstatic	ekisetnko	edgar	ejngan
ecthyma	ekiyihoms	edge	ejnge
ecto-	ekita	edging	ejngegnni
ectocrine	ekitaknrain	edgy	ejngesi
ectoderm	ekitajnramo	edible	ejijebe
ectogenous	ekitaginsi	edict	ejnko
ectomere	ekitamure	edifice	ejnfesi
ectomorph	ekitamophan	edify	ejnfe
-ectomy	ekitemo	edit	ejnto
ectoparasite	ekitapanrasosi	editio	ejntokn
ectophyte	ekitapheyo	edition	ejntosi
ectopia	ekitapan	editor	ejntoran
ectoplasm	ekitapanson	editorial	ejntoraijo

WORD (x)	EQUIVALENT (y)	WORD (x)	EQUIVALENT (y)
edmonton	ejnmenitin	efficient	efiseto
edmund	ejnmudain	effigy	efigun
educate	ejnkoyo	efflation	efanyoon
educated	ejnkoyode	effleurage	efijnragun
education	ejnkoyoon	effloresce	efonraisekn
educational	ejnkoyoonjo	efflorescence	efonraiseknsi
educationist	ejnkoyoonsi	effluence	efolusi
educatory	ejnkoyorai	effluent	efoluto
educe	ejnko	effluvium	efoluwinma
educt	ejnkote	efflux	efolusi
eduction	ejnkotesi	effluxion	efolusoon
edulcorate	ejnkiraiyo	effort	efonto
edward	ejnwegba	effortless	efontolabo
edwardian	ejnwegbahn	effrontery	efontnrai
-ee	eso	effulge	efunjogn
eel	esejn	effulgent	efunjoginte
een	esosi	effuse	efunsi
-eer	erai	effusion	efunsoon
eerie	eraise	effusive	efunsowin
ef-	ef	eft	efia
efface	efansi	egad	egbejn
effect	efnkoi	egal	egbejo
effective	efnkoiwin	egalitarian	egberatorain
effector	efnkoiran	eger	egnran
effectual	efnkoijo	egeria	egnransi
effectuate	efnkoiyo	egerton	egnratin
effeminate	efnminiyo	egest	egnsia
effendi	efinijn	egesta	egnsita
efferent	efiroinyo	egg1	egbn
effervesce	efirownsekn	egg2	egbn
effervescent	efirownseknti	egg3	egbn
effete	efntn	egger	egbnsi
efficacious	efnsekisi	eggle	egbnjn
efficacy	efnsekn	egis	egbso

WORD (x)	EQUIVALENT (y)	WORD (x)	EQUIVALENT (y)
eglantine	egbnlesitin	eisemes	enserinsi
ego	egbain	eisteddfod	ensetojnfijo
egocentric	egbainkntiraiko	either	ensira
egoism	egbainmosi	ejaculate	ejankoleyo
egoist	egbainsi	ejaculation	ejankoleyoon
egomania	egbainmohan	eject	ejnkn
egotism	egbaintesi	ejecta	ejnknte
ego-trip	egbain-taraipo	ejector	ejnknran
egregious	egiragonsi	ejido	ejnde
egress	egiraso	eke	ekn
egret	egirate	ekistics	ekinsikosi
egypt	egunpnti	ekka	ekia
egyptian	egunpntihn	el	ele
egyptology	egunpntilogbon	elaborate	elebooraiyo
eh	eh/ah	elan	elesi
eident	enjnto	eland	eledain
eider	enjnra	elapid	elepnjo
eido	enjo	elapse	elepnse
eidolon	enjojnsi	elasmosaur	elesimosanra
eiffel	enfijn	elastic	elesunko
eight	engbe	elasticity	elesunkotn
eighteen	engbetoon	elasticize	elesunkose
eightfold	engbefonjo	elasticated	elesunkoyode
eighth	engbesi	elastine	elesunhun
eightieth	engbetnsi	elastomer	elesuntomara
eighty	engbetn	elastoplast	elesunpansia
eigon	engon	elate	eleyo
eikon	enkin	elater	eleyora
eild	enjnra	elaterid	eleyoraijo
einkom	enknran	elaterin	eleyorain
eirene	enroin	elaterite	eleyoraito
einsteinium	ensitnnima	elaterium	eleyoraima
eisegesis	ensegnso	elation	eleyosi
eisenhower	ensesihinwo	elative	eleyowin

WORD (x)	EQUIVALENT (y)	WORD (x)	EQUIVALENT (y)
elayer	eleyinsi	electron	eleknroin
elbow	elebowo	electronic	eleknroinko
elder1	elejnra	electronics	eleknroinkosi
elder2	elejnra	electroplate	eleknronpantue
elderly	elejnralo	electrostatic unit	enite eleknronsetntiko
eldest	elejnsi	electrotherapeutics	eleknronsinranponkoss
eldorado	elejnrade	electrothermal	eleknronsinronjo
eldritch	elejnraite	eelectrotonus	eleknrontinsi
elea	ejnsi	electuary	eleknrai
eleatic	elesiko	eleemosynary	elemosirain
elecampane	elekompanun	elegance	elegunsi
elect	elekn	elegant	elegunte
election	eleknyoon	elegiac	elegunki
electioneer	eleknyoonsi	elegist	elegunsi
elective	eleknwin	elegit	elegunte
elector	eleknran	elegy	elegun
electoral	eleknranjo	element	elemutto
electorate	eleknraiyo	elemental	elemuttojo
electra	eleknra	elementary	elemuttorai
electret	eleknrate	elemi	elemun
electric	eleknrako	elena	elehun
electrical	eleknrakojo	elenchus	elekhnsi
electric eel	eleknrako esejn	elephant	elephitn
electrician	eleknrakohn	elephantiasis	elephitnso
electricity	eleknrakitn	elephantine	elephitin
electric shock	eleknrako sknki	eleusinia	elewasinsi
electrify	eleknraife	elevate	eleweyo
electro-	eleknron	elevation	eleweyoon
electrocute	eleknronkunte	elevator	elewerin
electrode	eleknronji	eleven	elewini
electrolyse	eleknronjinse	elevenses	elewinsesi
electrolysis	eleknronjinso	eleventh	elewinisi
electrolyte	eleknronjinyo	elevon	elewnsi
electrolyze	eleknronjinse	elevsis	elewnso

WORD (x)	EQUIVALENT (y)	WORD (x)	EQUIVALENT (y)
elf	elefe	el shadai	elo sugbain
elfin	elefesi	elsie	elosua
elfish	elefese	elucidate	elukunjnyo
elicit	elekiti	elude	elujin
elide	elejn	eluent	eluto
eligible	eleganbe	elusive	elusewin
elijah	elejia	elute	eluyo
eliminate	eleminayo	elutriate	elutaraiyo
elisabeth	elesuabe	eluviation	eluwinyoon
elisha	elesia	eluvium	eluwinma
elision	elesoon	elver	eluwesi
elite	eleto	elves	eluwnsi
elitism	eletomosi	ely	ejin
elixir	eleserai	elysian	ejinsinhn
elizbethan	elesuabe	elysium	ejinsinmi
elk	elekn	elytra	ejintnre
ell	elelo	elytroid	ejintnrejo
ellas	elelose	em	em
ellen	elelosi	emaciate	emakweyo
ellice	elelokn	email	emaajn
ellipse	elelopose	emanate	emuhunyo
ellipsis	eleloposo	emancipate	emukinpanyo
ellipsoid	eleloposejo	emancipation	emukinpanyoon
elliptic	elelopoko	emasculate	emusekuoleyo
elliptical	elelopokojo	embankment	embohaknmutto
ellipticity	elelopokitn	embar	embora
elm	elemo	embarcadero	emborakojinro
elocution	eloknyoon	embargo	emboralo
eloign	elogini	embark	emborakn
elongate	elogunyo	embarkation	emboraknyoon
elope	elopn	embarrass	emborrase
eloquence	elokunso	embassador	embosoojnran
eloquent	elokunto	embassage	embosoogun
else	elosia	embassy	embosoose

WORD (x)	EQUIVALENT (y)	WORD (x)	EQUIVALENT (y)
embathe	embotesn	embroil	emboinlo
embay	emboyo	embryo	emborain
embed	embeje	embryogeny	emborainginse
embellish	embejjnsua	embryology	emborainlogbon
ember	embena	embryonic	emborainko
embezzle	embesunji	embusque	embusakun
emblazon	embansua	emcee	emso
emblazonry	embansuarai	eme	emu
emblem	emgbnle	emend	emudan
emblematic	emgbnleko	emerald	emuranjo
emblematize	emgbnlese	emerge	emuragba
emblematic	emgbnleko	emergence	emuragbasi
emblematize	emgbnlese	emergency	emuragbasn
emblements	emgbnletosi	emergent	emuragbato
emblemize	emgbnlesi	emeritus	emuratnsi
embody	embojain	emersed	emurasnde
embolden	emboojonsi	emersion	emurasnsi
embolectomy	embooletemo	emery	emurai
embolism	emboolemosi	emery-board	bugba emurai
embololalia	emboolojnjan	emesis	emubiso
embolus	emboolesi	emetic	emubiko
embosom	embosinmi	emigrant	emugunraite
emboss	embosin	emigrate	emugunraiyo
embouchure	embounkhnrai	émigré	emugunran
embow	embowo	eminence	eminasi
embower	embowosi	eminence grise	girase eminasi
embrace	embanso	eminent	eminatn
embracery	embnsorai	emir	emuran
embranchment	embainkhomutto	emirate	emuraito
embrangie	embangan	emissary	emusoonrai
embrasure	embansorai	emission	emusoon
embrocation	embonkoyoon	emissivity	emusoonwotn
embroider	emboinjnra	emit	emutn
embroidery	emboinjnrai	emitter	emutnse

WORD (x)	EQUIVALENT (y)	WORD (x)	EQUIVALENT (y)
Emmanuel	emmaye	empyrean	emporain
emmenagogue	emminigonko	emu	emu
emmenthal	emminisinjo	emulate	emujoyo
emmer	emmurai	emulation	emujoyoon
emmetropia	emmutnrapan	emulous	emujosi
emmy	emmumo	emulsify	emujosoofe
emollient	emojjnto	emulsion	emujosoon
emolument	emojnmutto	emunctory	emukitirai
emote	emotn	en-1	en
emotion	emotusi	en-2	en
emotional	emotusijo	-en	ni
emotive	emotuwin	enable	enbesi
empanel	empanjo	enact	enknti
empathize	empansiose	enactment	enkntimutto
empathy	empansio	enamel	enmujo
emperor	empnra	enamor	enmuran
emperor penguin	pingini empnra	enamour	enmuran
empery	empnrai	enantiomorph	entnmophan
emphasis	emphnso	enrathrosis	enransnraso
emphasize	emphnsose	enate	enyo
emphatic	emphnko	en bloc	en bonkn
emphysema	emphesoma	encamp	enkompn
empire	emporan	encapsulate	enkopnsnleyo
empirical	emporaikojo	encase	enkoso
emplacement	empanknmutto	encaustic	enkoinsuko
employ	emponse	-ence	si/sun/su
employee	emponsesi	enceinte	enknnitn
employment	emponsemutto	enceladus	enknlejnsi
empoison	empinsise	encephalin	enknphijnsi
empoider	empinjnra	encephalitis	enknphijnso
emporium	empinraima	encephalogram	enknphijnganmo
empower	emowara	encephalograph	enknphijnganpha
empress	empesiso	enchant	enkhote
empty	empitn	enchanter	enkhotesi

WORD (x)	EQUIVALENT (y)	WORD (x)	EQUIVALENT (y)
enchiridion	enkhiraijo	endocarp	enjuakopan
enchondroma	enkhigbainma	endocrine	enjuaknrain
encipher	enkiphira	endocrinology	enjuaknrainlogbon
enclave	enkanwo	endogenous	enjuaginsi
enclitic	enkiunko	endometrium	enjuamutoraima
enclose	enkonsn	endomorph	enjuamophan
enclosure	enkonsnran	endoplasm	enjuapanson
encode	enkidie	endorse	enjuasi
encomiast	enkimuseyo	endorsee	enjuasise
encomium	enkimuma	endoscope	enjuasokipon
encompass	enkimpanso	endow	enjuan
encore	enkiran	endowment	enjuanmutto
encounter	enkaleyosi	endue	endisan
encroach	enknrakho	endurance	endiraisi
encumber	enkuobesi	endure	endirai
encumbrance	enkuoberaisi	enema	eninimi
-ency	nse/sn/sin	enemy	eninimo
encyclical	ensnkonkojo	energetic	enrailokun
encyclopedia	ensnkonpnjina	energize	enrailose
encyclopedic	ensnkonpnjnko	energy	enrailo
end	enjn	enervate	enraiweyo
endear	enjnran	en face	en fansi
endearment	enjnranmutto	en famille	en fanmujjn
endeavor	enjnwnran	enfeeble	enfinibe
endeavour	enjnwnrai	enfeoff	enfioffe
endemic	enjnmuko	en fete	en fntn
enderby	enjnrabe	enfilade	enfijanjin
ending	enjngnni	enfranchise	enfankhnse
endive	enjnwo	engage	engigun
endless	enjnlabo	engaged	engigunde
endo-	enjua	engagement	engigunmutto
endocardial	enjuakogbajo	engaging	engigungnni
endocarditis	enjuakogbaso	engarde	engirade
e ndocardium	enjuakogbama	engender	engnjnran

WORD (x)	EQUIVALENT (y)	WORD (x)	EQUIVALENT (y)
engine	engbihun	enormous	enraimosi
engineer	engbihunse	enough	enkngan
engineering	engbihunsegnni	en passant	en pansote
enginery	engbihunrai	enprint	enpante
england	engbiledain	enquire	enkunran
english	engbileso	enquiry	enkunrai
englishman	engbilesomoye	enrage	enrangun
englishism	engbilesomosi	enrapture	enranpnti
englishry	engbilesorai	enrich	enraikho
engorged	enjinrede	enrol	enrolo
engraft	enganfia	enroll	enrollo
engrave	enganwo	en route	en roota
engraving	enganwognni	ensconce	ensekins
engross	engonsoo	ensemble	ensnmberon
enhance	enhunsi	enshrine	ensurain
enigma	engbimo	enshroud	ensurajn
enigmatise	engbimose	ensign	ensoogan
enjambment	enjanmbemutto	enslave	ensanwin
enjoin	enjosi	ensnare	ensiaran
enjoy	enjinyo	ensue	ensunse
enjoyment	enjinyomutto	en suite	en suite
enkindle	enkinjoron	ensure	ensurai
enlace	enleso	ent	ento/yo
enlarge	enlegan	entablature	entebanyoran
enlarger	enlegansi	entail	entele
enlighten	enlighesi	entangle	entehagon
enlightenment	enlighesimutto	entanglement	entehagonmutto
enlist	enlisi	entasis	enteso
enliven	enliyesi	entelechy	entojnkho
enmass	enmasoo	entellus	entojjnsi
enmesh	enmuso	entente	entinto
enmity	eninitn	entente cordiale	entinto kigbajain
ennui	ennuyo	enter	entnra
enormity	enraimutn	enteric	entnraiko

WORD (x)	EQUIVALENT (y)	WORD (x)	EQUIVALENT (y)
entero	entnrain	entr'acte	entnraknto
enteron	entnrain	entrails	entnrejosi
enterprise	entnrapese	entrain	entnreto
enterprising	entnraesegnni	entrance1	entnrasi
entertain	entnrayo	entrance2	entnrasi
entertainer	entnrayosi	entrant	entnrate
entertaining	entnrayognni	entrap	entnraipo
entertainment	entnrayomutto	entreat	entasitn
enthalpy	ensinjopo	entreaty	entasitnso
enthetic	ensinko	entrecote	entasikite
enthral	ensinrejn	entrée	entasia
enthrall	ensinrejjn	entrench	entasinkho
enthrone	ensinrain	entrepot	entasipote
enthuse	ensunsi	entrepreneur	entnranpese
enthusiasm	ensunsiase	entropy	entnraipo
enthusiast	ensunsiasi	entrust	entnranse
enthusiastic	ensunsiasiko	entry	enterai
enthymeme	ensiomumo	entryphone	enteraiphohun
entice	entisi	entwine	entwinni
entire	entinran	e-number	e-yunmbe
entirely	entinranlo	enumerate	eyunmuraiyo
entirety	entinranto	enumerator	eyunmuraiyoran
entitle	entitoron	enunciate	eyunkinyo
entity	entotn	enure	eyunrai
entomb	entombo	enuresis	eyunraiso
entomic	entomuko	envelop	enwinlopo
entomo	entoma	envelope	enwinlopon
entomology	entomalogbon	enviable	enjowube
entomostracan	entomasetnrakin	envious	enjowusi
entophyte	entopheyo	environment	enjowaraimutto
entopic	entopnko	environmentalist	enjowaraimuttolesi
entourage	entooraigun	environs	enjowaraisi
entozoic	entosinko	envisage	enjowosegun
entozoon	entosinsi	envision	enjowosesi

WORD (x)	EQUIVALENT (y)	WORD (x)	EQUIVALENT (y)
envoy	enjown	ephah	ephihun
envy	enjowu	epharmone	ephanmo
enwrap	enwapan	epharmony	ephanmose
enzyme	ensaimn	ephebe	ephnbe
enzymology	ensaimologbon	ephebus	ephnbesi
enzymolysis	ensaimojinso	ephedra	ephnjnra
eoanthropus	enisinrapnsi	ephedrine	ephnjnrain
eobiont	enibarinte	ephemera	ephnmura
eocene	eniknsa	ephemeral	ephnmurajo
eohippus	enihipnsi	ephemerid	ephnmurjo
eolian harp	hapan enilehn	ephemeris	ephnmuraso
eolipile	enileporon	ephemeron	ephnmurasi
eolopile	eniloporon	ephesians	ephnsinsi
eolithic	enilisiko	ephesus	ephnsin
eolitropic	enilitnrapnko	ephesian	ephnsinhn
eon	enihun	ephiates	ephonyosi
eonism	enihun	ephod	ephnjo
eonism	enihunmosi	ephor	ephnran
ep	ep	ephraim	ephnraimo
epact	epankiti	ephraimite	ephnraimosi
eparch	epnknra	epi-	eepo
eparchy	epnknran	epiblast	eepobansia
epatant	epantayo	epiboly	eepobulo
epaulet	apanleto	epic	eepokn
epaulette	epanletin	epicalyx	eepokojinsi
epee	epnun	epicanthus	eepokosinsi
epeeist	epnunsi	epcardium	eepokogbama
epeirogeny	epnraiginse	epicarp	eepokopan
epencephalon	epnknphijnsi	epicedium	eepoknjnma
ependyma	epndainmo	epicene	eepoknsa
epenthesis	epnsinso	epicenter	eepokntirai
epergne	epnragini	epicenter	eepokntiran
epexegesis	epnsiginiso	epicotyls	eepokitilo
eph	epha	epicrisis	eepokoraiso

WORD (x)	EQUIVALENT (y)	WORD (x)	EQUIVALENT (y)
epicure	eepokunsn	epimorpha	eepomophan
epicurean	eepokunsnhn	epimorphosis	eepomophanso
epicurus	eepokunsnsi	epimysium	eepomusoma
epicycle	eeposnkuo	epinasty	eepohesito
epicyclic	eeposnkuoko	epinephrine	eepohunphirain
epicycloids	eeposnkuojo	epineurium	eepohunraima
epideictic	eepojinkitiko	epinosis	eepoknso
epidemic	eepojinmuko	epiontology	eepontelogbon
epidemiology	eepojinmulogbon	epiphany	eepophinse
epidermis	eepojnramuso	episcopacy	eeposekipansn
epidiascope	eepojinasokipon	Episcopal	eeposekipanjo
epididymis	eepodidainmuso	episcopalian	eeposekipanjohn
epidote	eepodeyo	episcopate	eeposekipanyo
epidural	eepodiraijo	episcope	eeposokipon
epifocal	eepofoonknjo	episematic	eeposemuko
epigamic	eepogimuko	episiotomy	eeposutemo
epigastrium	eepogisutnramo	episode	eeposoojo
epigeal	eepognjo	episodic	eeposoojokn
epigene	eepognhun	epispastic	eeposepansinko
epigenesis	eepognhunso	episperm	eeposepnron
epigenous	eepoginsi	epistasis	eeposetnso
epiglottis	eepogontiso	epistaxis	eeposetnsanso
epigoni	eepogonsi	epistemic	eeposutomako
epigram	eepoganmo	epistemology	eeposutomalogbon
epigraph	eepoganpha	episternum	eeposutoran
epigynous	eepoloyunsi	epistle	eeposetoron
epilate	eepoleyo	epistolary	eeposetojnrai
epilepsy	eepolepnso	epistrophe	eeposrtnraphn
epileptic	eepolepnko	epitaph	eepotephe
epileptoid	eepolepnjo	epitasis	eepoteso
epilogue	eepologbiso	epitaxy	eepotesin
epimere	eepomura	epithalamium	eeposanjoma
epimerism	eepomuraimosi	epithelioma	eeposinletoma
epimetheus	eepomusinsi	epithelium	eeposinlema

WORD (x)	EQUIVALENT (y)	WORD (x)	EQUIVALENT (y)
epithet	eeposetn	equilateral	ekunletnrajo
epitome	eepotemo	equlibrant	ekunliberaitn
epitomize	eepotemuse	equilibrate	ekunliberaiyo
epizoic	eeposinko	equilibrist	ekunliberaisi
epizoon	eeposinle	equilibrium	ekunliberaima
epizootic	eeposinleko	equine	ekunhun
epoch	eepokhn	equinoctial	ekuniknkitijo
epode	eepojin	equinox	ekunknsi
eponym	eeposuma	equip	ekunpn
eponymy	eeposumase	equipage	ekunpngun
epopee	eepopnse	equipment	ekunpnmutto
epos	eeposi	equipoise	ekunpinsun
epoxide	eeposinji	equitable	ekuntobe
epoxy	eeposian	equitation	ekuntoyoon
epsilon	eeposojnsi	equity	ekuntn
epsom	eeposnmi	equivalence	ekunwajose
equable	ekunbe	equivalent	ekunwajotn
equador	ekunjnra	equivocal	ekunwnkojo
equal	ekunjo	equivocate	ekunwnkoyo
equality	ekunjotn	equuleus	ekunronwa
equalize	ekunjose	-er1	si
equalizer	ekunjosesi	-er2	si
equally	ekunjosi	-er3	se
equanimity	ekunminitn	era	eeran
equanimous	ekunminisi	eradiate	erangbiyo
equate	ekunto	eradicate	erangbakoyo
equation	ekuntosi	erase	eransn
equator	ekuntora	eraser	eransnsi
equatorial	ekuntoraijo	erasure	eransnra
equerry	ekunrrai	erbium	eranbema
equestrian	ekunsetnrain	ere	erai
equi-	ekun	erect	ereto
equiangular	ekunnigunjnra	erectile	eretoron
equidistant	ekundisitatn	erection	eretoyoon

WORD (x)	EQUIVALENT (y)	WORD (x)	EQUIVALENT (y)
erector	eretoran	erotogenic	eraitoginko
erethism	eresumosi	erotology	eraitologbon
erg	eraisi	erotomania	eraitomohan
ergasthenia	eraisisinhun	err	errai
ergative	eraisiyowin	errancy	erraisn
ergo	eraise	errand	erraijn
ergogenic	eraiseginko	errant	erraitn
ergograph	eraiseganpha	erratic	erraiteko
ergonomics	eraiseknmukosi	erratum	erraitema
ergophile	eraisepheron	erroneous	erraisise
ergot	eraisete	error	erraisi
ergotism	eraisetemosi	ersatz	eraisise
eric	erako	erse	eraise
erica	eraiki	erstwhile	eraisiwholo
erie	eraisn	eruct	eraiknte
erigeron	eraignron	eructation	eraiknteyoon
erin	eraito	erudite	erigbonyo
erinaceous	erainsuwa	erupt	eraipiyo
eriometer	eraimuto	eruptive	eraipiyowin
eris	eraisi	ery	erai
eristic	eraisuko	-ery	ery
erlang	erailegun	Erymanthian	erymosinhn
ermine	eraimini	erymanthus	erymosinsi
ernie	eransi	erymology	ermologbon
erode	eraijin	eryngo	eryingon
erogenous	eraiginsi	erysipelas	erysoopnlesi
eros	eraisi	erysipeloid	erysoopnlejo
erose	eraiso	erythema	erypipan
erosion	eraisoon	erythrism	erypipanmo
erotic	eraitiko	erythrite	erypipanyo
erotica	eraitiki	erythritol	erypipanyojin
eroticism	eraitikomosi	erythro	erypupa
erotism	eraitimosi	erythrocyte	erypupasnyo
eroto	eraito	erythrocytometer	erypupasnyomuto

WORD (x)	EQUIVALENT (y)	WORD (x)	EQUIVALENT (y)
erythromycin	erypupamunkin	esoteric	esetnrako
erythroplesis	erypupapinjnso	espadrille	esepangbejnra
es	esa/su	espaller	esepanjnra
esau	esanun	esparto	esepantin
escalate	esekojnra	especial	esepnkijo
escalator	esekojnran	especially	esepnkijin
escallonia	esekojnrain	esperance	esepnrasi
escalope	esekojnpon	esprerato	esepnrato
escapade	esekopnjin	espial	eseponjn
escape	esekopn	espionage	esepooragn
escapee	esekopnse	esplanade	esepanjnmi
escapement	esekopnmutto	espousal	eseposijo
escapism	esekopnmosi	espouse	eseposi
escapology	esekopnlogbon	espresso	esepesisoo
escarpment	esekopanmutto	esprit	esepoora
escent	eseknti	espy	esepe
eschatology	esekhotnlogbon	-esque	esekun
escheat	esekhnte	esquire	esekunra
eschew	esekhnwe	-ess	eso/bo
escolar	esekijnra	essay	esooyo
escort	eseknrato	essayist	esooyosi
escribe	esekoraibe	essence	essetin
escritoire	esekorairan	essential	essetinjo
escrow	eseknrawa	-est	esesi
escudo	esekunde	establish	esetnberonsi
esculent	esekunjeto	establishment	esetnberonsimutto
escurial	esekunsnjo	estate	esetnyo
escutcheon	esekuntekhnsi	estate agent	aginte esetnyo
esemplastic	esempansuiko	estate car	kosi esetnyo
eserine	eserain	esteem	esetnmo
esker	eseknra	ester	esetnra
eskimo	esekimo	esterase	esetnrase
esky	eseko	esterification	esetnraifikoyoon
esophagus	esephijesi	esterity	esetnraitn

WORD (x)	EQUIVALENT (y)	WORD (x)	EQUIVALENT (y)
esther	esesinra	etape	etipan
esthesia	esesinsia	etch	etikho
esthesiometer	esesinsiamuto	etching	etikhognni
esthete	esesuwa	eteocles	etnkuosi
esthetic	esesuwako	eternal	etnrahunjo
esthetics	esesuwakosi	eternity	etnrahuntn
estimable	esetinmbe	eternity ring	rogan etnrahuntn
estimate	esetinmuyo	eternize	etnrahunse
estimation	esetinmuyoon	etesian	etnsoon
estivate	esetinweyo	,-eth	esi
estoile	esetonjn	ethanol	esanjo
estonia	esetoni	ethane	esanhun
estoppel	esetopnlo	ethanol	esanjin
estovers	esetowinsi	ether	esunra
estrade	esetnrejn	ethereal	esunraijo
estrange	esetnragbun	ethernet	esunrante
estray	esetnreya	ethic	esinko
estreat	esetasito	ethical	esinkojo
estrogen	esetnragin	ethics	esinkosi
estron	esetnran	ethiope	esipon
estrone	esetnrain	ethiopia	esiponsi
estrus	esetorai	ethiopian	esiponsihn
estuarine	esetnrain	ethmoid	esinmujo
estuary	esetnrai	ethnarch	eseyaknra
estufa	esetnfo	ethnic	eseyako
esurient	esuraito	ethnicity	eseyakitn
et	eti	ethno	eseyakn
eta	eto	ethnocentrism	eseyakntiraimosi
et al	eto jo	ethnogenic	eseyaknginko
et cetera	eto kitiran	ethnogeny	eseyaknginse
etaerio	etirain	ethnology	eseyaknlogbon
etagere	etigiran	ethology	esinlogbon
etalon	etijnsi	ethos	esinse
etamine	etimini	ethyl	esiole

WORD (x)	EQUIVALENT (y)	WORD (x)	EQUIVALENT (y)
ethylacetate	esiolekntiyo	eunuch	ewakura
ethylate	esioleyo	euonymus	ewasinmosi
ethylene	esiolena	eupatorium	ewapantnraima
ethylurethane	esioluraisunhun	eupatrid	ewapantnjo
etiolate	etinkoleyo	eupatridae	ewapantnjoin
etiology	etinkologbon	eupepsia	ewapnposia
etiquette	etokuntin	eupheme	ewaphnmo
eton	etosi	euphemism	ewaphanmosi
etruscan	etoraisuko	euphemise	ewaphnmuse
et se quens	eto se kunsn	euphonium	ewaphohunma
-ette	etn	euphony	ewaphohun
etude	etujin	euphorbia	ewaphirabua
etul	etujn	euphoria	ewaphirain
etymology	etiemologbon	euphoriant	ewaphiraite
etymon	etiemosi	euphotic	ewaphinko
eu	ewa	euphrasy	ewaphansn
eucaine	ewakoin	euplastic	ewapansuiko
eucalyptol	ewakojinpnti	euploid	ewaponjo
eucalyptus	ewakojinpntisi	eupnea	ewapnmi
eucharis	ewakhiranse	eurasia	ewarassia
eucharist	ewakhiransi	eureka	ewariko
eudemon	ewajinmoha	eurhythmy	ewarhaimosi
eudemonia	ewajinmohan	euro-	ewara
eudemonic	ewajinmohako	Europe	ewarapn
eudemonism	ewejainmohanmos	european	ewarapnhn
eudiometer	ewajomuto	europium	ewarapnma
eugenics	ewaginkosi	eurus	ewarasi
eugenol	ewaginjin	eury	ewary
euglena	ewagironhe	eurydice	ewarydisi
eukaryote	ewakirainyo	euryon	ewaryn
eulogia	ewalogbonsi	eurypterid	ewarypntijo
eulogize	ewalogbonse	eurystheus	ewarysinsi
eulogy	ewalogbon	eurythermal	ewarysinronjo
eunice	ewanike	eurythmics	ewarysimukosi

WORD (x)	EQUIVALENT (y)	WORD (x)	EQUIVALENT (y)
eurythmy	ewarrysimo	even2	ewini
eurytropic	ewarytnrapnko	evening	ewinignni
eustace	ewasetnsi	evens	ewinisi
eustachiantube	ewasetnkhihn tubo	event	ewinta
euthanasia	ewasankusi	eventide	ewintajin
euthenics	ewasunwnkosi	eventing	ewintagnni
eutheria	ewasurain	eventual	ewintajo
eutrophic	ewatnrapheko	eventuality	ewintajotn
eutrophication	ewatnraphekoyoon	eventuade	ewintiyo
euxenite	ewasinyo	ever	ewinra
evacuate	ewaikuoyo	everest	ewinrasn
evacuee	ewaikuosi	everett	ewinratn
evade	ewaijin	evergreen	ewinragirain
evaginate	ewagiheyo	everlasting	ewinralesngnni
evaluate	ewajoinyo	every	ewinrai
evanesce	ewainsekn	everybody	ewinraibujain
evanescent	ewainseknti	everday	ewinraidase
evangel	ewaingba	everyman	ewinraimaye
evangelical	ewaingbakojo	everyone	ewinraileni
evangelism	ewaingbamosi	every one	ewinrai ohun
evangelist	ewaingbasi	everything	ewinraisingn
evangelistic	ewaingbasuko	everywhere	ewinraiwhnrai
evangelize	ewaingbase	evict	ewoknyo
evanish	ewainsi	evidence	ewodasi
evans	ewainsi	evident	ewodato
evaporate	ewaipnraiyo	evidential	ewodatojo
evaporite	ewaipnranyo	evidently	ewodatolo
evaporimeter	ewaipnramuto	evil	eeworo
evasion	ewaisoon	evildoer	eeworodesi
evasive	ewaisowin	evil eye	eyiri eeworo
eve	ewin	evince	ewoinsi
evectics	ewinkntikosi	eviscerate	ewoseknraiyo
evection	ewinkntisi	evocation	ewnkoyoon
even1	ewini	evocative	ewnkoyowin

WORD (x)	EQUIVALENT (y)	WORD (x)	EQUIVALENT (y)
evoke	ewnko	excellent	esnknjjnto
evolution	ewnjnyoon	except	esnknpnti
evolutionist	ewnjnyoonsi	excepting	esnknpntignni
evolve	ewnjnwa	exception	esnknpntisi
ewe	ewe	exceptionable	esnknpntisibe
eweneck	ewehunko	exceptional	esnknpntisijo
ewer	ewesi	excerpt	esnknrate
ex	esn	excess	esnknsoo
exacerbate	esnknrabuyo	excessive	esnknsoowin
exact	esnknti	exchange	esnkhohign
exacting	esnkntignni	exchequer	esnkhnkunsi
exaction	esnkntiyon	excide	esnkijin
exactitude	esnkntitujin	excipient	esnkipnto
exactly	esnkntilo	excise1	esnkise
exaggerate	esngunraiyo	excise2	esnkise
exalt	esnjyo	excitable	esnkitibe
exam	esnmo	excite	esnkiti
examination	esnmoheyoon	excitement	esnkitimutto
examine	esnmohe	exciting	esnkitignni
example	esnmpon	exclaim	esnkanmo
examinate	esnmoheyo	exclamation	esnkanmoyoon
exanimo	esnhunmo	exclamatory	esnkanmoyorai
exanthema	esnhunsumo	exclaustration	esnkansetnreyoon
exarch	esnknra	exclave	esnkanwin
exarate	esnraiyo	exclosure	esnkonsnran
exrachate	esnrankheyo	exclude	esnkorajin
exasperate	esnsepnrayo	exclusion	esnkorasoon
ex cathedral	esn kosingbanle	exclusive	esnkorsoowin
excavate	esnkoweyo	excogitate	esnkignteyo
exceed	esnknjin	excoriate	esnkiraiyo
exceedingly	esnknjingnnilo	excrement	esnknramutto
excel	esnknjn	excrescent	esnknraseknti
excellence	esnknjjnsi	excreta	esnknraya
excellency	esnknjjnsn	excrete	esnknrayo

WORD (x)	EQUIVALENT (y)	WORD (x)	EQUIVALENT (y)
excruciate	esnkoraikiyo	exhibitioner	esnhigbeyoonsi
exculpate	esnkuopanyo	exhibitionism	esnhigbeyoonmosi
excursion	esnkuosoon	exhibitive	esnbigbeyowin
excuse	esnkuose	exhibitor	esnhigbeyoran
exeat	esnyo	exhilarate	esnhiloraiyo
exec	esnkn	exhort	esnhito
execrate	esnknrayo	exhortation	esnhitoyoon
executable	esnkunyobe	exhume	esnhumo
execute	esnkunyo	exigency	esnginsn
execution	esnkunyoon	exigent	esnginte
executioner	esnkunyoonsi	exiguous	esngiunsi
executive	esnkunyowin	exile	esnjia
executor	esnkunyoran	eximious	esnminisi
exegesis	esngnso	exist	esnse
exegete	esngnyo	existence	esnsesi
exegetic	esngnko	existential	esnsetojo
exemplar	esnmpanra	existentialism	esnsetojomosi
exemplary	esnmpanrai	exit	esnyo
exemplify	esnmpanrafe	exitance	esnyosi
exempt	esnmpnti	exo-	esnyn
exercise	esnraikise	exocentric	esnynkntiraiko
exerciser	esnraikisesi	exocrine	esnynknrain
exercitation	esnraikitiyoon	exoderm	esnynjnramo
exergue	esnraigan	exodontis	esnyndeyoso
exert	esnraiyo	exodus	esnynjn
exeunt	esnwata	exogamy	esnyngimo
exfoliate	esnfonjioyo	exogenous	esnynginsi
ex gratia	esn gnraite	exonerate	esnynraiyo
exhale	esnhajn	exopeptidase	esnynpnpojnse
exhaust	esnhaunyo	exoplasm	esnynpanson
exhaustion	esnhaunyoon	exorable	esnynrabe
exhaustive	esnhaunyowin	exorbitant	esnynrabetn
exhibit	esnhigbeyo	exorcize	esnynrase
exhibition	esnhigbeyoon	exordium	esnynrajoma

WORD (x)	EQUIVALENT (y)	WORD (x)	EQUIVALENT (y)
exosmosis	esnynsemiso	experiment	esnpnraimutto
exostosis	esnynsetoso	experimental	esnpnraimuttojo
exoteric	esnyntnrako	expert	esnpnra
exotic	esnynko	expertise	esnpnrase
exotica	esnynkon	expiate	esnpoyo
expand	esnpanjn	expire	esnpora
expanse	esnpanso	expirty	esnporase
expansible	esnpansobe	explain	esnpanto
expansion	esnpansoon	explanation	esnpantoyoon
expansionism	esnpansoonmosi	explanatory	esnpantoyorai
expansive	esnpansowin	expletive	esnpojnwin
exparte	esnpantn	explicable	esnpojnkibe
expatiate	esnpantnyo	explicate	esnpojnkiyo
expatriate	esnpantnraiyo	explicit	esnpojnkiti
expect	esnpnto	explode	esnpojoin
expectancy	esnpntosn	exploit	esnpote
expectant	esnpntotn	explore	esnporai
expectation	esnpntoyoon	explosion	esnposoon
expectorant	esnpntorantn	explosive	esnposoowin
expectorate	esnpntoraiyo	expo	esnpin
expedient	esnpnjnto	exponent	esnpinseto
expedite	esnpnjnyo	exponential	esnpinsetojo
expedition	esnpnjnyoon	export	esnpinta
expeditionary	esnpnjyoonrai	exportation	esnpintayoon
expeditious	esnpnjnyosi	expose	esnpinsi
expel	esnpnlo	expose	esnpinsi
expend	esnpnjon	exposition	esnpinsiyoon
expendable	esnpnjonbe	expostulate	esnpinsetoleyo
expenditure	esnpnjonrai	exposure	esnpinsirai
expense	esnpnson	expound	esnpojoin
expensive	esnpnsonwin	express	esnpesiso
experience	esnpnraise	expression	esnpesisoon
experienced	esnpnraisede	expressionism	esnpesisoonmosi
experiential	esnpnraitojo	expressive	esnpesisowin

WORD (x)	EQUIVALENT (y)	WORD (x)	EQUIVALENT (y)
expresso	esnpesisoo	extract	esntnrekyo
expressway	esnpesisowelo	extraction	esntnrekyoon
expropriate	esnponpanyo	extractive	esntnrekyowin
expulsion	esnpujnsoon	extractor	esntnrekyoran
expunge	esnpugba	extraditable	esntnrejnyobe
expurgate	esnpuragiyo	extradite	esntnrejnyo
exquisite	esnkunsuyo	extramarital	esntnremuraitojo
exsect	esnseknte	extramural	esntnremurajo
exsert	esnserate	extraneous	esntnrainsi
exstrophy	esnsetnraphe	extrapolate	esntnrepoleyo
extant	esntetn	extrasensory	esntnresesnrai
extemporaneous	esntompirihunsi	extravagant	esntnrewagantn
extemporary	esntompirirai	extravaganza	esntnrewaganse
extempore	esntompiri	extreme	esntasimo
extemporize	esntompirise	extremist	esntasimosi
extend	esntinjo	extremity	esntasimutn
extension	esntinsoon	extricate	esntaraikoyo
extensive	esntinsowin	extrinsic	esntaraisnko
extent	esntinto	extrovert	esntnrawinte
extenuate	esntinyo	extrude	esntnraijn
exterior	esntnrairan	extruder	esntnraijnsi
exterminate	esntnronhunyo	exuberant	esnberaitn
external	esntnranjo	exude	esnjin
externalize	esntnranjose	exult	esnjia
extinct	esntinyo	exuviae	esnwoin
extinction	esntinyoon	exuviate	esnwanyo
extinguish	esntingbasi	-ey	yin/in
extinguisher	esntingbasin	eye	eyiri
extirpate	esntaraipnyo	eyeball	eyirirobo
extol	esntojn	eyebrow	bonwoeyiri
extort	esntorati	eyelet	eyiritn
extortion	esntoratisi	eyelid	eyirilijo
extortionate	esntoratisiyo	eye-liner	eyiri-lehunsi
extra	esntnre	eyesight	eyirisogbe

WORD (x)	EQUIVALENT (y)	WORD (x)	EQUIVALENT (y)
eyewitness	eyiriwinsonisi	fad	fanjin
eyrie	eyiran	faddy	fanjinse
ezekiel	eseki	fade	fanjia
ezra	eseran	fado	fanjinkn
fa	fan	faecal	fansujo
fab	fanbe	faeces	fansusi
fable	fanbesi	faerie	fanuran
fabled	fanbeside	faeroes	fanrainsi
fabric	fanberaiko	faff	fanfo
fabricate	fanberaikoyo	fag1	fangi
fabulous	fanbejnsi	fag2	fangi
façade	fankojin	faggot	fangignti
face	fansi	fagot	fangnti
facer	fansise	fahrenheit	fanherainyo
facet	fansito	faience	fansun
facetious	fansitosi	fail	fanle
facia	fansia	failed	fanlede
facial	fansijo	failing	fanlegnni
facile	fansiron	failure	fanlerai
facilitate	fansironteyo	fain	fanni
facility	fansirontn	fainéant	fannitn
facing	fansignni	faint	fantue
facsimile	fansimujn	far1	fan
fact	fankyo	fair2	fanrai
faction	fankyoon	fair dos	fanrai desi
factious	fankyosi	fairy	fanra
factitious	fankyotesi	fait accompli	fansn akkimpan
factor	fankyorai	faitour	fansnwa
factorial	fankyoraijo	faith	fansn
factorize	fankyoraise	faithless	fansnlabo
factory	fankyoran	fake	fankwe
factotum	fankyotoma	fakir	fankira
factual	fankyojo	fakle	fankuo
faculty	fankunjia	falange	fanjngini

WORD (x)	EQUIVALENT (y)	WORD (x)	EQUIVALENT (y)
falcate	fanjnkoyo	fanagalo	fanyegan
falchion	fanjnkhoon	fanatic	fanyekn
falcon	fanjnkin	fancier	fanyesnsi
falconer	fanjnkinsi	fancy	fanyesn
falconet	fanjnkinte	fand	fandaa
falcongentle	fanjnkinginteron	fandance	fandajo
falconiform	fanjnkinfoon	fandangle	fandagiron
falconine	fanjnkinhun	fandango	fandagnta
falconry	fanjnkinrai	fanfare	fanfirai
falderal	fanjnrajo	fang	fangia
fald	fanjnra	fangle	fangiron
falk	fanjnko	fango	fangita
fall	fanjnra	fanion	fanyoon
fallacy	fanjnrasn	fannel	fanhunlo
fallible	fanjnrabe	fanner	fanhunran
fallopian tube	tbe fanjnrapon	fanny	fanyese
fallow	fanjnrawa	fannyadams	fanyesedamosi
false	fanjai	fantail	fantele
falsetto	fanjaito	fantan	fanteha
falsies	fanjaise	fantasia	fantesia
falsify	fanjaife	fantasize	fantesiase
falsity	fanjaitn	fantasm	fantesimo
falter	fanletn	fantasmagoria	fantesimagirain
fame	fanmo	fantast	fantesi
familial	fanmojnjo	fantastic	fantesiko
familiar	fanmojnran	fantasy	fantesn
familiarize	fanmojnraise	fantoccini	fantokini
family	fanmojn	fantod	fatojo
famine	fanmini	far	fan
famish	fanminisi	farad	fanda
famous	fanmosi	faraday	fandase
fan1	fanye	faradic	fandako
fan2	fanye	faradism	fandamosi
fans	fanyesi	faradise	fandasi

WORD (x)	EQUIVALENT (y)	WORD (x)	EQUIVALENT (y)
farandine	fanjoin	fascinate	fansekinyo
farandole	fanjnjain	fascinator	fansekinyoran
farce	fansia	fascine	fansekini
farceur	fansiaran	fascism	fansekimo
farcical	fansiakojo	fashion	fansehoon
farcy	fansiase	fashionable	fansehoonbe
fard	fanjn	fast1	fansa
fadel	fanjnjo	fast2	fansa
fare	fanra	fasten	fansasi
farewell	fanrawinjnro	fastening	fansasignni
farina	fanrain	fastidious	fansajnsi
farinaceous	fanrainsuwa	fastigiate	fansagiyo
farinose	fanrainse	fastness	fansanisi
farm	fanmo	fat	fantn
farmer	fanmosi	fatal	fantnjo
farming	fanmognni	fatalism	fantnjomosi
faro	fanro	fatality	fantnjotn
farouche	fanrokhn	fate	fanse
farrago	fanrraigon	father	fansira
farrier	fanrraisii	fatherly	fansiralo
fariery	fanrrai	fathom	fansimo
farrow	fanrrau	fathomless	fansimolabo
farsi	fansoo	fatidic	fantnjnko
far-sighted	fan-sogbede	fatigate	fantngiyo
fart	fanso	fatigue	fantngan
farther	fansunsi	fatima	fantnmo
farthest	fansunsii	fatimid	fantnmuda
farthing	fansugnni	fatten	fanttnsi
farthingale	fansugnnijn	fatty	fanttnse
fasces	fansekn	fatuity	fantotn
fascia	fansiki	fatuoid	fantnjo
fasciate	fansekiyo	fatuous	fantnsi
fasciation	fansekiyoon	faucal	fanknjo
fascicle	fansekikuo	fauces	fanknsi

WORD (x)	EQUIVALENT (y)	WORD (x)	EQUIVALENT (y)
faucet	fankiti	fealty	fnjotn
faugh	fangan	fear	fneru
fault	fanjia	fear	fneru
faultless	fanjialabo	fearless	fnerulabo
faulty	fanjiase	feasible	fnsebe
faun	fanhun	feasor	fnseran
fauna	fanhun	feast	fnseto
faunus	fanhunsi	feat	fnse
faust	fanseta	feather	fnsera
fausta	fanseto	feathering	fnseragnni
faustine	fansetin	feature	fnserai
faustus	fansetosi	feaze	fnsia
fautenti	fantinto	febri	fngban
fauves	fanwinse	febrifuge	fngbanfungbi
faux pas	fanssi pase	febrile	fngbanron
favela	fanwinjin	february	fngbanrai
faveolate	fanwinleyo	feces	fnsusi
favonian	fanwnni	fecht	fnkhiti
fave	fanwa	feck	fnki
favor	fanware	fecket	fnkite
favorable	fanwarebe	feckless	fnkilabo
favorite	fanwarete	fecula	fnknjn
favoritism	fanwaretemosi	feculence	fnknjnsi
favour	fanwaire	feculent	fnknjnto
favourable	fanwairebe	fecund	fnkunjn
favourite	fanwairete	fecundate	fnkunjnyo
favouritism	fanwairetemosi	fecundity	dnkunjntn
favus	fanwosi	fed	fnjn
fawn1	fanwn	federal	fnjnranjn
fawn2	fanwn	federacy	fnjnransn
fax	fansun	federate	fnjoraiyo
fay	fannu	federation	fjnoraiyoon
faze	fansn	fee	fnsan
feal	fnjo	feeble	fnsabe

WORD (x)	EQUIVALENT (y)	WORD (x)	EQUIVALENT (y)
feed	fnsaje	felsite	fnjusooyo
feedback	fnsajeboki	felspar	fnjusopan
feeder	fnsajesi	felt1	fnjia
feel	fnsajo	felt2	fnjia
feeler	fnsajosi	felucca	fnjnki
feeling	fnsajognni	felwort	fnjnwoole
feet	fnte	female	fnmale
feeze	fnsio	feme	fnmni
feign	fngini	feme fatale	fnmni fantejn
feint	fnnite	femesole	fnmnisoole
feisty	fnsotn	feminacy	fnminisn
feld	fnjon	feminality	fnminijotn
feldspar	fnjonsepan	feminie	fnminisi
felicitate	fnjokitiyo	feminine	fnminihun
felicitation	fnjokitiyoon	feminism	fnminimosi
felicitious	fnjokitisi	feminity	fnminitn
felicity	fnjokitn	feminise	fnminise
felix	fnjeese	femme	fnmmo
feline	fnjehun	femto	fnmnto
fell1	fnjnra	femoral	fnmnorajo
fell2	fnjnra	femur	fnmora
fell3	fnjnra	fen	fn
fell4	fnjnra	fence	fnko
fell5	fnjnra	fencing	fnkognni
fella	fnjnran	fencer	fnkosi
fellah	fnjnrai	fencible	fnkobe
fellatio	fnjnrantio	fend	fnjn
feller	fnjnrasi	fender	fnjnsi
felloe	fnjnrase	fenelon	fnjnsi
fellow	fnjora	fenestella	fnsetojnran
felly	fnjoran	fenestra	fnsetnre
fe lo de se	fnjokeku	fenestrated	fnsetnreyode
felon	fnjusi	fenestration	fnsetnreyoon
felony	fnjusise	fenian	fnhunhn

WORD (x)	EQUIVALENT (y)	WORD (x)	EQUIVALENT (y)
fenland	fnmiledain	fermatian	fnrontnhn
fennec	fnkin	ferment	fnrontto
fennel	fnhunjo	fermentation	fnronttoyoon
feny	fnmi	fermion	fnronsi
fenrir	fnrai	fermi	fnroin
fens	fnsi	fermium	fnroinma
fent	fnta	fermidirac	fnroindiko
fenugreek	fnkogirakn	fern	fnren
feod	fndon	femandez	fnrendainse
feodor	fnkojnra	femando	fnrendainko
feoff	fnofan	fernery	fnrenrai
feoffee	fnofanse	ferocious	fnrinkisi
feoffer	fnofansi	ferocity	fnrinkitn
feoffment	fnofanmutto	-ferous	fnrinsi
fer	fnra	ferralium	fnrinjoma
feracious	fnrakisi	fcrrari	fnrrinrai
feral	fnrajo	ferrate	fnrrinyo
ferbam	fnrabonun	ferreous	fnrrinsi
ferber	fnrabe	ferrero	fnrrairo
ferdelance	fnrajinlekosi	ferret	fnrrite
ferdinand	fnradidain	ferri	fnrrin
fere	fnra	ferriage	fnrraigun
ferencze	fnrainsese	ferric	fnrrinko
feretory	fnratorai	ferricy	fnrrinsn
fergus	fnragbisi	ferricyanic	fnrrinsnknko
ferguson	fnragbisin	ferricyanide	fnrrinsnknji
feria	fnrai	ferrier	fnrraisi
ferial	fnraijo	ferriferous	fnrrinfirosi
ferine	fnrain	ferrite	fnrrinyo
feringi	fnrigin	ferretin	fnrrintie
ferity	firaito	ferro	fnrm
ferlo	firailo	ferrocene	fnrinknsa
fermanagh	fnronheghan	ferroconcrete	fnrrnkinknrato
fermata	fnrontn	ferrol	fnrrnjn

WORD (x)	EQUIVALENT (y)	WORD (x)	EQUIVALENT (y)
ferrous	firrnsi	fetch	fntekhn
ferruginious	fnrrnginsi	fetch	fntekhn
ferrule	fnrrinron	fetching	fnteskhngnni
ferry	fnrrai	fete	fnta
fertile	fnratejo	feterita	fntaraite
fertility	fnratejotn	fetial	fntajo
fertilize	fnratejose	fetiales	fntajosi
fertilizer	fnratejosesi	feticide	fntakeku
ferula	fnrojn	fetid	fntabu
ferule	fnrojan	fetiparous	fntapanrunsi
fervent	fnranata	fetish	fntase
fervid	fnranajn	fetishism	fntasenosi
fervidor	fnranajnse	fetlock	fntalokn
fervor	fnranasi	fetor	fntorun
fervour	fnranaran	fetter	fnttosi
fescennine	fnseknnihun	fettle	fnttoron
fescue	fnsekunse	fettling	fnttognni
fess	fnse	fettucine	fnttokkihun
fesse	fnsoo	fetus	fntosi
festal	fnsejo	feu	fnan
fester	fnsetu	feud1	fndan
festinate	fnsetinyo	feud2	fndan
festination	fnsetinyoon	feudal	fndanjo
festival	fnsetowajo	feudalist	fndanjosi
festive	fnsetowin	feudalism	fndanjomosi
festivity	fnsetowiti	feudalise	fndanjose
festoon	fnsetoon	feudality	fndanjotn
festoonery	fnsetoonrai	feudatory	fndantorai
festschrify	fnsetosekhiraife	feudist	fndansi
fet	fnte	feuillant	fnanjnratn
feta	fnto	feuillet	fnanjnrate
fetal	fntejo	feuilleton	fnanjnrantin
fetation	fnteyoon	fever	fnwora
fetch	fntekhn	feverblister	fnworabiunsia

WORD (x)	EQUIVALENT (y)	WORD (x)	EQUIVALENT (y)
feverish	fnworase	fibrosis	fiberonso
feverous	fnworasi	fibrositis	fiberonsiso
few	fnwe	fibrous	fiberonsi
fey	fnsia	fibula	fibeji
fey	fnsia	-fic	fiko
fez	fnse	-fication	fikoyoon
fiacre	fiknra	fice	fisi
fiancé	fiyankn	fiche	fikhn
fiancée	fiyanknsi	fichte	fikhnte
fiar	firan	fichu	fikhun
fiasco	fiasekn	fickle	fikiron
fiat	fiate	fico	fiki
fib	fibe	fictile	fikotiron
fiber	fiberai	fiction	fikoyoon
fiberboard	bugbafiberai	fictional	fikoyoonjo
fiberform	fiberaifon	fictionlist	fikoyoonjosi
fibonacci	fibooheki	fictitious	fikoteyosi
fibre	fiberan	fictive	fikotewin
fibril	fiberaijn	ficus	fikunsi
fibrilla	fiberaijnra	fid	fidi
fibrillar	fiberaijnran	fiddle	fididuo
fibrillate	fiberaijnranyo	fiddle-faddle	fididuo-fandiduo
fibrillation	fiberaijnranyoon	fiddler	fididuosi
fibrilliferous	fiberaijnranfirosi	fiddling	fididuognni
fibrilliform	fiberaijnranfon	fiddly	fididuose
fibrillose	fiberaijnranse	fidejussion	fidejusoon
fibrin	fiberin	fidelcommissary	fidejnkimmusinrai
fibrinogen	fiberingin	fidelia	fidejnsi
fibrinolysin	fiberinlosoon	fidelity	fiderontn
fibrionsis	fiberinso	fidget	fadita
fibrinous	fiberinsi	fiducial	fidikijo
fibroid	fiberaijo	fiduciary	fidikirai
fibroin	fiberoin	fie	fise
fibroma	fiberonmo	fief	fifin

WORD (x)	EQUIVALENT (y)	WORD (x)	EQUIVALENT (y)
field	fisajo	filicinene	fijnkinhun
fielder	fisajosi	filicoid	fijnkijo
fiend	fisejn	filiform	fijnfoonmo
fiendish	fisejnsi	filigree	fijngirai
fierce	fisesia	filing	fijangnni
fierifacias	fiseraifansise	filipino	fijonpokn
fiery	fiserai	fill	fijjo
fiesta	fiseto	filler	fijjosi
fife	fifin	fillet	fijjote
fifteen	fifitoon	filling	fijjognni
fifth	fifisi	fillip	fijjopn
fifty	fifitn	filly	fijjose
fig1	figi	film	fijimo
fig2	figi	filmy	fijimn
fig.	figi.	filofax	fijinfansun
fight	fighe	filoplume	fijinpoluma
fighter	figheta	filter	fijito
figment	figimutto	filth	fijisu
figuration	figiraiyoon	filthy	fijisuo
figurative	figiraiyowin	filtrate	fijitnreyo
figure	figirai	filtration	fijitnreyoon
figurine	figirain	filum	fijima
filament	fijomutto	fimble	fimbe
filar	fijnra	fimbria	fimberai
filaria	fijnran	fimbriate	fimberaiyo
filariasis	fijnranso	fin	fini
filature	fijntoran	finacle	finikuo
filbert	fijnbua	finagle	finigiron
filch	fijnkhn	final	finijo
file1	fijan	finale	finijn
file2	fijan	finalist	finijosi
filial	fijnjo	finality	finijotn
filibuster	fijnbusiasi	finalize	finijose
filicide	fijnkeku	finally	finijin

WORD (x)	EQUIVALENT (y)	WORD (x)	EQUIVALENT (y)
finance	fininase	firl1	firoin
financial	fininasejo	firl2	firoin
financier	fininasesi	firmament	firoinmutto
finch	finkho	firmware	firoinwerai
find	finjn	firry	finnarai
finder	finjnsi	first	firai
fin de sie cle	fihun de soon kuo	first aid	aajo firai
finding	finjngnni	first-born	boran-firai
fine1	finni	first class	kansoo firai
fine2	finni	fiscal	fisankojo
fine arts	etesi finni	fish1	fisun
finery	finnirai	fish2	fisun
finesse	finnisoo	fishy	fisunse
finger	fingnra	fissile	fissiajn
fingering	fingnragnni	fission	fissiase
finial	finnijo	fissure	fissiarai
finicky	finnikoin	fist	fisu
finis	finniso	fisticuffs	fisukunfi
finish	finnisi	fistula	fisujn
finite	finitn	fit1	fite
fink	finko	fit2	fite
finn	finhe	fitment	fitemutn
finnan	finheye	fitted	fitede
finnic	finheko	fitter	fitesi
finnish	finhesua	fitting	fitegnni
finny	finse	five	fiwin
fino	finkn	fiver	fiwinra
finochio	finknkhio	fives	fiwinsi
finorin	finknran	five-star	fiwin setan
fipple	fiporon	fix	fisn
fir	firau	fixate	fisnyo
fir-cone	firau-kinnu	fixation	fisnyo
fire	finna	fixation	fisnyoon
fiream	aromu finna	fixative	fisnyowin

WORD (x)	EQUIVALENT (y)	WORD (x)	EQUIVALENT (y)
fixedly	fisndelo	flame	fanmana
fixed star	setan fisnde	flamenco	fanmakoi
fixer	fisnsi	flaming	fanmanagnni
fixings	fisngnni	flamingo	fanmagon
fixity	fisnto	flammable	fanmmanabe
fixture	fisntoran	flan	fanun
fizz	fisufe	flander	fanunjnra
fizzle	fisufon	flange	fanungbi
fizzy	fisufesi	flank	fankn
flab	fanbo	flanker	fanknra
flabby	fanbolo	flannel	fanhunlo
flabellate	fanbejjnyo	flannelette	fanhunlotin
flabellum	fanbejjnma	flap	fanpn
flabbergast	fanboraigiyo	flapdoodle	fanpndeinduo
flaccid	fankijo	dlapper	fanpnposi
flag1	fangn	flare	fanrai
flag2	fangn	flare-path	fanrai-panho
flag3	fangn	flash	fansia
flagellant	fangnjinte	flashback	bokifansia
flagellate	fangnjinyo	flasher	fansiasi
flagellum	fangnjinma	flash-gun	gunta-fansia
flageolet	fangnlote	flashing	fansiagnni
flaggy	fangnse	flashy	fansiase
flagitious	fangntesi	flask	fansikn
flagon	fangnsi	flat1	fante
flagrant	fangante	flat2	fante
flail	fanlu	flat-iron	irin-fante
falair	fanrai	flatmate	fantemote
flak	fanko	flatten	fanttnsi
flake	fankuo	flatten	fanttnsi
flaky	fankuosi	flatter	fanttnra
flam	fanma	flattery	fanttnrai
flambé	fanmabona	flatulent	fantejnto
flamboyant	fanmbuyote	flaunch	fankhn

WORD (x)	EQUIVALENT (y)	WORD (x)	EQUIVALENT (y)
flaunt	fantan	fletcher	fonjnkhira
flaunty	fantanse	fleur-de-lis	fonjnrie-jinle
flautist	fantusi	flew	fonjnwo
flava	fanwe	flews	fonjnwosi
flavin	fanwnni	flex1	fonjnsi
flavor	fanwnrin	flex2	fonjnsi
flavoring	fanwnringnni	flexible	fonjnsibe
flavour	fanwnrin	flexion	fonjnsilo
flavouring	fanwnringnni	flexitime	fonjnsitinmo
flaw1	fanwn	flexo	fonjnsin
flaw2	fanwn	flexor	fonjnsiran
flax	fanse	flexuous	fonjnsia
flaxen	fansesi	flibbertigibbet	fiunbetognbeyo
flax-seed	segbn fanse	flick	fiunko
flay	fanyo	flicker	fiunkosi
flea	fonjie	flick-knife	fiunko-kunfin
fleam	fonjnmo	flier	folosi
fleche	fonjn	flight1	fologbe
fleck	fonjnki	flight2	fologbe
flection	fonjnkoyoon	flightless	fologbelabo
fled	fonjnlo	flighty	fologbesi
fledge	fonjngbn	flimsy	fiunmosi
fledgling	fonjngbngnni	flinch	fiunko
flee	fonjnse	flinders	fiunjnra
fleece	fonjnsesi	fling	fiungan
fleet	fonjnte	flint	fiuntan
fleeting	fonjntegnni	flintlock	lokifiuntan
fleming	fonjnmugnni	flip1	fiunpo
flemish	fonjnmuso	flip2	fiunpo
flense	fonjnse	flippant	fiunpote
flesh	fonjnsn	flipper	fiunposi
fleshly	fonjnsnlo	flipping	fiunpognni
fleshy	fonjnsnse	flip side	soojo fiunpo
fletch	fonjnkhi	flirt	fiunte

WORD (x)	EQUIVALENT (y)	WORD (x)	EQUIVALENT (y)
flirtation	fiunteyoon	floret	fonraite
flit	fiunta	floribunda	fonraibujn
flitch	fiuntasi	floriated	fonraiyode
flite	fiunto	florid	fonraijin
flitter	fiunttnra	florida	fonrajina
float	fonta	florigen	fonraigin
floatation	fontayoon	florilegium	fonraijogbi
floating	fontagnni	florin	fonrain
floaty	fontase	florist	fonraisi
flocculant	fonkunlete	floristic	fonraisiko
flocculate	fonkunleyo	floristics	fonraisikosi
floccule	fonkunle	floruit	fonraite
flocculent	fonkunleto	flory	fonrai
flocculus	fonkunlesi	flosferri	fonsefnrai
floccus	fonkunsi	floss	fonsin
flock1	fonki	floatage	fontagun
flock2	fonki	flotation	fontayoon
flodden	fonjoin	flotilla	fontajnra
floe	fonre	flotsam	fontajnra
flog	fonlu	flotsam	fontamosi
flood	fonjin	flounce1	fonunsi
floodgate	fonjingiyo	flounce2	fonunsi
floor	fonrin	flounder1	fonunjnra
floorboard	bugbafonrin	flunder2	fonunjnra
flooring	fonringnni	flour	fonyere
floozie	fonlosi	flourish	fonyeresi
flop	fonpi	floury	fonyerese
floppy	fonpipo	flout	fontue
flora	fonrai	flow	fonwan
floral	fonraijo	flowage	fonwangun
florence	fonrainsi	flower	fonwara
florentine	fonraintin	flowery	fonwarai
flores	fonransi	flowing	fonwangnni
florescence	fonranseknsi	flown	fonwai

WORD (x)	EQUIVALENT (y)	WORD (x)	EQUIVALENT (y)
flu	folu	flush1	folusin
flube	folube	flush2	folusin
fluctuate	folukitiyo	flush3	folusin
flue	foluse	fluster	foluseto
fluent	flout	flute	foluto
fluff	folufn	flutter	folutosi
flugelhom	folugnhuran	fluvial	foluwojo
fluid	folujo	flux	folusi
fluidics	folujokosi	fly1	folo
fluidize	folujose	fly2	folo
fluke1	folukn	fly3	folo
fluke2	folukn	flyer	folosi
fluke3	folukn	flying	folognni
flume	folumi	flyover	folownra
flummery	folummirai	flywheel	folowhinlo
flummox	folummosi	foal	foojo
flung	folugan	foam	foomo
flunk	folukn	fob1	foobe
flunkey	foluknse	fob2	foobe
fluor	foluran	focaccia	foonkokia
fluorene	foluraun	focal	foonknjo
fluoresce	foluranse	focale	foonkojn
fluorescence	foluransekn	focus	foonknsi
fluorescent	foluranseknti	fodder	foojnra
fluoridate	foluraijiyo	foe	foose
fluoride	foluraiji	foe	foose
fluorinate	folurainyo	foetus	foosetosi
fluorine	folurain	fog	fongeu
fluorite	foluraiyo	fogey	fongeusi
fluorocarbon	foluraukosibu	foggy	fongeulo
fluorospar	folurausupan	foghom	fongeuran
fluoro	folurau	fogy	fongeuse
florried	folurraide	foible	foobe
flurry	folurrai	foie	fooni

WORD (x)	EQUIVALENT (y)	WORD (x)	EQUIVALENT (y)
foil1	fonlo	font2	fonte
foil2	fonlo	fontanel	fontelulo
foil3	fonlo	fontanelle	fontelulle
foin	fonhn	food	foonje
foist	fonsn	foodie	foonjesi
fold1	fonjo	fool1	fonjia
fold2	fonjo	fool2	fonjia
folder	fonjosi	foolery	fonjiarai
foliaceous	fonjiosuwa	foolish	fonjiase
foliage	fonjiogun	foolscap	fonjiasekopn
foliar	fonjioran	foos	fonsi
foliate	fonjioyo	foot	fontn
foliation	fonjioyoon	footage	fontngun
folic	fonjiko	football	robofontn
folie a deux	fonjise jinsi	footing	fontngnni
folio	fonjio	footle	fontnron
folialate	fonjioleyo	footrest	fontnresin
foliose	fonjiose	footsie	fontnsie
folium	fonjioma	fop	foopn
folk	fonliki	for-	fon/foon
folklore	fonlikilorai	forage	fongun
folksy	fonlikiso	forage cap	kopn fongun
follicle	fonjnrakuo	foray	fonyo
follow	fonjora	forbade	fongbejn
follower	fonjorasi	forbear1	fonberan
following	fonjoragnni	forbear2	fonberan
folly	fonjorau	forbearance	fonberansi
foment	fonmutto	forbid	fongbejn
fomentation	fonmuttoyoon	forbidden	fongbejnsi
fond	fondun	forbore	fonborai
fondant	fondunte	forborne	fonboroin
fondle	fondue	force1	foonsi
fondue	dondise	force2	foonsi
font1	fonte	forceps	foonkiposi

WORD (x)	EQUIVALENT (y)	WORD (x)	EQUIVALENT (y)
forcible	foonsiberon	formality	foonmojotn
ford	fonjn	formalize	foonmojose
fore	fonrai	format	foonmoyo
fore and aft	afitn ati fonrai	formation	foonmoyoon
forearm1	fonraiaraimu	formative	foonmoyowin
forearm2	fonraiaraimu	forme	foonmu
forebear	fonranberan	forme	foonmora
foreboding	fonraibojngnni	formerly	foonmoralo
forego	fonrailo	formica	foonmoko
foreign	fonraigan	formic acid	akijo foonmoko
foreigner	fonraigansi	formidable	foonmodainbe
foreign legion	jngbile fonraigan	formless	foonmolabo
forensic	fonraiseko	formula	foonmole
foresee	fonraiso	formulaic	foonmoleko
forest	fonraisi	formulary	foonmolerai
forever	fonraiwnsi	formulate	foonmoleyo
forewoman	fonraiwinmoye	formyl	foonmolo
foreword	fonraiwijo	fornicate	foonhekoyo
forfeit	fonfnyo	fornication	foonhekoyoon
forgather	fongisira	fomix	fonmolu
forge1	foongbe	forsake	foonsankn
forge2	foongbe	forsaken	foonsanknsi
forgery	foongberai	forseti	foonseye
forget	foongnyo	forsook	foonsokn
forget-me-not	foongnyo mi niti	forster	foonseto
forgo	foonlo	forsterite	foonsetoraiyo
forgot	foongonte	forswear	foonsewinwo
forgotten	foongonttin	forsyth	foonsosi
fork	foonko	forsythia	foonsosia
forlom	foonloran	fort	foonto
-form	foonmo	fortalice	foontojosi
formal	foonmojo	forte1	foonte
formalin	foonmojoin	forte2	foonte
formalism	foonmojomosi	forth	foonsi

WORD (x)	EQUIVALENT (y)	WORD (x)	EQUIVALENT (y)
fortieth	foontnsi	foundry	fonjorai
fortification	foontofikoyoon	fount1	fonunte
fortify	foontofe	fount2	fonunte
fortis	foontosi	fountain	fonuntelu
fortissimo	foontosoomo	fountain-pen	fonuntelu-pnya
fortitude	foontotujin	four	foora
fort knox	foonto knknsi	fourchette	foorakhntin
fortran	foontoran	fourteen	fooratoon
fortress	foontosin	fourth	foorasi
fortuitism	foontotemosi	fourth estate	foorasi esetnyo
fortuitous	foontotesi	fovea	fowini
fortuity	foontotn	foveola	fowinjn
fortuna	foontohe	fowl	fonwejn
fortunate	foontoheyo	fowling	fonwejngnni
fortune	foontohun	fox	fonsia
forty	foontn	foxtrot	fonsiatnra
forum	foonron	foxy	fonsian
forward	foonwegba	foy	fonye
forwarder	foonwegbase	foyer	fonyerai
forwardness	foonwegbanisi	fracas	fankasi
forwards	foonwegbasi	fractal	fankyojo
fossa	fonssi	fraction	fankyoon
fosse	fonsoo	fractionate	fankyoonyo
fossick	fonsooki	fractious	fankyosi
fossil	fonsnle	fractocumulus	fankyokunmujnsi
foster	fonseto	fracture	fankyorai
fought	fonghe	frag	fangi
foul	fonjan	fragile	fanghe
found1	fonjoin	fragment	fangimutto
found2	fonjoin	fragmentation	fangimuttoyoon
found3	fonunjo	fragrance	fangiraisi
foundation	fonjoinyoon	fragrant	fangiraite
founder	fonjoinsi	frail	fanjie
foundling	fonjoingnni	frailty	fanjietn

WORD (x)	EQUIVALENT (y)	WORD (x)	EQUIVALENT (y)
fraise	fansise	frau	fannu
framboesia	fanmbusesia	fraud	fanjua
framboise	fanmbusun	fraudster	fanjuaseto
frame	fanmu	fraudulent	fanjuajnto
franc	fankn	fraught	fanghan
france	fanknsi	fraulein	fanjainte
franchise	fankhnse	fraunhofer	fannihinfiro
franchisee	fankhnsesi	fraxinella	fansinhunjjn
franchisor	fankhnseran	fray1	fanya
francis	fanknso	fray2	fanya
franciscan	fanknsoko	frazzle	fansun
francium	fanknma	frazil	fansulo
franco-	fanki	freak	fesiako
fangible	fangnbe	freaky	fesiakn
franger	fangnsi	freckle	fesiakojn
franglais	fangbileso	free	fesia
frank	fankin	freely	fesialo
frankenfood	fanknnifoonje	freebie	fesiabon
franklinite	fankinlikotn	freeboard	fesiabugba
frankly	fankinlo	freedom	fesiademo
frankenstein	fankinseto	freelance	fesialekosi
frankincense	fankinknsun	fressia	fesisia
frantic	fantnko	freeze	fesiasn
frap	fanpo	freezer	fesiasnsi
frappe	fanpon	freight	fesiagbe
fraser	fansesi	freighter	fesiagbesi
frass	fanso	freightliner	fesiagbelehunsi
frat	fanti	frend	fesijn
fratchy	fantikho	french	fesiko
frater	fantira	frenchify	fesikofe
fraternal	fantirajo	frenetic	fesinko
fraternity	fantirato	frenzy	fesinse
fraternize	fantirase	freon	fesise
fratricide	fantirakeku	frequency	fesikunran

WORD (x)	EQUIVALENT (y)	WORD (x)	EQUIVALENT (y)
frequent	fesikunra	frigidity	fangijotn
frequentative	fesikunrayowin	frill	fanjnra
fresco	fesiseki	frilly	fanjnrase
fresh	fesisn	fringe	fangnni
freshen	fesisnse	fringilline	fangnnijnrain
fresher	fesisnsi	frippery	fanpnrai
freshet	fesisnte	frippet	fanpnti
freshman	fesisnmaye	Frisbee	fansibese
fresnet	fesisunjo	fries	fansue
fret1	fesita	frisette	fansuetin
fret2	fesita	frisian	fansian
fret3	fesita	frisk	fansia
freudian	fesidainhn	frisket	fansiate
fri.	fan	frisky	fansiase
fribble	fanbo	frisson	fansnsin
friable	fanbe	frit	fanti
friar	fanrai	frith	fantisi
friary	fanraisn	fritillary	fantijjnrai
fricassee	fankasesi	fritter1	fanttisi
fricative	fankayowin	fritter2	fanttisi
friction	fanknrasi	friuli	fanlele
friday	fandase	friulian	fanlelehn
fridge	fandign	frivol	fanwnjn
friend	fanjose	frivolity	fanwnjntn
friendly	fanjoselo	frivolous	fanwnjnsi
frier	fanra	frizz	fansuin
friesian	fansesuhn	frizzle1	fansuinron
frieze	fansesi	frizzle2	fansuinron
frig	fangi	frizzy	fansuin
frigate	fangiyo	fro	fon
fright	fangban	frock	ffonki
frighten	fangbansi	frog1	fogn
frigid	fangijo	frog2	fogn
frigidaire	fangijorai	frog3	fogn

WORD (x)	EQUIVALENT (y)	WORD (x)	EQUIVALENT (y)
frogman	fognmoye	fruiterer	foraterasi
frogmarch	fognmurakho	fruition	foratesi
frolic	fonjnke	fruitless	foratelabo
from	fonwa/lati	fruity	foratese
frome	fonwo	frumntaceous	foramuttosuwa
fromage frais	fonwagun fanso	frumenty	foramutto
froment	fonwato	frump	forampn
frond	fonjo	frustrate	forasiraiyo
front	fontn	frustration	forasiraiyoon
frontage	fontngun	frustum	forasimo
frontal	fontnjo	frutescent	forateseknti
frontier	fontnrai	fruiticose	foratekise
frost	fonsn	fry1	ferai
frostbite	fonsnbate	fry2	ferai
frosty	fonsnto	fryer	feraisi
froth	fonsi	fuchsia	funkosia
frother	fonsira	fuchsin	funkosin
frothy	fonsise	fuck	funki
frounce	fonkoi	fucoid	funkijo
frow	fonwe	fucus	funkn
froward	fonwegba	fuddle	funjiduo
frown	fonwn	fuddy duddy	funjide dijide
frowsty	fonwnsitn	fudge	funjian
frowzy	fonwnse	fuegian	fungnhn
froze	fonsin	fuehrer	funhnrai
frozen	fonsinsi	fuel	funna
fructify	forakntife	fug	fungn
fructose	forakntose	fugacious	fungnkisi
frugal	foragn	fugacity	fungnkito
frugality	foragnleto	fugal	fungnjo
frugivorous	foragnwnrunsi	fugato	fungnto
fruit	forate	fuge	fungbi
fruitage	forategun	fugio	fungbiko
fruitarian	foraterain	fugitive	fungbiyowin

WORD (x)	EQUIVALENT (y)	WORD (x)	EQUIVALENT (y)
fugue	fungan	fundamentalism	funjainmuttojomosi
fuhrer	funhasi	fundi	funjin
fuji	funjin	funeral	funsinjo
,-ful	funjn	funerary	funsinrai
fulcrum	funjnkarai	funereal	funsinrajo
fulfil	funjnfijo	fungicide	fungikeku
fulfill	funjnfijjo	fungoid	fuugijo
full1	funjjn	fungus	fungisi
full2	funjjn	funicle	funkuo
full board	bugba-funjjn	funicular	funkuoran
fuller	funjjnse	funiculus	funkuosi
fullness	funjjnnisi	funk1	funkn
fully	funjjnsi	funk2	funkn
fulmar	funjnmura	funky	funknse
fulminant	funjnmohetn	funnel	funyoro
fulminate	funjnmoheyo	funnies	funyosesi
fulmine	funjnmohun	funny	funyose
fulsome	funjnsoomo	fur	funre
fumble	funmibe	furan	funrein
fume	funmi	furbelow	funrebejn
fumigate	funmigiyo	furbish	funrebesi
fumitory	funmitorai	furbrigade	funrebangidie
fumulus	funmijnsi	furcal	funrekn
fumy	funmise	furcate	funreknyo
fun	funyo	furcraea	funreknran
funaluti	funhuntn	furcula	funreknjn
funambulist	funhunmbejnsi	furculum	funreknjnma
funchal	funkhnjo	furfur	funrefunre
function	funknyoon	furfural	funrefunrejo
functional	funknyoonjo	furfuraceous	funrefunresuwa
functionalism	funknyoonjomosi	furies	funraise
functionary	funknyoonrai	furioso	funraisoo
fund	funjan	furious	funraisi
fundamental	funjainmuttojo	furl	funrelo

WORD (x)	EQUIVALENT (y)	WORD (x)	EQUIVALENT (y)
furlong	funrelogun	fusible	funsebe
furlough	funrelogan	fusiform	funsefoonmo
furm	funremo	fusil	funsnle
furmenty	funremutto	fusile	funseron
furnace	funransi	fusilier	funsejnransi
furnish	funranse	fusillade	funsejnrade
furnished	funransede	fusion	funsiase
furnisher	funransesi	fuss	funsia
furnishings	funransegnnisi	fusspot	funsiapote
furniture	funrantosi	fussy	fusiase
furor	funreran	fust	fusia
furor loquendi	funreran lokunjn	fustanella	fusiahunjn
furor seribendi	funraisi seraibejn	fustian	fusiahn
furore	funrerai	fustic	fusiako
furphy	funrephe	fustigate	fusiagiyo
furred	funrrede	fustin	fusiasi
furrier	funrrese	fustle	fusiaron
furriery	funrrerai	fusty	fusiatn
furring	funrregnni	futile	futeron
furrow	funrresi	futilitarian	futeronterain
furry	funrrai	futility	futerontn
further	funrese	futon	futesi
furtherance	funresesi	futtock	funttoki
furthest	funresesii	future	funtnrai
furtive	funretewin	futurism	funtoraimosi
furuncle	funrekuo	futuristic	funtoraisuko
fury	funrai	futurity	funtoraitn
furze	funsia	futurology	funtorailogbon
fusain	funsuin	futz	funtese
fuse1	funse	fuze	fuse
fuse2	funse	fuzz	fuse
fusee	funsesi	fuzzy	fusese
fusel	funsijn	,-fy	fe
fuselage	funselogbi	Fyke	fekn

WORD (x)	EQUIVALENT (y)	WORD (x)	EQUIVALENT (y)
fyide	fejin	gaelic	gileko
fyifot	fefitin	gaff1	gifan
fyn	fehun	gaff2	gifan
fyrd	fegba	gaffi	gifon
gab	gibe	gaffe	gife
gabardine	gibegbain	gaffer	gifiro
gabble	fibo	gag	gigbi
gabbro	fiboun	gaga	gigan
gabby	fibose	gage1	gigun
gabelle	gibejnron	gage2	gigun
gabardine	gibegbain	gager	gigunsi
gaberlunzie	gibejoinsun	gaggle	giganron
gabfest	gibofnsi	gahnite	gihunyo
gabion	giboin	gaiety	gisuato
gabionade	giboinjin	gaillardia	gijnragbasi
gable	giboron	gaily	gisualo
gablet	gibotn	gain	gini
gabon	gibosi	gainer	ginisi
gabriel	giborai	gainful	ginifunjjn
gabrielle	giboraijn	gainsay	ginisanwi
gad	gijn	gair	girie
gadabout	gijnbounta	gait	gite
gadara	gijnrai	gaiter	gitesi
gadarene	gijnrain	gaiting	gitegnni
gadfly	fijnfolo	gal	gijo
gadget	fijnto	gal.	gijo
gadgeteer	gijntosi	gala	gije
gadgetry	gijntorai	gala	gile
gadoid	gijnjo	galactagog	gileketegon
gadolinium	gijnlehunma	galactan	gileketin
gadroon	gijnroon	galactic	gilekeko
gae	gisa	galacto	gileketo
gaea	gisan	galactocele	gileketoknjn
gael	gile	galactolipin	gileketoliposi

WORD (x)	EQUIVALENT (y)	WORD (x)	EQUIVALENT (y)
galactometer	gileketomuto	gal-in-gale	gijo-ni-gile
galactopoietic	gileketopinseko	galiot	gileta
galactose	gileketose	galipot	gilepote
galactoscope	gileketosokipon	gall1	gijoro
galactosemia	gileketosemua	gall2	gijoro
galactotherapy	gileketosinranpo	gall3	gijoro
galago	gilegon	gall.	Gille
galahad	gilehunjn	galla	gillese
galalith	gilelesi	gallant	gijnrantn
galangal	gileganjo	gallantry	gijnrantnrai
galant	gilete	galleass	gijnransoon
galantine	giletehun	galleon	gijnransi
galanty	giletese	galleria	gijnroran
galapagos	gilepangnsi	gallery	gijnrorai
galata	gileta	galley	gijnroin
galatea	giletosi	galliambic	gijnranmbuko
galati	gileti	galliard	gijnrangbaa
galatia	giletie	gallic	gijnranko
galatians	giletiehnsi	gallican	gijnrankojn
galax	filesia	Gallicism	gijnrankomosi
galaxy	gilesiasi	gallinaceous	gijnranhesuwa
galbanum	gilebaunma	gallinazo	gijnranhesin
gale	gile	galling	gijnrangnni
galea	gilesi	gallinipper	gijnranpansi
galena	gilehun	gallinule	gijnranjn
galenic	gilehunko	gallion	gijnrain
galenism	gilehunmosi	gallipoli	gijnranpinle
galeopithecus	gileposinkunsi	gallipot	gijnranpote
galere	gilerai	gallium	gijnranma
galeropia	gileraipan	gallivant	gijnranwntn
Galicia	gilekin	gallo-	gijnron
galilee	gilejnse	gallon	gijnronsi
galileo	gilejnko	galloon	gijnronse
galimatisa	gilemutose	gallop	gijnronpn

WORD (x)	EQUIVALENT (y)	WORD (x)	EQUIVALENT (y)
gallous	gijnronsin	gamic	gimuko
gallows	gijnronwo	gamin	gimun
gallstone	gijnronsetole	gamine	gimini
gallup poll	gijnronpn pojnra	gamma	gamma
galluses	gijnronsosi	gammadion	gimmajnle
galloot	gijnrontoo	gammer	gimmura
gallore	gijnronrai	gammon	gimmeni
gallop	gijnronpn	gamo	gimokn
galosh	gijosue	gamogenesis	gimokngnhunso
galumph	gijompha	gamomania	gimoknmohan
galvanic	gijowainko	gamophyllus	gimoknphewes
galvanize	gijowainse	gamous	gimosi
galvano	gijowain	gammy	gimmo
galvanometer	gijowainmuto	gamp	gimpn
galvo	gijown	gamut	gimuto
gam	gima	gamy	gimo
gamaliel	gimalelo	gan	gin
gamashes	gimasunsi	gander	ginjnra
gamb	gimbe	gandy	ginjnse
gambit	gimbeyo	gang	gigan
gamble	gimbeta	ganger	gigansi
gamboge	gimbegun	gangling	gignjognni
gambol	gimbejn	ganglion	giganjoin
gambrel	gimbejo	gangly	giganlo
game1	gimo	gangplank	giganpankn
game2	gimo	gangrel	giganrailo
gamelan	gimojin	gangrene	giganrain
gamer	gimorai	gangsta	gigansita
gamester	gimoseto	gangster	giganseto
gamete	gimuta	gangue	gigansi
gameto	gimuto	gang up	gigan pake
gametophore	gimutophiran	gannet	gante
gametophyte	gimutopheyo	ganister	ganseto
gamey	gimose	ganja	ganjo

WORD (x)	EQUIVALENT (y)	WORD (x)	EQUIVALENT (y)
ganold	ganjo	garment	giramutto
gansey	gansise	gamer	giransi
gantlet	ganteyo	garnet	girante
gantry	ganterai	garnierite	giranraiyo
ganymede	gansemojin	garnish	giransua
gaol	gijin	garnishee	giransuase
gaoler	gijinsi	garniture	girantorai
gap	gipn	garpike	girapokn
gape	gipin	garret	girraite
gappy	gipnpo	garrison	girraisi
gaptony	gipntose	garrote	girrante
garage	giragun	garrotte	girrantn
garammasala	girammusejn	garruline	girrailehun
garb	girabo	garrulity	girraileto
garbage	girabogbn	garrulous	girraileso
garbanzo	girabosin	garter	giratn
garble	girabe	garth	girasn
garboard	girabugba	garvey	girawain
garcon	girakin	gary	girase
garden	giragba	gas	gisun
garden centre	giragba kntiran	gaseous	gisunsi
garden city	giragba kito	gash	gisa
gardener	giragbase	gasify	gisunfe
gardenia	giragbasi	gasket	gisukiti
garfish	girafisun	gaskin	gisunkin
garganey	giragain	gaslight	gisunlighe
gargantuan	giragantan	gasman	gisunmoye
garget	giragnyo	gas mask	gisun mosia
gargle	giragan	gasogene	gisungini
gargoyle	giralojain	gasoline	gisunlehun
garibaldi	giraibojoin	gasometer	gisunmuto
garish	giraisu	gasometry	gisunmutorai
garland	giraledain	gasp	gisunpi
garlic	giraleko	gas ring	gisun rogan

WORD (x)	EQUIVALENT (y)	WORD (x)	EQUIVALENT (y)
gassy	gisunse	gaunt	gitie
gastero	gisekun	gauntlet1	gitietn
gasteropod	gisutnrapindie	gauntlet2	gitietn
gastralgia	gisutnrajigan	gauss	gisue
gastrectomy	gisutnratemo	gauze	gisia
gastric	gisutnrako	gauzy	gisiase
gastritis	gisutnrso	gave	giwin
gastro-	gisutnra	gavel	giwnlo
gastro-enteritis	gisutnra-entnraiso	gavial	giwinjo
gastroenterology	gisutnraentnralogbon	gavotte	giwntin
gastroenterostomy	gisutnraentnrasutemo	gawd	gidiwa
gastrolith	gisutnralesi	gawk	gikwo
gastrology	gisutnralogbon	gawky	gikwose
gastronome	gisutnraknmn	gawp	gipnwo
gastronomy	gisuntnraknmo	gay	giya
gastropod	gisutnrapindie	gay	giya
gastrotomy	gisutnratemo	gaya	giya
gastrotrich	gisutnratekhe	gayal	giyajo
gastrula	gisutnraile	gayety	giyatn
gate	giyo	gayomart	giyamurate
gateau	gitiele	gaze	giso
gatha	gisan	gazebo	gisobua
gather	gisira	gazelle	gisojjn
gatherer	gisirasi	gazette	gisoto
gathering	gisiragnni	gazetteer	gisotorai
gauche	gikwe	gazillion	gisojnransi
gaucherie	gikweran	gazpacho	gisipankhin
gaucho	gikweko	gazump	gisumpn
gaud	gidie	gazunder	gisujnra
gaudy	gidese	ge	gn
gauge	gigbaa	geanticline	gntekihun
gauger	gigbaasi	gear	gnran
gaul	gijee	gearbox	gnranbosi
gaulish	gijeese	gearing	gnrangnni

WORD (x)	EQUIVALENT (y)	WORD (x)	EQUIVALENT (y)
gearwheel	gnranwhinlo	gem	gnmi
gecko	gnkoin	gemara	gnmiran
gecrol	gnknra	gemel	gnmilo
gedact	gndaknti	geminate	gnminiyo
gedion	gnjnle	gemini	gnmini
gee1	gnsia	gemma	gnmmu
gee2	gnsia	gemmate	gnmmote
gee-gee	gnsia-gnsia	gemmiparous	gnmmopnran
geek	gnsiakn	gemmulation	gnmujnyoon
geese	gnsiasi	gemmule	gnmmujn
geest	gnsiasi	gemmy	gnmimo
geezer	gnsiasesi	gemology	gnmilogbon
gefilte	gnfijite	gemot	gnmuto
gegenschein	gnginsekhn	gemsbok	gnmisebuki
gehenna	gnhena	gemstone	gnmisetole
gehlenite	gnhejinyo	gemutlich	gnmuyokhn
geiger	gngira	gen	gin
geisha	gnsihun	gendarme	ginjnramu
geissier	gnsisoorai	gendamerie	ginjnramuran
gel	gnjo	gender	ginjnra
gelada	gnjojn	gene	gnhun
gelande	gnjoinjin	generalogy	gnhunlogbon
gelatin	gnjotin	genera	gnhunrai
gelatinate	gnjotinyo	general	gnhunraijo
gelatinoid	gnjotinjo	generalissimo	gnhunrailemosi
gelatinous	gnjotinsi	generality	gnhunraileto
gelation	gnjoyoon	generalize	gnhunraijose
geld	gnjon	generally	gnhunraijjn
gelding	gnjongnni	generate	gnhunraiyo
gelead	gijogba	generation	gnhunraiyoon
gelid	gnjojn	generative	gnhunraiwin
gelignite	gnjogbinayo	generator	gnhunrairan
gelsemium	gnjosemu	generic	gnhunraiko
gelt	gnjia	generous	gnhunraisi

WORD (x)	EQUIVALENT (y)	WORD (x)	EQUIVALENT (y)
genesis	gnhunso	gent	ginte
geneva	gnhunwa	genteel	gintejn
genevan	gnhunwain	gentian	gintehn
geneve	gnhunwin	gentianaceous	gintehunsuwa
genevieve	gnhunwowin	gentianella	gintehunjjn
genfersee	gnfirosun	gentile	gintijo
genet	gnhunte	gentilesse	gintijose
genetic	gnhunteko	gentilism	gintijosi
genetic code	gnhunteko kidie	gentility	gintileto
genetics	gnhuntekosi	gentle	ginteron
genevali	gnhunwele	getleoflk	ginteronfonliki
genial	gnhunjo	gentleman	ginteronmoye
genic	ginko	gentlemanly	ginteronmoyelo
geniculate	gnhunknleyo	gentoo	gintoo
genie	gnhunse	gentrification	ginteraifikoyoon
genioplasty	gnhunpansuito	gentry	ginterai
genital	ginitejo	gents	gintesi
genitalia	ginitejosi	genty	gintese
gentive	gnnitewin	genu	ginle
genito	ginito	genuflect	ginlefonjnko
genitor	ginitoran	genuine	ginlehun
genius	ginise	genus	ginlesi
geniusloci	giniseloki	geny	ginse
genizah	ginsehun	geo-	gbile
genlyon	ginlosi	geocentric	gbilekntiraiko
genoa	ginisi	geode	gbilejin
genocide	ginikeku	geodesic	gbilejinsiko
genoiese	ginisise	geodesic line	lehun gbilejinsiko
genome	ginimo	geodesy	gbilejinso
genotype	ginitnpon	geodetic	gbilejinko
-genous	ginsi	geodynamic	gbiledainsemuko
genre	giniran	geognosy	gbileginiso
genro	giniro	geographical	gbileganphekojo
gens	ginsi	geographical mile	mulele gbileganphekoy

WORD (x)	EQUIVALENT (y)	WORD (x)	EQUIVALENT (y)
geography	gbileganphe	gerald	gnrajon
geoid	gbilejo	geraldine	gnrajojoin
geology	gbilelogbon	geraniaceous	gnrainsuwa
geomancy	gbilemoyesn	geranial	gnrainjo
geometric	gbilemutoraiko	geraniol	gnrainjin
geometry	gbilemutorai	geranium	gnrainma
geomorphic	gbilemophanko	gerard	gnragba
geomorphology	gbilemophanlogbon	geratology	gnratologbon
geonomy	gbileknmo	gerbil	gnrabajn
geophagy	gbilephije	gerda	gnrajn
geophysics	gbilephekososi	geremia	gnremua
geophyte	gbilepheyo	gerent	gnreto
geoponics	gbileponkosi	gereology	gnrelogbon
geordie	gbilegansi	gerfalcon	gnrafanjnkin
georelle	gbileduo	gernuk	gnrakun
george	gbilegan	geriatric	gnretnrako
George cross	gbilegan konso	geriatrics	gnretnrakosi
georgette	gbilegantn	gericault	gnrekunjia
georgian1	gbileganhn	germ	gnron
georgian2	gbileganhn	german	gnroin
georgic	gbileganko	germander	gnroinjnra
geosciences	gbilesisunse	germane	gnronhun
geostatic	gbilesetntiko	germanic	gnroinko
geostrategy	gbilesetnretogbon	germanium	gnroinma
geostrophic	gbilesetnraphiko	germane-	gnroinkn
geosyncline	gbilesosekihun	germany	gnroinse
geotaxis	gbiletesanso	germen	gnronsi
geotectonic	gbiletokntiko	germicide	gnronkeku
geothermal	gbilesinronjo	germinal	gnronhunjo
geotropism	gbiletnrapnmosi	germinant	gnronhunte
geraniaceous	gnrahnsuwa	germinate	gnronhunyo
gera	gnra	geronto	gnranto
gerah	gnrahun	gerontocracy	gnrantokansn
geraint	gnrainta	gerontology	gnrantologbon

WORD (x)	EQUIVALENT (y)	WORD (x)	EQUIVALENT (y)
gerous	gnrasi	ghostly	ghosilo
gerry	gnrrai	ghoul	ghoje
gerrymander	gnrraimujnra	ghurry	ghunrrai
gertrude	gnratorai	ghyll	ghngbn
gerund	gnrajoin	gi	gbi
gerundive	gnrajoinwin	giant	gbiga
gesso	gnsesoo	giaour	gbira
gest	gnse	gib	gbibo
gestalt	gnsejia	gibber	gbibora
gestapo	gnsepo	gibberellic	gbiboraijjnko
gestate	gnseyo	gibberellin	gbiboraijjn
gestation	gnseyoon	gibberish	gbiboraisi
gestic	gnseko	gibbet	gbibote
gesticulate	gnsekunleyo	gibbon	gbiboun
gesture	gnserai	gibbosity	gbibounseto
gesundheit	gnsujnheyo	gibbous	gbibosi
get	gnte	gibbste	gbibesuyo
get-out	gnte-nita	gibe	gbibo
geyser	gnserai	gibeon	gbibesi
geyserite	gnseraiyo	gibeonite	gbibesiyo
gharry	ghirrai	giblets	gbibetnsi
ghastly	ghisialo	gibraltar	gbibejiaran
ghat	ghite	gibson	gbibesin
ghaut	ghiunte	gid	gbide
ghee	ghnse	giddy	gbidese
ghent	ghnto	gideon	gbidain
gherkin	ghnrakn	gidgee	gbidegnse
ghetto	ghntto	gle	gbilo
ghettoize	ghnttose	gift	gbifia
ghibelline	ghibejnroin	gifted	gbifiade
ghibli	ghibiun	gig1	gbign
ghillie	ghijnrase	gig2	gbign
ghost	ghosi	giga-	gbigan
ghosting	ghosignni	gigahertz	gbiganheraise

WORD (x)	EQUIVALENT (y)	WORD (x)	EQUIVALENT (y)
gigantic	gbigantokn	gine	gbihun
gigantism	gbigantomosi	ginger	gbignran
giganto	gbiganto	ginger group	gonpo gbignran
gigantomachy	gbigantomukho	gingerly	gbignranlo
giggle	gbignron	gingery	gbignrai
gigolo	gbignlo	gingham	gbignmo
gigot	gbignte	gingili	gbigile
gigue	gbignso	gingiva	gbigiwu
gila	gbijn	gingivitis	gbigiwuso
gilbert	gbijnbe	ginglymus	gbigbiynmasi
gild1	gbidon	gink	gbikn
gild2	gbidon	ginkgo	gbikngon
gilder	gbidonsi	ginnel	gbisilo
gilding	gbidongnni	ginner	gbisiran
gill1	gbinjn	gin palace	gbisi panjosin
gill2	gbinjn	gin rum	gbisi runmo
gill3	gbinjn	gin rummy	gbisi runmo
gillie	gbinjnse	ginormous	gbiranmosi
gillion	gbinjnsi	ginrummy	gbirunmmo
gillyflower	gbinjnfonwarasi	ginseng	gbisegan
gilolo	gbinlolo	gioconda	gbikokinjn
gilt1	gbijia	giorgi	gbirangan
gilt2	gbijia	giotto	gbikottn
gilt-edged	ajngede-gbijia	gip	gbipn
gimbals	gbimbejo	gippy tummy	gbipnse tummo
gimcrack	gbimkanko	gipps	gbipnsi
gimel	gbimlo	gipsy	gbipnso
gimlet	gbimte	giraffe	gbiraife
gimlet eye	eyiri gbimte	girandole	gbiraijnjain
gimme	gbimmo	gird	gberodi
gimmick	gbimmukin	girder	gberodisi
gimp	gbimpn	girdle1	gberoduo
gin1	gbisa	girdle2	gberoduo
gin2	gbisa	girdler	gberoduosi

WORD (x)	EQUIVALENT (y)	WORD (x)	EQUIVALENT (y)
girl	gberojn	gladden	gandunsi
girlie	gberojnsi	gladdon	gandunse
girlish	gberose	glade	gande
giro	gberon	glad eye	eyiri gandun
giron	gberoin	gladiate	gandute
gironde	gberoinde	gladiator	ganduteran
girondist	gberoindes	gladiatorial	ganduteraijo
gironny	gberoinse	gladiolus	gandunjinsi
girt	gberote	gladly	gandunlo
girth	gberosi	gladstone	gandunseto
gisarme	gbesaroin	glagol	gangijn
gismo	gbesimo	glaik	gankoi
gissing	gbesignni	glaikit	gankoito
gist	gbiso	glair	ganrai
git	gbiti	glaireous	ganraisi
gitalin	gbitejin	glairy	ganraise
gite	gbito	glaive	ganwain
gittern	gbittoran	galizie	gansesi
give	gbewain	glam	ganmo
given	gbewainsi	glamor	ganmora
gizmo	gbisemo	glamorize	ganmoraise
gizzard	gbisegbaa	glamour	ganmoran
glabella	ganbejjn	glance	ganso
glabrate	ganberayo	gland	gandain
glabrous	ganberasi	glanders	gandainsesi
glace	gankn	glandular	gandainjnra
glacial	ganknjo	glandule	gandainron
glacial period	pnraijo ganknjo	glare	ganran
glaciated	ganknyode	glare	ganran
glaciation	ganknyoon	glaring	ganrangnni
glacier	ganknrai	glarus	ganransi
glaciology	ganknlogbon	glary	ganranse
glacis	ganknso	glasnost	gansita
glad	gandun	glass	gansin

WORD (x)	EQUIVALENT (y)	WORD (x)	EQUIVALENT (y)
glassy	gansinse	glissando	giunsoondie
glaston	gansitin	glisten	giunton
Glaswegian	gansiwingihn	glister	giuntonsi
glauber	ganunbesi	glitch	giuntesi
glaucine	ganunkihun	glitter	giunttonsi
glauco	ganunki	glitterati	giunttonye
glaucoma	ganunkimo	glittery	giuntonrai
glauconite	ganunkinyo	glitz	giuntese
glaucous	ganunkisi	glitsy	giuntesn
glaze	ganse	gloaming	gonmugnni
glazier	gansesi	gloat	gonte
gleam	gnunmo	glob	gonbn
glean	gnunhun	global	gonbonjo
gleanings	gnunhungnnisi	globalize	gonbonjose
glebe	gnunbe	globate	gonbonto
glede	gnunjin	globe	gonbon
glee	gnunse	globin	gonbin
gleed	gnunjo	globold	gonbonjon
gleet	gnunte	globose	gonbuse
gleization	gnunseyoon	globular	gonbonjnra
glen	gnuni	globule	gonbnron
glengarry	gnunigirrai	globulicide	gonbnronkeku
glib	giunbo	globulin	gonbnronsi
glide	giunjin	glocal	gonkojo
glider	giunjinsi	glockenspiel	gonkosinpolo
gliff	fiunfo	glochidium	gonkhijoma
glim	giunmo	glogg	gongin
glimmer	giunmo	glom	gonmu
glimmer	giunmosi	glomerate	gonmuraiyo
glimpse	giunpnso	glomeration	gonmuraiyoon
glint	giuntan	glomerule	gonmuraijo
glioma	giunknma	glomerulus	gonmuraijosi
gliosa	giunknso	glomma	gonmomi
glissade	giunsoojin	glonoin	gonkns

WORD (x)	EQUIVALENT (y)	WORD (x)	EQUIVALENT (y)
gloom	gonmua	glow	gonyo
gloomy	gonmuase	glower	gonyosi
glop	gonpi	glowing	gonyognni
gloria	gonraisi	gloxinia	gonsihan
glorification	gonraifikoyoon	gloze	gonso
glorify	gonraife	glucagon	gbilekogon
gloriole	gonraijain	glucocorticold	gbilekikitekijon
glorious	gonraisi	gluconeogenesis	gbilekinnugnhunso
glory	gonrai	glucose	gbilekise
gloss1	gonsua	glucosuria	gbilekisuran
gloss2	gonsua	glue	gbile
glossa	gonsuan	glum	gbilema
glossal	gonsuajo	glumaceous	gbilemasuwa
glossarist	gonsuaraisi	glume	gbilemi
glossary	gonsuarai	gluon	gbilesi
glossator	gonsuaran	glut	gbileto
glossectomy	gonsuatemo	glutamate	gbiletomuyo
glosseme	gonsuamo	glutamic	gbiletomuko
glossina	gonsuahun	glutamine	gbiletomini
glossitis	gonsuaso	glutathione	gbiletosinleni
glosso	gonsun	gluteal	gbiletejo
glossography	gonsunganphe	glutelin	gbiletejan
glossolalia	gonsunjnjan	gluten	gbiletin
glossology	gonsunlogbon	gluteus	gbiletesi
glossopharyngeal	gonsunphisognjo	glutinous	gbiletinsi
glossy	gonsuase	glutton	gbileton
glottal	gonttojo	gluttonous	gbiletonsi
glot	gonto	gluttony	gbiletonse
glottis	gonttosi	glycerin	giloknran
glottic	gonttoka	glycerine	giloknrain
glottochronology	gonttokhironlogbon	glycerol	giloknrajin
glottology	gonttologbon	glycogen	gilokigin
glove	gonwe	glycogenesis	gilokignhunso
glover	gonwesi	glycolysis	gilokijinso

WORD (x)	EQUIVALENT (y)	WORD (x)	EQUIVALENT (y)
glyconeogenesis	gilokinungnhunso	gnu	giaun
glycosuria	gilokisuran	go1	lo
glyndebourrie	gilojnbonunran	go2	gon
glyoxaline	gilosinlehun	goa	gonsi
glyph	gilophin	goad	gonjan
glyphography	gilophinganphe	goal	gonjn
glyptal	gilopntijo	goalie	gonjasi
glyptic	gilopntiko	goalpost	gonjopinsi
glyptodont	gilopntideyo	goat	gonte
glyptography	gilopntiganphe	goatee	gontese
gnar	giaran	goatish	gontesi
gnarled	giaranjnde	goanna	gonhun
gnarly	giaranjnse	goave	gonwo
gnash	giase	gob1	gonbu
gnat	giate	gob2	gonbu
gnathic	giatako	gobang	gonbugn
gnathion	giatasi	gobbet	gonbute
gnathite	giatayo	gobble1	gonburon
gnatho	giatosi	gobble2	gonburon
gnathonic	giatosiko	gobbledygook	gonburondaingonko
gnathous	giatose	gobbler	gonburonsi
gnaw	giawe	goblet	gonbutn
gneiss	giasoo	goblin	gonbejan
gneissoid	giasoojo	gobioid	gonbujo
gnocchi	ginikhi	gobo	gonbo
gnome	ginimo	goby	gonbuse
gnomic	ginimuko	god	godi
gnomon	ginimosi	godard	godigba
gnomy	ginimose	godavari	godiwarai
gnosiology	giniselogbon	godden	godisi
gnosis	giniso	goddess	godibo
gnostic	giniseko	godel	godijo
gnosticism	ginisekomosi	godetia	goditie
gnosticize	ginisekose	godless	godilabo

WORD (x)	EQUIVALENT (y)	WORD (x)	EQUIVALENT (y)
godly	godilo	golon	gonjnsi
godparent	godipanrato	goltz	gonjiase
godroon	godiroon	gombroom	gonmberain
godson	godisin	gomel	gonmulo
goer	lorai	gomera	gonmuran
goering	loraignni	gomez	gonmuse
goeth	losesi	gomorrah	gonmurrhan
goethite	gonsinyo	gomphosis	gonmphiso
goffer	fonfiro	gomuti	gonmute
goggle	gongiron	gon	gun
goggle-box	bosi-gongiron	gon	goon
gogglet	gongitn	gon	gon
go-go	go-go	gonad	gondi
go go	go go	gondola	gondejn
going	lognni	gondolier	gondejnra
going	gongnni	gondwana	gonjnwain
goiter	gontnra	gone	gonlo
goitre	gontnran	goner	gonlosi
go kart	gon korate	gonfalon	gonfanjn
golconda	gonleki	gonfalonier	gonfnjnsi
gold	gondon	gong	gongbo
golden	gondonsi	gongorism	gongnraimosi
golden age	agba gondonsi	gonidium	goonjoma
golem	gonlema	gonio	goonko
golf	gonfia	goniometer	goonkomuto
golgi	gonjngi	gonion	goonsi
golgotha	gonjngonsin	gonium	goonma
gollard	gonjjngba	gonk	gonki
gollardery	gonjjngbarai	gono	goons
goliath	gonjnrasi	gonococcus	goonsokikisi
golliwog	gonjjnwngbi	gonocyte	goonsosnyo
gollop	gonjjnpn	gonophore	goonsophiran
golly1	gonjjn	gonopoietic	goonsopoteko
golly2	gonjjn	gonopore	goonsoporai

259

WORD (x)	EQUIVALENT (y)	WORD (x)	EQUIVALENT (y)
gonorrhea	goonsorhain	gore3	gbare
gonorrhoea	goonsorhoin	goree	gbarese
gony	gonse	gorge	gbagun
goo	gon	gorgeous	gbagunsi
good	gonjo	gorgerin	gbagunran
goodby	gonjobeo	gorget	gbagunto
goodbye	gonjobeyin	gorgias	gbagunse
goodie	gonjosi	gorgon	gbagon
goodish	gonjose	gorgoneion	gbagonsesi
goodly	gonjolo	gorgonian	gbagonhn
goodness	gonjonisi	gorgonzola	gbagonsinle
goody	gonjon	gorilla	gbaraijnran
goody-goody	gonjon goonjon	gorky	gonrako
gooey	gonki	gormand	gbamadain
goof	gonfo	gormandize	gbamadainse
goofy	gonfose	gormless	gbamolabo
google	gogoron	gorno	gbarain
googly	gogolo	gorse	gbase
googol	gogojin	gorsedd	gbasejo
gook	gonko	gory	gbarai
goon	gosi	gosh	gonso
gooney	gosise	goshawk	gonsohakwo
goosander	gonsoojnra	goshen	gonsooan
goose	gonsoo	gosling	gonsognni
goosy	gonsoose	gospel	gonsipn
goop	gopon	gospeller	gonsipnjjn
goover	gonwnra	gospodin	gonsipnjoin
gopher	gonphira	gossamer	gonsoomurai
goral	gbajo	gossan	gonsooe
gordian	gbagbain	gossip	gonso
gordon	gbagbasi	got	gonto
gordus	gbagbaso	goth	gontosi
gore1	gbare	gotham	gontomosi
gore2	gbare	gothio	gontosio

WORD (x)	EQUIVALENT (y)	WORD (x)	EQUIVALENT (y)
gothic	gontosiko	gradation	gandieyoon
gotten	gontotn	grade	gandie
gotterdammerung	gontotnradammurign	grader	gandiesi
gouache	gonkhun	gradient	gandieto
gouda	gongba	gradin	gandieni
goudy	gongbain	gradual	gandiejo
gouge	gongbe	gradualism	gandiejomosi
goulash	gonlese	graduand	gandiedain
gounder	gonjnra	graduate	gandieyo
gourami	gonrami	graduation	gandieyoon
gourd	gongba	gradus	gandiesi
gourmand	gongbamujn	graeae	gannini
gourmandise	gongbamujnse	graecism	gansemosi
gourmet	gongbamuto	graeme	gannimo
gout	gonti	graffiti	ganffita
goutte	gontti	graft1	ganfia
gouty	gontise	graft2	ganfia
governante	goonwato	grail	ganla
govern	goonwa	grain	gansn
governance	goonwasi	grainer	gansnsi
governess	goonwabo	grainy	gansnse
government	goonwamutto	grainge	gansngn
governor	goonwaran	graith	gantesi
gown	goonwn	grallatorial	ganjjntoraijo
goy	gose	gram	ganmo
grab	ganbo	grama	ganma
grabble	ganborao	gramary	ganmarai
grace	ganson	gramicidin	ganmikekusi
graceless	gansonlabo	graminaceous	ganminisuwa
gracile	gansonjn	gramineous	ganminiwa
gracious	gansonsi	graminivorous	ganminiwnrunsi
grackle	gankiron	grammar	ganmmuro
grad	gandi	grammarian	ganmmurosi
gradate	gandieyo	grammatical	ganmutokojo

WORD (x)	EQUIVALENT (y)	WORD (x)	EQUIVALENT (y)
grammatology	ganmutologbon	grantee	gantnse
gramme	ganmmo	grant of probate	gantn ti pongbayo
grammolecule	ganmmojnkuo	granth	gantnsi
grammy	ganmmose	grantor	gantnran
gramophone	ganmuphohun	granturismo	gantnraimosi
Grampians	ganmpnhn	granular	ganrejnra
grampus	ganmpnsi	granularity	ganrejnrato
gran	ganhn	granulate	ganreleyo
granadilla	ganhunjojjn	granule	ganrele
granadillo	ganhunjojjain	granulite	ganreleto
granary	ganhunrai	granulocyte	ganrelesnyo
grand	ganjn	granuloma	ganreloma
grande	ganjin	granulose	ganrelose
grandee	ganjnse	grape	ganpan
grandeur	ganjnrai	graph	ganpha
grandiloquent	ganjnlokunto	grapheme	ganphnmo
grandiose	ganjainse	-grapher	ganphasi
grandma	ganjnmo	graphic	ganphako
grandpa	ganjnpan	graphic arts	etesi ganphako
grandparent	ganjnpanrato	graphics	ganphakosi
grand tour	ganjn toorai	graphite	ganphuyo
grange	gangini	graphitise	ganphuyose
grangerize	ganginiraise	grapho	ganphin
graniferous	ganrefirosi	graphology	ganphinlogbon
granite	ganretn	-graphy	ganphe
granitite	ganretnyo	grapnel	ganpanlo
granitoid	ganretnjo	grappa	ganpan
granivorous	ganrewnrunsi	grapple	ganporon
granny	ganreya	graptolite	ganpotaleyo
grano	ganrekn	grasp	gansupo
granola	ganreknjn	grasping	gansupognni
granolith	ganreknlesi	grass	gansu
granophyre	ganreknpherai	grassland	ledaingansu
grant	gantn	grassy	gansuse

WORD (x)	EQUIVALENT (y)	WORD (x)	EQUIVALENT (y)
grate1	gante	gray	gansio
grate2	gante	grayling	gansiognni
grater	gantesi	graze1	ganje
grateful	gantefunjn	graze2	ganje
graticule	gantikuo	grazier	ganjesi
gratification	gantifikoyoon	grazing	ganjegnni
gratify	gantife	grease	giransue
gratin	gantisi	greaser	giransuesi
grating	gantignni	greasy	giransuese
gratis	gantison	great	girantn
gratitude	gantitujin	greatly	girantnlo
gratuitous	gantitnsi	greave	giranwn
gratuity	gantitn	grebe	giranbe
gratulate	gantileyo	grecian	girankihn
graupel	ganpnlo	grecism	girankimosi
grav	ganwa	greco	giranki
gravamen	ganwamuye	gree	giran
gravel	ganwo	greece	giransi
grave2	ganwo	greed	giranjn
grave3	ganwo	greedy	giranjnse
gravel	ganwolo	greek	girankn
gravelly	ganwolosi	green	girain
graven	ganwini	greenery	girainrai
graver	ganwosi	greengage	giraingigun
graves	ganwose	greengrocer	giraingonknra
gravettian	ganwotnhn	greengrocery	giraingonknrai
graveyard	gandanganwo	greenthorn	girainhuran
gravid	ganwojn	greet1	giranki
gravimeter	ganwomuto	greet2	giranki
gravitate	ganwoteyo	greeter	girankisi
gravitation	ganwoteyoon	greeting	girankignni
gravity	ganwoto	gregarious	girangansi
gravure	ganworai	gregorian	girangbarain
gravy	ganwose	gregory	girangbarai

WORD (x)	EQUIVALENT (y)	WORD (x)	EQUIVALENT (y)
greige	girangn	grim	ganmo
greisen	giransin	grimace	ganmosia
gremial	giranmujo	grimaldi	ganmojn
gremlin	giranmojan	grimalkin	ganmojnkin
grenade	girainjin	grime	ganmu
grenadier	girainjinsi	grimy	ganmun
grenadine	girainjoin	grin	ganrin
grendel	giranjinlo	grind	ganrun
gresham	giransuemo	grindelia	ganrunjoin
gressorial	giransoonraijo	grinder	ganrunsi
grew	giranwe	grindery	ganrunrai
grey	giranju	gringo	ganrinlo
gribble	ganbe	grip	ganpo
grid	ganda	gripe	ganpon
griddle	gandaduoduo	gripe water	wetomi ganpon
gride	gandn	grippe	ganponse
gridiron	gandnrain	griqua	gankun
grief	ganfu	grisaille	ganseron
grievance	ganwusi	griseofulvin	gansefujnwan
grieve	ganwu	griseous	gansesi
grievous	ganwusi	grisette	gansetin
griff	ganfo	griskin	gansukin
griffe	ganfon	grisly	ganselo
griffin	ganfofn	grison	gansin
griffon	ganfosi	grist	gansi
grafter	ganfiasi	gristle	gansiron
grig	gangn	grit	ganti
grignard	gangngba	grith	gantisi
grigri	gangira	grits	gantisi
grill	ganjara	gritter	ganttisi
grill	ganjara	gritty	ganttise
grillage	ganjaragun	grivation	ganwayoon
grille	ganjaran	grivet	ganwnti
grilse	ganjase	grizzle	gansuron

264

WORD (x)	EQUIVALENT (y)	WORD (x)	EQUIVALENT (y)
grizzled	gansuronde	groundsel	gonjoinsun
grizzly	gansulo	groundwater	gonjoinwetnra
groan	gonhu	group	gonpo
groat	gontie	groupie	gonposi
groats	gontiesi	grouse1	gonse
grocer	gonknra	grouse2	gonse
grocery	gonknrai	grout	gontn
grockle	gonkiron	grouty	gontnsi
grog	gonlu	grove	gonwn
groggy	gonlulo	grovel	gonwalo
groin1	gonso	grovet	gonwnti
groin2	gonso	grow	gonwin
grolier	gonlerai	grower	gonwinsi
grommet	gonmmuto	growl	gonwinjn
gromwell	gonmwinjjo	grown	gonwini
groom	gonmoin	growth	gonwinse
groove	gonwini	groyne	gonyun
groovy	gonwinise	grub	girabe
grope	gonpn	grubber	girabesi
grosgrain	gonsogansn	grubby	girabn
gross	gonsoo	grudge	giragbaa
grosz	gonsise	grue	girase
grot	gonti	gruel	giralo
grote	gontie	grueling	giralognni
grotesque	gontiekun	gruelling	giralognni
grotesquery	gontiekunrai	gruesome	girasoomo
grotto	gontto	gruff	girafi
grotty	gonttose	grumbe	girambo
grouch	gonkun	grume	giramo
grouchy	gonkunse	grumose	giramose
ground1	gonjoin	grumous	giramosi
ground2	gonjoin	grump	girampn
grounding	gonjoingnni	grumphie	giramphise
groundless	gonjoinlabo	grumpy	girampnse

WORD (x)	EQUIVALENT (y)	WORD (x)	EQUIVALENT (y)
grund	girajn	guarani	gunrain
grundy	girajnse	guarantee	gunrantnse
grunge	giragba	guarantor	gunrantnran
grunion	girainsi	guaranty	gunrantn
grunt	girato	guard	gungba
grunter	giratosi	guardant	gungbate
gruntled	giratoronde	guarded	gungbade
grus	girasi	guardian	gungbasi
gruyere	girayoran	guardsman	gungbamaye
g/string	gn/suraign	guarneri	gunranrai
gryphon	giriphon	guatemala	gunyomujn
grysbok	giraibu	guava	gunwe
guacamole	gunkomojn	guaviare	gunworain
guacharo	gunkhorain	guayule	gunyunjo
guadalcanal	gunjalekunjo	gubernatorial	gunwarantoraijo
guadiana	gunjinaho	gubbin	gunbahn
gualacol	gunlekijo	guck	gunki
gualacum	gunlekuo	gude	gundaa
guam	gunmo	gudgeon1	gungbesi
guandalajara	gunjnlejara	gudgeon2	gungbesi
guandeloupe	gunjnlopo	gudgeon pin	gungbesi poha
guan	gunhun	guilder rose	gunlojnra
guanabara	gunhebora	guelph	gunlophe
guanaco	gunheki	guenon	gunhnsi
guanajuato	gunhejanto	guerdon	gunjain
guanase	gunhese	guernsey	gunransn
guanidine	gunhejoin	guerrilla	gunrraijjo
guanine	gunhehun	guess	gunso
guano	gunkn	guesstimate	gunsotemuyo
guanocine	gunknkihun	guest	gunsn
guantanamo	guntnhemo	guff	gunfo
guaiacol	gunsikojin	guffaw	gunfe
guaiacum	gunsikuo	guidance	gunjuwesi
guapore	gunporai	guide	gunde

WORD (x)	EQUIVALENT (y)	WORD (x)	EQUIVALENT (y)
guidebook	bookogunde	gullible	gunjnrebe
guideline	gundelehun	gulliver	gunjnrewin
guider	gundesi	gully	gunjnresi
guidon	gundesi	gulosity	gunjnseto
guild	gunjo	gulp	gunjnpo
guilder	gunjora	gulpereel	gunjnpnranlo
guile	gunjua	gum1	gunma
guillemot	gunjjuamuta	gum2	gunma
guilloche	gunjjukhn	gum3	gunma
guillotine	gunjjuatin	gumbo	gunmbo
guilt	gunjia	gumlie	gunmajnsi
guiltless	gunjialabo	gummy1	gunmmasi
guilty	gunjiase	gummy2	gunmmasi
guimpe	gunmpn	gumption	gunmpnyoon
guinea	gunmini	gun	gunta
guinness	gunminisi	gunge	gungn
guinevere	gunwinrai	gung-ho	gungan-hin
guipure	gunpurai	gunnar	gunran
guise	gunse	gunnel	guntahun
guit guit	gunte gunte	gunner	guntasi
guitar	guntero	gunnery	guntarai
guitry	gunterai	gunny	guntasi
gujarat	gunjara	gunsel	guntase
gujarati	gunjarato	gunter	guntatnra
gunla	gunjn	gunther	guntasira
gulag	gunjngbn	gunwale	guntawejn
gular	gunjnra	guppy	gunpnpo
gulch	gunjnkho	gupta	gunpnti
gules	gunronsi	gurgle	gunrogn
gulf	gunfia	gurkha	gunrokha
gull1	gunjnre	gurnard	gunrangba
gull2	gunjnre	gurney	gunrain
gullet	gunjnrete	guru	gunrai
gulley	gunjnrese	gush	gunsun

WORD (x)	EQUIVALENT (y)	WORD (x)	EQUIVALENT (y)
gusher	gunsunrai	gyges	lognsi
gusset	gunseto	gym	loma
gust	gunsi	gymbals	lombejisi
gustation	gunsitoyoon	gym bunny	loma bunhn
gustavus	gunsitowan	gymkhana	lomkhahun
gusto	gunsito	gymnasiarch	lomhunsikhnra
gusty	gunsitn	gymnasium	lomhunsikma
gut	gunte	gymnast	lomhunsi
gutenberg	guntesibegan	gymnastic	lombunsiko
gutless	guntelabo	gymnastics	lomhunsikosi
gutrune	gunterain	gymno	lomhoho
gutsy	guntese	gymnosophist	lomhohosoophnsi
gutta	guntte	gymnosperm	lomhohosepnron
guttapercha	gunttepnrakho	gymp	lompn
guttate	guntteyo	gymslip	lomsiunpn
gutte	gunttesi	gyn	loyan
gutted	gunttude	gynae	loyann
gutter	gunttesi	gynaeceum	loyankinnsuma
guttering	gunttesignni	gynaecol	loyankinjin
gutter press	pesiso gunttesii	gynaecology	loyankinlogbon
guttural	gunttesijo	gynaecologist	loyankinlogbonsi
gutturalize	gunttesijose	gynander	loyanjnra
gutty	gunttese	gynandroid	loyangbainjo
guv	gunwa	gynandromorphic	loyangbainmophanko
guy1	gunye	gynandrous	loyangbainsi
guy2	gunye	gynarchy	loyankhnran
guyenne	gunyehun	gyneceum	loyunknma
guyot	gunyeto	gyneco	loyunkin
guzzle	gunsunron	gynecology	loyunkinlogbon
gwalior	gweloran	gynecocracy	loyunkinkansn
gwinnett	gwinhuntte	gynecoid	loyunkinjo
gwyn	gwain	gynecology	loyunkinlogbon
gyangtse	loganse	gynecomorphous	loyunkinmophansi
gybe	lobe	gyniatrics	loyanteraikosi

WORD (x)	EQUIVALENT (y)	WORD (x)	EQUIVALENT (y)
gyno	loyon	habanero	hagbehunro
gynoecium	loyonkinma	habbaniya	hagbeboye
gynogenesis	loyongnhunso	habeas corpus	hagbesi kipansi
gynopathy	loyonpansio	habendum	hagbejnma
gynophore	loyonphiran	haber	hagbe
gynous	loyoonsi	haberdasher	hagbedasunra
gyp	logba	haberdashery	hagbedasunrai
gypsophila	lopnsoophijn	habitable	hagbewaron
gypsum	logbaasumo	habitat	hagbewayo
gypsy	logbaasi	habitation	hagbewayoon
gyral	loraijo	habit-forming	hagbewa fonmognni
gyrate	loraiyo	habitual	hagbewajo
gyration	loraiyoon	habituate	hagbewayo
gyratory	loraitoran	habitué	hagbewase
gyre	lorai	habitus	hagbewasi
gyrfalcon	lorafanjnkin	habu	habua
gyro	loroin	hacek	hasiro
gyrocompass	loroinkimpanso	hachures	hakhunrai
gyrodynamics	loraindainsemukosi	hacienda	hakinjina
gyron	loroinsi	hack1	hakin
gyronny	loroinse	hack2	hakin
gyroscope	loroinsokipon	hackberry	hakinberrai
gyrostat	loroinsetnti	hackbut	hakinbute
gyrus	loraisi	hacker	hakinra
gyve	lowin	hackery	hakinrai
ha1	ha	hackle	hakinle
ha2	ha	hackly	hakinlo
haabal	haabejo	hackney	hakinsi
haakon	haakin	hackneyed	hekinside
haar	harai	hacksaw	hakinsawe
haarlem	harailema	had	hajn
habakkuk	hagbekkuo	haddin	hajndan
habana	hagbehun	haddington	hajndaintin
habanera	hagbehunrai	haddle	hajnduo

WORD (x)	EQUIVALENT (y)	WORD (x)	EQUIVALENT (y)
haddock	hajndekin	haematology	haumitologbon
hade	hajin	haematolysis	haumitojinso
hades	hajinsi	haematoma	haumitoma
hadith	hajosi	haematopolesis	haumitopinjnso
hadj	hajnsin	haematosis	haumitoso
hadji	hajnse	haematothermal	haumitosinronjo
hadjia	hajnbo	haematoxylin	haumitosinsejan
hadley	hajnroin	haematoxylon	haumitosinsejnsi
hadnt	hajnti	haematozoon	haumitosinhn
hadramaut	hajnramute	haematuria	haumitoran
hadrian	hajnrain	haemic	haumiko
hadron	hajnroin	haemin	haumisi
hadrosaur	hajnronsanra	haemo	hauje
hae	hau	haemocoel	haujekilo
haecceity	hauknto	haemocyanin	haujesnknsi
haechel	haukinlo	haemocyte	haujesnsu
haeju	haujo	haemocytometer	haujesnsumuto
haem	haumi	haemodialysis	haujejinajinso
haemacytometer	haumisntomuto	haemoglobin	haujegonbnsi
haemagglutinate	haumigbiletanyo	haemophilia	haujepheran
haemagogue	haumigonko	haemophiliac	haujepheranko
haemal	haumijo	haemoptysis	haujepntiso
haematein	haumiyoto	haemorrhage	haujerhoingun
haematemesis	haumiyomuso	haemorrhoids	haujerhoinjosi
haematic	haumiko	haemostasis	haujesetnso
haematin	haumitie	haemostatic	haujesetntiko
haematinic	haumutieko	haen	hauni
haematite	haumitieyo	haeremal	hauranmojn
haemato	haumito	haffet	hafito
haematocele	haumitoknjn	hafiz	hafisi
haematocryal	haumitokoraijo	hafnium	hafinima
haematogenesis	haumitognhunso	haft	hafia
haematogenous	haumitoginsi	haftarah	hafiaran
haematoid	haumitojo	hag	hagio

WORD (x)	EQUIVALENT (y)	WORD (x)	EQUIVALENT (y)
hagar	hagioran	hail1	hanjn
hagberry	hagioberrai	hail2	hanjn
hagen	hagiosi	haile	hansin
haggadah	hagiojnhun	hain	hansn
haggadic	hagiojnko	hainaut	hanheyo
haggadist	hagiojnsi	haiphong	hanphigan
haggai	hagiosi	hair	harun
haggard	hagiogbaa	hairline	harunlehun
haggis	hagiose	hairy	harunsi
haggle	hagioron	haiti	hanto
hagiarchy	hagikokhnran	haj	hajn
hagio-	hagio	haje	haje
hagiocracy	hagiokansn	hake	hakn
hagiographa	hagioganpha	hakenkreuz	hakinknrasun
hagiographer	hagioganphasi	hakim	hakimo
hagiography	hagioganphe	hakea	hakue
hagiolatry	hagioletorai	hakodate	hakojnte
hagiology	hagiologbon	halacha	hajnkho
hagoscope	hagiosokipon	halachist	hajnkhosi
haglet	hagiotn	halal	hajnjo
hagridden	hagiragbain	halation	hajnyoon
hague	hagbiso	halberd	hajnbeduo
hah	ha	halberdier	hajnbeduosi
haha	haha	halcanrnassus	hajnkoransoosi
hahn	hahun	halcyon	hajnsnsi
hahne	hahun	haldane	hajndain
haida	hanjn	hale	hajn
haidar	hanjnra	haleakala	hajnkiji
haiduk	hanjnko	halevi	hajnwi
haifa	hanfe	halevy	hajnwisi
haig	hanga	half	haji
haik	hanka	halfwit	hajiwinso
haiku	hanko	halibut	hajnbayo
haikwan	hankwin	halic	hajnko

WORD (x)	EQUIVALENT (y)	WORD (x)	EQUIVALENT (y)
halide	hajoji	halogenate	hajoginyo
halidom	hajnmo	haloid	hajojo
halifax	hajnfansi	halomancy	hajomoyesn
haliplankton	hajnpanknti	halon	hajosi
halitosis	hajnmiso	haloperidol	hajopnrajojin
halitus	hajnmisi	halophilous	hajopheronsi
hall	hajnra	halophyte	hajopheyo
hall	hajnra	halse	hajnse
hallan	hajnrain	halsey	hajnsise
halleck	hajnranki	halothane	hajosihun
hallel	hajnranlo	halsingbarg	hajnsibegan
hallelujah	hajnranlohun	halt1	hajia
halley	hajnroin	halt2	hajia
halliard	hajnrangba	halter	hajiasi
hallmark	hajnramurako	haltere	hajiasn
hallion	hajnransi	halting	hajiagnni
hallo	hajnro	halutz	hajnse
halloo	hajnroo	halva	hajiwa
hallow	hajnramo	halve	hajiwin
hallowed	hajnramode	halves	hajiwinsi
hallowe'en	hajnramosin	haly	hamo
hallowmass	hajnramomusn	halyard	hamogba
hallucinate	hajnrakinyo	ham	hamo
hallucination	hajnrakinyoon	hamadryad	hamojnrai
hallucinogen	hajnrakingin	hamadryas	hamojnraise
hallucinosis	hajnrakinso	hamburger	hambugansi
hallux	hajnransi	hamal	hamojn
hallux valgus	hajnransi wajngbun	hamamelidaceus	hamomujnjosuwa
halma	hajnma	hamamelis	hamomujnsi
halo	hajo	hamate	hamoyo
halo	hajo	hambletonian	hambejntoni
halobios	hajobako	hame	hamni
halobiont	hajobakote	hamein	hamnisi
halogen	hajogin	hamehung	hamnihungn

WORD (x)	EQUIVALENT (y)	WORD (x)	EQUIVALENT (y)
hamersley	hamniroin	handmaid	handemoaajo
Hamilton	hamijntin	handout	handenita
hamite	hamuyo	handrail	handerailo
hamitic	hamuyoka	hands	handesi
hamito	hamuto	handsel	handesojn
hamlet	hamlet	handset	handeseton
hammer	hammrai	handsome	handesoomo
hammock	hammkin	handson	handesesi
hammurabi	hammranbo	handy	handese
hammy	hammse	handyman	handesemoye
hamper1	hampnra	hang	hagan
hamper2	hampnra	hangar	haganran
hampstead	hampnsetogba	hanger	hagansi
hampton	hampntisi	hanger-on	hagansile
hamshakle	hamsueknron	hanging	hagangini
hamster	hamseto	hank	hakuo
hamstring	hamsetnrin	hanker	hakuosi
hamsun	hamsun	hankie	hakuosi
hamulate	hamujnyo	hanky	hakuose
hamulus	hamujnsi	hanky-panky	hakuo/pankuo
hamza	hamso	hanna	hanhun
han	han	hannah	hanhunsi
hanaper	hanpnra	Hannibal	hanhunbejn
hance	hansi	hanno	hankn
hand	hande	hannotaux	hankntisi
handball	handerobo	hanover	hanknwinra
handbell	handebejnro	hanoverian	hanknwinrain
handcuff	kunfihande	hansard	hansogbaa
handgun	handegunta	hanse	hansia
handicap	kopnhande	hansom	hansomo
handle	handuo	hants	hantesi
handlebar	handuoboosn	hanukkah	hanniran
handler	handuosi	hannuman	hannimoye
handmade	handemojain	hap	hapn

WORD (x)	EQUIVALENT (y)	WORD (x)	EQUIVALENT (y)
hapax	hapnsi	hare	harain
haphazard	hapnhasegba	harebell	harinbejnro
hapless	hapnlabo	harelip	harainlepo
haplite	hapnleyo	harem	haraima
haploid	haponjo	haricot	haraikiti
haplography	haponganphe	hark	haran
haplosis	haponso	hark back	haran bokn
haply	hapnlo	harken	haransi
happen	hapnsi	harl	harajn
happer	hapnra	harlem	haranjnma
happily	hapnpolo	harlequin	haranjnkun
happyness	hapnponisi	harlequinade	haranjnkunjo
happy	hapnpo	harlot	haranjnte
haptene	hapntini	harlotry	haranjnterai
hapteron	hapntirain	harm	hara
haptic	hapntiko	harmless	haralabo
haptophobia	hapntiphobua	harmattan	hanmooye
haptophore	hapntiphiran	harmature	hanmootnrai
haptotrap	hapntitaraipo	harmonic	hanmeniko
harakiri	hara-kiri	harmonica	hanmenike
haram	harami	harmonious	hanmenisi
harangue	harangan	harmonium	hanmenima
harass	haranse	harmonize	hanmenise
harbin	hagbe	harmony	hanmeni
harbinger	hagbegnsi	harness	hannisi
harbor	hagbebo	harney	hannise
harbour	hagbebo	harp	hanpn
hard	hagbaa	harper	hanpnrai
hardback	hagbaaboki	harpist	hanpnsi
hardboard	hagbaabugba	harpoon	hanpanun
harden	hagbaasi	harpsichord	hanpnsokhijora
hardly	hagbaalo	harpy	hanpnse
hardness	hagbaanisi	harridan	harraijn
hardy	hagbaase	harrier	harraisi

WORD (x)	EQUIVALENT (y)	WORD (x)	EQUIVALENT (y)
harriet	harraite	hatbox	hatebosi
harris	harraiso	hatch1	hatesi
harrison	hanraisin	hatch2	hatesi
harrogate	harraigiyo	hatch3	hatesi
harrow	harraiwa	hatchback	hatesiboki
harry	harrai	hatchet	hatesia
harsh	harasia	hate	hatn
hart	harote	hatpin	hatepoha
hartal	harotejo	hatred	hatnra
hartebeest	harotnbesesi	hatter	hatnran
hartle	harotnron	haugh	haughe
harum-scarum	haro-sekosima	haughty	haugbetn
haruspex	harowapnsi	haul	haullo
harvard	hawanjn	haulage	haullogun
harvest	hawinse	haulier	haullorai
harvester	hawinsesi	haulm	haulloma
harvey	hawini	haunch	haunkhn
harz	hasu	haunt	haunto
has	hasi	haunting	hauntognni
hasdrubal	hasegbirobe	haunse	haunsi
hash1	hasia	haunsen	haunsin
hash2	hasia	haustellum	haunsetojjnma
hashish	hasiase	haustorium	haunsetoma
hask	hasoro	haute couture	haunto kiletoran
haslet	hasotn	haute cuisine	haunto kunsehun
hasp	hasopo	hauteur	hauntorai
hassle	hasoron	have	hawa
hassock	hasooki	haven	hawasi
hastate	hasetayo	haver	hawase
haste	hasa	haver sack	saka hawase
hasten	hasasi	haverslancanal	hawasesankojnle
hasty	hasase	havoc	hawnko
hat	hate	haw1	hawo
hatband	hatebohnjo	haw2	hawo

WORD (x)	EQUIVALENT (y)	WORD (x)	EQUIVALENT (y)
hawai	hawoin	heart	hetantn
hawk1	hakwo	hearth	hetansi
hawk2	hakwo	hearty	hetanse
hawk3	hakwo	heartily	hetanlo
hawker	hakwosi	heartland	hetanledain
hawk-eyed	hakwo-eyiride	heartless	hetanlabo
hawser	hawosnra	heat	henasi
hawthorn	hawosinran	heated	henaside
hay	hase	heater	henasise
haycock	hasekiko	heath	hesin
hazard	hasugbaa	heathen	hesinsi
hazardous	hasugbaasi	heathenish	hesinsise
haze	hasu	heather	hesinse
hazel	hasujo	heating	henatngnni
hazy	hasuse	heave	hewain
he	he	heaven	hewaini
head	hegbi	heavenly	hewainilo
headband	hegbibohajo	heavy	hewainse
hedbanger	hegbibogansi	hebdomadal	hebedemojnjo
headboard	hegbiboogba	hebe	hebe
headrest	hegbiresin	hebephrenia	hebephirain
headline	hegbilehun	hebetate	hebetiyo
headset	hegbisetn	hebetic	hebetiko
heady	hegbise	hebetude	hebetujin
heal	hejo	hebraic	hegbanko
health	hejosi	hebraism	hegbanmosi
healthy	hejosise	hebraise	hegbansun
heap	hepan	hebraist	hegbansi
hear	heran	hebrew	hegbeswa
hearing	herangnni	hebrides	hegbanjinsi
hearing-aid	aajo herangnni	hebron	hegbonjn
hearken	herankin	hecate	heknyo
hearsay	heransanwi	heck	hekn
hearse	heranso	heckelphone	heknlophohun

WORD (x)	EQUIVALENT (y)	WORD (x)	EQUIVALENT (y)
heckle	hekuo	heidelbergman	heijinjobeganmoye
hectare	hekntirai	heifer	heifer
hectic	hekntiko	heigh-ho	heighi-lu
hector-	heknto	height	heigha
hectocotylus	hekntokitilosi	heighten	heighasi
hectogram	hekntoganmo	height to paper	heigha si panpnra
hectograph	hekntoganpha	heimdall	heimudajjn
hector	hekntiran	heineken	heihunkin
heddle	hejnduo	heinous	heiknsi
heder	hejnra	heir	heiran
hedge	hejnge	heiress	heiranbo
hedgerow	hejngeraiwe	heirloom	heiranloomo
hedonics	hedunkosi	heisenberg	heisibegan
hedonism	hedunmosi	heisman	hesimoye
hedonist	hedunsi	heist	heisi
hedral	hejnrajo	heitle	heitoron
hedron	hejnra	hekistothermic	hekisetosinronko
heebie-jeebies	hegbain-jigbainsi	hel	hejo
heed	hesejo	helcosis	hejokiso
heel1	hesejn	held	hejora
heel2	hesejn	heldentenor	hejoraintinran
heel3	hesejn	helen	hejosi
heelball	robohesejn	helena	hejohun
heeler	hesejnra	helgoland	hejogonledain
heel in	hesejn nu	heliacal	hejokajo
heft	hefia	helianthus	hejosesi
hefty	hefiase	heliast	hejose
hegel	hegunlo	helical	hejokasi
hegeliandialectic	hegunlojinakntiko	helices	hejokase
hegemony	hegunmeni	helichrysum	hejokhiraisumo
hegira	hegirai	helico	hejoka
hegumen	hegunmuye	helicograph	hejokaganpha
hegumene	hegunmini	helicoid	hejokajo
hegumeny	hegunminise	helicon	hejokin

WORD (x)	EQUIVALENT (y)	WORD (x)	EQUIVALENT (y)
helicopter	hejokipnti	hello	hejora
helicotrema	hejokitimosi	helluva	hejorowa
heligo	hejolo	helm	hejoma
helio-	hejokn	helmet	hejomuto
heliocentric	hejoknkntiraiko	helmholtz	hejomahinjia
heliograph	hejoknganpha	helminth	hejominise
heliogravure	hejoknganworai	helminthiasis	hejominisiaso
heliolatry	hejoknletorai	helminthic	hejominisiko
heliolithic	hejoknlesiko	helminthology	hejominisilogbon
heliopolis	hejoknpinjnsi	helmsman	hejomamuye
helios	hejoknse	helot	hejote
heliostat	hejoknsetnti	helotism	hejotemosi
heliotaxis	hejokntesanso	helotry	hejoterai
heliotrope	hejokntnrapon	help	hejopn
heliozoa	hejoknsia	helping	hejopngnni
heliport	hejopinta	helpless	hejopolabo
helium	hejoma	helpline	hejopolehun
helix	hejokoi	helpmate	hejopomote
hell	hejjo	helter-skelter	hejota-seknjota
helladic	hejjojinko	helve	hejowin
hellas	hejjose	helvetia	hejowintan
hellbent	hejjobehnte	hem1	hemn
helle	hejjose	hem2	hemn
hellebore	hejjoborai	hemal	hemnjo
helleborine	hejjoborain	heman	hemnhn
hellen	hejjosi	hemapolesis	hemnpinjnso
hellene	hejjohun	hematal	hemntejo
hellenism	hejjohunmosi	hematein	hemntehn
hellenistic	hejjohunsiko	hematinic	hemntieko
hellenise	hejjohunse	hematite	hemnteyo
heller	hejjora	hemato	hemnto
hellery	hejjorai	hematocele	hemntoknjn
hellion	hejjorain	hematocryal	hemntokoraijo
hellish	hejjosi	hematoid	hemntojo

WORD (x)	EQUIVALENT (y)	WORD (x)	EQUIVALENT (y)
hematology	hemntologbon	hemocyanin	heminsnknhn
hematoma	hemntoma	hemoglobin	hemingonbin
hematose	hemntose	hemohyperoxia	heminhopnrasia
hematosis	hemntoso	hemohypoxia	heminhopnsia
hematoxylin	hemntosinsejan	hemoid	heminjo
hemelytron	hemulotnran	hemoleukocyte	heminjnwakosnyo
hemerolopia	hemurailopan	hemolysin	heminjinsie
hemerophyte	hemuraipheyo	hemolysis	heminjinso
hemi-	hemi	hemophilia	heminpheran
hemialgia	hemijigan	hemophiliac	heminpheranki
hemianopsia	hemiknpnsia	hemophilic	heminpheranko
hemicellulose	hemiknjjnlose	homophobia	heminphobua
hemichordate	hemikhinrajoyo	hemoptysis	heminpntiseso
hemicrany	hemiknrase	hemorrhage	heminrhoingun
hemicycle	hemisnkuo	hemorrhoids	heminrhoinjosi
hemidemisemiquave	hemijinmusemikunwin	hemospasia	heminsepansia
hemidome	hemidemo	hemostasia	heminsetnsia
hemielytron	heminlotnran	hemostat	heminsetnti
hemignathous	hemigntosi	hemostatic	heminsetnko
hemignathous	hemihejnrajo	hemothorax	heminsinrase
hemimetabolic	hemimitoboojinko	hemp	hempn
hemimorphite	hemimophanyo	hempen	hempnsi
hemin	hemisi	hempy	hempo
hemiola	hemitole	hemstitch	hemsetinhun
hemiparasite	hemipanrasosi	hen	heya
hemipterous	hemipntiraisi	henbane	heyabohun
hemisphere	hemisephirai	hence	heyasi
hemisystole	hemisosetoron	henceforth	heyasifonsi
hemitepene	hemitopnhun	henchman	heyaknmoye
hemitrope	hemitnrapn	hencoop	heyakipon
hemline	hemlehun	hendeca	heyajinko
hemlock	hemlokn	hendecagon	heyajinkogun
hemmer	hemmorai	hendecahedron	heyajinkohejnrasi
hemo	hemin	hendecasyllable	heyajinkosollebe

WORD (x)	EQUIVALENT (y)	WORD (x)	EQUIVALENT (y)
hendiadys	heyajindinsi	heptarchy	hepntokhnran
henequen	heyakunsi	heptastich	hepntosetinhun
henge	heyagn	heptateuch	hepntotnkhun
henley	heyaroin	heptode	hepntojin
henna	heyahun	heptose	hepntise
hennery	heyarain	her	hera
henotheism	heyasinmosi	heraclea	herankuoni
hen-party	heya panteni	heracles	herankuosi
hen peck	heya pnkiti	herald	heranjnra
henrietta	heyaraito	heraldic	heranjnrako
henry	heyarai	heraldry	heranjnrai
hensard	heyasogba	herb	herabe
hent	hetn	herbaceous	herabesuwa
hep	hepn	herbage	herabegun
hepar	hepan	herbal	herabejo
heparin	hepanrie	herbalist	herabejosi
hepatic	hepanko	herbarium	heraberaima
hepatica	hepanka	herbary	heraberai
hepatitis	hepanso	herbennet	herabehnto
hepatization	hepanseyoon	herbert	herabeta
hepato	hepanto	herbescent	herabeknti
hepatogenic	hepantoginko	herbicide	herabekeku
hephaestus	hephisesi	herbivore	herabewnrun
hepta-	hepnto	herby	herabese
heptachior	hepntokhiran	herculean	herainkuo
heptachord	hepntokhinrajo	herecules	heraikuosi
heptad	hepntojo	hercynite	heraisnknyo
heptaglot	hepntoganto	herd	herejo
heptagon	hepntogun	herdsman	herejomoye
heptahedron	hepntohejnrain	herder	herejosi
heptamerous	hepntomuraisi	herdic	herejoka
heptameter	hepntomuto	here	herai
heptane	hepntohun	hereabouts	heraibounta
heptanglar	hepntonigunsi	hereditable	heraijntebe

WORD (x)	EQUIVALENT (y)	WORD (x)	EQUIVALENT (y)
hereditary	heraijnterain	herodotus	heraknjosi
heredity	heraijnto	heroic	heraknko
herein	heraini	heroin	heraknsn
heres	heraisi	heroine	heraknbo
heresiarch	heraisikhnran	heroism	heraknmosi
heresy	heransi	heron	herin
heretic	heransiko	heronry	herinrai
hereto	heraito	herophilus	heraknpheronsi
heriot	heraite	herpes	heraipnsi
heritable	heraitebe	herpes labialis	heraipnsi lebejoso
heritage	heraitegun	herpes zoster	heraipnsi sinseto
heritor	heraitesi	herpetology	heraipntilogbon
herl	herailo	herr	herrai
herm	heron	herring	herraign
hermaic	heronko	herring bone	herraign boin
herman	heronsi	herriot	herraite
hermaphrodite	heronphonjnyo	herry	herrai
hermaphrodites	heronphanjnyosi	hers	herasi
hermeneutic	heronhunko	hertz	heratesi
hermes	heronse	hertzian	heratesin
hermetic	herontnko	herzegovina	herasegonwini
hermione	heroin	heshwan	hesuwa
hermit	herontn	hesiod	hesejo
hermitage	herontngun	hesione	heseknni
hermod	heronjo	hesitancy	hesetisn
hermon	heronhn	hesitant	hesetite
herne	herann	hesitate	hesetiyo
hernia	herain	hesitation	hesetiyoon
hernio	herankn	hesp	hesepn
herniorrhaphy	heranknrhanphe	hesperia	hesepnran
herniotomy	herankntemo	hesperian	hesepnrain
hero	herakn	hesperides	hesepnraijosi
herod	heraknjo	hesperidia	hesepnraijina
herodias	heraknjose	hesperidium	hesepnraijoma

WORD (x)	EQUIVALENT (y)	WORD (x)	EQUIVALENT (y)
hesperornis	hesepnrainsi	heterolysis	hetnrojinso
hesperus	hesepnrasi	heteromerous	hetnromuraisi
hess	heso	heteromorphic	hetnromophanko
hesse	hesoo	heteronomous	hetnronimosi
hessian	hesoohn	heteronym	hetnromosi
hessite	hesooyo	heteroousian	hetnrotowahn
hessonite	hesoonyo	heterophony	hetnrophohun
hest	hesi	heterophyllous	hetnrophewesi
hester	heseto	heterophyte	hetnropheyo
hetetia	hesetan	heteroplasia	hetnropansia
hesychast	hesnkhosi	heteroplasty	hetnropansuito
het	hete	heteroscedasticity	hetnrosekndasukito
hetaera	heterai	heterosexual	hetnrosesiajo
hetaerism	heteraimosi	heterosexuality	hetnrosesialeto
hetero-	hetnro	heterosis	hetnroso
heterocercal	hetnroknrakojo	heterosporous	hetnroseporaisi
heteroclite	hetnrokiunyo	heterostyly	hetnrosetnlo
heterodont	hetnrodeyo	heterotaxis	hetnrotesanso
heterodox	hetnrojosin	heterotaxy	hetnrotesansi
herterodyne	hetnrodain	heterotopia	hetnrotopan
heteroecism	hetnrokimosi	heterotrichous	hetnrotaraikhisi
heteroecious	hetnrokkisi	heterotrophic	hetnrotnrapheko
heterogamete	hetnrogimuta	heterotrophy	hetnrotnraphe
heterogamous	hetnrogimosi	heterotypic	hetnrotnponko
heterogamy	hetnrogimo	heterousia	hetnrotosia
heterogeneous	hetnrognhunsi	heteroussian	hetnrosoohn
heterogenesis	hetnrognhunso	heterozygosis	hetnrosaijoso
heterogenous	hetnrognsi	heterozygote	hetnrosaijotn
heterogony	hetnrogonse	heterozygous	hetnrosaijosi
heterognynous	hetnroloyoonsi	heth	hese
heterokinesis	hetnrokihunso	heuristic	hewaraiseko
heterolecithal	hetnrojnkisujo	hew	hewa
heterologous	hetnrologbonsi	hex	heso
heterology	hetnrologbon	hexa-	heso

WORD (x)	EQUIVALENT (y)	WORD (x)	EQUIVALENT (y)
hexad	hesojin	hibernia	hiberansi
hexadecane	hesojinknhun	hibernian	hiberain
hexadecimal	hesojinknmulu	hibernianism	hiberainmosi
hexaemeron	hesomurain	hibernicize	hiberankise
hexagon	hesonigun	hibiscus	hibesikun
hexagram	hesoganmo	hibokhibok	hibokhikun
hexahedron	hesohejnran	hiccup	hikokun
hexamerous	hesomuraisi	hicetubique	hikitikunbe
hexameter	hesomuto	hicjacet	hikojnknti
hexane	hesohun	hick	hikoi
hexangular	hesonigunran	hackney	hikoise
hexanoic	hesoknko	hickok	hikoiki
hexapia	hesopan	hickory	hikoirai
hexapod	hesopindie	hicpochee	hikopnkhun
hexapody	hesopindiese	hicsepultus	hikosipnjia
hexastich	hesosetinhun	hid	hijn
hexastyle	hesosetnron	hidalgo	hijualegon
hexateuch	hesotekhn	hiddekel	hijuaknlo
hexenbesen	hesoenbesu	hidden	hijuase
hexo	heson	hidden agenda	aginjn hijuase
hexone	hesonhun	hiddenite	hijuaseyo
hexosan	hesonsin	hide1	hijua
hexose	hesonse	hide2	hijua
hexyl	hesolo	hideous	hijuasi
hey	hesun	hiding1	hijuagnni
heyday	hesundase	hiding2	hijuagnni
hezekiah	hesekia	hidrosis	higbnso
hiatus	hitesi	hidrotic	higbnko
hiawatha	hitewansi	hie	hise
hibachi	hibekona	hielaman	hisejnmoye
hibernacle	hiberankuo	hiemal	hisemojn
hibernaculum	hiberankuoma	hierach	hisekhnra
hibernal	hiberanjo	hierarchy	hisekhnran
hibernate	hiberanyo	hieratic	hiseraiko

WORD (x)	EQUIVALENT (y)	WORD (x)	EQUIVALENT (y)
hieratica	hiseraika	hilltop	hijjotopn
hiero	hiseran	hilly	hijjose
hierocracy	hiserankansn	hilt	hijia
hierodule	hiserandejn	hilum	hilema
hieroglyph	hiserangilopha	hilus	hijnse
hieroglyphic	hiserangilophiko	hilux	hijnsi
hierogram	hiseranganmo	him	himo/re/si
hierology	hiseranlogbon	himachal	himokhojo
hieromancy	hiseranmoyesn	himalayas	himojnyun
hieronymus	hiserainmosi	himation	himoyoon
hierophant	hiseranphetn	himeji	himujn
hierophobia	hiseranphobua	himmler	himmojnra
hierosolyma	hiseransnlemo	hin	hin
hierotherapy	hiseransinranpo	hind1	hijn
hierro	hiserran	hind2	hijn
hi-fi	hi-fi	hinder1	hijnsi
higgle	higioron	hinder2	hijnsi
higgled piggledy	higioron pogioron	hindi	hijnso
high	higha	hindrance	hijnrasi
highball	higharobo	hindsight	hijnsogbe
highbrow	highabonwo	hindu	hinduo
higher	highasi	hinduism	hinduomosi
highfalutin	highafanjntin	hindustani	hinduosetin
highlander	highaledainsi	hinge	hingn
highly	highalo	hinny	hinse
hijab	hijuba	hint	hitn
hijack	hijakuo	hinterland	hitnraledain
hijra	hijnra	hip1	hipn
hike	hikn	hip2	hipn
hilarious	hijoraisi	hip3	hipn
hilarity	hijoraito	hip4	hipn
hill	hijjo	hip hop	hipn-hinpn
hillary	hijjorai	hipparch	hipnpankhn
hillock	hijjokin	hipparchus	hipnpanchnsi

WORD (x)	EQUIVALENT (y)	WORD (x)	EQUIVALENT (y)
hippeastrum	hipnpnsetnra	his	hise
hipped	hipnpnde	hiskia	hisekia
hippet	hipnpnti	hisn	hisn
hippie	hipnposi	hispanic	hisepanko
hippish	hipnpose	hispaniola	hisepanjain
hippo	hipnpo	hispid	hisepnjo
hippocampus	hipnpokompnsi	hiss	hisio
hippocrates	hipnpoknatosi	hissel	hisoojo
Hippocratic oath	hipnpokantoka otesi	hist	hisetn
hippocrene	hipnpoknrain	histaminase	hisetnminise
hippodrome	hipnpoghnmo	histamine	hisetnmini
hippogriff	hipnpoganfo	histidine	hisetnjoin
hippolyta	hipnpojnto	histiocyte	hisetnsnyo
hippolytus	hipnposetosi	histiod	hisetnjo
hippomenes	hipnpomuhunsi	histo	hiseto
hippophagist	hipnpophijesi	histogen	hisetogin
hippophagy	hipnpophije	histogenesis	hisetognhunso
hippopotamus	hipnpopitimosi	histogram	hisetoganmo
hippous	hipnposi	histoid	hisetojo
hippy1	hipnpose	histology	hisetologbon
hippy2	hpnpose	histolysis	hisetojinso
hipster1	hipnseto	histone	hisetole
hipster2	hipnseto	histopathology	hisetopansiologbon
hiram	hiraimo	histoplasmosis	hisetopansonso
hiran	hirau	historian	hisetorain
hire	hire	historic	hisetoraiko
hirereling	hirelognni	historical	hisetoraikojo
hiro	hiknra	historicism	hisetoraikomosi
hirohito	hiknrato	historicity	hisetoraikito
hiroshima	hiknramosi	historiography	hisetoraiganphe
hirsel	hirasujo	history	hisetorai
hirsute	hirasuto	histrionic	hisetoraihnko
hirudineea	hirajoinsi	hit	hita
hirundine	hiranjoin	hitch	hitase

WORD (x)	EQUIVALENT (y)	WORD (x)	EQUIVALENT (y)
hither	hitasi	hock3	hinko
hitherto	hitasito	hockey	hinkoin
hit list	hita lesi	hocus-pocus	hinkuosi pinkuosi
hit man	hita moye	hod	hinjin
hitler	hitajnra	hodden	hinjingba
hittite	hittoyo	hodeida	hinjingba
hittorf	hittofe	hoder	hinjinra
hiv	hiwa	hodgepodge	hingbe pinjinge
hive	hiwin	hodgkin's disease	hingbekin
hives	hiwinsi	hodiernal	hindiranjo
hwassee	hiwasoon	hodograph	hindeganpha
hiya	hiyan	hodometer	hindemuto
hoar	hiran	hodocsope	hindesokipon
hoard	hiranjn	hoe	hinse
hoarding	hiranjngnni	hofer	hinfiro
hoarse	hiranse	hog	hingbe
hoarsen	hiransesi	hogan	hingbesi
hoary	hiranse	hogarth	hingirasi
hoast	hisita	hogg	hingbe
hoatch	hitei	hoggish	hingbese
hoatzin	hitesun	hogmanay	hingbemoyun
hoax	hisai	hogshead	hingbehegbi
hob	hingbi	hogue	hingbeso
Hobart	hingbeta	hogwash	hingbewesi
hobble	hingberon	hohum	hinhu
hobby	hingbese	hoick	hinleki
hobby-horse	hingbese hiso	hoi polloi	hinle pollo
hobgoblin	hingbegonbejan	hoiden	hinlejin
hobnail	hingbehelo	hoist	hinlesi
hobnob	hingbebin	hoity-toity	hinleto-toleto
hobo	hingbekn	hoke	hinkn
hobson's choice	hingbesin	hokey-cokey	hinknsi-kiknsi
hock1	hinko	hokum	hinkuo
hock2	hinko	hol	hinle

WORD (x)	EQUIVALENT (y)	WORD (x)	EQUIVALENT (y)
holard	hinlegba	holocaust	hilaukoinsi
holarctic	hinleknrako	holocene	hilauknsa
hold1	hinjo	holofernes	hilaufiransi
hold2	hinjo	hologram	hilauganmo
holdall	ajjohinjo	holograph	hilauganpha
holding	hinjognni	holography	hilauganphe
holding company	hinjognni kimpanse	holohedral	hilauhejnrajo
hold-up	hinmu-pake	holophrasis	hilauphiranso
hole	hinlu	holophrastic	hilauphiransuko
holey	hinluse	holophytic	hilaupheko
holiday	himodase	holoplankton	hilaupankiti
holiday camp	himodase kompn	holothurian	hilausunrain
holier	himosi	holotrichida	hilautaraikhijn
holily	himolo	holotype	hilautnpon
holiness	himonisi	holozoic	hilausinko
holism	himosi	holp	hilepn
holistic	himosiko	holpen	hilepnsi
holistically	himosikojjn	hols	hilese
holk	himoki	holstein	hilesetin
holland	hileledain	holster	hileseto
hollandaise sauce	hileledainse sansi	holt	hiletn
hollandia	hileledainsi	holus-bolus	himosi-booojnsi
holler	hileloso	holy	himose
hollo	hilelo	holy rood	himose rojn
hollow	hilelowai	hom	himini
holly	hilelo	homage	himinigun
hollyhock	hilelohinki	homburg	himinibugan
hollywood	hilelowoogi	home	himini
holm	hilemi	homeland	himiniledain
holmes	hilemiso	homeless	himinilabo
holmia	hilemisi	homely	himinilo
holmium	hilemima	home-made	himini-mojain
holo	hilau	homeo	hinmini
holoblastic	hilaubansia	homeopathy	hinminipansio

WORD (x)	EQUIVALENT (y)	WORD (x)	EQUIVALENT (y)
homeoplasia	hinminipansia	homologize	himologbonse
homeostasis	hinminisetnso	homologous	himologbisi
homer	himinisi	homology	himologbon
homeric	himinisiko	homonym	himomeni
home rule	himini rinron	homonymy	himomenise
homespun	himinisepoyi	homoousian	himotowahn
homestead	himinisetngba	homophobia	himophobua
homeward	himiniwegba	homophone	himophohun
homework	himiniwinsise	homophony	himophohunse
homey	himinise	homophyly	himophelo
homicide	himinikeku	homoplastic	himopansuiko
homiletics	himinijnkosi	homoptera	himopntiran
homilist	himinijinsi	homopterous	himopntiransi
homily	himinijin	homorganic	himorogbnko
homing	himinignni	homosapiens	himosanphnsi
hominid	himinijo	homoscedastic	himoseknjnsuko
hominoid	himiniknjo	homosexual	himosesuajo
hominy	himinise	homozygote	himosaijotn
homo-	himo	homozygous	himosaijosi
homodyne	himodain	homy	himnisi
homoeopathy	himopansio	hon.	Hini
homogamy	himogimo	honan	hinihun
homogenate	himognhunyo	honda	hijnna
homogeneity	himognhunto	hone	hihun
homogeneous	himognhunsi	honest	hihunsi
homogenize	himognse	honestly	hihunsilo
homogeny	himogn	honesty	hihunsito
homogony	himogonse	honey	hihunyin
homograde	himogandie	honeydew	hihunyinjinwa
homograph	himoganpha	honeyed	hihunyinde
homograft	himoganfia	honeymoon	hihunyinmoyin
homolog	himologbi	hong	hingan
homologate	himologbiyo	honiara	hinnirai
homologic	himologbonko	honk	hinkese

WORD (x)	EQUIVALENT (y)	WORD (x)	EQUIVALENT (y)
honor	hiniyi	hoop	hinpo
honorable	hiniyibe	hoop-la	hinpo-jn
honorarium	hiniyiraima	hoopoe	hinpose
honorary	hiniyirai	hooray	hurai
honore	hiniyira	hoord	hingbe
honorific	hiniyifiko	hoosac	hinsikn
honour	hinniyi	hoose	hinsesi
honourable	hinniyibe	hoosler	hinsejnra
honshu	hinnisua	hoot	hintoo
hooch	hinkhoin	hootenanny	hintoonihn
hoochie	hinkhoinsi	hooter	hintoosi
hood1	hinjo	hoover	hinwnrai
hood2	hinjo	hooves	hinfiose
,-hood	hinjo	hop1	hipo
hooded	hinjode	hop2	hipo
hooder	hinjosi	hopcallite	hipokoleyo
hoodle	hinjole	hope	hipon
hoodlum	hinjolema	hopi	hipe
hoodoo	hinjoin	hop in to	hipo le to
hoodwink	hinjowonkn	hopkins	hipokinsi
hooey	hinise	hoplite	hipoleyo
hoof	hinfio	hoplology	hiponlogbon
hoofer	hinfiosi	hopper1	hiposi
hook	hinkoi	hopper2	hiposi
hookah	hinkoihe	hopping	hipognni
hooke	hinkoin	hopple	hiporon
hooked	hinkoide	hops	hiposi
hooker	hinkoisi	hop sack	hipo saka
hookey	hinkoise	hopscotch	hiposekitisi
hook, lin, and sink	hinkoi, lehun ati sooknu	hor	hira
		hora	hirai
hook-up	hinkoi-pake	horace	hiraisi
hooky	hinkoisi	horacio	hiraisikn
hooligan	hinjigan	horae	hirain

WORD (x)	EQUIVALENT (y)	WORD (x)	EQUIVALENT (y)
horal	hiraijo	horrid	hinrraijo
horary	hirairan	horrific	hinrraifiko
horatii	hiranyan	horrify	hinrraife
horatio	hiranyato	horripilation	hinrraipoleyoon
horatius	hiranyasi	horror	hinrraisi
horde	hirajin	horsa	hinsa
hordein	hirajie	horsconcours	hinsakinkira
hordenine	hirajinhun	horse	hiso
horadeum	hirajinma	horse	hiso
horeb	hirebo	horseback	hisoboki
horicon	hiraikin	horsebox	hisobosi
horizon	hiraisnle	horseradish	hisorangbase
horizontal	hiraisnlejo	horsey	hisose
horizontalism	hiraisnlejomosi	horst	hisosi
horme	hiranmi	horsy	hinsose
hormone	hiranmini	horta	hitan
horn	huran	hortatory	hitantorai
horn	huran	hortense	hitanse
hornbill	huranbajjn	Horthy	hitansio
horned	hurande	horticulture	hitankunjiaran
hornet	hurante	hortussiccus	hitansooknsi
hornito	huranto	horus	hiransi
horny	huranse	hosanna	hisinhu
horo	hinrai	hose	hinse
horologe	hinrailogn	hosea	hinsesi
horologic	hinrailogbonko	hosier	hinsirai
horologist	hinrailogbonsi	hosiery	hinsirain
horologium	hinrailogbonma	hospice	hinsipo
horology	hinrailogbon	hospitable	hinsiponbe
horoscope	hinraisokipon	hospital	hinsiponjo
horoscopy	hinraisokipo	hospitaler	hinsiponjorai
horrendous	hinrraijnsi	hospitality	hinsiponleto
horrent	hinrraito	hospitalisation	hinsiponjoseyoon
horrible	hinrraibe	hospitalize	hinsiponjose

WORD (x)	EQUIVALENT (y)	WORD (x)	EQUIVALENT (y)
hospitaller	hinsiponjjorai	hound	hinjoin
hospitium	hinsiponma	hour	hinwa
hospodar	hinsiponjnra	hours	hinwasi
hossanah	hinsinhoo	houri	hinwai
host1	hinsi	hourly	hinwalo
host2	hinsi	house	hinlese
host3	hinsi	house-agent	aginte-hinlese
hosta	hinsia	houseleek	hinleselorin
hostage	hinsigun	house maid	hinlese maajo
hostel	hinsitojn	housey-housey	hinlesun-hinlesun
hosteling	hinsitojngnni	housie	hinlesio
hosteller	hinsitojjnra	housing	hinlesegnni
hostelling	hinsitojjngnni	houston	hinlesetin
hostelry	hinsitojnrai	houstonia	hinlesetinsi
hostess	hinsibo	houting	hinletognni
hostile	hinsitinron	hove	hiwin
hostility	hinsitinleto	hovel	hiwinjo
hostler	hinsijnra	hover	hiwinrai
hot	hitu	hovercraft	hiwinraikanfia
hot	hitu	hoverport	hiwinraipinta
hotchpotch	hitusipintesi	how	hinwo
hot dog	hitu degbi	howard	hinwogba
hotel	hitujo	howbeit	hinwobeto
hotelier	hitujosi	howdah	hinwodan
hothead	hituhegbi	howdle	hinwoduo
hotie	hituse	howdy	hinwodain
hot line	hitu lehun	howe	hinwin
hottentot	hitutinto	howel	hinwinlo
hottie	hittuse	however	hinwowinra
houdan	hinduhn	howitzer	hinwotnsi
houdini	hindain	howk	hinkwo
houdon	hindun	howl	hinwojn
hough	hinghun	howler	hinwojnra
houmous	hinmunsi	hoy	hinlo

WORD (x)	EQUIVALENT (y)	WORD (x)	EQUIVALENT (y)
hoyden	hinlodain	huggins	hungbihn
hoyle	hinloron	hugh	hungha
hoyte	hinlote	hughes	hunghasi
hradee	hiranjn	hughie	hunghan
huallaga	hunjjngan	hugmetight	hungbamutigbe
huambo	hunmboo	hugo	hungon
huarache	hunraikhn	hugues	hungbain
huascar	hunsunkosi	huguenot	hungbaintin
huascaran	hunsunkosia	huh	hunha
hub	hunbe	hula	hunjn
hubbard	hunbegbaa	hula hoop	hunjn hinpo
hubble-bubble	hunberon buberon	hulk	hunjnki
hubbub	hunbobu	hulking	hinjnkignni
hubby	hunbobn	hulla	hunjnran
hubris	hungbansi	hull1	hunjnra
huckleberry	hunkojnberai	hull2	hunjnra
hucklebone	hunkojnboun	hullabaloo	hunjnranboolo
huckster	hunkoseto	hullo	hunjnkn
hud	hundi	hum	humo
huddle	hundiduo	human	hunmaye
hudibrastic	hundibaunko	human being	begnni hunmaye
hudson	hundisin	humane	hunmayin
hue	hule	humanism	hunmayesi
hue and cry	hule ati korai	humanitarian	hunmayetorain
hued	hulede	humanitarianism	hunmayetorainmosi
huelva	hulewa	humanity	hunmayetn
huesca	hulekosi	humanize	hunmayese
huff	hunfio	humanly	hunmayelo
huffish	hunfiose	humanoid	hunmayejo
huffy	hunfiosi	human rights	hunmaye raighesi
hug	hungba	humber	hunmbesi
huge	hungbi	humbert	hunbeto
hugely	hungbile	humble	hunmbn
hugger-mugger	hungbira mugbira	humble pie	hunmbn pon

WORD (x)	EQUIVALENT (y)	WORD (x)	EQUIVALENT (y)
humboldt	hunmbojia	hunmphrey	hunmphirain
humbug	hunmbugbi	humpy	hunmpnse
humdinger	hunmjngnnisi	humus	humisi
humdrum	hunmgbiro	hun	hunsa
hume	hunmi	hunan	hunsaun
humectant	hunmikiti	hunch	hunkhe
humeral	hunmiraijo	hunchback	hunkhiboki
humerus	hunmiraisi	hundred	hunjnra
humic	hunmiko	hundredth	hunjnrasi
humicolous	hunmikojosi	hung	hungbn
humid	hunmijn	hungarian	hungbnrain
humidifier	hunmijnfirai	hungary	hungbnrai
humidify	hunmijnfe	hunger	hungbesi
humidity	hunmijnto	hungry	hungberai
humidor	hunmijnra	hunk	hunkn
humiliate	hunmijiayo	hunker	hunknra
humility	hunmijiato	hunks	hunknsi
humit	hunmitn	hunky	hunknse
humiture	hunmitnran	hunkydory	hunknsejnrai
hummel	hunmmulo	hunt	hunta
hummer	hummosi	hunter	huntasi
humming	hummognni	hunter's moon	huntasi moyin
hummock	hunmmokin	huntsman	huntamoye
humongous	hunmogansi	hunting	huntagnni
humor	hunmorin	huonpine	hunhnpo
humoral	hunmoranjo	hupeb	hunpobe
humoresque	hunmorankun	hurcheon	hunrakhnsi
humorism	hunmorinse	hurdle	hunraduo
humorist	hunmorinsi	hurdler	hunraduosi
humorous	hunmorinsi	hurdy-gurdy	hunradie gunradie
humour	hunmorin	hurl	hurajn
hummus	hunmisn	hurley	hurajnse
hump	hunmpo	hurly-burly	hunrajia burajia
humph	hunmphi	huron	hunrasi

WORD (x)	EQUIVALENT (y)	WORD (x)	EQUIVALENT (y)
hurrah	hurran	hyalo	honlo
hurray	hurrain	hyalogen	honlogin
hurricane	hunrraikojan	hyaloid	honlojo
hurry	hunrrai	hyaloplasm	honlopanson
hurt	hunrate	hyaluronic	honluranko
hurtle	hunratejn	hyaluroniidase	honluranjnse
husband	hunsibojn	hybla	hobejn
husbandry	hunsibojnri	hybalacan	hobejnko
hush	husn	hybrid	hobajo
hush-hush	husn husn	hybridism	hobajomosi
husk	hunsia	hybridize	hobajose
husky1	hunsiase	hybris	hobansi
husky2	hunsiase	hydantoin	hojntosi
huss	hunsun	hydathode	hojnsinde
hussar	hunsunrai	hydatid	hojnntojo
hussy	hunsunse	hydatogenesis	hojntognhunso
hustings	hunsiagnni	hyde	hojn
hustle	hunsiajn	hyderabad	hojnrabe
hustler	hunsiajnra	hydno	hojnkn
hut	huntn	hydnocarpate	hojnknkopanyo
hutch	huntnsi	hydr	hogb
hutment	huntnmutto	hydra	hogban
huxley	hunseroin	hydracid	hogbankijo
huzzah	hunsuha	hydragog	hogbangonko
huzzy	hunsuse	hydrangea	hogbangini
huy	hunye	hydrant	hogbante
hyacinth	honkhunsu	hydranth	hogbansi
hyacinthus	honkhunsuwa	hydrargyrum	hogbanganraima
hyaden	honjinna	hydrargyrism	hogbanganraimosi
hyades	honjnsi	hydrargyric	hogbanganraiko
hyaena	honihun	hydrastine	hogbansetin
hyalin	honlisi	hydrastinine	hogbasetinhun
hyaline	honlehun	hydrate	hogbanyo
hyalite	honliyo	hydraulic	hogbanleko

WORD (x)	EQUIVALENT (y)	WORD (x)	EQUIVALENT (y)
hydraulics	hogbalekosi	hydrothorax	hogbnsinransi
hydrazine	hogbansun	hydrous	hogbnsi
hydrazoic	hogbansinko	hydrovize	hogbnwose
hydria	hogbansi	hydroxide	hogbnsinji
hydric	hogbanko	hydroxonium	hogbnsinlema
hydride	hogbanji	hydroxy	hogbnsin
hydriodic	hogbainjnko	hydroxyl	hogbnsinlo
hydro-	hogbn	hydroxylamine	hogbnsinlomini
hydrobromic	hogbnbonmuko	hydrus	hogbisi
hydrocarbon	hogbnkosibu	hyena	horehun
hydrocele	hogbnknjn	hyeres	horesi
hydrocephalus	hogbnknphejnsi	hyetal	hotejo
hydrocoral	hogbnkiranjo	hyeto	hotekn
hydrocortisone	hogbnkiratesohun	hygela	hognbo
hydrodynamic	hogbdainsemuko	hygiene	hogini
hydrogen	hogbngin	hygienic	hoginiko
hydrogenate	hogbnginyo	hygienic	hoginikosi
hydrogen bomb	hogbngin boobon	hygienist	hoginisi
hydrography	hogbnganphe	hygristor	hogansiran
hydroid	hogbnjo	hygro	hognro
hydrology	hogbnlogbon	hygrometer	hognromuto
hydrolyse	hogbnjinse	hygroscope	hognrosokipon
hydrolysis	hogbnjiso	hygroscopic	hognrosokiponko
hydrolyze	hogbnjinse	hyksos	hoknso
hydromel	hogbnmulo	hyla	hole
hydropathy	hogbnpansio	hylas	holese
hydrophilic	hogbnpheronko	hylic	holeki
hydrophobia	hogbnphobua	hylicist	holekisi
hydrophobic	hogbnphobuako	hylism	holemosi
hydrophone	hogbnphohun	hylo	hole
hydroponics	hogbnponkosi	hylotheism	holesinmosi
hydroscopic	hogbnsokipon	hylozoism	holesinmosi
hydrosere	hogbnserai	hymen	homiki
hydrotheca	hogbnsinko	hymeneal	homikijo

WORD (x)	EQUIVALENT (y)	WORD (x)	EQUIVALENT (y)
hymenium	homikima	hyperbole	hopnraboojn
hymeno	homikn	hyperboloid	hopnraboojnjo
hymenophore	homiknphiran	hyperborean	hopnraboorain
hymenoptera	homiknpntiran	hypercatalectic	hopnrakotijnkyoko
hymenopterous	homiknpntiraisi	hyperemesis gravid	hopnramuso ganwojnr
hymettus	homittnsi	hyperemia	hopnramua
hymn	homini	hyperesthesia	hopnrasunwnsia
hymnal	hominijo	hyperesthetic	hopnrasunwnko
hymnist	hominisi	hypereutectic	hopnrawatntoko
hymnody	hominidun	hyperextention	hopnraesntinyoon
hymnology	hominilogbon	hyperfine	hopnrafinni
hyoid	hokoijo	hyperfocal	hopnrafoonkijo
hyoscine	hokoisekihun	hyperglycaemia	hopnragilokoinmo
hyoscyamine	hokoisesnmini	hypergolic	hopnragbinako
hyoscyamine	hokoisesnmini	hyperhidrosis	hopnrahigbnso
hyoscyamus	hokoisesnmisi	hyperion	hopnraisi
hyp	hopa	hypermetro	hopnromutnra
hypabyssal	hopabesoojn	hypermnesia	hopnronhunsia
hypaesthesia	hopasunwnsia	hyperon	hopnrain
hypallage	hopajjngun	hyperopia	hopnranpan
hypanthium	hopansinma	hyperosmia	hopnransoomua
hypatia	hopansua	hyperostosis	hopnransootoso
hype	hopn	hyperoxia	hopnransia
hyper	hopnra	hyperparasite	hopnrapanrasosi
hyperactive	hopnrakitiyowin	hyperphenomenal	hopnraphiknmuhunjo
hyperacusia	hopnrakunsia	hyperpiesia	hopnraponsia
hyperadrenia	hopnragbainsi	hyperpituitarism	hopnrapotuntoraimosi
hyperadulia	hopnradijan	hyperplane	hopnrapanyun
hyperaemia	hopnramua	hyperplasia	hopnrapansia
hyperalgesia	hopnrajognsia	hyperploid	hopnraponjo
hoperalgesis	hopnrajognso	hyperpnoea	hopnrapnhn
hyperbaric	hopnraboosiako	hyperprosexia	hopnraponsesia
hyperbarism	hopnraboosiamosi	hyperpyrexia	hopnraporansia
hyperbola	hopnraboojo	hypersensitive	hopnrasesntowin

WORD (x)	EQUIVALENT (y)	WORD (x)	EQUIVALENT (y)
hypersonic	hopnrasonko	hypobaric	hopinboosiako
hypersthene	hopnrasesinhun	hypobarism	hopinboosiamosi
hypersthenia	hopnrasesinhan	hypoblast	hopinbansia
hypertension	hopnratinsesi	hypocapnia	hopincopnhan
hyperthymic	hopnrasiomuko	hypocaust	hopinkoinsu
hyperthyroid	hopnrasioraijo	hypocenter	hopinkntiran
hypertonic	hopnratoniko	hypochondria	hopinkhojnran
hypertrophy	hopnratnraphe	hypochondriac	hopinkhojnranko
hyperventilation	hopnrawintaleyoon	hypochondrium	hopinkhojnraima
hypervitamin	hopnrawotemo	hypocorism	hopinkiraimosi
hypesthesia	hopnsunwnsia	hypocotyls	hopinkitilo
hypethral	hopnsnralo	hypocrisy	hopinknrase
hypha	hophan	hypocrite	hopinknra
hypheme	hophimo	hypocycloid	hopinsnkuojo
hyphen	hophini	hypoderm	hopinjnramo
hyphenate	hophiniyo	hypoderma	hopinjnramu
hypna	hopiko	hypodermal	hopinjnramujo
hypnagogic	hopikogonko	hypodermic	hopinjnramuko
hypnic	hopiknko	hypodermis	hopinjnramuso
hypno	hopikn	hypodorian	hopinderain
hypnogenesis	hopikngnhunso	hypoentectic	hopinentntoko
hypnoid	hopiknjo	hypogastrium	hopingisetnraima
hypnology	hopiknlogbon	hypogeal	hopingnjo
hypnopaedia	hopiknpanjina	hypogene	hopingnhun
hypnophobia	hopiknphobua	hypogenous	hopingnhunsi
hypnopompic	hopiknpinmponko	hypogeous	hopingnsi
hypnos	hopiknsi	hypogeum	hopingnma
hypnosis	hopiknso	hypoglossal	hopingonsoojo
hypnotic	hopiknko	hypoglyceamia	hopingilokoinma
hypnotism	hopiknmosi	hypognathous	hopingnsansi
hypnotize	hopiknse	hypogynous	hopinloyunsi
hypo1	hopin	hypolimnion	hopinjnmule
hypo2	hopin	hypolydian	hoposejain
hypoacidity	hopinakijotn	hypomania	hopinmayisi

WORD (x)	EQUIVALENT (y)	WORD (x)	EQUIVALENT (y)
hyponasty	hopinhesitn	hypsography	hopakeganphe
hyponitrite	hopinnitaraiyo	hypsometer	hopakemuto
hyponitrous	hopinnitnrasi	hypsometry	hopakemutorai
hypophosphate	hopinphosephiyo	hysophillum	hopakephewema
hypophosphite	hopinphosephito	hyracold	horaikijon
hypophosphorous	hopinphosephiransi	hyrax	horaisi
hypophyge	hopinphegn	hyson	hosin
hypophysis	hopinpheso	hyssop	hosoopn
hypopituitarsm	hopinpotuntomosi	hysterectomy	hositnrantemo
hypoplasia	hopinpansia	hysteresis	hositnranso
hypoploid	hopinponjo	hysteria	hositnran
hypopnoea	hopinpohn	hysteric	hositnranko
hypopodium	hopinpindiema	hysterical	hositnrankojo
hypopyon	hopinposi	hysterio	hositnrain
hypostasis	hopinsetnso	hystero	hositnra
hypostasize	hopinsetnsose	hysterogenic	hositnraginko
hypostatic	hopinsetnko	hysteroid	hositnrajo
hyposthenia	hopinsetnhun	hysteron	hositnran
hypostoma	hopinsetoma	hysteropexy	hositnrapnse
hypostyle	hopinsetnron	hysterophyte	hositnrapheyo
hypotaxis	hopintesanso	hysterotomy	hositnratemo
hypotenuse	hopintinse	hystricomorph	hosetaraikimophan
hypothalamus	hopinsanjnmosi	hyte	hote
hypothallus	hopinsanjjnsi	hyther	hosnra
hypothec	hopinsiko	hyzone	hoserun
hypothecate	hopinsikoyo	I	I mo e
hypothenar	hopinsirai	I	to form words ilarin
hypothermal	hopinsinronjo	;-ial	ijo
hypothesis	hopinsiso	iambic	imbeko
hypothetical	hopinsikojo	iambus	imbeso
hypothyroid	hopinsioranjo	,-ian	ihn
hypoxia	hopinsia	iasis	iseso
hypped	hopapode	iatrics	itaraikosi
hypso	hopake	iatrogenics	itnraginkosi

WORD (x)	EQUIVALENT (y)	WORD (x)	EQUIVALENT (y)
iatry	iterai	ichthyo	ikhoisun
ibague	ibogbi	ichthyoid	ikhoisunjo
i/beam	i/bemo	ichthyol	ikhoisunjin
iberia	iberan	ichthyology	ikhoisunlogbon
ibex	ibesn	ichthyosaurus	ikhoisunsanra
ibicui	ibankun	ichthyophagous	ikhoisunphijesi
ibid.	ibajo	ichthyosis	ikhoisunso
ibidem	ibajoma	-ician	ikohn
-ibility	ibeleto	icicle	iknkuo
ibis	ibaso	icily	iknlo
-ible	iberon	iciness	iknnisi
-ibly	ibelo	icing	ikngnni
ibn	omo	icon	akin
iboga	iboogi	iconic	akinko
-ic	iko	icono	akinkn
,-ical	ikojo	iconoclast	akinknkansi
icaria	ikorai	iconography	akinknganphe
icarian	ikorain	iconolatry	akinknletorai
icarus	ikoronsi	iconology	akinknlogbon
ice	aki	iconomania	akinknmohan
ice age	agun aki	iconomatic	akinknmuko
ice-axe	aake aki	iconostasis	akinknsetnso
iceberg	akibegan	icosahedron	akisohegbile
ice cap	aki kopn	icosi	akise
ice-cream	aki kesimo	-ics	ikosi
ichabod	ikhobajo	icteric	ikntirako
ickhin	ikhognni	icterus	ikntirasi
ichneumon	ikhunmeni	ictinus	ikntinsi
ichnite	ikhunyo	ictus	ikntisi
ichnography	ikhunganphe	icy	isn
ichnology	ikhunlogbon	id	ijo
ichor	ikhiran	ida	ijn
ichorous	akhiransi	idaho	ijnhin
ichyic	ikhoiko	ide	ide

WORD (x)	EQUIVALENT (y)	WORD (x)	EQUIVALENT (y)
idea	idesi	idiot	iditie
ideal	idejo	idiotic	iditieko
idealism	idejomosi	idiotism	iditiemosi
idealist	idejosi	idle	idile
ideality	ideleto	idle	iduo
idealize	idejose	idleness	iduonisi
ideate	ideyo	idler	idilesi
ideatum	ideyoma	idler	iduosi
idem	idemo	idlesse	iduosoo
idempotent	idempotinto	idol	idejo
ident	ideto	idolater	idejotnsi
identical	idetokojo	idolatrous	idejotnrasi
identification	idetofikoyoon	idolatry	idejotorai
identify	idetofe	idolism	idejomosi
identity	idetotn	idolize	idejose
ideo	idekn	idoloclast	idejokansi
ideogram	ideknganmo	idolum	idejoma
ideograph	ideknganpha	idoneous	idehunsi
ideography	ideknganphe	idun	ideun
ideolect	ideknjokyo	idyl	idejn
ideologist	ideknlogbonsi	idyll	idejnra
ideologize	ideknlogbonse	idyllic	idejnrako
ideologue	ideknlogbise	idyllically	idejnrakojin
ideology	ideknlogbon	-if	bi, boya, ti.
ideomotor	ideknmotu	iffy	ife/fife
ideophone	ideknphohun	igloo	igbele
ides	idesi	ign	igbi
idio	iditie	ignatia	igbinatie
idioblast	iditiebansia	igneous	igbinasi
idiocy	iditiesn	ignescent	igbinaseknti
idiom	iditiem	ignify	igbinafe
idiomatic	iditiemokn	ignis	igbinaso
idiopathic	iditiepansioko	ignite	igbinayo
idiosyncrasy	iditiesoseknra	igniter	igbinayosi

WORD (x)	EQUIVALENT (y)	WORD (x)	EQUIVALENT (y)
signition	igbinayoon	iliad	ilijn
ignitor	igbinaran	ilium	ilima
ignitron	igbinatnran	ilk	iloki
ignoble	igbiknbu	ill	illo
ignominy	igbiknmeni	illation	illoyoon
ignominious	igbiknmenisi	illative	illoyowin
ignoramus	igbiknramosi	illegal	illognjo
ignorance	igbiknrasi	illegalise	illognjose
ignorant	igbiknrate	illegible	illognberon
ignoratioelenchi	igbiknraiyatojnkhi	illegitimate	illogntomuyo
ignore	igbiknra	illiberal	illiberanjo
ignotumperignotius	igbihntompnragntowa	illicit	illikiti
igorot	igonraito	illimani	illimuhn
igrain	iganrain	illimitable	illimutnbo
iguana	igunhun	illiquid	illikunjo
iguanodon	igundebu	illinois	illiknso
iguassu	igunsun	illiterate	illitnraiyo
ihram	ihnramu	illness	illonisi
ijssel	ijnsoojo	illocal	illoknjo
ikaria	ikorai	illocution	illokunyoon
ikebana	ikunyebe	illogical	illogbonkojo
ikhnaton	ikhnyotin	illmened	illomuyede
ikon	akin	illude	illujin
il-	ilo	illume	illuma
ileitis	ilouso	illuminance	illumanasi
ileo	ilouni	illuminant	illumanate
ileostomy	ilousootemo	illuminate	illumanayo
ilerda	iloraijn	illuminati	illumanaye
iles du sa lut	ilosi de sa loto	illumination	illumanayoon
ileum	iloma	illuminative	illumanayowin
ileus	ilosi	illumine	illumana
ilex	ilosn	illuminism	illumanamosi
ilia	ijan	illuminist	illumanasi
iliac	iliko	illuse	illuse

WORD (x)	EQUIVALENT (y)	WORD (x)	EQUIVALENT (y)
illusion	illusoon	imbrue	imbomisi
allusionism	illusoonmosi	imbrute	imburutn
illusionist	illusoonsi	imbue	imbemu
illusive	illusewin	imidazole	imujnsinle
illusory	illuserai	imide	imuji
illustrate	illuseranyo	imido	imujikn
illustration	illuseranyoon	imine	imuhun
illustrative	illuseranyowin	imino	imukn
illustrious	illuseransi	imitate	imutnyo
illuviation	illuwonyoon	mitation	imutnyoon
illyria	illorai	imitative	imutnyowin
illyrian	illorain	immaculate	immoknleyo
illyricum	illoraikuo	immanakle	immohunkun
ilmen	illomini	immane	immohun
ilmenite	illominiyo	immanence	immohunsi
image	imogun	immanent	immohunto
imagery	imogunrai	immanuel	immohunlo
imaginal	imogunjo	immaterial	immoteraijo
imaginary	imogunrai	immature	immotnra
imagination	imogunyoon	immeasurable	immusunraibo
imaginative	imogunhyowin	immediacy	immujiasn
imagine	imogun	immediate	immujiayo
imagism	imogunmosi	immediately	immujiayolo
imago	imogon	immedicable	immujinkebo
imam	imomu	immelmann	immulomohn
imamate	imomuyo	immemorial	immumoraijo
imaret	imorantn	immense	immusua
imbalance	imbojosi	immensely	immusualo
imbecile	imbekue	immensity	immusuato
imbed	imbeje	immerse	immuraisn
imbibe	imbobe	immersion	immuraisnle
imbibition	imbobeyoon	immethodical	immutojnkn
imbricate	imberaikoyo	immigrant	immagunraite
imbroglio	imbejigan	immigrate	immagunraiyo

WORD (x)	EQUIVALENT (y)	WORD (x)	EQUIVALENT (y)
imminent	imminato	impanation	impanhunyoon
immingle	immnignron	impanel	impanhunjo
immiscible	immusikibo	imparadise	impanrajnse
immit	immutn	imparipinnate	impanraipohayo
immitigable	immutngibo	imparisyllabic	impanraisollebeko
immobile	immobajn	imparity	impanraito
immobilize	immobajnse	impart	impante
immoderate	immodieraiyo	impartial	impantejo
immodest	immodiesi	impassable	impansobo
immolate	immoleyo	impasse	impansoo
immoral	immorunjo	impassible	impansobo
immorality	immorunleto	impassioned	impansoonde
immortal	immositn	impassive	impansowin
immortelle	immositnjjn	impaste	impansitn
immovable	immowainbo	impasto	impansinkn
immune	immuhun	impatience	impatetansi
immunity	immuhuntn	impatiens	impatetan
immunize	immuhunse	impeach	impnkho
immune	immuhunkn	impeccable	impnkkobe
immunoassay	immuhunknsoon	impeccant	impnkkote
immunogenetics	immuhunkngnhunkosi	impecunious	impnkuesi
immunogenic	immuhunkngnko	impedance	impndisi
immunoglobulin	immuhunkngonbujan	impede	impndi
immunology	immuhunknlogbon	impediment	imopndimutto
immure	immurau	impedimenta	impndimutta
immutable	immutnbo	impel	impnlo
immutableness	immutnbonisi	impellent	impnlloto
imode phone	imodie phohun	impeller	impnllosi
imp	impn	impend	impnjon
impact	impanknti	impenetrable	impnyuntnrabo
impair	impanra	impennate	impnyayo
impala	impanja	impenitent	impntinto
impale	impanjn	imperative	impnrayowin
impalpable	impanjopibee	imperator	impnrayoran

WORD (x)	EQUIVALENT (y)	WORD (x)	EQUIVALENT (y)
imperceptible	impnraknpobe	implead	impojnde
imperceptive	impnraknpowin	implement	imporonmutto
imperfect	impnrafnkn	implicate	imponlokoyo
imperfection	impnrafnknyoon	implication	imponlokoyoon
imperfective	impnrafnknwin	implicit	imponlokiti
imperforate	impnrafonyo	implied	imponlode
imperial	impnraijo	implode	imponnjin
imperialism	impnraijomosi	implore	imponrai
imperil	impnralo	implosion	imponsoon
imperio	impnrain	implosive	imponsowin
imperious	impnrainsi	imply	imponlo
imperishable	impnrasebo	impolder	impinjonsi
imperium	impnrama	impolicy	impinjnsn
impermanent	impnronhunto	impolitic	impinjntokn
impermeable	impnronbo	imponderable	imponjnrabo
impermissible	impnramusoobo	imponderabilia	imponjnrabojan
impersonal	impnrasinjo	impone	impinse
impersonate	impnrasinyo	imponent	impinseto
impertinence	impnratinsi	import	impinta
impertinent	impnratinto	important	impintatn
imperturbable	impnraturabo	importation	impintayoon
impervious	impnrawosi	impose	impinsi
impetigo	impntigon	imposition	impinsiyoon
impetrate	impntiraiyo	impossible	impinssebo
impetuous	impntisi	impossibility	impinsseboleto
impetus	impntise	impost	impinseto
impiety	imponbotn	impostor	impinsetoran
impinge	impingun	impostumate	impinsetomuyo
impious	imponbosa	impostume	impinsetomu
impish	impnsue	imposture	impinsetorai
implacable	impanknbo	impotent	impintitan
implant	impantn	impound	impinjoin
implantation	impantnyoon	impoverish	impinwnra
implausible	impanlesebo	impower	impowara

WORD (x)	EQUIVALENT (y)	WORD (x)	EQUIVALENT (y)
impracticable	impankiobo	improvement	imponwinmutto
imprecate	impesikoyo	improvident	imponwindato
imprecation	impesikoyoon	improvise	imponwinse
imprecise	impesikise	imprudence	imporajinsi
impreg	impesigi	imprudent	imporajinto
impregn	impesigini	impudence	impudasi
impregnable	impesiginibo	impudent	impudato
impregnate	impesiginiyo	impudicity	impudakito
impregnation	impesiginiyoon	impugn	impugn
impresa	impesise	impulse	impulese
impresario	impesiserain	impulsive	impulesewin
imprescriptible	impesisekoraipnbo	impunity	impuhuntn
imprese	impesisia	impure	impurai
impress	impesiso	impurity	impuraito
impressible	impesisobe	imputation	imputoyoon
impression	impesisoon	imputative	imputoyowin
impressionable	impesisoonbe	impute	impute
impressionism	impesisoonmosi	imputrescible	imputasisebo
impressionist	impesisoonsi	in-1	ini pron in
impressive	impesisowin	in-2	ini ninu
impressments	impesisomutto	inability	iniaboleto
impressure	impesisorai	in absentia	ini abesesita
imprest	impesite	inaccessible	iniaknsobo
imprimatur	impanmute	inaccuracy	iniakunrasn
imprimis	impanmeni	inaccurate	iniakunrayo
imprint	impante	inachus	iniakunsi
imprison	impansnsn	inaction	iniakntiyon
imprisonment	impansnlemutto	inactivate	iniakntiweyo
improbable	impongbabo	inactive	iniakntiwinyo
improbity	impongbati	inadequate	iniadikunyo
impromptu	imponmpiti	inadmissible	iniadimusinbo
improper	imponpnra	inadvertence	iniadiwintesi
impropriate	imponpanyo	inadvertent	iniadiwintetin
improve	imponwin	inadvisable	iniadiwosebo

WORD (x)	EQUIVALENT (y)	WORD (x)	EQUIVALENT (y)
inae	inni	inca	iniko
inaeternum	innitnranma	incalculable	inikojokunbo
inalterable	iniajotnrabo	incalescent	inikojnseknti
inamorato	iniamoranto	incamera	inikomura
inane	inini	incandesce	inikojnsekn
inanimate	ininimuyo	incandescence	inikojnseknsi
inanition	ininiyoon	incantation	inikoteyoon
inanity	ininito	incapable	inikopnbo
inappellable	iniapinllobo	incapacitate	inikopnkitoyo
inappetence	iniapntisn	incapacity	inikopnkito
inapplicable	iniapanlokobo	incapsulate	inikopnsuyo
inapposite	iniapinseyo	incarcerate	inikosiknra
inappreciable	iniapesiknbo	incardinate	inikosijnyo
inapprehensive	iniapesihesnwin	incarnadine	inikosihunjoin
inapproachable	iniaponkhobo	incarnant	inkosihuntn
inappropriate	iniaponpanyo	incarnate	inikosihunyo
inapt	iniapnti	incarnation	inikosihunyoon
inarch	iniaknra	incase	inikoso
inarticulate	inietekunleyo	incautious	inikoinyosi
inartificial	inietefisjo	incavation	inikowoyoon
inartistic	inietesuko	incendiarism	iniknjoraimosi
in as much as	ini se mukhi se	incendiary	iniknjorai
inattentive	iniatintowin	incense1	iniknsun
inaudible	inigbobo	incense2	iniknsun
inaugural	inigunrajo	incentive	inikntiwin
inaugurate	inigunraiyo	incentivize	inikntiwinse
inauguration	inigunraiyoon	incept	iniknpo
inauspicious	inisepokisi	inception	iniknposi
inbeing	inibegnni	inceptive	iniknpowin
inboard	inibugba	incertitude	iniknratetujin
inborn	iniboran	incessant	iniknsotn
inbound	inibojoin	incest	iniknsia
inbox	inibosi	incestuous	iniknsiasi
inc.	inikn	inch	inikhn

WORD (x)	EQUIVALENT (y)	WORD (x)	EQUIVALENT (y)
inchmeal	inikhnmuje	incommode	inikimmoda
inchoate	inikhinyo	incommodious	inikimmodawa
inchoative	inikhinyowin	incommodity	inikimmodato
inichon	inikhihn	incommunicable	inikimmuhunkobo
incidence	inikidasi	incommunicado	inikimmuhunkode
incident	inikidato	incommunicative	inikimmuhunkoyowin
incidental	inikidatojo	incommutable	inikimmutnbo
incidentally	inikidatojin	incomparable	inikimpanrabo
incinerate	inikisunraiyo	incompartible	inikimpantebo
incinerator	inikisunrairan	incomplete	inikimporontn
incipient	inikipito	incompliant	inikimponlotn
incipit	inikipiti	incomprehensible	inikimpesihesnbo
incise	inikisa	incomprehension	inikimpesihesoon
incision	inikisasi	incompressible	inikimpesisobo
incisive	inikisawin	incomputable	inikimpntebo
incisor	inikisaran	inconceivable	inikinknwinibo
incite	inikito	inconclusive	inikinkorasowin
incitation	inikitoyoon	incondensable	inikindainsebo
incivility	inikiwoleto	incondite	inikindeti
inclination	inikihunyoon	inconformity	inikinfonmuto
incline	inikiun	incongruity	inikingiraito
include	inikunrajin	inconsecutive	inkinsnkuntewin
inclusion	inikunrasoon	inconsequential	inikinsekunrajo
inclusive	inikunrasowin	inconsiderable	inikinsoojorabo
incoercible	inikiraisobo	inconsiderate	inikinsoojorayo
incogitable	inikigitobe	inconsistency	inikinsoosisn
incogitant	inikigitote	inconsistent	inikinsoositin
incognito	inikiginito	inconsolable	inikinsinlebo
incognizant	inikiginisunte	inconsonant	inikisoseto
incoherent	inikiherato	inconstant	inikinsetntn
income	inikimwa	inconsumable	inikinsumobo
incoming	inikimwagnni	incontestable	inikintnsibo
incommensurable	inikimmusunraibo	incontinent	inikintihunto
incommensurate	inikimmusunriayo	incontrollable	inikintnrajnbo

WORD (x)	EQUIVALENT (y)	WORD (x)	EQUIVALENT (y)
incontrovertible	inikintnrawintobo	incult	inikunjia
inconvenience	inikinwinisi	incumbency	inikunbesn
inconvenient	inikinwinito	incumbent	inikunbeto
inconvertible	inikinwintobo	incumber	inikunbesi
inconvincible	inikinwokinbo	incunabula	inikunhunbejn
incoordinate	inikiorojnyo	incur	inikunra
incorporable	inikiraporanbo	incurable	inikunrabo
incorporate	inikiraporanyo	incurious	inikunraisi
incorporated	inikiraporanyode	incurrent	inikunrraito
incorporator	inikiraporaran	incursion	inikunrasoon
incorporeal	inikiraporejo	incurvate	inikuowinyo
incorporeity	inikiraporeto	incus	inikusi
incorrect	inikirreto	incuse	inikunse
incorrigible	inikirraignbo	indaba	inijinbe
incorrupt	inikirranpi	inidagate	inijingiyo
incorruptible	inikirranpibo	indamines	inijinmini
incrassate	iniknrasiyo	indebted	inijigbesede
increase	iniknranse	indecent	inijinknti
increate	iniknranyo	indeciduosu	injinkndisi
incredible	iniknranjnbo	indecipherable	inijinkiphirabo
incredulity	iniknranjnleto	indecisive	inijinkisowin
incredulous	iniknranjnlesi	indeclinable	inijinkihunbo
increment	iniknranmutto	indecorous	inijinkirasi
incremental	iniknramuttojo	indeed	inijinde
increscent	iniknranseknti	indefatigable	inijinfanteganbo
incretion	iniknranyoon	indefeasible	inijinfnsesibo
incriminate	inikoranminiyo	indefectible	inijinfnkobo
incubate	inikuobeyo	indefensible	injinfnsebo
incubation	inikuobeyoon	indefinable	inidafinnibo
incubator	inikuoberan	indefinite	inidafinite
incubus	inikuobesi	indehiscent	inijinhiseknti
inculcate	inikunjnko	indeliable	inijinjobo
inculpable	inikunjnpanbe	indelicate	inijinjokoyo
inculpate	inikunjnpanyo	indenify	inidaamufe

WORD (x)	EQUIVALENT (y)	WORD (x)	EQUIVALENT (y)
indemnity	inidaamuto	indigenous	inidiginsi
indemonstrable	inijumoserainbo	indigent	inidiginte
indene	inijini	indigestion	inidigintesi
indent	inidato	indign	inidign
indentation	inidatoyoon	indignant	inidigntn
indenture	inidatorai	indignation	inidignyoon
independence	inidipnjonsi	indignity	inidignto
independency	inidipnjonsn	indigo	inidigio
independent	inidipnjonto	indirect	inidireto
indescribable	inidisekoraibo	indirection	inidiretosi
indestructible	inidisetnrankobo	indiscernible	inidisiknranbo
indeterminable	inijintnronhunbo	indiscreet	inidisiknra
indeterminate	inijintnronhunyo	indiscretion	inidisiknrayoon
indeterminism	inujintnronhunmosi	indiscriminate	inidisikoraminiyo
index	inijinsi	indispensable	inidisipnyasebo
indexation	inijinsiyoon	indispose	inidisipinsi
india	inijina	indisputable	indisiputobo
indian	inijinahn	indissoluble	indisisinlebo
indiana	inijinahun	indistinct	inidisitinko
indican	inidikohun	indistinctiive	inidisitinkowin
indicate	inidiknyo	indistinguishable	inidisitingbisubo
indicative	inidiknyowin	indite	inidito
indicator	inidiknyoran	indium	inidima
indicatory	inidiknyorai	indivertible	inidiwintebo
indices	inidisesi	individual	inidawajnjo
indices	inidisesi	individualism	inidawajnjomosi
indict	inidikn	individuality	inidawajnleto
indictable	inidiknbe	individualize	inidawajnjose
indictment	inidiknmutto	individuate	inidawajnyo
indies	inidilesi	indivisible	inidawasebo
indifference	inidifirosi	indo-	inijn
indifferent	inidifiroto	indoor	inideinsi
indifferentism	inidifirotomosi	indocile	inidekue
indigene	indignhun	indoctrinate	inidekitirainyo

WORD (x)	EQUIVALENT (y)	WORD (x)	EQUIVALENT (y)
indole	inidile	industrial	inidisitnraijo
indolence	inidilesi	industrialise	inidisitnraijose
indolent	inidileto	industrous	inidisitnraisi
Indonesia	inidihunsia	industry	inidisitnrai
indophenol	indiphinjin	,-ine	ihun
indorse	inijinrase	inebriant	iniebante
indorsee	inijinrasun	inebriate	iniebanyo
indoxyl	inijnsinlo	inedible	iniejijebo
indra	inigban	inedited	iniejnyode
indraugbt	inigbaungbe	indeducable	iniejnkobo
indrawn	inigbanwn	ineffable	iniefanbo
indris	inigbanso	ineffaceable	iniefansibo
indubitable	inidibonbo	ineffective	iniefnkyowin
induce	inidisi	ineffectual	iniefnkyojo
inducement	inidisimutto	inefficacious	iniefikokisi
induct	inidiki	inefficient	iniefikito
induactance	inidikisi	inelastic	iniejnsunko
inductee	inidikise	inelegant	inielegante
inductile	inidikitiron	ineligible	inielegnbo
induction	inidikitiyoon	ineloquent	inielokunto
inductive	inidikiwin	ineluctable	inieluknbo
inductor	inidikiran	ineludible	inislujnbo
indue	inidisan	inept	iniepnti
indulge	inidijign	inequable	iniekunbo
indulgence	inidijiginsi	inequality	iniekunjote
indulgent	inidijiginto	inequitable	iniekuntebo
induline	inidijihun	inequity	iniekunti
indult	inidejia	ineradicable	inieraijnkobo
induna	inidihun	inerrable	inierraibo
induplicate	inidipankoyo	inerrancy	inierraisn
indurate	inidipankoyo	inert	inieranti
indurate	inidiraiyo	inertia	inirantisi
indus	inidise	inertial	inirantijo
indusium	inidisoma	inescapable	iniesekopnbo

WORD (x)	EQUIVALENT (y)	WORD (x)	EQUIVALENT (y)
inescutcheon	iniesekuntekhn	infante	inifantn
inesse	iniesse	infantile	inifanteron
inessential	iniessetijo	infantilism	inifanteronmosi
inessive	iniessewin	infantry	inifanterai
inestimable	iniesetinmubo	infaret	inifansanyo
inevitable	iniewintnbo	infaretion	inifansanyoon
inexact	iniesnaknti	infare	inifansan
inexcuasable	iniesnkunsebo	infatuate	inifatnyo
inexist	iniesnsi	infect	inifnkn
inexorable	iniesnranbo	infection	inifnknyoon
inexpedient	iniesnpnjnto	infectious	inifnknsi
inexpensive	iniesnpinsanwin	infective	inifinknwin
inexperience	iniesnpnraisi	infecund	inifnkuojin
inexpert	iniesnpnra	infelicitous	inifnjokitisi
inexplicable	iniesnpankobo	infelicity	inifnjokito
inexplicit	iniesnpankiti	infer	inifiro
inexpressible	iniesnpesisobo	inference	inifirosi
inexpressive	iniesnpesisowin	inferior	inifiroran
inexpugnable	iniesnpugnbo	inferiority	inifiroranto
inexpungible	iniesnpurabo	infernal	inifirunjo
inextensible	iniesntinsebo	inferno	inifirun
inextenso	iniesntinsi	infertile	inifnratejn
inextinguishable	iniesntingbisebo	infest	inifnsi
inextirpable	iniesntirapanbo	infeudation	inifndanyoon
inextremis	iniesntasimo	infidel	inifijinle
inextricable	iniesntaraikobo	infidelity	inifijinleto
infallible	inifanjnrabo	infield	inifirojn
infamies	inifanmise	infielder	inifirojnra
infamous	inifanmisi	infighting	inifighegnni
infamy	inifanmi	infill	inifijjo
infancy	inifansn	infiltrate	inifijitnrayo
infant	inifante	infinite	inifinitn
infanticide	inifantekeku	infinitesimal	inifinitnsemujo
infanta	inifanta	infinitive	inifinitnwin

WORD (x)	EQUIVALENT (y)	WORD (x)	EQUIVALENT (y)
infinity	inifinitn	informer	inifoonmosi
infirm	inifiron	infra	inifan
infirmary	inifironsi	infract	inifankyo
infirmity	inifirontn	infradig	inifandign
inflame	inifanmana	infralapsarian	inifanjoperain
inflammable	inifanmanabe	infrangible	inifangnbo
inflammation	inifanmanayoon	infrasonic	inifansonko
inflammatory	inifanmanarai	infrastructure	inifansetnrakosi
inflatable	inifanyobe	infrequent	inifesikunra
inflate	inifanyo	infringe	inifangini
inflation	inifanyoon	infulae	inifujoin
inflationary	inifanyoonrai	infundibuliform	inifunjnbulefoonmo
inflationism	inifanyoonmosi	infundibulum	inifnjnbulema
inflect	inifojnko	infuriate	inifunraiyo
inflection	inifojnkosi	infuscate	inifunsekoyo
inflexed	inifojnside	infuse	inifunsi
inflexible	inifojnsibo	infuser	inifunsise
inflict	inifiunkn	infusible	inifusibo
inflight	inifologbe	infusion	inifunsoosi
inflorescence	inifonranseknsi	infusorian	inifunsoorain
inflow	inifonwa	.-ing1	gnni
influence	inifolusi	.-ing2	gnni
influent	inifoluto	in3	gnni
influential	inifolutojo	ingather	inigisirai
influenza	inifolusan	ingeminate	inignminiyo
influx	inifolusia	ingenerate	inignhunraiyo
infold	inifonjo	ingenious	inignnisi
inform	inifoonmo	ingénue	iniginlese
informal	inufoonmojo	ingenuity	iniginleto
nformality	inufoonmoleto	ingenuous	iniginlesi
informant	inifoonmote	ingest	inignsetn
information	inifoonmoyoon	ingesta	inignsetn
informative	inifoonmoyowin	ingle	inignron
informed	inifoonmode	inglorious	inigoraisi

312

WORD (x)	EQUIVALENT (y)	WORD (x)	EQUIVALENT (y)
ingoing	inilognni	inhesion	inihesoon
ingot	inigitn	inhibit	inihigbeyo
ingraft	iniganfia	inhibition	inihigbeyoon
ingrain	inigansn	inhibitor	inihigbeyoran
ingrate	inigante	inhomogeneous	inihimognhunsi
ingratiate	iniganteyo	inhospitable	inihinsiponlebo
ingratiatory	iniganteyorai	inhospitality	inihinsiponleto
ingratitude	inigantetujin	inhouse	inihinlese
ingravescent	iniganwoseknti	inhuman	inihumaye
ingredient	inigiraidieto	inhumane	inihumayin
ingress	inigiraiso	inhumanity	inihumayeto
ingressive	inigiraisowin	inhume	inihumi
ingroup	inigonpo	inigo	inigon
ingrown	inigonwn	inimical	inimikojo
ingrowth	inigonwasi	inimitable	inimutebo
inguinal	inigunhnjo	inini	inini
inguino	inigunhn	inion	iniso
ingulf	inigunjnfe	iniquity	inikuntn
ingurgitate	inigunregiteyo	initial	initejo
inhabit	inihagbesi	intialise	initejosi
inhabitant	inihagbesite	initiate	initeyo
inhalant	inihajnte	intiation	initeyoon
inhalation	inihajnyoon	initiative	initeyowin
inhalator	inihajnyoran	inject	inijnkn
inhale	inihajn	injection	inijnknyoon
inhaler	inihajnsi	injector	inijnknran
inharmonious	inuhanmenisi	injudicious	inijugbonkisi
inhaul	inihallo	injun	inijoni
inhere	iniheran	injunction	inijoknyoon
inherence	iniheransi	injure	inijuran
inherent	iniheranto	injurious	inijuraisi
inherit	iniheraite	injury	inijurai
inheritable	iniheraitebe	injustice	inijusesi
inheritance	iniheraitesi	ink	iniki

WORD (x)	EQUIVALENT (y)	WORD (x)	EQUIVALENT (y)
inkin	inikihn	innumerable	iniyunmuraibo
inkle	inikijn	innumerate	iniyunmuraiyo
inkling	inikijngnni	innutrition	iniyuntaraiyoon
inky	inikise	inoculate	inikileyo
inlace	inilekoi	inoculum	inikilema
inlaid	inilejo	inodorous	iniodirunsi
inland	iniledain	inoperative	iniopnranyowin
in-law	ini-leewo	inosculate	iniosekunleyo
inlet	inijntn	inositol	iniosetojin
inlay	inileyn	inotropism	iniotnrapnmosi
inlier	inilerai	inoxidize	inosinjnse
inloco	inilokn	in-patient	ini-patetan
inly	inilo	in put	ini puto
inmate	inimote	inquest	inikunyo
inmemoriam	inimumoraisi	inquiline	inikunlehun
inmigrant	inimogunraite	inquire	inikunran
inn	inni	inquiry	inikunrai
innards	innigbasi	inquisition	inikunsiyoon
innate	innite	inquisitive	inikunsiyowin
inner	innirai	inquisitor	inikunsiyoran
innervate	inniraiweyo	inquisitiorial	inikunsiyoraijo
innerve	inniraiwin	in re	ini re
inness	innisi	in road	ini ronjn
innings	innignnisi	insalivate	inisanjnweyo
innocence	inniknsi	insalubrious	inisanjnbansi
innocent	inniknti	insane	inisanunti
innocuous	innikunsi	insanitary	inisanuntorai
innominate	innimohunyo	insanity	inisanunto
innomine	innimohun	insatiable	inisantinbo
innovate	inniweyo	inscribe	inisukorai
innovation	inniweyoon	insect	iniseknte
innoxious	inniswa	insectivorous	inisekntewnrunsi
innuendo	ininide	insecure	inisekunra
innuit	iniyato	inselberg	inisejnbegan

WORD (x)	EQUIVALENT (y)	WORD (x)	EQUIVALENT (y)
inseminate	iniseminiyo	insomnious	inisoonmnusi
insensate	inisesnsnyo	insonate	inisoseyo
insensible	inisesnsnbo	insouciance	inisoosiasi
insensitive	inisesnsnyowin	insouciant	inisoosiate
insentient	inisesitato	inspan	inisepan
inseparable	inisepnrabo	inspect	inisepnto
insert	iniserai	inspector	inisepntoran
insertion	iniseraiyoon	inspiration	iniseporaiyoon
insessorial	inisesooraijo	inspire	iniseporai
inset	inisetn	inspirit	inisepoora
inshore	inisuinran	inspissate	iniseposooyo
inside	inisoojo	instability	inisetnboleto
insidious	inisoojosi	install	inisetnran
insight	inisogbe	installant	inisetnrante
insignia	inisoogansi	installment	inisetnranmutto
nsignificant	inisooganfikote	installation	inisetnranyoon
insinuate	inisoteyo	nstalment	inisetnramutto
insinuation	inisoteyoon	instance	inisetnsi
insipience	inisoopnsi	instant	inisetnte
insist	inisoosi	instantaneous	inisetntehunsi
insistent	inisoosito	instanter	inisetntesi
in situ	ini sootn	instantiate	inisetnteyo
insnare	inisiarai	instantly	inisetntelo
insobriety	inisoobnraitn	instar	inisetan
insofar	ini soo fan	instate	inisetnyo
insolate	inisinleyo	nstatuquo	inisetntunkue
insolation	inisinleyoon	instauration	inisetnraiyoon
insole	inisinle	instead	inisitngba
insolent	inisinleto	instep	inisitnpi
insoluble	inisinlebo	instigate	inisetingiyo
insolvable	inisinlewnbo	instil	inisetiele
insolvent	inisinlewinta	instill	inisetielle
insomenia	inisoonmnu	instinct	inisetinkyo
insomniac	inisoonmnuko	instinctive	inisetinkyowin

WORD (x)	EQUIVALENT (y)	WORD (x)	EQUIVALENT (y)
institute	inisetintuyo	intarsia	initesia
institution	inisetintuyoon	integer	initognra
institutional	inisetintuyoonjo	integral	initoganjo
institutionalize	inisetintuyoonjose	integrand	initoganjn
institutive	inisetintuyowin	integrant	initogante
instruct	inisetnranko	integrate	initoganyo
instruction	inisetnrankoyoon	integration	initoganyoon
instrument	inisetnranmutto	integrator	initoganran
instrumental	inisetnramuttojo	integrity	initogantn
nstrumentalist	inisetnramuttojosi	integument	initogbnmutto
instrumentality	inisetnramuttojotn	intellect	initojjnkn
insubstantial	inisnbesetntejo	intellenctual	initojjnknjo
insufficient	inisnfiknto	intelligence	initojjngnsi
insuffiate	inisnfiayo	intelligent	initojjngntan
insula	inisnle	intelligentsia	initojjngntansia
insular	inisnleran	intelligible	initojjngnbo
insulate	inisnleyo	intelsat	initojnsantn
insulation	inisnleyoon	intemerate	initomuraiyo
insulator	inisnleyoran	intemperate	initompnrayo
insulin	inisnlesi	intend	initinjo
insult	inisnjia	intended	initinjode
insuperable	inisupnrabo	intense	initinse
insupportable	inisupintabo	intensifier	initinsefesi
insurance	inisuraisi	intensify	initinsefe
insure	inisurai	intensity	initinseto
insured	inisuraide	intensive	initinsewin
insurer	inisuraisi	intent	initinyo
insuragence	inisuralesi	intention	initinyoon
insurgent	inisuraleto	intentional	initinyoonjo
insusceptible	inisusiknpntibo	inter-	initnra
intact	initnkan	interact	initnraknti
intaglio	initngiun	interactive	initnrakntiwin
intake	initekn	inter alia	initnra ajoni
intangible	initegnbo	intercede	initnraknjin

WORD (x)	EQUIVALENT (y)	WORD (x)	EQUIVALENT (y)
intercept	initnraknpo	interfuse	initnrafunsi
interceptor	initnraknporan	interglacial	initnragansejo
intercession	initnraknsoon	intergrade	initnragandie
interchange	initnrkhogini	interim	initnramo
interchangeable	initnrakhoginibe	interior	initnraran
inter-city	initnrakitn	interiorize	initnraranse
interclavicle	initnrakanwokuo	interjacent	initnrajaknti
intercolumniation	initnrakijomoyoon	interject	initnrajnkn
intercom	initnrakia	interjection	initnrajnknyoon
intercommunicate	initnrakimmuhunkoyo	interlace	initnralekoi
intercommunion	initnrakimmuhunsi	interlard	initnralejnra
intercontinental	initnrakintihuntojo	interlay	initnraleyn
intercostal	initnrakisitajo	interleave	initnrajnwini
intercourse	initnrkiraise	interline	initnralehun
intercrop	initnrakonpo	interlinear	initnralehunran
intercross	initnrakonso	interlingua	initnraikogun
intercut	initnrakunte	interlink	initnraliko
interdental	initnradatojo	interlock	initnrlokn
interdict	initnradikn	interlocution	initnralokunyoon
interdiction	initnradiknyoon	interlocutor	initnralokunran
interdigitate	initnradigitoyo	interloper	initnralopnra
interdisciplinary	initnradisikipanrai	interlude	initnralujin
interest	initnrasi	interlunation	initnralujnyoon
interesting	initnrasigini	intermarry	initnramurrai
interface	inifnrafansi	intermediary	initnramujirai
interfere	inifnrafiro	intermediate	initnramujiyo
interference	inifnrafirosi	interment	initnramutto
interferometer	initnrafiromuto	intermezzo	initnramuseni
interferon	initnrafiroin	interminable	initnramibo
interfertile	initnrafnraite	intermission	initnramusinse
interfile	initnrafijan	intermit	initnramutn
interflow	initnrafonwa	intermittent	initnramutnto
interfluent	initnrafoluto	intern	initnran
interfluve	initnrafoluwin	internal	initnranjo

WORD (x)	EQUIVALENT (y)	WORD (x)	EQUIVALENT (y)
internalise	initnranjose	interrelate	initnrrejoyo
international	initnraheyoonjo	interrex	initnrresn
internationale	initnraheyoonjn	interrogate	initnrrogiyo
internationalism	initnraheyoonjomosi	interrogative	initnrrogiyowin
internationalist	initnraheyoonjosi	interrogatories	initnrrogiyoransi
internationalize	initnraheyoonjose	interrupt	initnrranpi
interne	initnrain	interrupter	initnrranpisi
internecine	initnrainkisun	intersect	initnraseknte
internee	initnranse	intersection	initnraseknteyoon
internet	initnrante	intersex	initnrasesia
internist	initnransi	intersperse	initnrasepnrasi
internment	initnranmutto	interstadial	initnrasetngbajo
internode	initnrande	interstate	initnrasetnyo
internos	initnrasoo	interstice	initnrasetinsi
internship	initnransunpn	interstitial	initnrasetintejo
internuncial	initnranknjo	interstratify	initnrasetnrefe
internuncio	initnrankio	intertidal	initnratijinjo
interoceptor	initnrakiporan	intertrigo	initnrataraigon
interosculate	initnrasekunleyo	intertwine	initnratwehun
interpellant	initnrapnllote	interval	initnrawajo
interpellate	initnrapnlloyo	intervene	initnrawini
interpenetrate	initnrapnyuntnraiyo	intervention	initnrawinyoon
interpersonal	initnrapnrasinjo	interventionist	initnrawinyoonsi
interphone	initnraphohun	intervertebral	initnrawintobajo
nterplay	initnrapansie	interview	initnrawowin
interplead	initnrapojngba	intervocalic	initnrawnkojnko
interpol	initnrapinjn	interweave	initnrawinwe
interpolate	initnrapinjnyo	interstate	initnrasiyo
interpolation	initnrapinjnyoon	intestine	initnsihun
interpose	initnrapinsi	intima	initima
interpret	initnrapesito	intimacy	initimasn
interpretive	initnrapesitowin	intimate1	initimayo
interradial	initnrrangbajo	intimate2	initimayo
interregnum	initnrregnma	intimidate	initimujiyo

WORD (x)	EQUIVALENT (y)	WORD (x)	EQUIVALENT (y)
intinction	initinknyoon	introgression	initnragiraisoon
intine	initini	introit	initnrato
intitule	inititoron	introject	initnrajnkn
into	inito	introjection	initnrajnknyoon
intolerable	initojnrabo	intromission	initnramusinse
intolerant	initojnrate	intromit	initnramutn
intonation	initoniyoon	introrse	initnranse
intone	initoni	introvert	initnrawinto
intorsion	initorasoon	intrude	initnranjin
in toto	ini toto	intrusion	initnransoon
intoxicant	initoosikote	intrusive	initnransowin
intoxicate	initoosikoyo	intrust	initnranse
intra-	initnre	intubate	initubeyo
intracardiac	initnrekogbakn	intuit	inituti
intracellular	initnreknjjnran	intuition	initutiyoon
intractable	initnrekobo	intuitive	initutiwin
intracutaneous	initnrekuntelusi	intuitivism	initutiwinmosi
intradermal	initnrejnrama	intumesce	initumosesi
intrados	initnredesi	intumescence	initumoseknsi
intransigent	initnresunginte	intussuscept	initusoosiknpiti
intransitive	initnrasunyowin	intwine	initwehun
intrauterine	initnreutnrain	inuct	inknyo
intravasation	initnrewaseyoon	inuction	iniknyoon
intravenous	initnrewinsasi	inundant	iniunjntn
intray	initnreya	inundate	iniunjnyo
intrepid	initasipnjo	inuk	iniunkn
intricate	initaraikoyo	inulin	iniunjan
intrigant	initaraigantn	inure	iniunrai
intrigue	initaraigan	inurn	iniunran
intrinsic	initaraiseko	inutile	iniuntiron
intro-	initnra	invacuo	iniwakuo
introduce	initnradikn	invade	iniwajin
introduction	initnradikitiyoon	invasion	iniwasoon
introductory	initnradikitirai	invaginate	iniwaganyo

WORD (x)	EQUIVALENT (y)	WORD (x)	EQUIVALENT (y)
invalid1	iniwajngbe	invigorate	iniwogonraiyo
invalid2	iniwajngbe	invincible	iniwoknbo
invalidate	iniwajngbeyo	inviolable	iniwokojnbo
invalidism	iniwajngbemosi	inviolate	iniwokojnyo
invaluable	iniwajoinbo	inivisible	iniwosaibe
invar	iniwarai	invitation	iniwoteyoon
invariable	iniwaraibo	invite	iniwote
invariant	iniwaraite	inviting	iniwotegnni
invasion	iniwasoon	in vitro	ini wotnra
invasive	iniwasoowin	in vi vo	ini wo wn
invective	iniwinkntiwin	invocation	iniwnkoyoon
inveigh	iniwingan	invoice	iniwnniso
inveigle	iniwingiron	invoke	iniwnko
invent	iniwinti	involucel	iniwnjnknjn
invention	iniwintiyoon	involucre	iniwnjnknra
inventive	iniwintiwin	involuntary	iniwnjnterai
inventory	iniwintirai	involute	iniwnjnwe
inveracity	iniwinrankito	involution	iniwnjnyoon
inverse	iniwinso	involve	iniwnjnwa
inversion	iniwinsoon	invulnerable	iniweleranbo
invert	iniwinte	invultuation	iniweletnyoon
invertebrate	iniwinteberaiyo	inward	iniwegba
invest	iniwnsn	inwardly	iniwegbalo
investigate	iniwnsngiyo	inwards	iniwegbasi
investigation	iniwnsngiyoon	inweave	iniwinwe
investitive	iniwnsntowin	inwrap	iniwapan
investiture	iniwnsntoran	inwrought	iniwongbe
investment	iniwnsnmutto	io	iko
investor	iniwnsnran	ioannina	ikoinnihun
inveteracy	iniwntiraisn	iodate	ikodeyo
inveterate	iniwntiraiyo	iodic	ikodako
inviable	iniwobo	iodide	ikodaji
invidious	iniwojowu	iodine	ikodain
invigilate	iniwogbileyo	iodize	ikodase

WORD (x)	EQUIVALENT (y)	WORD (x)	EQUIVALENT (y)
iodo	ikode	iraqi	iraiki
iodoform	ikodefoon	irate	iraiyo
iodometry	ikodemutorai	irascible	iraisekibo
iodous	ikodesi	iratamente	iraitamutto
iolcus	ikojnkn	ire	irau
iomoth	ikomosi	ireland	irauledain
ion	ikoin	irene	irauni
iona	ikoini	irenic	irauniko
ionia	ikoini	iridaceous	iraijnsuwa
ionian	ikoinhn	iridectomy	iraijintemo
ionic	ikoinko	iridescent	iraijinseknti
ionium	ikoinma	iridic	iraijnko
ionization	ikoinseyoon	iridium	iraijnma
ionize	ikoinse	irido	iraide
ionizer	ikoinsesi	iridoplegia	iraidepojngan
ionogenic	ikoinginko	iridosmine	iraidesimini
ionone	ikoinhun	iridotomy	iraidetemo
ionopause	ikoinpanlese	iris	iraiso
ionosphere	ikoinsephirai	irisdiaphragm	iraisojinaphiragon
iontophoresis	ikointophiranso	irish	iraisoo
iota	ikote	irishry	iraisoora
iou	ikown	iritis	iraiso
iowa	ikowa	irk	iriko
ipecacuanha	ipnkokunhan	irksome	irikosoomo
iphigenia	ipheginsi	irkutsk	irikunsi
ipomoea	ipnmoni	iron	irin
ipsissimaverba	ipnsosoomawinbe	iron age	agba irin
ipso facto	ipnso fanto	ironclad	irinkandi
ipso jure	ipnso joran	iron cross	konso irin
iquique	ikunkuo	irone	irinni
iracund	iraikunjn	ironic	irinsiko
iran	iraini	ironing	iringnni
iranian	irainihn	ironing-board	bugba-iringnni
iraq	iraiko	ironmonger	irinmenignra

WORD (x)	EQUIVALENT (y)	WORD (x)	EQUIVALENT (y)
irony	irinsi	irretention	irretinyoon
irony	irinsi	irretraceable	irretnreknbo
iroquoian	irikunhn	irretrievable	irretaraiwinbo
iroquois	irikunsi	irreverence	irrewnsinsi
irradiant	irranjinatn	irreversible	irrewinsobo
irradiance	irranjinasi	irrevocable	irrewnkobo
irradiate	irrranjinayo	irrigate	irraigiyo
irradiation	irranjinayoon	irriguous	irraigunsi
irrational	irrayoonjo	irritable	irraitebo
irrationality	irrayoonleto	irritant	irraitetn
irrawaddy	irrawagbn	irritate	irraiteyo
irreclaimable	irrekanlemubo	irrupt	irranpn
irreconcilable	irrekinkunbo	irtish	iratusi
irrecoverable	irrekiwnrabo	irving	irawognni
irrecusable	irrekunsebo	is	ise ni ire re
irredenta	irredate	isaac	iseko
irredentist	irredatosi	isabella	isebejnran
irreducible	irrediknbo	isacoustic	isekisitako
irrefragable	irrefangibo	isagoge	isegngon
irrefragible	irrefangnbo	isagogic	isegngonko
irrefutable	irrefuntebo	isaiah	isehan
irregular	irregnjnra	isallobar	isejjoboosia
irregularity	irregnjnratn	isandrous	isejnrasi
irrelative	irrejoyowin	isanomal	isenimujn
irrelevant	irrejowintn	isantherous	isesinraisi
irrelievable	irrejowinibo	isantherous	isesinrasi
irreligious	irrejogbisinsi	isar	iserai
irremeable	irremubo	isatine	isetin
irremediable	irremudanbo	isauria	iserain
irremissibility	irremusinboleto	isba	isebo
irremoveable	irremowainbo	iscariot	isekosi
irreparable	irrepanrabo	ischaemia	isekhinmo
irreplaceable	irrepanknbo	ischia	isekhin
irrepressible	irrepesisobo	ischium	isekhima

WORD (x)	EQUIVALENT (y)	WORD (x)	EQUIVALENT (y)
,-ise	si/su/se	isocosm	isinkiseto
isentropic	isesitnrapnko	isocracy	isinkansn
isere	iseroin	isocrates	isinknranyo
iseult	isewajia	isocyanine	isinsnknhun
,-ish	si/sn/su	isocyclic	isinsnkuoko
isherwood	isurawinijo	isodef	isinjinfi
ishim	isumi	isodesmic	isinjinsemuko
ishmael	isumijn	isodiametric	isinjinamutoraiko
ishtar	isutnra	isodimorphism	isinjimophanmosi
isiac	isinko	isodose	isindese
isidore	isinderan	isoengenol	isinenginjin
isinglass	isingansan	isogamete	isingimuta
isis	isinse	isogamy	iingimo
island	isnledain	isogenous	isinginsi
islander	isnledainsi	isogeotherm	isingbilesinron
islay	isnleyin	isogonic	isingonko
isle	isnle	isogriv	isinganwa
islet	isnletn	isohel	isinhilo
ism	imosi	isohyet	isinhote
iso-	isin	isolate	isinleyo
isoagglutination	isingbiletinyoon	isolationism	isinleyoonmosi
isoagglutinin	isngbiletinsi	isolative	isinleyowin
isoantigen	isintngin	isolead	isinjngba
isobar	isinboosia	isolecithal	isinjngba
isobaric	isinboosiako	isolecithal	isinjnkisijo
isobath	isinbowe	isoleucine	isinjnkihun
isocandle	isinkoduoran	isolex	isinlesi
isochasm	isinkhisemo	isolog	isinlogbi
isocheim	isinkhnmo	isologous	isinlogonsi
isochors	isinkhira	isolux	isinlusua
isochore	isinkhiran	isomagnetic	isinmogbiteko
isochronal	isinkironjo	isomer	isinmura
isoclinal	isinkiunjo	isomerism	isinmuraimosi
isoclines	isinkiunsi	isomerous	isinmuraisi

WORD (x)	EQUIVALENT (y)	WORD (x)	EQUIVALENT (y)
isometric	isinmutoraiko	isothere	isinsinran
isometropia	isinmutnrapan	isotherm	isinsinron
isometry	isinmutorai	isotone	isintoni
isomorphism	isinmophanmosi	isotonic	isintoniko
isoneph	isinhunphn	isotope	isintopn
isoniazid	isinhnsejo	isotron	isintnran
isonomy	isinknmo	isotropic	isintnrapnko
isonzo	isinsan	israeli	isnraile
isopathy	isinpansio	israelite	isnraileyo
isophene	isinphini	issuable	isunsebe
isophone	isinphohun	issuant	isesunte
isophotic	isinphotinko	issue	isunse
isophylly	isinphewe	issus	isunsi
isopiestic	isinponsuko	.-ist	isi
isopleth	isinpojnsi	istic	isuko
isopod	isinpindie	isthmus	isosimowa
siopolity	isinpinjnto	istle	isetoron
isopor	isinpinra	it	ite, nit e to
isoprat	isinpante	it	ite
isoprene	isinpesihun	itabira	iteburan
isopropyl	isinponpnlo	itabirite	iteburaiyo
isopterous	isinpntiransi	itacolumite	itekijomuyo
isorhythmic	isinrhaimosiko	itaconic	itekinko
isosceles	isinseknjnsi	italian	itejnhn
isoseismal	isinsesunmujn	italianate	itejnhnyo
isoseimic	isinsesunmuko	italic	itejnko
isospory	isinsepinrai	italicize	itejnkose
isospondylous	isinsepinjnlosi	Italy	itejn
isostasy	isinsetnso	itch	itesi
isostemonous	isinsetomenisi	itchy	itesia
isostere	isinsitnran	.-ite	ito/yo
isosteric	isinsitnranko	item	itemo
isosterism	isinsitnranmosi	itemize	itemose
isotactics	isintekankosi	iterate	iteraiyo

WORD (x)	EQUIVALENT (y)	WORD (x)	EQUIVALENT (y)
ither	itesirai	jacana	jakahun
ithyphallic	itesinphanjjnko	jacinth	jakisin
.-itic	iko	jack	jakuo
,itinerant	itehunraitn	jackal	jakuojn
itinerary	itehunranrai	jackanapes	jakuohunpnsi
itinerate	itehunraiyo	jackaron	jakuorain
.-it is	iteso/so	jackass	jakuosoo
itol	itejin	jackdaw	jakuodawa
its	itesi	jacket	jakuote
itself	itesejo	jackplane	jakuopanyun
,-ity	ito itn tin	jackpot	jakuopinte
Ivan	iwain	jackson	jakuosin
ivanhoe	iwainhinse	jackstay	jakuosetnsi
ivanovo	iwainwn	jacquard	jakungba
ive	iwini	jacob	jakibe
ivory	iworai	jacobean	jakibehn
ivory tower	iworai toowaro	jacobin	jakiban
ivy	iwoin	jacobite	jakibeyo
ivy league	iwoin jngbiso	jaconet	jakiunte
ixia	isia	jacqueminot	jakunminte
ixion	iseun	jacquerie	jakunran
ixodiasis	isekojinso	jactation	jakitiyoon
izabal	isubeejn	jactitation	jakititoyoon
iznik	isukin	jacuzzi	jakunse
izard	isngbaa	jade1	jadie
ize	ise	jade2	jadie
izzard	isungba	jaded	jadiede
jab	jabe	jadoube	jadiunbe
jabber	jabesi	jaeger	jangnra
jabiru	jaburon	jael	jalo
jaborandi	jaburainjo	jag1	jagi
jabot	jabeto	jag2	jagi
jacaranda	jakarainde	jaga	jagin
jacamar	jakamura	jagged	jagide

WORD (x)	EQUIVALENT (y)	WORD (x)	EQUIVALENT (y)
jagger	jagisi	jangle	jangiron
jagery	jagirai	janiculum	jankunlema
jaghir	jaghirai	janitor	jantoran
jaguar	jagirain	janizary	janserai
jaguarundi	jagiraingbe	jansenism	jansemosi
jah	jahin	januar	januran
jahbulon	jahinbule	january	janurai
jahovah	jahinwa	janus	januso
jail	janjn	japaconitine	janpankitihun
jailer	janjnra	japan	janpan
jailor	janjnran	japanese	janpanse
jain	jain	jape	janpn
jainism	jainmosi	japonica	janponko
jakarta	jankata	japonism	janponmosi
jakes	janknsi	jar1	jaro
jalap	janlepa	jar2	jaro
jalapin	janlepan	jar3	jaro
jalopy	janlopn	jarabe	jarobe
jalousie	janlosunse	jarabub	jarobu
jam1	jam	jardinière	jarojnron
jam2	jam	jargon	jarogon
jamaica	jamakoi	jargonelle	jarogonlle
jamb	jambe	jargonize	jarogonse
jambalaya	jambeloyn	jarina	jarain
jambean	jambehun	jari	jarai
jamboree	jamberain	jarosite	jaronsooyo
james	jamse	jarp	jaropn
jamjar	jamjaro	jarrah	jarrohun
jammy	jammo	jarret	jarroto
jamshid	jamasujo	jarrow	jarrosi
janata	janto	jarvis	jarowaso
jan	janu	jarvey	jarowa
jane	jani	jasmine	jasimini
janet	janite	jason	jasin

WORD (x)	EQUIVALENT (y)	WORD (x)	EQUIVALENT (y)
jasp	jasipn	jefferson	jnfnrosin
jasper	jasepnra	jeffrey	jnfnroin
jaspidean	jasipnjoin	jehad	jnghangba
jass	jaso	jehovah	jnhoonwa
jat	jantn	jehovist	jnhoonwasi
jatropha	jantnraphn	jehu	jnhun
jaud	janundie	jejune	jnjuasi
jauk	janunkn	jejunum	jnjuama
jaunder	janunjnra	jekyll and hyde	hojin ati jnkoijo
jaundice	janunjnsi	jell	jnrro
jaunt	janunta	jellaba	jnrrobo
jaunting car	kosi januntagnni	jellify	jnrrofe
jaunty	jauntase	jello	jnrrosn
java	jawa	jelly	jnrrose
javanese	jawanse	jelutong	jnrotegn
javelin	jawinjn	jemadar	jnmojnra
jaw	jawi	jemima	jnmoma
jawbone	jawiboin	jimmy	jnmmo
jay	jasn	jena	jnna
jaycee	jasnsin	jennesais	jnhunsesi
jazerant	jasuraite	jenkins	jnhunkisi
jazz	jasun	jenner	jnhunran
jazzman	jasunmaye	jennet	jnhunte
jazzy	jasunsi	jenny	jnhunyun
jealous	jnjowu	jeopardize	jnpangbainse
jealousy	jnjowuse	jeopardy	jnpangbain
jean	jnyi	jephthah	jnpisin
jeans	jnyisi	jequirity	jnkunraitn
jebel	jnbelo	jerabmeel	jnramulo
jeddart	jnjnrate	jerboa	jnrabo
jeep	jnpn	jeremiad	jnradaro
jeepers	jnpnrasi	jeremiah	jnradarose
jeer	jnran	jericho	jnraikho
jeef	jnfn	jerid	jnrajo

WORD (x)	EQUIVALENT (y)	WORD (x)	EQUIVALENT (y)
jerk1	jnraka	jetty	jnttn
jerk2	jnraka	jeu	jnsie
jerkin	jnrakasi	jeudesprit	jnsie de panto
jerky	jnrakase	jeunesse doree	jnsiansoo derain
jeroboam	jnramogbe	jew	jnwa
jerom	jnramo	jewel	jnwan
jerry	jnrran	jeweler	jnwansi
jerrycan	jnrranko	jeweller	jnwannsi
jersey	jnrasua	jewellery	jnwannrai
jerusalem	jnrasnle	jewess	jnwabo
jervine	jnrawoin	jewish	jnwase
jervis	jnrawosi	jewry	jnwarai
jess	jnso	jezial	jnsialo
jessamine	jnsomini	jezebel	jnsegbain
jessant	jnsotn	jezreal	jnsegbile
jesse	jnsoo	jib1	jibn
jesselton	jnsoojian	jib2	jibo
jessica	jnsooako	jibba	jibbo
jessie	jnsooan	jibboom	jibboomo
jest	jnsie	jibe1	jibe
jester	jnsieran	jibe2	jibe
jesu	jesu	jibuti	jibute
jesuate	jesuyo	jicama	jikunmo
jesuati	jesuyon	jiff	jifn
jesuit	jesute	jiffy	jifnni
jesuitic	jesuteko	jig	jigbi
jesuitical	jesutekojo	jigger	jigbiran
jesuitism	jesutemosi	jiggered	jigbirande
jesuitry	jsuterai	jiggle	jigbiron
jesus	jnsnso	jigsaw	jigbisawn
jet1	jntu	jihad	jighangba
jet2	jntu	jill	jijore
jettison	jnttusin	jillet	jijorete
jetton	jnttusi	jillion	jijoresi

WORD (x)	EQUIVALENT (y)	WORD (x)	EQUIVALENT (y)
jilt	jijia	job	jogbe
jim	jimo	job	jose
jim cro	jimo knra	jobber	jogbesi
jim jam	jimo janma	jobbery	jogberai
jimmy	jimmo	jobbing	jogbegnni
jimp	jimpn	jock	joki
jimson	jimosin	jockey	jokise
jingal	jignjo	jocko	jokiko
jingle	jignron	jocose	jokwese
jinglet	jigntn	jocular	jokwejnra
jingo	jingbo	jocund	jokwejn
jingoism	jingbomosi	jocundity	jokwejntn
jingoist	jingbosi	jodhpur	jojnpnra
jink	jinkn	joel	josele
jinnee	jinhnni	joey	joseyin
jinni	jinhn	jog	jingn
jinny	jinyun	jogger	jingnra
jinriksha	jinraikasi	joggle	jingnron
jinrikisha	jinraikisi	jogtrot	jingntnran
jinx	jinso	john	john
jipijapa	jipijanpa	johnson	johnsin
jissom	jisoomo	johnsonese	johnsinse
jitney	jitnun	johnston	johnsetin
jitter	jittnra	join	josi
jitters	jittnrasi	joiner	josiran
jittery	jittnrai	joint	josita
jive	jiwin	jointure	jositaran
jizera	jiserai	joist	josian
joab	jogbi	joke	jokwe
joad	jogba	joker	jokwesi
joan	johun	jollify	jojofe
joannes	johunsi	jollity	jojoleto
joao	join	jollof	jojofn
joe	jose	jolly1	jojoran

WORD (x)	EQUIVALENT (y)	WORD (x)	EQUIVALENT (y)
jolly2	jojoran	jour	jinran
jolt	jojia	journal	jinranjo
jonah	johun	journalese	jinranjose
jonathan	johunsi	journalism	jinranjomosi
jones	johunse	journalist	jinranjosi
jonglery	johungnrai	journey	jinrainse
jongleur	johungnrain	journeyman	jinransemoye
jonquil	johunkunjo	joust	jonunsi
jonson	johunsin	jove	jojown
jook	jokoi	jovial	jojowa
joppa	jopan	joviality	jojowaleto
jordan	jorodan	jow	jowi
jornada	joronjn	jowl1	jowin
jorum	joromu	jowl2	jowin
joseph	josephin	joy	jinyo
josephien	josephini	joyance	jinyosi
josephite	josephinyo	joyous	jinyowa
josephus	josephinsi	joyride	jinyoraijin
josh	josua	juan	juhn
joshua	josuan	jube	jube
josiah	josign	jubilant	jubejnte
joskin	josikin	jubilate	jubejnyo
joss	josin	jubilation	jobejnyoon
jostle	josiaron	jubilee	jubejnse
jot	jote	judaic	jugbiko
jota	jota	judaism	jugbimosi
jotham	jotesimo	judies	jugbesi
jotter	jottesi	judas	jugbase
jotting	jottegnni	judder	jugbaran
jotun	jotusi	judge	jugbon
jotunheim	jotusihema	judgement	jugbonmutto
jouk	jonunko	judgemental	jugbonmuttojo
joule	jonunle	judicable	jugbonkobe
jounce	jonuns	judicative	jugbonkowin

WORD (x)	EQUIVALENT (y)	WORD (x)	EQUIVALENT (y)
judicatory	jugbonkorain	jump	jumpn
judicature	jugbonkoran	jumper1	jumpnsi
judicial	jugbonkojo	jumper2	jumpnsi
judiciary	jugbonkorai	jumpy	jumpnsi
judicious	jugbonkosi	jun.	juhn
judith	jugbnsi	junction	joknyoon
judo	jude	junction box	joknyoon bos
judoka	judeko	juncture	joknyorai
judy	judun	june	juhun
jug	jugba	jungian	juhungihn
jugal	jugbajn	jungle	jugbun
jugate	jugbayo	junior	juran
juggemaut	jugbaranto	juniper	jupnra
juggle	jugbaron	junk1	juakn
juggler	jugbaronsi	junk2	juakn
juggling	jugbarongnni	junker	juaknra
juglandaceous	jugbaledainsuwa	junket	juaknte
jugoslav	jugbasoolewa	junkie	juaknse
jugular	jugbajnra	junta	juata
jugulate	jugbaleyo	jupiter	juapiti
juice	jumise	jupon	juapon
juicy	jumisn	jura	juaran
jujitsu	jujnta	jural	juaranjn
ju-ju	juju	jurassic	juaransooko
jujube	jujube	jurat	juranto
juke box	juko bosi	jure	jura
jul.	julo	jurel	juralo
julep	julopn	juridical	juraigbonknjo
julian	julohn	jurisdiction	juraisegbonknyoon
julienne	julohun	jurisprudence	juraiseporajinsi
julius	julosi	jurist	juraisi
july	julo	juristic	juraisuko
jumble	jumberon	juror	juraran
jumbo	jumboo	jurua	jurain

WORD (x)	EQUIVALENT (y)	WORD (x)	EQUIVALENT (y)
juruena	jurainhun	k	k
jury	jurai	ka	kho
jus	jusi	kabalega	kholega
juscanonicum	jusikoyelekuo	kabbala	kholebo
jusgentium	jusigintema	kabob	khobnbe
jossanguinis	jusoogunwinsi	kabuki	khobeki
jussive	jusoowin	kabul	khobejn
jussoli	jusoonjn	kabyle	khobnron
just	juse	kachina	khokhihn
justice	jusesi	kadara	khojnra
justiciable	jusesiberon	kaffir	khorofo
justiciary	jusesirai	kaffiyeh	khoifon
justifiable	jusefiberon	kafir	kofirai
justification	jusefikoyoon	kafka	khofiki
justifier	jusefisi	Kafkaesque	khofikihun
justify	jusefe	kaftan	khofian
jistin	jusetin	kagera	khognrai
justina	jusehn	kago	khogbi
justitia	jusetan	kagu	khogun
justness	jusenisi	kaiak	khoiko
justus	jusesi	kain	khoite
jut	jutu	kainite	khoiteyo
jute	jute	kainogenesis	khoitegnhunso
jutty	jututn	kaka	khoko
juvenal	jowinisi	kakapo	khokopin
juvenescent	jowinseknti	kakemono	khoknmohn
juvenile	jowiniron	kaki	khoki
juvenilia	jowinijan	kalamata	khojomuto
juvenility	jowinileto	kalashnikov	khojosunkin
juvenitia	jowinitan	kalazar	khojoseran
jusxta	joseto	kalahari	khojoharai
juxtapose	josetopinsi	kalamazoo	khojomusoo
juxtaposition	josetopinsiyoon	kalamkari	khojomkorai
jyland	jinledain	kale	khojo

WORD (x)	EQUIVALENT (y)	WORD (x)	EQUIVALENT (y)
kaleidoscope	khojoraisokipon	kapok	khopinki
kalends	khojojn	kappa	khopa
kalevala	khojowajn	kaput	khopati
kaleyard	khojoyandan	kara	khoran
kali	kholo	karabiner	khoranbahunsi
kolian	kholohn	karachi	khoranki
kalif	kholofa	karaite	khoraite
kalium	kholoma	karakul	khorankun
kalmia	kholomini	karakum	khorankuo
kalong	khologun	karaoke	khoranke
kalpa	kholopan	karat	khorante
kalsomine	kholosoomini	karate	khoranta
kalyptra	kholopotnra	karma	khoramo
kama	khomi	karnataka	khorantaka
kamala	khomijn	karnatak	khorantaku
kame	khomin	kaross	khorasoo
kami	khomi	karroo	khorara
kamikaze	khomikuse	karri	khorarai
kana	khoihe	karst	khorasi
kanaka	khoiheka	kart	khoratn
kanara	khoiheran	karyo	khoroin
kanarese	khoiheranse	karyogamy	khoroingimo
kanga	khoigan	karyolysis	khoroinjinso
kangaroo	khoiganrin	karyosome	khoroinsoomo
kantar	khoitnra	karyotin	khorointie
kanoon	khoihihun	karyotype	khorointnpon
kanpur	khoinpnrai	kasha	khosua
kansas	khoisnsn	kasher	khosuran
kantianism	khoitnhnmosi	kashruth	khosuraisi
kaolinag	kholefungn	kat	khote
kaolin	kholefun	katabasis	khotabosnso
kaolinite	kholefunyo	katabatic	khotabosnko
kapelimetster	khopnlomuseto	katabolism	khotabujinmosi
kapenaar	khopnran	katakana	khotakohe

WORD (x)	EQUIVALENT (y)	WORD (x)	EQUIVALENT (y)
katarina	khotarain	keep	knpon
katharsis	khosiranso	keeper	knponsi
katydid	khotndijo	keeping	knpongnni
katzenjammer	khosunjanmusi	keeve	knwini
kauri	khorai	kef	knfa
kava	khowa	keffiheh	knfihn
kavass	khowaso	kefir	knfiran
kawi	khowi	keg	kngbi
kay	khoha	kegler	kngbiran
kayak	khohaka	keister	knseto
kayles	khohasi	keitloa	kntejoin
kayo	khoyo	kekule	knkunron
kazakh	khosaka	kellar	knlleran
kazoo	khosiun	keller	knllerai
kea	knso	kelodi	knlejo
keamy	knrain	kelp	knlepo
keat	knta	kelpie	knlepan
kebab	knbu	kelson	knlesin
kebble	knbojn	kelt	knjia
kebbor	knboran	kilter	knjiasi
keck	knkobi	kelvin	knlewin
keckle	knkojn	kemal	knmujo
kedar	knjara	Kemble	knmberon
keddah	knjaha	kempt	knmpiti
kedge	knjngn	ken	knhn
kedgeree	knjngnra	kench	knkho
kedron	knjnran	kendal	kndanjo
keek	knkn	kendo	knhnde
keel	knllo	kenedy	knhunde
keelage	knllogun	kennel	knhnlo
keeley	knlloun	Kenneth	knhunsi
keelson	knllosin	kenning	knhungnni
keen1	knse	kenny	knhunse
keen2	knse	keno	knhn

WORD (x)	EQUIVALENT (y)	WORD (x)	EQUIVALENT (y)
kenogenesis	knhngnhunso	kem	knran
kenosis	knhnso	kernel	knranjn
kenotic	knhnko	kernite	knranyo
kenotron	kntiran	kerosene	knrasun
Kensington	knsoogntin	kerr	knrra
kenspeckle	knsepnkuo	Kerry	knrrai
kent	knot	kersey	knraso
kentish	kntosi	kerub	knrabo
kentledge	kntojngbon	kestrel	knserai
kentuchy	kntokhun	ketamine	kntemini
kep	knpn	ketch	kntikho
kepi	knpnn	ketchup	kntikhunpn
kepler	knpejnra	ketene	kntihun
kept	knponu	keto	knto
ker	knra	ketoenoltautomerisn	kntoenjintetomuramoss
kerala	knrajn	ketoform	kntofoon
keramics	knramukosi	ketone	kntohun
keratin	knratie	ketosis	kntoso
keratinize	knratiese	ketoxime	kntosinmi
keratitis	knratieso	kettering	knttiragnni
kerato	knrato	kettle	knttiron
keratogenous	knratoginsi	keuka	knkun
keratoid	knratojo	kevel	knwinlo
keratol	knratojin	kew	knwa
keratose	knratose	kew pie	knwa pon
keratosis	knratieso	kex	knsn
kerb	knrabe	key1	knsi
kerchief	knrakhifin	key2	knsi
kerching	knrakhignni	keyboard	bugbaknsi
kerf	knrafe	keyhole	knsihinlu
kerfuffle	knrafefijn	keynesian	knsisinhn
kerkyra	knrakoiran	keyway	knsiwelo
kerman	knramoye	khaddar	khodira
kermes	knramosi	khaki	khodira

WORD (x)	EQUIVALENT (y)	WORD (x)	EQUIVALENT (y)
khaki	khoki	kiddle	kijoduo
khamsin	khomusun	kiddo	kijode
khan	khohn	Kiddush	kijosue
khanate	khohnyo	Kiddy	kijosi
khania	khohan	kidnap	kijopan
khnaty	khohnto	kidney	kijose
kharif	khirafe	kidult	kijoijia
khatanga	khotengba	kier	kirai
khazi	khosoo	kierkegaard	kiraikngigba
khedive	khnjnwo	kieselgurh	kiselogun
khenem	khnmun	kiserite	kiseraiyo
kherson	khnrasin	kiester	kiseto
khidmutgar	khijogira	kike	kikue
khiva	khiwa	kikuyu	kikunyo
khmer	khimurai	kilderkin	kijonjnra
khnum	khnma	kilim	kijanmo
khoisan	khoiso	Kilimanjaro	kijanmujnra
khond	khojn	kilkenny	kijnkinhn
khuskhus	khunsekhiwa	kill	kinjan
kiaat	kiayo	killerney	kijanrain
kiang	kiagan	killer	kijansi
kiaugh	kiagbun	kilijoy	jinyokijan
kibble	kibuje	killock	kijanko
kibitzer	kibatisi	kiln	kijona
kiblah	kibolu	kiln dry	kinjona gbe
kibotz	kibose	kilo	kilo
kibosh	kibosn	kilocycle	kilosnkuo
kick	kikon	kilograme	kiloganmo
kick back	kikon boki	kiloton	kilotin
kicker	kikonsi	kilt	kijia
kicky	kikonse	kilter	kijnto
kid1	kijo	kiltie	kijiase
kid2	kijo	kimberley	kimbesiroin
kiddie	kijodie	kimberlite	kimbesileyo

WORD (x)	EQUIVALENT (y)	WORD (x)	EQUIVALENT (y)
kimmer	kimmurai	kinkinic	kinkinko
kimono	kimolu	kinsman	kinsemaye
kin	kini	kioga	kiogbn
-kin	kinropo	kiosk	kioko
Kinabelu	kinibelu	kioto	kioto
kinaesthesia	kinisunwnsia	kiowan	kiowin
kinase	kinnise	kipper	kipnra
kincald	kinkojon	kirchhoff	kirakhinfo
kincardine	kinkogbain	kirghitz	kiragbnsi
kind	Kinjo	kiria	kiran
kindergarten	kinjoragiratn	kirigami	kiraigimo
kindergartner	kinjosegiratnsi	kirin	kirain
kinderspiel	kinjorasipo	kirk	kirasn
kindle	kinjoron	kirk caldy	kirasn kojoin
kindling	kinjorongnni	kirk-session	kirasn sesoon
kindly1	kinjose	kirkman	kirasnmoye
kindly2	kinjose	kirn	kiran
kindness	kinjonisi	kirov	kirawn
kindred	kinjorai	kirsch	kirasekhi
kinematics	kihunmukosi	kirten	kirasetin
kinephantom	kihunphitnmo	kirtle	kiratoron
kinesiatrics	kihunsiatnraikosi	kish	kisu
kinesimeter	kihunsimuto	kishke	kosukn
kinesthesia	kihunsunwnsia	kiska	kisuko
kinetic	kihunko	kismet	kisomu
kinetics	kihunkosi	kiss	kiso
king	kinga	kissagram	kisooganmo
kingdom	kingademo	kisser	kisosi
kinglet	kingatn	kissogram	kisoganmo
kingpin	kingapoha	kist	kisi
Kingston	kingasitin	kit	kiti
kinin	kinhn	kitchen	kitikhin
kink	kinko	kitchenette	kitikhintn
kinky	kinkoin	kite	kite

WORD (x)	EQUIVALENT (y)	WORD (x)	EQUIVALENT (y)
kitemark	kitemurokn	knack	knkho
kitenge	kitegini	knacker	knkhosi
kith	kitisi	knag	kngi
kithe	kitisi	knaggy	kngisi
kitsch	kitisesi	knap	knpn
kittel	kittijo	knar	knran
kitten	kittin	knave	knwnni
kittenish	kittinse	knavery	knwnrai
kittiwake	kittiwekn	knavish	knwnse
kittle	kittiron	knead	kngbo
kittool	kittoojo	knee	knse
kitty1	kitito	kneel	knlo
kitty2	kitito	knell	knjiro
kiva	kiwa	kneller	knjirosi
kiver	kiwnra	knelt	knsejia
kivu	kiwe	knesset	knsoote
kiwi	kiwn	knew	knmo
kizil	kisun	knibblack	knbebakki
klamath	kanmosi	knickers	knkisi
klaxon	kanhusi	knife	knfe
klebs	kijibe	knight	kngba
kleenex	kijinsn	knight head	kngba hegbi
klein	kijihn	knish	knsun
Kleist	kijisi	knit	knta
kleagle	kijignron	knitting	kntagnni
klepht	kijiphe	knives	knwesi
kleptomania	kijipntimohan	knob	knboo
kleg	kijigon	knobbly	knbolo
klingsor	kijigonsiran	knock	knkon
klondike	kolujonko	knock-down	knkon juan
kloof	kolufn	knock out	knkon nita
kluane	koluhun	knocker	knkonsi
dludge	kolugbn	knoll	knlle
klystron	kolotnran	knot1	knta

WORD (x)	EQUIVALENT (y)	WORD (x)	EQUIVALENT (y)
knot2	knta	kohoutek	kohitako
knotty	kntasi	koine	koihun
know	knmo	kokanee	kokoyin
know-how	knmo-hinwo	kokobeh	kokinbe
knowing	knmognni	kokomo	kokinmo
knowingly	knmognnilo	kola	kole
knowledge	knmojngbon	kolinsky	kojinsuko
knowledgeable	knmojngbonberon	kolkhoz	kolekhunsi
known	knmosi	kol ni dre	kolegbain
knox	knso	kolo	kojoin
knubbly	knbujo	Kolyma	kojinmo
knuckle	knkiron	komatik	komutnka
knurl	knrejo	komodo	komude
knut	kntan	koodoo	koondein
k		kondo	koonde
k o	kunkon sita	kongo	koongon
koa	koo	kook	kokoi
koala	koojn	kookaburra	kokoiburara
koan	koohn	kooky	kokoin
kob	koba	kooteney	koontin
kobe	kobe	kop	kopin
kobold	kobojon	kopek	kopinka
kocher	kokhnsi	koph	kophn
kochi	kochi	kopje	kopinjn
Kodak	kojnki	koppie	kopan
kodiak	kojnkin	kor	korai
koel	kose	koran	Koran
kofta	kofia	korea	korain
kofta gar	kofia gan	Korean	korainhn
koheleth	kohejnsi	koritsa	koraitosi
kohinoor	kohirain	korma	koraimo
kohl	kohijn	kornelis	koranlose
kohler	kohijnra	koruna	koraina
kohlrabi	kohijnrabe	kos	kosu

WORD (x)	EQUIVALENT (y)	WORD (x)	EQUIVALENT (y)
kosher	kosua	krieg	knrangn
kosice	kososi	kriegspiel	knrangnsepo
kossovo	kosoown	krill	knraijjn
kossuth	kosoosi	krimmer	knraimmosi
kostroma	kositnramo	krio	knrain
kotabaru	koteboosi	kris	knraisi
kotka	kotaka	krishna	knraisuan
koto	koto	kriss kringle	knraiso knraignron
kotor	kotiran	krk	knrako
koulibiaca	kobaunjnka	kromesky	knramuseknu
kousso	kosoowa	krona	knrana
kowhai	kownhan	krone	knrahun
kowtow	kownwa	kronos	knrasin
kra	knra	kronstadt	knransetnjo
kraal	knrajo	kroon	knrain
kraepelin	knranpnjan	kropotkin	knrapintekin
kraft	knrafia	krubi	knrabe
krag	knragi	kruger	knragnra
krait	knratu	krugerrand	knragnrranjn
krakatoa	knrakoto	krummhorn	knrammhuron
kraken	knrakin	krupp	knrapo
Krakow	knrakun	kryolite	knraileyo
krameria	knramuran	krypton	knraipntin
krans	knrase	ku	kun
krasnodar	knrasejnra	kuala	kunjn
k ration	kn raiyoon	kuan yin	kunhn yin
kraut	knrate	kuban	kunbaun
krebbiel	knranboojn	kuchen	kunkhin
krebs	knranbe	kudos	kundesi
Kreisler	knransejnra	kudus	kunjosi
kreister	knranseto	kudzu	kunjnsun
kremlin	knranmojan	kufic	kunfiko
kreutzer	knrantosi	kufle	kunfijn
kreuzer	knransesi	kufra	kunfan

WORD (x)	EQUIVALENT (y)	WORD (x)	EQUIVALENT (y)
kukenaam	kunknmo	Kyoto	koiknto
ku klux klan	kun kolusi	kyphoscoliosis	koiphisekijinso
kukri	kunknrai	kyphosis	koiphiso
kula	kunjn	kyrieeleison	koiraijnsin
kulak	kunjnke	l	l li
kultur	kunjiaran	la	le la
kumiss	kunmusin	laager	legunran
kummel	kunmoin	lab	lebe
kumquat	kunmkunte	labarum	leberon
kundry	kunjorai	lab danum	lebedan
kung fu	kunpa fun	labefantion	lebefanyoon
kunzite	kunseyo	label	lebejn
kura	kunra	labellum	lebejjnma
kurd	kunrajo	labial	lebejo
Kurdish	kunrajose	labialize	lebejose
kuria	kunran	labia	lebesi
kurile	kunraijn	labia majora	lebesi mojinra
kursaal	kunrasujo	labia minora	lebesi miniran
kurtosis	kunrateso	labiates	lebeyo
kvass	kunwaso	labiche	lebekhn
kuvaaz	kunwase	labile	lebajn
Kuwait	kunwate	labio	lebekn
kuznetsk	kunsntosi	labio dental	lebekn jinhatojo
kvaaz	kwesia	labio velar	lebekn winjnra
kwashiorkor	kwesuknra	labium	lebema
ky	koi	lab lab	legbn lebe
kyanite	koihunyo	labor	legbnrai
kyanize	koihunse	laboratory	legbnraitosi
kye	knun	laborer	legbnraise
kyle	koijn	laborious	legbnrisi
kylix	koijnsi	labour	legbnran
kyloe	koilose	laborism	legbnraimosi
kymograph	koimiganpha	laborist	legbnraisi
kyoga	koikngbn	laborite	legbnraiyo

WORD (x)	EQUIVALENT (y)	WORD (x)	EQUIVALENT (y)
labor omnia	legbnran omuhn	lackaday	lakoidase
labrador	legbnsejnra	lackey	lekoin
labradorite	legbnsejnraiyo	lacking	lekoignni
labret	legbnseto	lackluster	lekoiluseto
labroid	legbnsujo	laconic	lekinko
labrum	legbesimo	laconism	lekinmosi
Labuan	legbuhun	lacquer	lekekunra
Laburnum	legburanma	lacrimal	lekomijejo
labyrinth	legbunraisi	lacrimal duct	lekomijejo dikiti
labyrinthine	legbunraisun	lacrimation	lekomijeyoon
labyrinthodont	legbunraidebuyo	lacrimtor	lekomijeyoran
lac	leke	lacrimatory	lekomijeyorai
laccadive	lekekojnwo	lacrosse	lekorasoon
laccate	lekekoyo	lactalbumin	leketejobumin
laccolith	lekekilisi	lactam	leketemo
lace	lekoi	lactary	leketerai
lacer	lekoisi	lactase	leketese
lacerant	leloisitn	lactate1	leketeyo
lacerate	lekoisiyo	lactate2	leketeyo
lacerta	lekoito	lactation	lekeyoon
lacertilian	lekoitajain	lacteal	leketejo
laches	lekhnsi	lactescent	leketeseknti
lachesis	lekhnso	lactic	leketeko
lachish	lekhisu	lactiferous	leketefirosi
lachryma	lekhoraimo	lacto	leketo
lachrymal	lekhoraimojn	lactobacillus	leketobokunsi
lachrymator	lekhoraimotnran	lactoflavin	leketofanwin
lachrymatory	lekhoraimotnrai	lactogenic	leketoginko
leachrymose	lekhoraimose	lactometer	leketomuto
lacing	lesognni	lactone	leketoni
lacinate	lesohunyo	lactoprotein	leketoponyoto
lack	lekoi	lactoscope	leketosokipon
lackadaisical	lekoidasekojo	lactose	leketose
lackadaisy	lekoidaso	lacuna	lekuosi

342

WORD (x)	EQUIVALENT (y)	WORD (x)	EQUIVALENT (y)
lacunar	lekuoran	lagena	legnhun
lacunose	lekuose	lager	legasi
lacustrine	lekunsirain	lager lout	legasi lonita
lacy	lesose	laggard	legagbaa
lad	ledie	lagging	legagnni
ladakh	ledikho	lagniappe	legnponsi
ladanum	ledima	lagomorphs	legonmophan
ladder	lediesi	lagophthalmia	legonphitimosi
ladder-back	lediesi boki	lagoon	legoon
laddism	lediemosi	lagos	legonsi
lade	ledi	lah	lehi
lading	ledaingnni	la hogue	le hingbi
laden	ledisi	lahore	lehinrai
ladette	ledietn	laic	laiki
ladida	lediejo	laicise	laikise
ladies	ledansi	laid	laijo
ladin	ledieso	laigh	laigba
ladino	lediekn	laika	laikun
ladle	leduo	lain	leisi
ladoga	ledigbi	lair	lerai
ladon	ledoin	laird	leraijo
ladrone	lediroin	laissez-faire	laisusi-fanroin
lady	ledan	laity	laito
lady day	ledan dase	lake1	lekun
laertes	leraitosi	lake2	lekun
laetare	lanitorai	laky	lekunse
laevo	leniwn	lala	lele
laevorotation	leniwnraitoyoon	lalang	lelegn
laevulose	leniwelese	lalia	lelolo
lag1	lega	laliatry	leloloterai
lag2	lega	lallans	lelolosi
lag3	lega	lallation	leloloyoon
lagan	legahun	lalo	lelolo
lagash	legase	laloneuresis	lelolohunraiso

WORD (x)	EQUIVALENT (y)	WORD (x)	EQUIVALENT (y)
lalopathology	lelolopanselogbon	lamina	lemahun
lalophobia	lelolophobua	laminate	lemahunyo
lam	lemlu	lamination	lemahunyoon
lama	lemsn	laminiferous	lemahunfirosi
lamaism	lemsnmosi	laminitis	lemahunso
lamancha	lemsnkho	lammas	lemmaso
lamanche	lemsnkhn	lammastide	lemmasojin
lamarck	lemaraki	lammergeier	lemmaraignran
lamarckism	lemarakimosi	lammy	lemma
lamasery	lemasera	lamp	lempon
lamb	lembe	lampas	lemponse
lambaste	lembesia	lampedusa	lemponjinsi
lambda	lembaso	lampern	lemponran
lambdacisms	lembasokimosi	lampion	lemponsi
lambdoid	lembasojo	lamplight	lemponleghe
lambent	lembeta	lampoon	lemponsn
lambert	lembeto	lamppost	lemponpinsi
lembeth	lembesi	lamprey	lempesise
lambkin	lembekin	lamprophyre	lemponphirain
lambrequin	lemberaikun	lamyik	lemuyika
lamdan	lemodan	lan	leko
lame	lema	lanai	lekosi
lame	lema	lanark	lekoknra
lamella	lemajnra	lanary	lekorai
lamellae	lamajnran	lanate	lekoyi
lamellar	lemajnransi	lancashire	lekosuran
lamelli	lemajnra	lancaster	lekoseto
lamelli rostral	lemajnra rontnrejo	lancastrian	lekosetorain
lamelloid	lemajnrajo	lance	lekosi
lamellose	lemajnranse	lancelet	lekokitn
lament	lemasun	lancelot	lekoknte
lamentable	lemasunbe	lanceolate	lekoknteyo
lamentation	lemasunyoon	lancer	lekokisi
lamia	lemasi	lancet	lekosesiti

WORD (x)	EQUIVALENT (y)	WORD (x)	EQUIVALENT (y)
lacinate	lekinyo	lanneret	lekorante
land	ledain	lanolin	lakojan
land-agent	aginte-ledain	lanose	lakose
landau	ledanun	lansdowne	lekosejuan
lande	ledainsa	lansquenet	lekosekunte
landed	ledainde	lant	lekoto
landing	leadaingnni	lantana	lekotohun
landler	ladainjnra	lantern	lekoton
landloper	ledainlopnra	lanthanide	lekotehunji
landlubber	ledainlubesi	lanthanum	lekotehunma
landscape	ledainsekopon	lanthopine	lekotepohun
land scrip	ledain seknrapo	lanuginous	lekoginsi
lane	lekosi	lanugo	lekogon
lang	lekogn	lanyard	lekoyandan
langley	lekognroin	lanzarote	lekoserate
langobardi	lekognbegbain	lao	leki
langshan	lekognsuhn	laocoon	lekikoon
langsyne	lekognsohun	laodicean	lekijnkoin
language	lekogngun	laos	lekisi
langue	lekognni	lap1	lepn
languet	lekognte	lap2	lepn
languid	lekognjo	lap3	lepn
languish	lekognse	laparo	lepnro
languor	lekognran	laparoscope	lepnrosekipon
languorous	lekognransi	laparotomy	lapnrotemo
langur	lekognrai	lapel	lepnlo
lanyard	lekoyandan	lapidary	lepnjnra
laniary	lekorai	lapidate	lepnjnyo
laniferous	lekofirosi	lapidify	lepnjnfe
lanital	lekotejo	lapillus	lepnjjnsi
lank	lekora	lapis	lepnsi
lankester	lakoraseto	lapislazuli	lepnsijnsulo
lanky	lekorasi	lapithae	lepnnise
lanner	lekoran	lapp	lepnpo

WORD (x)	EQUIVALENT (y)	WORD (x)	EQUIVALENT (y)
lapper	lepnsi	larnax	leransi
lappet	lepnti	larrigan	lerraigan
lapsation	lepnseyoon	larrikin	lerraikin
lapse	lepnse	larum	leranma
lapsi	lepnso	larva	lerawe
lapstrake	lepnsetnrako	larvate	leraweyo
lapsus	lepnsunsi	larvicide	lerawekeku
laputa	lepnti	larvipositor	leraweposeran
larache	lerakhn	laryngeal	leraisognjn
larboard	lerabugba	laryngaphone	leraisogiphohun
larcener	leraknran	laryngeal	leraisognjo
larceny	leraknse	laryngismus	leraisogimusesi
larch	lerakhi	laryngitis	leraisogiso
lard	lerajo	laryngo	leraisogin
lardacein	lerajosuhn	laryngology	leraisoginlogbon
lardaceous	lerajosuwa	laryngotomy	leraisogintemo
larder	lerajora	larynx	leraisosi
lardon	lerajosi	lasa	lesn
lardy	lerajose	lasagne	lesungini
large	leragan	lascar	lesunkosi
largesse	leraganbo	lascivious	lesiawosi
larghetto	leraighntto	lase	lese
larghissimo	leraghnsoomo	laser	leserai
largish	leraganse	lash	lesia
largo	leragn	lasher	lesiasi
lariat	leraite	lashings	lesiagnnisi
larine	lerain	lasket	lesiato
la rio ja	le rain jn	lass	lesua
larisa	leraise	lassle	lesuaran
larithmics	leraimosukosi	lassafever	fnwora lesue
lark1	lerako	lassen	lesuase
lark2	lerako	lassitude	lesuatujin
larky	lerakose	lasso	lesuakn
larn	leran	last1	lesn

WORD (x)	EQUIVALENT (y)	WORD (x)	EQUIVALENT (y)
last2	lesn	latin	letnso
last3	lesn	latinate	letnsoyun
lastex	lesnki	latinism	letnsomosi
lasting	lesngnni	latinist	letnsosi
lastly	lesnlo	latinity	letnsotn
lat	leto	Latinize	letnsose
latakia	letokosi	latino	letnsokn
latania	letohun	latish	letnse
latch	letokhi	latitude	letntujin
latchet	letokhiti	latitudinarian	letntujinraihn
latchkey	letokhiknsi	latium	letoma
late	leyo	latona	letohun
late	letn	latria	letnran
latecomer	letnkiawasi	latrine	letnrain
lateen	letnsi	latry	letnrai
lately	letnlo	latten	letntosi
latensification	letnsunfikoyoon	latter	letnto
latent	letnto	latterly	letntolo
later	letnra	lattice	letntoso
lateral	letnraijo	latus	letnsi
lateran	letnrain	latvia	letnwa
laterite	letnraiyo	latvian	letnwahn
lateritious	letnraiyosi	laud	leunro
latex	letnki	laudable	leunrobe
lath	letnsi	laudanine	leunronni
lathe	letnsun	laudanum	leunronma
lather	letnsiasi	laudation	leunroyoon
lathi	letnsin	laudatory	leunroyorai
lathy	letnsunse	lauder	leunrosi
lattices	letnkisi	laugh	leunrin
laticiferous	letnkifirosi	laughable	leunrinbe
laticlave	letnkanwo	laughing	leunringnni
latifoliate	letnfonjiayo	laughter	leunrinsi
latifundium	letnfunjnma	launch1	leunsi

WORD (x)	EQUIVALENT (y)	WORD (x)	EQUIVALENT (y)
launch2	leunsi	lawn2	lewini
launcher	leunsi	Lawrence	leeworansi
launder	leungbesi	lawrencium	leeworansima
laundering	leungbegnni	lawsone	leewosoohun
launderette	leungbetin	lawsuit	leewosnto
laundress	leungbebo	lawyer	leeworan
laundry	leungberai	lawyer	leeworan
launfal	leunfnjo	lax	lesn
laura	leunran	laxation	lesnyoon
lauraceous	leunransuwa	laxative	lesnyowin
laureate	leunrade	lay1	leyn
laurel	leunrai	lay2	leyn
laurence	leunransi	lay3	leyn
laurent	leunranto	lay4	leyn
laurentian	leunrantoni	layabout	abonuntaleyn
laurus	leunrasi	layer	leynsi
laurustien	leunrasetin	layette	leyntin
lava	lewe	layman	leynmoye
lavabo	lewebn	lay out	leyn nita
lavage	lewegun	lazar	lesuerun
lavalava	lewejnwe	lazaretto	lesueretto
lavaliere	leweorunrai	lazarist	lesueraisi
lavation	leweyoon	lazarus	lesueransi
lavatorial	leweyoraijo	laze	lesue
lavatory	leweyorai	lazulite	lesueleyo
lave	lewesn	lazurite	lesueraiyo
lavender	lewesnjnra	lazy	lesuesi
laver	lewesnra	lazzarone	lesueroin
lavish	lewonsia	lea	jnsi
lavishment	lewonsiamutto	lea	jnsi
law	leewo	leach	jnsikho
law	leofin	lead1	jngba
lawine	leewohun	lead2	jngba
lawn1	lewini	leaden	jngbainse

WORD (x)	EQUIVALENT (y)	WORD (x)	EQUIVALENT (y)
leader	jngbasi	leatheroid	jnyiranjo
leading1	jngbagnni	leathery	jnyirai
leading2	jngbagnni	leave1	jnwini
lead pencil	jngba pnyakun	leave2	jnwini
leaf	jnfan	leaved	jnwinide
leaflet	jnfantn	leaven	jnwini
leafty	jnfanse	leaves	jnwinisi
league1	jngbiso	leavings	jnwinignnisi
league2	jngbiso	leavy	jnwinise
league table	teberon jngbiso	leavy	jnwinise
leaguer	jngbisosi	lebanon	jnbonini
leah	jnha	leben	jnbehn
leak	jnkuo	lebensraum	jnbesunraima
leakage	jukuogun	lebkuchen	jnbekunkoin
leaky	jnkuose	lech	jnkhn
leal	jnjo	lecher	jnkhnra
lean1	jntesi	lecherous	jnkhnrasi
lean2	jntesi	lechery	jnkhnrai
leander	jntesijnra	lecithin	jnkiyora
leaning	jntesignni	lecithinase	jnkiyorase
leant	jntetn	lectern	jnkayoran
leap	jnpaun	lection	jnkayoon
lear	jnnira	lectionary	jnkayoonrai
learn	jnniran	lector	jnkaran
learned	jnnirande	lecture	jnkatorai
learner	jnniransi	lecturer	jnkatoraisi
learning	jnnirangnni	led	jngbe
lease	jnsesi	lederhosen	jngbesihinsin
leash	jnsosi	ledge	jngbon
least	jnsnsi	ledger	jngbonsi
leat	jnyi	lee	jnsi
leather	jnyiran	leech	jnsikho
leatherette	jnyirantn	leeds	jnsiduo
leathern	jnyiran	leek	jnsiki

WORD (x)	EQUIVALENT (y)	WORD (x)	EQUIVALENT (y)
leer	jnsiran	legionary	jngbilerai
leery	jnsirai	legionnaire	jngbilehnse
lees	jnsise	legislate	jngnsoleyo
leet	jnsito	legislation	jngnsoleyoon
leeward	jnsiwegba	legislative	jngnsoleyowin
leeway	jnsiwelo	legislature	jngnsoleyorai
left1	jnfia	legistlator	jngnsoleyoran
left2	jnfia	legit	jngnto
leftie	jnfiase	legitimate	jngntomutn
leftist	jnfiasi	legitimatize	jngntomutnse
leftward	jnfiawegba	legitimize	jngntomuse
lefty	jnfiasi	legless	jngnlabo
leg	jngn	lego	jngon
legacy	jngnse	legume	jngnmi
legal	jngnjo	legumin	jngnmini
legalese	jngnjose	leguminous	jngnminisi
legalis homo	jngnjosi himo	leh	jnho
legalism	jngnjomosi	lehua	jnhun
legalistic	jngnjosuko	lei	jnsi
legality	jngnleto	leicester	jnsiknseto
legalize	jngnjose	leinster	jnsiseto
legal tender	jngnjo tinjnra	leishmania	jnsiunmohan
legate	jngnyo	leishmaniasis	jnsiunmohanso
legatee	jngnyosi	leister	jnsieta
legation	jngnyoon	leisure	jnsierai
legato	jngnte	leisured	jnsieraide
legator	jngnran	leisurely	jnsierailo
legend	jngnnito	leith	jntesi
legendary	jngnnitorai	leitha	jntesan
legerdemain	jngngbamorai	leitmotif	jntemotefe
legging	jngngnni	leitrim	jntaraimo
leggy	jngngun	lekker	jnknkn
legible	jngnron	leman	jnmoin
legion	jngbile	lemma	jnmmo

WORD (x)	EQUIVALENT (y)	WORD (x)	EQUIVALENT (y)
lemming	jnmmgnni	lenticular	jnsokuoran
lemnian	jnmnihn	lentiform	jnsofoonmo
lemons	jnminisi	lentiginose	jnsoginse
lemniscates	jnmnisekoiyo	lentigo	jnsogn
lemniscus	jnmnisekunsi	lentil	jnsoje
lemon	jnmini	lentissimo	jnsosoomo
lemonade	jnminijo	lento	jnsoki
lemonverbena	jnminiwinbehun	lentoid	jnsokijo
lemony	jnminise	lentor	jnsoran
lempira	jnmpnra	leo	jnko
lemuel	jnmulo	leon	jnkon
lemur	jnmura	leonard	jnkongba
lemurs	jnmurasi	leonardesque	jnkongbakun
lemuria	jnmurase	leonardo	jnkongbain
lemuroid	jnmurajo	leonid	jnkonjo
lena	jnhe	leonidas	jnkonjose
lenard	jnhegba	leonine	jnkonhun
lend	jnwin	leontiasis	jnkotanso
lenetic	jnhunko	leopard	jnkopngba
length	jngansi	leopardi	jnkopngba
lengthen	jngansii	leopold	jnkopnjo
lengthy	jnganse	leotard	jnkotngba
lenient	jnhunto	lepanto	jnpanto
lenin	jnhunsi	leper	jnpnra
lenis	jnhunse	lepido	jnpnde
lenitive	jnhuntowin	lepidolite	jnpndeleyo
lenity	jnhuntn	lepidopteran	jnpndepntirain
leno	jnhn	lepidopteron	jnpndepntiroin
lens	jnso	lepidopterous	jnpndepntiransi
lent	jnsa	lepidopterist	jnpndepntiraisi
lentamente	jnsominito	lepidosiren	jnpndesirain
lentando	jnsodehn	lepidote	jnpndeyo
lenten	jnsosn	lepidus	jnpndesi
lenticels	jnsokuo	leporid	jnpnranjo

WORD (x)	EQUIVALENT (y)	WORD (x)	EQUIVALENT (y)
leporide	jnpnranjan	let2	jntn
leporine	jnpnrain	lethal	jntnjo
leprechaun	jnpnrankhun	lethality	jntnleto
leprosarium	jnpnrasnranma	lethargic	jntnraganko
leprose	jnpnrasi	lethargy	jntnragun
leprosy	jnpnrase	lethe	jntnsi
leprous	jnpnrasia	letheferous	jntnsifirosi
lepto	jnpnto	leticia	jntnkoon
leptocephalus	jnpntoknphijosi	letitia	jntntoon
leptome	jnpntomo	letter	jntnto
lepton	jnpntosi	lettered	jntntode
leptophyllous	jnpntophewesi	lettic	jntntiko
leptorrhine	jnpntorrhain	lettuce	jntntesi
leptosomatic	jnpntosommuko	leu	jnwa
leptosome	jnpntosoomo	leucas	jnwakosi
leptospirosis	jnpntoseporaiso	leucine	jnwakihun
leptotene	jnpntotnun	leucite	jnwakiyo
lepus	jnpnso	leuco-	jnwaki
lequear	jnkunran	leucocratic	jnwakikanko
lerna	jnrahe	leucocyte	jnwakisnyo
lesbian	jnsabahn	leucocytosis	jnwakisnyoso
lesbianism	jnsabahnmosi	leucoderma	jnwakijnramo
lesbos	jnsabosi	leucoma	jnwakimo
lesemajesty	jnsemojinseto	leucomaine	jnwakimohun
lesion	jnsoon	leucomelanous	jnwakimelonisi
less	labo	leucopenia	jnwakipnhan
lessee	jnsun	leucoplastid	jnwakipansujo
lessen	labose	leucopolesis	jnwakipinjnso
lesser	labosi	leucorrhoea	jnwakirhoin
lesser	jnsesi	leucosin	jnwakisie
lesson	jnsesin	leucosticte	jnwakisetinto
lessor	jnsesiran	leucotomy	jnwakitemo
lest	jnsi	leud	jnwajo
let1	jntn	leukaemia	jnwakoinmua

WORD (x)	EQUIVALENT (y)	WORD (x)	EQUIVALENT (y)
leukemia	jnwaknmua	levy	jnwo
leuko	jnwako	levyist	jnwosi
leukocythemia	jnwakosnsinmoon	lewd	jnwojo
leukocytosis	jnwakosnyoso	lewis	jnwose
leukoma	jnwakoma	lewisite	jnwoseyo
lev	jnwa	lewiston	jnwosetin
levalloisian	jnwajoinsoohn	lex	jnso
leva nt	jnwanta	lexeme	jnsomu
levanter	jnwantasi	lexical	jnsokojo
levantine	jnwantahun	lexicog	jnsokign
levator	jnwayoran	lexicography	jnsokiganphe
levee	jnwasn	lexicology	jnsokilogbon
level	jnwajo	lexicon	jnsokin
leveler	jnwajora	lexico	jnsoki
leveller	jnwajjora	lexis	jnsose
leventis	jnwatosi	ley	jnse
lever	jnwarai	ley	roin
leverage	jnwaraigba	leydenjar	jnsedain
leveret	jnwaraite	li	le
leviable	jnwanbe	li	li
leviathan	jnwansanra	li	li
levigate	jnwangiyo	liability	ligbirontn
levin	jnwansi	liable	ligbibe
levirate	jnwanraiyo	liaise	ligbise
levis	jnwanso	liaison	ligbisin
levitate	jnwanteyo	liana	ligbihe
levitation	jnwanteyoon	liao	ligbihn
levite	jnwante	liaoning	ligbihngnni
leviticus	jnwantekunsi	liar	lirosi
levity	jnwante	liard	ligbaa
levo	jnwain	lias	lisn
levorotatory	jnwainroteyorai	lib	libo
levulinic	jnwejanko	libation	liboyoon
levulose	jnwejose	libau	libonun

WORD (x)	EQUIVALENT (y)	WORD (x)	EQUIVALENT (y)
libeccio	libekoon	lichen-in	likhisi-nu
libel	libejia	lichenology	likhisilogbon
libellant	libejiatn	lich-gat	likhi giyo
libelee	libejiase	licht	likho
liberal	liberaijo	licit	likito
liberality	liberaileto	lick	likila
liberalize	liberaijose	lickerish	likilaraisi
liberate	liberaiyo	lickety	likilato
liberation	liberaiyoon	licking	likilagnni
liberee	liberain	licorice	likiraisn
liberia	liberan	lector	likiran
libertine	liberaitin	lid	lijo
libertinism	liberaitinmosi	lidia	lijoin
liberty	liberaito	lidice	lijosi
libidinous	libejoinsi	lido	lijnko
libido	libejoin	lie1	liro
libra	ligba	lie2	liro
librarian	ligbanraihn	lied	lirode
library	ligbanrai	liederkranz	lirojnrakorai
librate	ligbaraiyo	life	lifn
libration	ligbaraiyoon	liefer	lirofiro
libretto	ligbareto	liege	lirogn
libriform	ligbaraifoon	lie-in	liro-nu
libya	libeso	lien	liron
libyan	libesohn	lienal	lironjo
lice	likn	lientery	lirontnrai
licence	liknsun	lierne	liroin
license1	liknse	lieto	liroto
license2	liknse	lieu	lirou
licensee	liknsesi	lieut.	lironti
licentiate	likntiyo	lieutenant	liroutinte
licentious	likntisi	life	lifn
lichee	likhise	life	lifn
lichen	likhisi	lifebelt	lifnbejia

WORD (x)	EQUIVALENT (y)	WORD (x)	EQUIVALENT (y)
lifeless	lifnlabo	like1	likn
lift	lifia	like2	likn
ligament	liganmutto	,-like	likn
ligate	ligiyo	likeable	liknberon
ligature	legiyorai	likely	liknlo
ligeance	legnsi	liken	liknsi
liger	legnra	likeness	liknnisi
light1	lighe	lilac	lileko
light2	lighe	lilith	lilesi
light	lighe	liliaceous	lilesuwa
lighten1	lighesi	lilian	lilehn
lighten2	lighesi	lilith	lilesi
lighter1	ligheran	lillibullero	lillebullero
lighter2	ligheran	lilliput	lillepnti
lights	lighese	lilliputian	lillepntiun
lignaloes	liginijoinsi	lillypilly	lillese pollese
ligneous	liginisi	lilo	lilo
ligni	ligini	lilt	lijia
lignify	liginife	lily	lilese
lignin	liginihn	lilyiron	lilese irin
lignite	liginiyo	lima	limo
lignivorous	liginiwnrunsi	limacine	limokihun
lignocaine	liginikoin	limacon	limokin
lignose	liginise	limb1	limbe
lignum vitae	liginiwa woton	limb2	limbe
ligny	liginise	limbate	limbeyo
ligroin	ligirain	limbed	limbede
ligula	ligunle	limber1	limbesi
ligulate	ligunleyo	limber2	limbesi
ligule	ligunron	limbo1	limbo
liguorist	ligunransi	limbo2	limbo
ligure	ligunrai	limbus	limbusi
liguria	ligunran	lime1	limi
likable	liknbe	lime2	limi

WORD (x)	EQUIVALENT (y)	WORD (x)	EQUIVALENT (y)
lime3	limi	linchpin	likhnpon
limen	limisi	lincoln	liknjnna
limenade	limijin	linconnu	likinnu
limerick	limiraiko	linctus	likntisi
limes	limusi	lincrusta	liknraisita
limey	limise	lind	lijn
limit	lemutn	lindane	lijnhun
limit	limutn	linden	lijnsi
limitarian	limutnrain	lindsay	lijnsan
limtary	limutnrai	line1	lehun
limitation	lemutnyoon	line2	lehun
limited	limutnde	lineage	lehungun
limiter	limutnra	lineal	lehunjo
limn	limini	lineament	lehunmutto
limnetic	liminiko	linear	lehunran
limnology	liminilogbon	lineate	lehunyo
limonene	limenihun	lineation	lehunyon
limonite	limeniyo	linen	lehunni
limo	limnni	liner1	lehunsi
limousine	limnnisun	liner2	lehunsi
limp1	limpn	linesman	lehunmoye
limp2	limpn	ling1	legnni
limpte	limpnte	ling2	legnni
limpid	limpnjo	-ling	lignni
limpkin	limpnkin	linga	likogn
limpsy	limpnse	linger	likognsi
limuloid	limulujo	lingerie	likognran
limulus	limulusi	lingo	likogin
limy	limise	lingua franca	likogun fanka
limulus	limulusi	lingual	likogunjo
limy	limise	linguist	likogunsi
lin	liko	linguistic	likogunsuko
linage	lehungun	linguistics	likogunsukosi
linalool	likunlojin	lingulate	likogunleyo

WORD (x)	EQUIVALENT (y)	WORD (x)	EQUIVALENT (y)
liniment	likunmutto	lipolysis	lipojinso
linin	likunsi	lipoma	lipoma
lining	lehungnni	lipophilic	lipopheronko
link	liko	lipoprotein	lipoponyoto
linkage	likogun	lippe	lipopn
linkman	likomaye	lipped	lipode
links	likosi	lippie	lipopon
linn	likun	lipton	lipotin
linnaean	likunhn	liquate	likunyo
linnet	likunto	liquefacient	likunfanseto
lino	likosn	liquefy	likunfe
linocut	likosnkunte	liquesce	likunsnkn
linodendron	likosnhagbn	liquescent	likunsnknti
linoleate	likosnjeyo	liqueur	likunrai
linoleic	likosnjeko	liquid	likunjn
linoleum	likosnjema	liquidate	likunjnyo
linotype	likotnpon	liquidation	likunjnyoon
linpipe	likopopon	liquidator	likunjnyoran
linsang	likosangn	liquidity	likunjnto
lint	likote	liquidize	likunjnse
lintel	likotejn	liquor	likunran
linter	likotesi	lira	lira
linters	likotesi	liri	lirai
lion	lile	lisa	lise
lioness	lilebo	lisle	lisia
lionize	lilese	lisp	lisopo
lip	lipn	lispendens	lisopindainsi
liparoid	lipnranjo	lissajous	lisoojinsi
lipase	lipnse	lissome	lisooemo
lipid	lipnjo	list	lisi
lipo	lipo	listel	lisijo
lipocaic	lipokako	listen	lisitin
lipocyte	liposnyo	lister	lisitnra
lipoid	lipojo	listerine	lisitnrain

WORD (x)	EQUIVALENT (y)	WORD (x)	EQUIVALENT (y)
listerism	lisitnramosi	lithophytes	lisikopheyo
listing	lisignni	lithosphere	lisikosephirai
listless	lisilabo	lithosol	lisikosnjin
lists	lisise	lithotomy	lisikotemo
lit	lito	lithotrity	lisikotaraito
litany	litose	litigable	litegiberon
litchi	litokhi	litigant	litegita
lite	leto	litigate	litegiyo
lite	leyo	litigation	litegiyoon
lite	liyo	litigious	litegisi
liter	litnra	litimus	litemosi
litre	litiran	litotes	litoyosi
literacy	litoransn	littre	littiran
literal	litoranjo	litter	littnra
literalism	litoranjomosi	litterateur	littnrantorai
literary	litoranrai	litterlout	littnralonita
literate	litoranyo	little	littnron
literati	litoraiye	littoral	littnranjo
literatim	litoraiyemu	liturgical	littosnlokojo
literature	litoraiyoran	liturgy	littosnlo
lith	lisi	littuus	littosun
litharge	lisirangi	livid	liwonjn
lithe	lisin	livable	liwabe
lithemia	lisinmua	live	liwa
lithia	lisinni	lively	liwalo
lithiasis	lisinniso	liven	liwasi
lithic	lisiko	liver	liwaran
lithium	lisima	liverish	liwaranse
litho	lisiko	livery	liwarai
lithography	lisikoganphe	living	liwagnni
lithoid	lisikojo	livonia	liwnhun
lithology	lisikologbon	livraison	liwaraisin
lithomarge	lisikomuragn	livre	liwaran
lithometeor	lisikomutoran	lixiviate	lisuewnyo

WORD (x)	EQUIVALENT (y)	WORD (x)	EQUIVALENT (y)
lixiviation	lisuewnyoon	lobelia	loobele
lixivium	lisuewnma	lobeline	loobeleni
lizard	lisungba	loblolly	loobelojin
llama	lilamo	lobectomy	loobetemo
llanelly	lilahunjin	lobeline	loobeleni
llano	lilakn	lobelolly	loobelojin
llewellyn	lilewinjjoin	lobo	loobu
lloyd's	lilosejnsi	lobola	loobujn
lo	lo	lobotomy	loobutemo
lo	loo lu	lobscouse	loobesnkilese
loach	lokho	lobster	loobesia
load	logbi	lobule	loberan
loaded	logbide	lobworm	loobeworon
loader	logbide	local	loknjo
loader	logbisi	locale	loknjn
loaf1	lofan	localism	loknjomosi
loaf2	lofan	locality	loknleto
loafer	lofansi	localize	loknjose
loam	lomini	locate	loknyo
loan	lowin	location	loknyoon
loanda	lowinjn	locative	loknyowin
loasis	losinsi	locator	loknyoran
loath	lotisi	loc. Cit.	lokn kite
loathe	lotinsi	loch	lokhun
loaves	loowusi	lochia	lokhue
lob	loobn	loci	loki
lobar	loobnran	lock1	lokkn
lobate	loobnyo	lock2	lokkn
lobby	loobebe	lockage	lokkngun
lobbyism	loobebemosi	locke	lokknn
lobbyist	loobebesi	locker	lokknsi
lobe	loobe	locket	lokknte
lobectomy	loobetemo	lock up	lokkn pake
lobed	loobede	loco1	loki

WORD (x)	EQUIVALENT (y)	WORD (x)	EQUIVALENT (y)
loco2	loki	logarithmic	logiraimosiko
loco citato	loki kiteto	logbook	logibooko
locofoco	lokifooki	loge	logn
locomotion	lokimotusi	logger	logignra
locomotive	lokimotuwin	loggerhead	logignrahegbi
locomotor	lokimotu	loggia	logbonso
locris	lokiraisi	logging	logignni
locular	lokuoran	logic	logbonko
locule	lokuo	-logic	logbonko
locum tenens	lokuo tnnisi	logical	logbonkojo
locus	lokunso	-logist	logbonsi
locus sigilli	lokunso soogbijjn	logistic	logbisiko
locust	lokunsi	logistics	logbisikosi
locution	lokunyoon	logiion	logbile
lode	logba	loglog	logilogi
loden	logbain	logo	logbo
lodestar	logbasetan	logogram	logboganmo
lodestone	logbasetole	lgography	logboganphe
lodge	logbn	logogriph	logboganpho
lodger	logbnsi	logomachy	logbomukhn
lodging	logbnggni	logopaedics	logboponjnkosi
lodgement	logbnmuyo	logorrhea	logborrhoin
lodicules	logbakuo	logon	logbosi
loess	losoo	logos	logbosi
loft	lofia	logopathy	logbopansio
lofter	lofiasi	logothete	logbosinte
lofty	lofiase	logotypy	logbotnpo
log1	logi	logue	logbiso
log2	logi	-logy	logbon
logan	logini	lohengrin	lohegnrin
loganiaceous	loginisuwa	loin	losn
logaoedic	logisejinko	loins	losnsi
logarithm	logiraisiro	loir	lorai
logarithm	logiraimosi	loire	lorain

WORD (x)	EQUIVALENT (y)	WORD (x)	EQUIVALENT (y)
loiter	lotnra	longi	logunsi
loki	lokoi	longing	logungnni
loll	lojan	longitude	loguntujin
lollard	lojagba	longitudinal	loguntujinjo
loller	lojansi	longtom	loguntimo
lollipop	lojanpipo	loo	loo
lollop	lojanpn	loo	lu
lolly	lojanse	looby	lobn
lomami	lomanmi	loof	loofi
lombard	lombegba	loofah	loofin
lombardy	lombegbain	look	loowo
lomblem	lomgbnle	loom1	loomo
lombok	lomgbnki	loom2	loomo
lombrosian	lomgbnrasuhn	looming	loomognni
lome	loma	loon	loosi
loment	lomutto	loony	loosise
lomond	lomidan	looniest	loosisesii
london	lounjo	loop	loopo
londoner	lounjosi	loophole	loopohinlu
london pride	lounjo panjin	loopy	loopose
londonderry	lounjojnrrai	loose	loose
lone	lohun	loosen	loosesi
lonely	lohunlo	loot	loote
loner	lohunsi	lop	lopn
long1	logun	lope	loopn
long2	logun	lopho	lopnho
long	logun	lophotrichous	lopnhotaraikhosi
longan	logunse	loppy	lopnpo
loganimity	logunsemutn	lopsided	lopnsoojode
longboat	logunbute	loquacious	lokunsosi
longbow	logunbowo	loquat	lokunte
longe	logunrai	loquitur	lokuntorai
longeron	logunrain	loran	lorain
longevity	logunwnto	lord	lojoin

WORD (x)	EQUIVALENT (y)	WORD (x)	EQUIVALENT (y)
lordly	lojoinsi	louden	loodunsi
lore	loran	lough	logbun
lorelei	loranjn	Louis	loosun
lorgnette	lorangntin	louisa	loosua
lorgnon	lorangnsi	louise	loosunse
lorica	loraikn	louisiana	loosuahn
lorication	loraiknyoon	louis seize	loosun sesnsi
lorient	loraito	lounge	logbede
lorikeet	loraiknto	lounge bar	boosn logbede
lorimer	loraimura	loup	loopan
loris	loraisi	loup	loopn
lorn	lorau	lour	loran
lorne	loraun	lourengo	lorangbin
lorrain	lorrain	louse	losise
lorraine	lorraini	lousy	losisoo
lorry	lorrai	lout	lote
lory	lorai	louth	lotesi
lose	loosia	louther	loteran
loser	loosiasi	loutish	lotese
loss	losai	louver	lownran
lost	loosai	louvre	lownrai
lot	lotu	lovable	lowonberon
lota	loto	lovage	lowongun
loth	lotusi	lovat	lowonte
lothair	lotusirai	love	lowon
lothario	lotusirain	loveable	lowonberon
lothians	lotusia	loveless	lowonlabo
lotion	lotunse	lovelorn	lowonlorau
lotophagi	lotuphije	lovely	lowonse
lottery	lotturai	love-nest	lowon-hunsi
lotto	lottu	lover	lowonsi
lotus	lotusi	loving	lowongnni
louch	lookhn	low1	lowe
loud	loodun	low2	lowe

WORD (x)	EQUIVALENT (y)	WORD (x)	EQUIVALENT (y)
low-born	lowe boran	Lucca	lukoka
lowbrow	lowebonwo	Luce	lukn
lower1	lowesi	Lucent	luknti
Lower2	lowesi	Lucemal	luknranjo
Lower3	lowesi	Luceme	luknrain
Lowest	lowesitn	Lucia	lukoon
Lowland	loweledain	Lucid	lukojo
Lowly	lowese	Lucifer	lukofiro
Lox	losun	Luciferase	lukofirose
Loyal	losnjo	Luciferous	lukofirosi
Loyalist	losnjosi	Luciform	lukofonmo
Loyalty	losnjotn	Lucina	lukonu
Loyola	losnjoin	Lucite	lukoyo
Lozenge	losuegbun	Lucius	lukosi
Lu	lu	Lucivee	lukownse
Lualaba	luhobe	Luck	luki
Luanda	luhojn	Luckless	lukilabo
Luangwa	luhogunwa	Luckner	lukiran
Luau	luhun	Lucky	lukise
Lubber	lubesi	Lucrative	lukiranyowin
Lubber	lubesi	Lucre	lukiran
Lube	lube	Lucretia	lukirantan
Lubeck	lubeki	Lucrezia	lukiransia
Lublin	lubejin	Lucubrate	lukunberaiyo
Lubra	lubera	Lucubration	lukunberaiyoon
Lubric	luberaiko	Luculent	lukunjnsi
Lubricant	luberaikote	Lud	luri
Lubricate	luberaikoyo	Luddite	lurinte
Lubricator	luberaikoran	Ludicrous	lurinknrasi
Lubricious	luberaikiwa	Ludo	lude
Lubricity	luberaikito	Lues	lusi
Lubritorium	luberairanma	Luff	lufin
Lucan	lukosi	Luftwaffr	lufiaweffo
Lucame	lukorain	Lug	lugbe

WORD (x)	EQUIVALENT (y)	WORD (x)	EQUIVALENT (y)
Lug aid	lugbe aajo	Luminosity	lumanaseto
Luge	lugn	Luminous	lumanasi
Luger	lugnra	Lumisterol	lumasetojin
Luggage	lugbegun	Lummex	lummosn
Lugged	lugbede	Lump1	lumpo
Lugger	lugbesi	Lump2	lumpo
Luggle	lugbejn	Lumpectomy	lumpotemo
Lugubrious	lugbnberaisi	Lumper	lumposi
Lugworm	lugnwnron	Lumpish	lumposia
Luigia	lugoon	Lumpy	lumpose
Luke	luka	Luna	lujn
Lukewarm	lukaweron	Lunacy	lujnse
Lull	lujnra	Lunar	lujnran
Lullaby	lujnranbe	Lunary	lujnrai
Lully	lujnransi	Lunate	lujnyo
Lulu	lulo	Lunatic	lujnyoka
Lum	lumo	Lunation	lujnyoon
Lumachelle	lumokhnjjn	Lunch	lujnje
Lumbago	lumbngbn	Luncheron	lujnjesi
Lumbar	lumbnran	Luncheonette	lujnjesitn
Lumber	lumbesi	Lundy	lujndain
Lumbering	lumbesignni	Lune	lujnse
Lumberjack	lumbesijako	Lunette	lujnsetn
Lumbricalis	lumberaikajn	Lung	lugn
Lumbricold	lumberaikijon	Lunger	lugnsi
Lumia	lumoon	Lungi	lugnni
Lumen	lumaye	Lung wort	lugn winjo
Lumen	lumaye	Luni	luni
Luminance	lumanasi	Lunik	lunikn
Luminary	lumanarai	Lunt	lunite
Luminesce	lumanasesi	Lunula	lunijn
Luminescence	lumanaseknsi	Lunular	lunijnra
Luminescent	lumanaseknti	Lunulate	lunijnyo
Luminiferous	lumanafirosi	Luny	lunise

WORD (x)	EQUIVALENT (y)	WORD (x)	EQUIVALENT (y)
Lupercalia	lupnrakojan	Lute1	lute
Luperel	lupnralo	Lute2	lute
Lupin	luposn	Luteal	lutejo
Lupine	lupohun	Lutein	luteni
Lupulin	lupnjan	Lutenist	lutenisi
Lupus	lupnsi	Luteolin	lutejin
Lupuserythematosus	lupnseraipipansnso	Lutetium	lutetima
Lupus vulgaris	lupnsi wujogiraso	Luther	lutesnra
Lur	lurai	Lutheran	lutesnrain
Lurch1	luraika	Luthem	lutesnran
Lurch2	luraika	Luting	lutegnni
Lurcher	luraikasi	Lutist	lutesi
Lure	lurai	Lux	lusua
Lurex	luraisi	Luxate	lusuayo
Lurid	luraijo	Luxe	lusuase
Lurk	luraiki	Luxmeter	lusuamuto
Lusatia	lusetan	Luxor	lusuaran
Luscious	lusesuwa	Luxulianite	lusuajainto
Lush1	lusemi	Luxuriance	lusuaraisi
Lush2	lusemi	Luxuriant	lusuaraite
Lusher	lusemisi	Luxuriate	lusuaraiyo
Lushy	lusemin	Luxurious	lusuaraisi
Lusitania	lusetinni	Luxury	lusuarai
Lust	luse	,-1y1	lo
Luster	luseto	,1y2	jin
Lustihood	lusehinjo	1yard	logba
Lustral	luseranjo	Lycanthrope	lokoinsnrapon
Lustrate	luseranyo	Lycanthropy	lokoinsnrapo
Lustration	luseranyoon	Lycaonia	lokoinni
Luster	luseran	Lycee	loknse
Lustrum	luseranma	Lyceum	loknma
Lusty	lusetn	Lychnis	lokhnnisi
Lusus	lusesi	Lycia	lokoon
Lutanist	lutechesi	Lycian	lokoonhn

WORD (x)	EQUIVALENT (y)	WORD (x)	EQUIVALENT (y)
Lycidas	lokijose	Lyophilic	loknphobanko
Lycomedes	lokimujinsi	Lyra	loran
Lycopod	lokopindi	Lyrate	loraiyo
Lycopodium	lokipindima	Lyre	loranlyric
Lycra	loknra	Lyric	loraiko
Lyddite	lodainyo	Lyrical	loraikojo
Lydia	lojina	Lyriciam	loraikomosi
Lydie	lojie	Lyricist	loraikosi
Lye	lose	Lysergic	loseraignko
Lying	lognni	Lysi	losi
Lyme	lomi	Lysimeter	jinsomuto
Lymph	lomiphn	.-lysis	jinso
Lymphadenitis	lomiphndainso	Lysine	jinsohn
Lymphangial	lomiphngunjo	Lysine	losun
Lymphangitis	lomiphngunso	Lysis	jinso
Lymphatic	lomiphnko	Lyssa	lossa
Lymphatism	lomiphnmosi	Lysso	lossia
Lymphatitis	lomiphnso	Lyssosome	lossiasoomo
Lymphato	lomiphnto	Lyssozyme	lossiaimo
Lymphatolysis	lomiphntojinso	Lyster	loseto
Lymphnode	lomiphnjoin	Lyte	loyo
Lympho	lomiphnko	Lytic	loyoko
Lymphoid	lomiphnkojo	Lytta	lotte
Lymphoma	lomiphnkopinjnso	Ma	ma
Lymphorrhea	lomiphnkorrhain	Maam	mama
Lyn	loo	Martens	maratinsi
Lyncean	looknso	Maas	masa
Lynch	lookhn	Mab	mabe
Lynch law	lookhn leewo	Mabel	mabejn
Lynx	looso	Mabinogion	mabekngboin
Lynx-eyed	looso eyiri	Mac	makn, omo
Iyo	lokn	Macabre	maknbonu
Iyon	lokin	Macaco	maknki
Lyonnaise	lokinhnse	Macadam	maknjnra

WORD (x)	EQUIVALENT (y)	WORD (x)	EQUIVALENT (y)
Macadamia	maknjnran	Machination	makihunyo
Macadamize	maknjnrase	Machine	makhihun
Macao	maknni	Machinery	makhihunrai
Macaque	maknkun	Machinist	makhihunsi
Macaroni	maknrain	Machismo	makhise
Macaronic	maknrainko	Machmeter	makhimuto
Macaroon	maknroon	Macho	makho
Macassar	maknsooran	Machree	makhora
Macaulay	maknjnse	Machupicchu	makhunpokhun
Macaw	maknwa	Machy	makhise
Macbeth	maknbesi	Macie	maknse
Maccabees	maknkobese	Macintosh	makntonise
Macaroni	maknkorain	Mack	makki
Mccarthyism	maknransemosi	Mackenzee	makkinsun
Macdonald	makndainjo	Mackerel	makkiranjo
Mace 1	masia	Machinac	makkhinko
Mace 2	masia	Machinaw	makkhinwa
Macedonia	massaidainni	Mackintosh	makkintose
Macedoine	masiadainse	Mackle	makkira
Macedon	masiadain	Maclaren	maknjnrain
Macelo	masialo	Maclauren	maknlerain
Macer	masiasi	Macle	maknron
Macerate	masiaraiyo	Macleod	maknronjo
Maceration	masiaraiyoon	Maclura	maknlura
Mach	makhi	Macmillian	maknmujnran
Machado	makhide	Macon	makin
Machere	makhiran	Macpherson	maknphirosin
Machete	makhite	Macquarie	maknkunrain
Machiavelli	makhiwinjnra	Macramé	maknresi
Machiavellian	makhiwinjnrain	Macrencephaly	maknranknphijin
Machiavellianism	makhiwinjnrainmosi	Macro-	maknra
Machicolate	makhikileyo	Macrobiosis	maknrabakoso
Machicolation	makhikileyoon	Macrobiotic	maknrabahnko
Machination	makhihunyoon	Macrocarpa	maknrakopan

WORD (x)	EQUIVALENT (y)	WORD (x)	EQUIVALENT (y)
Macrocephaly	maknraknphijin	Madame	majinse
Macrochemistry	maknrachnmusorain	Madaringay	majinraingise
Macroclimate	maknrakiunmote	Madcap	majiakopn
Macrocosm	maknrakiseto	Madden	majiajn
Macrocyst	maknrasnsu	Madder	majiajnra
Macrocyte	maknrasnyo	Made	majain
Macrocytosis	maknrasnyoso	Madeira	majainran
Macrodome	maknrademo	Madeleine	majainjohun
Macroeconomics	maknraekinknmukosi	Mademoiselle	majainmusnlle
Macrogamete	maknragimuta	Madero	majainra
Macrogamy	maknragimo	Madison	majainsi
Macrograph	maknraganpha	Madly	majialo
Macrography	maknraganphe	Madman	majiamaye
Macrometer	maknramuto	Madoera	majinrain
Macrometeorology	maknramutoranlogbon	Madonna	majaini
Macromolecule	maknramojnkuo	Madras	majiaransi
Macromorphology	maknramophanlogbon	Madrasa	majiaranse
Macron	maknran	Madre	majiaran
Macrophage	maknraphije	Madreporarian	majiaranpinsirain
Macropodian	maknrapindiesi	Madrepore	majiaranpinsi
Macropsia	maknraposia	Madrigal	majiaraignjo
Macrosporangium	maknraseporaigunma	Madrilène	majiaraijeun
Macroscopic	maknrasekiponko	Madrona	majiarain
Macrospecies	maknrasepnsesi	Madrone	majiaroin
Macrosporangium	maknraseporaignma	Madura	majiaran
Macrospore	maknraseporai	Madurai	majiarai
Mactation	maknteyoon	Maduro	majiaro
Macula	makunle	Madwort	majiawinyo
Maculalutea	makunletie	Mae	mase
Macule	makuo	Maeander	masejnra
Macumba	makuobe	Maelstrom	masetnra
Mad	majia	Maenad	masedan
Madagascar	majingankosi	Maeter	maseto
Madam	majinsi	Maestoso	

WORD (x)	EQUIVALENT (y)	WORD (x)	EQUIVALENT (y)
Maestoso	masetosin	Magnacumlaude	magansnkunjin
Maestro	masetnra	Magnanimity	magansnmuto
Maewest	masewinsi	Magnanimous	magansnmosi
Maffick	mafanko	Magnate	maganyo
Mafia	mafia	Magnesia	magansia
Mafioso	mafiase	Magnesite	magansuyo
Mafoi	mafia	Magnesium	magansuma
Maga	magia	Magnet	magante
Mag	magi	Magnetic	maganteko
Magazine	magisun	Magnetism	magantemosi
Magdalen	magidijoin	Magnetize	magantese
Magdalena	magidijnna	Magneto	maganto
Mage	magn	Magnetolysis	magantojinso
Magellanic	magnjnrainko	Magnetometer	magantemuto
Magendie	maginise	Magneton	magantesi
Magenta	maginito	Magnetron	maganteran
Magersfontein	magnrafontelu	Magni	magan
Maggie	magigan	Magnific	maganfiko
Magpie	magipan	Magnificat	maganfikota
Maggot	magite	Magnification	maganfikoyoon
Maggoty	magitn	Magnificent	maganfiknti
Magi	magba	Magnifico	maganfiki
Magic	magbako	Magnify	maganfe
Magical	magbakojo	Magnigying glass	gansue maganfegnni
Magician	magbakohn	Magnitude	magantujin
Maginot	maginto	Magnolia	maganjan
Magisterial	magisetoraijo	Magnolianceous	maganjansuwa
Magistery	magisetorai	Magnox	maganisin
Magistracy	magisetosi	Magnum	maganma
Magistrate	magisetoyo	Magnumopus	maganmapnsi
Magistrature	magisetotnran	Maggot	magite
Maglemose	magiranmuse	Magpie	magipan
Magma	magbina	Maguey	magunse
Magna carta	magansn koseto	Magus	magunwa

WORD (x)	EQUIVALENT (y)	WORD (x)	EQUIVALENT (y)
Magyar	magbnran	Maine	maraisi
Mahabharata	maheberaito	Mainmast	maraimasitn
Mahala	mahejn	Mainstay	maraisetnwa
Mahalla	mahejjn	Maintain	maraitelu
Mahanadi	mahejn	Maintenance	maraitinsi
Maharaja	maheraijn	Mair	maresi
Maharani	maheraini	Maist	massua
Maharanee	maherainse	Maisonette	masehuntn
Maharishi	maherosua	Maitre d hotel	matnran jn hintujo
Mahatma	mahetnsi	Maize	masifn
Mahdi	mahejo	Majestic	majnsitnko
Mahjong	mahejingan	Majesty	majnsitn
Mahler	mahejnra	Majolica	majnleko
Mahi	maha	Major	majura
Mahogany	mahungan	Majorca	majurako
Mahoria	mahunhan	Majordomo	majuradeo
Mahout	mahunta	Majorette	majnratn
Maia	maasi	Majority	majnraito
Maid	maajo	Majorscule	majurasekuo
Maidan	maajoin	Makatea	makintie
Maidanek	maajokin	Make	makn
Maiden	maajosi	Maker	maknsi
Maieutic	maawako	Mal-	maji
Maiger	maagiran	Malacca	majiko
Mail1	maajn	Malachite	majikhiti
Mail2	maajn	Malaco	majiki
Mailer	maajnra	Malacold	majikilogbon
Maillot	maajntu	Malacophyllous	majikiphewesi
Maim	malema	Malacopterous	majikipntiransi
Main	marai	Malacopterygian	majikipntiraigan
Mainland	marailedain	Malacostracan	majikisetnreko
Mainline	marailehun	Malacostracous	majikitnrekosi
Main line	marai lehunb	Maladjusted	majiadijoside
Mainly	marailo	Maladminister	majiadiminiseto

WORD (x)	EQUIVALENT (y)	WORD (x)	EQUIVALENT (y)
Maladroit	majiagbainto	Maletic	maletiko
Malady	majidin	Malevolent	malewnjnto
Malafide	majinfijo	Malfeasance	majifnsesi
Malaga	majigan	Mmalfeasant	majifnsete
Malagasy	majiganse	Malformation	majifonmoyoon
Malaise	majisise	Malgrelui	majigiranlo
Malaita	majiseto	Mali	majan
Malamute	majinmutn	Malic	majanko
Malanders	majijnrasi	Malice	majanse
Malapert	majipnra	Malicious	majansesi
Malaprop	majiponpe	Malign	majangn
Malapropism	majiponpemosi	Malignant	majangnte
Malar	majira	Malignancy	majangnsn
Malaria	majiran	Malignity	majangnto
Malaria	majiran	Malihini	majanhiyo
Malarkey	majirakn	Malinger	majanhunsi
Malate	majiyo	Malinger	majangnra
Malathion	majinsinsi	Malison	majansin
Malawi	majinwa	Malkin	majikwo
Malay	majinso	Mall	majnra
Malaya	majinson	Mallard	majnragba
Malayopolynesian	majinsoposehunso	Malleable	majnrabe
Malaysia	majinsosia	Mallee	majnrase
Malcolm	majinkira	Mullein	majnrain
Malcontent	majikintinto	Mallemuck	majnramuki
Malde mer	majijin mura	Mallet	majntn
Male	male	Malleus	majnrasi
Malea	malesi	Mallow	majnrawe
Maleate	maleniyo	Malm	majimi
Maledict	maledikiti	Malmsey	majimisun
Malediction	maledikitisi	Malnourished	majiyuntnraisuade
Male factor	male fanknran	Malnutrition	majiyuntnraiyoon
Maleficent	malefiknti	Malocclusion	majiokikolusoon
Malentendu	maletindi	Malo	malo

WORD (x)	EQUIVALENT (y)	WORD (x)	EQUIVALENT (y)
Malodor	malodium	Mammalian	mammijosi
Malodorous	malodirunsi	Mammaliferous	mammijofirosi
Malonic	maleniko	Mammalogy	mammilogbon
Malonylurea	malenilorain	Mammary	mammirai
Malpais	majipanso	Mammate	mammiyo
Malpighi	Majipoghi	Mammatus	mammiyosi
Malpighiaceous	majipoghisuwa	Mammer	mammirai
Malpractie	majipnrankiko	Mammering	mammiraignni
Malt	majia	Mammie	mammise
Malta	majiato	Mammiferous	mammifirosi
Maltase	majiatose	Mammilla	mammijjo
Maltese	majiatnse	Mammillary	mammijjorai
Maltha	majiahun	Mammillate	mammijjotn
Malthus	majiasi	Mammilliform	mammijjofon
Mnalthusian	majiasihn	Mammitis	mammiso
Maltose	majiase	Mammock	mammukin
Maltreat	majitasito	Mammogram	mammuganmo
Maltster	najiaseto	Mammography	mammuganphe
Malty	majiasi	Mammology	mammulogbon
Malvaceous	majiwnsuwa	Mammon	mammusi
Malvasia	molewnsia	Mammoth	mammosi
Malversation	majiwinsoyoon	Mammy	mammi
Malvolsie	majiwnjosie	Mampara	mampnara
Malwa	majiwa	Man	maye
Mam	mami	Mana	mayahe
Mama	mama	Manacle	mahunkuo
Mamba	mambu	Manage	mayegun
Mambo	mambn	Management	mayegunmutto
Mamelle	mamujnra	Manager	mayegunsi
Mamelon	mamujnsi	Manageress	mayegunsibo
Mameluke	mamujnkin	Managerial	mayegunraijo
Mamey	mamuse	Managing director	diraikeran
Mamma	mammi		mayegungnni
Mammal	mammijo	Managua	mayegun

WORD (x)	EQUIVALENT (y)	WORD (x)	EQUIVALENT (y)
Manakin	mayekin	Mandrel	madainranlo
Manana	mayehe	Mandrill	madainrailo
Manasarowar	mayesunrowa	Manducate	madainjeyo
Manassas	mayesoon	Mane	mayun
Manasseh	mayesooa	Manege	mayungn
Man-at-arms	maye-asumusi	Manes	mayunsi
Manatee	mayetuse	Manetho	mayunkosi
Manaus	mayesi	Maneuver	mayunwara
Manavelins	mayewinjansi	Maneuvers	mayunwarasi
Manavilins	mayewojansi	Man Friday	maye fandase
Manchester	mayekhnta	Manga	magbun
Manchet	mayekhn	Mangabey	magbunbe
Manchineel	mayekhihunjo	Manganate	magbunyo
Manchu	mayekhun	Manganic	magbunko
Manchukuo	mayekhunkuo	Manganin	magbunsi
Manchuria	mayekhunran	Manganite	magbunyo
Mancipium	mayekipoma	Manganous	magbunsi
Manciple	mayekiporon	Mange	magbunse
Mancunian	mayekunhn	Mangel	magbunjo
Mancus	mayekunsi	Manger	magbunsi
Mancy	mayesi	Mange-tout	magbunse_toote
Mandala	madainjn	Mangel1	magbunlo
Mandalay	madainjnse	Mangle2	magbunron
Mandamus	madainmuwa	Mangler	magbunronsi
Mandan	madainsi	Mango	magbunko
Mandarin	madainran	Mangonel	magbunkolo
Mandate	madainyo	Mangosteen	magbunkositoon
Mandatory	madainyorai	Mangrove	magbunrawo
Mandible	madainbujeran	Mangy	magbunse
Mandibulate	madainbujeyo	Manhandle	mayehanduo
Mandola	madainjn	Manhood	mayehinjo
Mandolin	madainjan	Mania	mayisi
Mandoria	madainran	Maniac	mayiko
Mandrate	madainranyo	Manicheism	mayikhnmosi

373

WORD (x)	EQUIVALENT (y)	WORD (x)	EQUIVALENT (y)
Manicotti	mayikiti	Mannose	moyehnse
Manicure	mayikunra	Manocryometer	mayekoraimuto
Manifest	mayifnse	Manoeuvre	mayewara
Manifestation	mayifnsetoyoon	Manometer	mayemuto
Manifesto	mayifoonjo	Manon	mayesi
Manikin	mayikin	Manor	mayeran
Manila	mayijn	Manorial	mayeraijo
Manilla	mayijnra	Manpower	mayepowara
Manille	mayijjo	Manqué	mayekue
Manioc	mayiki	Mansard	mayesegba
Maniple	mayiporon	Manse	mayese
Manipular	mayipoleran	Manservant	mayeseraiwnte
Manipulate	mayipoleyo	Mansion	mayesesi
Manipulative	mayipoleyowin	Mansuetude	mayesuetujin
Manipur	mayiporai	Manta	mayeto
Manis	mayisi	Manteau	mayetiele
Mantissa	mayitisoo	Mantel	mayetojn
Manito	mayito	Mantelet	mayetojntn
Manitoba	mayitobe	Mantelletta	mayetojjntie
Manitoulin	mayitojan	Mantelpiece	mayetojnpansi
Manizales	mayisejnsi	Mantelshelf	mayetojnsuefe
Manjack	maye jako	Mantic	mayeko
Manky	mayekn	Mantilla	mayetijjo
Manly	mayelo	Mantis	mayetisi
Mann	mayehi	Mantissa	mayetisoo
Manna	mayehe	Mantle	mayetin
Manned	mayehunse	Man to man	maye to (si) maye
Mannequin	mayehunkun	Mantoux	mayetose
Manner	mayeran	Mantra	mayeto
Mannered	mayerande	Mantrap	mayetnrapo
Mannerism	mayeraimosi	Mantua	mayetnun
Mannerly	mayeranlo	Manual	mayejo
Mannish	mayehisi	Manubrium	mayegbamu
Mannitol	mayetojin	Manufacture	mayefanknran

WORD (x)	EQUIVALENT (y)	WORD (x)	EQUIVALENT (y)
Manufacturer	mayefanknransi	Marasca	muraseko
Manure	mayerai	Maraschino	murasekhini
Manuka	mayeki	Marasmus	murasemo
Manumit	mayemutn	Marathon	murainsa
Manus	mayese	Marathoner	murainsasi
Manuscript	mayesekoraipn	Maraud	muraujn
Manx	mahnsi	Marauder	muraujnsi
Many	mayi	Maravedi	murawinjn
Manzanares	mayesehunraisi	Marble	murabo
Manzanilla	mayesehunjjo	Marbleize	murabnronsi
Manzanita	mayesehunta	Marbling	murabnrongnni
Maoism	makomosi	Marc	muraka
Maori	makorai	Marcasite	murakosuyo
Map	mapo	Marcel	muraknjo
Maple	maporon	Marcella	muraknjjo
Maquette	makuntin	Marcellus	muraknjjosi
Maquillage	makunjjogun	Marcescent	murakosiknti
Maqui	makun	March	murakhi
Maquis	makunso	Marches	murakhisi
Mar.	mura	Marchen	murakhini
Mara	mura	Marcher	murakhisi
Marabou	muraboun	Marchesa	murakhnsa
Marabout	murabounta	Marchese	murakhnse
Marabunta	murabounto	Marcionism	murakoonmosi
Maraca	murako	Marcia	murakoon
Maracaibo	muracoibo	Marco	muraki
Maracanda	murakodain	Marconi	murakini
Maracay	murakose	Marcottage	murakitigun
Maracas	murakosi	Marcus	murakunsi
Marage	muragun	Mardi gras	murade gansi
Maraginig	muragungnni	Marduk	muradeko
Maranatha	muraintose	Mardy	muradie
Maranon	murainsi	Mare1	muran
Marante	murainto	Mare2	muran

WORD (x)	EQUIVALENT (y)	WORD (x)	EQUIVALENT (y)
Mareclausum	murankansumo	Marinade	muramijin
Mareliberum	muranlebema	Marinate	muramiyo
Maremma	muranmmo	Marine	murami
Marengo	murainlo	Mariner	muramisi
Marestail	muransetnlo	Marinism	muramimosi
Margaric	muragiraiko	Marion	murain
Margaret	muragirate	Marionette	muraintn
Margarita	muragiraito	Mariolatry	murainleterai
Margarite	muragiraite	Mariology	murainlogbon
Margate	muragiyo	Mariposa	muraipinsa
Margarine	muragirain	Marish	murasue
Margay	muragise	Marist	muranisi
Marge	muragn	Maritage	muratogun
Margin	muragin	Maritain	muratelu
Marginal	muraginjo	Marital	muratejo
Marginalia	muraginjoin	Maritime	muratimi
Marginalize	muraginjose	Maritza	muraisun
Marginate	muraginyo	Marjoram	murajiranmu
Margrative	muraganweyo	Mark1	murako
Margrave	muraganwo	Mark2	murako
Margraviate	muraganwoyo	Marked	murakode
Margravine	muraganwohun	Marker	murakosi
Marguerite	muragnraiyo	Market	murakia
Maria	muran	Marketable	murakiaberon
Mariachi	murankhi	Marketer	murakiaran
Mariachi	muranikhi	Mark-up	murako pake
Marian	muraihn	Markhor	murakohiran
Marianao	Muraihnko	Markka	muraka
Mariculture	muraikunjiaran	Markov	murakowa
Marie	murase	Marl	murajo
Marigold	muraigondon	Marlborough	murajoboroungba
Marijuana	muraijona	Marley	murajoin
Marimba	muranmbe	Marlin	murajan
Marina	muramn	Marline	muralehun

WORD (x)	EQUIVALENT (y)	WORD (x)	EQUIVALENT (y)
Marlite	muraleyo	Mars	murase
Marmalade	muramijin	Marsala	murasin
Mamara	muramarai	Marseillaise	murasinjjose
Marmion	muramuse	Marseille	murasinjjo
Marmite	muramuto	Marsh	murasu
Marmolada	muramolejn	Marshal	murasujo
Marmoreal	muramoraijo	Marshalling yard	yandan murasujjognni
Marmoset	muramoseto	Marshland	murasuledain
Marmot	muramote	Marston	murasetin
Mame	murahun	Marsupial	murasupnjo
Marocain	murokoin	Marsupium	murasupnma
Maroni	muroin	Mart	murate
Maronite	murosiyo	Martaban	muratebn
Maroon1	murosi	Martagon	murategon
Maroon2	murosi	Maetello	muratejjoin
Maroquin	murokun	Maten	muratin
Marquee	murakunse	Martensite	muratinsuyo
Marquesas	murakunsi	Martha	murasua
Maquess	murakunse	Martial	muratnjo
Marqetry	murakunterai	Martial arts	etesi muratnjo
Marquis	murakuosi	Martial law	meofin muratnjo
Marquise	murakuose	Martial	muratnjo
Marquisette	murakunsetin	Martian	muratnsi
Marram	murranmo	Martin	muratin
Marrano	murrain	Martinet	muratinte
Marriage	murraigun	Martingle	muratingijon
Marriageable	muraigunbe	Martini	muratini
Married	murraide	Martinmas	muratinmosn
Marron glace	murran ganse	Martinique	muratinikun
Marron	murran	Martyr	muratnra
Marrow	murra	Martyrdom	muratnradeo
Marrowbone	murra	Martyrize	muratnrase
Marrowbone	murra boin	Martyrlogy	muratnralogbon
Marry	murrai	Martyr	muratnra

WORD (x)	EQUIVALENT (y)	WORD (x)	EQUIVALENT (y)
Marvel	murawanlo	Masseur	masoorai
Marvelous	murawanlosi	Massicot	masookiti
Marx	murasa	Massif	masoofan
Marxism	murasamosi	Massine	masaoohun
Mary	murasi	Massinger	masooginisi
Marzipan	murasepan	Massive	masoowin
Mascara	masekosi	Mass media	masoo mujina
Mascle	masekuo	Mast1	masi
Mascon	masekin	Mast2	masi
Mascot	masekiti	Mastaba	masibo
Masculine	masekuohun	Mastax	masitesi
Masculinity	masekuohunto	Mastectomy	masitetemo
Maser	maserai	Master	masitn
Mash	masue	Mastery	masitnrai
Mashie	masueni	Mastic	masiko
Mashlin	masuejan	Masticate	masitekoyo
Mask	masia	Masticatory	masitekoyorai
Masochism	mallekhimosi	Mastiff	masitefe
Mason	mallesi	Mastigophoran	masitegonphiran
Masonia	mallesini	Mastitis	masiteso
Masonic	mallesiko	Masto	masito
Masonite	mallesitn	Mastodon	masitojain
Masonry	mallesirai	Mastoid	masitojo
Masora	masoran	Mastoisitis	masitojoso
Masque	masekun	Mastoidectomy	masitojotemo
Masquerade	masekunrajin	Mat1	mate
Mass1	masoo	Mat2	mate
Mass2	masoo	Matabele	matnbejn
Massacre	masooknra	Matador	matndera
Massage	masoogbo	Matameros	matnmurosi
Massasauga	masoosagan	Matanuska	matnsunka
Masse	masoo	Matapan	matnpan
Masses	masoosi	Match1	matora
Masseter	masootnra	Match2	matora

WORD (x)	EQUIVALENT (y)	WORD (x)	EQUIVALENT (y)
Matchboard	matorabugba	Matricide	matnraikeku
Matchbox	matorabosi	Matriculate	matnrakunleyo
Matchless	matoralabo	Matrimony	matnraimeni
Matchmaker	matoramaknsi	Matrix	motnrasi
Mate	muyo	Matron	matnran
Mate1	mate	Matronage	matnrangun
Mate2	mate	Matronly	matnranlo
Mater	matera	Matte	matte
Material	materaijo	Matter	matto
Materialism	materaijomosi	Mattery	mattorai
Materialist	materaijosi	Matthew	mattosn
Materiality	materaileto	Matthias	mattosn
Materialize	materaijose	Matting	mattegnni
Materially	materaijjn	Mattins	mattesn
Materia medica	materan mujinko	Mattock	mattekin
Materiel	materailo	Mattoid	mattejo
Maternal	materanjo	Mattress	matterai
Maternalize	materanleto	Maturate	matnraiyo
Maternity	materantn	Maturation	matnraiyoon
Matey	matere	Mature	matnran
Math	matesi	Matutinal	matntunjo
Mathematical	matesikojo	Maty	matnsi
Mathematical table	matesikojo teberon	Matzo	matnse
Mathematics	matesikosi	Matzoon	matnsesi
Maths	mosise	Mauby	munbe
Matico	mateki	Maud	maunde
Matilda	matejo	Maudlin	maundejan
Matinee	matehun	Maul	maunjan
Matins	matesn	Maulana	maunjnhn
Matrass	matnreso	Maumet	maunmuto
Matri	matnra	Mau	maun
Matriarch	matnraknra	Maund	maunjn
Matriarchy	matnraknran	Maunder	maunjnra
Matrices	matnraiknsi	Maundy	maunde

WORD (x)	EQUIVALENT (y)	WORD (x)	EQUIVALENT (y)
Maungy	maungn	Mayoralty	maynranjotn
Maurist	maunraisi	Mayoress	maynranbo
Mauser	maunserai	Maypole	maynpinjn
Mausoleum	maunsoonjn	May queen	mayn kuneni
Mauve	maunwin	Maze	mase
Maverick	mawinraiko	Mazagan	masegbi
Maw	mawi	Mazard	masegbaa
Mawger	mawignra	Mazarin	maseran
Mawkin	mawikin	Mazarine	maserain
Mawkish	mawikisue	Mazaruni	maseroin
Max	malu	Mazda	masire
Maxi	malusi	Maze	masia
Maxilla	malujawi	Mazeppa	masiapan
Maxillary	malujawirai	Mazer	masnra
Maxim	malumso	Mazuma	masuma
Maxima	maluma	Mazurka	masuajo
Maximal	malumojn	Mazuru	masurai
Maximite	malumoyo	Mazut	masute
Maximize	malumose	Mazzard	masiasegba
Maximum	malumo	Mc carthyism	mkn kosnsnmosi
Maxixe	malusun	Mc coy	mkn kise
May	mayn	Me1	mi
Maya	maya	Me2	mu
Mayari	mayarai	Mea culpa	mu kuopan
Maybe	maynbe	Mead	mugba
Mayday	mayndase	Meadow	mugbawa
Mayence	maynsi	Meager	mugnra
Mayhap	maynhapn	Meager	mugnran
Mayhem	maynheu	Meall	muje
Mayo	mayoko	Meal2	muje
Mayotte	mayotn	Maelie	mijese
Mayon	mayohi	Meals on wheels	muje le whinlo
Mayonnaise	mayohunsia	Meal-ticket	tikiyo muje
Mayor	maynran	Mealy	mujelo

WORD (x)	EQUIVALENT (y)	WORD (x)	EQUIVALENT (y)
Mean1	muhn	Medalist	mujinjosi
Mean2	muhn	Medallion	mujinjjosi
Mean3	muhn	Medallist	mujinjjosi
Means	muhnsi	Medan	mudeun
Meant	miuhnte	Meddle	mujiduo
Meany	muhnsi	Meddlesome	mujiduosoomo
Meander	muhnjnra	Media	mujina
Meanie	mihnse	Medevac	mujinwako
Meaning	muhngnni	Media	mujina
Measles	musuronsi	Mediacy	mujinase
Measly	musurain	Mediaeval	mujinawinjo
Measure	muwonrai	Medial	mujijo
Measure	muwonraide	Median	mujiun
Measureless	muwonrailabo	Mediastinum	mujisetima
Measurement	muwonraimutto	Mediate	mujinyo
Meat	mutan	Mediator	mujinyoran
Meatball	mutanrobo	Medic	mujinko
Meaty	mutansi	Medical	mujinkojo
Mecate	mukiyo	Medicament	mujinkomutto
Mecca	mukko	Medicate	mujinkoyo
Meccano	mukkoin	Medication	mujinkoyoon
Mechanic	mikhohiknjo	Medicinal	mujinkinjo
Mechanics	mukhohiknsi	Medicine	mujinkin
Mechanism	mukhohimosi	Medieval	mujinwinjo
Mechanize	mukhohise	Mediocre	mujinkioran
Mechanist	mukhohisi	Mediocrity	mujinkiorantn
Mechanistic	mukhohisuko	Meditate	mujinteyo
Mechanotherapy	mukhohisinranpo	Meditate	mujinteyo
Mechlin	mukjojan	Meditative	mujinteyowin
Meck	muki	Mediterranean	mujitnrarain
Meconism	mukinmosi	Medium	mujinma
Mecopterous	mukipntisi	Medlar	mujiran
Med	mujin	Madley	mujiroin
Medal	mujinjo	Medulla	mujijjo

WORD (x)	EQUIVALENT (y)	WORD (x)	EQUIVALENT (y)
Medulla oblongata	obngunta mujijjo	Megapode	muganpindie
Medullary	mujijjorai	Megara	muganra
Medullated	mujijjoyode	Megaris	muganran
Medusa	mujise	Megaron	muganran
Medusoid	mujise	Megastar	mugansetan
Meed	munjin	Megasporangium	muganseporaignma
Mee	misn	Megasporophyll	muganseporaiphewe
Meek	misnko	Megathere	mugansirai
Meer	misnsn	Megaton	mugantin
Meerkat	misnko	Megatron	mugantnran
Meerschaum	misnsekho	Megavitamin	muganwintnmi
Meet1	misnto	Megavolt	muganwnjia
Meet2	misnto	Megawatt	mughisun
Meeting	misntognni	Megiddo	mugndo
Mega	mugan	Megohm	mugonhnmo
Mega-	mugan	Megohm	mugonhnmo
Megabyte	muganbeyo	Megrim	mugiron
Megaphilic	muganphejnko	Mein kampt	muhn kanpo
Megacephaly	muganknphejn	Meiny	muhnse
Megadeath	muganjinsi	Meiosis	mukoso
Megagamete	mugangimuta	Mel	melo
Megahertz	muganheraise	Melaena	melohunje
Megalith	muganlesi	Melaleuca	melojnko
Megalithic	muganlesiko	Melamine	melomini
Megalo	muganlo	Melancholia	melohunkhijan
Megalocardia	muganlokogbain	Melancholy	melohunkhijin
Megalocephaly	muganloknphejn	Melanemia	melodudumo
Megalomania	muganlomohan	Melanesia	melohunsia
Megalopolis	muganlopinjnsi	Mélange	melogini
Megalopsia	muganlopnsia	Melanian	melodudusi
Megalosaur	muganlosanra	Melanic	melodudusi
Megaloptera	muganlopntnran	Melanin	melodudu
Meganthropus	mugansinrapnsi	Melanism	melodudumosi
Megaphone	muganphohun	Melanite	meloduyo

WORD (x)	EQUIVALENT (y)	WORD (x)	EQUIVALENT (y)
Melano	meloduko	Mellite	mellote
Melanochroi	melodukokhi	Mellon	mellosi
Melanocratic	melodukokanko	Mellophone	mellophohun
Melanocyte	melodukosnyo	Mellow	mellose
Melanoid	melodukojo	Melodeon	melodunni
Melanoma	melodukoma	Melodia	melodungi
Melanosis	melodukoso	Melodic	melodunko
Melanoous	melodukosi	Melodious	melodunsii
Melanthaceous	melotesuwa	Melodist	melodunsi
Melaphyre	melopherai	Melodize	melodunse
Melatonin	melotodu	Melodrama	melogbanma
Melba	melobe	Melodramatics	melogbamakosi
Melboume	meloburain	Melody	melodun
Melchior	melokhiran	Meloid	melojo
Melchisedec	melokhijnke	Meloidae	melojoin
Melchite	melokhiyo	Melolonthinae	melojnlesihun
Meld	melojn	Melomania	melomohan
Melee	melose	Melon	meloni
Melee	melosia	Melt	meloyo
Meliaceous	melosuwa	Meltage	meloyogun
Melic	meloko	Melton	melotin
Melilia	melojan	Melungeon	meluginisi
Melilot	melojnte	Melville	melowojjn
Melinite	meloheyo	Melvin	melowan
Meliorate	melorainyo	Member	mumora
Meliaoration	melorainyoon	Membership	mumorasunpn
Meliorism	melorainmosi	Membrane	memorahun
Meliority	melorainto	Membraneous	mumorahunsi
Melisma	melosua	Memento	muminito
Melita	meloto	Memento mori	muminito moorai
Mell	mello	Memnon	muminisi
Melliferous	mellofirosi	Memo	mumo
Mellifluous	mellofolusi	Memoirs	mumoraisi
Mellophagous	mellophijesi	Memorabilia	mumoraibejan

WORD (x)	EQUIVALENT (y)	WORD (x)	EQUIVALENT (y)
Memorable	mumoraibe	Menendez	musiajnse
Memorandum	mumeraijnsi	Menes	musiasin
Memorial	mumoraijo	Menhaden	musehungbain
Memorialize	mumoraijose	Menhir	musiahun
Memorize	mumoraise	Menial	musiajo
Memory	mumorai	Meniere	musiaran
Memory lane	mumorai lehasi	Meninges	musiaginisi
Memphis	mumphesi	Meningitis	musiaginiso
Memsahib	mumosewa	Meningocele	musiaginikojn
Men	muye	Meniscus	musiasekun
Men	muye	Menispermaceous	musiasipnronsuwa
Menace	muyosia	Mennonite	museniniyo
Menacme	muyemosi	Meno	minkn
Menad	muyedan	Menology	miniknlogbon
Menadione	muyegun	Menominee	miniknmise
Ménage a trios	muyegun a tnraso	Menopause	miniknpanlese
Menagerie	muyegunrai	Menorah	miniknrhan
Menander	muyejnra	Menorrhagia	minikrrhangia
Menaquineone	muyekunuhun	Menotti	minikntto
Menarche	muyekhnra	Mensa	minisa
Menchen	muyekhin	Mensal	minisayo
Mend	mudan	Mensch	minisekhi
Mendacity	mudankito	Mense	minise
Mendacious	mudankisi	Menses	minisesi
Mendel	musdannle	Mens rea	minisi rein
Mendelevium	mudanlewinma	Menshevic	minisuawinko
Mendelian	mudanlehn	Menstrual	minisetnrajo
Mendelism	mudanlemosi	Menstrual cycle	snkuo minisetnrajo
Mendicant	mudannte	Menstruate	minisetnrayo
Mendigo	musdangon	Menstruation	minisetnrayoon
Mending	mudangnni	Mensurable	museraibe
Mendocino	musejnkinko	Mensural	museraijo
Mendoza	mudannko	Mensuration	museraiyoon
Mene	musia	Ment	mutto

WORD (x)	EQUIVALENT (y)	WORD (x)	EQUIVALENT (y)
Mental	minitojo	Mercer	muraknra
Mental age	agun minitojo	Mercerize	muraknraise
Mentalism	minitojomosi	Mercery	muraknrai
Mentality	minitojotn	Merchandise	murakhojnse
Menthaceous	minisesuwa	Merchant	murakhota
Menthane	minisehun	Merchantable	murakhotaberon
Menthene	minisinhun	Merchant bank	bonkn murakhota
Menthol	minisejin	Merchantman	murakhotamoye
Mentholated	minisejintode	Merchet	murakhnti
Menticide	minitokeku	Merci	muraki
Mention	minitosi	Mercia	murakin
Menton	minitin	Mercian	murakinsi
Mentor	minitnra	Merciless	murasnlabo
Mentum	minitnma	Mercurate	muraknrayo
Menu	minisi	Mercurialism	muraknrajomosi
Mepacrine	mupakahun	Mercurialize	muraknrajose
Meperidine	mupanrajoin	Mercuric	muraknrako
Mephasistophelean	muphisetophiroin	Mercurous	muraknrasi
Mephitic	muphitnnko	Mercury	muraknra
Mephitis	muphitnso	Mercy	murasn
Meprobamate	muponbeyo	Mere1	muran
Mer	mura	Mere2	murai
Merak	murako	Meredith	muraijosi
Merbromin	murabonmoin	Meringue	muraigini
Mercantile	murakotajn	Meretricious	muraitasiasi
Mercantilism	murakotajnmosi	Merganser	muragisi
Mercator projection	ponjnknyoon	Merge	muragbi
	murakoran	Merger	muragbisi
Mercaptan	murakopntin	Meridian	muraijoin
Mercaptide	murakopntijin	Meridional	muraijoinjo
Mercapto	murakopnto	Meringue	muraigan
Mercaptopurine	murakopnpuroin	Merino	muraihn
Mercator	muraknya	Merit	muratn
Mercenary	muraknrain	Meritocracy	muratnkansn

385

WORD (x)	EQUIVALENT (y)	WORD (x)	EQUIVALENT (y)
Meritorious	muratnransi	Mesic	misoko
Merie	murase	Mesotylene	misosilohun
Merkin	murakin	Mesmerism	misomuraimosi
Merlin	murajan	Mesmerize	misomuraise
Merlon	murajnsi	Mesne	misohun
Memaid	murameja	Meso-	miso
Merman	muramole	Mesobenthos	misobehntesi
Mero	mure	Mesocarp	misokopan
Meroblast	murebansia	Mesocephalic	misoknphejnko
Meroblastic	murebansiako	Mesocratic	misokanko
Merope	murepn	Mesocratic	misokanko
Meroplankton	murepankntin	Mesoderm	misojnramo
Merovingian	murewognsi	Mesogastrium	misogisuraima
Merozoite	muresinyo	Mesoglea	misogeron
Merrimark	murraiko	Mesognathous	misogbnhesi
Merry	murrai	Mesolithic	misolesiko
Merse	murase	Mesology	misologbon
Mersey	murasun	Mesomorph	misomophan
Mesa	musn	Meson	misosi
Misalliance	musnjjosi	Mesonephros	misohunphiran
Mesarach	musnranki	Mesopause	misopanlese
Mescal	musnkojo	Mesophyll	misophewe
Mescaline	musnkolehun	Mesophyte	misopheyo
Mesdames	musndamora	Mesosphere	misosuphirai
Mesdemoiselles	musndamorasejjn	Mesopotamia	misopintoma
Mesembryanthemum	musnembroinsinma	Mesorrhine	misorrhain
Mesencephalon	musnenknphijnsi	Mesosere	misoserai
Mesenchyme	musnenkhoinmo	Mesothelioma	misosinjonmo
Mesenteritis	musnentnraso	Mesothelium	misosinjoma
Mesentron	musnentnrain	Mesotron	misotnran
Mesentery	musnentnrai	Mesozoic	misosinko
Meseta	museto	Mescuit	musnkunte
Mesh	muso	Mess	musoo
Mesial	misojo	Message	musogun

WORD (x)	EQUIVALENT (y)	WORD (x)	EQUIVALENT (y)
Messalina	musoonleni	Metalize	mitollese
Massaline	musoonlehun	Metallo	mitolleko
Messene	musoonhun	Metallography	mitollekoganphe
Messenger	musoongunsi	Metalloid	mutallekojo
Messenia	musoohan	Metallurgy	mitollegbon
Messiah	mussehau	Metalwork	mitolewinro
Messianic	mussehauko	Metamale	mitomole
Messidor	musoodera	Metamer	mitomurai
Messieurs	musooraisi	Metamerism	mitomuraimosi
Mess mate	musoo mote	Metamorphosis	mitomophanso
Messrs	mussose	Metaphase	mitophanse
Messuage	musoosngun	Metaphor	mitophiran
Messy	musoosi	Metaphrase	mitophanso
Mesta	musnto	Metaphrast	mitophansi
Mestee	musnte	Metaphysic	mitophekoso
Mestizo	musetosin	Metaplasia	mitopansia
Mestranol	musurainjin	Metaplasm	mitopanson
Met1	mite	Metapsychology	mitopfiyekhologbon
Met2	mite	Metasomatism	mitosoomosi
Meta-	mito	Metastable	mitosetnberon
Metabolism	mitobujinmosi	Metastasis	mitosetnso
Metabolite	mitobujinyo	Metatarsal	mitotesnjo
Metabolize	mitobujinse	Metatarsus	mitotesnwa
Metacarpus	mitokopanwa	Metatheria	mitosinran
Metacentre	mitokntiran	Metatherian	mitosinrain
Metachromatic	mitokisinmosi	Metathesize	mitosinsose
Metacinnabarite	mitokiheboosnyo	Metathorax	mitosinrase
Metafemale	mitofnmole	Metatrophy	mitotnraphe
Metage	mitogun	Metaxylem	mitosonlomi
Metagenesis	mitognhunso	Metazoan	mitosinhn
Metal	mitole	Mete	mutn
Metalanguage	mitoletogngun	Metampirical	mutnemporaikojo
Metallic	mitoleko	Metempiricism	mutnemporaikomosi
Metalline	mitollehun	Metampsychosis	mutnemphiyekhoso

WORD (x)	EQUIVALENT (y)	WORD (x)	EQUIVALENT (y)
Meteor	mutnran	Methlene	musiolehun
Meteoric	mutnranko	Methylsobutylketone	musiolesoobutekntohun
Meteorite	mutnranyo	Methylmeth	musiolemutn akoraileyo
Meteoroid	mutnranjo	acrylate	
Meteorology	mutnranlogbon	Methylthionine	musiolesinlehun
Meter1	mutosi	Metic	mutiko
Meter1	muto	Meticulous	mutikunsi
Meter2	muto	Métier	mutiran
Meterage	mutogun	Metiff	mutifn
Metestrus	mutnsetorai	Metis	mutiso
Methacrylate	mutnakoraileyo	Metochy	mutikhoin
Methacrylic	mutnakoraileko	Metodontiasis	mutidebuyoso
Methadone	mutnjoin	Metoestrus	mutisetorai
Methamphetamine	mutnamphntemini	Metol	mutijin
Methanol	mutnhunjin	Metonic	mutinko
Methaqualone	mutnkunlohun	Metonym	mutinmo
Methedrine	mutngbain	Metonymy	mutinmose
Metheglin	mutngnjan	Metooism	mutoonmosi
Methinks	musinknsi	Metope	mutinpon
Methionine	musinlehun	Metopic	mutinponko
Method	musejn	Metralgia	mutnrejngan
Methodical	musejnkojo	Metrazol	mutnrasejin
Methodism	musejnmosi	Metre1	mutoran
Methodist	musejnsi	Metre2	mutoran
Methodize	musejnse	Metric	mutoraikojo
Methodology	musejnlogbon	,metrical	mutoraikojo
Methotrexate	musetasiseyo	.metricate	mutoraikoyo
Methought	musinragbe	Metrify	mutoraife
Methuselah	musunjnse	Metrist	mutoraisi
Methys	musiose	Mutritis	mutoraiso
Methyl	musiole	Metro	mutnra
Methylal	musiolejo	Metrology	mutnralogbon
Methlate	musioleyo	Metronome	mutnranmo
Methldopa	musioledepan	Metronymic	mutnrainmuko

WORD (x)	EQUIVALENT (y)	WORD (x)	EQUIVALENT (y)
Metropolis	mutnrapinjnso	Micawber	makwebesi
Metropolitan	mutnrapinjntan	Mice	makn
Metrorrhagia	mutnrarrhangi	Micelle	maknjjn
-metry	mutorai	Michaelmas daisn	machnlomusan dainsn
Mettle	muttoron	Michigan	makhigan
Mettled	muttoron	Mick	maki
Mettled	muttoronde	Mockery	makirai
Meum	muumi	Mickey	makisi
Meuniere	muwaniran	Mickle	makiran
Meurthe	muraisun	Micky	makise
Meuse	muwasun	Micra	maknre
Mew1	mewn	Micrify	muknraife
Mew2	mewn	Micro	muknra
Mew3	mewn	Microanalysis	muknranijinso
Mew4	mewn	Microbarograph	muknrabosiaganpha
Mews	mewnsi	Microbe	muknrabe
Mewl	mewnjo	Microbicide	muknrabakeku
Mexcan	mesiakin	Microbiology	muknrabalologbon
Mexico	mesiaki	Microbiota	muknrabakote
Meyer	mesesi	Microcephaly	muknraknphejo
Mezereon	meserain	Microchip	muknrakhipn
Mezuzah	messosi	Microclimate	muknrakiunmote
Mezzanine	messehnhun	Microclimatology	muknrakiunmote-logbon
Mezzo	messe		
Mezzotint	messetito	Microcline	muknrakihun
Mho	mhn	Micrococcus	muknrakikisi
Mi	mi	Microcopy	muknrakipe
Miami	mamini	Microcosm	muknrakiseto
Miarolitic	maranjinko	Microcrystalline	muknrakoraitnjjohun
Miasma	mamisia	Microcyte	muknrasnyo
Mib	mabe	Microdont	muknradebuyo
Mica	mako	Microdot	muknradeti
Micaceous	makosuwa	Microfiche	muknrafikhn
Mica diorite	mako diraiyo	Micrograph	muknraganpha

WORD (x)	EQUIVALENT (y)	WORD (x)	EQUIVALENT (y)
Microgroove	muknragonwini	midas	midanse
Microlith	muknralesi	midden	midadain
Micrometeorite	muknramutnranyo	middle	midaduo
Micrometeorology	muknramutnran-logbon	middling	midaduognni
		middy	midade
Micrometer	muknramuto	midgard	midagngba
Micron	muknran	midge	midagn
Micronesia	muknrahunsia	midget	midagnyo
Micronesian	muknrahunsianh	midgut	midagunte
Micronutrient	muknrayunteraito	midi	midi
microorganism	muknraorogbnmosi	midianite	midihunyo
Micropalaeontology	muknrapanjoinon-tologbon	midinette	midihuntin
		midiron	midairin
Microphone	muknraphohun	midland	midaledain
Micropyle	muknraperon	midmost	midamosua
Micropyrometer	muknraporoinmuto	midpoint	midapinoni
Microscope	muknrasokipon	midrash	midaransua
Microscopic	muknrasekiponko	midriff	midaraife
Microscopy	muknrasekipe	midst	midasi
Microseism	muknsesun	midterm	midatnramo
Microsome	muknrasoomo	midaway	midawelo
Microsporangium	muknraseporaigima	midweek	midawiniko
Microspore	muknraseporai	midwicket	midawokoto
Microsporophyll	muknraseporaiphewe	midwife	midawofin
Microstomatous	muknrasetomitesi	mien	misn
Microtome	muknratemu	miff	mifan
Microtomy	muknratemo	might1	magbe
Microtone	muknratoni	might2	magbe
microsurgery	muknrasugbilerai	mighty	magbetn
microwave	muknrawewin	mightily	magbetolo
micrurgy	muknraigbon	mightily	magbetolo
micturate	mukyoraiyo	mignon	magnsi
micturition	mukyoraiyoon	mignonette	magnsitin
mid	mida	migraine	magnrain

WORD (x)	EQUIVALENT (y)	WORD (x)	EQUIVALENT (y)
migrant	magnraitn	Militarize	malletaraise
migrate	magnraiyo	Military	malletarai
migration	magnraiyoon	Militate	malletayo
migratory	magnraiyoran	Militia	malletie
Miguel	magunran	Millium	mallema
Mikado	maknde	Milk	maliki
Mike	makn	Milk round	maliki rojoin
Micron	maknran	Milker	malikisi
Mil	male	Milko	maliko
Milady	maledn	Milky	malikise
Milage	malelegun	Mill	mujnra
Milan	maleto	Millay	mujnrase
Milch	malekhi	Milled	mujnrade
Mild	malejn	Millefiori	mujnrafirai
Milden	malejnsi	Mille fleurs	mujnra fijnrai
Mildew	malejnwa	Mille fleurs	mujnra fijnrai
Mildly	malejnse	Millefeuille	mujnrafnwajjn
Mildred	malejnra	Millenarian	mujnrainrain
Mile	malele	Millenarianism	mujnrainrainmosi
Mileage	malelegun	Millenary	mujnrainrai
Mileometer	malelemuto	Millennium	mujnrainhunma
Milepost	malelepintn	Millipede	mujnranpndie
Miler	malelesi	Miller	mujnrasi
Miles	malelesi	Millerite	mujnraraiyo
Milesgioriosus	malelesugiransnso	Millesimal	mujnrasoomojn
Milestone	malelesetole	Millet	mujnratn
Milliaria	mallerain	Milli-	mujnran
Millarision	malleraisoon	Milliard	mujnrangbaa
Milliary	mallerai	Millibar	mujnranbo
Milliary fever	mallerai finwosi	Miller	mujnrasi
Millicent	malleknti	Milligram	mujnranganmo
Milieu	mallewa	Milliliter	mujnranlitnra
Militant	malletate	Milliliter	mujnranlitnran
Militarism	malletaraimosi	Millimeter	mujnranmuto

391

WORD (x)	EQUIVALENT (y)	WORD (x)	EQUIVALENT (y)
millimetre	mujnranmutoran	Mine2	mihun
millimicron	mujnranmuknran	Miner	mihunran
milline	mujnrain	Mineral	mihunranjo
milliner	mujnrainsi	Mineralize	mihunranjose
millinery	mujnrainrai	Mineralogy	mihunranlogbon
million	mujnransi	Minerva	mihunranwa
millionth	mujnransi	Minestrone	mihunsuroini
millionaire	mujnransirai	Ming	mihungi
millipede	mujnranpndie	Minge	mihunng
mill run	mujnra rian	Mingle	mihungiron
milo	mulo	Mingrelian	mihungirejohn
milometer	mulomuto	Mingy	mihungise
milt	mujia	Mini	mini
milter	mujiasi	Miniature	minitoran
Miltonic	mujiatinko	Miniaturize	minitoraise
Mime	mimi	Minibus	minibusa
Mimeograph	mimiganpha	Minibo	minibon
Mimesis	mimiso	Minicu	minikun
Mimetic	mimiteko	Minify	minife
Mimetite	mimiteyo	Minikin	manikin
Mimic	mimiko	Minim	minimo
Mimosa	mimiosan	Minimal	minimojn
Mina	far	Minimalism	minimojnmosi
Mina	mina	Minimize	minimuse
Minacious	minaknsi	Minimum	minimuse
Minaret	minaranyo	Minion	minisi
Minas	minase	Minipill	minipolle
Minatory	minayorai	Meningitis	minigainso
Mince	minisi	Minister	miniseto
Mind	minijn	Ministration	minisetoyoon
Minded	minijnde	Ministry	minisetorai
Mindel	minijnjo	Minitrack	minitnreko
Mindless	minijnlabo	Minium	minima
Mine1	mihun	Minimus	minimasi

WORD (x)	EQUIVALENT (y)	WORD (x)	EQUIVALENT (y)
Mining	minignni	Miocene	minknhun
Miniver	miniwinra	Miombo	minmbu
Minivet	miniwnti	Miosis	minkoso
Mink	minkn	Miquelet	mukunlo
Minkowski	minknwakisi	Mirabile dictum	muraibajn dikiti
Minnow	miniwa	Mirabilia	miraibajan
Minoan	minihn	Miracidium	muraikijnma
Minor	miniran	Miracle	muraikun
Minorca	miniranko	Miraculous	muraikunsi
Minorist	miniransi	Mirador	muraijnra
Minorite	minirante	Mirage	muraigun
Minority	minirantn	Miranda	muraijina
Minotaur	minitorai	Mire	muere
Minsk	minseki	Mirepoix	muerepile
Minster	minseto	Mirex	mueresi
Minstrel	minsetoran	Mirinda	muraijn
Mint1	minate	Mirk	murakn
Mint2	minate	Mirror	muraran
Mintage	minategun	Mirth	muraisi
Mintjulep	minatejoran	Nus-1	musi
Minton	mintele	Mis-2	musi
Minuend	minwajin	Misadventure	musiadiwintaran
Minuet	minwata	Misalliance	musiajjosi
Minus	miniyo	Misapply	musiaponlo
Minuscule	miniyokuo	misapprehend	musiapesihejn
Minute1	miniti	Misappropriate	musibekiawa
Minute2	minite	Misbehave	musibehawin
Minutely	minitilo	Miscall	musikolle
Minuthesis	minisiaso	miscarry	musikosirai
Minutia	minitie	Miscast	musikosoto
Minutiae	minitiese	Miscegenation	musiknginyoon
Minx	minsia	Miscellaneous	musknijjnhunsi
Minyan	minyin	Miscellany	musiknjjnhun
Miocardio	minkogbako	Miscellanist	musiknjjnhunsi

WORD (x)	EQUIVALENT (y)	WORD (x)	EQUIVALENT (y)
Mischance	musikhohunkn	Mishna	musuhn
Mischievous	musikhiwinsi	Misjoinder	musijotojnra
Mischmetal	musikhimitole	Misjudge	musijugbon
Miscible	musikibe	Mislay	musilesn
Misconceive	musikinknwini	Misnomer	musihnmurai
Misconception	musikinknpnyoon	Misogyny	musiloyon
Misconduct	musikindikiti	Misology	musilogbon
Miscopy	musikipe	Misoneism	musihunmosi
Miscount	musikaleyo	Misprision	musipansoon
Miscreance	musiknrasi	Miss1	musin
Miscreant	musiknrate	Miss2	muso
Miscue	musikunse	Missal	musinjo
Misdeal	musijinjo	Missay	musinso
,osdeed	musijindi	Missel	musinlo
Misdemean	musijinmihun	Missile	musoonjn
Misdemeanant	musijinmihunte	Missilery	musoonjnrai
Misdemeanor	musijinmihunsi	Missing	musoongnni
Mise	muse	Mission	musinse
Miseen scene	musesi seknsa	Missionary	musinserai
Miseno	musekn	Missis	musinsi
Miser	musera	Mississippi	musinsipo
Miserable	muserabe	Missive	musinwin
Miserere	muserairan	Missolonghi	musinlogbin
Misericorde	museraikigban	Missouri	musinrai
Misericordia	museraikigbain	Missout	musinnita
Misety	muserau	Missus	musinsi
Misfeasance	musifnsesi	Missy	musinse
Misfire	musifinna	Mist	misi
Misfit	musifito	Mistake	musitekn
Misfortune	musifontnni	Mistaken	musiteknsi
Misgovern	musigoonwa	Mistate	musitnyo
Misguide	musigunjuwe	Mistal	misitnjo
Mishap	musihapn	Mister	misitn
Mishmash	musumosia	Mistigris	misitngansi

WORD (x)	EQUIVALENT (y)	WORD (x)	EQUIVALENT (y)
Mistletoe	misitoronton	Mixolydian	mulujindain
Mistletoe	misitoronton	Mizar	museran
Mistral	musitnranjo	Mizzen	museni
Mistreat	musitnrante	Mizzle	musejn
Mistress	musitnrabo	Mnemme	momeni
Mistrial	musiteraijo	Mnemonic	momeniko
Mistryst	musiteraisi	Mnemonics	momenikosi
Misty	msise	Mnemosyne	momenisohun
Misunderstand	musinujnrasetndan	Mo	mo
Misuse	musilese	Moa	mohe
Misventure	musiwinyoran	Moan	mohu
Mitchell	mutnkhnllo	Moat	moyika
Mite1	mutn	Mob	mobu
Mite2	mntn	Mob-cap	mobu-kopn
Miter	mutnra	Mobile	mobajn
Mither	mutnsira	Mobility	mobajnto
Mithra	mutnseran	Mobilize	mobajnse
Mithridates	mutnraidatosi	Mobus strip	mobusa
Miticide	mutnkeku	Mobile	mobajn
Mitigate	mutngiyo	Mobocracy	mobukansan
Mitigation	mutngiyoon	Mobster	mobuseto
Mitis	mutnse	Moccasin	mokikosun
Mitosis	mutiso	Mocha	mokho
Mitrailleuse	mutnrellojnse	Mock	mokio
Mitral	mutnrejo	Mocker	mokiosi
Mitre	mutnran	Mockery	mokiorai
Mitt	mutnti	Mock-up	mokio-pake
Mitten	mutntin	Mod	modi
Mittimus	mutntima	Mod	modi
Mitzvah	mutnsuwan	Modal	modijo
Mix	mulu	Modality	modileto
Mixed	mulude	Mod cons	modi kinsi
Mixer	mulusi	Mode	modie
Mixture	mulutnran	Model	modiejo

WORD (x)	EQUIVALENT (y)	WORD (x)	EQUIVALENT (y)
Momentum	momuttnma	Mom	momo
Momism	momosi	Moment	momuto
Momma	momma	Momentary	momutorai
Mommy	mommi	Momentous	momutosi
Momoson	momisi	Molder	mojorasi
Momus	momusi	Molding	mojoragnni
Mon	meni	Moldy	mojorase
Mon.	meni	Mole 1	moju
Monacetin	menisintie	Mole 2	moju
Monaco	meniki	Mole3	moju
Monarchism	menikhnmosi	Mole4	moju
Monad	menijn	Molecular	mojukunra
Monadelphous	menijnjophisi	Molecule	mojukuo
Monadism	menijnmosi	Molest	mojusie
Monadnock	menojnkho	Moliere	mojurai
Monaghan	menighain	Moline	mojuhun
Mona lisa	menilesi	Moll	molele
Monami	menimi	Mullah	molelerain
Monandrous	menigbainsi	Molle	molele
Mollusk	mojnrasia	Mollescent	moleleseluntri
Molly	mojnrase	Mollify	molelefe
Mollycoddle	mojnrasekididuo	Mollities	moleletosi
Moloch	molokhia	Molluscum	molelesekuo
Moloney	moloyun	Mother	mosira
Molt	moloyo	Mojarra	mojarra
Molten	moloyin	Mojave	mojawin
Molto	moleto	Mojeur	mojnra
Molucca	molukko	Moji	mojan
Moly	molau	Mocha	monkho
Molybdae	molaubudiyo	Mokpo	moppo
Molybdenite	molaubudainte	Mojo	monjo
Molybdenum	molaubudainma	Moke	mokoi
Molybdic	molaubudiko	Mol	mojn
Molybdous	molaubudisi	Mola	mojin

WORD (x)	EQUIVALENT (y)	WORD (x)	EQUIVALENT (y)
Molal	mojnjo	Moe	more
Molar	mojnre	Moellon	mollesi
Molasses	mojnsunsi	Moerae	morein
Mold1	mojora	Moesia	moresia
Mold2	mojora	Moesogoth	mosesiagonto
Mold3	mojora	Mofette	mofntn
Moldavia	mojorawa	Mofussil	mofunsoojo
Moldavite	mojorawote	Mog	mogn
Mohave	mohawin	Mogador	mogndera
Mohawk	mohakwo	Mogendavid	mogindawojn
Mohegan	Mohegan	Mogul	mogunjo
Mohenjodaro	mohinjodaro	Mohair	moharun
Mohican	mohiko	Modem	modimu
Mohock	mohinka	Moderate	modieyo
Mohole	mohinlu	Moderation	modieyoon
Mohorovicic	mohinraiwoki	Moderato	modieto
Mhs	mohasi	Moderator	modieran
Moidore	mojnrain	Modern	modiran
Moiety	mojito	Modemism	modiranmosi
Moil	moji	Modernize	modiranse
Moiral	mojirajo	Modest	modiesi
Moiré	mojiran	Modesty	modiesitn
Moiré	mojimi	Modicum	modikuo
Moist	mojimi	Modification	modiefikoyoon
Moisten	mojimisi	Modifier	modiefesi
Moisture	mojimiran	Modify	modiefe
Moisturize	mojimiraise	Modillion	modiellesi
Modular	modieransi	Modiolus	modiejinsi
Modulate	modieranyo	Modish	modiesua
Modulation	modieranyoon	Modiste	modieseto
Module	modieran	Modjokerto	modijoknrato
Modulus	modiejnsi	Modular	modieransi
Modus operandi	modiesi opnranjo	Modulate	modieranyo
Modus Vivendi	modiesi wonwinjo	Modulation	modieranyoon

WORD (x)	EQUIVALENT (y)	WORD (x)	EQUIVALENT (y)
Module	modieran	Moither	mojitesi
Modulus	modiejnsi	Mojarra	mojarra
Modus operandi	modiesi opnranjo	Mojave	mojawin
Modus Vivendi	modiesi wowinjo	Mojeur	mojnran
Moe	more	Moji	mojan
Moellon	morellesi	Mokha	monkho
Moerae	morein	Mokpo	moppo
Moesia	moresia	Mojo	monjo
Moesogoth	moresiagonto	Moke	mokoi
Mofette	mofntn	Mo1	mojn
Mofussil	mofunsoojo	Mola	mojin
Mog	mogn	Mola1	mojnjo
Mogador	mogndera	Molar	mojnre
Mogendavid	mogindawojn	Molasses	mojnsunsi
Mogul	mogunjo	Mold1	mojora
Mohair	moharun	Mold2	mojora
Mohave	mohawin	Mold3	mojora
Mohawk	mohakwo	Moldavia	mojorawa
Mohegan	Mohegan	Moldavite	mojorawote
Mohenjodaro	mohinjodaro	Molder	mojorasi
Mohican	mohiko	Molding	mojoragnni
Mohock	mohinka	Moldy	mojorase
Mohole	mohinlu	Mole1	moju
Mohorovicic	mohinraiwoki	Mole2	mojn
Mhs	mohasi	Mole3	moju
Moidore	mojirain	Mole4	moju
Moiety	mojito	Molecular	mojukunra
Moil	mojia	Molecule	mojukun
Moiral	mojarajo	Molest	mojusie
Moiré	mojiran	Moliere	mojurai
Moiré	mojimi	Moline	mjuhun
Moisten	mojimisi	Moll	molele
Moisture	mojimiran	Mullah	moleleran
Moisturize	mojimiraise	Molle	molelesi

WORD (x)	EQUIVALENT (y)	WORD (x)	EQUIVALENT (y)
Mollescent	molelesiseknti	Monadnock	menojnkho
Mollify	molelefe	Monaghan	menigbain
Mollities	moleletosi	Monalisa	menilesi
Molluscum	molelesekuo	Monami	menimi
Mollusk	molelesia	monandrous	menigbainsi
Molly	molelese	Monandry	menigbainse
Mollycoddle	molosekididuo	Monanthous	menisinsi
Moloch	molokhia	Monarch	meniknra
Moloney	moloyun	Monarchianism	meniknrainmosi
Molt	moleto	Monarchical	meniknrakojo
Molucca	molukko	Monarchism	meniknrakojo
Moly	molau	Monarchy	meniknran
Molybdate	molaubudiyo	Monarda	menijora
Molybdenite	molaubudainte	Monas	menise
Molybdenum	molaubudainma	Monastery	menisetnrai
Molybdic	molaubudiko	Monastic	menisetnko
Molybdous	molaubudisi	Monastism	menisetnmosi
Mom	momo	Monaural	meniranjo
Moment	momuto	Monazite	menisuyo
Momentary	momutorai	Moncher	menikhnra
Momentous	momuttnsi	Monck	meniki
Momentum	momuttnma	Moncton	menikitin
Momism	momosi	Mond	menijn
Momma	momma	Monday	menidase
Mommy	mommi	Monde	menijin
Momoson	momusi	Mondial	menijinjo
Mon	meni	Monetarism	menisanraimosi
Mon.	meni	Monetary	menisanrai
Monacetin	menisintie	Monetize	menisanse
Monaco	meniki	Money	menisan
Monarchism	menikhranmosi	Moneyed	menisande
Monad	menijn	Monger	menignra
Monadelphous	menijnjophisi	Mongol	menigbun
Monadism	menijnmosi	Mongolia	menigbunhn

WORD (x)	EQUIVALENT (y)	WORD (x)	EQUIVALENT (y)
Mongolism	menigbunmosi	Monoclinous	meniknkiunsi
Mongoloid	menigbunjo	Monocoque	meniknkun
Mongoose	menigonse	Monocracy	meniknkansn
Mongrel	menignranjo	Monocular	meniknkuoran
Mongrelize	menignranjose	Monocycle	meniknsnkuo
Monies	menisansi	Monocylic	meniknsnkuoko
Mongst	menignsi	Monocyte	meniknsnyo
Moniker	meniknra	Monodrama	menikngbanma
Monism	menimosi	Monody	meniknkinsi
Moniliasis	menijanso	Monofilament	meniknfilemutto
Moniliform	menijanfonmo	Monogamy	menikngimo
Monish	menise	Monogenesis	menikngnhunso
Monism	menimosi	Monogenetic	menikngnhun
Monition	menitosi	Monogenic	menikngin
Monitor	menitoran	Monogeny	meniknginse
Monitorial	menitoraijo	Monogram	meniknganmo
Monitory	monitorai	Monograph	meniknganpha
Monk	meniko	Monogyny	meniknloyun
Monkery	menikorai	Monohull	meniknhunlle
Monkey	menikoin	Monolatry	meniknleyorai
Monshood	menisoojo	Monolingua	meniknlikogunjo
Monmouth	menimounsi	Monolith	menknlesi
Mono-	menikn	Monologue	meniknlogbiso
Monoacetin	meniknsintie	Monomania	meniknmuhan
Monoacid	meniknboosoko	Monomark	meniknmurako
Monocacy	meniknkosn	Monomer	meniknmurai
Monocarpellary	meniknkopanllorai	Monomerous	meniknmuraisi
Monoceros	meniknknra	Monometalism	meniknmitolemosi
Monochasium	meniknhosuma	Monometer	meniknmuto
Monochord	meniknkhigba	Monomial	meniknmujo
Monochromatic	meniknkisinmu	Monomorphic	meniknmophanko
Monocle	meniknkuo	Monopetalous	meniknpntijosi
Monocline	meniknkihun	Monophagous	meniknphijesi
Monoclinic	meniknkiunko	Monophobia	meniknphoban

WORD (x)	EQUIVALENT (y)	WORD (x)	EQUIVALENT (y)
Monophonic	meniknphohun	Monotreme	menikntosimo
Monophithong	meniknphisi	Monotrichous	menikntaraikhasi
Monophyllous	meniknphewesi	Monotrophic	menikntnraphiko
Monophysite	meniknphesuyo	Monotropy	menikntnrapo
Monoplane	meniknpanyun	Monotype	menikntnpon
Monoplegia	meniknpojngan	Monovalent	meniknwajnto
Monopode	meniknpinjoma	Monoxide	meniosinji
Monopole	meniknpinjn	Monroe	meniron
Monopolist	meniknposi	Monrovia	menironwa
Monopolize	meniknpose	Mons	menise
Monopoly	meniknpose	Monseigneur	meniseganran
Monopropellant	meniknponpnllote	Monsieur	menisooran
Monopteros	meniknpntiransi	Monsignor	menisooganran
Monopsony	meniknpnson	Monsoon	menisoon
Monorail	meniknrailo	Monster	menisiatn
Monosaccharide	meniknsankhiraijin	Monstrance	menisetnsi
Monosemy	meniknsemo	Monstrosity	menisiatntn
Monosepalous	meniknsepanjosi	Monstrous	menisiatnsi
Monosome	meniknsoomo	Montage	menitegun
Monospermous	meniknsipnronsi	Montagnard	menitegngba
Monosilane	meniknsojnhun	Montagu	menitegn
Monosodium	meniknsoojoma	Montague	menitegnse
Monostich	meniknsetiko	Montaigne	menitegini
Monostichous	meniknsetikosi	Montale	menitejn
Monostome	meniknsetomu	Montana	menitelo
Monostrophe	meniknsetnraphn	Montane	menitelu
Monostylous	meniknsetnronsi	Montanic	meniteluko
Monosyllable	meniknsojnranbe	Montanism	menitelumosi
Monosymmetric	meniknsommutoraiko	Montauk	menitekn
Monotheism	meniknsinmosi	Mont bretia	menite besitie
Monothemia	meniknsintn	Mont de pie te	menite jin pon to
Monotone	menikntini	Monte casino	menita kosoon
Monotonous	menikntisi	Monteith	menitasi
Monotony	menikntise	Montenegro	menitahungnra

401

WORD (x)	EQUIVALENT (y)	WORD (x)	EQUIVALENT (y)
Monterey	menitarain	Mool	moojn
Monterrey	menitarrain	Moolah	moolehn
Montero	menitara	Mooley	moojnse
Montespan	menitasipan	Moon	moyin
Montesquieu	menitakusuwa	Moonie	moyinse
Montessori	menitasoorai	Moonlight	moyinlighe
Monteux	menitase	Moonlit	moyinleto
Monte verdi	menita winjn	Moony	moyinsi
Monte video	menia wojinko	Moop	mopan
Monte zuma	menita snmo	Moorl	mooro
Montagolfier	menitegonjafe	Moor2	mooro
Montgomery	menitegonmurai	Moore	mooron
Month	menisi	Moorea	mooroin
Monthly	menisilo	Mooring	mooroledain
Monticello	menitiknjjoin	Moorish	moorose
Monticule	menitikuo	Moory	moorosn
Montmartre	menitemuratn	Moose	moosua
Montmorency	menitemorainsi	Moot	mooto
Montpeller	menitepnllosi	Mop	mopn
Montreal	menitnranjo	Mope	mopi
Montreux	menitnransi	Moped	mopnde
Montrose	menitnrase	Mopoke	mopokin
Monument	menimutto	Moquette	mokuntin
Monumental	menimuttojo	Moqui	mokun
Mony	mensie	Mora	moran
Mony	menise	Moraceous	morasuwa
Monza	menise	Moraine	moraini
Monzonite	menisesita	Moral	moranjo
Monzonitic	menisesitako	Morale	moranjon
Moo	moo	Moralist	moranjosi
Mooch	mookha	Morality	moranleto
Mood1	moodi	Moralize	moranjose
Mood2	moodi	Moral law	moranjo leewo
Moody	moodise	Morass	morasoo

WORD (x)	EQUIVALENT (y)	WORD (x)	EQUIVALENT (y)
Moratorium	moratoraima	Morganatic	moragbainko
Moratory	moratorai	Morgen	moragan
Morava	morawo	Morgue	moragun
Moravia	morawa	Moriah	moaihun
Moravian	morawain	Moribund	moraibojn
Moray	morain	Morin	morie
Morbid	morabu	Morion	morain
Morbidity	morabutn	Morisco	moraiseki
Morbific	morabufiko	Morison	moraisin
Morbille	morasujose	Morituri	moraitnra
Morbilli	morasujo	Moritz	moraita
Morbillous	morasujosi	Morland	moraledain
Morceau	moraknun	Morley	morajnse
Morcha	morakho	Mormon	morameni
Mordacious	morejekisi	Morn	moran
Mordancy	morejesn	Mornay	morain
Mordant	morejetn	Morning	morangnni
Mordecai	morejekoi	Morocco	morooki
Mordent	morejeto	Moron	moroon
Mordavian	morejewini	Moronism	moroonmosi
Mordred	moreje	Moropus	moroopnsi
More	mosii	Morose	moroose
Morea	moren	Morphallaxis	mophijjosi
Moreau	moreun	Morpheme	mophimo
Moreen	morein	Morpheus	mophisun
Moreish	morese	Morphic	mophanko
Morel	morejo	Morphine	mophini
Morelia	moreijn	Morphinism	mophinimosi
Morello	moreillo	Morpho	mophnko
Morelos	morelosi	Morphogenesis	mophnkognhunso
Mores	morese	Morphology	mophnkologbon
Moresnet	moreisnte	Morpholysis	mophnjinso
Moresque	moresekun	Morpnhophoneme	mophnkophohunmo
Morgan	`	Morphosis	mophnkoso

WORD (x)	EQUIVALENT (y)	WORD (x)	EQUIVALENT (y)
Morphous	mophansi	Mosasaur	mosusanra
Morphy	mophe	Mosby	mosnbe
Morrigu	morraigbun	Moschate	mosnkhotn
Morrion	morrain	Moschate1	mosnkhtnjo
Morris	morraisi	Moscow	mosnki
Morrison	morraisin	Moseley	mosnjnse
Morro	moorro	Moselle	mosnjjn
Morrow	moorrawa	Moses	mosnsi
Mors	morasn	Mosey	mosnse
Morse	moraso	Moskva	mosikwo
Morsel	morasu	Mosley	mosijn
Mort	morate	Mosque	mosikun
Mortal	moratejo	Mosquito	mosikiti
Mortality	morateleto	Mosquitp-net	hunte mosnkiti
Mortal sin	moratejo sote	Moss	mosu
Mortar	moratnra	Moss agate	agiyo mosu
Mortarboard	bugbamoratnra	Mossad	mosujn
Mortgage	morategigun	Mossbaure	mosubaunsi
Mortgagee	morategigunse	Mossbunker	mosubuknra
Mortgager	morategigunsi	Mosssie	mosuse
Mortgagor	morategigunran	Mosso	mossuko
Mortice	moratesi	Most	mosua
Mortician	moratesihn	Mostly	mosualo
Mortification	moratefikoyoon	Mostar	mosuaran
Mortify	moratefe	Moste	mosuasi
Mortimer	moratemurai	Mot	moti
Mortise	moratese	Mote	mote
Mortise lock	moratese lokn	Motel	motejo
Mortmain	moratemorai	Motet	moteti
Morton	moratn	Moth	mosi
Mortuary	moratunrai	Mothball	mosirobo
Morula	morajn	Mother	mosira
Mosaic	mosuako	Motherland	mosiraledain
Mosander	mosunjnra	Motherly	mosiralo

WORD (x)	EQUIVALENT (y)	WORD (x)	EQUIVALENT (y)
Motherhood	mosirahinjo	Moulding	mounjoragnni
Motherlode	mosiralojin	Mouldy	mounjoran
Mothy	mosise	Moulin	mounjan
Motif	motefe	Mouline	mounjahun
Motile	motujn	Moult	mounjayo
Motion	motusi	Moulton	mounjatin
Motivate	motuweyo	Moultrie	mounjatnran
Motive	motuwin	Mound	mounjo
Motley	moturoin	Mount1	mounte
Motor-cross	motu-konso	Mount2	mounte
Motor	motu	Mountain	mountelu
Motorcade	motukojin	Mountain ash	asun mountelu
Motorist	motusi	Mounte	mounta
Motorize	motuse	Mounted	mounted
Motorman	motumoye	Mountie	mountese
Motown	motown	Mounting	mountegnni
Mott	motti	Mounty	mountesi
Motte	mottn	Mourn	mundaro
Mottle	mottoron	Mourn	mounsaro
Motto	motto	Mourner	mounsarosi
Motty	moottose	Mourning	mounsarognni
Mou	moun	Mouse	mounsia
Mouch	mounkho	Mouser	mounsiasi
Mouchoir	mounkhorai	Moussaka	mounsooka
Moudle	mounduo	Mousse	mounsoo
Moue	mounsa	Mouterian	mountetorain
Mouflon	mounfonsi	Mousy	mounsise
Mouille	mounlle	Mouth	mounsi
Moul	mounjn	Mouth-organ	mounsi orogbn
Moulage	mounjngun	Mouthpiece	mounsiponsi
Mould1	mounjora	Mounthy	mounsise
Mould2	mounjora	Move	mowain
Mould3	mounjora	Moveable	mowainbe
Moulder	mounjorasi	Movement	mowainmutto

WORD (x)	EQUIVALENT (y)	WORD (x)	EQUIVALENT (y)
Mover	mowainsi	Mucous	mukoonsi
Movie	mowainse	Mucro	muknre
Moving	mowaingnni	Mucronate	muknreyo
Mow	mowi	Mucus	mukunsi
Mow	mowi	Mud	mujo
Moxa	mosana	Muddle	mujoduo
Moxie	mosanase	Muddler	mujoduosi
Moyen	mooyin	Muddy	mujodain
Mozarab	mosesin	Mudguard	mujogungba
Mozart	moseto	Mudpie	mujopon
Mozzarella	mossewara	Mudpuppy	mujopupo
Mr	mtn misitn	Muenster	munsnto
Mrs	mbe misibe	Muesli	munsnle
Ms	mb misibo	Muezzin	muntosin
Mu	mu	Muff1	mufu
Much	mukhi	Muff2	mufu
Much	mukhi	Muffin	muffusi
Mucic	mukiko	Muffle	mufuran
Mucid	mukijo	Muffler	mufuran
Mucilage	mukilegun	Mufti	mufnra
Mucin	mukihn	Mug1	mugba
Muck	mukki	Mug2	mugba
Muck about	mukki abounta	Mugger	mugbasi
Mucker	mukkisi	Mugger	mugbaran
Muckle	mukkiron	Muggings	mugbasn
Muckrake	mukkirakn	Muggy	mugbain
Mucky	mukkise	Mug wort	mugba winyo
Muco	mukoon	Mug wump	mugba wumpn
Mucoid	mukoonjo	Muhu	muha
Mucopoly	mukoonpose	Muir	muran
Mucoprotein	mukoonponyoto	Muirapuama	muraipanmo
Mucopurulent	mukoonpuraituyo	Muk luk	muka luka
Mucorales	mukoonraijnsi	Mulada	mujnjo
Mucosa	mukoonse	Mulatto	mujntto

WORD (x)	EQUIVALENT (y)	WORD (x)	EQUIVALENT (y)
Mulberry	mujnberrai	Multifarious	mujntefanraisi
Mulch	mujnsi	Multifid	mujntefijo
Mule1	mujn	Miltifoil	mujntefonlo
Mule2	mujn	Multifold	mujntefoonjo
Mulet	mujntn	Multiform	mujntefoonmo
Muleta	mujnte	Multigravida	mujnteganwojn
Muleteer	mujntosi	Multilateral	mujnteletnraijo
Muley	mujnsn	Multimedia	mujntemujina
Mulhacen	mujnhukin	Multimillionaire	mujntemujnranrai
Mulheim	mujnhunmo	Multinational	mujnteheyoonjo
Mulga	mujngin	Multinomial	mujntenimojo
Muliebrity	mujnberaito	Multipara	mujntepanra
Mulish	mujnse	Multiparous	mujntepanrasi
Mulki	mujnki	Multipartile	mujntepanteyo
Mull1	mujnre	Multipede	mujntepndie
Mull2	mujnre	Multiphase	mujntephanse
Mull3	mujnre	Multiplane	mujntepanyun
Mulla	mujnren	Multiple	mujnteporon
Mullah	mujnrehun	Multiplet	mujntepote
Mullen	mujnrein	Multiplex	mujnteposi
Muller	mujnresi	Multiplicand	mujntepokojn
Mullet	mujnretn	Multiplicate	mujntepokoyo
Mulligan	mujnregan	Multiplication	mujntepokoyoon
Mulligatawny	mujnregitewnse	Multiplicity	mujntepokito
Mulligrubs	mujnreganbu	Multiplier	mujnteporan
Mullingar	mujnregnra	Multiply	mujntepo
Mullion	mujnresi	Multipropellant	mujnteponpnllote
Mullite	mujnreyo	Multipurpose	mujntepupinse
Mullock	mujnreki	Multisection	mujntesekntesi
Mules	mujnson	Multistage	mujntesetngun
Multi-	mujnte	Multitude	mujntetujin
Multi-access	mujnte akknso	Multitudinous	mujntetujinsi
Multicipital	mujntekipntejo	Multiverse	mujntewinso
Mutifacet	mujntefansite	Multiversity	mujntewinseto

WORD (x)	EQUIVALENT (y)	WORD (x)	EQUIVALENT (y)
Multivocal	mujntewnkojn	Munificent	muyefiknti
Multivoltine	mujntewnjiani	Munition	muyeyoon
Multum	mujntema	Munnion	muyehnsi
Multure	mujnteran	Munro	muyeran
Mum1	mumo	Munsel	muyesejo
Mum2	mumo	Munster	muyeseto
Mumble	mumbe	Munt	muyete
Mumbo jumbo	mumbo jumboo	Muntenia	muyetehan
Mummeson	mummosin	Muntin	muyetie
Mummer	mummoran	Muntz	muyese
Mummery	mummorai	Muon	munsia
Mummify	mummofe	Muonio	munsiako
Mummy1	mummio	Mur	murau
Mummy2	mummo	Muraena	murauni
Mump	mumpn	Murage	muraugun
Mumpish	mumpnse	Mural	muraujo
Mumps	mumpnsu	Murder	murauku
Mun	muye	Murderous	muraukusi
Mun	muye	Mure	murau
Muna	muyena	Murex	murausn
Munch	muyekho	Murgeou	muraugnsi
Munchen	muyekhn	Muriate	murauyo
Munchausen	muyekhoinse	Murine	murausi
Muncle	muyekuo	Murk	murauki
Munda	muyedan	Murky	muraukin
Mundane	muyedain	Murmur	muraunmo
Mundic	muyeko	Murmurous	muraunmosi
Mundungo	muyegbun	Murphy	murauphe
Munga	muyegin	Murrain	murraun
Mungo	muyegon	Murray	murrain
Munich	muyekhn	Murre	murrai
Municipal	muyekiponjo	Murrelet	murraitn
Municipality	muyekiponleto	Murrey	murraisu
Municipalise	muyekiponjose	Murrshine	murrasunene

WORD (x)	EQUIVALENT (y)	WORD (x)	EQUIVALENT (y)
Murrine	murraunni	Musleteer	musiatesi
Murrumbidgee	murrambegunse	Musketry	musiaterai
Musaceous	musnsuwa	Muskhogean	musiahogun
Musca	musnko	Muskrat	musiaraite
Muscadel	musnkojinjo	Musky	musiase
Muscadine	musnkojoin	Muslin	muselewe
Muscarine	musnkorain	Muso	muson
Muscaevolitantes	musnkoin wnjntetnsi	Musquash	musikunse
Muscat	musunkoti	Muss	mussu
Muscatel	musunkotilo	Mussel	mussujo
Muscid	musunkijo	Mussy	mussuse
Muscle	musunkuo	Must1	muse
Muscovite	musunkiwa	Must2	muse
Muscovy	musunkiwn	Mustache	musetnmu
Muscow	musunkiwo	Mustang	musetngan
Muscular	musunkuoran	Nustard	musetngba
Musculature	musunkuotiran	Muster	musetnra
Muse1	musun	Muster	musetira
Muse2	musun	Musth	musesi
Musette	musuntn	Musty	musetie
Museum	musungbn	Mutable	mutunberon
Museology	musunkilogbon	Mutagen	mutungin
Muses	musunsi	Mutant	mutunte
Mush	musue	Mutate	mutunyo
Mushroom	musueroomo	Mutation	mutunyoon
Mushy	musuese	Mutatis mutandis	mutunso mutnjnso
Music	musunko	Mutch	mutnkho
Musical	musunkojo	Mutchkin	mutnkhokin
Musician	musunkhn	Mute	mutn
Musicology	musunkologbon	Muticious	mutnsiwa
Musk	musia	Mutilate	mutnleyo
Muskey	musiagn	Mutineer	mutnhunran
Muskellunge	musiallogun	Mutinous	mutnhunsi
Musket	musiate	Mutiny	mutnsi

WORD (x)	EQUIVALENT (y)	WORD (x)	EQUIVALENT (y)
Mutism	mutnmosi	Mycorrhiza	munkirhaise
Mutt	mutte	Mycosis	munkiso
Mutter	mutteran	Mycostatin	munkisitatan
Mutton	muttesi	Mycotrophism	munkitnraphemosi
Mutual	mutujo	Mydriasis	mungbaaso
Mutualism	mutujomosi	Mydriatic	mungbaako
Mutualise	mutujose	Myel	munlo
Mutule	mutujn	Myelencephalon	munlonuknphejnsi
Muumuu	mummu	Myelin	munloni
Muzark	museko	Myelitis	munlokoso
Muzhik	musokhi	Myelo	munloko
Muzzey	mussose	Myeloid	munlokojo
Muzzle	mussoron	Myeloma	munlokoma
Muzzy	musso	Mylasis	munleso
My	mi	Mylonite	munloseyo
My	mun	Myna	munhn
Myalgia	munjoingn	Myo	munkn
Myallism	munjjomosi	Myocardial	munknkogbajo
Myall	munjjo	Myocardiograph	munknkogbakoganpha
Myasthenia	munsunwnni	Myocarditis	munknkogbaso
Myasthenia gravis	munsunwnni ganwosi	Myocardium	munknkogbama
Mycale	munkojn	Myogenic	munknginko
Mycelium	munknjnma	Myoglobin	munkngonbin
Mycenae	munkinni	Myogram	munknganmo
Mycenaean	munkinnihn	Myograph	munknganpha
Mycete	munknte	Mycology	munknlogbon
Mycetes	munkntesi	Myoma	munknma
Myceto	munknto	Myope	munknpn
Mycetogenic	munkntoginko	Myopia	munknpan
Mycetoma	munkntoma	Myosin	munknsin
Mycetozoan	munkntosinhn	Myosotis	munknsinso
Mycin	munkin	Myotic	munknko
Myco	munki	Myotome	munkntemu
Mycology	munkilogbon	Myotonia	munkntohan

WORD (x)	EQUIVALENT (y)	WORD (x)	EQUIVALENT (y)
Myriad	munrai	Mythopoeia	munsnkopinsesi
Myriad	munraijn	Mythopoeic	munsnkopinseko
Myriapod	munraipindie	Mythos	munsnkosi
Myrica	munraiko	Myxo	munkun
Myristic	munraisiko	Myxoedema	munkunjinmo
Myrmeco	munronkin	Myxoma	munkunmo
Myrmecology	munronkinlogbon	Myxomatosis	munkunmotinso
Myrmecophagous	munronkinphijesi	Myxomycete	munkunmoknyo
Myrmecophile	munronkinpheron	myxovirus	munkunworasi
Myrmidon	munronjoin	Mzee	minisu
Myrobalan	munrabejin	Nab	hegbe
Myron	munran	Nabataean	hegbetiehn
Myrrh	munrara	Nabis	hegbesi
Myrtaceous	munratosuwa	Nablus	hegbelesi
Myrtle	munratoron	Nabob	hegbebe
Myself	munsejo	Naboth	hegbesi
Mysia	munsia	Nacarat	hekoraite
Mysore	munsoran	Nacelle	henjjn
Mystagog	munseogon	Nacho	hekho
Mysterious	munsetnrasi	Nacre	heknran
Mystery	munsetnra	Nacreous	heknransi
Mystic	munsetnko	Nadir	hejnra
Mystical	munsetnkojo	Nae	heu
Mysticism	munsetnkomosi	Naevoid	heuwajo
Mystify	munsetnfe	Naevus	heuwasi
Mystique	munsetnkun	Nafud	hefujo
Myth	munsn	Naff	helo
Mythical	munsnkojo	Nafrantiti	hefantosi
Mythicize	munsnkose	Nag1	hegbo
Mytho	munsnko	Nag2	hegbo
Mythological	munsnkologbonkojo	Naga	hegbn
Mythologist	munsnkologbonsi	Nagana	hegbnhn
Mythology	munsnkologbon	Nagari	hegbnrai
Mythomania	munsnkomohan	Nagasaki	hegbnkosi

WORD (x)	EQUIVALENT (y)	WORD (x)	EQUIVALENT (y)
Nageli	hegnlo	Nancy	henusi
Naguya	hegunyan	Nanda	henujn
Nagpur	hegnposi	Nankeen	henuknni
Naha	hehun	Nanking	henukinga
Nahua	nehun	Nanny	henuse
Nahuati	hehunto	Nano-	henkn
Nahuatian	hehuntohn	Nanogram	henknganmo
Nahum	hehumo	Nanonetre	henknmutoran
Naiad	hejnmi	Nanoplankton	henpankntin
Nail	helo	Nanook	henknko
Nail-file	helo-fijn	Nansemond	hensemojn
Nain sook	herai sooki	Nansen	hensesi
Naim	herain	Nantes	hentesi
Nairobi	herainbe	Nautuchet	hentekoto
Naissant	hesoote	Naomi	hekomi
Naïve	hewini	Naos	hekosi
Naivete	hewinito	Nap1	hepn
Naked	hoho	Nap2	hepn
Naked eye	eyiri hoho	Nap3	hepn
Naker	hohosi	Napalm	hepnjomu
Makhichivan	hekhikhiwa	Nape	hepon
Naktong	hekitigun	Napery	heponrai
Mamangan	hemogini	Naphtali	hephito
Namaqualand	hemokunledain	Naphtha	hephisan
Namaycush	hemosekunsi	Naphthalene	hephisanhun
Namby-pamby	hembn-panmbn	Naphthene	hephisinhun
Name	hemo	Naphthol	hephisinjin
Nameless	hemolabo	Naphthyl	hephisinlo
Namely	hemolo	Napiers	heponrasi
Nameplate	hemopautue	Napiform	heponfonmo
Namesake	hemosankn	Napkin	heponkin
Namur	hemurai	Naples	heporonsi
Nan	henu	Napoleon	hepinronse
Nana	henuni	Napoleonic	hepinronseko

WORD (x)	EQUIVALENT (y)	WORD (x)	EQUIVALENT (y)
Nappa	hepnpan	nascent	hesiknti
Nappe	hepnpn	naseberry	hesebesn
Napper	hepnpnra	Naseby	hesebn
Nappy	hepnpo	Nash	hesue
Naprapathy	hepanpnsio	Nashville	hesuewollo
Narbaba	herobojn	Nasion	hesoosi
Narbonne	heroboun	Naso	hesun
Narc	heroki	Nasofrontal	hesunfontnjo
Narceine	heroknun	Nasopharynx	hesunphiraiso
Marcissiam	herokisuamosi	Nasoscope	hesunsekipon
Narcissus	herokisua	Nassau	hesisoo
Narco	heroki	Nastic movement	hesiko mosamutto
Narcolepsy	herokijnpnse	Nastitis	hesisunso
Narcomania	herokimohan	Nasturtium	hesiraitima
Narcosis	herokiso	Nasty	hesitn
Narcotic	herokiko	Nat.	heyo
Narcotine	herokihun	Natal	heyojo
narcotism	herakiomosi	Natality	heyoleto
narcotize	herokise	Natant	heyotn
nard	heragba	Natation	heyoyoon
nardoo	heragbain	Natatorium	heyoyoraima
nares	herasi	Natatory	heyoyorai
narghile	heraghijn	Natch	heyokho
narial	heraijo	Nates	heyosi
nark	heraki	Nation	heyoon
narrate	herraijo	National	heyoonjo
narration	herraiyoon	National grid	ganjn heyoonjo
narrative	herraiyowin	Nationalism	heyoonjomosi
narrow	herrawn	Nationality	heyoonleto
narthex	herasinsi	Nationalize	heyoonjose
narwhal	herawhujo	Native	heyowin
nary	herai	Nativism	heyowinmosi
nasal	hesunjn	Nativity	heyowinto
nasalize	hesunjnse	Natrium	heyoraima

WORD (x)	EQUIVALENT (y)	WORD (x)	EQUIVALENT (y)
Natrolite	heyoraleyo	Navigator	hewegiyoran
Natron	heyoran	Navigation	hewegiyoon
natter	heyora	Navy	hewese
Natterjack	heyorajako	Navy	hewese
Natty	heyotn	Navy cut	kunte hewese
Natural	heyoraijo	Naxalite	hesanleyo
Naturalism	heyoraijomosi	Nay	hesn
Naturalist	heyoraijosi	Nazarene	hesairan
Naturalize	heyoraijose	Nazareth	hesairansi
Nature	heyorai	Nazarite	hesairante
Natured	hetnraide	Nazi	hese
Naturism	hetnraimosi	Nazify	hesefe
Naturopathy	hetnrapansio	Nazism	hesemosi
Naught	heungbe	Ne	hun
Naughty	heungbeto	Neanderthal	hunjnrasejo
Naumachia	heunmukho	Neap	hunpn
Nauplius	heunpansi	Neapolitan	hunpnjintan
Nausea	heunsia	Near	hunra
Nauseate	heunsiayo	Nearby	hunrabeo
Nauseous	heunsiasi	Nearly	hunralo
Naut	heunte	Neat	huntoni
Nautch	heuntesi	Neaten	huntonisi
Nautical	heuntekojo	Neath	huntosn
Nautiloid	heuntejnjo	Neb	hunbo
Nautilus	heuntejn+si	Nebiim	hunboma
Naval	hewejn	Nebo	hunboo
Navar	hewerai	Nebuchadnezzar	hunboknijnrai
Navorino	hewerain	Nebula	hunbojn
Nave1	hewe	Nebular	hunbojnran
Nave2	hewe	Nebulizer	hunbojnse
Navel	hewelo	Nebulose	hunbojnse
Nevel orange	oraigini hewinlo	Nebulosity	hunbojnseto
Navigable	hewegibe	Nebulous	hunbojnseto
Navigate	hewegiyo	Nebulous	hunbojnsi

WORD (x)	EQUIVALENT (y)	WORD (x)	EQUIVALENT (y)
Necessaries	hunknsooraisi	Need	hunde
Necessarily	hunknsoorailo	Needle	hunduo
Necessitarianism	hunknsooterainmosi	Needless	hunduolabo
Necessitate	hunknsooteyo	Needs	hundesi
Necessitous	hunknsootesi	Needy	hundese
Necessity	hunknsootn	Neengatu	hunginito
Neck	hunko	Nefarious	hunfanraisi
Necker	hunkosi	Neeze	hunsin
Neckline	hunkolehun	Nefertiti	hunfnraito
Necktie	hunkotise	Negate	hungiyo
Necrectomy	hunknrantemo	Negation	hungiyoon
Necremia	hunknranmi	Negative	hungiyowin
necrencephalous	hunknranknphijnsi	Negativism	hungiyowinmosi
Necro-	hunknra	Negator	hungiyoran
Necromancy	hunknramoyesi	Negatory	hungiyorai
Necromania	hunknramohan	Neglect	hungiunto
Necrophagous	hunknraphijesi	Negligee	hungiungnse
Necrophilia	hunknrapheran	negligence	hungiungnsi
Necrophobia	hunknraphobua	negligent	hungiungnto
Necropolis	hunknrapinjnsi	negotiable	hungntobe
Necropsy	hunknrapnso	negotiant	hungntote
Necrose	hunknrase	negotiate	hungntoyo
Necrosis	hunknraso	negress	hungirabo
Necrotic entiritis	hunknrako entnraso	negrillo	hungnraillo
Necrotomy	hunknratemo	negritude	hungnraitujin
Nectar	hunkitiran	negrito	hungnraito
Nectariferous	hunkitiranfirosi	negro	hungnra
Nectarine	hunkitirain	negroid	hungnrajo
Nectar	hunkitirai	negroness	hungnranisi
Ned	hunjn	negros	hungnrasi
Neddy	hunjnde	negus	hungunsi
Neder	hunjnra	Nehemiah	hunhemosi
Nee	hunse	Neigh	hunlegbe
Neebour	hunsegbe	Neighbor	hunlegbero

415

WORD (x)	EQUIVALENT (y)	WORD (x)	EQUIVALENT (y)
Neighborhood	hunlegberohinjo	Neogaea	hunkngini
Neighborly	hunlegberolo	Neogene	hunkngnun
Neighbour	hunlegbera	Neolithic	hunknlesiko
Neighbourhood	hunlegberahinjo	Neologism	hunknlogbonmosi
Neighbourly	hunlegberalo	Neomycin	hunknmunkin
Neilson	hunlosin	Neon	hunknsi
Neisse	hunsoon	Neonatal	hunknhetnjo
Neisserosis	hunsoonraso	Neonate	hunknheyo
Neist	hunsi	Neophyte	hunknpheyo
Neither	hunsnra	Neoplasm	hunknpanson
Nekton	hunkntin	Neoprene	hunknpesile
Neleus	hunjosi	Neoteny	hunkntinse
Nell	hunjnra	Neoteric	hunkntnrako
Nelly	hunjnrase	Neotype	hunkntnpon
Nelson	hunjnsin	Nepal	hunpnjo
Nelumbo	hunjnmbo	Nepenthe	hunpinsin
Nemathelminth	hunmisinjomini	Nepenthes	hunpinsinsi
Nematic	hunmiko	Neper	hunpnra
Nemato	hunmito	Nephele	hunphele
Nematode	hunmitojin	Nepheline	hunphelehun
Nemcon	hunmikin	Nephelinite	hunphelehunyo
Nemea	hunmni	Nephelometer	hunphelemuto
Nenean	hunmnisi	Nephew	hunphewn
Nemertean	hunmuraite	Nephogram	hunphekoganpha
Nemesia	hunmusia	Nephrology	hunphekologbon
Nemesis	hunmuso	Nephralgia	hunphanjngan
Nemine	hunmihun	Nephrectomy	hunphantemo
Nemoral	hunmoorajo	Nephric	hunphanka
Nemorose	hunmoorase	Nephridium	hunphanjnma
Nene	hunsia	Nephritic	hunphanko
Neo-	hunkn	Nephritis	hunphanso
Neocene	hunknknsa	Nephro	hunphon
Neoclassicism	hunknkansookomosi	Nephrogenous	hunphonginsi
Neodymium	hunkndaimuwa	Nephroid	hunphonjo

WORD (x)	EQUIVALENT (y)	WORD (x)	EQUIVALENT (y)
Nephrolysis	hunphonjinso	Nester	hunsnsi
Nephron	hunphonsi	Nestle	hunsnron
Nephropathy	hunphonpansio	Nestling	hunsnrongnni
Nephrosis	hunphonso	Nestor	hunsnran
Nephrotomy	hunphontemo	Nestorianism	hunsnrainmosi
Nepotism	hunpintemosi	Net1	hunte
Neptune	hunpntini	Net2	hunte
Neptunian	hunpntinihn	Netball	hunterobo
Neptunium	hunpntinima	Nether	hunsira
Neral	hunrajo	Netherland	hunsiraledain
Nereid	hunranjo	Nett	huntte
Nereis	hunranso	Netting	hunttegnni
Nereus	hunransi	Nettle	huntteron
Neritic	hunraiko	Netty	huntetn
Nero	hunro	Network	huntewinsise
Neroli	hunrolo	Neu	hunwe
Nerd	hunrajn	Neuchatel	hunwekhotejo
Nervate	hunraiyo	Neufchatel	hunwefunkhotejo
Nervation	hunraiyoon	Neuk	hunwekn
Nerve	hunrai	Neume	hunwemo
Nerve-cell	hunrai knjjn	Neuqueu	hunwekun
Nerveless	hunrailabo	Neural	hunwerajo
Nervine	hunraini	Neuralgia	hunwerajogan
Nervosity	hunraiseto	Neurectomy	hunwerantemo
Nervous	hunraisi	Neurasthenia	hunwerasunwnsi
Nerves	hunraisn	Neurath	hunweraisi
Nervure	hunrairan	Neuration	hunweraiyoon
Nervy	hunraise	Neuraxis	hunweraisiso
Nescience	hunsisunse	Neurectomy	hunwerantemo
.-ness	nisi bo/so	Neurenteric	hunweraintoko
Nessler	hunsinjra	Neurilemma	hunwerajnmma
Nessus	hunsise	Neuritis	hunweraso
Nest	hunsn	Neuro-	hunwerai
Nest egg	hunsn egbn	Neurology	hunwerailogbon

WORD (x)	EQUIVALENT (y)	WORD (x)	EQUIVALENT (y)
Neuroma	hunweraimo	Newly	hunwalo
Neuropath	hunweraipanho	News	hunwasi
Neuropathology	hunweraipanhologbon	Newsagent	agintohunwasi
Neuropathy	hunweraipansio	Newscast	hunwasikosoto
Neurophysiology	hunweraiphesoologbon	Newscaster	hunwasikosotosi
Neuropter	hunweraipntira	Newsy	hunwase
Neuropteran	hunweraipntiran	Newt	hunwiti
Neuropterous	hunweraipntirasi	Newton	hunwatin
Neuron	hunwerain	Next	hunsio
Neurosis	hunweraiso	Nexus	hunsosi
Neurosurgery	hunweraiknsuraleran	Ney	hunye
Neurotic	hunweraiko	Ngami	ngimi
Neurotomy	hunweraitemo	Ngandong	ngidainko
Neuter	hunweto	Niagara	ngirain
Neutral	hunwetnrejo	Nias	nisio
Neutralism	hunwetnrejomosi	Nib	nibe
Neutrality	hunwetnreleto	Nibble	niberon
Neutralize	hunwetnrejose	Nibelungenlied	nibelugnnilode
Neutreto	hunwetnranto	Nibs	nibesi
Neutrino	hunwetnrain	Nicaea	nikoin
Neutriphil	hunwatnraiphero	Nicaragua	niknrangun
Neutron	hunwatnran	Nicaria	niknrain
Neutron bomb	bubon hunwatnran	Niccolite	nkkileyo
Neva	hunwe	Nice	nike
Navada	hunwejn	Nicety	niketo
Neve	hunwn	Nicene	niknsa
Never	hunwnra	Niche	nikhn
Nevertheless	hunwnrasinlabo	Nicholas	nikhijinse
Nevus	hunwnsi	Nick	nikn
New	hunwa	Nickel	niknlo
New	hunwa	Nickelferous	niknlofirosi
New age	agun hunwa	Nickelodeon	niknlojnsi
Newel	hunwalo	Nicker	niknsi
Newfangled	hunwafangironde	Nick-nack	nikn-heki

WORD (x)	EQUIVALENT (y)	WORD (x)	EQUIVALENT (y)
Nickname	niknhemo	Nightie	nigheuse
Nicobar	nikibosi	Nightly	nigheulo
Nicodemus	nikijinmosi	Nightingale	nigheugile
Nicolson	nikijnsin	Nightmare	nigheumuran
Nicopolis	nikipinjnsi	Nignog	nignlo
Nicosia	nikisia	Nigrscent	nigiranseknti
Nicotine	nikitihun	Nigrify	nigiraife
Nicotinism	nikitihunmosi	Nigritia	nigitaitie
Nictitate	nikyoteyo	Nigritian	nigiraitihn
Nictitation	nikyoteyoon	Negritude	nigiraitujin
Niddering	nijinragnni	Nigrosine	nigirasun
Niddle-nodle	nijinduo-nknduo	Nihil	nigbu
Nide	nijin	Nihilism	nigbumosi
Nidicolous	nijinkojinsi	Nihility	nigbuleto
Nidifugous	nijinfegunsi	Nihilobstart	nigbubosetn
Nidify	nijinfe	Nihon	nihisi
Nid-nod	nijin-hnjin	Nijmegen	nijnmogin
Nidus	nijinsi	,-nik	niki/kin/kan
Niece	niyosi	Nike	nikn
Niello	niyollo	Nikolaev	nikjinwa
Nieve	niyowo	Nikolayevsk	nikijnsuwasi
Niff	nifin	Nil	nirau
Niffer	nifiro	Nile	nijn
Nifihelm	nifinhejo	Nilgal	nijngala
Nifty	nifinto	Nilgiri	nijngarai
Niger	nigira	Nill	nijnra
Nigeria	nigirasi	Nilometer	nijnmuto
Niggard	nigigbaa	Nilotic	nijnko
Niggardly	nigigbaalo	Nim	nim
Nigger	nigira	Nimble	nimbe
Niggle	nigiron	Nimbo	nimnu
Niggling	nigirongnni	Nimbus	nimbusa
Nigh	nighe	Nimby	nimbeyo
Night	nigheu	Nimiety	niminito

WORD (x)	EQUIVALENT (y)	WORD (x)	EQUIVALENT (y)
Niminypiminy	niminipomini	Nish	nisua
Nimonic	nimeniko	Nisi	niso
Nimrod	nimorudu	Nisiprius	nisopansi
Nimrod	lamurudu	Nissen hut	nisoon
Nimwegen	nimownjin	Nisus	nisosi
Nina	nihe	Nit	niti
Nincompoop	ninikwepipo	Nitchie	nitnkhoi
Nine	nihe	Nite	nitn
Ninepin	nihepohn	Niter	nitnra
Nineteen	nihetoon	Nitrate	nitnraiyo
Nineteenth	nihetoonsi	Nitre	nitnran
Ninety	nihetn	Nitric	nitnraiko
Ninetieth	nihetnsi	Nitride	nitnraji
Ninny	nihese	Nitrify	nitnraife
Ninon	nihesn	Nitrite	nitnraito
Ninth	nihesi	Nitro-	nitnra
Nineveh	nihewa"	Nitrogen	nitnragin
Ninus	nihewa	Nitroglycerin	nitnragiloknran
Niobe	nikobe	Nitroglycerine	nitnragiloknrain
Niobic	nikobeko	Nitromethane	nitnramutohun
Niobite	nikobeyo	Nitroso	nitnrasoo
Niobium	nikobema	Nitrous oxide	nitnrasi osinji
Niobous	ninibesi	Nitty-gritty	nititn-ganttn
Nip	nipn	Nitwit	nitn-winso
Nip1	nipn	Nival	niwajo
Nip2	nipn	Nivation	niwayoon
Nip and tuck	nipn ati tunki	Niveous	niwinsi
Nipa	nipan	Nix	nisia
Nipper	nippnra	Nixer	nisiasi
Nipple	nipporon	Nixie	nisiase
Nippy	nipnpo	Nixon	nisinle
Nivana	niwahun	Nizza	nisua
Nisan	nisehn	Njord	nijingban
Nisei	nisue	No1	nko

WORD (x)	EQUIVALENT (y)	WORD (x)	EQUIVALENT (y)
No2	nko	Nogg	nigbi
Nob1	nkobe	Noggin	nigbign
Nob2	nkobe	Nogging	nigbignni
No-ball	nko-robo	No go	nko lo
Nobble	nkoboron	Noise	niso
Nobelium	nkobejnma	Noiseless	nkisolabo
Nobel prize	panyio nkobejn	Noisome	nisoomo
Nobiliary	nknbolerai	Noisy	nisosia
Noble	nknbo	Nolimetangere	nijinmutegnron
Nobleman	nknbomoye	Nolleprosequi	nijjoponkunse
Noblesse oblige	nkobojnsoo	Nolocontendere	nijoinkintojinsi
Nobody	nkobodain	Noma	nima
Nociceptive	nkokiknpntiwin	Nomad	nimajia
Nock	nkoki	Nomadize	nimajiase
Noctambulism	nkunkunmbejnmosi	No man's land	nko moyesi ledain
Nocti	nkunkuntn	Nomen	nimuye
Noctiluca	nkunkunluko	Nomenclature	nimuyekantorai
Noctilucent	nkunkunluknti	Nominal	nimohejo
Noctuid	nkunkuntjo	Nominalism	nimohejo
Noctule	nkunkunron	Nominate	nimoheyo
Noctum	nkunkunmo	Nominative	nimoheyowin
Noctumal	nkunkunmojo	Nominee	nimoheyun
Noctume	nkunkunmo	Nomism	nimomosi
Nod	niji	Nomo	nimoko
Noddle	nijiduo	Nomocracy	nimokokansn
Noddy	nijidain	Nomography	nimokoganphe
Node	nijia	Nomology	nimokologbon
Nodical	nijiakojo	Nomy	nimose
Nodule	nijiaron	Non-	nini
Nodous	nijiasi	Nona	nihe
Nodus	nijiawa	Nonagenarian	nihegbarain
Noel	nkolo	Nonagon	nihegun
Noesis	nkoseso	Nonaligned	niniajognde
Noetic	nkoseko	Nonanoic	niheniko

WORD (x)	EQUIVALENT (y)	WORD (x)	EQUIVALENT (y)
Nonce	ninisi	North	nirose
Nonce-word	winjo-ninisi	Northerly	niroseralo
Nonchalant	ninikhorate	Northern	niroseran
Non-com	nini-kia	Northemer	niroseransi
None	nini	Northward	nirosewegba
Nonentity	ninitotn	Nothumberland	nirosunmbeledain
Nones	ninisi	Nose	nisun
Nonetheless	ninisilabo	Nosh	nisue
Noni	nihi	Nosh-up	nisue-pake
Nonillion	nihijnrain	Noso	nisoo
Noodle1	ninaduo	Nosography	nisooganphe
Noodle2	ninaduo	Nosology	nisoologbon
Nook	nikoin	Nostalgia	nisujngan
Noon	nina	Nostril	nisunmi
Noonday	ninadase	Nostrum	nisunrama
No one	nko ohun	Nosy	nisunse
Noose	nisose	Not	nkoti
Nor	niro	Notability	nkotebeleto
Nor'	niro	Notable	nkotebe
Noradrenaline	nirangbainlehun	Notarise	nkoteraise
Nordic	nirojnko	Notary	nkoterai
Noria	niroin	Notation	nkoteyoon
Noricum	niraikuo	Notch	nkotehun
Norite	niraijo	Note	nkote
Norm	niron	Notebook	nkotebooko
Normal	nironjo	Nothing	nkosignni
Normalize	nironjose	Nothingness	nkosignnibo
Normally	nironjjn	Notice	nkotesi
Norman	nironye	Noticeable	nkotesiberon
Normative	nironyowin	Notice-board	bugba nkotesi
Norn	nirun	Notifiable	nkotefeberon
Norncotine	nirunkitihun	Notify	nkotefe
Noro	nirakn	Notion	nkoteyoon
Norse	niroso	Notional	nkoteyoonjo

WORD (x)	EQUIVALENT (y)	WORD (x)	EQUIVALENT (y)
Notitia	nkotetie	Noviciate	nkowoknyo
Noto	nkoti	Now	niwai
Notogaea	nkotigin	Now	niwayi
Notoriety	nkotiraintn	Nowadays	niwaidasesi
Notorious	nkotiraisi	Nowhere	nwaiwhinsi
Notomis	nkotiranso	No-win	nko-winla
Nototherium	nkotisinraima	Nowt	niwaita
Notour	nkotoorai	Nox	nkosu
Notre dame	nkotiran daramo	Noxious	nkosusi
Nottingham	nkottighan	Noyade	nkoyanjin
Notum	nkotima	Nozzle	nisunron
Notus	nkotisi	Nauance	yunkoisi
Nougat	nkogi	nub	yungbi
Nought	nkogbu	Nubbin	yungbisi
Noun	nkonn	Nubble	yungbi
Noumenon	nkomunini	Nubia	yungbasi
Nourish	nkoraise	Nubile	yungbajn
Nourishment	nkoraisemutto	Nucha	yunkho
Nous	nkosin	Nuclear	yunkojnra
Nouveau riche	nkowini raikhn	Nucleate	yunkojnyo
Nova	nkowa	Nucleon	yunkojnsi
Novaculite	nkowakunleyo	Nucleus	yunkojnwa
Novation	nkowayoon	Nude	yunhoho
Novel1	nkowinjo	Nudge	yungbun
Novel2	nkowinjo	Nudicaul	yunhohokojn
Novelese	nkowinjose	Nudism	yunhohomosi
Novelette	nkowinjotin	Nudist	yunhohosi
Novelist	nkowinjosi	Nudity	yunhohotn
Novelization	nkowinloseyoon	Nudumpactum	yunhohopankyoma
Novella	nkowinjjo	Nuffield	yunfinronjo
Novelty	nkowinloto	Nugatory	yungbiyorain
November	nkowinmbe	Nuggar	yungbiran
Novena	nkowinhun	Nugget	yungbite
Novice	nkowose	Nuggety	yungbitn

WORD (x)	EQUIVALENT (y)	WORD (x)	EQUIVALENT (y)
Nuisance	yunsiasi	Nuptial	yunpntijo
Nuke	yunkoi	Nurse	yunsan
Null	yunjnra	Nurseling	yunsangnni
Nullah	yunjnrahun	Nursemaid	yunsanmaajo
Nullarbor	yunjnrabua	Nursery	yunsanrai
Nullification	yunjnrafikoyoon	Nurseryman	yunsanraimoye
Nullifidian	yunjnrafijoin	Nursery rhyme	rhaimo yunsanrai
Nullify	yunjnrafe	Nurture	yunsantnra
Nullipara	yunjnrapanra	Nut	yunti
Nullipore	yunjnraporai	Nutcase	yuntikoso
Nullity	yunjnratn	Nutcracker	yuntikankosi
Numb	yunmbn	Nutmeg	yuntimule
Number	yunmbe	Nutria	yuntnrain
Numberless	yunmbelabo	Nutrient	yuntnraito
Numerable	yunmoraiberon	Nutriment	yuntnraimutto
Numeral	yunmoraijo	Nutrition	yuntnraiyoon
Numerate	yunmoraiyo	Nutritious	yuntnraitosi
Numeration	yunmoraiyoon	Nutritive	yuntnraitowin
Numerator	yunmoraiyoran	Nuts	yuntisi
Numerical	yunmoraikojo	Nuts and bolts	yuntisi ati bojia
Numerology	yunmorailogbon	Nutter	yunttnra
Numerous	yunmoraisi	Nutty	yunttn
Numinous	yunminisi	Nux vomica	yunmuko yunsi
Numismatic	yunmosiko	Nuzzle	yunsunron
Numismatics	yunmosikosi	Nyanza	yunsanse
Nummular	yunmmuleran	Nyala	yunjn
Nummulite	yunmuleyo	Nyctaginaceous	yunnuteginsuwa
Numptie	yunmpntie	Nyctalopia	yunnutejopan
Nun	yunjn	Nyctinasty	yunnutehesito
Nunatak	yunjnteka	Nyctitropism	yunnutetnrapnmosi
Nunciature	yunjnkuntnran	Nyctophobia	yunnutophobua
Nuncio	yunjnkun	Nye	yunnu
Nuncle	yunjnrai	Nyeman	yunnumoye
Nunnery	yunjnrai	Nylon	yunjnsi

WORD (x)	EQUIVALENT (y)	WORD (x)	EQUIVALENT (y)
Nymph	yunmphn	Obelize	obejnse
Nympha	yunmpha	Obelus	obejnsi
Nymphaeceous	yunmphansuwa	Oberammergau	oberammuraigan
Nymphalid	yunmphejnjo	Oberland	oberoledain
Nymphet	yunmphnte	Oberon	oberon
Nympho	yunmphe	Obese	obesanra
Nympholepsy	yunmphejnpnsn	Obesity	obesanratn
Nympholept	yunmphejnpnti	Obey	obegbo
Nymphomania	yunmpemayisi	Obfuscate	obefusekoyo
Nystatin	yunsetntin	Obi	obein
Nyx	niyisi	Obituary	obeinturai
O	o in ni to	Object	obejnknyo
Oaf	ofu	Objectify	obejnknyofe
Oak	oki	Objection	obejnknyoon
Oak-apple	aporon oki	Objectionable	obejnknyoonbe
Oaken	okilo	Objective	obejnknyowin
Oakum	okima	Objectivity	obejnknyowinto
Oar	obele	Objetdart	obejndete
Oarsman	obelemoye	Objettrouve	obejnttrawin
Oasis	osunso	Objurgate	obejuagiyo
Oast	osunyo	Oblanceolate	obejnkisunleyo
Oat	ote	Oblate	obejnyo
Oaten	oteni	Oblation	obnjnyoon
Oatcake	otekoki	Obligate	obnjngbayo
Oath	otesi	Obligation	obnjngbayoon
Oatmeal	otemuje	Obligatory	obnjngbayorai
Ob	obe	Oblige	obejngba
Obbligato	obejngito	Obliging	obejngbagnni
Obconic	obekinko	Oblique	obejnkue
Obdurate	obederaiyo	Obliquity	obejnkueto
Obedient	obegbotn	Obliterate	obejntnrayo
Obedientiary	obesetorai	Oblivion	obejnwasi
Obeisance	obegbasi	Oblivious	obejnwasn
Obelisk	obejnsikn	Oblong	obelogun

WORD (x)	EQUIVALENT (y)	WORD (x)	EQUIVALENT (y)
Obloquy	obelokue	Obstinate	obesiayo
Obmutescence	obemutnseknsi	Obstipation	obesetipanyoon
Obnoxious	obekosesi	Obstreperous	obesetosiapnra
Obnubilate	obenugbileyo	Obstruct	obesetnra
Oboe	obon	Obstruction	obesetnrasi
Oboedaddacacia	obonkojnkoon	Obstructive	obesetnrawin
Obolus	obonkojnsi	Obtain	obetelu
Obovate	obonkowuyo	Obtect	obeteto
Obovoid	obonkowujo	Obtrude	obetnrajin
Obreption	oberaipnyoon	Obtrusion	obetnrasoon
Obscene	obeseknsa	Obtrusive	obetnrasuwin
Obscenity	obeseknsato	Obtund	obetujn
Obscurant	obeseknra	Obdurate	obeturaiyo
Obscurantism	obeseknramosi	Obtuse	obetuse
Obscure	obeseknra	Obverse	obewinso
Obscurity	obeseknrato	Obvert	obewinte
Obsecrate	obeseknrayo	Obviate	obewanyo
Obsequy	obesekue	Obvious	obewasi
Observance	obesowasi	Obvolute	obnwnleyo
Observance	obesowasi	Ocarina	oknrain
Observant	obesowwatn	Occasion	okknsesi
Observation	obesowayoon	Occasional	okknsesijo
Observatory	obesowayorai	Occident	okkijindato
Observe	obesowa	Occidental	okkijinhatojo
Observer	obesowase	Occipital	okkipatejo
Obsess	obesesoo	Occipito	okkipateko
Obsession	obesesoosi	Occiput	okkipako
Obsidian	obesesoojoin	Occlude	okknjain
Obsolescent	obesinlesiknti	Occluded	okknjainde
Obsolete	obesinleyo	Occlusion	okknsoon
Obstacle	obesitako	Occlusive	okknsowin
Obstetrician	obesigbebihn	Occult	okkunjia
Obsterics	obesigbebisi	Occupant	okkunpnte
Obstinacy	obesiasn	Occupation	okkunpnyoon

WORD (x)	EQUIVALENT (y)	WORD (x)	EQUIVALENT (y)
Occupational	okkunpnyoonjo	Octahedron	okntahejnrain
Occupier	okkunpnsi	Octalnotation	okntajonkntoyoon
Occupy	okkunpn	Octamerous	okntamuraisi
Occur	okkunra	Octameter	okntamuto
Occurrence	okkunrrasi	Octane	okntahun
Ocean	okun	Octant	okntale
Oceanarium	okunraima	Octave	okntawin
Occeania	okunni	Octavia	okntawan
Oceanic	okunko	Octavo	okntawn
Oceanid	okunjo	Octennial	okntahunjo
Oceano	okunko	Octet	okntate
Oceanography	okunkoganphe	Octillion	okntillesi
Oceanology	okunkologbon	Octo-	oknto
Oceanus	okunsi	October	okntobe
Ocellus	oknjjnsi	Octogenarian	okntogbarain
Ocelot	oknjo	Octonary	okntoserai
Och	okhi	Octopod	okntopindie
Ocher	okhisi	Octopus	okntopinsi
Occlesis	okkiranso	Octoroon	okntorain
Ochlocracy	okhirankansn	Octrol	okntnrajin
Ochlophobia	okhiranphobua	Octuple	okntopon
Ochone	okhiun	Ocular	oknworan
Ochre	okhiran	Ocularist	oknworansi
Ochrea	okhirain	Oculist	oknwosi
Ock	okiun	Oculo	oknwoka
O,clock	o konko	Oculomotor	oknwokamotu
Ocotillo	okitijo	Odalisque	odijosikwe
Ocrea	okiran	Odd	oddi
Ocreate	okiranyo	Oddball	oddirobo
Oct.	oknta	Oddity	oddito
Octa-	oknta	Oddment	oddimutto
Octagon	okntagun	Odds	oddisi
Octahedral	okntahejnrajo	Odds-on	oddisi/le
Octahedrite	okntahejnraiyo	Ode	ojoin

WORD (x)	EQUIVALENT (y)	WORD (x)	EQUIVALENT (y)
Odeum	ojoinma	Oestrin	onsetnran
Odious	odisi	Oestriol	onsetnraijin
Odium	odima	Oestrogen	onsetnragin
Odoacer	odeknra	Oestrone	onsetnrain
Odograph	odeganpha	Oestrous	onsetnrasi
Odometer	odemuto	Oestrus	onsetorasi
Odont	odebuyo	Oeuvre	owawnrai
Odontalgia	odebuyogan	Of	ofa si afi ni fun
Odonto	odebuyo	Off.	Offan
Odontoblast	odebuyobansia	Offal	offajo
Odontoglossum	odebuyogonsuama	Offence	offinsi
Odontograph	odebuyoganpha	Offend	offinjn
Odontoid	odebuyojo	Offense	offinse
Odontology	odebuyologbon	Offensive	offinsewin
Odontophore	odebuyophiran	Offer	offiro
Odor	odirun	Offering	offirognni
Odoriferous	odirunfirosi	Offertory	offirorai
Odour	odirun	Office	offanse
Odra	odira	Officer	offansesi
Odyl	odainlo	Official	offansejo
Odynia	odainhun	Officialese	offansejosi
Odyssey	odainsoon	Officiate	offanseto
Oecist	onkisi	Officious	offansesi
Oecology	onkilogbon	Offing	offangnni
Oecumecial	onkunmuyekojo	Oft	ofiti
Oedema	ondiro	Often	ofitin
Oedipus complex	ondipasi	Ogden	ogidain
Oeillade	onwojin	Ogdoad	ogidejn
Oenology	onilogbon	Ogee	ogise
Oenomel	onimole	Ogham	ogiha
Oenone	onini	Ogive	ogiwo
Oersted	onraiside	Ogle	ogiwo
Oesophagus	onsoophijesi	Ogre	ogirun
Oestradiol	onsetnrejinle	Ogygian	ogilohn

WORD (x)	EQUIVALENT (y)	WORD (x)	EQUIVALENT (y)
Ohio	ohiko	Oldie	ojnrase
Ohm	ohnmo	Oleaceous	ojesuwa
,-oid	onjo/jo	Oleaginous	ojeginsi
Oidea	ojina/ojinre	Oleander	ojejnra
Oil	oje	Oleaster	ojeseto
Oilcan	ojekohun	Oleate	ojeyo
Oiled	ojede	Olecranon	ojeknran
Oily	ojesi	Olefiant	ojefinte
Oink	onko	Olefine	ojefinni
Ointment	ontonimutto	Oleic	ojeko
Oireachtas	orainkhitosi	Olein	ojeran
Oka	okwe	Olekma	ojeknma
Okanogan	okwogini	Olenek	ojekin
Okapi	okwepo	Oleo	ojeko
Okay	o kn o daa	Oleograph	ojekoganpha
Okey doke	oknsi deron	Oleooil	ojekooje
Okecchohee	oknkhnboo	Oleoresin	ojekoraisun
Okeeffe	oknffin	Oleron	ojeran
Okefinakee	oknfinikun	Oleum	ojema
Okelleu	oknllese	Olfactle	ojnfanknko
Okie	okise	Olfaction	ojnfanknyoon
Okinawa	okisewa	Olfactory	ojnfanknrai
Oklahoma	okilehnmo	Olga	ojngba
Okle	okuo	Oli	ojn
Okra	oknla	Olifants	ojnfante
Okta	oknte	Oligarch	ojngiknra
,-ol	ojn/jn/lo	Oligarchy	ojngiknran
Olaf	olefn	Oligo	ojngn
Olav	olewa	Oligocene	ojngnknsa
Ole	oje	Oligochaete	ojngnkhointe
Old	ojnra	Oligohydraminous	ojngnhogbnminisi
Old age	agba ojnra	Oligopoly	ojngnpose
Old boy	ojnra boyn	Oligopsony	ojngnpora
Olden	ojnrasi	Oligotrophic	ojngntnraphiko

WORD (x)	EQUIVALENT (y)	WORD (x)	EQUIVALENT (y)
Oliguria	ojngunran	Omicron	omuknran
Olimbos	ojnmbusi	Ominous	omuhunsi
Olio	ojnko	Omission	omusinse
Oliphant	ojnphantn	Omit	omutn
Olivary	ojnwnrai	Ommatidium	ommutinjn
Olive	ojnwini	Ommatophore	ommutnphiran
Olive branch	ojnwini banyasi	Ommaid	ommaajo
Olivine	ojnwnni	Omni-	omini
Olla	ojnran	Omnibus	ominibusa
Olla podrida	ojnran pindirai	Ominifarcious	ominifanraisi
Olm	ojnmu	Omnific	ominifiko
Olylogy	ojnlogbon	Omniferous	ominifirosi
Olyroso	ojnrainso	Omniparous	ominipanraisi
Olympia	ojnmpan	Omnipotent	ominipintinto
Olympaid	ojnmpan	Omnipresent	ominipesisetin
Olympiad	ojnmpnde	Omnirange	ominiraigini
Olympian	ojnmpnhn	Omniscient	ominisisunto
Olympic	ojnmpnko	Omniumgatherum	ominimugisirama
Olympus	ojnmpnsi	Omnivorous	ominiwnrunsi
Oma	oma	Omolon	omojnsi
Omadhaun	omadehaun	Omophagia	omophijesi
Omaha	omahan	Omphale	omphijn
Oman	omahn	Omphalos	omphijn
Omasum	omasue	Omphalos	omphijosi
Omber	ombesi	On	ohn si le lo ini ni
Ombro	ombemi	Onager	ohungunsi
Ombrophilous	ombemipheransi	Onagraceous	ohungansuwa
Ombudsman	omgbejamoye	Onanism	onhunmosi
Omega	omugan	Once	ohunkan
Omegaminus	omuganmosi	Once over	ohunkan ownra
Omelette	omujotin	Oncer	ohunknra
Omen	omuse	Oncidium	onkijnma
Omentum	omuttoma	Onco	onki
Omer	omurai	Oncogene	onkignhun

WORD (x)	EQUIVALENT (y)	WORD (x)	EQUIVALENT (y)
Oncogenesis	onkignhunso	Ontogeny	ontogini
Oncogenic	onkiginko	Ontology	ontologbon
Oncology	onkilogbon	Onus	ohunsn
Oncoming	onkimwagnni	Onus pro bandi	ohunsn pon bohnjn
Oncost	onkisito	Onward	ohunwegba
Ondogram	ondeganmo	Onychophoran	onyinsekhophirain
Ondometer	ondemuto	Onym	onynsemo
One	ohun ookan eni okan	Onymous	onynsemosi
One another	ohun ahnsinra	Onyx	oynsesi
Onega	ohungan	Oo	owu
Oneida	ohunjn	Oocyte	owusnyo
Oneiro	ohunlala	Oodles	owuduosi
Oneiromancy	ohunlalamoyesn	Oof	owufi
Oneness	ohunnisi	Oogamy	owuganmo
One-off	ohun-offan	Oogenesis	owugnhunso
Oner	ohunra	oogonium	owugonma
Onerous	ohunraisi	oolite	owuleyo
Onery	ohunrai	oology	owulogbon
One-self	ohun sejo	oolong	owulogun
One-sided	ohun soojode	oomica	owumuko
One-step	ohun setopn	oomph	owumpha
Ongoing	nilognni	oont	owute
Onion	ohunsi	oophorectomy	owuphirantemo
Online	nilehun	oophoritis	owuphiranso
Onlooker	niloowosi	oophoro	owuphiro
Only	ohunlo	oophyte	owupheyo
Ono	onko	oose	owuse
Onomasiology	onkomuselogbon	oosperm	owusepnron
Onomastic	onkomuseko	oosephere	owusephirai
Onomatopoeia	onkomutopinsi	oospore	owuseporai
Onscreen	nisoknre	Oostende	owusetinjin
Onset	nisetn	Ootheca	owusinko
Onshore	nisoorai	Ootid	owutijo
Onto	leto	Oozel	owuse

WORD (x)	EQUIVALENT (y)	WORD (x)	EQUIVALENT (y)
Ooze2	owuse	Ophiology	ophikologbon
Oozy	owusia	Ophite	ophiyo
Opacity	opankwetn	Ophitic	ophiyoko
Opah	opanha	Ophiuchus	ophikhunwa
Opal	opanjo	Ophthalmia	ophisojnmi
Opalesce	opanjosekn	Ophthalmitic	ophisojnmiko
Opalescent	opanjoseknti	Ophthalmitis	ophisojnmiso
Opaline	opanjohun	Ophthalmo	ophisojnmo
Opaque	opankwe	Ophthalmologist	ophisojnmologbonsi
Open	opnya	Ophthalmology	ophisojnmologbon
Opener	opnyasi	Ophthalmoscope	ophisojnmosekipon
Opening	opnyagnni	Ophthalmoscopy	ophisojnmosekipe
Openly	opnyalo	Opia	oposi
Opera1	opnran	Opiate	opoyo
Opera2	opnran	Opine	opohun
Operable	opnranbe	Opinion	opohunsi
Operand	opnranjn	Opinionated	opohunsiyode
Operant	opnrante	Opinionative	opohunsiyowin
Operate	opnrante	Opistho	oposisa
Operatic	opnrantn	Opisthognathous	oposisagnsuwa
Operatics	opnrankosi	Opisthograph	oposisaganpha
Operation	opnranyoon	Opisthotonous	oposisatonisi
Operational	opnranyoonjo	Opium	opomu
Operationalism	opnranyoonjomosi	Opiumism	opomumosi
Operations	opnranyoonsi	Opossum	opinsoma
Operative	opnranyowin	Oppilate	oppileyo
Operator	opnranyoran	Opponent	oppinhunto
Operculum	opnratto	Opportune	oppintahun
Operon	opnrain	Opportunism	oppintahemosi
Operose	opnrase	0pportunity	oppintaheto
Ophella	ophnjjo	Opposable	oppinsiberon
Ophicieide	ophikorinjin	Oppose	0ppinsi
Ophidian	ophijoin	Opposite	oppinsiyo
Ophiolatry	ophikojnterai	Opposition	oppinsiyoon

WORD (x)	EQUIVALENT (y)	WORD (x)	EQUIVALENT (y)
Oppress	oppesiso	Oracular	oroknran
Oppressive	oppesisowin	Oracy	orosn
Opprobrious	opponbuwa	Oral	orojo
Opprobrium	opponbuma	Orange	orogini
Oppugn	oppugn	Orangeade	oroginijin
Oppugnant	oppugnte	Orangeism	oroginimosi
Opsimath	opnsumosi	Orangeman	oroginimoye
Opsis	opnso	Orangery	oroginirai
Opsonic	opnsinke	Orang-utan	orogntuhun
Opsonin	opnsinsi	Oration	oroyoon
Opsonise	opnsinse	Orator	oroyoran
Opt	opnti	Oratorio	oroyorain
Optative	opntiyowin	Oratory	oroyorai
Optic	opntiko	Orb	orobe
Optical	opntikojo	Orbicular	orobekojnran
Optical art	ete opntikojo	Orbit	orobewa
Optician	opntikohn	Orbital	orobewajo
Optics	opntikosi	Orbiter	orobewasi
Optimal	opntimojo	Orc	oroka
Optimism	opntimosi	Orca	oroko
Optimize	opntimuse	Orcein	oroknra
Optimum	opntimuma	Orch.	Orokh
Option	opntise	Orchard	orokhogba
Optional	opntisejo	Orchardman	orokhogbamoye
Opulence	opuposi	Orchestra	orokhnseran
Opulent	opupoto	Orchestrate	orokhnseraiyo
Opuntia	opuansi	Orchestrina	orokhnserain
Opus	opuso	Orchid	orokhijo
Opuscule	opusokuo	Orchidaceous	orokhijosuwa
Oquassa	okunsue	Orchil	orokhile
Or1	ora	Orchis	orokhisi
Or2	oro	Orchitis	orokhiso
Orache	orokhn	Orcinol	orokinjn
Orache	orokhn	Ordain	orojain

WORD (x)	EQUIVALENT (y)	WORD (x)	EQUIVALENT (y)
Ordeal	orojinle	Organogenesis	orogbnkognhunso
Order	orojnra	Organogram	orogbnkoganmo
Orderly	orojnralo	Organography	orogbnkoganphe
Ordin	orojnhun	Organoleptic	orogbnjoinpntiko
Ordinal	orojnhunjo	Organology	orogbnkologbon
Ordinance	orojnhunsi	Organometallic	orogbnmitolleko
Ordinand	orojnhunse	Organon	orogbnsi
Ordinant	oojnhunte	Organum	orogbnma
Ordinary	orojnhunrai	Orgasm	orogbnmo
Ordinate	orojnhunyo	Orgeat	orognte
Ordination	orojnhunyoon	Orgy	orogbon
Ordinance	orojinsi	Oribi	oraibe
Ordonnance	orojnhunsi	Oriel	orailo
Ordovican	orojnwnkosi	Orient	oraito
Ordure	orojnran	Oriental	oraitojo
Ore	ore	Orientate	oraitoyo
Oread	orejn	Orientation	oraitoyoon
Orectic	orekyoko	Oriente	oraite
Oregano	oregbnko	Orienteering	oraitesignni
Oregon	oregun	Orifice	oraifesi
Orense	orese	Origami	oraigimo
Oresund	oraisujn	Origan	oraigbn
Orfe	orofin	Origen	oraign
Organ	orogbn	Origin	oraigin
Organdie	orogbnjnse	Original	oraiginjo
Organelle	orogbnlle	Originality	oraiginleto
Organic	orogbnko	Originally	oraiginjin
Organicism	orogbnkomosi	Originate	oraiginyo
Organism	orogbnmosi	Orinasal	oraihesujo
Organist	orogbnsi	Oriole	oraijoin
Organization	orogbnseyoon	Orion	oraisi
Organize	orogbnse	Orison	oraisin
Organza	orogbnsan	Orie	oraise
Organo	orogbnko	Ormolu	oromolu

WORD (x)	EQUIVALENT (y)	WORD (x)	EQUIVALENT (y)
Ornament	orohemutto	Orsini	orosoohe
ornate	oroheyo	Ortanique	orotuekun
Ome	omu	Ortho-	oorose
Omery	omurai	Orthicon	oorosekin
Omis	ominisa	Orthodontics	oorosedeyokosi
Omith	ominafo	Orthodox	oorosedesi
Omithic	ominifoko	Orthodoxy	oorosedesian
Omithine	ominifohun	Orthoepy	oorosesepo
Omithischian	ominifosikhi	Orthognthous	oorosegnsinsi
Omitho	ominafo	Orthogonal	oorosegunjo
Omithomancy	ominafoknmoyesn	Orthography	ooroseganphe
Omithopod	ominafoknpindi	Orthopeadics	oorosepandiekosi
Omithopter	ominafopnti	Orthopedics	oorosepndiekosi
Omithoscopy	ominafosekipe	Orthophony	oorosephohun
Omithosis	ominafoso	Orthopteran	oorosepntirain
Oro	orokn	Orthoptic	oorosepntiko
Orobanchaceous	oroknbounkhisuwa	Orthorhombic	ooroserhonmbuko
Orogeny	oroknginse	Orthoscope	oorosesekipon
Orography	oroknganphe	Orthositichy	oorosesetinhun
Oroide	oroknji	Orthotone	oorosetoni
Orometer	oroknmuto	Orthotropous	oorosetnrapnko
Orotund	orotnjoin	Ortles	orotoronsi
Orphan	orukan	Ortolan	orotejain
Orphanage	orukangun	Ortis	orotesi
Orpharion	orukanrain	Orwell	orowinjjo
Orphean	orophnye	,-ory	orain
Orphic	orophiko	Oryx	oraisi
Orphism	orophimosi	Os	ose
Orphrey	orophiroin	Osage	osegun
Orpiment	oropomitto	Oscar	osekosi
Orpine	oropohun	Oscillate	osekunleyo
Orpington	oropogntin	Oscillator	osekunleyoran
Orrery	orranrai	Oscilloscope	osekunlosekipon
Orris	orraisi	Oscine	osesun

WORD (x)	EQUIVALENT (y)	WORD (x)	EQUIVALENT (y)
Oscitancy	osekitisn	Ostensive	osetinsunwin
Osculant	osekuote	Ostentation	osetintoyoon
Oscular	osekuoran	Osteo-	osetnko
Osculate	osekuoyo	Osteoarthritis	osetnkoranrhaiso
Osculation	osekuoyoon	Osteoblast	osetnkobansia
Osculum	osekuoma	Soteclasis	osetnkoikanso
-osier	oserai	Osteoclast	osetnkokanta
,-osis	seso/so	Osteology	osetnkologbon
,-osity	seto	Osteoma	osetnkomu
Osler	osejnra	Osteomalacia	osetnkomolekoon
Osmic	osemiko	Osteomyelitis	osetnkomunjokoso
Osmious	osemisi	Osteopath	osetnkopanho
Osmium	osemima	Osteopathy	osetnkopansio
Osmometer	osemimuto	Osteoplastic	osetnkopansuiko
Osmose	osemise	Osteoplasty	osetnkopansuito
Osmosis	osemiso	Osteoporosis	osetnkoporaiso
Osmotic	osemiko	Osteotome	osetnkotemu
Osmous	osemisi	Osteotomy	osetnkotemo
Osmunda	osemijina	Ostiary	osetirai
Osnaburg	osehebugan	Ostinato	osetiheto
Osprey	osepesin	Ostiole	osetijoin
Ossa	osoo	Ostium	osetima
Ossein	osooyo	Ostler	osetijnra
Osseous	osoosi	Ostosis	osetoso
Ossetia	osootie	Ostracize	osetnrekose
Ossetic	osootiko	Ostracod	osetnrekijn
Ossicle	osookuo	Ostracoderm	osetnrekijnramo
Ossiferous	osoofirosi	Ostracon	osetnrekin
Ossification	osoofikoyoon	Ostrich	osetnraiki
Ossify	osoofe	Ot	oti, tin
Ossuary	ossorai	Other	osira
Osteal	osetnjo	Otic	oteti
Ostensible	osetinsunbe	Otiose	otese
Ostensory	osetinsunrai	Oto	oteti

WORD (x)	EQUIVALENT (y)	WORD (x)	EQUIVALENT (y)
Otitis	otetisi	Ova	owe
Otocyst	otetisnsu	Oval	owejo
Otolarymgology	otetijnrasognlogbon	Ovary	owerai
Otolith	otetilesi	Ovate	oweyo
Otology	otetilogbon	Ovation	oweyoon
Otoscope	otetisokipon	Oven	ownna
Ott	otta	Over	ownre
Ottar	ottan	Over-	ownre
Ottava	ottowa	Overlord	ownreyinsnjo
Ottavarima	ottoweraima	Overly	ownrelo
Otter	ottosi	Ovi-	owin
Otto	otto	Oviduct	owindikn
Ottoman	ottomoye	Oviferous	owinfirosi
Ouabain	ounbuto	Oviform	owinfoon
Ouananiche	ounyekhn	Oviaparous	owinpansi
Ouch	ounki	Ovoid	owejo
Oubliette	ounbiuntin	Ovolo	owolo
Ought	oungba	Ovofestis	owofinsuso
Ouija	ounjo	Ovoviviparous	owowopansi
Ounce	ounsi	Ovulate	oweleyo
Our	wa. Awa	Ovule	owejn
Ours	was. Tiwa	Ovum	owema
.-ous	wa;si	Owe	owin
Ouse	ounse	Owing	owingnni
Oust	ounyo	Owl	owiwi
Out	nita ita/nita/ode/ gbagede	Owlet	owitn
		Own	own
Out-	nita gbangba	Owner	ownsi
Outlet	nitatn	Owt	ownte
Outage	nitagun	Ox	osin
Out and about	nita ati abounta	Oxalate	osinleyo
Outward	nitawegba	Oxalic acid	osinleko
Ouzel	osunlo	Oxalis	osinleso
Ouzo	osesu	Oxidant	osianjitn

WORD (x)	EQUIVALENT (y)	WORD (x)	EQUIVALENT (y)
Oxidase	osianjinse	Paca	pako
Oxide	osianji	Pace1	pase
Oxidation	osianjiyoon	Pace2	pase
Oxidize	osianjise	Pace setter	pase settnra
Oxford	osinfonjn	Pacha	pankho
Ox-heart	osin hetan	Pachalic	pankhisi
Oxime	osinmo	Patchouli	pankhile
Oxo	osinko	Pachuca	pankhunko
Oxon	osinye	Pachuco	pankhunki
Oxonian	osinyehn	Pachy	pankhin
Oxtail	osintele	Pachyderm	pankhinjnramo
Oxter	osinto	Pachymenia	pankhinmuhan
Oxy	osian	Pachyrizid	pankhinraisujo
Oxyacetylene	osiankntilohun	Pachysandra	pankhinsanjnra
Oxygen	osiangin	Pacific	pasefiko
Oxygenate	osianginyo	Pacification	pasefikoyoon
Oxymoron	osianmoron	Pacifico	pasefiki
Oxytocic	osiantokiko	Pacifier	pasefise
Oxytocin	osiantokin	Pacifism	pasefimosi
Oxytone	osiantoni	Pacifist	pasefisi
Oyer	oynro	Pacify	pasefe
Oyez	oynso	Pacinian	pasekinhn
Oyster	oynseto	Park1	panki
Ozalid	oselijo	Park2	panki
Ozena	osehun	Package	pankigun
Ozocerite	osinknrayo	Packaging	pankigungnni
Ozonation	osinhunyoon	Packer	pankisi
Ozone	osinhun	Packet	pankiti
Ozonide	osinhunji	Packing	pankignni
Ozonise	osinhunse	Pact	panko
Ozonolysis	osinhunjinso	Pad 1	pangbi
Ozonosphere	osinhunsephirai	Pad2	pangbi
Pabulum	panbnje	Padang	pangbigan
Pac	paka	Padauk	pangbika

WORD (x)	EQUIVALENT (y)	WORD (x)	EQUIVALENT (y)
Paddle1	pangbiron	Paginal	pangnhunjo
Paddle2	pangbiron	Paginate	pangnhunyo
Paddock	pangbiki	Pagination	pangnhunyoon
Paddy	pangbisi	Pagoda	pangonjn
Paddy1	pangbisi	Pagoplexia	pangonposia
Paddy2	pangbisi	Pagurian	pangnrain
Pademelon	pangbimujoin	Paguriadae	pangnraijn
Padishah	pangbisua	Pahlavi	panhunsi
Padlock	pangbilokkh	Pahoehoe	panhinsise
Padre	pangbira	Paid	pesan
Padrone	pangbnhun	Paid-up	pesan pake
Paduasoy	pangbisanyo	Paideutics	pesanunkosi
Paean	panyo	Paidle	pesanjn
Paederast	pandieransi	Paidology	pesielogbon
Paederasty	pandieranto	Paigle	pangilo
Paediatrics	pandietnrakosi	Paignton	panginitin
Paedo-	pandie	Pail	panlo
Paedogenesis	pandiegnhunso	Paillasse	panllosoon
Paedology	pandielogbon	Pain	panta
Paedomorphosis	pandiemophanso	Painless	pantalabo
Paedophile	pandiepheron	Paint	pantone
Paedophilia	pandiepheransi	Paintbox	pantonibosi
Paella	panjerai	Painter1	pantonisi
Paeon	pansio	Painter2	pantonisi
Paeony	pansiosi	Painterly	pantonisilo
Paestum	pansetoma	Painting	pantonignni
Pagan	pangisi	Painty	pantonise
Paganise	pangisise	Pair	panrai
Page1	pangn	Pais	panse
Page2	pangn	Pairsley	panseroin
Pageant	pangnte	Pajamas	panjosun
Pageantry	pangnterai	Pajero	panjnrai
Paget	pangnti	Pakeha	pankeha
Pager	pangnsi	Pal	panjo

439

WORD (x)	EQUIVALENT (y)	WORD (x)	EQUIVALENT (y)
Palace	panjosin	Palenque	panjoinkun
Palcio	panjokio	Paleo-	panjonko
Paladin	panjodain	Paleopadology	panjonkopndelogbon
Palaeanthropic	panjounsinrapnko	Palestine	panjositin
Palaearctic	panjounrankako	Palestra	panjosirain
Palaeethnology	panjouneseyahn-logbon	Palet	panjonte
		Paletot	panjontin
Palaeo	panjounko	Palette	panjottn
Palaeoanthropology	panjounansnrapin-logbon	Palfrey	panjofisin
		Palgrave	panjoganwo
Palaeocene	panjounkoknsa	Palikar	pamjokira
Palaeogene	panjounkognhun	Palimony	panjomenise
Palaeography	panjounkoganphe	Palimpsest	panjompnsesi
Palaeolithic	panjounkolesiko	Palindrome	panjoingbnmo
Palaeontology	panjounhntologbon	Palindromia	panjoingbnmu
Palaeozoic	panjounsinko	Paling	panjoingn
Palaestra	panjounsetnre	Palingenesis	panjoingnhunso
Palais	panjoso	Palinode	panjoinjo
Palamedes	panjomujnsi	Palinurus	panjoinsunra
Palames	panjomosi	Palisade	panjosejin
Palanquin	panjoinkun	Palissy	panjosuwa
Palatable	panjotebe	Pall1	panjnra
Palatal	panjotele	Pall2	panjnra
Palatalize	panjotelese	Palladian	panjnragbain
Palate	panjote	Palladic	panjnragbako
Palatial	panjotelo	Palladio	panjnragboin
Palatinate	panjoteheyo	Palladium	panjnragbasi
Palatine	panjotehun	Pallas	panjnrase
Palau	panjole	Pallbearer	panjnra beransi
Palaver	panjowinsi	Pallet	panjnrate
Palay	panjosia	Pallet2	panjnrate
Pale1	panjon	Palletize	panjinratese
Pale2	panjon	Pallette	panjnratte
Palea	panjoin	Palliasse	panjnrasoon

WORD (x)	EQUIVALENT (y)	WORD (x)	EQUIVALENT (y)
Palliate	panjnratie	Paltry	panjetnrai
Palliative	panjnrajo	Paludal	panjonjo
Pallor	panjnraran	Paludism	panjonmosi
Pally	panjnrasi	Pal up	panjo pake
Palm1	panjema	Paly	panjia
Palm2	panjema	Palynology	panjiaknlogbon
Palmaceous	panjemasuwa	Pam	panmo
Palmate	panjemayo	Pamir	panmorai
Palmation	panjemayoon	Pamlico	panmjnki
Palmer	panjemasi	Pampas	panmpnse
Palmette	panjematn	Pamper	panmpnra
Palmetto	panjemato	Pampero	panmpnran
Palmi	panjemo	Pamph	panmphn
Palmiped	panjemopnjn	Pamphlet	panmphntn
Palmistry	panjemoterai	Pamphleteer	panmphntosi
Palmitate	panjemoteyo	Pan	panu
Palmic	panjemuko	Pan1	panu
Palmitin	panjemotie	Pan2	panu
Palmy	panjemu	Pan-	panu
Palmyra	panjemuran	Panacea	panusin
Palolo	panjelo	Panache	panukhn
Palomar	panjemura	Panada	panujo
Palomino	panjemuhn	Panama	panumi
Palooka	panjereka	Panatela	panuto
Palp	panjepn	Panathenaea	panusinhunsi
Palpable	panjepnbe	Panatrophy	panutnraphe
Palpate	panjepnyo	Pancake	pankoki
Palpitate	panjepntiyo	Panchax	pankhosi
Palpitation	panjepntiyoon	Panchromatic	pankhironmuko
Palpus	panjepnsi	Pancosmism	pankisetomosi
Palsgrave	panesiganwo	Pancratium	panknraitoma
Palstave	panjesitnwin	Pancreas	panknranse
Palsy	panjeso	Pancreatic	panknranko
Palter	panjetnra	Panda	panjnna

WORD (x)	EQUIVALENT (y)	WORD (x)	EQUIVALENT (y)
Pandacar	panjnnakosi	Paniculate	payakoleyo
Pandanus	panjnnasi	Panjandrum	panjaingbiro
Pandarus	panjnnaransi	Panjnad	panjainjo
Pandean	panjinhun	Panmixia	panmisia
Pandect	panjinknyo	Pannage	pannigun
Pandemic	panjinmuko	Panne	panhn
Pandemonium	panjinmulema	Pannier	panhnsi
Pander	panjinra	Pannikin	panhnkin
Pandit	pandete	Pannonia	panhnhan
Pandora's box	panderansi bosi	Panocha	panhnkho
Pandore	panderai	Panoply	pankopn
Pandour	panderain	Panoptic	pankopnko
Pandowdy	pandewajo	Panorama	pankoraima
Pandurate	pandiraiyo	Panoramic	pankoraimuko
Pandy	panjnse	Pan out	panu nita
Pane	panhun	Panpaychism	panjnpansekhimosi
Panegyric	panhunloraiko	Panpipes	panpoponsi
Panegyrise	panhunloraise	Pansophy	pansoophe
Panel	panhunjo	Pansy	pansai
Paneling	panhunjognni	Pant	pantie
Panelist	panhunjosi	Pantagruel	pantogirailo
Panelling	panhunjjognni	Pantalet	pantotn
Panellist	panhunjjosi	Pantaloons	pantolosesi
Panatela	panhuntojn	Pantar	pantora
Pang	pangn	Pantechnicon	pantokhinikin
Panga	pangan	Pantellaria	pantojjnran
Pangaea	pangini	Pantheism	pantosinmosi
Pangamy	pangimo	Pantheon	pantosin
Pangenesis	pangnhunso	Panther	pantosira
Pangolin	pangonjan	Panties	pantisi
Panhandle	panhaduo	Pantile	pantiron
Panic	payako	Pantisocracy	pantisookansin
Panicle	payakuo	Panto	panton
Panic stations	payako setnyoon	Pantofle	pantonfijn

WORD (x)	EQUIVALENT (y)	WORD (x)	EQUIVALENT (y)
Pantograph	pantonganpha	Papoose	panpoonse
Pantomime	pantonmimi	Pappus	panposi
Pantothenic	pantonsinko	Pappy	panpnpo
Pantoum	pantonma	Paprika	panpanko
Pantry	pantierai	Pap test	panpn tnsi
Pants	pantiesi	Papua	panpnko
Panty	pantiese	Papule	panpnkuo
Panung	pangun	Papyraceous	panpnraisuwa
Panzer	panserai	Papyrology	panpnrailogbon
Pap1	panpo	Papyrus	panpnraisi
Pap2	panpo	Par	pan
Papa	panpe/baba	Para-1	panra
Papacy	panpesn	Para-2	panra
Papain	panpetie	Paramino	panramukn
Papal	panpejo	Parabasis	panrabooso
Paparazzo	panperaisi	Parabiosis	panrabakoso
Papaveraceous	panpewnrasuwa	Parablast	panrabansia
Papaw	panpanwai	Parable	panralowe
Papaya	panpanya	Parable	panraron
Papen	panpnya	Parabola	panraboojo
Paper	panpnra	Parabole	panraboojn
Paperback	panpnraboki	Parabolic	panraboojnko
Papery	panpnrai	Parabolise	panraboojnse
Papeterie	panpntiron	Paraboloid	panraboojnjo
Paphian	panphesi	Parabrake	panrabankn
Papier mache	panpnra mukke	Paracasein	panrakoso
Papilionaceous	panpojnsesuwa	Paracel	panraknjn
Papilionidae	panpojnsedie	Paracenesthesis	panraknsunwnso
Papilla	panpojnran	Paracentric	panrakntiranko
Papilloma	panpojnranmo	Paracetamol	panrakntimujin
Papillon	panpojnrain	Parachronism	panrakhironmosi
Papillote	panpojnrante	Parachute	panrakhunyo
Papist	panpesi	Paraclete	panraknra
Papistry	panpesirai	Paracme	panraknmo

WORD (x)	EQUIVALENT (y)	WORD (x)	EQUIVALENT (y)
Parade	panrajin	Paralogism	panralogbonmosi
Parade-ground	gonjoin panrajin	Paralyse	panrajnsia
Paradiddle	panrajinduo	Paralysis	panrajnso
Paradigm	panrajingbi	Paralytic	panrajnsiako
Paradise	panrajinse	Paralyze	panrajnsia
Paradisiacal	panrajinsekojo	Paramatta	panramatto
Parados	panrajinso	Paramecin	panramukin
Paradox	panrajinsin	Paramecium	panramukima
Paradoxical	panrajinsinkojo	Paramedic	panramujinko
Paradrop	panragbnpe	Paramedical	panramujinkojo
Paraesthesia	panrasunwnsai	Parameter	panramuto
Paraffin	panrafin	Parametric	panramutoraiko
Paraffine	panrafini	Paramnesia	panraminisia
Paraform	panrafonmo	Paramo	panramo
Parafrag	panrafangi	Paramorph	panramophan
Paragenesis	panragnhunso	Paramorphism	panramophansi
Paragoge	panragonko	Paramount	panramounte
Paragon	panragun	Paramour	panramoran
Paragonite	panragunyo	Parana	panrain
Paragraph	panraganpha	Paranaiba	panrainbe
Paragraphia	panraganphan	Paranephric	panrahunphanko
Paraguay	panragunse	Paranephros	panrahunphansoo
Paraheliotropism	panrahejntnrapnmosi	Paranoia	panrakoin
Paraiba	panraibe	Paranoiac	panrakoinka
Parakeet	panraknte	Paranoid	panrakoinjo
Parakinesia	panrakihunsia	Paranosis	panrakoiso
Paralanguage	panralehagngun	Paranormal	panranironjo
Paraldehyde	panjojinhoji	Paranymph	panrayunmpha
Paraleipsis	panrajnpnso	Parapet	panrapnti
Paralipomena	panrajopinmuhe	Paraph	panrapha
Parallax	panrajnranse	Paraphenalia	panraphnnijo
Parallel	panrajnran	Paraphone	panraphohun
Parallelism	panrajnranmosi	Paraphrase	panraphanso
Parallelogram	panrajnranloganmo	Paraphysis	panrapheso

WORD (x)	EQUIVALENT (y)	WORD (x)	EQUIVALENT (y)
Paraplegia	panpojngan	Parbukle	panbukuo
Parapodium	panrapinjoma	Parcae	pankoin
Parapraxis	panpansiso	Parcel	panknjo
Paraprofessional	panraponfnsoonjo	Parcenary	pankinrai
Paraquat	panrakuite	Parcener	pankinra
Paraque	panrakun	Parch	pankhn
Parasang	panrasungn	Parcheesi	pankhnsesi
Paraselene	panrasejoin	Parchment	pankhnmutto
Parashah	panrasua	Pard	pangba
Parasieve	panrasoowin	Pardi	pangba
Parasite	panrasosi	Pardner	pangbaron
Parasitism	panrasosimosi	Pardon	pangbain
Parasitise	panrasosise	Pardoner	pangbainsi
Parasitology	panrasosilogbon	Pare	panra
Parasol	panrasinle	Pare	panra
Parasphenoid	pansephinijo	Paragon	panragun
Parastichy	panrasetinhun	Paregoric	panragonko
Parasympathe	panrasompansio	Pareira	panraran
Parasympathetic	panrasompansioko	Parenchyma	panraikhnmo
Parasynapsis	panrasosepanso	Parent	panrato
Parasynthesis	panrasosesinso	Parentage	panratogun
Parasyphilis	panrasopherosi	Parental	panratojo
Parataxic	panratesanko	Parentalia	panratojain
Parataxis	panratesanso	Parenteral	panratoranjo
Parathion	panrasiose	Parenthesis	panrasinso
Parathyroid	pansioraijo	Parenthesize	panrasinse
Paratroops	panratnraposi	Parenthetical	panrasinkojo
Paratyphoid	pantnphojo	Parenting	panratognni
Paraunit	panraenite	Paresis	panraso
Paravane	panrawain	Paresthesia	panrasunwnsia
Parazoan	panrasinhn	Paretic	panratoko
Par avion	pan awwosi	Pareto	panrato
Parazoan	pansinye	Pareu	panrau
Parboil	panbole	Pareve	parewin

WORD (x)	EQUIVALENT (y)	WORD (x)	EQUIVALENT (y)
Par excellence	pan esnknjjnsi	Parlance	panjoinso
Parfait	panfante	Parlando	panjoinde
Parfleche	panfijnkhn	Parlatoria	panjoteran
Parget	pangnyo	Parlay	panjose
Parhelic	panhejoko	Parley	panjoso
Parhelion	panhejosi	Parliament	panjomutto
Pari	panrai	Parliamentarian	panjomuttorain
Paria	panrai	Parliamentary	panjomuttorai
Pariah	panraiha	Parlor	panjnran
Parian	panraihn	Parlous	panjnrasi
Paries	panraisi	Parma	panma
Parietal	panraitnjo	Parmenides	panminijosi
Paring	panraignni	Parmesan	panmusn
Parillin	panraijjnsi	Parmigiana	panminigan
Parimutuel	panraimutnlo	Pamaiba	panmubaun
Paring	panraigini	Pamassian	panmusoon
Paripassu	panraipansoo	Pamell	panmujin
Paris	panraisi	Parochial	panrokhnjo
Parish	panraisin	Parochialism	panrokhnjomosi
Parishad	panraisinjn	Parody	panrodun
Parishioner	panraisinsi	Paroecous	panroknsi
Parison	panraisnle	Parol	panrojo
Paritor	panraitnran	Parole	panrolo
Parity	panraito	Paronomasia	panrosimosai
Pariviscular	panraiwoknjnra	Paronym	panrosin
Park	panka	Paroral	panronjo
Parka	pankn	Paros	panrosi
Parker	panknsi	Parotic	panrotiko
Parkin	pankata	Parotid	panrotijo
Parkinson	pankatasi	Parotitis	panrotiso
Parking-lot	pankagnni lote	Parotoid	panrotijo
Parkland	pankaledain	Parous	panrosi
Park way	pankawelo	Paroxysm	panrosianma
Parky	pankase	Paroxysmal	panrosiansemojn

WORD (x)	EQUIVALENT (y)	WORD (x)	EQUIVALENT (y)
Paroxytone	panrosiansetoni	Partial	pantejo
Parpend	panpnjon	Partible	pantebe
Parquet	pankunte	Participant	pantekopa
Parquetry	pankunterai	Participate	pantekopayo
Parquine	pankunhun	Participatory	pantekopayorai
Parr	panrre	Participial	pantekopanjo
Parrel	panrrejo	Participle	pantekopan
Parricide	panrraikeku	Particle	pantekun
Parritch	panrraihun	Particular	pantekunjnra
Parrot	panrraito	Particularity	pantekunjnraito
Parry	panrrai	Particularize	pantekunjnraise
Parse	pansoo	Particularly	pantekunjnralo
Parsee	pansooa	Particulate	pantekunjnyo
Parsee	pansooa	Partim	pantemo
Parsfal	pansofan	Parting	pantegnni
Parsimony	pansoomeni	Parti pris	pante pansi
Parsley	pansoroin	Partisan	pantesin
Parsnip	pansopan	Partite	panteyo
Parson	pansnle	Partition	panteyoon
Parsonage	pansnlegun	Partitive	panteyowin
Parsons	pansnlesi	Partizan	pantesan
Part	pante	Partlet	pantetn
Partake	pantekn	Partly	pantelo
Partan	pantera	Partner	pantira
Parted	pantede	Partnership	pantirasunpn
Parterre	panterrai	Partridge	panteraigbon
Parthenocarpy	pantekinikopan	Parturient	panteraito
Parthenogenesis	pantekinignhunso	Parturition	panteraiyoon
Parthenon	pantekini	Party	pantesi
Parthenopeaus	pantekinipansi	Party line	pantesi lehun
Parthenope	pantekinipn	Parulis	panroinsi
Parthenos	pantekinisi	Parure	panroin
Parthia	pantesia	Parve	panwin
Parthian	pantesiahn	Parvenu	panwini

WORD (x)	EQUIVALENT (y)	WORD (x)	EQUIVALENT (y)
Parvis	panwosi	Passant	pansotn
Parvoline	panwnjnmi	Passband	pansobohajn
Parzival	pansuwajo	Passbook	pansobooko
Pas	pansa	Pass by	panso beo
Pasadena	pansajina	Passé	pansose
Pasargadae	pansagiranjn	Passel	pansolo
Passay	pansase	Passementerie	pansosnminito
Pascal	pansaknjo	Passaenger	pansoongnsi
Pasch	pansakhn	Passepartout	pansopantenita
Paschal	pansakhnjo	Passepied	pansopnde
Pascual	pansakunjo	Passer-by	pansosi-beo
Pasdecalais	pansajinkojo	Passeriformes	pansosifoonmo
Pasdedeux	pansajijisi	Passerine	pansorain
Pase	panse	Passero	pansoknra
Pash	pansua	Passeul	pansoji
Pasha	pansuan	Passible	pansobe
Pashlik	pansuankn	Passifloraceous	pansofonraisuwa
Pashka	pansuako	Passim	pansoma
Pashm	pansuamo	Passing	pansognni
Pashto	pansuto	Passion	pansonsi
Pasiphae	pansephini	Passional	pansonsijo
Paso doble	pansoo deran	Passionate	pansonsiyo
Pasque-flower	pansekun	Passivate	pansoweyo
Pasquin	pansekue	Passive	pansowin
Pasquinade	pansekuejin	Passivism	pansowinmosi
Pass1	panso	Passivity	pansowinto
Pass2	panso	Passkey	pansoknsi
Passable	pansobe	Passover	pansownra
Passably	pansobe	Passport	pansopinta
Passacaglia	pansokogan	Passus	pansosi
Passade	pansojin	Password	pansowijo
Passage	pansogun	Passy	pansose
Passageway	pansogunwelo	Past	pansin
Passaic	pansoko	Pasta	pansinte

WORD (x)	EQUIVALENT (y)	WORD (x)	EQUIVALENT (y)
Paste	pansintn	Patamar	patemura
Pasteborad	boogbapansintn	Patapsen	patepnsun
Pastel	pansinlo	Patch	patekhun
Paster	pansinsi	Patchboard	boogbapatekhun
Pastem	pansinmo	Patchouli	patekhnjin
Pasteurella	pansinwalle	Patchouly	patekhnlo
Pasteurism	pansinwamosi	Patchy	patekho
Pasteurization	pansinwaseyoon	Pate	pato
Pasteurizer	pansinwasesi	Pate	patn
Pasticcio	pansitekio	Pate	pate
Pastiche	pansitekhn	Patella	patelle
Pastille	pansitelle	Patellate	patelleto
Pastime	pansitinmo	Patelliform	patellefoonmo
Pastiness	pansitinsi	Paten	patesi
Pastis	pansinso	Patency	patesn
Pasto	pansinkn	Patent	pateto
Pastor	pansinran	Patentee	patetose
Pastoral	pansinranjo	Patentor	patetoran
Pastorale	pansinranjn	Pater	pantnra
Pastoralist	pansinranjosi	Patera	paterai
Pastorate	pansinranto	Paternal	pantnranjo
Pastorium	pansinraima	Paternalism	pantnranjomosi
Past participle	pansin pantekipan	Paternity	pantnranto
Pastrami	pansinrami	Paternoster	pantnranseto
Pastry	pansinrai	Paterson	pantnrasin
Pasturage	pansinraigun	Path	panho
Pasture	pansinrai	Pathan	panssue
Pasty1	pansinse	Pathetic	pansioko
Pasty2	pansinse	Pathic	pansuko
Pat.	Patn	Patho	patesia
Pat1	patn	Pathogen	patesiagin
Pat2	patn	Pathogenesis	patesiagnhunso
Patagium	pategima	Pathogenic	patesiaginko
Patagonia	pategonsi	Pathognomonic	patesiagonmeniko

WORD (x)	EQUIVALENT (y)	WORD (x)	EQUIVALENT (y)
Pathognomy	patesiagonmo	Patriot	panknrato
Pathological	patesialogbonkojo	Patriotic	panknratokn
Pathology	patesialogbon	Patriotism	panknratomosi
Pathomimosis	patesiamophanmosi	Patristic	panknrasuko
Pathos	patesin	Patrol	pantnrajn
Pathy	patesio	Patrol car	kosi pantnrajn
Patiala	patejn	Patron	Pantnra
Patience	patetansi	Patronage	pantnragun
Patient	patetan	Patronize	pantnrase
Patina	patehun	Patron saint	santoni pantnrasi
Patino	patehn	Patronymic	pantnramuko
Patio	pateko	Patroon	pantnrain
Patisserie	patesooran	Pattee	pattese
Patmore	patemosii	Patten	pattesi
Patmos	patemosi	Patter1	patteso
Patna	patohun	Patter2	patteso
Patois	patoso	Pattern	patteran
Patola	patojn	Patton	pattesa
Patos	patosi	Pattu	patteu
Patras	pantnresi	Patty	patteni
Patri	panknra	Patulous	patejnsi
Patriarch	panknrasi	Paucity	pankueto
Patriarchal	panknraranjo	Pau	pane
Patriarchate	panknraranto	Paul	panle
Patriarchy	panknraran	Pauldron	panlegbain
Patricia	panknrasua	Paulin	panlesi
Patrician	panknrasuan	Pauline	panlehun
Patriciate	panknrasuato	Paulinus	panlehunsi
Patricide	panknrakeku	Paulist	panlesi
Patrick	panknraki	Paulownia	panlewini
Patriclinous	panknrakiunsi	Paulus	panlese
Patrilineal	panknralehunjo	Paunch	pankhun
Patrilocal	panknraloknjo	Pauper	panpaisi
Patrimony	panknrameni	Pauperies	panpairaise

WORD (x)	EQUIVALENT (y)	WORD (x)	EQUIVALENT (y)
Paurometabolous	panraumitoboojnsi	Payload	panyiologbi
Pausanias	pansaihnse	Payment	panyiomutto
Pause	pansai	Payne	panyioni
Pavan	panwain	Paynim	panyionimo
Pavage	panwaigun	Payola	panyiojn
Pavane	panwain	Pay phone	panyio phohun
Paver	panwaisi	Pea	pnn
Pave	panwai	Peace	pnnsin
Pavement	panwaimutto	Peaceable	pnnsinberon
Pavement artist	etesi panwaimutto	Peach1	pnnkho
Pavia	panwini	Peach2	pnnkho
Pavid	panwinjo	Peach melba	mujobo pnnkho
Pavilion	panwinlesi	Peachy	pnnkhose
Paving-stone	panwingnni	Peacoat	pnnkite
Paviour	panwinran	Peacock	pnnkiko
Pavis	panwnse	Peag	pngi
Paviser	panwinsera	Peahen	pnnhesi
Pavlova	panwnwa	Peak1	pnke
Pavlovian	panwnwahn	Peak2	pnke
Pavo	panwn	Peak-load	pnke-logbi
Pavonine	panwoinhun	Peaky	pnkesi
Paw	panwo	Peal	pnjan
Pawky	panwoko	Peale	pnjain
Paw1	panwo	Pean	pnhun
Pawn1	panwn	Peanut	pnhunte
Pawn2	panwn	Pear	pnruan
Pawnbroker	pawnbonknra	Pearl	pnruanjo
Pawnee	panwnse	Pearler	pnruanjosi
Pawner	panwnsi	Pearlite	pnruanleyo
Pawpaw	panwowo	Pearly	pnruanlo
Pax	panse	Pearse	pnruanse
Pay	panyio	Pearson	pnruansin
Payable	panyiobe	Peart	pnruante
Pay-as-you-earn	panyio eran-se yin	Peary	pnruan

451

WORD (x)	EQUIVALENT (y)	WORD (x)	EQUIVALENT (y)
Peasant	pnsetn	Peculiarity	pnkuojnraito
Peasantry	pnsetnrai	Peculiarly	pnkuojnranlo
Peascod	pnsekidi	Peculium	pnkuojnma
Pease	pnsesi	Pecuniary	pnkuonirai
Peat	pnte	Ped	pndie
Peaty	pntese	Pedagog	pndiegonko
Peaudesole	pnnijinsinle	Pedagogue	pndiegonkun
Peavey	pnwinse	Pedagogic	pndiegonko
Pebble	pnbnbe	Pedagogics	pndiegonkosi
Pecan	pnkoin	Pedagogism	pndiegonkomosi
Peccable	pnkobe	Pedagogy	pndiegonkose
Peccadillo	pnkodillo	Pedal	pndiejn
Peccant	pnkotn	Pedalfer	pndiejnfiro
Peccary	pnkorai	Pedalier	pndiejnran
Peccavi	pnkowi	Pedalo	pndielo
Pech	pnkha	Pedant	pndiete
Pechan	pnkhun	Pedantic	pndieteko
Pechenga	pnkhngan	Pedantry	pndieterai
Pechora	pnkhoran	Pedate	pndieyo
Peck1	pnke	Pedati	pndieya
Peck2	pnke	Pedatifid	pndieyafijo
Pecker	pnkesi	Pedatisect	pndieyaseknte
Peckish	pnkese	Peddle	pndieron
Pecktase	pnketese	Peddler	pndieronsi
Pecos	pnkoonsi	Peddling	pndiegnni
Pectate	pntoyo	Pede	pndie
Pecten	pnton	Pederast	pndieranse
Pectic	pntoko	Pederasty	pndieranseto
Pectin	pntohn	Pedestal	pndiesijo
Pectinate	pntohnyo	Pedestrian	pndiesirain
Pectise	pntose	Pedestrianise	pndiesirainse
Pectoral	pntoranjo	Pedi	pndi
Pectus excarinatus	pntosi esnkorainyosi	Pediatrics	pndigbebi
Peculate	pnkuojnran	Pediatrics	pnditnraiko

WORD (x)	EQUIVALENT (y)	WORD (x)	EQUIVALENT (y)
Pedicab	pndikobe	Peep1	pnpn
Pedicel	pndiknle	Peep2	pnpn
Pedicelate	pndiknleyo	Peer1	pnsira
Pedicle	pndikuo	Peer2	pnsira
Pedicular	pndikunleran	Peerage	pnsiragun
Pediculate	pndikunleyo	Peeress	pnsirabo
Pediculosis	pndikunleso	Peer group	gonpo pnsira
Pedicure	pndikunrai	Peerless	pnsiralabo
Pedigree	pndigirain	Peeve	pnwini
Pediment	pndimutto	Peevish	pnwinisi
Pedipalp	pndipanjo	Peewe	pnwere
Pedlar	pndijnra	Peewit	pnwote
Pedo-	pnde	Peg	pngi
Pedocal	pndekojo	Pegasus	pngisesi
Pedology	pndelogbon	Pegboard	bugbapngi
Pedometer	pndemuto	Peg matite	pngi motnyo
Pedophile	pndepheron	Peignioir	pnginirai
Pedophilia	pndepherain	Pegu	pngun
Pedregal	pndiregijo	Peinotherapy	pnkinisinranpo
Pedro	pndiro	Peiping	pnpinign
Pedule	pndiron	Peipus	pnposun
Peduncle	pndikun	Peiraiers	pnrairainsi
Pedunculate	pndiekunleyo	Peirce	pnraisi
Pee	pnse	Peiree	pnraise
Peebeen	pnbnsin	Peixotto	pnsuatto
Peebles	pnbnsi	Pejoration	pnjinraiyoon
Peek	pnkoi	Pejorative	pnjinraiyowin
Peel	pnbo	Pekalongan	pnkologunsi
Peele	pnbose	Pekan	pnkusi
Peeler	pnbosi	Pekin	pnkini
Peeling	pnbognni	Pekingese	pnkiginise
Peelie-wally	pnbose-wanlle	Peking	pnkigini
Peen	pnsi	Pekoe	pnknse
Peenge	pnsign	Pelage	pnyngbaa

WORD (x)	EQUIVALENT (y)	WORD (x)	EQUIVALENT (y)
Pelagianism	pnyngbaamosi	Pelon	pnynrun
Pelagic	pnyngbaako	Pelophyte	pnynknpheyo
Pelagius	pnyngbaasi	Peloponnese	pnynknponsinse
Pelargonic	pnyngbunko	Peloponnesian	pnynknponsinhn
Pelargonium	pnyngbunma	Peloponnesus	pnynknponsinsi
Pelasgi	pnyngise	Pelops	pnynknpa
Pele	pnyo	Peloria	pnynknran
Pelecypod	pnyosnpinjo	Pelorus	pnynknransi
Pelee	pnyose	Pelota	pnynknta
Pelerine	pnyorain	Pelotas	pnyntasi
Peleus	pnyosi	Pelt1	pnynte
Pelf	pnynfn	Pelt2	pnynte
Pelham	pnynhaun	Pelta	pnynte
Pelias	pnynse	Peltast	pnyntesi
Pelican	pnynkoin	Peltate	pnynteyo
Pelican crossing	konsognni pnynkoin	Peltier	pnynteran
Pelides	pnyndesi	Peltry	pnynterai
Pelion	pnynsi	Pelvic fin	pnynwoko fihe
Pelisse	pnynsoo	Pelvimeter	pnynwomuto
Pelite	pnynyo	Pelvimetry	pnynwomutorai
Pella	pnynra	Pelvis	pnynwosi
Pellagra	pnynragan	Pemba	pnmibe
Pellagrin	pnynragbaran	Pembroke	pnmibonkn
Pelleas	pnynrase	Pemmican	pnmmikin
Pellet	pnynrato	Pemphigus	pnmiphignsi
Pelletierine	pnynratorain	Pen1	pnya
Pellicle	pnynrankuo	Pen2	pnya
Pellitory	pnynrantorai	Pen3	pnya
Pell-mell	pnynran mulle	Penal	pnyajo
Pellotine	pnynraknti	Penalize	pnyojose
Pellucid	pnynrakijo	Penalty	pnyajoin
Pelly	pnynrain	Penalty area	aria pnyajoin
Pelmanism	pnynmoyemosi	Penance	pnyakini
Pelmet	pnynmuto	Penang	pnyangan

WORD (x)	EQUIVALENT (y)	WORD (x)	EQUIVALENT (y)
Penates	pnyayosi	Peninsula	pnyasunjn
Pence	pnyasi	Peninsular	pnyasunjnra
Pencel	pnyaknjn	Peninsularity	pnyasunjnraito
Penchant	pnyakhote	Peninsulate	pnyasunjnyo
Pencil	pnyakun	Penis	pnyasi
Pend	pnjon	Penitence	pnyatunse
Pendant	pnjontn	Penitent	pnyatunto
Pendent	pnjonto	Penitential	pnyatuntojo
Pendent	pnjonto	Penitentiary	pnyatuntorai
Pendentelite	pnjontoleyo	Penki	pnyaki
Pendentive	pnjontowin	Penman	pnyamoye
Pending	pnjongnni	Penmanship	pnyamoyesunpn
Pendragon	pnjongini	Penna	pnyayun
Pendulous	pnjongnsi	Pennant	pnyayntn
Pendulum	pnjongnma	Pennate	pnyaynyo
Pene	pnyun	Pennel	pnyaynlo
Penelope	pnyunlopon	Penni	pnyayn
Peneplain	pnyunpanto	Penniless	pnyaynlabo
Penetralia	pnyunteraijan	Pennines	pnyaynhunsi
Penetrance	pnyunteraisi	Pennine way	pnyaynhun welo
Penetrant	pnyunteraitn	Penninite	pnyaynhunyo
Penetrate	pnyunteraiyo	Pennon	pnyasise
Penetration	pnyunteraiyoon	Pennoncel	pnyasiseknjn
Penetrative	pnyunteraiyowin	Pennsylvania	pnyasijnwain
Penetrometer	pnyuntnramuto	Penny	pnyayn
Peneus	pnyunsi	Pennyaliner	pnyaynlehunsi
Penghu	pnyaghn	Pennycress	pnyaynkesiso
Pengo	pnyalo	Pennywork	pnyaynwinsise
Penguin	pnyagbain	Peno	pnyakn
Penicillate	pinyakunleyo	Ponobscot	pnyaknbosikiti
Penicillin	pinyakunlesi	Ponology	pnyaknlogbon
Penicillium	pinyakunlema	Penpal	pnyapanjo
Penile	pnyaron	Penrhyn	pnyarhain
Penillion	pnyaroin	Pensacola	pnyasekile

WORD (x)	EQUIVALENT (y)	WORD (x)	EQUIVALENT (y)
Pensemon	pnyasemeni	Pentheus	pnyatohinlese
Pensile	pnyasooron	Pentimento	pnyatomutn
Pension1	pnyasoon	Pentium	pnyatoma
Pension2	pnyasoon	Pentlandite	pnyatoledainto
Penisionable	pnyasoonberon	Pentobarbitone	pnyatobobantoni
Pensionary	pnyasoonrai	Pentode	pnyatojain
Pensioner	pnyasoonsi	Pentoid	pnyatojo
Pensive	pnyasoowin	Pentomic	pnyatomuko
Pensremon	pnyasetomeni	Pentosan	pnyatosie
Penstock	pnyasetoki	Pentose	pnyatose
Pent	pnyato	Pentoxide	pnyatosianji
Penta-	pnyate	Pentstmon	pnyatosimeni
Pentacle	pnyatekuo	Pentyl	pnyatojin
Pentad	pnyatejo	Petylacetate	pnyatojinkntiyo
Pentadactyl	pnyatedakntilo	Pentylenetetrazol	pnyatojinhuntnresijin
Pentagon	pnyategun	Penuche	pnyakhn
Pentahedron	pnyatehejnran	Penuchle	pnyakhnjn
Pentamerous	pnyatemurasi	Penult	pnyajn
Pentagram	pnyateganmo	Penultimate	pnyajnmuyo
Pentameter	pnyatemuto	Penumbra	pnyambora
Pentane	pnyatehun	Penurious	pnyaraisi
Pentanoic	pnyatehunko	Penury	pnyarai
Pentapolis	pnyatepnjinsi	Penutian	pnyatan
Pentaprism	pnyatepanmosi	Penza	pnyasn
Pentaquine	pnyatekuihun	Penzance	pnyasnsi
Pentarchy	pnyatekhran	Peon	pneni
Pentastich	pnyatesetinsi	Peonage	pnenigun
Pentateuch	pnyatetokhun	Peony	pnenise
Pentathlon	pnyatesejn	People	pnenipo
Pentatonic	pnyatetoniko	Peoria	pneniran
Pentecost	pnyatokisi	Pep	pnpo
Pentelikon	pnyatolokin	Pephedo	pnphede
Pentene	pnyatnna	Peplos	pnpolaso
Penthesilea	pnyatosunajin	Peplum	pnpolema

WORD (x)	EQUIVALENT (y)	WORD (x)	EQUIVALENT (y)
Pepo	pnpin	Per cent	pnra knti
Pepper	pnpota	Percent	pnraknti
Pepper com	kia pnpota	Percentage	pnrakntigun
Pepperidge	pnpotagbn	Percentile	pnrakntiron
Peppermint	pnpotamutin	Percept	pnraknpyo
Peppery	pnpotase	Perceptible	pnraknpyobe
Pep pill	pnpo pojnra	Perception	pnraknpyosi
Peppy	pnpose	Perceptive	pnraknpyowin
Pepsin	pnposie	Perceptual	pnraknpyojo
Pepsinate	pnposieto	Perceval	pnraknwajo
Pepsinogen	pnposiegin	Perch1	pnrakhun
Peps	pnposi	Perch2	pnrakhun
Peptic	pnpotiko	Perchance	pnrakhunsi
Peptidase	pnpotijise	Perche	pnrakhn
Peptide	pnpotiji	Percher	pnrakhnsi
Peptise	pnpotise	Percheron	pnrakhnran
Peptone	pnpotoni	Perchlorate	pnrakhonraiyo
Peptonise	pnpotonise	Perchloride	pnrakhonraiji
Pepys	pnpesi	Perchloron	pnrakhonran
Pequot	pnkuote	Percipient	pnrakipanto
Per	pnra	Percival	pnrakiwajo
Per-	pnra	Percoid	pnrakijo
Pera	pnran	Percolate	pnrakijnyo
Peraicid	pnrakijo	Percolator	pnrakijnran
Peracidity	pnrakijotn	Percontra	pnrakintnre
Peradventure	pnradiwintarai	Percurrent	pnrakunrraito
Perambulate	pnrambejnyo	Percuss	pnrakunso
Perambulator	pnrambejnyoran	Percussion	pnrakunsose
Peraborate	pnraboraiyo	Percussion cap	kopn pnrakunsose
Peraboric	pnraboraiko	Percussionist	pnrakunsosesi
Percale	pnrakojn	Percussive	pnrakunsowin
Peracaline	pnrakojnhun	Percutaneous	pnrakuntehunsi
Per capita	pnra kopnte	Percy	pnrasn
Perceive	pnraknwin	Perdido	pnradide

457

WORD (x)	EQUIVALENT (y)	WORD (x)	EQUIVALENT (y)
Perdiem	pnradise	Perfumery	pnrafunmirai
Perdition	pnradiyoon	Perfunctory	pnrafunknyorai
Perdu	pnradi	Perfuse	pnrafunsi
Perdue	pnradisn	Pergamum	pnragimo
Perdurable	pnradiraibe	Pergola	pnragonjn
Pere	pnran	Pergolesi	pnragonjnsi
Peregrination	pnragnrainyoon	Perhaps	pnrahun
Peregrine	pnragnrain	Peri-	pnrai
Pereira	pnranrai	Periander	pnrainjnra
Pereirine	pnranrain	Perianth	pnrainsi
Peremptory	pnranmpntirai	Perianthritis	pnrainsiraiso
Perennate	pnrainhunyo	Periapt	pnraipnti
Perennial	pnrainhunjo	Periastron	pnraisetnran
Perez	pnranse	Periblem	pnraigbile
Perestroika	pnrasetaki	Periblepsis	pnraigbipeso
Perfect	pnrafnkn	Pericardial	pnraikogbajo
Perfectionism	pnrafnknyoomosi	Pericardiectomy	pnraikogbakitemo
Perfectionist	pnrafnknyoonsi	Pericardiotomy	pnraikogbakotemo
Perfective	pnrafnknwin	Pericarditis	pnraikogbaso
Perfectly	pnsinfnknlo	Pericardium	pnraikogbama
Perfect pitch	potikho pnrafnkn	Pericarp	pnraikopan
Perfecto	pnrafnknko	Perichondrium	pnraikhingbnma
Perfervid	pnrafirowin	Periclase	pnraikanse
Perfidious	pnrafijansi	Periclean	pnraikojnsi
Perfidy	pnrafidon	Pericles	pnraikojn
Perfoliate	pnrafonjiayo	Periclinal	pnraikiunjo
Perforate	pnrafonraiyo	Pericline	pnraikiun
Perforation	pnrafonraiyoon	Pericope	pnraikipon
Perforce	pnrafoonse	Pericrane	pnraiknrain
Perform	pnrafoonmo	Pericranium	pnraiknrainma
Performance	pnrafoonmosi	Pericycle	pnraisnkuo
Performing arts	etesi pnrafoonmognni	Pericynthion	pnraisnsinle
Perfrigeration	pnrafangnraiyoon	Priderm	pnraijnramo
Perfume	pnrafunmi	Peridium	pnraijnma

WORD (x)	EQUIVALENT (y)	WORD (x)	EQUIVALENT (y)
Peridot	pnraidetn	Periosteum	pnrainsetnma
Peridotite	pnraidetnyo	Periostitis	pnrainsetnso
Perigee	pnraignse	Periotic	pnrainko
Periglacia	pnraigankin	Peripatetic	pnraipoyako
Perigon	pnraigun	Peripetia	pnraipntisi
Perigonium	pnraigunso	Peripheral	pnraphiraijo
Perigord	pnraigongba	Periphery	pnraphirai
Perigordian	pnraigongbain	Periphrasis	pnraiphanso
Perigueux	pnraigunwasi	Periphrastic	pnraiphansuko
Perigynous	pnrailoyunsi	Periphton	pnraiphetin
Perihelion	pnraihejosi	Periplocin	pnraiponsie
Peril	pnraija	Peripteral	pnraipntiraijo
Perilous	pnraijasi	Perique	pnraikue
Perim	pnraimo	Perisare	pnraisuran
Perimeter	pnraimuto	Periscope	pnraisekipon
Perimetry	pnraimutorai	Perish	pnraisn
Perimorph	pnraimophan	Perishable	pnraisnberon
Perimysium	pnraimunsoma	Perisher	pnraisnsi
Perinatal	pnraihuntejo	Perishing	pnraisngnni
Perinephritis	pnrainphanso	Perisperm	pnraisupnron
Perinephrium	pnrainphanma	Perispomenon	pnraisupinmini
Perineum	pnrainma	Perisscodactyl	pnraisoodakntilo
Perineuritis	pnrainraiso	Peristalsis	pnraisetnjnso
Period	pnraijo	Peristasis	pnraisetnso
Periodate	pnraijoyo	Peristome	pnraisetomi
Periodic	pnraijoko	Peristyle	pnraisetnron
Periodical	pnraijokojo	Perithecium	pnraisinkima
Periodic table	teberon pnraijoko	Peritoneum	pnraitonima
Periodide	pnraijoji	Peritonitis	pnraitoniso
Periodisation	pnraijoseyoon	Peritricha	pnrataraikho
Periodontal	pnraindeyojo	Perivisceral	pnraiwosekuojo
Periodontics	pnraindeyokosi	Periwig	pnraiwogbi
Periomania	pnrainmohan	Periwinkle1	pnraiwoknron
Perionychium	pnrainsekhima	Periwinkle2	pnraiwoknron

WORD (x)	EQUIVALENT (y)	WORD (x)	EQUIVALENT (y)
Perjure	pnrajoran	Peron	pnroin
Perjury	pnrajoro	Peroneal	pnroinjo
Perk1	pnrake	Peronist	pnroinsi
Perk2	pnrake	Perorate	pnronraiyo
Perkin	pnrakese	Peroration	pnronraiyoon
Perkins	pnrakesesi	Peroxide	pnrosianji
Perky	pnrakesi	Perpend	pnrapnjon
Perlis	pnralesi	Perpendicular	pnrapnjonkuoran
Perlite	pnraleyo	Perpetrate	pnrapntiraijo
Perlocution	pnralokunyoon	Perpetual	pnrapntijo
Perm1	pnramo	Perpetuity	pnrapntito
Perm2	pnramo	Perpignan	pnrapogini
Permafrost	pnramifonsi	Perplex	pnraporu
Permanence	pnramisi	Perplexity	pnraporutn
Permanent	pnramito	Perquisite	pnrakunseyo
Permanent wave	wewin pnramito	Perron	pnraran
Permanganate	pnramignhunyo	Perry	pnrrai
Permanganic	pnramignko	Persalt	pnrasanjyo
Permeable	pnramube	Per se	pnra se
Permeability	pnramubeleto	Persecute	pnrasekunyo
Permeate	pnramuyo	Persecution	pnrasekunyoon
Permian	pnramuhn	Perseids	pnrasejnsi
Permill	pnramujnra	Persphone	pnrasephohun
Permissible	pnramusnbe	Persepolis	pnrasepnjinsi
Permission	pnramusnse	Perseus	pnrasesi
Permissive	pnramusnwin	Perseverance	pnrasewnraisi
Permit	pnramutn	Perseveration	pnrasewnraiyoon
Permittivity	pnramuttnwinto	Persevere	pnrasewnrai
Permutation	pnramutoyoon	Pershing	pnrasegnni
Permute	pnramuto	Persia	pnrasia
Pernambuco	pnrahunmbeki	Persian	pnrasiahn
Pernicious	pnrahunkisi	Persicaria	pnrasookoran
Pernickety	pnrahunkhito	Persicary	pnrasookorai
Pernod	pnrahunjo	Persiennes	pnrasoonhun

WORD (x)	EQUIVALENT (y)	WORD (x)	EQUIVALENT (y)
Persiflage	pnrasoofangn	Pertain	pnratelu
Persimmon	pnrasoommeni	Perth	pnrasn
Persis	pnraso	Pertinacious	pnratinsuwa
Persist	pnrasoosi	Pertinent	pnratinto
Persistence	pnrasoosise	Perturb	pnratuban
Persistent	pnrasoosito	Perturbation	pnratubanyoon
Persnichety	pnrasunkhnto	Pertussis	pnratusiso
Person	pnrasin	Peru	pnrau
Persona	pnrasinse	Peruke	pnraukn
Personable	pnrasinbe	Peruse	pnrause
Personage	pnrasingun	Peruvian	pnrauwohn
Persona grata	pnrasinse ganto	Peruzzi	pnrausua
Personal	pnrasinjo	Perv	pnrawn
Personality	pnrasinleto	Pervade	pnrawajin
Personalize	pnrasinjose	Pervasive	pnrawasoowin
Personally	pnrasinjin	Perverse	pnrawinso
Personalty	pnrasinjotn	Perversion	pnrawinsesi
Personate	pnrasinyo	Perversity	pnrawinseto
Personification	pnrasinfikoyoon	Pervert	pnrawinsete
Personify	pnrasinfe	Perverted	pnrawintede
Personnel	pnrasinhun	Pervious	pnrawosi
Perspective	pnrasepntowin	Pes	pnse
Perspex	pnrasepnsi	Pesach	pnsekho
Perspicacious	pnrasepokokunsi	Pesade	pnsejn
Perspicacity	pnrasepokokito	Pesaro	pnserain
Perspicuous	pnrasepokunsi	Pescara	pnsekoran
Perspicuity	pnrasepokunto	Pescadores	pnsekojnrasi
Perspiration	pnraseporaiyoon	Peseta	pnseto
Perspire	pnraseporai	Peshawar	pnsuanwa
Persuade	pnrasuejin	Peshito	pnsuanto
Persuasion	pnrasuesoon	Pesky	pnseke
Persuasive	pnrasuewin	Peso	pnson
Persulfate	pnrasnlefanyo	Pessary	pnsoorai
Pert	pnrate	Pessimism	pnsoomosi

WORD (x)	EQUIVALENT (y)	WORD (x)	EQUIVALENT (y)
Pest	pnsia	Petiolule	pntijoinran
Pestalozzi	pnsialosi	Petite	pntite
Pester	pnsiasi	Petit	pntiti
Pesticide	pnsiakeku	Petite	pntiyo
Pestiferous	pnsiafirosi	Petition	pntiyoon
Pestilence	pnsiajnsi	Petitioner	pntiyoonsi
Pestlent	pnsiajnto	Petition principii	pntition pankinipon
Pestilential	pnsiajntojo	Petit jury	pntite jorai
Pestle	pnsiaron	Petit mal	pntiti mujn
Pesto	pnsiakn	Petit point	pintiti pintoni
Pestszenterzsebe	pnsiasuntnrasesi	Petit pois	pintiti pinso
Pet1	pnti	Petitry	pntitirai
Pet2	pnti	Petnapping	pntipangnni
Petain	pntelu	Petra	pntire
Petal	pntejo	Petrarchan	pntirekho
Petaliferous	pntejofirosi	Petrel	pntirelo
Petaline	pntejohun	Petri	pntirai
Petalody	pntejodun	Petrifaction	pntiraifanknyoon
Petalody	pntejodie	Petrify	pntiraife
Petaloid	pntejojo	Petrine	pntirain
Petalous	pntejosi	Petro	pntiro
Petard	pntegbaa	Petroglyph	pntiroganpha
Petasus	pntesesi	Petrol	pntirojn
Petcock	pntikiko	Petrolatum	pntirojnyoma
Pete	pnto	Petroleum	pntirojnma
Petechia	pntokhan	Petrology	pntirologbon
Peter	pntosi	Petrol station	setnyoon pntirojn
Peterkin	pntosikin	Petronel	pntiroinlo
Peterman	pntosimoye	Petronious	pntiroinsi
Petermann	pntosimo	Petropavlovsk	pntiropanwinlo
Peterpan	pntiranpan	Petropolis	pntiropojinsi
Petersham	pntiransuemo	Petrosal	pntirosejo
Pethidine	pntihijoin	Petrous	pntirosi
Petiole	pntijoin	Petrozavodsk	pntirosewinsi

WORD (x)	EQUIVALENT (y)	WORD (x)	EQUIVALENT (y)
Petrus	pntirosi	Phagolysis	phijeknjinso
Petticoat	pnttikitie	Phagomania	phijeknmohan
Pettifogger	pnttifongnsi	Phagophobia	phijeknphobua
Pettish	pnttise	Phagia	phijesia
Pettle	pnttiron	Phagous	phijesi
Pettitoes	pnttitose	Phagy	phijese
Petto	pnttini	Phainopepla	phiponpnjn
Petty	pnttisi	Phalange	phijngini
Pettulance	pnttijnsi	Phalangeal	phijnginijo
Petulant	pntijnte	Phalanger	phijnginisi
Petunia	pntihan	Phalanstery	phijnsitorai
Petuntze	pntitese	Phalanx	phijnsi
Peu	pnun	Phalarope	phijnropn
Pew	pnwn	Phallic	phijnsinko
Pewee	pnwnni	Phallin	phijnsinsi
Pewter	pnwnto	Phallism	phijnsinmosi
Pewterer	pnwntosi	Phallus	phijnsinse
Peyerian	pnserain	Phanar	phiniran
Peyote	pnsetie	Phanariots	phinirantosi
Pfennig	pnfangin	Phane	phini
Ph	phi	Phanner	phinisi
Phaeacia	phinkin	Phaneric	phiniraiko
Phaeacian	phinkinse	Phanero	phiniran
Phaedra	phinjn	Phanerocrytaalline	phinirankoraitoroin
Phaedrus	phinjnso	Phanerogam	phinirangimo
Phaenogam	phinganmo	Phanerogamia	phinirangimoji
Phaephycean	phinphekun	Phanerophyte	phiniranpheyo
Phaethon	phinsunsi	phanerozoic	phinisisinko
Phage	phije	Phantasm	phintemosi
Phagedaena	phijejinna	Phantasmagoria	phintemosigonran
Phago	phijekn	Phantasy	phintese
Phagocyte	phijeknsnyo	Phantom	phintemo
Phagocytic	phijeknsnko	Phany	phinse
Phagocytosis	phijeknsnso	Pharamond	phisinmodan

WORD (x)	EQUIVALENT (y)	WORD (x)	EQUIVALENT (y)
Pharaoh	phisinle	Phelps	phnjopn
Pharisaic	phisinseko	Phen	phn
Pharisaism	phisinsemosi	Phene	phnni
Pharisee	phisinsa	Phenacaine	phnnikoihun
Pharmaceutical	phisankntikojo	Phenacetin	phnnikntie
Pharmaceutics	phisankntikosi	Phenacite	phnnikiyo
Pharmacist	phisankinsi	Phenakisto	phnnikiseto
Pharmaco	phisanki	Phenanthrene	phinitesirain
Pharmacognosy	phisanbkigbonsn	Phenazine	phnnisehun
Pharmacology	phisankilogbon	Phonetic	phnniteko
Pharmacomania	phisankimohan	Phenetidine	phnnitejohun
Pharmacy	phisankin	Phenetidine	phnnitejohun
Pharos	phisansi	Phenetole	phnnitejoin
Pharsala	phisansejn	Phenformin	phnnifoonmoin
Pharyngeal	phisognjo	Phenicia	phnnikin
Pharyngealtonsil	phisognjotosnje	Phenix	phnnisi
Pharyngitis	phisogonso	Pheno	phnkn
Pharyngo	phisogon	Phenobarbitone	phnknboosnbutoni
Pharyngology	phisogonlogbon	Phenocopy	phnknkipe
Pharyngoscope	phisogonsokipon	Phenocryst	phnknkoraitn
Pharyngotomy	phisogontemo	Phenol	phnknle
Pharynx	phisosi	Phenolate	phnknleyo
Phase	phanse	Phenolic	phnknleko
Phasia	phansia	Phenology	phnknlogbon
Phasine	phansun	Phnolphthalein	phnknlephisanrain
Phasmid	phansemujo	Phenomena	phnknmuhun
Phatic	phanko	Phenomenal	phnknmuhunjo
Pheasant	phnsuatn	Phenomenology	phnknmuhunlogbon
Pheidippile	phnjopipojin	Phenomenon	phnknmuhunsi
Phebe	phnbe	Phenothiazine	phnknsinsehun
Phelim	phnjoma	Phenotype	phnkntnpon
Phellem	phnjoinma	Pheny	phnse
Phellodem	phnjoinjnramo	Phenyl	phnlo
Phellogen	phnjoingin	Phenylalanine	phnlolenihe

WORD (x)	EQUIVALENT (y)	WORD (x)	EQUIVALENT (y)
Phenylene	phnlohun	Philocteles	pherankntisi
Phenylamine	phnlomoin	Philodendron	pheranjinhagbn
Phenylkeyonuria	phnloknsihunran	Philigyny	pheranloyun
Phoebe	phnnibe	Philology	pheranlogbon
Pheromone	phnranmini	Philoprogenitive	pheranponginyowin
Phew	phnwa	Philosopher	pheransoophnsi
Phd	phejn	Philosophical	pheransoophnkojo
Phi	phe	Philosophist	pheronsoophnsi
Phial	phejo	Philosophistic	pheronsoophnseko
Phibetakappa	phebntokhopa	Philosophize	pheransoophnse
Phidias	phejnse	Philosophy	pheransoophe
Philadelphia	pheronjinlephnsi	Philous	pheronsi
Philae	pheronse	Philter	pheronto
Philander	pheronjnra	Phimosis	phemuso
Philanthropic	pheronsirapnko	Phiphenomenon	phephnnmini
Philanthropize	pheronsirapose	Phineas	phehunse
Philanthropy	pheronsirapo	Phineus	phehunsi
Philately	pherontelo	Phintias	phetnse
.-phile	pheron	Phips	phepnsi
Philemon	pheronmeni	Phiz	phese
Philharmonic	pheronhanmeniko	Phlebitis	phijnbeso
Philhellene	pheronhejjohun	Phlebo	phijnbe
Philia	pheronsi	Phlebosclerosis	phijnbesikuoranso
Philip	pheropn	Phlebotomize	phijnbetemuse
Philippa	pheropan	Phlegethon	phijngnse
Philippe	pheropin	Phlegm	phijnguo
Philippi	pheropon	Phlegmasia	phijnguosia
Philippic	pheropnko	Phlegmatic	phijnguoko
Philippopolis	pheropopinjnsi	Phlegmy	phijnguose
Philistia	pherosetan	Phloem	philomi
Philistine	pherosetin	Phlogistic	philogbinako
Phillips	pherropnsi	Phlogiston	philogbina
Phillumenist	pherromuyesi	Phlogopite	philogbiponyo
Philo-	pheran	Phlogosis	philogbiso

WORD (x)	EQUIVALENT (y)	WORD (x)	EQUIVALENT (y)
Phlorizin	philoraisie	Phonolite	phohnleyo
Phlox	philosi	Phonology	phohnlogbon
Phlyctena	philokitimi	Phonomania	phohnmohan
.-phobe	phobe	Phonometer	phohnmuto
,phobia	phobua	Phonoscope	phohnsokipon
Phobos	phobusi	Phonon	phohnsi
Phoca	phoko	Phonotactics	phohntekankosi
Phocine	phokini	Phonotype	phohntnpon
Phocis	phokisi	Phonotypy	phohntnpe
Phocomelia	phokimujan	Phony	phohunse
Phoebe	phinibe	Phoney	phohnse
Phoebus	phinibesi	Phore	phorai
Phoenicia	phinikin	Phorcus	phoraikn
Phoenix	phinisi	Phoresis	phoraiso
Phon	phohn	Phoresy	phoraisn
Phonate	phohunyo	Phorous	phoraisi
Phonantograph	phohunteganpha	Phosgene	phosegini
Phone	phohun	Phosgenite	phoseginyo
Phone book	booko phohun	Phosphatase	phosephayose
Phonecard	phohunkogba	Phosphate	phosephayo
Phone-in	phohun-sinu	Phosphaturia	phosephayoran
Phoneme	phohunmo	Phosphide	phosephiji
Phonemic	phohunmuko	Phosphine	phosephihun
Phonendoscope	phohunjnsekipon	Phosphite	phosephiyo
Phonetic	phohunteko	Phospho	phosephn
Phonetician	phohuntekohn	Phosphocreatine	phosephnknratin
Phonetics	phohuntekosi	Phospholipid	phosephnlepojn
Phoney	phohunse	Phosephonium	phosephnhunma
Phonic	phohunko	Phosphoprotein	phosephnponyoto
Phono-	phohn	Phosphor	phosephnran
Phonodeik	phohnjinki	Phosphorate	phosephnraiyo
Phonogram	phohnganmo	Phosphoresece	phosephnransesi
Phonogrammic	phohnganmmuko	Phosphorescence	phosephnranseknsi
Phonograph	phohnganpha	Phosphorescent	phosephnranseknti

WORD (x)	EQUIVALENT (y)	WORD (x)	EQUIVALENT (y)
Phosphoreted	phosephnrantode	Phraseology	phansoknlogbon
Phosphorite	phosephnraiyo	Phratry	phanterai
Phosphorous	phosephnransi	Phreatic	phiranmiko
Phosphorlase	phosephnrailese	Phrenetic	phirainmiko
Phossy	phosoo	Phrenic	phirainko
Phot	phote	Phrenitis	phirainmiso
Photic	photeko	Phreno	phirainkn
Photius	photesi	Phrenology	phirainknlogbon
Photo	photin	Phrensy	phirainso
Photoactinic	photinkntiko	Phryne	phiroin
Photoactive	photinkntiwin	Phrygia	phiraigan
Photoautotrophic	photinauntotnraphiko	Phthalein	phisanjnse
Photobiotic	photinbaknko	Phthalic	phisanjnko
Photocell	photinknjjn	Phthalin	phisanjn
Photocomposer	photinkimpinsesi	Phthalocyanin	phisajnknsnnini
Photocomposition	photinkimpinseyoon	Phthiriasis	phisinraiso
Photoconduction	photinkindeknyoon	Phthisic	phisinsuko
Photocopier	photinkipesi	Phthisical	phisinsukojo
Photocopy	photinkipe	Phthisis	phisinsuso
Photocurrent	photingbanma	Phut	phuto
Photodynamic	photindainhemuko	Phyceae	pheknni
Photogenic	photinginko	Phyco	pheki
Photograph	photinganpha	Phycoerythrin	phekiraiseran
Photography	photinganphe	Phycology	phekilogbon
Photogravure	photinganwerai	Phycomycete	phekimuknti
Photokinesis	photinkihunso	Phycophaein	phekiphikun
Photon	photinsi	Phycophyfe	phekiphefn
Photophobia	photinphobua	Phyla	phewa
Photopia	photinpan	Phylactery	phewaknterai
Photoplay	photinpansie	Phyle	phewn
Photoproton	photinpontin	Phyletic	phewnko
Photostat	photinsetnti	Phyll	phewe
Phrase	phanso	Phyllis	pheweso
Phraseograph	phansoknganpha	Phyllite	pheweyo

WORD (x)	EQUIVALENT (y)	WORD (x)	EQUIVALENT (y)
Phyllo	phewekn	Physostomous	phesoosetomosi
Phylloclade	pheweknkanjin	Phyte	pheyo
Phyllode	pheweknjin	Phytin	phetie
Phyllody	phewekndie	Phyto	pheto
Phylloid	phewejo	Phytobenthon	phetobesnle
Phyllome	pheweknmo	Phytogenesis	phetoginiso
Phyllophore	pheweknphirai	Phytogenic	phetoginko
Phyllopod	pheweknpindi	Phytoid	phetojo
Phyllopoda	pheweknpinde	Phytology	phetologbon
Phylloquinone	pheweknkuinini	Phytophagous	phetophijesi
Phyllotaxis	phewekntesanso	Phyton	phetosi
Phyllous	pheweknsi	Phytoplankton	phetopanknti
Phylloxera	pheweknseran	Phytosterol	phetosetnrajn
Phyllogeny	pheweknginse	Phytotron	phetotnran
Phyligenesis	phewagnhunso	Pi	po
Phylum	phewama	Piacenza	ponkinse
Phyre	pherai	Piacular	ponkuoran
Physiatrics	phesitaraikosi	Piaffe	ponffi
Physic	phesiko	Piaffer	ponffiro
Physical	phesikojo	Piamater	ponmutnra
Physician	phesikohn	Pianissimo	ponhusoomo
Physicist	phesikosi	Pianist	ponhusi
Physico	phesikokn	Piano1	ponhu
Physics	phesikosi	Piano2	ponhu
Physio	phesito	Pianoforte	ponhufonyo
Physiocracy	phesitokansn	Pianola	panhujn
Physiognomy	phesitogonmo	Piano trio	ponhu tarain
Physiography	phesitoganphe	Piarist	ponraisi
Physiological	phesitologbonkojo	Piassava	ponsoowa
Physiology	phesitologbon	Piaster	ponseto
Physiotherapy	phesitosinranpo	Piaui	ponse
Physique	phesikun	Piave	ponwin
Physoclistous	phesookiunsesi	Piazza	ponssi
Physostigmine	phesoosetigbihun	Pibal	pobejn

WORD (x)	EQUIVALENT (y)	WORD (x)	EQUIVALENT (y)
Pibroch	poberosi	Pico-	ponki
Pica	poko	Picoline	ponkilehun
Picacho	pokokhin	Picong	pokingn
Picador	pokodera	Picot	ponkiti
Picard	pokogba	Picotee	ponkitise
Picardy	pokogbaa	Picrate	ponraiyo
Picaresque	pokoraikun	Picric	ponraiko
Picaroon	pokoroon	Picro	ponra
Picasso	pokosooa	Picrol	ponrajo
Piccadilly	pokojnllo	Picrotoxin	ponratoosia
Piccalilli	pokojolle	Pict	ponknti
Piccaninny	pokoinyun	Pictish	ponkntiso
Piccard	pokkogba	Pictograph	ponkntiganpha
Piccolo	pokkelo	Pictor	ponkntiran
Pice	posun	Pictorial	ponkntiraijo
Piceous	posunsi	Picture	ponkntirai
Pichiciago	pokhikinlo	Picturesque	ponkntiraikun
Pick1	ponki	Picul	ponknjn
Pick2	ponki	Piddle	pondeduo
Pickaback	ponkinboki	Pidduck	pondediki
Pickaninny	ponkinniyun	Pidgin	pondegin
Pickaxe	aake ponki	Pie1	ponse
Picker	ponkira	Pie2	ponse
Pickerel	ponkiralo	Piece	ponso
Picket	ponkiti	Piecemeal	ponsomuje
Picket line	lehun ponkiti	Piecer	ponsosi
Pickett	ponkitti	Pied	ponjia
Pickings	ponkignni	Pier	ponri
Pickle	ponkiron	Pierce	ponrisi
Pick-me-up	ponki-mi-pake	Pieria	ponran
Pick-up	ponki pake	Pierian	ponrain
Picky	ponkise	Pierides	ponraijnsi
Pick-your-own	ponki own yin	Pieridine	ponraijnhun
Picnic	ponkkiko	Pierre	ponrrai

WORD (x)	EQUIVALENT (y)	WORD (x)	EQUIVALENT (y)
Pierrot	ponrrato	Pilch	pojnkho
Pierus	ponrasi	Pilchard	pojnkhogbaa
Piet	ponte	Pilcomayo	pojnkunyo
Pieta	pontie	Pile1	pojn
Pietemaritzeburg	pontnramuraise	Pile2	pojn
Pietism	pontnmosi	Pile3	pojn
Piety	pontn	Piles	pojnsi
Piezo	ponsu	Pileate	pojnnayo
Piezometer	ponsumuto	Pileous	pojnsi
Piffle	poffijn	Pileum	pojnma
Piffling	poffijngnni	Pile-up	pojn-pake
Pig	pogbn	Pilfer	pojnfe
Pigeon	pognsi	Pilferage	pojnfegun
Piggery	pogbnrai	Pilgarlic	pojngirako
Piggin	pogbnni	Pilgrim	pojngirai
Piggish	pogbnsi	Pilgrimage	pojngiraigun
Piggy	pogbnse	Pili	pojia
Pig-iron	irin-pogbn	Piliferous	pojiafirosi
Piglet	pogbntn	Piliform	pojiafon
Pigment	pogbnmutto	Piling	pojngnni
Pigmentation	pogbnmuttoyoon	Pillia	pojian
Pigmy	pogbnmo	Pill	pojnra
Pignus	pogbnsn	Pillage	pojnragun
Pigsty	pogbnsito	Pillar	pojnran
Pigtail	pogbntele	Pillion	pojnrain
Pika	poka	Pilliwinks	pojnranwinknsi
Pike	pokn	Pillory	pojnrai
Piker	poknsi	Pillow	pojnwn
Pikestaff	pokn setnfin	Pillowcase	pojnwnkoso
Pilar	pojnran	Pilocarpine	pojnkopanhun
Pilaster	pojnseto	Pilose	pojnse
Pilate	pojnyo	Pilot	pojntu
Pilatus	pojnyosi	Pilotage	pojntugun
Pilau	pojnnu	Piloting	pojntugnni

WORD (x)	EQUIVALENT (y)	WORD (x)	EQUIVALENT (y)
Pilsner	pojnsnsi	Pindus	pohajnsi
Pil down man	moye pojia juan	Pine1	pohun
pilule	pojio	Pine2	pohun
Piman	pomain	Pineal	pohunjo
Pimelosis	pomjnso	Pineapple	pohunaporon
Pimento	pomito	Pine cone	pohun kinnu
Pimeson	pomisi	Pine nut	yunti pohun
Pimiento	pominito	Pinel	pohunlo
Pimola	pomjain	Pinene	pohunni
Pimp	pompn	Pinery	pohunrai
Pimpemel	pompnranlo	Pinetum	pohuntema
Pimple	pompa	Pinery	pohunse
Pin	poha	Ping	pogan
Pina	pohn	Ping-pong	pogan-pingan
Pinaceae	pohnknni	Pinhead	pohahegbi
Pinaceous	pohnsua	Pinhole	pohahinlu
Pina colada	pohn kijojn	Pinhole camera	pohahinlu komura
Pinafore	pohnfonre	Pinion1	pohasi
Pinang	pohngn	Pinion2	pohasi
Pinar	poharan	Pinite	pohayo
Pinaster	pohnseto	Pink1	ponki
Pinball	poharobo	Pink2	ponki
Pince-nez	pohakn-hunse	Pink3	ponki
Pincer movement	pohaknra-mosunmutto	Pinkerton	ponkiratin
Pincers	pohaknra	Pink gin	gijn ponki
Pinch	pohakhn	Pinkie	ponkini
Pinchbeck	pohakhnbeki	Pinky	ponkise
Pinchney	pohakhnse	Pinkle	ponkiron
Pinchot	pohakhnti	Pinko	ponkikn
Pincurl	pohakuojo	Pin-money	poha-menisan
Pincushion	pohakunsoon	Pinkster	ponkiseto
Pindar	pohajnran	Pinkstem	ponkisetnran
Pindaric	pohajnranko	Pinna	pohahun
Pindliing	pohaduognni	Pinnace	pohahunsi

WORD (x)	EQUIVALENT (y)	WORD (x)	EQUIVALENT (y)
Pinnacle	pohahunkun	Pinxit	pohaseto
Pinnate	pohahunyo	Piny	pohunsi
Pinnati	pohahunye	Pinzon	posunsi
Pinnatifid	pohahunyefijn	Pion	pounse
Pinnatilobe	pohahunyeloobe	Pioneer	pilehunsi
Pinnatipartite	pohahunyepanteyo	Pioneer	pounhunsi
Pinnatiped	pohahunyepndie	Pious	pounsin
pinnatisect	pohahunyeseknte	Pip1	popn
Pinner	poharan	Pip2	popn
Pinnigrade	pohahungandie	Pip3	popn
Pinniped	pohahunpndie	Pip4	popn
Pinnula	pohahunjo	Pip5	popn
Pinnule	pohahunjn	Pipage	popongun
Pinny	pohase	Pipal	poponjo
Pinochle	pohakokuo	Pipe	popon
Pinole	pohakoje	Pipeclay	poponkanyin
Pinon	pohaje	Pipeline	poponlehun
Pinpoint	pohapintoni	Piper	poponsi
Pinprick	pohapanki	Piperacean	poponraknni
Pin rail	poha railo	Piperaceous	poponrasuwa
Pinscher	pohasekhnra	Piperazine	poponrasehun
Pinsk	pohasia	Piperidine	poponraijoin
Pinson	pohasin	Piperine	poponrain
Pint	pohate	Piperonal	poponranjo
Pinta	pohata	Pipette	popontn
Pin-table	poha-teberon	Piping	popongini
Pintado	pohatade	Pipkin	poponkin
Pintail	pohatele	Pippin	poponsi
Pintano	pohatakn	Pipsqueak	poponsekunko
Pintle	pohatoron	Pipy	poponse
Pintsch	pohatokhn	Piquant	pokinte
Pinturicchio	pohatoraikkhn	Pique	pokun
Pin-up	poha-pake	Piquet	pokunti
Pin-wheel	poha whinlo	Piracy	poraisn

WORD (x)	EQUIVALENT (y)	WORD (x)	EQUIVALENT (y)
Piraeus	porainsn	Piassarro	posorran
Piragua	poraigun	Pissed	posode
Pirandello	porainllo	Piss-up	poso pake
Piranha	poraihun	Pistachio	posikhio
Pirate	poraite	Pistareen	posirain
Pirithous	poraisin	Piste	posisn
Pirm	poron	Pistil	posile
Pirog	porangbi	Pistilate	posileyo
Pirogue	porangun	Pistol	posijn
Pirouette	poraintin	Pistola	posijain
Pirozhaki	poranseki	Pistole	posijoin
Pisa	posa	Pistoleer	posisejoinsi
Pisaller	posallesi	Piston	posise
Pisano	posako	Pit1	poti
Piscary	possnkerai	Pit2	poti
Piscatology	possnkejalogbon	Pita	potie
Piscator	possnkejaran	Pital	potijo
Pisces	possnke	Pitch1	potikho
Pisci	possnki	Pitch2	potikho
Pisciculture	possnkikunjiaran	Pitcher1	potikhosi
Piscina	possnkimi	Pitcher2	potikhosi
Piscine	possnkhun	Pitchometer	potikhomuto
Piscivorous	possnkiwnrunsi	Pitchy	potikhose
Pisgah	posnga	Pitch-pine	potikho pohun
Pish	posoo	Piteous	potise
Pishogue	posoogun	Pith	potisi
Pisidia	posoojina	Pithecanthropus	potisinkosiranpn
Pisiform	posoofoonmo	Pithy	potise
Pisistratus	posoositnre	Pitiable	potibe
Pismire	posoomere	Pitiless	potilabo
Pismoclam	posoomokan	Pitman	potimoye
Pisolite	posooleyo	Piton	potisi
Piss	poso	Pitot	potito
Piss artist	etesi poso	Pitt	potti

473

WORD (x)	EQUIVALENT (y)	WORD (x)	EQUIVALENT (y)
Pitta	pottie	Placet	panknti
Pittance	pottisi	Placeta	panknte
Pitter patter	pottirai panttesi	Placid	panknjo
Pituitary	potuntorai	Plack	panki
Pity	poti	Placket	pankiti
Pityriasis	potiraiso	Placoderm	pankijnramo
Piu	possi	Placoid	pankijo
Pius	posin	Plafond	panfonjn
Pivot	pownta	Plagal	pangiajo
Pivotal	powntajo	Plage	pangia
Pix	posua	Plagiarism	pangiaimosi
Pixel	posuajo	Plagiarize	pangiaraise
Pixie	posuan	Plagiary	pangiarai
Pixilated	posualeyo	Plagio	pangio
Pixy	posuase	Plagioclase	pangiokiunmolu
Pize	pose	Plagioclimax	pangiokiunmolu
Pizza	posse	Plagiotropism	pangiotnrapnmosi
Pizarro	posserro	Plague	pangbun
Pizzazz	possesun	Plaguy	pangbunse
Pizza	posse	Plaice	panlase
Pizzeria	posseran	Plaid	panlajo
Pizzicato	possekito	Plain	panto
Pizzle	posseron	Plaint	pantone
Placable	panknberon	Plaintiff	pantoniffo
Placard	pankngbaa	Plaintive	pantoniwin
Placate	panknto	Plait	pantwe
Placatory	pankntorai	Plan	panye
Place	pankn	Planar	panyunran
Placebo	panknbu	Planarian	panyunrain
Placenta	pnakinto	Planchet	pankhnti
Placental	pankintojo	Planchette	pankhntin
Placentation	pankintoyoon	Plane1	panyun
Placentia	pankintie	Plane2	panyun
Placer	panknsi	Plane3	panyun

WORD (x)	EQUIVALENT (y)	WORD (x)	EQUIVALENT (y)
Planer	panyunsi	Plash	pansue
Planet	panyato	Plashy	pansuese
Planetable	panyatobe	Plasia	pansia
Planetarium	panyatoraima	Plasm	panson
Planetary	panyatorai	Plasma	pansonsi
Planetary nebula	panyatorai hunbejn	Plasmin	pansonte
Planetesimal	panyatosemujn	Plasma	pansonkn
Planetoid	panyatojo	Plasmodesma	pansonknjinmi
Plan form	panye fonmo	Plasmodium	pansonknjnma
Planetology	panyatologbon	Plasmoid	pansonjo
Plangent	panyeginto	Plasmolyse	pansonjinse
Plangorous	pangnransi	Plasmolysis	pansonjinso
Planicopter	panyunkipnti	Plasmon	pansonse
Planimeter	panyunmuto	Plasmosome	pansonsoomo
Planimetry	panyunmutorai	Plassey	pansoose
Planish	panyunsi	Plast	pansui
Plank	pankn	Plastein	pansuite
Planking	pankngnni	Plaster	pansuito
Planksheer	panknsuasi	Plasterboard	bugbapansuito
planography	panyinganphe	Plaster cast	kosoto pansuito
Planometer	panyinmuto	Plastic	pansuiko
Planosol	panyinsoojn	Plastic arts	etesi pansuiko
Planning	panyegnni	Plasticine	pansuikoin
Planner	panyeran	Plasticity	pansuikotn
Plant	pantn	Plasticizer	pansuikosesi
Plantagenet	pantngunte	Plastid	pansuijo
Plantain1	pantelu	Plastisol	pansuisejin
Plantar	pantnran	Plastomer	pamsuitnmurai
Plantation	pantnyoon	Plastometer	pansuitnmuto
Planter	pantnsi	Plastron	pansuitnran
Plantigrade	pantngandie	Plasty	pansuito
Plantocracy	pantnkansn	Plat	pantwn
Planula	panyinjn	Plata	pantwa
Plaque	pankun	Plataea	pantwan

WORD (x)	EQUIVALENT (y)	WORD (x)	EQUIVALENT (y)
Plate	pantwe	Platts	panttusi
Platelet	pantwele	Platy	pante
Plated	pantwede	Platyhenminth	pantehejomini
Platen	pantweni	Platypus	pantepnsi
Plater	pantwesi	Platyrrhine	panterhain
Platetectonics	pantwetokntinkosi	Plaudit	paundan
Platform	pantwnfon	Plauen	paunni
Platie	pantwnse	Plausible	paunsebe
Platilla	pantwnlle	Plausive	paunsewin
Platina	pantwnhe	Plautus	pauntosi
Palatinate	pantwnheyo	Play	pansie
Plating	pantwngnni	Play-act	pansie-aknti
Platinic	pantwnheko	Play-back	pansie-boki
Plainiferous	pantwnhefirosi	Player	pansiesi
Platiniridium	pantwnherajnma	Playgoer	pansielosi
Platinise	pantwnhese	Playground	pansiegonjoin
Platino	pantwnkn	Playgroup	pansiegonpo
Platinocyanide	pantwnknsnhunji	Playlet	pansietn
Platiniod	pantwnlnjo	Playmate	pansiemote
Platinous	pantwnknsi	Playwright	pansiewangba
Platinum	pantwnknma	Plaza	pansira
Platinum blonde	pantwnknma-bonjini	Playa	pansnmi
Platitude	pantwntujin	Plea	poron
Platitudinise	pantwntujinse	Pleach	poronkhi
Platitudinous	pantwntujinsi	Pleached	poronkhide
Plato	panton	Plead	poronbe
Platonic	pantonko	Pleading	poronbeginni
Platonism	pantonmosi	Pleasance	poronsnsi
Platoon	pantonsi	Pleasant	poronsnte
Platt	pantto	Pleasantry	poronsnterai
Plattensee	panttose	Please	poronsn
Platter	panttosi	Pleasing	poronsngnni
Platte	panttu	Pleasurable	poronsnraibe
Platting	panttognni	Pleasure	poronsnrai

WORD (x)	EQUIVALENT (y)	WORD (x)	EQUIVALENT (y)
Pleat	poronji	Pleocroism	poronkakironmosi
Pleater	poronjisi	Pleomophism	poronkamophansi
Pleb	poronbn	Pleonasm	poronkahunso
Plebby	poronbnse	Pleonexia	poronkahunsia
Plebe	poronbin	Pleopod	poronkapindie
Plebeian	poronbnhn	Plerome	poronramo
Plebiscite	poronbndibo	Plesiosaur	poronsiasanra
Plebs	poronbnsi	Plessor	poronbsiran
Plecopteran	poronkipntiran	Pleasure	poronsnrai
Plecetognath	poronkitigan	Plethora	poronsirai
Plectrum	poronkitiran	Plethoric	poronsiraiko
Pled	poronbe	Plethysmograph	poronsisemoganpha
Pledge	porongbe	Pleura	poronrai
Pledge	porongbe	Pleurisy	poronraiso
Pledger	porongbese	Pleura	poronro
Pledget	porongbeti	Pleurodont	poronrodeyo
Pledgon	porongbesi	Pleudynia	poronrodainsia
Plegia	porongo	Pleuron	poronroin
Pleiad	porongbon	Pleurotomy	poronrotemo
Pleiades	porongbonsi	Pleuropneumonia	poronropohunmoha
Pleinair	poronsiarie	Pleaston	poronsutin
Pleio	poronte	Pleven	poronwini
Pleiosyllabic	porontesollebeko	Plexiform	poronsefon
Pleistocene	poronsetoknsa	Plexiglas	poronsegan
Plen	poroin	Pleximeter	poronsemuto
Plenary	poroinrai	Plexor	poronseran
Plenipotent	poroinpintito	Plexus	poronsesi
Plenipotentiary	poroinpintitorai	Pliable	polobe
Plenish	poroinse	Pliant	polote
Plenitude	porointujin	Plica	polokn
Plenteous	porointesi	Plicate	poloknyo
Plenty	porointo	Plier	polose
Plenum	poroinma	Pliers	polosesi
Plenism	poroinmosi	Plight1	pologbe

WORD (x)	EQUIVALENT (y)	WORD (x)	EQUIVALENT (y)
Plight2	pologbe	Plugugly	ponlegbnlo
Plimsoll	polomusnle	Plum	ponlema
Plinth	polosin	Plum	ponlema
Pliny	polose	Plumage	ponlemagun
Plio	polokn	Plumate	ponlemayo
Pliocene	poloknsa	Plumb	ponlebo
Plisse	polosoo	Plumbaginaceous	ponlebogunsuwa
Plod	ponjn	Plumbago	ponlebu
Plodder	ponjnra	Plumbbob	ponlebobe
Plodge	pongbon	Plumbeous	ponlebesi
Ploesti	ponseto	Plumber	ponlebosi
Ploid	ponjo	Plumbery	ponleborai
Plok1	ponki	Plumbic	ponleboko
Plonk2	ponki	Plumbicon	ponlebokin
Plonker	ponkisi	Plumbiferous	ponlebognni
Plop	ponpi	Plumb-line	lehun-ponlembo
Plosion	ponsoon	Plumbo	ponlebu
Plosive	ponsowin	Plumbous	ponlembusi
Plot	ponti	Plumbum	ponlembuma
Plotinus	pontinsi	Plume	ponlemo
Plotter	ponttisi	Plummet	ponlemmutn
Plotty	ponttise	Plummy	ponlemmo
Plough	ponghia	Plump1	ponlepo
Ploughman	ponghiamoye	Plump2	ponlepo
Plover	ponwnrai	Plumper	ponleposi
Plow	ponwan	Plumule	ponlemuron
Plowman	ponwanmoye	Plumy	ponlemase
Plowshare	ponwansueran	Plunder	ponlejnra
Ploy	ponse	Plunderage	ponlejnragun
Plu	ponle	Plunge	ponlejn
Pluck	ponlekn	Plunger	ponlejnsi
Plucky	ponleknse	Plunk	ponleko
Plug	ponlegbn	Pluperfect	ponlepnrafnko
Plug-in	ponlegbn si	Plural	ponlera

WORD (x)	EQUIVALENT (y)	WORD (x)	EQUIVALENT (y)
Pluralism	ponleramosi	Pneumatolytic	pohunmitojinko
Pluralist	ponlerasi	Pneumatometer	pohunmitomuto
Plurality	ponleraleto	Pneumatophore	pohunmitophiran
Pluralize	ponlerase	Pneumectomy	pohunmitemo
Pluri	ponlerai	Pneumo	pohunmo
Plus	ponlesi	Pneumobacillus	pohunmobokijjnsi
Plus fours	ponlesi foora	Pneumococcus	pohunmokikoonsi
Plush	ponlesua	Pneumoconiosis	pohunmokinso
Plushy	ponlesuan	Pneumodynamics	pohunmodainsem-ukosi
Plutarchy	ponletankho		
Pluto	ponletin	Pneumoectasis	pohunmokitiso
Plutocracy	ponletinkansn	Pneumoedema	pohunmoknjinmi
Plutocrat	ponletinkanta	Pneumoencephalogram	pohunmoenknphijn-ganmo
Pluton	ponletinse		
Plutonic	ponletinko	Pneumogastric	pohunmogisunraiko
Plutonium	ponletinma	Pneumograph	pohunmoganpha
Plutus	ponletinsi	Pneumonectomy	pohunmohunkintemo
Pluvial	ponlewnjo	Pneumonia	pohunmoha
Pluvio	ponlewnmi	Pheumonic	pohunmohako
Pluviometer	ponlewnmimuto	Pneumono	pohunmokn
Pluviose	ponlewnmise	Pnom penh	pohnmo pnhn
Pluvious	ponlewnmi	Pnys	poynso
Ply1	ponlo	Po	pin
Ply2	ponlo	Poaceous	pinsuma
Plywood	ponlowinjo	Poach1	pinkhese
Pneu	pohun	Poach2	pinkhese
Pneostenosis	pohunsetinse	Pocahontas	pinkhointesi
Pneuma	pohunmi	Pochard	pinkhigba
Pneumatic	pohunmiko	Poacher	pinkhesesi
Pneumatics	pohunmikosi	Pock	pinko
Pneumato	pohunmito	Pocket	pinkoto
Pneumatography	pohunmitoganpha	Pocketbook	pinkotobooko
Pneumatology	pohunmitogbon	Pockety	pinkotose
Pneumatolysis	pohunmitojinso	Pocky	pinkose

WORD (x)	EQUIVALENT (y)	WORD (x)	EQUIVALENT (y)
Poco	pinkin	Poetics	pinsetokosi
Poco a poco	pinkin si pinkin	Poetize	pinsetose
Pococurante	pinkinmkunrate	Poet justice	josesi pinseto
Pocosin	pinkinsin	Poetry	pinsetorai
Pod	pindi	Po-faced	pin-fanside
Pod	pindi	Pogamoggan	pingimogbain
Pod	pindie	Pogany	pinginse
Poda	pindie	Pogey	pingnse
Podagra	pindiegira	Pogge	pingbn
Podconus	pindikinsi	Pogonia	pinginisi
Poddy	pindisi	Pogonip	pinginipo
Podesta	pindiseto	Pogo	pingin
Podgy	pindisi	Pogrom	pingirun
Podiatry	pinditerai	Pogy	pingnse
Podiatrist	pinditeraisi	Poi	pini
Podismos	pindisemosi	Poiesis	piniseso
Podium	pindima	Poietic	piniteko
Podolia	pindijia	Poignant	pinignte
Podolsk	pindijnsi	Poikilothermic	pinikilosinronko
Podophyllin	pindipheroin	Poilu	pinirun
Podous	pindisi	Poincare	pinnikosi
Podsol	pindisujin	Poinciana	pinnikinun
Podsolise	pindisujinse	Poind	pinnijn
Podunk	pindikn	Poinsettia	pinnisettin
Podurid	pindieniru	Point	pintoni
Podzol	pindiesnle	Point-blank	pintoni-bainko
Podzolization	pindisinleseyoon	Point device	pintoni jinwose
Poe	pinse	Point-duty	pintoni-deto
Poem	pinseto	Pointe a piter	pinteni si pitiran
Poenology	pinsekologbon	Pointed	pintonide
Poesy	pinseso	Pointer	pintonise
Poet	pinseto	Pointers	pintonisesi
Poetaster	pinsetotnra	Pointes	pintonisi
Poetic	pinsetoko	Pointillion	pintonijjnsi

WORD (x)	EQUIVALENT (y)	WORD (x)	EQUIVALENT (y)
Pointillism	pintonijjnmosi	Pole2	pinjn
Pointing	pintonignni	Poleaxe	aakepinjn
Pointless	pintonilabo	Pole cat	pinjn koti
Poise	pintise	Polemic	pinjnmuko
Poised	pintisede	Polemicist	pinjumukosi
Poison	pintisn	Polemics	pinjnmukosi
Poisonous	pintisnsi	Polemoniaceous	pinjnmenisuwa
Poison sumac	pintisn snmko	Polenta	pinjnnta
Poitiers	pintiran	Poler	pinjnse
Poitou	pintito	Pole star	pinjn setan
Poitrel	pintiralo	Pole vault	pinjn wajia
Poke1	pokuo	Poleyn	pinjnyin
Poke2	pokuo	Police	pinjnsi
Poker1	pokuosi	Policeman	pinjnsimoye
Poker2	pokuosi	Police state	pinjnsi setnyo
Pokerish	pokuosise	Police station	pinjnsi setnyoon
Poky	pokuose	Policlinic	pinjnkiunko
Pola	pole	Policy1	pinjnsn
Polacca	polekko	Policy2	pinjnsn
Polack	poleki	Polillo	pinjnllo
Polacre	poleknra	Polio	pinjnkn
Poland	poledain	Polioencephalitis	pinjnenknphijnso
Polander	poledainsi	Poliomyelitis	pinjnknmuloso
Polar	pinjnra	Polish	pinjnsua
Polar axis	asosi pinjnra	Polished	pinjnsuade
Polar bear	pinjnra beran	Politburo	pinjntobin
Polarimeter	pinjnraimuto	Polite	pinjnto
Polaris	pinjnrasi	Politesse	pinjntosi
Polarization	pinjnraiseyoon	Politic	pinjnko
Polarize	pinjnraise	Political	pinjnkojo
Polaroid	pinjnrajo	Political asylum	asnlema pinjnkojo
Polder	pinjnjora	Politician	pinjnkohn
Pole	pinjn	Politicize	pinjnkose
Pole1	pinjn	Politicking	pinjnkignni

WORD (x)	EQUIVALENT (y)	WORD (x)	EQUIVALENT (y)
Politico	pinjnki	Pollux	pojnrasi
Politics	pinjnkosi	Polly	pojnrase
Polity	pinjntn	Pollyanan	pojnrasenana
Polje	pinjnde	Polo	polo
Polk	pinjnka	Polonaise	polohunse
Polka	pinjnkan	Polo-neck	polo-hunko
Polkadot	pinjnkande	Polonium	polohunma
Poll	pojnra	Polonius	polohunsi
Pollack	pojnraki	Polska	polosia
Pollan	pojnrahn	Poltava	polotanwa
Pollard	pojnragba	Poltergeist	polotnragnsi
Polled	pojnrade	Poltroon	polotnrain
Pollee	pojnrase	Poly-	pose
Pollen	pojnrain	Poluadelphous	poseajinjophisi
Pollen count	pojnrain kaleyo	Polyamide	poseamuji
Pollex	pojnrasn	Polyandry	posegbainro
Pollice	pojnransi	Polyanthus	poseasinsi
Pollinate	pojnrainyo	Polyarchy	poseknran
Pollination	pojnrainyoon	Polyatomic	poseatimuko
Polliniferous	pojnrainfirosi	Polybasite	poseboosuyo
Pollinium	pojnrainma	Polybius	posebooso
Pollinosis	pojnrainso	Polybrid	posebajo
Pollio	pojnranko	Polycarp	posekopan
Polliverso	pojnranwnrasoo	Polycarpellary	posekopanllerai
Polliwog	pojnranwingio	Polycarpic	posekopanko
Pollock	pojnraki	Polycarpous	posekopansi
Pollster	pojnraseto	Polycentrism	posekntiraimosi
Poll tax	pojnra tesan	Polychaete	posekhokntisi
Polling	pojnragnni	Polychasium	posekhesema
Pollucite	pojnrukiyo	Polychrome	posekhironma
Pollutant	pojnruyotn	Poluchromy	posekhironmase
Pollute	pojnruyo	Polyclinic	posekiunko
Polluted	pojnruyode	Polyclitus	posekiuntesi
Pollution	pojnruyoon	Polyconic	posekinnuko

WORD (x)	EQUIVALENT (y)	WORD (x)	EQUIVALENT (y)
Polycrates	poseknratesi	Polymorph	posemophan
Polycrystal	posekoraitnjo	Polymorphism	posemophansi
Polycythemia	posesnsinmo	Polymorphous per	posemophansi pnra
Polydactyl	posedakntilo	Polynesia	posehunsia
Polydemic	posejinmuko	Polynesian	posehunsiahn
Polydeuces	posejinsesi	Polyneuritis	posehunraiso
Polydipsia	posedipnsia	Polyneuropathy	posehunraiknpansio
Polyembryony	poseemborainse	Polynics	posenikesi
Polyergic	poseraileko	Polynomial	posenimojo
Polyester	posesito	Polynya	poseni
Polyethene	posesinhun	Polynymous	posenimosi
Polyethylene	posesinlohun	Polyose	posese
Polygala	posegije	Polyp	posepn
Polygamous	posegimosi	Polypary	posepnrai
Polygamy	posegimo	Polypeptide	posepnpotiji
Polygenesis	posegnhunso	Polypetalous	posepntijosi
Polyglot	posegonte	Polyphagia	posephijesi
Polygon	posegun	Polyphagic	posephijeko
Polygonaceous	posegunsuwa	Polyphase	posephanse
Polygonal	posegunjo	Polyphemus	posephimusi
Polygonum	posegunma	Polyphonic	posephohunko
Polygony	posegunse	Polyphony	posephohunse
Polygraph	poseganpha	Polyphylesis	posephejnso
Polygraphy	poseganphe	Polypidom	posepndeo
Polygynous	poseloyunsi	Polyploidy	poseponjo
Polygyny	poseloyun	Polypod	posepindie
Polyhedral	posehejnrajo	Polypody	posepindiese
Polyhedron	posehejnran	Polypous	posepinsi
Polyhydraminous	posegbanmisi	Polyropene	poseponpnhun
Polymath	posemosi	Polypropylene	poseponpnlohun
Polymer	posemura	Polyptych	posepntikho
Polymerism	posemuramosi	Polypus	posepnsi
Polymeriazation	posemuraseyoon	Polysaccharide	posesankkhoraijo
Polymerous	posemurasi	Polysepalous	posesepnajosi

WORD (x)	EQUIVALENT (y)	WORD (x)	EQUIVALENT (y)
Polysperm	posesepnron	Pomiferous	pomofirosi
Polyspermy	posesepnronse	Pommel	pommolu
Polystelic	posesitnjnko	Pommenm	pommoran
Polystyrene	posesitnrain	Pommy	pommose
Polysulfide	posesnlefiji	Pomology	pomologbon
Polysyllable	posesojnranbe	Pomona	pomohun
Polysydeton	posesojintin	Pomp	pompon
Polysynthetic	posesosesinko	Pompadour	pomponjnwa
Polytechnic	posetokhiniko	Pompano	pompankn
Polytheism	posesinmosi	Pompeli	pomponlo
Polythene	posesinhun	Pompelmous	pomponlema
Polytrophic	posetnrapheko	Pompey	pomponse
Polytypic	posetnponko	Pompholyhemia	pomponhijinmo
Polyunsaturated	posenusatnraiyode	Pom-pom	pom-ponna
Polyurethane	poseuresanhun	Pompon	pompon
Polyuria	poseuran	Pomposity	pomponseto
Polyvalent	posewajnso	Pompous	pomponsi
Polyvinyl	posewinlo	Ponape	popan
Polyxena	posesiajn	Ponce	pokn
Polyzoan	posesinhn	Poncho	pokhnko
Polyzoarium	posesinraima	Pond	ponjn
Polyzoic	posesinko	Ponder	ponjnra
Pom	pomi	Ponderable	ponjnrabe
Pomace	pomise	Ponderous	ponjnrasi
Pomaceous	pomisesi	Pondicherry	ponjnkhnrrai
Pomade	pomijin	Pondokkie	ponjnkoin
Pomander	pominijnra	Pondoland	ponjnledain
Pombe	pombe	Pone	ponse
Pome	pomo	Ponent	ponseto
Pomegranate	pomogiranyo	Pong	pongi
Pomelo	pomolo	Pongee	pongini
Pomerania	pomorain	Pongid	pongijo
Pomeranian	pomorainhn	Poniard	pongbaa
Pomiculture	pomokunjiaran	Pons	ponse

WORD (x)	EQUIVALENT (y)	WORD (x)	EQUIVALENT (y)
Pons asinorum	ponsesoonraima	Poole	poojn
Ponselle	ponsello	Pools	pojin
Ponsvarolii	ponsnweraijn	Poon	poosi
Pontard	pontngbaa	Poona	posia
Pontes	pontesi	Poonce	posies
Pont	pontn	Poop	popoo
Ponatiac	pontnko	Poor	poran
Pontianak	pontnhunka	Poor law	poran leewo
Pontic	pontnko	Poorly	poranlo
Pontifex	pontnfnsi	Poor relation	poran rejoyoon
Pontiff	pontnffn	Pop1	popn
Pontifical	pontnfnkojo	Pop2	popn
Pontificate	pontnfnkoyo	Pop3	popn
Pontil	pontnlo	Pop art	ete popn
Pontine	pontnhun	Popcom	popnkinra
Pontinier	pontnhunsi	Pop culture	popn kunjiaran
Pontius	pontnsi	Pop gun	popn gunta
Pontonier	pontooran	Pope	popon
Pontoon1	pontoojn	Popery	poponrai
Pontoon2	pontoojn	Pop-eyed	popu-eyiride
Pontoppidan	pontopodan	Popinjay	popujinyo
Pony	posiun	Popish	popuse
Pony-tail	posiun-tele	Poplar	popujora
Poo	poo	Poplin	popujan
Poob	poobe	Popliteal	popujntojo
Pooch	pookhi	Popocatepeti	popukotapnti
Pood	poodi	Popover	popuwnra
Poodle	pooduo	Poppaea	popupan
Poof	poofe	Popper	popusi
Poohbah	poohuhan	Poppet	poputi
Pooh-pooh	poohu	Poppied	popude
Pook	pooko	Popple	popupon
Pool1	poojo	Poppy	popuse
Pool2	poojo	Popsicle	popusookuo

WORD (x)	EQUIVALENT (y)	WORD (x)	EQUIVALENT (y)
Popsy	popusn	Porphyroid	porapheraijo
Populace	popujnsi	Porphyropsin	porapheraipnsie
Popular	popujnran	Porphyry	porapherai
Popularity	popujnraitn	Porpoise	porapinsesi
Popularize	popujnraise	Porridge	porraigbo
Populate	popujnyo	Porringer	porraignsi
Population	popujnyoon	Porsche	porasekhn
Populist	popujnsi	Porsena	poraseun
Populous	popnjnse	Port1	pinta
Pop-up	popu-pake	Port2	pinta
Porcelain	porasejan	Port3	pinta
Porcelaneous	porasejansi	Port4	pinta
Porch	porakho	Portable	pintabe
Porcine	porahun	Portage	pintagun
Porcupine	porapohun	Portakabin	pintakobin
Pore1	porai	Porta	pintan
Pore2	porai	Portal	pintajo
Porgy	poralo	Portal to portal	pintajo si pintajo
Poriferan	poraifiron	Portal vein	pintajo wnsa
Poriferous	poraifirosi	Portamento	pintaminito
Porism	poraimosi	Portative	pintayowin
Pork	poraki	Portcullis	pintakunllesi
Porker	porakisi	Porte	pintan
Porky	porakn	Porte co chere	pintan ki khnrai
Pom	poran	Portee	pintase
Pomocracy	porankansn	Portend	pintinjo
Pomography	poranganphe	Portent	pintinto
Poromeric	poramuko	Portentous	pintintosi
Porosity	poraseto	Porter1	pintasi
Porous	porai	Porter2	pintasi
Porphyria	porapherain	Porterage	pintasigun
Porphyrin	porapherie	Porter house	pintasi hinlese
Porphyritic	porapheraiko	Port folio	pinta fonjia
Porphyrogenite	porapheraiginyo	Port hole	pinta hinlu

WORD (x)	EQUIVALENT (y)	WORD (x)	EQUIVALENT (y)
Portia	pintase	Positronium	pinsitnronma
Portico	pintaki	Posology	pinsilogbon
Portiere	pintarin	Poss	pinso
Portiledefire	pintaronjinfinna	Posse	pinse
Portion	pintasi	Possess	pinseso
Portly	pintalo	Possession	pinsesosi
Portmanteau	pintamotiele	Possessive	pinsesowin
Portmanteau word	pintamotiele wijo	Possessory	pinsesorai
Portland	pintaledain	Posset	pinsetn
Portly	pintalo	Possibility	pinsebeleto
Porto	pinto	Possible	pinseberon
Porto novo	pinto hunwa	Possibly	pinsebelo
Portrait	pintnreto	Possum	pinsema
Portraitist	pintnretosi	Post1	pinseto
Portraiture	pintnretoran	Post2	pinseto
Portray	pintnre	Post3	pinseto
Portrayal	pintnrejo	Post-	pinseto
Portress	pintabo	Postage	pinsetogun
Portugal	pintogunjo	Postal	pinsetogun
Portuguese	pintogunse	Postal	pinsetojo
Portulaca	pintojnka	Postal code	pinsetojo kidie
Portulakaceous	pintojnkasuwa	Postbag	pinsetobogbi
Posada	pinsijo	Postbox	pinsetobosi
Pose	pinsi	Postcard	pinsetokogba
Poseidon	pinsijoin	Postcode	pinsetokidie
Poser	pinsise	Post-coital	pinseto-kitejo
Poseur	pinsirai	Postdate	pinsetodayo
Posh	pinsua	Postdiluvian	pinsetojnlewnhn
Posit	pinsiyo	Post doctoral	pinseto dekntiranjo
Position	pinsiyoon	Posteen	pinsetoon
Positive	pinsiyowin	Poster	pinsetosi
Positivism	pinsiyowinmosi	Posterestant	pinsetoresintn
Positron	pinsiyowinmosi	Posterior	pinsetnraran
Positron	pinsitnron	Posterity	pinsetnratn

WORD (x)	EQUIVALENT (y)	WORD (x)	EQUIVALENT (y)
Postem	pinsetoran	Pot-belly	pote-bejnron
Poster paint	pinsetosi pantone	Poteen	potoon
Postgraduate	pinsetogandieyo	Potency	potinsn
Post haste	pinseto haseto	Potent	potinto
Pastiche	pinsetokhn	Potenatae	potintoyo
Posticous	pinsetoknsi	Potential	potintojo
Postil	pinsetira	Potentiality	potintoleto
Postilion	pinsetirain	Potentiate	potintoyo
Posting	pinsetognni	Potentilla	potintolle
Postle	pinsetoron	Potentiometer	potintoknmuto
Postliminium	pinsetoleminima	Potentize	potintose
Postliminy	pinsetolemini	Potheen	potehesi
Postlude	pinsetolejin	Pother	potesira
Postman	pinsetomoye	Potiche	potekhn
Postmeridiem	pinsetomuraijimo	Potdaea	potejina
Postmortem	pinsetomositn	Potion	potesi
Postnatal	pinsetohetnjo	Potiphar	potephiran
Postpone	pinsetopohun	Potlatch	potelehun
Postprandial	pinsetopanjnjo	Potsherd	potesuagba
Postscript	pinsetosekoraipn	Potomac	potemokn
Postulant	pinsetolete	Potometer`	potemuto
Postulate	pinsetoleyo	Potosi	potesi
Posture	pinsetorai	Potpourri	poteporrai
Posy	pinsue	Pott	potte
Pot1	pote	Pottage	pottegun
Pot2	pote	Potted	pottedpotterai
Potable	potebe	Potter2	potterai
Potage	potegun	Potter's wheel	potterai whinlo
Potash	potesue	Pottery	potterain
Potassium	potesooma	Pottle	potteron
Potation	poteyoon	Potto	potto
Potato	potato	Potty1	pottesi
Potatory	potetorai	Potty2	pottesi
Potaufen	potefini	Pouch	pokhun

WORD (x)	EQUIVALENT (y)	WORD (x)	EQUIVALENT (y)
Pouffe	poffun	Powerless	powaralabo
Pough	poghun	Power line	powara lehun
Polaine	pojuagbaa	Poweney	pownse
Poult	pojua	Powter	powntn
Poulter	pojuase	Powwow	pownwn
Poulterer	pojuasesi	Powys	pownso
Poultice	pojuasi	Pox	posai
Poultry	pojuarai	Poxy	posaise
Pounce	pounsi	Poyang	posngan
Pound1	pojoin	Poyon	posnsi
Pound2	pojoin	Pozzouli	possunjn
Pound3	pojoin	Praam	pnranmi
Poundage	pojoingun	Pracharak	pnrankhosun
Pounder	pojoinsi	Practic	pnrankiko
Pour	pinrai	Practicable	pnrankikobe
Pourboire	pinraiburon	Practical	pnrankikojo
Pourparler	pinraipanjnra	Practically	pnrankikjin
Pousse-café	pinssuekofn	Practice	pnrankiko
Poussette	pinssuetn	Practise	pnrankikose
Poussie	pinsuetn	Practitioner	pnrankikoyoonsi
Pousto	pinssotn	Prado	pnrande
Pout	pinsita	Prae	pnrau
Pouter	pinsitase	Praecipe	pnraukipon
Pouther	pinsitase	Praedial	pnraujinjo
Poutry	pinsitarai	Praemunire	pnraumuhunrai
Poverty	pownratn	Praenomen	pnrainmuye
Poverty line	pownratn	Praeposter	pnraupinseto
Pow	powa	Praesepe	pnrausepon
Powan	powasi	Praesidium	pnrausoojoma
Powder	powajnra	Praetexta	pnrautoson
Powdery	powajnrai	Praetor	pnrautoran
Powell	powajnro	Praetorian	pnrautorain
Power	powara	Praga	pnrangba
Powerboat	powaraboote	Pragmatic	pnrangbamuko

WORD (x)	EQUIVALENT (y)	WORD (x)	EQUIVALENT (y)
Pragmatical	pnrangbamukojo	Preachify	pesikhofe
Pragmatism	pnrangbamumosi	Preachment	pesikhomutto
Prague	pnrangan	Preadamite	pesiadimuto
Prairial	pnranraijo	Preagonal	pesiagunjo
Prairie	pnranpapa	Preamble	pesiamberon
Prairie	pnranrai	Preamplifier	pesiamponfesi
Praise	pnransa	Preaxial	pesiasosi
Prajna	pnranjina	Prebend	pesibesijn
Prakrit	pnrankiti	Prebendary	pesibesijnrai
Praline	pnranlehun	Precambrian	pesikomberain
Prall triller	pnranlle taraille	Precarious	pesikoraisi
Pram	pnranmo	Precast	pesikosoto
Prance	pnransi	Precative	pesikotiwin
Prandial	pnranje	Precaution	pesikoinyoon
Prang	pnrangan	Precede	pesiknjin
Prank	pnrankn	Precedence	pesiknjinsi
Prankster	pnranknseto	Predent	pesiknjinto
Prase	pnransn	Precedential	pesiknjintojo
Praseodymium	pnransndainmo	Precent	pesiknti
Prat	pnranti	Precentor	pesikntiran
Prate	pnranto	Precept	pesiknpo
Pratincole	pnrantoknjoin	Preceptor	pesiknporan
Pratique	pnrantokun	Preceptory	pesiknporai
Prattle	pnranttoron	Precession	pesiknsosi
Pravdinsk	pnranwajn	Precinct	pesikiknyo
Prawn	pnranwan	Preciosity	pesisuaseto
Praxis	pnransesi	Precious	pesisua
Praxiteles	pnransetojnsi	Precipe	pesikipn
Pray	pnranye	Precipice	pesikipnsi
Prayer1	pnranyesi	Precipitable	pesikipnti
Prayer2	pnranyesi	Precipitant	pesikipntite
Prayer-book	booko pnranyesi	Precipitate	pesikipntiyo
Pre-	pesi	Precipitation	pesikipntiyoon
Preach	pesikho	Precipitin	pesikipntie

WORD (x)	EQUIVALENT (y)	WORD (x)	EQUIVALENT (y)
Precipitous	pesikipntisi	Predicament	pesidiknmutto
Précis	pesikisi	Predicant	pesidiknte
Precise	pesikise	Predicate	pesidiknyo
Precisely	pesikiselo	Predicative	pesidiknyowin
Precian	pesikisn	Predict	pesidikn
Precision	pesikisesi	Predictable	pesidiknbe
Preclinical	pesikiunkojo	Prediction	pesidiknyoon
Preclude	pesikuojin	Predilection	pesidilekyoon
Precoial	pesikikunjn	Predispose	pesidisipinse
Precocious	pesikikunsi	Prednisone	pesidnsohun
Precognition	pesikignyoon	Predominant	pesideminatn
Preconceive	pesikinknwin	Predominate	pesideminayo
Preconception	pesikinknpoyoon	Pree	pesie
Preconcert	pesiknrate	Preemie	pesiemuse
Precondition	pesikindiyoon	Preeminent	pesieminato
Preconize	pesikinse	Pre-emption	pesi-empnyoon
Preconscious	pesikinsisesi	Pre-emptive	pesi-empnyowin
Precontract	pesikintnreko	Preen	pesijo
Precritical	pesikantakojo	Preexilian	pesiesnlo
Precursive	pesikuosewin	Prefab	pesifanbe
Precursor	pesikuoseran	Prefabricate	pesifanberaikoyo
Predacious	pesidasesi	Preface	pesifansi
Predate	pesidayo	Prefatory	pesifantorai
Predator	pesidayoran	Prefect	pesifnko
Predatory	pesidayorai	Prefecture	pesifnkorai
Predecease	pesikinknsise	Prefer	pesifiro
Predecessor	pesijinknsoran	Preferable	pesifirobe
Predella	pesijinjnra	Preference	pesifirosi
Predesignate	pesidesooganyo	Preferent	pesifirote
Predestinarian	pesijinsitinrain	Preferential	pesifirotejo
Predestinate	pesidesitinyo	Preferment	pesifiromutto
Predestine	pesijinsitin	Preferred	pesifirrode
Predetermine	pesidntnrahun	Prefiguration	pesifigiraiyoon
Predial	pesidile	Prefigure	pesifigirai

WORD (x)	EQUIVALENT (y)	WORD (x)	EQUIVALENT (y)
Prefix	pesifisn	Premises	pesimusesi
Preflight	pesifologbe	Premiss	pesimusin
Preflorate	pesifonraiyo	Premium	pesimusan
Prefoliation	pesifonjiayoon	Premolar	pesimojnra
Preformation	pesifoonmoyoon	Premorish	pesimose
Pregel	pesignlo	Premonition	pesimohunyoon
Pregi	pesigi	Premorse	pesimoknse
Pregnable	pesiginibe	Premundane	pesimujnhun
Pregnandiol	pesiginidijin	Premunition	pesimuhunyoon
Pregnant	pesiginitn	Prename	pesihemo
Preheat	pesihenasi	Prenatal	pesihetnjo
Prehensible	pesihesnbe	Prenomen	pesinimuye
Prehensile	pesihesnron	Pronominal	pesinimohejo
Prejudise	pesijogbonse	Prent	pesite
Prelacy	pesilesn	Preoccupy	pesiokunpn
Prelate	pesiletn	Prep	pesipn
Preletism	pesiletnmosi	Preparation	pesipanrayoon
Prelatist	pesiletnsi	Preparatory	pesipanrayorai
Prelect	pesijnkayo	Prepare	pesipanra
Preleech	pesijnsikho	Preparedness	pesipanradesi
Prelibation	pesiliboyoon	Prepay	pesipanyio
Prelim	pesilimo	Prepense	pesipnsan
Preliminary	pesilimorai	Preponderant	pesiponjnrate
Preliterate	pesilitoraiyo	Preponderate	pesiponjnraiyo
Prelude	pesilujin	Preposition	pesiposeyoon
Prelusion	pesilusoon	Prepositive	pesiposeyowin
Prelisove	pesilusowin	Prepositor	pesiposeyoran
Premature	pesimotnran	Prepossess	pesipinseso
Premed	pesimujin	Prepossession	pesipinsesosi
Premedication	pesimujinkoyoon	Preposterous	pesipinsetoraisi
Premeditate	pesimujinteyo	Prepotent	pesipotinto
Premier	pesimeni	Prepuce	pesipnsi
Premiere	pesimenirai	Preraphaelite	pesiranphinileyo
Premise	pesimuse	Prerequisite	pesirekunsooyo

WORD (x)	EQUIVALENT (y)	WORD (x)	EQUIVALENT (y)
Prerogative	pesirogiyowin	Press2	pesiso
Presa	pesisu	Press agent	aginte pesiso
Presage	pesisugun	Pressie	pesison
Presbycusis	pesosugbokunso	Pressing	pesisognni
Presbyophrenia	pesosugbophirain	Press-up	pesiso-pake
Presbyopia	pesosugbopan	Pressure	pesisorai
Presbyter	pesosugbotnra	Pressure group	gonpo pesisorai
Presbyterian	pesosugbotnrai	Pressurize	pesisoraise
Prescience	pesisunse	Prest	pesite
Prescient	pesisunto	Prestidigitation	pesitedigitoyoon
Prescind	pesisunjn	Prestel	pesitejo
Prescribe	pesisekorai	Prestige	pesitegbaa
Prescript	pesisekoraipn	Prestigious	pesitegbain
Prescription	pesisekoraipnyoon	Presto	pesito
Prescriptive	pesisekoraipnyowin	Preston	pesiton
Presence	pesisesi	Prestone	pesitoni
Present	pesiseto	Prestonpans	pesitonpnsn
Present1	pesiseto	Prestressed	pesitnransode
Present2	pesiseto	Presumably	pesisumbelo
Present3	pesiseto	Presume	pesisumo
Presentable	pesisetobe	Presumption	pesisumpntisi
Presentation	pesisetoyoon	Presumptive	pesisumpntiwin
Presentiment	pesisetomutto	Presumptuous	pesisumpntise
Presently	pesisetolo	Presuppose	pesisupinsi
Preservative	pesiserawinyo	Pre-tax	pesi-tesan
Preserve	pesiserawin	Pretence	pesitinsi
Pre-set	pesi-seton	Pretend	pesitinjo
Preside	pesisoojo	Pretender	pesitinjosi
Presidency	pesisoojosn	Pretense	pesitinse
President	pesisoojotn	Pretension	pesitinsoon
Presidio	pesisoojoin	Pretentious	pesitintosi
Presidium	pesisoojoma	Preterite	pesitnraiyo
Presignify	pesisooganfe	Pretermit	pesitnramutn
Press1	pesiso	Pretertion	pesitnrayoon

WORD (x)	EQUIVALENT (y)	WORD (x)	EQUIVALENT (y)
Pretematural	pesitnrahetnraijo	Pribilof	panbale
Pretext	pesitesio	Price	pankn
Pretonic	pesitoniko	Priceless	panknlabo
Pretor	pesito	Pricey	panknse
Pretoria	pesitoran	Prick	pankki
Pretorius	pesitoraisi	Pricker	pankkisi
Prettify	pesittofe	Pricket	pankkiti
Pretty	pesitto	Prickle	pankkiron
Pretty-pretty	pesittn-pesitto	Prickly	pankkilo
Pretzel	pesisio	Pride	panjin
Preussen	pesisun	Prie-dieu	panso-jowa
Prevail	pesiwajn	Priest	pansoto
Prevalent	pesiwajnto	Priest craft	pansoto kanfia
Prevaricate	pesiwaraikoyo	Priestess	pansotobo
Prevenient	pesiwinito	Priest-hood	pansoto-hinjo
Prevent	pesiwinta	Priestley	pansotoroin
Prevention	pesiwintasi	Prig	pangba
Preventative	pesiwintayo	Priggish	pangbase
Preventive	pesiwinitase	Priggism	pangbamosi
Preview	pesiwowin	Prill	panlloe
Previous	pesiwo	Prim	panme
Previse	pesiwose	Prima cord	panmeni kigba
Prevision	pesiwosesi	Prima ballerina	panmeni roborain
Prevocation	pesiwnkoyoon	Primacy	panmenisi
Provost	pesiwnseto	Prima donna	panmeni dejnna
Prevue	pesiwnso	Prima facie	panmeni fansi
Prexy	pesisian	Primage	panmenigun
Prey	peseje	Primal	panmenijo
Prezzie	pesesun	Primaquine	panmenikuihun
Priam	panlomo	Primarily	panmeniselo
Priapean	panlapini	Primary	panmenise
Priapic	panlapiniko	Primate	panmenito
Priapism	panlapinimosi	Primatology	panmenitologbon
Priapus	panlapinisi	Primavera	panmeniwinra

WORD (x)	EQUIVALENT (y)	WORD (x)	EQUIVALENT (y)
Prime1	panmeni	Principe	pankinipn
Prime2	panmeni	Principium	pankinipnma
Primer1	panmenise	Principle	pankinipnron
Primer2	panmenise	Principled	pankinipnronde
Primero	panmenise	Prink	panki
Primeval	panmeniwajo	Print	pante
Primigenial	panmeniginjo	Printer	pantesi
Primigravida	panmeniganwojn	Printing	pantegnni
Primine	panmeniso	Printout	pantenita
Priming	panmenign	Prior	panknra
Primipara	panmenipanra	Prioress	panknraibo
Primitive	panmenitown	Prioritize	panknraitose
Primitivism	panmenitownmosi	Priority	panknraito
Primogenitor	panmoginteran	Priory	panknrain
Primogeniture	panmoginterai	Pripet	panpnti
Primomo	panmoko	Prisage	pansigun
Primordial	panmenijo	Priscilla	pansikijjo
Primordium	panmenijoma	Priscillian	pansikijjoin
Primp	panmpn	Prise	pansui
Primrose	panmrosua	Prism	pansinmo
Primsie	panmise	Prism	pansinmo
Primula	panmule	Prismatic	pansinmuko
Primuleceous	panmulesuwa	Prismoid	pansinmujo
Primus	panmeni	Prison	pansnsn
Primus interpares	panmeni initopanse	Prisoner	pansnsnsi
Prince	pankini	Prissy	pansnse
Princeling	pankinilognni	Pristina	pansntinsi
Princely	pankinilo	Pristine	pansntin
Princess	pankinibo	Privacy	panwesn
Princesse	pankinisoo	Private	panweyo
Princess royal	pankinibo rosnjo	Privateer	panweyosi
Princeton	pankinitin	Privation	panweyoon
Principal	pankinipile	Privative	panweyowin
Principality	pankinipileto	Privatize	panweyose

WORD (x)	EQUIVALENT (y)	WORD (x)	EQUIVALENT (y)
Privatization	panweyoseyoon	Proceed	ponknjin
Privet	panwinti	Proceeding	ponknjingnni
Privilege	panwinlogn	Proceeds	ponknjinsi
Privily	panwinlo	Proceleusmatic	ponknjnmosiko
Privity	panwinto	Procelial	ponknjnjo
Privy	panwinse	Process1	ponknso
Prix fixen	pansi fisn	Process2	ponknso .
Prize1	pansian	Procession	ponknsoon
Prize2	pansian	Processional	ponknsoonjo
Prize3	pansian	Processor	ponknsoran
Prizefight	pansianfighe	Proclaim	ponkanlemo
Pro1	pon	Proclamation	ponkanmoyoon
Pro2	pon	Proclitic	ponkiunteko
Proa	ponsia	Proclivity	ponkiunwinto
Proactive	ponakntiwin	Procne	ponknun
Probabilism	pongbibnmosi	Proconsul	ponkinsle
Probable	pongbibe	Procopious	ponkipesi
Probands	pongbijnsi	Procrastinate	ponkansetiyo
Probang	pongbign	Procrastination	ponkansetiyoon
Probate	pongbiyo	Procreant	ponknrante
Probation	pongbiyoon	Procreate	ponknranyo
Probationer	pongbiyoonsi	Procreative	ponknranyowin
Probative	pongbiyowin	Procrustean	ponknraisetnhn
Probe	pongbi	Procrustes	ponknraisetnsi
Probity	pongbito	Procrayptic	ponkoraipnko
Problem	pongbile	Procto	ponknto
Problematic	pongbileko	Proctology	ponkntologbon
Probono	pongbini	Proctoplasty	ponkntologbon
Proboscidian	pongbisijoin	Proctor	ponkntoran
Proboscis	pongbisiso	Proctoscope	ponkntosokipon
Procambium	ponkomgbema	Proculus	ponkunlesi
Procathedral	ponkosingbanle	Procumbent	ponkunmbeto
Procedendo	ponkndainde	Procurable	ponkunrabe
Procedure	ponknjinrai	Procuracy	ponkunrasn

WORD (x)	EQUIVALENT (y)	WORD (x)	EQUIVALENT (y)
Procurance	ponkunrasi	Professionalism	ponfnsesijomosi
Procuration	ponkunrayoonb	Professor	ponfnseran
Procurator	ponkunraran	Professorate	ponfnseranyo
Procure	ponkunra	Professorial	ponfnseraijo
Procurement	ponkunramutto	Professoriate	ponfnseraiyo
Procurer	ponkunrasi	Professorship	ponfnseransunpn
Procyon	ponsnsi	Profer	ponfiro
Prod	ponjn	Proficience	ponfisesi
Prodigal	ponjnganjo	Proficient	ponfiseto
Prodigality	ponjnganleto	Profile	ponfijan
Prodigious	ponjngansi	Profit	ponfite
Prodigy	ponjngan	Profitable	ponfitebe
Prodrome	pongbnmo	Profiteer	ponfitesi
Produce	pondisi	Profiterole	ponfiteraijn
Producer	pondisise	Profligacy	ponfiungisn
Product	pondikiti	Profligate	ponfiungiyo
Productile	pondikitiron	Profluent	ponfoluto
Production	pondikitiyoon	Pro forma	pon foonma
Production line	lehun pondikitiyoon	Profound	ponfonjoin
Productive	pondikitiwin	Profoundity	ponfonjointo
Productivity	pondikitiwinto	Profuse	ponfunsi
Proem	ponmini	Profusion	ponfunsoosi
Pro et con	pon ati kin	Progenitor	ponginteran
Prof.	ponf	Progeny	ponginse
Profanation	ponfanyoon	Progeria	pongnran
Profane	ponfan	Progestation	pongnsetnyoon
Profanity	ponfanto	Progesterone	pongnsetnroin
Profanum vulgus	ponfanma welgnsi	Progestin	pongnsetie
Profert	ponfnrate	Proglottid	pongonttnjo
Profess	ponfnse	Proglottis	pongonttnsi
Professed	ponfnsede	Prognathous	ponginisesi
Professedly	ponfnsedelo	Prognosis	ponginiso
Profession	ponfnsesi	Prognostic	ponginisuko
Professional	ponfnsesijo	Prognosticate	ponginisukoyo

WORD (x)	EQUIVALENT (y)	WORD (x)	EQUIVALENT (y)
Prognostication	ponginisukoyoon	Proliferate	ponlefiraiyo
Program	ponganmo	Proliferous	ponlefirosi
Programme	ponganmmo	Prolific	ponlefiko
Progreso	pongiraisoon	Proline	ponlehun
Progress	pongiraiso	Prolix	ponlesi
Progression	pongiraisoon	Prolocutor	ponlokuntesi
Progressist	pongiraisosi	Prolog	ponlogn
Progressive	pongiraisowin	Prologue	ponlognso
Prohibit	ponhibeyo	Prolong	ponlogun
Prohibition	ponhibeyoon	Prolongation	ponlogunyoon
Prohibitive	ponhibeyowin	Prolonge	ponlogini
Project	ponjnkn	Prolusion	ponlusoon
Projectile	ponjnknron	Prom	ponme
Projection	ponjnknyoon	Promenade	ponmelojin
Projectionist	ponjnknyoonsi	Promethazine	ponmesansun
Projective	ponjnknwin	Promethean	ponmesinhun
Projector	ponjnknran	Prometheus	ponmesinsi
Prokofiev	ponkofanwin	Promethium	ponmesinma
Prolactin	ponleketie	Prominence	ponminato
Prolamine	ponlemihun	Prominent	ponmuhunto
Prolapse	ponlepnse	Promiscuity	ponmusikunto
Prolapsus	ponlepnsesi	Promiscuous	ponmusikunsi
Prolate	ponleyo	Promise	ponmuse
Prole	ponle	Promised land	ponmusede ledain
Proleg	ponlegn	Promising	ponmusegnni
Prolegomenon	ponlegonmini	Promissory	ponmuserai
Prolepsis	ponlepnso	Promo	ponmo
Proletarian	ponleyarain	Promontory	ponmootorai
Proletariat	ponleyaraita	Promote	ponmotie
Proletarist	ponleyaraisi	Promoter	ponmotiesi
Proletary	ponleyarai	Promotion	ponmotiesi
Proletcult	ponleyakunjia	Promotive	ponmotiewin
Proliferate	ponlefiroyo	Prompt	ponmpnti
Prolicide	ponlekeku	Prompter	ponmpntisi

WORD (x)	EQUIVALENT (y)	WORD (x)	EQUIVALENT (y)
Promptitude	ponmpntitujin	Proparoxytone	ponposiantoni
Promulgate	ponmuleganyo	Propatria	ponpotnran
Promulge	ponmulegan	Propel	ponpnlo
Pronate	ponleniyo	Propellant	ponpnllotn
Pronation	ponleniyoon	Propellent	ponpnlloto
Pronator	ponleniran	Propellence	ponpnllosi
Prone	ponleni	Propend	ponpnjon
Pronephros	ponleniphon	Propene	ponpnyun
Pronephrus	ponleniphones	Propenoic	ponpnyunko
Prong	pongun	Propensity	ponpnyunto
Pronominal	ponnomohejo	Proper	ponpnra
Pronoun	ponnkon	Properly	ponpnralo
Pronounce	ponnkonso	Propertied	ponpnratode
Pronounced	ponnknunsode	Property	ponpnrato
Pronouncement	ponnkonsomutto	Prophage	ponphije
Pronto	ponkia	Prophase	ponphanse
Pronunciamento	ponnknsomutto	Prophecy	ponphnsn
Pronunciation	ponnknsoyoon	Prophesy	ponphnso
Proof	ponfin	Prophet	ponphnto
Prop1	ponpo	Prophetic	ponphntokn
Prop2	ponpo	Prophylactic	ponpgeleknko
Prop3	ponpo	Prophylaxis	ponpheleseso
Propaedeutic	ponposejinko	Propine	ponpohun
Propaedeutics	ponposejinkosi	Propinquity	ponpohunkunto
Propagable	ponpoganbe	Propionate	ponpounyo
Propaganda	ponpoganjn	Propionic	ponpounko
Propagandium	ponpoganjnma	Propitheque	ponposikun
Propagandize	ponpoganjnse	Propitiate	ponpotnyo
Propagate	ponpoganyo	Propitiation	ponpotnyoon
Propagation	ponpoganyoon	Propitious	ponpotnsi
Propagator	ponpoganran	Propolis	ponpojinsi
Propagule	ponpoganron	Propone	ponpinse
Propane	ponpohun	Proponent	ponpinseto
Propanoic	ponpohunko	Proportion	ponpinyoon

WORD (x)	EQUIVALENT (y)	WORD (x)	EQUIVALENT (y)
Proportional	ponpinyoonjo	Prosecretin	ponseknratie
Proportionate	ponpinyoonyo	Prosect	ponseknte
Proposal	ponpinsijo	Prosector	ponseknteran
Propose	ponpinsi	Prosecute	ponsekunte
Proposition	ponpinsiyoon	Prosecution	ponsekuntesi
Propositus	ponpinsitosi	Prosecutor	ponsekunteran
Propound	ponpojoin	Proselyte	ponseloto
Propraetor	ponpantoran	Proselytize	ponselotose
Propranolol	ponpanhunjin	Prosencephalon	ponsesiknphijnsi
Proprietor	ponpansetoran	Prosenchyma	ponsesikhnma
Proprietary	ponpansetorai	Proser	ponsesi
Proprietor	ponpansetoran	Proserpine	ponsiapnsi
Propriety	ponpanseto	Prosimian	ponsomeni
Proprioceptor	ponpanknpntiran	Prosit	ponsotn
Proptosis	ponpntiso	Prosodemic	ponsojinmuko
Propulsion	ponpnjnsoon	Prosodiac	ponsodunka
Propyl	ponpelo	Prosodist	ponsodunsi
Propylaeum	ponpeloinma	Prosody	ponsodun
Propylene	ponpelohun	Prosopopoeia	ponsopipejo
Propylite	ponpeleyo	Prospect	ponsepnto
Propylon	ponpelosi	Prospective	ponsepntowin
Pro rata	pon raite	Prospector	ponsepntoran
Prorate	ponraiyo	Prospectus	ponsepntosi
Prore	ponrai	Prosper	ponsepnra
Prorogation	ponrogiyoon	Prosperity	ponsepnraito
Prorogue	ponrogan	Prosperous	ponsepnraisi
Prosaic	ponsiako	Prostaglandin	ponsetngandain
Prosaism	ponsiamosi	Prostate	ponsetnyo
Pros and cons	ponsi ati kinsi	Prostatectomy	ponsetnyotemo
Proscenium	ponsekinma	Prostatistics	ponsetntitosi
Prosciutto	ponsekitti	Prosthesis	ponsesinso
Proscribe	ponsekoraibe	Prosthetics	ponsesinkosi
Proscription	ponsekoraipnyoon	Prosthodontia	ponsesindeyosi
Prose	ponse	Prostitute	ponsetintuyo

WORD (x)	EQUIVALENT (y)	WORD (x)	EQUIVALENT (y)
Prostitution	ponsetintuyoon	Protestantism	pontasetnmosi
Prostomium	ponsetomuma	Protestation	pontasetnyoon
Prostrate	ponsetnraiyo	Protester	pontasesi
Prostration	ponsetnraiyoon	Proteus	pontasia
Prostyle	ponsetnron	Prothalamion	ponsanllemini
Prosy	ponsiase	Prothallium	ponsanllema
Protactinium	pontekanhunma	Prothallus	ponsanllesi
Protagonist	pontegonsi	Prosthesis	ponsinso
Protagoras	pontegonranse	Prothonotary	ponsinkntorai
Protamine	pontemihun	Prothorax	ponsinrasi
Protandrous	pontejnrasi	Prothrombin	ponsinranbajn
Protanopia	ponteknpan	Protist	pontesi
Protasis	ponteso	Protium	pontema
Protea	ponton	Proto-	ponto
Protean	pontohun	Protococcus	pontokikunsi
Protease	pontonse	Protocol	pontokijo
Protect	pontoknti	Protogene	pontognhun
Protectant	pontokntitn	Protogram	pontoganmo
Protection	pontoknyoon	Protogynous	pontoloyunsi
Protective	pontokntiwin	Protohippus	pontohiposi
Protector	pontokntiran	Protohominoid	pontohinmujo
Protectorate	pontokntiraiyo	Protolithic	pontolesiko
Protégé	pontogba	Protomorphic	pontomophanko
Protein	ponyoto	Proton	pontosi
Pro tem	pon toma	Protonema	pontosnma
Pro tempore	pon tompnsi	Protopathic	pontobpasiko
Protend	pontajn	Protophyte	pontopheyo
Protensity	pontaseto	Protoplasm	pontopanson
Proteolysis	pontajinso	Protoplast	pontopansi
Proteose	pontaknse	Protostele	pontosetnjo
Proterozoic	pontaraisinko	Prototheria	pontosinran
Protesilaus	pontasejnsi	Protetherian	pontosinrain
Protest	pontase	Prototrophic	pontotnrapheko
Protestant	pontasetn	Prototype	pontotnpon

501

WORD (x)	EQUIVALENT (y)	WORD (x)	EQUIVALENT (y)
Protoxid	pontosinji	Provincial	ponwaknjo
Protoxylem	pontosinlomi	Provision	ponwosesi
Protozoan	pontosinhn	Provisional	ponwosesijo
Protozoology	pontosinkologbon	Proviso	ponwoson
Protract	pontnreko	Provisory	ponwosonrai
Protractile	pontnrekoron	Provo	ponwn
Protrction	pontnrekoyoon	Provocation	ponwnkoyoon
Protractor	pontnrekosi	Provocative	ponwnloyowin
Protrude	pontnrajin	Provoke	ponwnko
Protrusion	pontnrasoon	Provolone	ponwnlohun
Protuberant	pontubete	Provost	ponwnsi
Protyle	pontnron	Prow	ponwo
Proud	ponjain	Prowess	ponwosia
Proudhon	ponjainhin	Prowl	ponwojn
Proust	ponsitn	Prox.	Ponsun
Proustite	ponsitnyo	Proxima	ponsunma
Prout	pontasi	Proximal	ponsunmajo
Prove	ponwin	Proximate	ponsunmatn
Provection	ponwinknyoon	Proximity	ponsunmato
Provector	ponwinknran	Proximo	ponsunnmo
Proven	ponwini	Proxy	ponsunse
Provenance	ponwinisi	Prude	porajin
Provencal	ponwinikojo	Prudery	porajinrai
Provender	ponwinjnra	Prudent	porajinto
Proverb	ponlowe	Prudential	porajintojo
Proverbial	ponlowejo	Prudish	porajinse
Provide	ponwajin	Pruinose	porainse
Provided	ponwajinde	Prunel	porahun
Providence	ponwajinsi	Prune2	porahun
Provident	ponwajinto	Prunella	porahunlle
Providential	ponwajintojo	Prunelle	porahunllo
Provident society	ponwajinto sookotn	Pruniferous	porahunfirosi
Providing	ponwajingnni	Prurient	porareto
Province	ponwaknsi	Prurigo	porareto

WORD (x)	EQUIVALENT (y)	WORD (x)	EQUIVALENT (y)
Pruritus hiemalis	poraresi himugnso	Pseudomutuality	pesediemutileto
Prusa	poransi	Pseudonym	pesediemosi
Prussia	poransia	Pseudopod	pesediepindie
Prussian	poransiahn	Pseudopodium	pesediepojnma
Prussiate	poransiayo	Psi	pesoo
Prussic acid	akijo poransiako	Psilocybin	pesoolosnbin
Prut	porate	Psilomelane	pesoolomulehun
Pry	porai	Psittaciform	pesoottokifoonmo
Pryer	poraisi	Psittacine	pesoottokiun
Prynne	poraihun	Psittacosis	pesoottokiso
Prytaneum	poraitehunma	Pskov	pesookown
Prsewalski	posewajosi	Psoas	pesoose
Psalm	peseko	Psocoptera	pesookipntiran
Psalmist	pesekosi	Psora	pesoora
Psalmody	pesekodun	Psoralea	pesooranjn
Psalms	pesekosi	Psoriasis	pesooraiso
Psalter	pesetoran	Psych	posiakhi
Psalterium	pesetoraima	Psychalgia	posiakhijogan
Psaltery	pesetorai	Psychasthenia	posiakhisesiha
Psammite	pesemmute	Psyche	posiakhn
Psammitic	pesemmuteko	Psychedelia	posiakhnjin
Psellism	pesellemosi	Psychedelic	posiakhnjinko
Psephite	pesephanyo	Psychiatrist	posiakhitiraisi
Psephitic	pesephanko	Psychistry	posiakhitirai
Psephology	pesephanlogbon	Psychic	posiakhiko
Pseud	pesedaa	Psychical	posiakhikojo
Pseudaxis	pesediesosi	Psycho	posiakho
Pseudepigrapha	pesediepngirapha	Psychoactive	posiakhokntiwin
Pseudo	pesedie	Psychoanalysis	posiakhohunjnsiaso
Pseudobuld	pesediebujnbe	Psychoanalyst	posiakhohunjosiasi
Pseudocarp	pesediekopan	Psychoanalyze	posiakhobakolosiase
Pseudoclassic	pesediekansooko	Psychobiology	posiaknogbanma
Pseudoisidore	pesediesooderai	Psychodynamics	posiakhodainsemukosi
Pseudomorph	pesediemophan	Psychogenesis	posiakhognhunso

WORD (x)	EQUIVALENT (y)	WORD (x)	EQUIVALENT (y)
Psychogenic	posiakhoginko	Psyllium	posiallema
Psychognosis	posiakhoginiso	Pt	piti
Psychograph	posiakhoganpha	Ptarmigan	pitiramugan
Psychography	posiakhoganphe	Pteridology	pitiraidielogbon
Psychohistory	posiakhisetorai	Pteridophyte	pitiraidiepheyo
Psychokinesis	posiakhokihunso	Pteridosperm	pitiraidiesepnron
Psychological	posiakhologbonkojo	Ptero	pitiron
Psychologism	posiakhologbonmosi	Pterodactyl	pitirondakntilo
Psychologist	posiakhologbonsi	Pteropod	pitironpindie
Psychologize	posiakhologbonse	Pterosaur	pitironsanra
Psychology	posiakhologbon	Pterosaurian	pitironsanrasi
Psychometry	posiakhomutorai	Pterous	pitironsi
Psychomotor	posiakhomoota	Pterygoid	pitiraignjo
Psychoneurosis	posiakhohunraiso	Ptesan	pitisi
Psychopath	posiakhopansio	Pteryla	pitiraijn
Psychopathology	posiakhopansiologbon	Ptochocracy	pntokhinkansn
Psychopathy	posiakhpansio	Ptolemaeus	pntojnmosi
Psychopharmacology	posiakhphisankilogbon	Ptolemaic	pntojnmuko
Psychophysics	posiakhphesikosi	Ptolemaist	pntojnmusi
Psychophysiology	posiakhophesitologbon	Ptolemy	pntojnmo
Psychosexual	posiakhosesiajo	Ptomaine	pntimohun
Psychosis	posiakhoso	Ptosis	pntoso
Psychosomatic	posiakhosomuko	Pty	petiya
Psychosurgery	posiakhosuralerai	Ptyalin	petiyajan
Psychotechnician	posiakhotokhinikohn	Ptyalism	petiyajnmosi
Psychotechnics	posiakhotokhinikosi	Pu	pu
Psychotherapy	posiakhosinranpo	Pub	pube
Psychotic	posiakhokn	Puberty	pubeto
Psychotomimetic	posiakhotomimiko	Pubes1	pubesi
Psychotropic	posiakhotnrapnko	Pubes2	pubesi
Psychro	posiakhiron	Pubescence	pubeseknti
Psychrometer	posiakhironmuto	Pubic	pubeko
Psychrotherapy	posiakhironsinranpo	Pubis	pubeso
Psyllic	posialleko	Public	pubejnko

WORD (x)	EQUIVALENT (y)	WORD (x)	EQUIVALENT (y)
Publican	pubejnkojn	Puerto	puranto
Publication	pubejnkoyoon	Puff	pufan
Public bar	boosn pubejnko	Puff-adder	pufan addisi
Publicist	pubejnkosi	Puffball	pufan robo
Publicity	pubekotn	Puffer	pufanro
Publicize	pubekose	Puffery	pufanrai
Publicily	pubekolo	Puffin	puffin
Publicness	pubejnkonisi	Puffy	pufanse
Publish	pubejnso	Pug	pugbn
Publisher	pubejnsosi	Puget	pugbnta
Puccini	pukkini	Pugilist	pugbnlesi
Puccoon	pukkoon	Pugilism	pugbnlemosi
Puce	pusi	Pugnacious	pugbnkisi
Pucelle	pusille	Pugnacity	pugbnkito
Puck1	puki	Pug-nose	pugbn-nisun
Puck2	puki	Pugree	pugbnra
Pucka	pukin	Puir	purai
Pucker	pukisi	Puisne	pusohun
Pud	podie	Puissance	pusoonsi
Pud	pudie	Puissant	pusoote
Pudding	pudiegnni	Puke	pukwo
Puddle	pudieron	Pukka	pukwokn
Pudler	pudiesi	Pula	pujn
Puddling	pudiegnni	Pulchritude	pujnkhiraitujin
Pudency	pudiesn	Pule	pujn
Pudendum	pudiejnma	Pulex	pujnsi
Pudgy	pudielo	Puli	pujan
Puebia	puseban	Pulicene	pujanknsa
Pueblo	pusejo	Puling	pujangnni
Puerile	puranjn	Pulitzer	pujansesi
Puerilism	puranjnmosi	Pulkha	pujnkha
Puerity	puranto	Pull	pujnra
Puerperal	puranpnrajo	Pulldoo	pujnradein
Puerperium	puranpnrama	Pullet	pujnte

WORD (x)	EQUIVALENT (y)	WORD (x)	EQUIVALENT (y)
Pulley	pujnroin	Puma	pumo
Pull-in	pujnra-nu	Pumice	pumose
Pullman	pujnramoye	Pummel	pummujo
Pull-out	pujnra-nita	Pump1	pumpo
Pullover	pujnra ownsn	Pump2	pumpo
Pullulate	pujnraleyo	Pumpemickel	pumpnmukijo
Pulmonmeter	pujnmimuto	Pumpkin	pumpokin
Pulmonary	pujnmisirai	Pun	puha
Pulmonate	pujnmisiyo	Puna	puhun
Pulmonic	pujnmisiko	Punce	puhunsi
Pulmotor	pujnmoturan	Punch1	pukhan
Pulp	pujnpn	Punch2	pukhan
Pulpit	pujnpnti	Punch3	pukhan
Pulpy	pujnpnse	Punchball	pukhanrobo
Pulque	pujnkun	Punch-line	pukhan lehun
Pulsar	pujnserai	Puncheon	pukhansesi
Pulsate	pujnseto	Puncher	pukhansi
Pulsatile	pujnsetinron	Punchinello	pukhanhunllo
Pulsatilla	pujnsetojjo	Punchy	pukhanse
Pulsation	pujnsetosi	Punctate	pukntiyo
Pulsative	pujnsetowin	Punctilio	pukntijn
Pulsator	pujnsetoran	Punctilious	pukntijnsi
Pulsatory	pujnsetorai	Punctual	pukntijo
Pulse1	pujnsi	Punctuate	pukntiyo
Pulse2	pujnsi	Punctuation	pukntiyoon
Pulsimeter	pujnsimuto	Puncture	pukntirai
Pulsometer	pujnsemuto	Pundit	pujnte
Pulcerable	pujnwinrabe	Pung	pugbun
Pulverane	pujnwinrain	Pungent	pugbunto
Pulverize	pujnwinraise	Punic	puyako
Pulverulent	pujnwinrajnto	Punish	puyase
Pulvillus	pujnwinllesi	Punishment	puyasemutto
Pulvinate	pujnwinto	Punitive	puyatewin
Pulvinous	pujnwinsi	Punjab	pujnbe

WORD (x)	EQUIVALENT (y)	WORD (x)	EQUIVALENT (y)
Punjabi	pujnba	Purana	puranhun
Punk	puke	Purblind	purabiunjn
Punka	pukefe	Purchase	purakhese
Punkah	pukehn	Purdah	puragbain
Punkie	pukesi	Pure	purai
Punky	pukese	Puree	purase
Punnet	puhunte	Purely	purailo
Punster	puseto	Purfle	purafijn
Punt1	pute	Purgation	puragiyoon
Punt2	pute	Purgative	puragiyowin
Punt3	pute	Purgatory	puragiyorai
Punt4	pute	Purge	puragin
Punter	putesi	Purification	puraifikoyoon
Puntilla	putelle	Purify	puraife
Punto	putinb	Purim	puraimi
Punty	putese	Purine	purain
Puny	pujie	Purism	puraimosi
Pup	pupe	Purist	puraisi
Pupa	pupan	Puritan	puraitin
Pupae	pupanse	Puritanical	puraitinkojo
Puparium	pupanraima	Purity	puraito
Pupate	pupanyo	Purkinje	purakinjn
Pupil1	pupolo	Purl1	purajn
Pupil2	pupolo	Purl2	purajn
Puppillage	pupollogun	Purler	purajnra
Pulippary	pupollorai	Purlieu	purajnwa
Pupin	puposn	Purlin	purajan
Pupiparous	pupopanrasi	Purloin	purajoin
Puppet	pupnte	Purple	purapon
Puppet state	setnyo pupnte	Purport	purapinta
Puppeteer	pupntesi	Purpose	purapinsi
Puppetry	pupnterai	Purposeless	purapinsilabo
Puppy	pupnse	Purposely	purapinsilo
Purace	puransi	Purpose-made	purapinsi mojain

WORD (x)	EQUIVALENT (y)	WORD (x)	EQUIVALENT (y)
Purposive	purapinsiwin	Pussy	pusinse
Purpura	purapuran	Pustulant	pusetorante
Purpurin	purapurie	Pustular	pusetoransi
Purr	purra	Pustulate	pusetoranyo
Purse	purase	Pustule	pusetoran
Purser	purasesi	Put	puto
Purslane	purasejnhun	Putamen	putomini
Pursue	purasun	Putative	putoyowin
Pursuance	purasunse	Put-on	puto-le
Pursuant	purasunte	Putrefaction	putnrunfanknyoon
Pursuit	purasunti	Putrefactive	putnrunfanknyowin
Pursuivant	purasunwnte	Putrefy	putnrunfe
Pursy	purasue	Putrescence	putnrunseknsi
Purtenance	puratinsi	Putrescent	putnrunseknti
Purtenant	puratinte	Putrescible	putrnrunsekibe
Purulent	purunjnte	Putrescine	putnrunseki
Purus	puraisi	Putrid	putnrunjo
Purvery	purawoin	Putsch	putako
Purveyance	purawoinse	Putt	putta
Purveyor	purawoinran	Puttee	puttasi
Purview	purawowin	Putter1	puttasi
Pus	pusu	Putter2	puttasi
Pusey	pususe	Putty	puttase
Push	pusun	Putumayo	putumuyo
Pusher	pusunsi	Puy	puyo
Pushing	pusungnni	Puzzle	pusiaron
Pushover	pusunownra	Puzzler	pusiaronsi
Push-start	pusun-setnte	Py	pe
Pushtu	pusuntu	Pydna	pejohun
Pushy	pusunse	Pyaemia	pesemoon
Pusillanimity	pusilleminito	Pyatigorsk	peyotegonsi
Pusillanimous	pusilleminisi	Pyelitis	pesejnso
Puss	pusin	Pyemia	pesemi
Pussley	pusinroin	Pyenidium	peseknjoma

WORD (x)	EQUIVALENT (y)	WORD (x)	EQUIVALENT (y)
Pyenometer	peseknmuto	Pyran	perain
Pyenospore	peseknseporai	Pyranometer	perainmuto
Pyeilitis	pesejnso	Pyrangyrite	perainloraiyo
Pyelogram	pesejngamo	Pyranzole	perainsinle
Pyelography	pesejnganphe	Pyre	peran
Pygidium	pegbijnma	Pyrene	peranhun
Pymalion	pemajoin	Pyreneer	peransi
Pygmy	pegbn	Pyrenoid	peranyo
Pyic	peko	Pyrenomycetes	peranmunknti
Pyin	pesu	Pyrethrum	peransinrama
Pyjamas	pejnmusun	Pyretic	peranko
Pyknic	pekinko	Pyretology	peranknlogbon
Pyknophrasia	pekinphansia	Pyretotherapy	peranknsinranpo
Pylades	pejojnse	Pyrex	peransi
Pyle	pejn	Pyrexia	peransia
Pylon	pejnsi	Pyrgeometer	peragbilemuto
Pylorectomy	peloratemo	Pyrtheliometer	perasinjomuto
Pylorus	pelorasi	Pyribenzamine	peraibesunmini
Pylos	pelosn	Pyridine	peraijoin
Pym	pemo	Pyridoxine	peraijosinhun
Pyo	peyo	Pyriform	peraifoomon
Pyogenesis	peyognhunso	Pyrimidine	peraimujoin
Pyoid	peyojo	Pyrite	peraiyo
Pyongyang	peyogungan	Pyrites	peraiyosi
Pyorrhea	peyorrhain	Pyro-	peron
Pyorrhoea	peyorrhoin	Pyrocatechol	peronkotikhnjin
Pyosis	peyoso	Pyrocellulose	peronknjjnlose
Pyr	pera	Pyroceram	peronknrama
Pyracantha	peraikona	Pyroclastic	peronkansuko
Pyralidid	peraijjnle	Pyroconductivity	peronkindikitiyowinto
Pyramid	peraimuin	Pyrocrystalline	peronkoraitnjjohun
Pyramidal	peraimujnjo	Pyroelectric	peroneleknrako
Pyramidalis	peraimujnjosi	Pyroelectricity	peroneleknrakitn
Pyramus	peraimosi	Pyrogallate	perongilleyo

WORD (x)	EQUIVALENT (y)	WORD (x)	EQUIVALENT (y)
Pyrogallic	perongilleko	Pyrrha	perrhan
Pyrogallol	perongillejin	Pyrrhic	perrhanko
Pyrogenic	peronginko	Pyrrhon	perrhonjn
Pyrognostics	peronginisukosi	Pyrrhonism	perrhonjnmosi
Pyrography	peronganphe	Pyrrhotine	perrhontin
Pyrogravure	peronganworai	Pyrrhotite	perrhontinyo
Pyrolignic	peronlegnko	Pyrrhuloxia	perrhulosia
Pyroligneous	peronlegihunsi	Pyrrhus	perrhusi
Pyrology	peronlogbon	Pyrrole	perronjn
Pyrolusite	peronlusooyo	Pyrrolidine	perronjnjoin
Pyrolysis	peronjinso	Pyruvic	peruwako
Pyromancy	peronmoyesn	Pythagoras	pesigunran
Pyromania	peronmohan	Pythagoreanism	pesigunrainmosi
Pyromantic	peronmoyeko	Pythia	pesia
Pyrometer	peronmuto	Pythaid	pesiajn
Pyromorphite	peronmophanyo	Pythian	pesiahn
Pyrone	peroin	Pythias	pesiase
Pyrope	peronpon	Pythogenesis	pesingnhunso
Pyrophoric	peronphiraiko	Pythogenic	pesinginko
Pyrophosphate	peronphesephayo	Python	pesinle
Pyrophosphoric	peronphosephnraiko	Pythoness	pesinlebo
Pyrophotometer	peronphotnmuto	Pythonic	pesinleko
Pyrophyllite	peronpheweyo	Pyx	posi
Pyrosis	peronso	Pyxides	posijosi
Pyrostat	peronsetnti	Pyxie	posisun
Pyroulfate	peronsnlefanyo	Pyxis	posiso
Pyrosulphate	peronsnlephanyo	Qandahar	kunjnhun
Pyrotechnic	perontokhiniko	Qatar	kuntnran
Pyrotechnics	perontokhinikosi	Qatara	kuntnra
Pyrotic	peronko	Qena	knhun
Pyrotoxin	perontoosia	Qishm	kisumo
Pyroxene	peronsinhun	Qishon	kisoon
Pyroxenite	peronsinhunyo	Qua	kun
Pyroxylin	peronsisejan	Quack1	kunkwe

WORD (x)	EQUIVALENT (y)	WORD (x)	EQUIVALENT (y)
Quack2	kunkwe	Quadroon	kunjoronsi
Quackery	kunkwerai	Quadraphonic	kunjoraphohunko
Quad1	kunjo	Quadrumanous	kunjoraumohunsi
Quad2	kunjo	Quadruped	kunjoraupndie
Quad3	kunjo	Quadruple	kunjoraupon
Quadragesima	kunjoragunsemo	Quadruplet	kunjorauponte
Quadragesimal	kunjoragunsemojn	Quadruplex	kunjorauponsi
Quadrangle	kunjoranigun	Quadruplicate	kunjoraupankoyo
Quadrant	kunjorate	Quaere	kunserai
Quadraphonic	kunjoraphohunko	Quaestor	kunseto
Quadrat	kunjoraiya	Quaff	kunfa
Quadrate	kunjoraiyo	Quag	kungbn
Quadratic	kunjoraiyako	Quagga	kungbngi
Quadrature	kunjoratnrai	Quaggy	kungbngn
Quadrennial	kunjoraihunjo	Quagmire	kungbnmere
Quadrennium	kunjoraihunma	Quahaug	kunhagan
Quadric	kunjoraiko	Quahog	kunhingbi
Quadricentennial	kunjoraikntihunjo	Quaidoresay	kunjnrase
Quadriceps	kunjoraiknposi	Quaigh	kunghn
Quadrifid	kunjoraifijo	Quail1	kunle
Quadriga	kunjoraigan	Quail2	kunle
Quadrilateral	kunjorailetoraijo	Quaiant	kuntoni
Quadrilingual	kunjorailetogunjo	Quake	kunka
Quadrille	kunjoraille	Quaker	kunkasi
Quadrillion	kunjoraillesi	Quaky	kunkase
Quadrinomial	kunjorainmujo	Quale	kunjo
Quadripartite	kunjoraipanteyo	Qualification	kunjofikoyoon
Quadriplegia	kunjoraipojigan	Qualify	kunjofe
Quadrisect	kunjoraiseknte	Qualitative	kunletoyowin
Quadrisyllable	kunjoraisojnranbe	Quality	kunleto
Quadrivalent	kunjoraiwajnso	Quality control	kintnrajo kunleto
Quadrivial	kunjoraiwonjo	Qualm	kunlo
Quadrivium	kunjoraiwonma	Quandary	kudierai
Quadrominium	kunjoronminima		

WORD (x)	EQUIVALENT (y)	WORD (x)	EQUIVALENT (y)
Quandmeme	kudiemimi	Quartile	kunlaron
Quandong	kudiegan	Quarto	kunlakn
Quango	kungnto	Quartz	kunssa
Quant	kuntte	Quartzite	kunssayo
Quanta	kunttesi	Quatziferous	kunssafirosi
Quantal	kunttejo	Quasar	kunsa
Quantic	kuntteko	Quash	kunsia
Quantifier	kunttefesi	Quasi-	kunsio
Quantify	kunttefe	Quaquicentennial	kunsekukntihunjo
Quantimeter	kunttemuto	Quassia	kunssia
Quantitative	kunttetoyowin	Quassin	kunssie
Quantity	kunttetn	Quartem	kunlaran
Quantise	kunttese	Quarter	kubnllarin
Quantum	kunttema	Quatemary	kunllaranrai
Quaquaversal	kunkuwinsejo	Quatemion	kunllarinsi
Quar	kunro	Quatemity	kunllarinto
Quarantine	kunrotehun	Quatrain	kunllarinjn
Quare	kunrai	Quatrefoil	kuntiesnfonjia
Quark1	kurukn	Quattrocento	kunttnraknto
Quark2	kurukn	Quaver	kunwinra
Quarrel	kunrrojo	Quay	kunso
Quarrelsome	kunrrojosoomo	Quayage	kunsogun
Quarrian	kunrainyan	Quayside	kunsoojo
Quarrier	kunraisi	Quean	kunhun
Quarry1	kunrrai	Queasy	kunse
Quarry2	kunrai	Quebec	kunbeki
Quart	kunla	Quebracho	kunbankhin
Quartan	kunlasi	Quechua	kunkhun
Quarte	kunlase	Queen	kuneni
Quarter	kunlarin	Quell	kunllo
Quarterback	kunlarinboki	Quelque	kunlokue
Quarterly	kunlarinlo	Quench	kunkhn
Quartet	kunlate	Quenelle	kunhunllo
Quartic	kunlako	Quentin	kunitin

WORD (x)	EQUIVALENT (y)	WORD (x)	EQUIVALENT (y)
Quercetin	kunraknti	Quid1	kuije
Quercine	kunrakihun	Quid2	kuije
Quercitin	kunrakitin	Quidde	kuijejin
Quercitron	kunrakitiroin	Quiddity	kuijejinto
Quercus	kunraknsi	Quid pro quo	kuije kuo pon
Queretaro	kunraitoro	Quidnune	kuijinahun
Querida	kunraijo	Quiescent	kuiseknti
Querist	kunraisi	Quiet	kuitn
Querl	kunranje	Quieten	kuitnsi
Querulous	kuerojnsi	Quietism	kuitnmosi
Query	kunrai	Quietly	kuitnlo
Queshie	kunsua	Quietude	kuitnjin
Quesnay	kunsan	Quietus	kuitnsi
Quest	kunyo	Quaff	kuifo
Question	kunyoon	Quill	kuillo
Questinable	kunyohunbe	Quillai	kuilloni
Questor	kunyoran	Quillal	kuillojo
Quetta	kuetto	Quiller	kuillosi
Quetzal	kunsuajo	Quillet	kuillote
Quetzalcoatl	kunsualokiti	Quillmes	kuillomosi
Queue	kunsesi	Quilt	kuileto
Quevoulez	kunlesewo	Quim	kuimo
Quezaltonango	kunsejotingan	Quin	kuini
Quezon	kunsejn	Quinary	kuinirai
Quibble	kuiboron	Quinate	kuiniyo
Quiche	kuikhn	Quince	kuinisi
Quiche	kuikhe	Quincuncial	kuinikunknjo
Quick	kuikia	Quincunx	kuinikunsi
Quicken	kuikiani	Quincy	kuinisn
Quickie	kuikiasi	Quindecagon	kuinijinkngun
Quicklime	kuikialemi	Quinine	kuinihun
Quickly	kuikialo	Quinnat	kuinihunya
Quick one	kuikia ihun	Quino	kuinikn
Quickset	kuikiasetopn	Quinoa	kuinikin

WORD (x)	EQUIVALENT (y)	WORD (x)	EQUIVALENT (y)
Quinoid	kuinijo	Quip	kuipn
Quinodine	kuinijohun	Quipter	kuipnseto
Quinoline	kuinijinhun	Quipu	kuipe
Quinone	kuinini	Quire	kuirai
Quinonimine	kuinimini	Quirinal	kuiranjo
Quinonoid	kuininijo	Quirino	kuirain
Quinoxaline	kuinisinlehun	Quirinus	kuiransi
Quinquagenarian	kuinikungbarai	Quirites	kuiraitesi
Quinquagesima	kuinikungbasemo	Quirk	kuirako
Quinquagesimal	kuinikungbasemojn	Quirky	kuirakose
Quinque	kuninikue	Quirt	kuirate
Quinquefoliate	kuinikuefonjiayo	Quisling	kuisoojognni
Quinquennial	kuinikuehunjo	Quist	kuisi
Quiniquennium	kuinikuehunma	Quit	kuita
Quinquereme	kuinikueraimo	Quite	kuitn
Quinquevalent	kuinikuewajnto	Quitch	kuitahun
Quinsy	kuiniso	Quite	kuitn
Quint	kuite	Quito	kuito
Quitain	kuitelu	Quitrent	kuitiranto
Quital	kuitejo	Quits	kuitasi
Quitan	kuiteni	Quittance	kuittnsi
Quitana	kuitehun	Quittor	kuittnran
Quitescent	kuitesiknti	Quitter	kuittnra
Quintessence	kuitesookini	Quiver1	kuiwnsi
Quintet	kuiteto	Quiver2	kuiwnsi
Quintic	kuiteko	Qui vive	kuiwawin
Quintile	kuiteron	Quixotic	kuisetiko
Quintilian	kuiteroin	Quiz	kuisia
Quintillion	kuitellesi	Quizzical	kuisiakojo
Quintin	kuitin	Quo	kuo
Quintuple	kuitnpon	Quod	kuojn
Quintuplet	kuitnponte	Quodlibet	kuojnbeto
Quintuplicate	kuitnpankoyo	Quoin	kuojan
Quinze	kuinise	Quoit	kuoti

WORD (x)	EQUIVALENT (y)	WORD (x)	EQUIVALENT (y)
Quo jure	kuo jorai	Rabble rouser	ranbnrai roosesi
Quoll	kuolle	Rabboni	ranboomi
Quo mo do	kuo mo de	Rabdomance	ranbndemoyesn
Quondam	kuojnma	Rabelais	ranbejnso
Quonset	kuoseto	Rabelaisian	ranbejnsohn
Quorate	kuoraiyo	Rabid	ranbujin
Quorum	kuoranmo	Rabies	ranbusi
Quota	kuote	Raccoon	rankkoon
Quotable	kuoteberon	Race1	ransa
Quotation	kuoteyoon	Race2	ransa
Quote	kuoto	Race3	ransa
Quoth	kuotosi	Racegoer	ransalosi
Quotha	kuotose	Raceme	ransamo
Quotidian	kuotedain	Racemic	ransamuko
Quotient	kuoteto	Racemism	ransamosi
Quo warranto	kuo warraito	Racemize	ransemuse
Ra	ran	Racemose	ransamose
Rabanna	ranbehun	Racer	ransase
Rabat	ranbeti	Rachel	rankhnlo
Rabaul	ranbaun	Rachis	rankhisi
Rabbath	ranbosin	Rachitis	rankhiso
Rabbet	ranbonte	Rachmanism	rankhimoyemosi
Rabbi	ranbo	Racial	ransajo
Rabbinate	ranbojnto	Racialism	ransajomosi
Rabbinic	ranbojnko	Racine	rankihun
Rabbinical	ranbojnkojo	Racing	ransagnni
Rabbinism	ranbojnmosi	Racism	ransamosi
Rabbinist	ranbojnsi	Racist	ransasi
Rabbit	ranbnte	Rack1	ranki
Rabbiter	ranbntesi	Rack2	ranki
Rabbitry	ranbnterai	Rack3	ranki
Rabble	ranbnrai	Racket1	rankiti
Rabble	ranbnrai	Racket2	rankiti
Rabblement	ranbnraimutto	Racketeer	rankitisi

WORD (x)	EQUIVALENT (y)	WORD (x)	EQUIVALENT (y)
Rackety	rankitise	Radiogenic	rangboginko
Rack-rent	ranki reya	Radiogenetics	rangbognhunkosi
Racon	rankin	Radiogram	rangboganmo
Raconteur	rankintosi	Radiograph	rangboganpha
Raccoon	rankoon	Radioimmunoassay	rangboimmuhunkn-
Racequet	rankikunti		soon
Racy	ransase	Radioisotope	rangboisotopon
Rad	rangba	Radiolarian	rangbolerain
Radar	rangbaro	Radiolocation	rangboloknyoon
Raddle	rangbaduo	Radiology	rangbologbon
Radeau	rangbaun	Radiolucent	rangboluknti
Radiac	rangbaka	Radioluminescence	rangbomanaseknsi
Radial	rangbajo	Radiometer	rangbomuto
Radian	rangbainni	Radiomimetic	rangbomimiko
Radiance	rangbainsi	Radiopaque	rangbopankuo
Radiant	rangbaintn	Radiophone	rangbophohun
Radiate	rangbainyo	Radiophonic	rangbphohunko
Radiation	rangbainyoon	Radioscopy	rangbosokipo
Radiator	rangbainyose	Radiosonde	rangbosoonjin
Radical	rangbainko	Radiostrotium	rangbosetnratema
Radicalism	rangbainkomosi	Radiostelegram	rangbosetnratemo
Radicalization	rangbainkoseyoon	Radiotelegraphy	rangbotojnganphe
Radicalize	rangbainkose	Radiotelephone	rangbotojnphohun
Radically	rangbainkojin	Radiorelescope	rangbotojnsokipon
Radicand	rangbainkojo	Radiotherapy	rangbosinranpo
Radicel	rangbainknlo	Radiothorium	rangbosinraima
Radicle	rangbainkuo	Radish	rangbasia
Radii	rangbainn	Radium	rangbama
Radio	rangbo	Radius	rangbaso
Radio-	rangbo	Radix	rangbasn
Radioactive	rangboakntiwin	Radome	rangbamu
Radioactivity	rangboakntiwinto	Radon	rangbasi
Radiod	rangbojo	Radula	rangbajn
Rqadioelement	rangboelemutto	Raeder	ransejnra

WORD (x)	EQUIVALENT (y)	WORD (x)	EQUIVALENT (y)
Raff	ranfan	Railing	railognni
Rafferty	ranfanto	Raillery	railosi
Raffia	ranffia	Railman	railomoye
Raffinate	ranfinyo	Raiment	raimutto
Raffinose	ranfinise	Rain	raise
Raffish	ranfansi	Rainproof	raiseponfin
Raffle	ranfijn	Rainy	raisese
Rafflesia	ranfijnsia	Raise	raiso
Raft	ranfia	Raisin	raisosi
Rafter	ranfiasi	Raising	raisognni
Rag1	rangi	Raison	raisin
Rag2	rangi	Raisonne	raisinhun
Rag3	rangi	Raj	ranjo
Raga	rangin	Raja	ranjon
Ragamuffin	ranginmofia	Rajput	ranjonpn
Rage	rangia	Rajputana	ranjonpntihun
Ragged	rangiade	Rake1	rankuo
Raggedy	rangiadie	Rake2	rankuo
Ragi	rangn	Rake3	rankuo
Raglan	rangbile	Raki	ranki
Ragnarok	ranginiknra	Rakish	rankinisi
Ragout	ranginita	Rakoczy	rankosi
Rag tag	rangi tegn	Raleigh	ranjngan
Ragtime	rangitinmo	Rallentando	ranlletode
Raguel	rangunlo	Ralliform	ranllofon
Ragusa	rangunsi	Ralline	ranllohun
Rahab	ranha	Rally1	ranllose
Raiatia	raintin	Rally2	ranllose
Raible	raibo	Ram	ranmo
Raid	raija	Ram	ranmo
Raid	raija	Ramachandra	ranmukhojnra
Rail1	railo	Ramadan	ranmodian
Rail2	railo	Raman	ranmojn
Rail3	railo	Ramapithecus	ranmopinikosi

WORD (x)	EQUIVALENT (y)	WORD (x)	EQUIVALENT (y)
Ramayana	ranmojnna	Ramshackle	ranmsuekuo
Ramble	ranmosia	Ramson	ranmsin
Rambler	ranmosiasi	Ramtil	ranmtira
Rambling	ranmosiagnni	Ramulose	ranmuyase
Ramboillet	ranmobounllo	Ramus	ranmuya
Rambunctious	ranmobountisi	Rana	rainba
Rambutan	ranmobaunte	Ranarium	rainraima
Ramee	ranmosi	Rance	rainsi
Ramekin	ranmokise	Ranch	rainkhun
Rament	ranminite	Rancher	rainkhunsi
Ramganga	ranmugungan	Ranchero	rainkhnra
Ramie	ranmusi	Rancho	rainkhunkn
Ramife	ranmufn	Rancid	rainkanjn
Ramification	ranmufikoyyon	Rancidity	rainkanjntn
Ramiform	ranmufoonmo	Rancor	rainkansi
Ramify	ranmufe	Rancour	rainkanse
Ramillies	ranmullosi	Rand	raindan
Rammish	ranmoosi	Randem	raindamo
Ramon	ranmeni	Random	raindemo
Ramose	ranmoya	Randy	raindesi
Ramous	ranmooya	Ranee	rainse
Rammish	ranmosi	Range	raingini
Ramp	ranmpn	Rangeley	rainginilosi
Rampage	ranmpngun	Ranger	rainginisi
Rampancy	ranmpnsn	Rangiron	raingiron
Rampant	ranmpnte	Rangoon	Raingoon
Rampart	ranmpante	Rangy	rainginse
Rampike	ranmpoku	Rani	raini
Rampion	ranmpnse	Rank1	rainkn
Rampur	ranmpnra	Rank2	rainkn
Ramrod	raimorojin	Ranke	rainknse
Ramsay	ranmso	Ranker	rainknsi
Ramsgate	ranmsogiyo	Rankine	rainknhun
Ramses	ranmsesi	Rankle	rainkuo

WORD (x)	EQUIVALENT (y)	WORD (x)	EQUIVALENT (y)
Ranoid	rainjo	Rapt	raipnti
Ransack	rainsaka	Rapti	raipnti
Ransom	rainsan	Raptor	raipntiran
Rant	rainto	Raptorial	raipntiranjo
Ranunculaceous	ranunkuosuwa	Rapture	raipntira
Ranunculus	ranunkuosi	Rapturous	raipntirasi
Rap1	raipe	Rare1	raira
Rap2	raipe	Rare2	raira
Rap3	raipe	Rarebit	rairabnte
Rapacious	raipnkisi	Raree	rairase
Rapacity	raipnkitn	Rarefaction	rairafanknyoon
Rapallo	raipnllo	Rarefy	rairafe
Rape1	raipn	Rarely	rairalo
Rape2	raipn	Rareripe	rairaraipon
Rape3	raipn	Raring	rairagnni
Raphe	raiphn	Raritan	rairatin
Raphide	raiphnji	Rarity	rairatn
Rapid	raipojn	Rarotonga	rairotingan
Rapidan	raipojina	Ras	raise
Rapidity	raipojntn	Rasbora	raisebua
Rapier	raipnsi	Rascal	raisekn
Rapine	raipnhun	Rascality	raisekntn
Rapist	raipnsi	Rascally	raiseknjjn
Raploch	raiponki	Ras da shan	raise jo sun
Rappa	raippn	Rase	raise
Rappahannock	raippnhunki	Rash1	raisun
Rapparee	raippnran	Rash2	raisun
Rappee	raippnse	Rasher	raisunsi
Rappel	raippnlo	Raskolnik	raisekikin
Rapper	raippesi	Rasmussen	raisemusoon
Rapport	raipinta	Rason	raisujo
Rapporteur	raipinteran	Rasorial	raisuranle
Rapprochement	raiponkhnmutto	Raps	raisepn
Rapscallion	raipnsekollsi	Raspatory	raisepnra

519

WORD (x)	EQUIVALENT (y)	WORD (x)	EQUIVALENT (y)
Rasputin	raisepnti	Rating	raiyognni
Raspy	raisepo	Ratio	raiyato
Rasselas	raisoojose	Ratiocinant	raiyatokinte
Rastafarian	raisetofanrain	Ratiocinate	raiyatokinyo
Raster	raiseto	Ratiocinative	raiyatokinyowin
Rasure	raisnra	Ratioing	raiyatognni
Rat	raite	Ration	raiyoon
Ratable	raitebe	Rational	raiyoonjo
Ratafia	raitefin	Rationale	raiyoonjn
Ratak	raiteka	Rationalism	raiyoonjomosi
Ratal	raitejo	Rationality	raiyoonleto
Rattan	raitesi	Rationalization	raiyoonjoseyoon
Ratany	raitese	Rationalize	raiyoonjose
Ratapian	raitepolu	Rations	raiyoonsi
Ratatattat	raitetesi	Ratite	raiteyo
Ratatouille	raitetellesi	Ratline	raitelehun
Ratbaggery	raitebogbira	Ratoon	raitoo
Ratch	raitekn	Rat race	raite ransa
Ratchet	raiteknti	Rats	raitesi
Rate1	raiyo	Rattan	raittesi
Rate2	raiyo	Ratteen	raitini
Rateable	raiyobe	Ratten	raittin
Ratel	raiyojn	Ratter	raittnra
Rater	raiyosi	Rattish	raittese
Rath	raisa	Rattle	raittoron
Ratha	raisan	Rattler	raittoronsi
Rathaus	raisansi	Rattling	raittorongnni
Rathe	raisia	Rattly	raitelo
Rathenau	raisiahun	Ratton	raittesi
Rather	raisasi	Ratty	raittese
Ratherest	raisasesion	Raucle	raikesi
Rathskeller	raisaseknjjn	Raucous	raikesi
Ratification	raitefeknyoon	Raunchy	raikhese
Ratify	raitefe	Rauwolffia	raiwnfan

WORD (x)	EQUIVALENT (y)	WORD (x)	EQUIVALENT (y)
Ravage	raiwingun	Re1	re
Rave	raiwin	Re2	rai
Ravel	raiwinlo	Re3	ran
Ravelin	raiwinlosi	Reach	rekhn
Ravelment	raiwinlomutto	Reacquaint	rekikuntoni
Raven	raiwini	React	reaknti
Ravenala	raiwinijn	Reactance	reakntisi
Ravening	raiwinignni	Reaction	reakntiyon
Ravenna	raiwinihun	Reactionary	reakntiyonrai
Ravenous	raiwinisi	Reactivate	reakntiweyo
Raver	raiwinra	Reactive	reakntiwin
Ravi	raiwi	Reactor	reakntira
Ravin	raiwisi	Read	regbo
Ravine	raiwihun	Readable	regbobe
Raving	raiwignni	Reader	regbosi
Ravioli	raiwile	Readership	regbosisunpn
Ravish	raiwisua	Readily	regboinlo
Ravishing	raiwisuagnni	Readiness	regboinsi
Ravishment	raiwisuamutto	Reading	regbognni
Raw	ranwi	Readjust	regbojuse
Raw deal	ranwi jinle	Ready	regboin
Rawalpindi	raiwijopinjo	Ready-made	regboin majain
Rawhide	ranwihijin	Read money	regbo menisan
Rawlinson	ranwijansi	Reagan	regini
Rax	ransia	Reagent	reginte
Ray1	ranse	Reak	rekin
Ray2	ranse	Real1	reinjo
Ray3	ranse	Real2	reinjo
Rayon	ransesi	Realgar	reinjogan
Raze	raise	Realia	reinjosi
Razee	raisesi	Realign	reinjognni
Razor	raiseran	Realism	reinjomosi
Razz	raissia	Realistic	reinjosuko
Razzia	raissiasi	Reality	reinleto

WORD (x)	EQUIVALENT (y)	WORD (x)	EQUIVALENT (y)
Realization	reinjoseyoon	Rebuff	rebufe
Realize	reinjose	Rebuke	rebukn
Reallocate	reinlloknyo	Rebus	rebusa
Really	reinjosi	Rebut	rebute
Realm	reinjoma	Rebutter	rebuttesi
Realschule	reinjosekhnran	Recalcitrant	rekojnkitite
Realtor	reinjotnra	Recalesce	rekojnsekn
Realty	reinjotn	Recalescence	rekojnseknsi
Ream	reinmo	Recall	rekojjn
Reamer	reinmosi	Recamier	rekomusi
Reap	reinpn	Recant	rekotn
Reaper	reinpnsi	Recap	rekopn
Reappear	reinpnran	Recapitalize	rekopntejose
Reapply	reinponlo	Recapitulate	rekopnteleyo
Rear1	reran	Recapitulation	rekopnteleyoon
Rear2	reran	Recapitulatory	rekopnteleyorai
Rearguard	rerangungba	Reception	rekopntiyoon
Rearguard action	akntiyon rerangungba	Recapture	rekopntirai
Rearm	rearaimu	Recast	rekosoto
Rearranage	rearraigini	Recode	rekidie
Reason	resnle	Receipt	reknpiti
Reasonable	resnlebe	Receive	reknwin
Reasoner	resnlesi	Receiver	reknwinsi
Reave	rewain	Receivership	reknwinsunpn
Rebate1	rebote	Recense	reknse
Rebate2	rebote	Recension	reknsoon
Rebec	rebeki	Recent	reknti
Rebecca	rebekko	Recept	reknpo
Rebel	rebejn	Receptacle	reknpokun
Rebellion	rebejnrosi	Reception	reknpoyoon
Rebellious	rebejnrose	Receptionist	reknpoyoonsi
Reboant	reboote	Receptive	reknpowin
Rebound	rebounjn	Recess	reknso
Rebozo	rebooso	Recession	reknsoon

WORD (x)	EQUIVALENT (y)	WORD (x)	EQUIVALENT (y)
Recessional	reknsoonjo	Recognizance	rekiginisesi
Recessive	reknsowin	Recognizee	rekiginisise
Rechabite	rekhobeyo	Recoil	rekilo
Recheat	rekhnte	Recollect	rekijjokn
Recherché	rekhnrakho	Recollection	rekijjoknyoon
Recidivist	rekijowasi	Recombination	rekimbahunyoon
Recidivous	rekijowase	Recommend	rekimmudan
Recife	rekife	Recommendation	rekimmudanyoon
Recipe	rekipon	Recommendatory	rekimmudanyorai
Recipience	rekiponsi	Recommit	rekimmutn
Recipient	rekiponto	Recompense	rekimpnsan
Reciprocal	rekiponrajn	Recompose	rekimpinse
Reciprocate	rekiponrayo	Reconcentrado	rekinkntnradie
Reciprocating	rekiponrayognni	Reconcentrate	rekinkntiraiyo
Reciprocation	rekiponrayoon	Reconcile	rekinkijo
Reciprocatory	rekiponrayorai	Reconcileable	rekinkijobe
Reciprocity	rekiponrato	Reconciliation	rekinkijotion
Recital	rekitojo	Recondite	rekindiyo
Recitation	rekitoyoon	Recondition	rekindiyoon
Recitative	rekitoyowin	Reconnaissance	rekinhunsoonsi
Recite	rekito	Reconsider	rekinsoojosi
Reck	rekin	Reconsign	rekinsoogan
Reckless	rekinlabo	Reconstitute	rekinsetintuyo
Reckon	rekinse	Reconstitution	rekinsetintuyoon
Reckoner	rekinsesi	Reconstruct	rekinsetnran
Reckoning	rekinsegnni	Reconsruction	rekinsetnranyoon
Reclaim	rekanlemo	Reconvey	rekinwinse
Reclamation	rekanlemoyoon	Recopy	recipe
Recline	rekihun	Record	rekigba
Recluse	rekuose	Recorder	rekigbasi
Reclusion	rekuosoon	Recount	rekaleyo
Reclusive	rekuosewin	Recountal	rekaleyojo
Recognize	rekiginise	Recoup	rekilepo
Recognition	rekiginiyoon	Recover	rekiwnra

WORD (x)	EQUIVALENT (y)	WORD (x)	EQUIVALENT (y)
Recoverable	rekiwnrabe	Recusant	rekunsete
Recovery	rekiwnrai	Recusation	rekunseyoon
Recreant	reknrante	Recucle	rekunkuo
Recreate	reknranyo	Red	reje
Recreation	reknranyoon	Redact	rejekn
Recrement	reknramutto	Redaction	rejeknyoon
Recriminate	rekoramihunyo	Redan	rejeni
Recriminiation	rekoramihunyoon	Redden	rejesi
Recrudesce	rekorajosekn	Reddle	rejeduo
Recrudescence	rekorajoseknsi	Redendum	rejejnma
Recruit	rekorati	Rede	rejn
Rectal	retojo	Redeem	rejnmu
Rectangle	retonigun	Redeemer	rejnmusi
Rectification	retofikoyoon	Redemptible	rejnmpnyobe
Rectifier	retofesi	Redemption	rejnmpnyoon
Rectify	retofe	Redemptor	rejnmpnran
Rectilinear	retolehunran	Redingote	redigonto
Rectitude	retotujin	Redound	redeinjn
Recto	retokn	Redowa	redewain
Rector	retoran	Reduce	redisi
Rectory	retorai	Reductase	redikitise
Rectum	retoma	Reductio	redikitio
Rectus	retosi	Reduction	redikitiyoon
Recubation	rekunbeyoon	Redress	rediraiso
Reculet	rekuntn	Redundant	redijointn
Recuperate	rekunpnrayo	Redundance	redijoinsi
Recuperation	rekunpnrayoon	Redundancy	redijoinsn
Recuperative	rekunpnrayowin	Reduplicate	redipankoyo
Recuperator	rekunpnrayoran	Reduplication	redipankoyoon
Recur	rekunra	Ree	ree
Recurrence	rekunrraisi	Reedmace	rejnmoeding
Recurrent	rekunrraito	Reedling	reejngnni
Recurring	rekunrraignni	Reeducate	reejnkoyo
Recurvate	rekunraweyo	Reef1	reffo

WORD (x)	EQUIVALENT (y)	WORD (x)	EQUIVALENT (y)
Reef2	reffo	Reflex	refonjnsi
Reefer	reffosi	Reflight	refologbe
Reek	rekon	Refluent	refoluto
Reeky	rekonse	Reform	refoonmo
Reel	relo	Reformation	refoonmuyoon
Rest	resin	Reformatory	refoonmoyorai
Reevel	rewosi	Refract	refankn
Reave2	rewosi	Refraction	refanknyoon
Reave3	rewosi	Refractometer	refanknmuto
Ref1	refi	Refractory	refanknrai
Ref2	refi	Refragable	refangbibe
Refect	refnko	Refrain1	refansi
Refection	refnkoyoon	Refrain2	refansi
Refectory	refnkoyorai	Refresh	refesisua
Refer	refiro	Refresher	refesisuasi
Referee	refirose	Refreshment	refesisuamutto
Referece	refirosi	Refrigerant	refangnraitn
Refrend	refirojn	Refrigerate	refangnraiyo
Referendum	refirojnma	Refrigerator	refangnraiyoran
Referent	refirotn	Refrigeratory	refangnraiyorai
Referral	refiranjo	Refrigency	refanginsn
Refill	refijjo	Reft	refia
Refine	refinni	Refuel	refunna
Refined	refinnide	Refuge	refungba
Refinement	refinnimutto	Refugee	refungbasi
Refiner	refinnirai	Refulgent	refujnte
Refit	refito	Refusal	refunsijo
Reflate	refanyo	Refuse1	refunsi
Reflect	refonjnko	Refuse2	refunsi
Reflection	refonjnkoyoon	Refusenik	refunsikin
Reflective	refonjnkowin	Refulgence	refunjnginsi
Reflectivity	refonjnkowintn	Refulgent	refunjnginto
Reflector	refonjnkosi	Refund	refunjn
Reflet	refonjnte	Regain	regini

WORD (x)	EQUIVALENT (y)	WORD (x)	EQUIVALENT (y)
Regal	regijo	Register	regiseto
Regale	regijn	Registered	regisetode
Regalia	regijoin	Registrant	regisetoraitn
Regality	regileto	Registrar	regisetoran
Regan	regisi	Registration	regisetoraiyoon
Regard	regigba	Registry	regisetorai
Regardant	regigbate	Regius	regisi
Regarding	regigbagnni	Reglet	regite
Regardless	regigbalabo	Regma	regima
Regatta	regitto	Regnal	reginijo
Regelate	regnleyo	Regnant	reignite
Regelation	regnleyoon	Regnauld	reginijon
Regency	regnsn	Regnier	reginisi
Regent	regnte	Regorge	regonragun
Regeneracy	regnhunraisn	Regrade	regandie
Regenerate	regnhunraiyo	Regrate	regante
Regeneration	regnhunraiyoon	Regress	regiraiso
Regenerator	regnhunrairan	Regression	regiraisoon
Regent	regnto	Regressive	regiraisowin
Reggae	regbede	Regret	regiraro
Regicide	regikeku	Regrettable	regirarobe
Regillus	regillosn	Regroup	regonpo
Regime	regbimo	Regrow	regonwin
Regimen	regimini	Regula	regijn
Regiment	regimutto	Regular	regijnra
Regimental	regimuttojo	Regularity	regijnraitn
Regimentation	regimuttoyoon	Regularize	regijnraise
Regin	regin	Regularly	regijnralo
Regina	regibo	Regulate	regijnyo
Reginal	regibojn	Regulation	regijnyoon
Region	regbile	Regulator	regijnyoran
Regional	regbilejo	Regulatory	regijnyorai
Regionalism	regbilejomosi	Regulus	regijnsi
Regisseur	regiseran	Regurgitate	regiraiteyo

WORD (x)	EQUIVALENT (y)	WORD (x)	EQUIVALENT (y)
Regurgitation	regiraiteyoon	Reinsure	reinisurai
Rehabilitate	rehabejntoyo	Reinvent	reiniwinti
Rehash	rehasia	Reinvest	reiniwinsn
Rehearsal	reheransojn	Reinwald	reiniwejon
Rehearse	reheranso	Reis	reisu
Reheat	rehesun	Reise	reisun
Rehnquist	rehnkunsi	Reissue	reisesun
Rehoboam	rehinboma	Reiterate	reiteraiyo
Rei	rei	Reiterative	reiteraiyowin
Reich	reikhn	Rejane	rejanhun
Reichsland	reikhnsnledain	Reject	rejnkn
Reichsrat	reikhnsnrato	Rejectamenta	rejnknminiya
Reichstag	reikhnsnto	Rejection	rejnknyoon
Reid	reijo	Rejoice	rejinyosi
Reif	reifn	Rejoin1	rejosi
Reify	reife	Rejoin2	rejosi
Reign	reigini	Rejoinder	rejosijnra
Reimburse	reimbusan	Rejuvenate	rejowiniyo
Reimplantation	reimpantnyoon	Rejuvenesce	rejowinisekn
Reimpression	reimpesisoon	Rejuvenescence	rejowiniseknsi
Reims	reimosin	Relabel	rejobejn
Rein	reini	Relape	rejopnse
Reinach	reinikho	Relate	rejoyo
Reincamate	reinikosnyo	Related	rejoyode
Reincamation	reinikosnyoon	Relation	rejoyoon
Reindeer	reinijnra	Relationship	rejoyoonsunpn
Reinfecta	reinifnkyo	Relative	rejoyowin
Reinforce	reinifoonsi	Relativity	rejoyowinto
Reinforcement	reinifoonsimutto	Relax	rejosia
Reinhardt	reinihagban	Relaxation	rejosiayoon
Reinhold	reinihinjo	Relay	rejose
Reins	reinise	Re-lay	re leyin
Reinstall	reinisetnran	Release	rejnnasi
Reinstate	reinisetnyo	Relegate	rejngiyo

WORD (x)	EQUIVALENT (y)	WORD (x)	EQUIVALENT (y)
Relent	rejnsa	Remagen	remogini
Relentless	rejnsalabo	Remain	remora
Re-let	re-jntn	Remainder	remoraijna
Relevant	rejnwinte	Remains	remoraisi
Reliable	rejnnabe	Reman	remoye
Reliance	rejnnasi	Remand	remodain
Reliant	rejnnate	Remanence	remoyunsi
Relic	rejnko	Remark	remurokn
Relict	rejnkyo	Remarkable	remuroknbe
Relief	rejnfin	Remarque	remurakue
Relier	rejnra	Remblal	rembonjo
Relieve	rejnwini	Rembrandt	rembaunte
Relieve	rejnwinkn	Remediable	remujiabe
Religieuse	rejnginiwase	Remedial	remujiajo
Religieux	rejnginieasi	Remediless	remujialabo
Religion	rejngnsin	Remedy	remujia
Religionism	rejngnsinmosi	Remember	remumora
Religiousity	rejngnsinto	Remembrance	remumoraise
Religious	rejngnsinsi	Remembrance	remumoraisi
Relinquish	rejnkunsn	Remix	remusia
Reliquary	rejnkunrai	Remind	reminijin
Relique	rejnkue	Remington	reminigntin
Reliquiae	rejnkusi	Reminisce	reminiseknsi
Relish	rejnsia	Reminiscent	reminiseknti
Relive	rejnwin	Remise	remuse
Reload	relogbi	Remiss	remusin
Relocate	reloknyo	Remissible	remusinbe
Reluctance	rekukntesi	Remission	remusinse
Reluctant	reluknte	Remit	remutn
Reluctivity	reluknwinto	Remittee	remuttnse
Relucuit	reluknti	Remittance	remuttnsi
Relume	relumana	Remittent	remuttnto
Rely	rejina	Remitter	remuttnsi
Rem	remo	Remnant	reminitn

WORD (x)	EQUIVALENT (y)	WORD (x)	EQUIVALENT (y)
Remodel	remodiejo	Renascent	resunknti
Remonetize	remenisanse	Renationalize	reheyoonjose
Remonstrance	remeniseransi	Rencontre	rekntiran
Remonstrant	remeniseraitn	Reencounter	reenkaleyosi
Remonstrate	remeniseraiyo	Rend	rejn
Remonstration	remeniseraiyoon	Render	rejnra
Remonstrative	remeniseraiyowin	Rendezvous	rejnrajowa
Remonta	remenito	Rendition	rejntosi
Remontant	remenitote	Rendeva	rejnwaki
Remontoir	remenitorai	Rene	rehun
Remora	remora	Renegade	rehungijin
Remorse	remurase	Renege	rehungn
Remote	remotie	Renew	rehunwajo
Remotion	remosunsi	Renewal	rehunwajo
Remoulade	remujodie	Renewed	rehunwade
Remount	remounte	Renfrew	rehifanran
Removable	remosunbe	Reni	rehi
Removal	remosunjo	Reniform	rehifonmo
Remove	remosun	Rennin	rehisi
Removed	remosunde	Renitent	rehitinto
Remscheid	remosikhnjo	Rennet	rehihunte
Remsen	remusesi	Renounce	reniunso
Remuda	remujo	Renovate	reniunweyo
Remunerate	remuhunraiyo	Rensselaerite	resoonleraiyo
Remuneration	remuhunraiyoon	Rent1	reya
Remunerative	remuhunraiyowin	Rent2	reya
Remus	remosi	Rent3	reya
Ren	rehun	Rental	reyajo
Renaisessance	rehunsoonsi	Rent-boy	reya-buo
Renal	rehunjo	Renter	reyasi
Rename	rehemo	Rente	reyun
Renan	rehunsi	Rentier	reyunsi
Renard	rehungba	Renunciation	renkunsoyoon
Renascence	resunknsi	Reorganize	reorogbnse

WORD (x)	EQUIVALENT (y)	WORD (x)	EQUIVALENT (y)
Rep1	repn	Repine	repohun
Rep2	repn	Replacement	repanknmutto
Repack	repanki	Replay	repansie
Repackage	repankigun	Repleader	repojnbesi
Repaint	repantoni	Replenish	repojnnase
Repair1	repnra	Replete	repojnte
Repair2	repnra	Replevin	repojnwon
Repairman	repnramoye	Replevy	repojnwin
Repand	repnjn	Replica	repojnko
Reparable	repnrabe	Replicate	repojnkoyo
Reparation	repnrayoon	Replication	repojnkoyoon
Repartee	repantese	Reply	reponlo
Repartition	repanteyoon	Repoint	repintoni
Repast	repansin	Repondez s ll vdus plait	reponjnse sajjnwasi
Repatency	repantinsi		
Repatriate	repantaraiyo	Report	repinto
Repay	repanyio	Reportage	repintogun
Repeal	repnjo	Reporter	repintosi
Repeat	repnti	Repose1	repinse
Repeater	repntisi	Repose2	repinse
Repechage	repnkhogn	Reposit	repinseto
Repel	repnlo	Repository	repinsetorai
Repellent	repnlloto	Repossess	repinseso
Repent	repetun	Repousse	repinsuwa
Repentance	repetunsi	Repot	repinte
Repentant	repetuntn	Repplier	reponlosi
Repercussion	repnrakunsosi	Reprehend	repesihejn
Repercussive	repnrakunsowin	Represent1	repesiseto
Repertoire	repnratoran	Represent2	repesiseto
Repertory	repnratorai	Representation	repesisetoyoon
Repetend	repntijo	Representative	repesisetowin
Repetition	repntiyoon	Repression	repesisoon
Repetitious	repntitesi	Repressive	repesisowin
Repetitive	repntitewin	Reprieve	repanwini

WORD (x)	EQUIVALENT (y)	WORD (x)	EQUIVALENT (y)
Reprimand	repnranmodain	Reputable	reputobe
Reprint	repante	Reputation	reputoyoon
Reprisal	repnrasejo	Repute	repute
Reprise	repnrase	Request	rekunyo
Repro	repon	Requiem	rekunmini
Reproach	reponkhn	Requiescat	rekunsikoti
Reprobate	repongbiyo	Require	rekunran
Reprobation	repongbiyoon	Requirement	rekunranmutto
Reprobative	repongbiyowin	Requisite	rekunseyo
Reprocess	reponknso	Requisition	rekunseyoon
Reprocessed	reponknsode	Requital	rekuntajo
Reproduce	repondikn	Requite	rekuntan
Reproducer	repondiknsi	Reradiation	reranjnnayoon
Reproduction	repondiknyoon	Reran	rerana
Reporogram	reponganmo	Reredos	rerejnna
Reprography	reponganphe	Reread	reregbo
Reproof	reponfin	Reremouse	reremosio
Reprove	reponwin	Resaca	reseko
Reptant	repititn	Resind	resekin
Reptile	repitiron	Rescissible	resekisoobe
Reptilian	repitiroin	Rescission	resekisoosi
Republic	repubeko	Rescissory	resekisoorai
Republican	repubekohn	Rescript	resekoraipn
Republicanism	repubekohnmosi	Rescue	resekuo
Republicanize	repubekohnse	Research	resetn
Republication	repubekoyoon	Reseat	resehun
Republish	repubekosi	Resect	reseknte
Repudiate	repujnnayo	Resection	resekntesi
Repudiation	repujnnayoon	Reseda	resejn
Repugnance	repoginisi	Resedaceous	resejnsuwa
Repugnant	repuginite	Resell	reseta
Repulse	repulesn	Resemblance	resembajosi
Repulsion	repulesnsi	Resemble	resembajo
Repulsive	repulesnwin	Resent	resesita

WORD (x)	EQUIVALENT (y)	WORD (x)	EQUIVALENT (y)
Resentment	resesitamutto	Resinous	resoonsi
Reserpine	reserapohun	Resiny	resoonse
Reservation	reserawinyoon	Resist	resoosi
Reserve	reserawin	Resistace	resoositn
Reserved	reserawinde	Resistant	resoosite
Reservist	reserawinsi	Resistencia	resoosikin
Reservoir	reserawnrai	Resistible	resoosibe
Reset	reseton	Resistive	resoosiwin
Resettle	resetonron	Resistivity	resoosiwinto
Resgesta	resignseto	Resistless	resoosilabo
Reshape	resuepo	Resistor	resoosira
Reship	resunpn	Resjudikata	resijogbonknti
Reshipment	resunpnmutto	Resit	resosi
Reside	resoojo	Resnatron	resntnron
Residence	resoojosi	Resoluble	resinlebe
Residency	resoojosn	Resolute	resinleyo
Resident	resoojotn	Resolution	resinleyoon
Residential	resoojotnjo	Resolve	resinlewin
Residentiary	resoojotnrai	Resolved	resinlewinde
Residual	resooduosi	Resolvent	resinlewinta
Residuary	resoodurai	Resonance	resosesi
Residue	resooduo	Resonant	resoseto
Residuum	resooduoma	Resonate	resosetn
Resign	resoogan	Resonator	resosetnra
Re-sign	re-soogan	Resorb	resinra
Resignation	resooganyoon	Resorcinol	resinrakinjin
Resile	resoojn	Resort	resinrate
Resilence	resoojnnasi	Re-sort	re-sinrate
Resilient	resoojnnatn	Resound	rersojoin
Resin	resoon	Resounding	resojoingnni
Resinate	resoonyo	Resource	resoorasi
Resiniferous	resoonfirosi	Respect	resipnto
Resinography	resoonganphe	Respectable	resipntobe
Resinoid	resoonjo	Respecting	resipntognni

WORD (x)	EQUIVALENT (y)	WORD (x)	EQUIVALENT (y)
Respective	resipntowin	Restrainer	resetnresi
Respectively	resipntowinlo	Restraint	resetnreyo
Respirable	resiporaibe	Restrict	resetnran
Respiration	resiporaiyosi	Restricted	resetnrande
Respirator	resiporaiyoran	Restriction	resetnranyoon
Respiratory	resiporaiyorai	Restrictive	resetnranwin
Respire	resiporai	Restyle	resetnraron
Respite	resipotn	Result	resnjia
Resplendence	resipojndansi	Resultant	resnjiate
Resplendent	resipojndanto	Resume	resumo
Resplendid	resipojndanjo	Resume	resuma
Respond	resiponjn	Resumption	resumposi
Respondent	resiponjnto	Resupinate	resupohunyo
Response	resiponse	Resupine	resupohun
Responser	resiponsesi	Resurface	resurafansi
Responsible	resiponseberon	Resurge	resurale
Responsion	resiponsoon	Resurgence	resuralesi
Responsive	resiponsewin	Resurgent	resuraleto
Responsory	resiponserai	Resurrect	resurrekn
Rest1	resin	Resurrection	resurreknyoon
Rest2	resin	Resurrectionary	resurreknyoonrai
Restart	resitete	Resurrectionist	resurreknyoonsi
Restate	resetnyo	Resuscitate	resusikitiyo
Restaurant	resinraite	Resuscitation	resusikitiyoon
Restaurateur	resinraitoran	Reszke	resuekn
Restiform	resinfoonmo	Ret	rete
Restitution	resintuyoon	Retable	reteberon
Restive	resinwin	Retail	retele
Restless	resinlabo	Retailer	retelesi
Restock	resetoki	Retain	retelu
Restoration	resetoranyoon	Retainer	retelusi
Restorative	resetoranwin	Retake	retekn
Restore	resetoran	Retaliate	raitejiayo
Restrain	resetnre	Retaliation	raitejiayoran

WORD (x)	EQUIVALENT (y)	WORD (x)	EQUIVALENT (y)
Retard	retigba	Retiree	retinrase
Retarded	retigbade	Retirement	retinramutto
Retch	retosi	Retort1	retorate
Rete	reto	Retort2	retorate
Retell	retojjn	Retortion	retorayoon
Retem	retima	Retouch	retokhan
Retene	retinsi	Retrace	retnresi
Retent	retinyo	Retract	retnre
Retention	retinyoon	Retractile	retnretiron
Retentive	retinyowin	Retractive	retnrewin
Retentively	retinyowinto	Retral	retnrejo
Retexture	retnsoran	Retread	retasijn
Rethink	resinki	Retreat	retasite
Rethondes	resinjosi	Retrench	retasinkho
Retiarius	retiraisi	Retrenchment	retasinkhomutto
Retiary	retirai	Retribution	retetaibeyoon
Reticence	retiknsi	Retributive	reteraibeyowin
Reticent	retiknti	Retrieval	reteraiwinjo
Reticle	retikun	Retrieve	reteraiwin
Reticulate	retikunyo	Retriever	reteraiwinsi
Reticulation	retikunyoon	Retro-	retnra
Reticule	retikunjn	Retroact	retnraknti
Reticulum	retikunjnma	Retroactive	retnrakntiwin
Retie	retinso	Retrocede	retnraknjin
Retina	retihun	Retrocession	retraknsoon
Retinaculum	retihunkunma	Retrochoir	retnrakhinro
Retinene	retinini	Retrofit	retnrafito
Retinite	retihunyo	Retroflex	retnrafonjnse
Retinitis	retihunso	Retroflexion	retnrafonjnsesi
Retinol	retihunjin	Retrograde	retnragandie
Retinoscopy	retihunsokipo	Retrogress	retnragiraiso
Retinue	retihunse	Retrogression	retnragiraisosi
Retire	retinra	Retrogressive	retnragbisisowin
Retired	retinrade	Retrolental fibroplasia	retnrajntojo fibonpansia

WORD (x)	EQUIVALENT (y)	WORD (x)	EQUIVALENT (y)
Retrorocket	retnraronkiti	Revere	rewnsin
Retroise	retnrase	Reverence	rewnsinsi
Retrospect	retnrasepnko	Reverend	rewnsinjn
Retrospection	retnrasepnkosi	Reverent	rewnsinto
Retrospective	retnrasepnkowin	Reverential	rewnsintojo
Retroussage	retnrasingun	Reverie	rewnsinse
Retroversion	retnrawinsoon	Revers	rewinsi
Retum	retunrai	Reversal	rewinsojn
Retumable	retunraibe	Reverse	rewinso
Retuse	retusn	Reversible	rewinsobe
Reuben	rebejn	Reversing light	leghe rewinsognni
Reuchlin	rekhejan	Reversion	rewinsoon
Reunion	reenise	Reversional	rewinsoonjo
Reunionism	reenisemosi	Reversionary	rewinsoonrai
Reunite	reenito	Reversioner	rewinsoonsi
Reuterdahl	retnrajo	Reverso	rewinsoo
Reuters	retnraso	Revert	rewinto
Reuther	resirai	Revest	rewinsn
Rev.	rewin	Revet	rewinti
Revalue	rewapoin	Revetment	rewintimutto
Revamp	rewampe	Review	rewowin
Reveal	rewnwo	Reviewal	rewowinjo
Revealment	rewinwojomutto	Reviewer	rewowinsi
Reveille	rewanille	Revile	rewojn
Revel	rewnwo	Revillagigedo	rewojnragndie
Revelation	rewnwoyoon	Revisal	rewosejn
Revelationist	rewnwoyoonsi	Revise	rewose
Revelator	rewnworan	Revision	rewosesi
Revelry	rewnworai	Revisionism	rewosesimosi
Revenant	rewnnitn	Revisit	rewoseto
Revenge	rewnnigba	Revisory	rewoserai
Revenue	rewnnise	Revital	rewintnjo
Reverberate	rewnraigbanyo	Revitalize	rewintnjose
Reverbratory	rewnraigbanyorai	Revival	rewinwajn

WORD (x)	EQUIVALENT (y)	WORD (x)	EQUIVALENT (y)
Revivalism	rewinwajnmosi	Rhaetia	rhaiseto
Revivalist	rewinwajnsi	Rhaetian	rhaisetohun
Revive	rewinwa	Rhaetic	rhaisetoka
Revivify	rewinwafe	Rhamnaceous	rhaiminasuwa
Reviviscence	rewinwaseknsi	Rhapsodist	rhaipnsodunsi
Reviviscent	rewinwasekoti	Rhapsodize	rhaipnsodunse
Revocable	rewinkobe	Rhapsody	rhaipnsodun
Revocation	rewnkoyoon	Ryatany	rhaitesi
Revoice	rewnso	Rhea	rheni
Revoke	rewnko	Rhein	rhenisi
Revolt	rewnjia	Rheingold	rhenigondan
Revolting	rewnjiagnni	Rhema	rhemo
Revolute	rewnjnwe	Rhematic	rhemuko
Revolution	rewnjnyoon	Rhenish	rhenise
Revolutionary	rewnleyoonrai	Rhenium	rhenima
Revolutionize	rewnleyoonse	Rheo	rhein
Revolve	rewnjnwa	Rheobase	rheinbooso
Revolver	rewnjnwasi	Rheology	rhinlogbon
Revue	rewesi	Rhemeter	rhinmuto
Revulsion	rewelesoon	Rheoscope	rheinsokipon
Reward	rewegba	Rheostat	rheinsetnti
Rewarding	rewegbagnni	Rheotaxis	rheintesanso
Rewind	rewojin	Rheotropism	rheintnrapnmosi
Reword	rewijo	Rhesus	rhesesi
Rework	rewinsise	Rhetor	rhetoran
Rewrite	rewanto	Rhetoric	rhetoraiko
Rex	resin	Rhetorical	rhetoraikojo
Rexine	resinhun	Rhetorician	rhetoraikohn
Reynard	reyngba	Rheum	rheunmu
Renolds	reynjosi	Rheumatic	rheunmuko
Rh	rha	Rheumatism	rheunmumosi
Rhabdomancy	rhanbndemoyesn	Rheumatoid	rheunmujo
Rhabdomyoma	rhanbndemuma	Rheumatology	rheunmulogbon
Rhadamanthus	rhanjnmosnsn	Rheumy	rheunmo

WORD (x)	EQUIVALENT (y)	WORD (x)	EQUIVALENT (y)
Rheydt	rhetedie	Rhododendron	rhondiejijnron
Rh	rha	Rhodolite	rhondieleyo
Rhuigolene	rhaigijinhun	Rhodonite	rhondiejnyo
Rhyinal	rhainjo	Rhodope	rhondiepn
Rhyinencephalon	rehainenknphijnsi	Rhodopsin	rhondipnsie
Rhinestone	rhainsetole	Rhodora	rhondiepnsise
Rhinitis	rhaimiso	Rhodora	rhondiero
Rhino	rhamuu	Rhombencephalon	rhonmbueknphijnsi
Rhinoceros	rhamuuknrasi	Rhomb	rhonmbu
Rhinology	rhamuulogbon	Rhombic	rhonmbuko
Rhinoplasty	rhamuupansuito	Rhomboid	rhonmboojo
Rhinoscopy	rhamuusokipo	Rhombohedron	rhonmboohegboin
Rhizo	rhasun	Rhombus	rhonmbusi
Rhizobium	rhasunboma	Rhondda	rhongba
Rhizocarpous	rhasunkopansi	Rhone	rhoin
Rhizocephalous	rhasunknphijnsi	Rhubarb	rhaibigba
Rhizogenic	rhasunginko	Rhumb	rhaubn
Rhizoid	rhasunjo	Rhumba	rhauban
Rhizome	rhasunmo	Rhus	rhause
Rhizomorph	rhasunmophan	Rhyme	rhaimo
Rhizomorphous	rhasunmophansi	Rhymester	rhaimuseto
Rhizophagous	rhasunphijesi	Rhynchocephalian	rhaikhnphijnhn
Rhizopod	rhasunpindie	Rhyolite	rhaikoleyo
Rhizotomy	rhasuntemo	Rhythm	rhaimose
Rho	rhon	Rhythmic	rhaimoseko
Rhoda	rhonjo	Rhythmic	rhaimosekosi
Rhodamine	rhonjomini	Rhythmist	rhaimosesi
Rhode	rhonjin	Rial	raira
Rhodes	rhonjinsi	Riralto	rairato
Rhodesia	rhonjinsia	Riant	rairin
Rhodic	rhondieko	Riata	raita
Rhodrum	mondiema	Rib	raibo
Rhodo	rhondie	Rib	raibo
Rhodochrosite	rhondiekironseto	Ribald	raibojon

WORD (x)	EQUIVALENT (y)	WORD (x)	EQUIVALENT (y)
Ribaldry	raibojonsi	Rickle	raiknron
Riband	raiboha	Rickrack	raiknraiki
Ribbed	raibode	Rickshaw	raiknsue
Ribbing	raibognni	Ricochet	raikikhnte
Ribbon	raibini	Ricotta	raikitti
Ribcage	raibokogn	Ricrac	raiknrako
Ribera	rabies	Rictus	raikntisi
Riboflavin	raibnfanwie	Rid	raijn
Ribonucleic acid	raibnyunkuoko	Ridable	raijnbe
Ribose	raibnse	Riddance	raijnnasi
Ribosome	raibnsoomo	Ridden	raijnna
Ricardo	raikogbain	Riddle1	raijaran
Rice	raise	Ride	raijin
Ricer	raisesi	Rider	raijinsi
Rich	raikhi	Ridge	raigban
Richard	raikhigba	Ridge-pole	raigban-pinjn
Richelieu	raikhnwa	Ridgy	raigbanse
Riches	raikhisi	Ridicule	raijnkuo
Richet	raikhite	Ridiculous	raijnkuosi
Richie	raikhise	Riding1	raijingnni
Richly	raikhilo	Riding2	raijingnni
Richmond	raikhimojn	Ridley	raigbasi
Richter scale	sikjn raikhitn	Ridotto	raidiette
Richthofen	raikhisefan	Ridpath	raijnpansi
Ricin	raikoro	Riemann	rainmohun
Ricinolein	raikorojnsi	Riemple	rainmpon
Rick1	raikn	Rienzi	rainse
Rick2	raikn	Riesengebirge	rainsejngan
Rickenhancker	raiknhaunsi	Riesling	rainsiungnni
Rickets	raikntisi	Riet	rainta
Rickettsia	raikntisia	Rifacimento	raifesiminito
Rickettsial	raikntisiajo	Rif	raife
Rickety	raikntise	Rife	raifan
Rickey	raiknse	Riff	raifo

WORD (x)	EQUIVALENT (y)	WORD (x)	EQUIVALENT (y)
Riff-raff	raifon ranfan	Rigmarole	raigbimurin
Riffle	raifonjn	Rigoletto	raigbiletto
Riffler	raifonjnsi	Rigor1	raigbiran
Rifle1	raifijn	Rigor2	raigbiran
Rifle2	raifijn	Rigorism	raigbiranmosi
Rifleman	raifijnmoye	Rigormortis	raigbiranmoratnsi
Rifling	raifijngnni	Rigorous	raigbiransi
Rifle range	raigini raifijn	Rigour	raigbiron
Riflery	raifijnra	Rig-out	raigbi nita
Rift	raifia	Rigsdag	raigbidaji
Rift-valley	raifia-eajnrase	Rigveda	raigbiwinjo
Rig1	raigbn	Rile	rale
Rig2	raigbn	Riley	ralese
Riga	raigbi	Rill	raille
Rigadoon	raigbidun	Rim	raimu
Rigatoni	raigbiyo	Rime1	raimo
Rigel	raigbnjo	Rime2	raimo
Rigged	raigbnde	Rimer	raimosi
Rigger	raigbnsi	Rimester	raimoseto
Rigging	raigbngnni	Rimini	raimini
Riggs	raigbisi	Rimose	raimise
Right	raigbe	Rimple	romipon
Right angle	anigun raigbe	Rimy	romisi
Right arm	araimu raigbe	Rind	roinjo
Righten	raigbeni	Rinderpest	roinjorapnsia
Righteous	raigbeniwa	Rine	roin
Righteousness	raigbeniwasi	Rinforzando	ronfoonsejn
Rightism	raigbemosi	Ring1	rogan
Rightly	raigbelo	Ring2	rogan
Rightness	raigbenisi	Ring-binder	rogan-bojnra
Righto	raigbeto	Ringed	rogande
Rigid	raigbijo	Ringer	rogansi
Rigidity	raigbijotn	Ringer	rogansi
Rigil	raigbile	Ringhal	roghnsinto

WORD (x)	EQUIVALENT (y)	WORD (x)	EQUIVALENT (y)
Ringlet	rogantn	Risibility	raisobeleto
Ringplover	roganponwnra	Rising	raisognni
Ringster	roganseto	Risk	raisia
Rink	ronkini	Risky	raisiase
Rinse	ronsin	Risorgimento	raisoragnmutto
Rio bravo	rain banwn	Risotto	raisootto
Rio bronvo	rain bankin	Risqué	raisekun
Rio de jenero	rain jin janhun	Riss	raisoo
Rio grande	rain ganjin	Rissole	raisoole
Riot	rainta	Rist	raisi
Riotous	raintasi	Risus	raisisoo
Rip	raipn	Ritardando	raitogbadie
Rip1	raipn	Rite	raito
Rip2	raipn	Rite of passage	raito fi pansogun
Rip3	raipn	Ritter	raitotnra
Riparian	raipnrami	Ritual	raitojo
Riparious	raipnramisi	Ritualism	raitojomosi
Ripe	raipon	Ritzy	raitose
Ripe	raipon	Rival	raiwajo
Ripen	raipnsi	Rivalry	raiwajora
Ripieno	raiponkn	Rive	raiwin
Ripley	raiponse	Riven	raiwini
Ripon	raipnse	River	raiwnra
Riposte	raipinseto	Rivera	raiwnran
Ripper	raipnsi	Riverine	raiwnrain
Ripple	raipnpo	Riverside	raiwnrasoojo
Ripplet	raipnpotn	Rivet	raiwinti
Ripply	raipnposi	Riviera	raiwinira
Rip rap	raipn raipe	Riviere	raiwnran
Riptide	raipntijin	Rivulet	raiwntn
Ripuarian	raipnrain	Rizal	raisejo
Rise	raiso	Rizzer	raisunsi
Riser	raisosi	Ro	ron
Risible	raisobr	Roach	ronkho

WORD (x)	EQUIVALENT (y)	WORD (x)	EQUIVALENT (y)
Road	ronjn	Robustious	robuseyosi
Roadie	ronjnse	Roc	ronkn
Roadstead	ronjnsetogbi	Roca	ronko
Roadster	ronjnseto	Rocambole	ronknmbejoin
Roadtest	ronjntnsi	Rochambeau	ronkhombehun
Roadway	ronjnwelo	Rochefort	ronkhnfoon
Roald	ronjon	Rochelle	ronkhnllo
Roam	ronma	Rochester	ronkhnseto
Roan	ronkun	Rochet	ronkhnti
Roanoke	ronkunko	Rocinante	ronkinite
Roar	ronke	Rock1	ronkn
Roarer	ronkesi	Rock2	ronkn
Roast	ronsun	Rockability	ronknballese
Roaster	ronsunsi	Rockaby	ronknsun
Roasting	ronsungnni	Rockhominy	ronknhinmini
Rob	rongbe	Rockefeller	ronknfnjjosi
Robalo	rongbelo	Rock air	ronkn aria
Roband	rongbejn	Rock and roll	ronkn ati rollo
Robber	rongbesi	Rocker	ronjnra
Robbery	rongberai	Rockery	ronknrai
Robbia	rongbesi	Rocket	ronknti
Robe	rongbn	Rocketry	ronkntirai
Robert	rongbito	Rockoon	ronkoon
Roberta	rongbite	Rocky1	ronknse
Robeson	rongbisin	Rocky2	ronknse
Robin	rongbese	Rococo	ronkiki
Robin hood	rongbese hinjo	Rod	rojn
Robinia	rongbesesi	Rode	ronjin
Robinson	rongbesesin	Rodent	ronjinte
Roble	rongbain	Rodeo	ronjinkn
Roborant	rongbarate	Roderick	ronjinrakn
Robot	rongbato	Rodger	rojngnra
Robotics	rongbatokosi	Rodman	rojnmoye
Robust	robuseyo	Rodney	rojnnase

WORD (x)	EQUIVALENT (y)	WORD (x)	EQUIVALENT (y)
Rodomontade	rojnmenitejin	Roller	rollosi
Rodrigue	rojnraign	Rollick	rollokn
Roe1	ronye	Rollo	rolle
Roe2	ronye	Roly poly	ropo pipo
Roe buck	ronye buki	Romgna	ronmogini
Roemer	ronyemo	Romaic	romako
Roentgen	ronyetogin	Romaine	romainhun
Roentgenize	ronyetoginse	Romains	romaraisi
Roentgeno	ronyetogini	Roman	romain
Roentgenogram	ronyetoginiganmo	Romance	romainse
Roentgenography	ronyetoginiganmo	Romancer	romainsesi
Roentgenology	ronyetoginilogbon	Romanesque	romainkun
Roentgenopaque	ronyetoginipankun	Romania	romaine
Roentegenitherapy	rontoginisinranpo	Romanian	romainihn
Roerick	ronyeraiki	Romanic	romainko
Rogation	rogiyoon	Romanism	romainmosi
Rogation days	rogiyoon dasesi	Romanize	romainse
Rogatory	rogiyorai	Roman law	romain leewo
Roger	rogira	Romano-	romainkn
Rogue	rogan	Romantic	romainteko
Roguery	roganrai	Romanticism	romaintekomosi
Roguish	roganse	Romanticist	romaintekosi
Rohypnol	rohopnjin	Romanticize	romaintekose
Roil	roleu	Romany	romainse
Roily	roleuse	Romaunt	romainto
Roister	rosiata	Rombion	rombesi
Roland	roledain	Rome	roma
Role	rolo	Romeo	romakn
Role model	rolo modiejo	Romford	romfonjn
Rolex	rolosi	Romish	romasin
Roll	rollo	Rommel	rommalo
Rolland	rollodain	Romney	romini
Rolled gold	rollode gondon	Romp	ronmpn
Rollander	rollodainsi	Rompers	ronmpnsi

WORD (x)	EQUIVALENT (y)	WORD (x)	EQUIVALENT (y)
Rompish	ronmpnse	Room-mate	roommote
Romulus	romujnsi	Room service	roomo serawnsi
Ronald	ronjain	Roomy	roomose
Rondeau	ronjnun	Roon	roonsi
Rondel	ronjnlo	Roop	roope
Rendelet	ronjnloto	Roor	rooran
Rondo	ronjne	Roose	roose
Rondonia	ronjnhan	Roosewelt	roosewinjia
Rondure	ronjnrai	Roost	roosn
Rone	roin	Rooster	roosnsi
Roneo	roinkn	Roostit	roosnte
Rongelap	rongnpan	Root1	rooyo
Rongerik	rongnrai	Root2	rooyo
Renion	ronkio	Rooter	rooyosi
Ronne	ronhun	Rooty	rooyose
Ronquil	ronkuilo	Rope	ronpo
Ronsard	ronsogbaa	ropery	ronporai
Rontgen	rontogin	ropery	ronporai
Roo	roo	ropy	ronpose
Rood	roojn	roque	ronkue
Roof	roofio	ronquefort	ronkuefoonth
Roofage	roofiogun	roquelaure	ronkuejnrai
Roofer	roofiosi	roquet	ronkunta
Roof-garden	roofio-giragbn	roraima	roraimo
Roofing	roofiognni	rorer	roraisi
Rook1	rookn	rorqual	rorakunjo
Rook2	rookn	ro-ro	ro-roi
Rookery	rooknrai	Rorschach test	tnsi rorasekhn
Rookie	rooknse	Rosa	rosin
Rooky	rooknso	Rosaceous	rosinsuwa
Room	roomo	Rosalie	rosinle
Roomer	roomosi	Rosalind	rosinlejn
Roomette	roomotn	Rosamond	rosinmodan
Roomier	roomosii	Rosa monte	rosin menita

WORD (x)	EQUIVALENT (y)	WORD (x)	EQUIVALENT (y)
Rosamunda	rosinmujina	Rostov	rosetowa
Rosaniline	rosinlehun	Rostral	rosetnjo
Rosario	rosinrain	Rosetrum	rosetnma
Rosary	rosinrai	Rosy	rosuan
Roscius	rosinki	Rot	roonte
Roscoe	rosinkn	Rota	rota
Rose1	rosua	Rotarian	Rotarian
Rose2	rosua	Rotary	rotarai
Rose	rosua	Rotate	rotayo
Roseate	rosuayo	Rotation	rotayoon
Rosebery	rosuaberai	Ratative	rotayowin
Rosecrans	rosuakansn	Rotator	rotayoran
Rosecross	rosuakonso	Rotania	rotayorin
Rosejericho	rosuajnrakhn	Rotatory	rotayorai
Rosemary	rosuamorai	Rotavator	rotaweyoran
Rosemoss	rosuamosi	Rotche	rotakhn
Rosenwald	rosuawnjon	Rote	rote
Roseola	rosuajain	Rote	rote
Rossetta	rosuatto	Rotenone	rotenini
Rosette	rosuattn	Rotgot	rotegon
Rosewood	rosuawitijo	Rotherham	roteraisi
Rosicrucian	rosinkorasuan	Roti	rota
Rosin	rosoon	Rotifer	rotafiro
Rosin oil	rosoon oje	Rotiform	rotafon
Rosolio	rosoojan	Rotisserie	rotasooron
Ross	roson	Rotl	rotejn
Rosetti	rosontte	Rotochute	rotokhunyo
Rossini	rosonhun	Rotograph	rotoganpha
Rossiya	rosooye	Rotogravure	rotoganworai
Rostand	rosetojn	Rotor	rotara
Rostellate	rosetojjnyo	Rotocraft	rotarakanfia
Rostellum	rosetojjnma	Rotovator	rotaweyo
Roster	rosetnra	Rototill	rotatijjn
Rostock	rosetoki	Rotten	roontesi

WORD (x)	EQUIVALENT (y)	WORD (x)	EQUIVALENT (y)
Rotter	roontnra	Roundlet	rojointn
Rotweller	roontewinjjosi	Roundly	rojoinlo
Rotuma	rotoma	Round robin	rojoin rongbese
Rotund	rotojoin	Roundsman	rojoinmoye
Rotunda	rotojoinsi	Round tabe	teberon rojoin
Rotundity	rotojointn	Round up	rojoin pake
Roture	rotorai	Roup	roopn
Roturier	rotoraisi	Roupet	roopnti
Rouble	roonberon	Rouphia	roophan
Rouche	roonkhn	Roupy	roonpnse
Roué	roose	Rouse	roose
Rouen	roonni	Rousement	rosemutto
Rouge	roogn	Rousing	rosegnni
Rough	roonghi	Rousseau	roosua
Roughage	roonghigun	Roussillon	roossollesi
Roughcast	roonghikosotn	Rout1	rooto
Roughen	roonghini	Rout 2	rooto
Roughly	roonghilo	Route	roota
Roughneck	roonghi-hunko	Router	rootosi
Roughshod	roonghisujo	Routh	roosia
Roulade	roonjoin	Routine	rootahun
Rouleau	roonjnum	Routinism	rootahunmosi
Roulers	roonjnrasi	Roux	roosoo
Roulette	roonjntn	Rove 1	raiwn
Roum	roonmo	Rove 2	raiwn
Rounce	roonsi	Rover 1	raiwnsi
Round	rojoin	Rover 2	raiwnsi
Roundabout	abountarojoin	Roving eye	raiwngnni eyiri
Roundel	rojoinlo	Row 1	raiwe
Roundelay	rojoinlose	Row 2	raiwe
Rounder	rojoinsi	Row 3	raiwe
Rounding	rojoingnni	Rowan	raiwin
Roundish	rojoinse	Row – boat	raiwin
Roundhead	rojoinhegbi	Rowdy	raiwedie

WORD (x)	EQUIVALENT (y)	WORD (x)	EQUIVALENT (y)
Rowel	raiweloo	Rube	rube
Rowen	raiweni	Rubefacient	rubefanseto
Rowland	raiweledain	Rubefy	rubefe
Rowlock	raiwelokn	Rubella	rubella
Roxana	rosuanse	Rubellite	rubelleyo
Roxane	rosuan	Rubens	rubesua
Roxasy	rosuase	Rubeola	rubekiji
Roxy	rosua	Rubesent	rubeseknti
Royal	ronsnjo	Rubiaceous	rubosuwa
Royalism	ronsnlemosi	Rubicon	rubokin
Royalist	ronsnlesi	Rubiocund	rubokunjn
Royalty	ronsnleto	Rubidium	rubojnma
Royce	ronsnsi	Rubiginous	ruboginsi
Rrhagia	rrhaigan	Rubigo	rubogon
Rrhaphy	rrhaiphe	Rubik's cube	runbuka kunbe
Rrhea	rrhain	Rubin	rubo
Ru	ru	Rubinstein	rubosetosi
Ruanda	rujina	Rubious	rubosi
Rub	rube	Ruble	ruberon
Rubadub	rubedigbi	Rubric	ruborako
Rubal	rubejo	Rubricate	ruborakoyo
Rubasse	rubesoo	Rubrician	runborakhn
Rubate	rubeto	Ruby	rubose
Rubato	rubeeto	Rucervine	ruknrawini
Rubber1	rubesi	Ruche	runkhn
Rubber2	rubesi	Ruching	rukhngnni
Rubber band	rubesi boha	Ruck1	runki
Rubberize	rubesise	Ruck2	runki
Rubbemeck	rubesihunko	Rucksack	runkisankhn
Rubbing	rubegnni	Ruckus	runkisi
Rubbish	rubeso	Ruction	runkeyoon
Rubbishy	rubesosi	Ructious	runkesi
Rubble	runberon	Rudaceous	runjasuwa
Rub-down	rube juan	Rudbleckia	runjabekia

WORD (x)	EQUIVALENT (y)	WORD (x)	EQUIVALENT (y)
Rudd	runja	Ruler	rinronsi
Rudder	runjajnra	Ruling	rinrongnni
Ruddle	runjaduo	Rum1	runmo
Ruddy	runjase	Rum2	runmo
Rude	runjin	Rumenia	runmoin
Ruderal	runjirajo	Rumanian	runmoinhn
Rudeshy	runjinsubo	Rumba	runmbe
Rudiment	runjinmutto	Rumble	runmbusiasi
Rubimentary	runjimuttorai	Rumelia	runmujia
Rudolf	rundefia	Rumen	runmini
Rue1	runse	Ruminant	runminite
Rue2	runse	Ruminate	runminiyo
Rueful	runsefunjn	Rummage	runmogun
Rufescent	rufiseknti	Rummer	runmmusi
Ruff1	runfia	Rummy	runmmo
Ruff2	runfia	Rumor	runmosi
Ruffian	runfiasi	Rumour	runmosi
Ruffle	runfijn	Rump	runmpn
Ruffler	runfijnra	Rumpelstiltiskin	runmpnlosetitikin
Rufous	runfnsi	Rumple	runmpon
Rug	rungn	Rumpus	runmpnsi
Rugate	rungnto	Run	ruin
Rugged	rungnde	Run	sare
Ruggedize	rungndese	Runabout	abonuntaruin
Rugose	rungonse	Run-around	ruin arojoin
Rugby	rungnbo	Runcible	ruinyabe
Ruggger	rungnsi	Runcinate	ruinyato
Ruhr	runho	Rund	ruindi
Ruin	run	Rundle	ruinduo
Ruinate	runyo	Rundlet	ruinduote
Ruination	runyoon	Rune	ruhun
Ruinous	runsi	Rung1	rugun
Ruiz	runsia	Rung2	rugun
Rule	rinron	Runic	ruhunko

WORD (x)	EQUIVALENT (y)	WORD (x)	EQUIVALENT (y)
Run-in	ruin-nu	Rut1	runto
Runlet	ruintn	Rut2	runto
Runnel	ruinlo	Rutabaga	runtobegan
Runner	ruinsi	Rutaceous	runtosuwa
Running	ruingnni	Ruth	runsn
Runny	ruinse	Ruthenia	runsinhun
Runnymede	ruinsemujin	Ruthenic	runsinko
Runt	runte	Ruthenoius	runsinsi
Runyon	runsnle	Ruthenium	runsinma
Rupee	runpnse	Ruthless	runsnlabo
Rupert	runpnto	Rutland	runtoledain
Rupiah	runpnhun	Rutilant	runtolete
Rupture	runpitirai	Rutile	runtole
Rural	runrajo	Rutledge	runtolegbon
Rurality	runralet	Rutish	runtosi
Ruralise	runrajose	Ruvuma	ruwinma
Ruse	runse	Rwanda	ruwejnna
Rush1	ruinse	Ry	rai
Rush2	ruinse	Ry	ry
Rusher	ruinsesi	Ryazan	raisehun
Rushy	ruinselo	Ryder	raijnra
Rusk	runseki	Rye	raise
Ruskin	runsekin	Ryegrass	raisegansu
Russel	rusoolo	Ryke	raikn
Russet	rusooto	Rynd	raijn
Russia	Russia	Ryot	raite
Russian	russiahn	S	s si sn se
Russo-	russun	Saale	sanjn
Rust	runsi	Saar	saran
Rustic	runsiko	Saare	sanrai
Rusticate	runsikoyo	Saaririen	sanrain
Rusticity	runsikito	Saba	sanbo
Rustle	runsiron	Sabadilla	sanbojnlle
Rusty	runsise	Sabaism	sanbomosi

WORD (x)	EQUIVALENT (y)	WORD (x)	EQUIVALENT (y)
Sabaoth	sanbosin	Sabe	sanbe
Sabarmati	sanboronye	Sabean	sanbehun
Sabbat	sanbote	Sabellian	sanbellosi
Sabbatarian	sanboterain	Sabenito	sanbehito
Sabbath	sanbotesi	Saber	sanbesi
Sabbatic	sanbote	Sabi	sanbn
Sabbatical	sanbotekojo	Sabin	sanbnjn
Sabe	sanbe	Sabine	sanbnhun
Sabean	sanbehun	Sabir	sanbnro
Sabellian	sanbellosi	Sable	sanbnron
Sabenito	sanbehito	Sabot	sanbati
Saber	sanbesi	Sabotage	sanbati
Sabi	sanbn	Saboteur	sanbatiran
Sabin	sanbnjn	Sabra	sanbnra
Sabine	sanbnhun	Sabre	sanberai
Sabir	sanbnro	Sabretache	sangbntokhn
Sable	sanbnron	Sabulous	sanbntesi
Sabot	sanbati	Sac	saka
Sabotage	sanbati	Sacaton	sakatin
S	s si sn se	Sacate	sakato
Saale	sanjn	Saccharate	sakakhnraiyo
Saar	saran	Saccharic	sakakhnrako
Saare	sanrai	Sacchariade	sakakhnraji
Saaririen	sanrain	Saccharify	sakakhnranfe
Saba	sanbo	Saccharimeter	sakakhnranmuto
Sabadilla	sanbojnlle	Saccharin	sakakhnran
Sabaism	sanbomosi	Saccharine	sakakhnrain
Sabaoth	sanbosin	Saccharo	sakakhnron
Sabarmati	sanboronye	Saccharoid	sakakhnronjo
Sabbat	sanbote	Saccharometer	sakakhnronmuto
Sabbatarian	sanboterain	Saccharomycetous	sakakhnromukntisi
Sabbath	sanbotesi	Saccharose	sakakhnrase
Sabbatic	sanbote	**WORD (x)**	**EQUIVALENT (y)**
Sabbatical	sanbotekojo	Sacco	sakaki

WORD (x)	EQUIVALENT (y)	WORD (x)	EQUIVALENT (y)
Saccophagus	sakakiphijesi	Sad	sangbi
Sacculate	sakakueyo	Sadden	sangbisi
Saccule	sakakue	Saddle	sangbiduo
Sacculus	sakakuesi	Saddler	sangbiduosi
Sacerdotal	sakaraidetnjo	Saddlery	sangbiduorai
Sachem	sakhamo	Sadducee	sangbidesi
Sachet	sakhate	Sadhu	sangbihun
Sachsen	sakhase	Sadiron	sangbirain
Sack1	sakakn	Sadism	sangbimosi
Sack2	sakakn	Sadomasochism	sangbimusookhimosi
Sack3	sakakn	Sadova	sangbiwini
Sackbut	sakaknte	Safari	sanfirai
Sacking	sakakngnni	Safe	sanfn
Sacque	sakakue	Safeguard	sanfngungba
Sacral	sakaranjo	Safety	sanfnto
Sacrament	sakaranmutto	Saffian	sanfnhun
Sacrementarian	sakaranmuttorain	Saffron	sanfannini
Sacramentary	sakaranmuttorai	Safrranine	sanfannini
Sacramento	sakaranmito	Safrole	sanfnrolo
Sacrarium	sakaraima	Saft	sanfia
Sacred	sakarande	Sag	sangi
Sacrifice	sakarunfise	Saga	sangbo
Sacrificial	sakarunfisejo	Sagacious	sangbokisi
Sacrilege	sakarunjo	Sagacity	sangbokito
Sacrilegious	sakarunjosi	Sagaman	sangbomoye
Sacring	sakarogan	Sagami	sangbomi
Sacrist	sakarosi	Sagamore	sangbomorai
Sacristan	sakarosetin	Sage1	sangbon
Sacristy	sakaroseto	Sage2	sangbon
Sacro	saknra	Saggar	sangbona
Sacroiliac	saknrajanko	Saginaw	sangiwa
Sacrosanct	saknrasankn	Saginaw	sangiwa
Sacrum	saknrama	Sagitta	sangitta
Sacrosciatic	saknrasekitiko	Sagittal	sangittajo

WORD (x)	EQUIVALENT (y)	WORD (x)	EQUIVALENT (y)
Sagittarius	sangittaraisi	Sake2	sankn
Sagittate	sangittayo	Saker	sanknsi
Sago	sangn	Sakhalin	sankhnjon
Saguache	sangunkhn	Sakishima	sankasunma
Saguaro	sangunro	Sakkara	sanknran
Saguenay	sangunsi	Sakti	sanknti
Saguinel	sangunle	Sakuntala	sankntijn
Sagurol	sangunmo	Sal	sanjn
Sagunto	sangunto	Salaam	sanjnmini
Sagy	sangbonsi	Salable	sanjnbe
Sahara	saheran	Salacious	sanjnkisi
Saharanpur	saheranpo	Salad	sanjnje
Sahib	sanhebo	Saladang	sanjnje
Said	sanwi	Salad days	sanjnje dasesi
Saida	sanjn	Saladin	sanjnjain
Saiga	sanga	Salade	sanjnjo
Sail	sanlo	Salado	sanjnjan
Sailboard	bugbasanlo	Salamander	sanjnmujora
Sailor	sanloran	Salami	sanjnmi
Sain	sanni	Salamis	sanjnmosi
Sainfoin	sanfoini	Salary	sanjnrai
Saint	santoni	Salazar	sanjnse
Sainted	santonide	Salchow	sanjnkhiwa
Sainte	santonise	Sale	sanjn
Saintly	santonilo	Saleable	sanjnbe
Saipan	sanpojn	Salesmn	sanjnmoye
Sair	saran	Salem	sanjnmo
Sair	saran	Salep	sanjnpa
Sairy	saransn	Saleratus	sanjnrato
Sais	sanso	Salemo	sanjnrain
Saith	sansi	Salesian	sanjnsuan
Saiva	sanwa	Sales	sanjnsi
Sakarya	sanknrai	Salford	sanjnfon
Sake1	sankn	Salian	sanjnhun

WORD (x)	EQUIVALENT (y)	WORD (x)	EQUIVALENT (y)
Salic	sanjnko	Sallow2	sajnlewa
Salicaceous	sanjnkosuwa	Sallowy	sajnlewase
Salicin	sanjnkoro	Sallust	sajnlesi
Salicine	sankihun	Sally	sajnlese
Salicylate	sanjnsnleyo	Sally lunn	sajnlese lujnsi
Salicylic acid	sanjnsnleko	Salmacis	sanjnmoknsi
Salicional	sanjnkoonjo	Salmagundi	sanjnmognunjo
Salicornia	sanjnkirain	Salmi	sanjnmi
Salience	sanjnnasi	Salmis	sanjnmisi
Salient	sanjnnato	Salmon	sanjnmeni
Salientian	sanjnnatan	Salmonberry	sanjnmeniberrai
Saliferous	sanjnfirosi	Salmonella	sanjnmenille
Salify	sanjnfe	Salomonellosia	sanjnmenilleso
Salimeter	sanjnmuto	Salmonoid	sanjnmenijo
Salina	sanjnbu	Salol	sanjnjo
Saline	sanjyo	Salome	sanjnmuse
Salinity	sanjyoto	Salon	sanjne
Salinization	sanjyoseyoon	Salonika	sanjnsekin
Salinometer	sanjyomuto	Saloon	sanjnsin
Salique	sanjnkue	Saloop	sanjnpn
Salisbury	sanjnberai	Salopatte	sanjnpantn
Salish	sanjnso	Salp	sanjnpe
Salishan	sanjnsosi	Salpa	sanjnpan
Saliva	sanjnwe	Salpicon	sanjnpokin
Salivary	sanjnwerai	Salpiglossis	sanjnpogonsueso
Salivate	sanjnweyo	Salpingectomy	sanjnpingntemo
Salivation	sanjnweyoon	Salpingitis	sanjnpingnso
Salk	sanjnki	Salpirix	sanjnpinsi
Salfe a manger	sanknfn moginisi	Salsa	sanjnse
Salee	sajnse	Salsify	sanjnsoofe
Sall	sajnle	Salsilla	sanjnsoolle
Sallenders	sajnlejnrasi	Salt	sanjiyo
Sallet	sajnletn	Salt	sanjnyo
Sallow1	sajnlewa	Salta	sanjnya

WORD (x)	EQUIVALENT (y)	WORD (x)	EQUIVALENT (y)
Saltant	sanjyate	Salvemini	sanjnwnmini
Saltarello	sanjyarello	Salver	sanjnwnra
Saltation	sanjyayoon	Salver regina	sanjnwnra regihun
Saltatorial	sanjyayoraijo	Salvia	sanjnwnsi
Salted	sanjyode	Salvin	sanjnwini
Salter	sanjyora	Salvo	sanjnwo
Salterm	sanjyoran	Salvor	sanjnwo
Saltigrade	sanjyagandie	Salween	sanjnwinni
Saltillo	sanjyallo	Salz	sanjnse
Saltine	sanjyahun	Samani	sanmuhun
Salting	sanjyognni	Samar	sanmura
Saltire	sanjyaran	Samara	sanmura
Salt rheum	sanjyo rhaima	Samaria	sanmurasi
Salton	sanjntin	Samaritan	sanmuratan
Saltus	sanjyosi	Samarium	sanmurama
Salty	sanjyose	Samrkand	sanmiknra
Salubrious	sanjnbaunsi	Samarskite	sanmurakiti
Saluki	sanjnka	Samba	sanmbe
Salus	sanjnle	Sambo	sanmbn
Salutary	sanjnkirai	Sambre	sanmbnra
Salutation	sanjnkiyoon	Sambuca	sanmbuko
Salutatorian	sanjnkiyorain	Sambur	sanmbura
Salutatory	sanjnkiyorai	Same	samo
Salute	sanjnki	Sameness	samonisi
Salvable	sanjnwabe	Samfoo	samfoo
Salvador	sanjnjoran	Samiel	samukn
Salvadorian	sanjnjorai	Samisen	samusun
Salvage	sanjnwagn	Samite	samuto
Salvagee	sanjnwagnse	Samizdat	samusita
Salvarsan	sanjnwarasi	Samlet	samutn
Salvation	sanjnwayoon	Samnite	samuhunto
Salvationist	sanjnwayoonsi	Samnium	samuhunma
Salve1	sanjnwn	Samoa	samosi
Salve2	sanjnwn	Samoan	samosin

WORD (x)	EQUIVALENT (y)	WORD (x)	EQUIVALENT (y)
Samogitia	samogbitan	Sanctus	sankntosa
Samos	samosn	Sancy	sansn
Samosa	samose	Sand	sangbn
Samothrace	samonsro	Sandal1	sangbnjo
Samovar	samowara	Sandal2	sangbnjo
Samoyed	samenide	Sandarac	sangbnrokn
Samoyedic	samenideko	Sandcast	sangbnkosoto
Samp	sampe	Sandcrack	sangbnkanko
Sampan	sampn	Sander	sangbnsi
Samphire	samphira	Sandhi	sangbnhi
Sample	sampo	Sand hurst	sangbn hunseto
Sampler1	samposi	San diego	san dilelo
Sampler2	samposi	San verbena	san winbehun
Sampson	samposin	Sandwich	sangbnwakhi
Samsara	samuserai	Sandy	sangbnse
Samson	samuse	Sane	sanun
Samuel	samulo	Sanford	sanfonjn
Samurai	samuro	Sanforize	sanfonse
San	san	Sang	sangan
Sanative	santowin	Sangamon	sangnmeni
Santorium	santoraima	Sangaree	sangirain
Sanatory	santorai	Sangay	sangisua
Sanbenito	sanbetoni	Sanger	sanganisi
San blas	san baunsi	Sang-froid	sangan-fonjo
Sancho panza	sankhiun panse	Sangha	sangba
Sanctified	sankntofede	Sangbihe	sangnhun
Sanctify	sankntofe	Sangreal	sangbisijo
Sanctimonious	sankntomenisi	Sangria	sangnran
Sanctimony	sankntomeni	Sanguicolous	sangbejekijosi
Sanction	sankntosi	Sanguiferous	sangbejefirosi
Sanctity	sankntotn	Sanguinaria	sangbejerain
Sanctuary	sankntorai	Sanguinary	sangbejerai
Sanctum santorum	sankntoma	Sanguine	sangbejehun
	sankntorama	Sanguineous	sangbejehunsi

WORD (x)	EQUIVALENT (y)	WORD (x)	EQUIVALENT (y)
Sanguiolent	sangbejejinto	Santalaceous	santojnsuwa
Sanhedrin	sanhegbo	Santalic	santojnko
Sanhedrim	sanhegboma	Santa maria	santo muran
Saniucle	sannikuo	Santana	santohun
Sanies	sannise	Satander	santojnra
Sanious	sannisi	Santayana	santosuan
Sanitarian	santonirain	Santee	santose
Sanitarium	santoniraima	Santiago	santogon
Sanitary	santonirai	Santo domingo	santo deminilo
Sanitate	santoniyo	Santonica	santonikn
Sanitation	santoniyoon	Santonin	santonini
Sanitize	santonise	Santos	santosi
Sanity	santoni	Sao	sakin
San joa quin	san jina kun	Saone	sakinni
Sank	sanki	Sao Paulo	sakin panlo
Sankey	sankise	Sao tiago	sakin tinlo
Sankhya	sanjhia	Sap1	sanpo
San luis	san lusi	Sap2	sanpo
San luis potosi	san lusi pintosi	Sap	soje
San marino	san murrain	Sapajou	sanpojua
Sans	sansa	Sapele	sanporan
Sansculotte	sansekunlotn	Saphena	sanphini
Sansculottides	sansekunlotnjosi	Sapid	sanpojn
Sansevieria	sanseworain	Sapience	sangbonto
Sanskrit	sansokiti	Sapiential	sangbontojo
Sanskritic	sansokitiko	Sapindaceous	sanpojnsuwa
Sansovino	sansoowini	Sapless	sanpolabo
Sans pareil	sansn panralo	Sapling	sanpognni
Sans sanci	sansn sookn	Sapodilla	sanpojnlle
Santa	santo	Sapondillo	sanpojnllo
Santa claus	santo kansi	Saponaceous	sanpohunsuwa
Santa cruz	santo korasi	Saponification	sanpohunfikoyoon
Santa fe	santo fe	Saponify	sanpohunfe
Santa Tenerife	santo tinraife	Saponin	sanpohinni

WORD (x)	EQUIVALENT (y)	WORD (x)	EQUIVALENT (y)
Saponite	sanpohunyo	Sarcina	sarekihun
Sapor	sanpora	Sarco	sareki
Sapotaceous	sanpotosuwa	Sarcocarp	sarekikopan
Sapper	sanposi	Sarcodina	sarekijohun
Sapphic	sanphike	Sarcogenic	sarekigiko
Sapphira	sanphira	Sarcolemma	sarekilemma
Sapphire	sanphirai	Sarcoma	sarekimo
Sapphirine	sanphirain	Sarcomatosis	sarekimotnso
Sappho	sanpho	Sarcophagus	sarekiphijesi
Sappy	sanpose	Sarcoplasm	sarekipanson
Sapremia	sanporami	Sarcous	sarekisi
Sapro	sanpora	Sard	sarejn
Saprobe	sanporabe	Sandanapalus	sarekipanson
Saprogenic	sanporaginko	Sarda	sarejnra
Saprolite	sanporaleyo	Sardine	sarejoin
Saprophagous	sanporaphijesi	Sardinia	sarejoinsi
Sapropel	sanporapnlo	Sardis	sarejosn
Saprophyte	sanporapnlo	Sardius	sarejosi
Saproplankton	sanporapanknti	Sardonic	sarejnhnko
Saprozoic	sanporasinko	Sardonyx	sarejnhnse
Sapsago	sanposegan	Sargasso	saregisoo
Saraband	sareboha	Sarge	saregn
Saracen	sarekin	Sergeant	sareginte
Saragossa	saregonsoo	Sargon	saregini
Sarah	sarerin	Sari	sanrai
Sarajevo	sarejnwo	Sark	sareko
Saran	sareni	Sarkit	sarekiti
Saranac	sarekun	Sarky	sarekise
Saratoga	saretogan	Sarmetia	saremotan
Saratov	saretowa	Sarment	sarekinto
Sarawak	sarewinko	Sarmentaceous	saremintosuwa
Sacresm	sareknsumo	Sarmentose	sareminitosi
Sarcastic	sareknsuko	Sarmentum	sareminitoma
Sarce	saresi	Sarmiento	saremenito

WORD (x)	EQUIVALENT (y)	WORD (x)	EQUIVALENT (y)
Sarmy	sanroin	Sassafras	sansoofanse
Sarong	sanrogan	Sassanid	sansoonjo
Saronic	sanronko	Sassanidae	sansoonjose
Saros	sanrosi	Sassenack	sansoonki
Sarod	sanrojn	Sassoon	sansoonsi
Sarong	sanrogn	Sassy	sansoosn
Saros	sanrosi	Sastruga	santnragan
Saroyan	sanroinsn	Sat	sati
Sarpedon	sarepanjn	Satan	satina
Sarracenia	sarrekinni	Satang	satigan
Sarraceniaceous	sarrekinnisuwa	Satanic	satinako
Sarrusophone	sarresophohun	Satanism	satinamosi
Sarsaparilla	saresepanlle	Satara	satiran
Sarsar	saresesi	Satchel	satikho
Sarsen	saresun	Sate	sato
Sarsenet	saresunte	Sateen	satoon
Sarto	sareto	Satellite	satojnrayo
Sartor	saretoranjo	Satellite dish	satojnrayo disu
Sartorial	saretoranjo	Satem	satoma
Sartorius	saretoransi	Satiable	satinbe
Sartre	saretnran	Satiate	satiny
Sarvodaya	sarewnjya	Satie	satinse
Sasebo	sasibo	Satiety	satinto
Saseno	sasikn	Satin	satihun
Sash1	sanso	Satinet	satihunte
Sash2	sanso	Satiny	satihunse
Sashay	sansose	Satire	satirai
Sashimi	sansomi	Satiric	satiraiko
Sasin	sansoo	Satirical	satiraikojo
Saskatchewan	sansekitokhn	Satirist	satiraisi
Saskatoon	sansekitosi	Satirize	satiraise
Sasquatch	sansekunkho	Satisfaction	satinsefanknyoon
Sass	sansoo	Satisfactory	satinfanknyorai
Sassaby	sansoonbe	Satisfy	satinfe

WORD (x)	EQUIVALENT (y)	WORD (x)	EQUIVALENT (y)
Satori	satorai	Saurian	sanrasun
Satrap	satoranpn	Saurischaian	sanraisekin
Satrapy	satoranpi	Saurus	sanrasi
Satsuma	satnranpi	Sauro	sanrase
Saturant	satnrate	Sanropod	sanrapindie
Saturate	satnrayo	Saury	sanrai
Saturation	satnrayoon	Sauszge	sansugn
Saturday	satnradase	Saussurite	sansunraiyo
Satum	satnran	Saut	sanyo
Satumalia	satnranjan	Sauté	sanyon
Satumian	satnrain	Sautermes	sanyonrainsi
Satumid	satnranjo	Sautoir	santorai
Satumine	satnrahun	Sauve qui peut	sanwini kun pnti
Satumism	satnranmosi	Savage	sanwngo
Satyagraha	satnseganhe	Savagery	sanwngorai
Satyagrahi	santnseganha	Savannah	sanwnhun
Satyr	satnrai	Savant	sanwnte
Satyriasis	satnrainso	Savate	sanwnyo
Satyromania	satnroinmohan	Save1	sanwin
Sauce	sansia	Save2	sanwin
Saucepan	sansiapan	Saved	sanwinde
Saucer	sansiasi	Saveloy	sanwinlo
Saucy	sansiase	Saver	sanwinsi
Saud	sangbe	Savile	sanwinjn
Saudi	sangbesi	Savin	sanwinsu
Sauerbraten	sansebantin	Saving	sanwingnni
Sauerkraut	sansekante	Savior	sanwiran
Sauger	sangera	Saviour	sanwara
Sauk	sanke	Savourless	sanwaralabo
Saul	sanle	Savoury	sanwarai
Sault	sanle	Savoy	sanwnsn
Sauna	sannawe	Savoyard	sanwnsngba
Saunter	santerin	Savvy	sanwnwn
Saurel	sanrejo	Saw1	sanwe

WORD (x)	EQUIVALENT (y)	WORD (x)	EQUIVALENT (y)
Saw2	sanwe	Scabious	sekobese
Saw3	sanwo	Scabrous	sekoberaisi
San buck	buki sanwe	Scaccography	sekokkiganphe
Sawn	sanwn	Scads	sekojosi
Sawyer	sanwnsnra	Scafell	sekofnjnra
Sax	sansi	Scaff	sekofon
Sax	sansi	Scaffold	sekofonjo
Saxatile	sansitiron	Scaffolding	sekofonjognni
Saxe	sansin	Scag	sekogbi
Saxocoburg	sansinkinugan	Scaglla	sekogbille
Saxe Weimar	sansin winimura	Scagllola	sekogbillejn
Sax horn	Sansi huran	Scalable	sekolebe
Saxicoline	Sansikinlehun	Scalade	sekolejn
Saxifragaceous	sansifangunsuma	Scalage	sekolegun
Saxifrage	sansifangun	Scalar	sekolera
Saxon	sanson	Scalare	sekolerai
Saxonism	sansonmosi	Scalariform	sekoleraifon
Saxonism	sansonsi	Scalawag	sekolewegn
Saxony	sansonse	Scald	sekojon
Saxophone	sansiphohun	Scale1	sekole
Saxtuba	sansitube	Scale2	sekole
Say	sanwi	Scale3	sekole
Say	sanwi	Scalene	sekolehun
Sayan	sanwini	Scalenus	sekolehunsi
Sayers	sanwisesi	Scaler	sekolesi
Sayid	sanwijn	Scall	sekolle
Saida	sanwijo	Scallion	sekollesi
Saying	sanwignni	Scallop	sekollepo
Say-so	sanwi-soo	Scallywag	sekollesewegn
Scab	sekobe	Scaloppini	sekolepohun
Scabbard	sekobegba	Scalp	sekolepn
Scabble	sekobejn	Scalpel	sekolepnlo
Scabbling	sekobegnni	Scalth	sekolesi
Scabies	sekobese	Scaly	sekojnse

WORD (x)	EQUIVALENT (y)	WORD (x)	EQUIVALENT (y)
Scam	sekomu	Scapula	sekopnjn
Scamander	sakomujnra	Scapular	sekopnjnra
Scamble	sekombe	Scar1	sekora
Scammony	sekommeni	Scar2	sekora
Scamp	sekompn	Scarab	sakorabe
Scamper	sekompnra	Scarabaeid	sekorabnjo
Scmpi	sekompi	Scaraboid	sekorabajo
Scan	sekoso	Scaramouch	sekoramokhun
Scandal	sekosojn	Scarborough	sekoraborongun
Scandalization	sekosojnseyoon	Scarce	sekorakn
Scandalize	sekosojnse	Scarcely	sekoraknlo
Scandalous	sekosojnsi	Scarcement	sekoraknmutto
Scandroon	sekosojnrain	Scarcity	sekoraknto
Scandent	sekosojnto	Scare	sekorau
Scandia	sekosojnna	Scare crow	sekorau knrawo
Scandic	sekosojnko	Scaremonger	sekorau menignra
Scandian	sekosojnhn	Scarf1	sekorafn
Scandinavia	sekosojnwa	Scarf2	sekorafn
Scandinavian	sekosojnwahn	Scarfpin	sekorafnpoha
Scandium	sekosojnma	Scarificator	sekorafikosi
Scanner	sekosoran	Scarifier	sekorafesi
Scansion	sekososoon	Scarify1	sekorafe
Scansorial	seksoosirailo	Scarify2	sekosrafe
Scant	sekote	Scarious	sekorausi
Scantling	sekotegnni	Scarlatina	sekopanto
Scanty	sekotesi	Scarlatinoid	sekopantojo
Scapa	sekopa	Scarlatti	sekopantto
Scape	sekopon	Scarlet	sekopan
Scape grace	sekopon ganson	Scarp	sekopan
Scaphoid	sekophijo	Scarpe	sekorapn
Scaphopod	sekophipindie	Scarper	sekorapnsi
Scapi	sekope	Scarron	sekorron
Scapolite	sekopnleyo	Scart	sekorate
Scapose	sekopnse	Scart	sekorate

WORD (x)	EQUIVALENT (y)	WORD (x)	EQUIVALENT (y)
Scarves	sekorawn	Schedule	sekhnduo
Scary	sekosia	Scheelite	sekhnleyo
Scat1	sekoti	Schema	sekhnma
Scat2	sekoti	Schematic	sekhnmako
Scathe	sekotise	Schematism	sekhunmamosi
Scathing	sekotignni	Schematize	sekhnmase
Scato	sekotin	Scheme	sekhnma
Scatology	sekotinlogbon	Schenk	sekhnki
Scatomancy	sekotinmoyesn	Scherzando	sekhnrasidie
Scatter	sekotnra	Scherzo	sekhnrasi
Scatter brain	sekotnra banto	Scheveningen	sekhnpanralle
Scattering	sekotnragnni	Schick	sekhiki
Scatty	sekotn	Schiedam	sekhijnma
Scaturient	sekotnraito	Schiller	sekhironsi
Scaup	sekopn	Schillerize	sekhironse
Scauper	sekopnra	Schilling	sekhirongnni
Scavenge	sekowngba	Schiuphel	sekhiphijin
Scavenger	sekowngbasi	Schipperke	sekhipnrako
Scenario	seknsarain	Schism	sekhimosi
Scend	seknjn	Schismatic	sekhimosiko
Scenarist	seknsaransi	Schist	sekhisi
Scene	seknsa	Schistaceous	sekhisisuwa
Scenery	seknsarai	Schisto	sekhisito
Scenic	seknsako	Schistosome	sekhisitosoomo
Scenography	seknsaganphe	Schistosomiasis	sekhisitosoomoso
Scent	seknti	Schizo	sekhisia
Sceptic	seknponko	Schizocarp	sekhisiakopan
Scepter	seknponsi	Schizogenesis	sekhisiagnhunso
Skeptical	seknponkojo	Schizogony	sekhisiagonse
Schacabac	sekhokibe	Schizoid	sekhisiajo
Schadenfreude	sekhodainfesi	Schizomycete	sekhisiamuknti
Schanz	sekhosn	Schizomycetes	sekhisiamukntisi
Scappe	sekhopipo	Schizont	sekhisiatn
Schatchen	sekhofekhn	Schizophrenia	sekhisiaphirain

WORD (x)	EQUIVALENT (y)	WORD (x)	EQUIVALENT (y)
Schizophyceous	sekhisiaphesuwa	School2	sekhoonjo
Schizophyte	sekhisiapheyo	School age	agba sekhoonjo
Schizopod	sekhisiapindie	Schoolmarm	sekhoonjokomora
Schizothymia	sekhisiasioma	Schooner	sekhoonran
Schlemiel	sekhuomulo	Schopenhauerism	sekhopinhauraimosi
Schlep	sekhuopn	Schorl	sekhorajo
Schley	sekhuosi	Schorlaceous	sekhorajosuwa
Schliere	sekhuoran	Schottische	sekhottikhn
Schlieren	sekhuorain	Schouton	sekhonita
Schlock	sekhuoki	Sachrik	sekhoraki
Schmaltz	sekhimusnto	Schrodinger	sekhoraijngnsi
Schmidt	sekhimujin	Schubert	sekhunbeto
Schmo	sekhimu	Schuit	sekhunte
Schmoose	sekhimooso	Schule	sekhunjn
Schmuck	sekhimuko	Schuman	sekhunmo
Schnabel	sekhnnibe	Schumann	sekhunmosi
Schnapps	sekhnnipo	Schurman	sekhunramo
Schnapper	sekhnnipnra	Schurz	sekhunrasi
Schnauzer	sekhnnisunsi	Schuschnigg	sekhunwagbn
Schnecken	sekhnknni	Schuss	sekhunsin
Schnitzler	sekhntojnra	Schuyler	sekhunjnra
Schnorkel	sekhnknrresi	Schwa	sekhwe
Schnozzle	sekhnknsun	Schweitzer	sekhwetosi
Schnook	sekhnknko	Schwetz	sechwesi
Scholar	sekhojn	Sciaenoid	sisunjo
Scholarch	sekhojnknra	Sciamachy	sisunmukho
Scholarship	sekhojnsunpn	Sciatic	sisunko
Scholarly	sekhojnlo	Sciatica	sisunsia
Scholastic	sekhojnkin	Science	sisunse
Scholasticate	sekhojnkinyo	Sciential	sisuntojo
Scholasticism	sekhojnkinmosi	Scientific	sisuntofiko
Scholiast	sekhojnseto	Scientism	sisuntomosi
Scholium	sekhojnma	Scientist	sisuntosi
School1	sekhoonjo	Scientologist	sisuntologbonsi

WORD (x)	EQUIVALENT (y)	WORD (x)	EQUIVALENT (y)
Scientology	sisuntologbon	Sclerite	sakuoranyo
Scifi	sisufe	Sclerites	sakuorunso
Scilicet	sisulokiti	Sclero	sakuoron
Scilla	sisulle	Scleroderma	sakuoronjnrama
Scilly	sisullo	Sclerodermatous	sakuoronjnramasi
Scimitar	sisumutnra	Scleroid	sakuoronjo
Scincold	sisunkijon	Scleroma	sakuoroma
Scintilla	sisuntilleyo	Sclerosis	sakuoronso
Scintillation	sisuntilleyoon	Sclerotic	sakuoontnko
Scintillator	sisuntillesi	Sclerotium	sakuorontnma
Sciolism	sisujnmosi	Sclerotomy	sakuorontemo
Sciolist	sisujnsi	Sclerous	sakuoronsi
Sciomancy	sisumoyesn	Scob	sokibo
Scion	sisuse	Scoff1	sokifo
Sciophilous	sisupheransi	Scoff2	sokifo
Sciophyte	sisupheyo	Scogger	sokigbnsi
Sciosophy	sisusoophe	Scold	sokijon
Scioto	sisuto	Scolecite	sokijnkiyo
Scire facias	sisurai fansise	Scolex	sokijnsi
Scirrhus	sisurhunsi	Scoliosis	sokijnso
Scissel	sisunlo	Scolopendrid	sokipindieraijo
Scissile	sisunla	Scombroid	sokimberaijo
Scission	sisunte	Sconce	sokinsi
Scissorer	sisunresi	Sconce	sokinsi
Scissor	sisunre	Scone	sokihun
Scissors	sisunrese	Sconner	sokihunsi
Scissortail	sisunretele	Scoop	sokipo
Scissure	sisunrein	Scoot	sokiti
Sciurine	sisunrain	Scooter	sokitisi
Sciuroid	sisunraijo	Scop	sokipn
Sclaff	sekanfo	Scope	sekipon
Sclera	sakuoran	Scopodromic	sokipongbimuko
Sclerenchyma	sakuorainkhoma	Scopolamine	sokiponlemini
Scleriasis	sakuoranso	Scopoline	sokiponlehun

WORD (x)	EQUIVALENT (y)	WORD (x)	EQUIVALENT (y)
Scopophilia	sokiponpheran	Scotophobia	sokitinphobua
Scopophobia	sokiponphobua	Scotopia	sokitinpan
Scopula	sokiponle	Scots	sokitise
Scopulate	sokiponleyo	Scott	sokitti
Scopus	sokipnsi	Scottish	sokittise
Scopy	sokipe	Scotticism	sokittikomosi
Scorbutic	sokirabuko	Scoundrel	sokijoinrejo
Scorbutus	sokirabusi	Scoundreldom	sokijoinrejodeo
Scorch	sokirakn	Scoundrelism	sokijoinrejomosi
Scorcher	sokiraknsi	Scoundrelly	sokijoinrejin
Scordato	sokirajnto	Scourl	sokiwe
Scordatura	sokirajntnra	Scour2	sokiwe
Score	sokiran	Scourer	sokiwesi
Scoreboard	bugbasokiran	Scourge	sokiwegi
Scoria	sokiran	Scourging	sokiwegignni
Scoriform	sokironfon	Scouse	sokise
Scarify	sokironfe	Scout	sokite
Scorn	sokiran	Scout	sokite
Scorpeanid	sokirunpinjo	Scouter	sokitesi
Scorper	sokirunpnsi	Scow	sokiwo
Scorpio	sokirunpo	Scowl	sokiwojn
Scorpioid	sokirunpnjo	Scabble	seknrabe
Scorpion	sokirunpn	Scrag	seknregi
Scot	sokiti	Scraggly	seknragilo
Scotch	sokitisi	Scraggy	seknragise
Scoter	sokitiran	Scraich	seknrake
Scot free	sokiti fesia	Scram	seknramo
Scotia	sokitini	Scramble	seknrambe
Scotie	sokitise	Scrambler	seknrambesi
Scotism	sokitimosi	Scrannel	seknrahun
Scotland	sokitiledain	Scranton	seknrantin
Scoto	sokitin	Scrap1	seknrapn
Scotoma	sokitinma	Scrap2	seknrapn
Scotophilia	sokitinpheron	Scrape	seknrapo

WORD (x)	EQUIVALENT (y)	WORD (x)	EQUIVALENT (y)
Scraper	seknraposi	Scripture	sekoraipnre
Scrapie	seknrapose	Scrive	sekoraiwn
Scrapple	seknrapon	Scrivello	sekoraiwnllo
Scrappy	seknrapo	Scrivener	sekoraiwinsi
Scratch	seknrate	Scrobiculate	seknrobnleyo
Scratchy	seknratesi	Scrod	seknrojo
Scrawl	seknrako	Scrofula	seknrofu
Scrawly	seknrakose	Scrofulous	seknrofusi
Scrawny	seknrakosi	Scroggy	seknrogn
Screak	seknranso	Scroll	seknrolo
Scream	seknranke	Scrolled	seknrolode
Screamer	seknrankesi	Scrooge	seknrogon
Scree	seknranse	Scroop	seknrope
Screech	seknranko	Scrophulariaceous	seknrophujnransuwa
Screed	seknranjin	Scrotum	seknropon
Screen	seknransi	Scrounge	seknrogbe
Screw	seknranwa	Scrounge	seknrongbe
Screwy	seknranwo	Scrouginig	seknrongbegnni
Scria	sekora	Scroungy	seknrongbese
Scribble	sekorairon	Scrub1	seknre
Scribbler	sekoraironsi	Scrub2	seknre
Scribe	sekorai	Scrubber	seknresi
Scrieve	sekoraiwn	Scrubby	seknrese
Scrim	sekoraimu	Scruff1	seknrefa
Scrimmage	sekoraimmugun	Scruff2	seknrefa
Scrimp	sekoraimpn	Scruffy	sekarefilo
Scrimshaw	sekoraimusue	Scrum	seknrem
Scrip	sekoraipa	Scrimmage	seknremogun
Scripps	sekoraipase	Scrump	seknrempo
Scripsit	sekoraipaseto	Scrumptious	seknremposi
Script	sekoraipn	Scrumpy	seknrempose
Scriptorium	sekoraipnrema	Scrunch	seknreunsi
Scriptural	sekoraipnrejo	Scruple	seknrepn
Scripturalism	sekoraipnrejomosi	Scrupulous	seknrepnsi

WORD (x)	EQUIVALENT (y)	WORD (x)	EQUIVALENT (y)
Scrutable	seknretebe	Scurry	sekuerrai
Scrutator	seknreteran	Scurvy	sekuewin
Scrutineer	seknretinsi	Scut	sekunte
Scrutinize	seknretinse	Scutage	sekuntegun
Scrutiny	seknretin	Scutari	sekunterai
Scrying	sekoraignni	Scutate	sekunteyo
Scuba	sekunmi	Scutch	sekuntesi
Scub	sekunjn	Scutcheon	sekuntesinle
Scudder	sekunjnra	Scute	sekunti
Scudery	sekunjnrai	Scutellate	sekuntilleyo
Scudo	sekunde	Scutellation	sekuntilleyoon
Scuff	sekunfan	Scutellum	sekuntillema
Scuffle	sekunfanjn	Scutter	sekunttesi
Sculdudder	sekunjnran	Scuttle1	sekuntteron
Scull	sekunjo	Scuttle2	sekuntteron
Scull	sekunjo	Scuttle3	sekuntteron
Sculler	sekunjosi	Scuttle	sekunttejosi
Scullery	sekunjorai	Scutum	sekuntema
Scullion	sekunjoin	Scutum	sekuntema
Sculp	sekuopa	Skuzzy	seknsuse
Sculpin	sekuopan	Scylla	sekojnra
Sculpt	sekuopn	Scyphistoma	sekophntoma
Sculptor	sekuopnran	Scypho	sekophn
Sculpture	sekuopnrai	Scyphozoan	sekophnsinhn
Sculpturesque	sekuopnraikun	Scyphus	sekophnsi
Scum	sekuo	Scythe	sekosi
Scumble	sekuobe	Scythia	sekosia
Scunthorpe	sekunsipon	Scythian	sekosiahn
Scup	sekuepn	Se	sei
Scupper1	sekuepnra	Sea	osa
Scupper2	sekuepnra	Sea anchor	akhiran osa
Scurf	sekuefe	Sea anemone	ahunmini
Scurrility	sekuerraitn	Seabed	sebeosa
Scurrilous	sekuerrailosi	Sea bird	barai osa

WORD (x)	EQUIVALENT (y)	WORD (x)	EQUIVALENT (y)
Seaboard	bugbaosa	Seaside	osasoojo
Seaborne	boroinosa	Season	osasin
Seagage	osagigun	Seasonable	osasinbe
Seagirt	osagiran	Seasonal	osasinjo
Seagull	osagunjjn	Seasoner	osasinsi
Seakale	osaknron	Seasoning	osasingnni
Seal1	sejain	Seat	setn
Seal2	sejain	Seat-belt	setnbejia
Selant	sejaintn	Seater	setnsi
Sealer	sejainsi	Seating	setngnni
Sealery	sejainrai	Seattle	setnron
Sea lion	lile osa	Seawan	osawin
Sea lord	lojain osa	Seaward	osawegba
Seam	semo	Seaway	osawelo
Seaman	moyeosa	Seaweed	osawinijn
Seamanship	moyeosaunpn	Seaworthy	osawinisan
Seamstress	semositnranbo	Sebaceous	segborasuwa
Seamy	semosi	Sebacic	segborako
Sean	sehun	Sebastian	segborasuan
Séance	sehunsi	Sebastopol	segboratopnjin
Seannachic	sehunkhinko	Sebi	segbora
Seaport	osapinta	Sebiferous	segborafirosi
Seaquake	osa kunknra	Seborrhea	segborarhain
Sear	sera	Seborrhoea	segborarhoin
Sear	sera	Sebum	segborama
Search	sekhnri	Sec1	seki
Searchlight	ligheseknri	Sec2	seki
Search-party	panteni-seknri	Secant	sekite
Search warrant	werraite seknri	Secateous	sekiteraisi
Sea room	roomo osa	Secco	sekki
Seal salt	sanjyo osa	Secede	seknjin
Seascape	osasakipon	Secem	seknran
Seashell	osasualle	Secesh	seknso
Seasick	osasokoi	Secession	seknsoon

WORD (x)	EQUIVALENT (y)	WORD (x)	EQUIVALENT (y)
Secessionism	seknsoonmosi	Sectionalism	sekntesijomosi
Seck	sekin	Sectionalist	sekntesijosi
Seckel	sekinlo	Sectionality	sekntesijotn
Seclude	sekorajin	Sectionalize	sekntesijose
Seclusion	sekorasoon	Sector	seknteran
Seclusive	sekoraso	Sectoral	seknteranjo
Second1	sekinjo	Secular	sekunjnra
Second2	sekinjo	Secularism	sekunjnramosi
Second3	sekinjo	Secularist	sekunjnrasi
Secondary	sekinjora	Secularity	sekunjnratn
Second-best	besii sekinjo	Secularize	sekunjnrase
Second class	kansoo sekinjo	Secund	sekunjo
Seconde	sekinjin	Secunderabad	sekunjorabe
Seconder	sekinjora	Secundine	sekunjoin
Secondly	sekinjolo	Secundumusum	sekunjomawama
Secondo	sekinjon	Secure	sekunrai
Secrecy	seknrasn	Security	sekunraitn
Secret	seknra	Sedan	sedasi
Seret agent	aginte seknra	Sedan	sedasi
Secretage	seknragun	Sedate	sedayo
Secretaire	seknaran	Sedation	sedayoon
Secretariat	seknrararainto	Sedative	sedayowin
Secretary	seknrarai	Sedentary	sedantorai
Secretary-general	gnhunraijo seknrarai	Seder	sejnra
Secretary of state	seknrarai ti setnyo	Sedge	sedagn
Secrete	seknrayo	Sedgemoor	sedagnmora
Secretin	seknratie	Sedile	sediron
Secretion	seknrayoon	Sediment	sedimutto
Secretive	seknrayowin	Sedimentary	sedimuttorai
Secretory	seknrarai	Sedimentation	sedimuttoyoon
Sect	seknte	Sedimentology	sedimuttologbon
Sectarian	seknterain	Sedition	sediyoon
Section	sekntesi	Seditionary	sediyoonrai
Sectional	sekntesijo	Seduce	sedikn

WORD (x)	EQUIVALENT (y)	WORD (x)	EQUIVALENT (y)
Seduction	sediknyoon	Seicento	seknnito
Seductive	sediknwin	Seiche	sekhiun
Seductress	sediknranbo	Seidlitz	segbileto
Sedulous	sedijnsi	Seigneur	seginiran
Sedum	sedima	Seigneury	seginirai
See1	seso	Seignior	segbainran
See2	seso	Seigniorage	segbainrangun
Seed	segbn	Seim	semi
Seed-bed	beje-segbn	Seine	sehun
Seeder	segbnsi	Seise	sesun
Seedling	segbngnni	Seism	sesunmi
Seed-pearl	segbn-pnranjo	Seismic	sesunmiko
Seedsman	segbnmoye	Seismo	sesunmo
Seedy	segbnni	Seismogram	sesunmoganmo
Seeing	sesognni	Seismograph	sesunmoganpha
Seek	sesoka	Seismology	sesunmologbon
Seem	semini	Seismometer	sesunmomuto
Seeming	seminignni	Seismometry	sesunmomutorai
Seemly	seminilo	Seismoscope	sesunmosekipon
Seen	sesosi	Seistan	sesuntin
Seep	semi	Seize	sesin
Seepage	semmigun	Seizer	sesinsi
Seer	sesosi	Seizing	sesinni
See-saw	seso-sanwe	Seizure	sesinran
Seethe	sesosi	Sejant	sejaute
Segment	segnmutto	Sejm	sejnma
Segmentation	segnmuttoyoon	Selachii	sejnkhi
Segno	segnkn	Selachian	sejnkhihn
Sego	segini	Selachiod	sejnkhijo
Segovia	seginwan	Selaginella	sejngninille
Segregate	segiraigiyo	Selah	sejnho
Segregation	segiraigiyoon	Selamjik	sejnlikima
Segue	segan	Selanga	sejngnran
Seguidilla	seganjnlle	Seldom	sejndeo

WORD (x)	EQUIVALENT (y)	WORD (x)	EQUIVALENT (y)
Select	sejnsa	Selves	sejnwin
Selectee	sejnsase	Semantic	semuyeko
Selection	sejnsayoon	Semanticist	semuyekosi
Selective	sejnsawin	Semantics	semuyekosi
Selectivity	sejnsawintn	Semaphore	semuphirai
Selectoman	sejnsamoye	Semarang	semuragn
Selector	sejnsaran	Semasiology	semusiologbon
Selene	sejnnu	Sematic	semuko
Selenate	sejnnuyo	Semblable	sembejora
Selenga	sejngini	Semblance	sembejorasi
Selenic	sejnnko	Semble	sembosi
Selnoius	sejnnusi	Seme	semua
Selenite	sejnnuto	Semele	semumo
Selenium	sejnnuma	Semen	semini
Seleno	sejnko	Semester	semiseto
Selenodont	sejnkodeyo	Semi	semi
Selenography	sejnkoganphe	Semi-bold	semi boojon
Selenologist	sejnkologbonsi	Semibreve	semibesiwin
Selenology	sejnkologbon	Semilunar	semilujnra
Seleucia	sejnwakin	Semimute	semimuto
Seleucid	sejnwakijo	Seminal	seminijo
Seleucus	sejnwakisi	Seminar	seminiran
Self	sejo	Seminary	seminirai
Selfish	sejofisun	Semination	seminiyoon
Seljuk	sejojoko	Seminiferous	seminifirosi
Selkirk	sejoknra	Seminivorous	seminiwnrunsi
Sell	sejnra	Seminole	semikojn
Seller	sejnrasi	Semiology	semikologbon
Sellotape	sejnratepon	Semiotics	semikotekosi
Sell-out	sejnra-nita	Semioviparous	semikownpanrasi
Seltzer	seijiasi	Semipalmate	semipnjomote
Selva	sejnwa	Semite	semite
Selvage	sejnwagun	Semitic	semiteko
Salvagen	sejnwagunsi	Semiticism	semitekomosi

WORD (x)	EQUIVALENT (y)	WORD (x)	EQUIVALENT (y)
Semitone	semitoni	Sennit	sesunto
Semolina	semojinna	Sennopia	seknpan
Sempach	sempanki	Serior	seknran
Semper	sempnra	Seriora	seknra
Simper paratus	sempnra panrasi	Seriorita	seknrate
Sempervirent	sempnravoraito	Sensate	sesnsnyo
Sempiternal	sempntiranjo	Sensation	sesnsnyoon
Semplice	sempansi	Sensational	sesnsnyoonjo
Sempre	sempesi	Sensationalism	sesnsnyoonjomosi
Sempstress	sempetnranbo	Sense	sesnsn
Sen	sesi	Senseless	snsnsnlabo
Senary	sesirai	Sensibility	snsnsnbetn
Senate	sesitn	Sensible	sesnsnbe
Senator	sesitnra	Sensitization	sesnsnteseyoon
Senatorial	sesitnraijo	Sensitive	sesnsntewinto
Senatus	sesitnsi	Sensitize	sesnsntese
Send	sesijn	Sensitometer	sesnsntemuto
Sandal	sesijnle	Sesnsor	sesnsnran
Seneca	sesinko	Sensorium	sesnsnraima
Senega	sesingi	Sensory	sesnsnrai
Senegal	sesingijo	Sensual	sesnsnjo
Senegambia	sesigimbua	Sensualism	sesnsnjomosi
Senescent	sesiseknti	Sensuality	sesnsnjotn
Seneschal	sesisekhojo	Sensualize	sesnsnjose
Senile	sesiijn	Sensuous	sesnsnsi
Senility	sesiijntn	Sent	sesita
Senilium	sesiijnma	Sentence	sesitinso
Senior	sesiiran	Sententious	sesitinsosi
Seniority	sesiiraito	Sentience	sesitasi
Senlac	sesijnko	Sentient	sesitato
Senna	sesun	Sentiment	sesitamutto
Sennar	sesunra	Sentimental	sesitamuttojo
Sennet	sesunte	Sentimentalism	sesitamuttojomosi
Sennight	sesungeu	Sentinel	sesitajo

WORD (x)	EQUIVALENT (y)	WORD (x)	EQUIVALENT (y)
Sentry	sesitarai	Septicemia	sepntiknmua
Sepal	sepnjo	Septic tank	tejnkn sepntiko
Separable	sepnraibe	Septicidal	sepntikijnjo
Separate	sepnraiyo	Septicity	sepntikito
Separation	sepnraiyoon	Septifragal	sepntifangnjo
Separatist	sepnraiyosi	Septilateral	sepntiletoraijo
Separator	sepnrairan	Septillion	sepntijnrasi
Separatrix	sepnraitnrasi	Septime	sepntimo
Separatum	sepnraima	Septuagenarian	sepntigbarain
Sephardi	sephisinjo	Septuagenary	sepntigbarai
Sepia	sepan	Septuagesima	sepntigbasemo
Sepix	sepako	Septuagesima	sepntigbasemo
Sepiolite	sepaknleyo	Septuagint	sepntigbatn
Sepoy	seposi	Septum	sepntima
Sepsis	sepnso	Septuple	sepntipon
Sept.	sepnt	Septuplicate	sepntipankoyo
Septangle	sepntenigun	Sepulcaher	sepujnjhnra
Septarium	sepnteraima	Sepulchral	sepujnkhnrajoi
Septate	sepnteyo	Sepulcher	sepujnkhnran
Septavalent	sepntewajnso	Sepulture	sepujntnrai
Septectomy	sepntetemo	Sequacious	sekunrasi
September	sepntembe	Sequel	sekunra
Septembrist	sepntembesi	Sequela	sekunran
Septemia	sepntemwirai	Sequence	sekunrase
Septenary	sepntehnrai	Sequencer	sekunrasesi
Septennate	sepntehunyo	Sequent	sekunrato
Septennial	sepntehunjo	Sequential	sekunratojo
Septennium	sepntehunma	Sequester	sekunsoto
Septentrio	sepntetorain	Sequestered	sekunsotode
Septemtrion	sepntetnrain	Sequestrant	sekunsotorai
Septet	sepnteto	Sequestrate	sekunsotoraiyo
Septi	sepnti	Sequestrum	sekunsotorun
Septic	sepntiko	Sequin	sekunso
Septicaemia	sepntikoinmua	Sequoia	sekuosi

WORD (x)	EQUIVALENT (y)	WORD (x)	EQUIVALENT (y)
Sequola	sekuojain	Serialism	seraijomosi
Ser	sera	Seriatim	seraitemo
Serac	serakn	Seriation	seraiyoon
Seraglio	seragiun	Sericeous	seraisuwa
Serai	serajo	Sericin	seraikin
Serajevo	serajnwn	Sericulture	seraikunjiaran
Serall	serajjo	Seriema	serainmo
Serape	serapon	Series	serainsi
Seraph	seraphn	Serif	seraifo
Seraphic	seraphnko	Serigraph	seraiganpha
Seraphim	seraphnmo	Serigraphy	seraiganphe
Seraphin	seraphini	Serin	serahn
Seraphine	seraphohun	Serine	serahun
Serapis	serapesi	Seringa	seraigin
Seraskier	serasiasia	Seringapatam	seraiginpntima
Serbia	serabua	Serio-comic	serain-kimuko
Serbian	serabuahn	Serious	seraisi
Serbo	seraboo	Serjeant	serajnte
Serbonian	seraboomi	Serjeant-at-arms	serajnte ni ariamu
Serdab	serajnbe	Sermon	serameni
Sere	serai	Sermonet	seramenite
Serein	seraijn	Sermonic	serameniko
Serena	seraihun	Sermonize	seramenise
Serenata	seraihunto	Sero	sero
Serendipity	serainjopiti	Serology	serologbon
Serene	serain	Seroon	serosia
Serf	serafe	Serosity	seroseto
Serge	seragan	Serotherapy	serosinranpo
Sergeant	seragante	Serotinous	serotiesi
Sergeant-major	seragante-mojuran	Serotonin	serotooni
Sergeant	seraganto	Serous	serose
Sergipe	seraganpn	Serow	serowa
Serial	seraijo	Serpens	serapnsi
Serialize	seraijose	Serpent	serapetun

WORD (x)	EQUIVALENT (y)	WORD (x)	EQUIVALENT (y)
Serpentine	serapetunsi	Sesqui-	sesakun
Serpento	serapetunse	Sesquiltera	sesakuijotnra
Serpigo	serapnlejo	Sesquicentennial	sesakuikntihunjo
Serra	serran	Sesquipedalian	sesakuipndiejoin
Serranoid	serrainjo	Sesquiplane	sesakuipanyun
Serrate	serraiyo	Sess	sesoo
Serration	serraiyoon	Sessile	sesoojn
Serrefile	serraifijan	Session	sesoon
Serried	serraide	Sesterces	sesitnra
Serriform	serraifon	Sestertium	sesitnratoma
Serraulate	serraileyo	Sestet	sesito
Serrulation	serraileyoon	Sestina	sesitohun
Sertorious	seratoraisi	Sestus	sesitn
Sertularian	seratojnrain	Set1	seton
Serum	seroma	Set2	seton
Serval	serawnjo	Set3	seton
Servant	serawnte	Seta	seta
Serve	serawn	Setaceous	setasuwa
Server	serawnsi	Set-back	seton-boki
Servery	serawnrai	Set piece	seton pansi
Servetus	serawntisi	Set square	seton sekunrai
Servia	serawnni	Sete	setn
Service	serawnsi	Setebos	setnbosi
Serviceable	serawnsibe	Seth	setnsi
Serviceman	serawnsimoye	Seti	setin
Servicewoman	serawnsiwinmoye	Setiferous	setinfirosi
Serviette	serawnti	Setiform	setinfoon
Servile	serawnjn	Seton	setinsi
Serving	serawngnni	Setose	setinse
Servitor	serawntosi	Sett	setton
Servitude	serawntujin	Settee	settonsn
Servo	serawe	Settee	settonsn
Sesame	sesame	Setter	settonsi
Sesamoid	sesamojo	Set theoy	seton sinrain

WORD (x)	EQUIVALENT (y)	WORD (x)	EQUIVALENT (y)
Setting	snttongnni	Sewer	sewerai
Settle1	settonron	Sewer	sewerai
Settle2	settonron	Sewerage	seweraigun
Settlement	settonronmutto	Sewerity	seweraito
Settler	settonronsi	Sewern	seweran
Setto	seta	Sewing	sewegnni
Setubal	setonbejo	Sewn	seweni
Setulose	setonlose	Sex	sesia
Set up	seton pake	Sex	sesia
Seurat	seriate	Sexagenarian	sesiagbarain
Sevan	sewain	Sexagenary	sesiagbarai
Seven	sewini	Sexagesima	sesiagbasomo
Seven seas	osasi sewini	Sexagesimal	sesiagbasomojn
Seventeen	sewinitoon	Sexangle	sesianigun
Seventeenth	sewinitoonsi	Sexcentenary	sesiakntirai
Seventh	sewinisi	Sexennnial	sesiahunjo
Seventy	sewinitn	Sexfid	sesiafijo
Sever	sewnra	Sexism	sesiamosi
Severable	sewnrabe	Sexless	sesialabo
Several	sewnraijo	Sexology	sesialogbon
Severally	sewnraijin	Sex symbol	sesia sombujn
Severalty	sewnraijotn	Sext	sesiatn
Severance	sewnrasi	Sextain	sesiatelu
Severance pay	panyio sewnraisi	Sextans	sesiatesu
Severe	sewnrai	Sextant	sesiatetn
Sevem	sewnrain	Sextarious	sesiateraisi
Sevemaya	sewnrainni	Sextet	sesiateto
Sevign	sewogini	Sextile	sesiatiron
Seville	sewolle	Sextillion	sesiatijnransi
Sevres	sewoora	Sexton	sesiatnsi
Sew	sewe	Sextuple	sesiatopo
Sewage	sewegun	Sextuplet	sesiatoposi
Sewall	sewejjo	Sextuplicate	sesiatopankoyo
Seward	sewegba	Sexual	sesiajo

WORD (x)	EQUIVALENT (y)	WORD (x)	EQUIVALENT (y)
Sexuality	sesialeto	Shahjehan	suehajnhun
Sexy	sesian	Shairp	sueranpo
Sey	sesn	Shake	suegbon
Seyhan	sesnhun	Shaker	suegbonsi
Sferics	sefiraikosi	Shakespeare	suegbonsopnran
Sh	su	Shake up	suegbon pake
Shabby	suebn	Shakhti	suekhito
Shabuoth	seubuyo	Shako	sueki
Shack	suekn	Shakti	suekiti
Shack	suekn	Shaky	suegbonse
Shackle	sueknron	Shale	suele
Shad	suejn	Shale	suele
Shadbelly	suejnbello	Shall	suejan
Shad berry	suejn berrai	Shalloon	suejansi
Shadbush	suejnbuso	Shallop	suejanpo
Shaddock	suejnkin	Shallot	suejanto
Shade	suejin	Shallow	suejanwa
Shading	suejingnni	Shalom	suejoma
Shadoof	suejnfoon	Shalt	suejia
Shadow	suejowa	Shalwar	suejanwo
Shadowgraph	suejowaganpha	Sham	suemo
Shadowy	suejowase	Shaman	suemoye
Shadrach	suejoraikn	Shamanism	suemoyemosi
Shady	suejnse	Shamanish	suemoyese
Shaft	suefio	Shamash	suemosin
Shaft	suefio	Shamateurism	suemotnraimosi
Shafting	suefiognni	Shamble	suembe
Shag1	suegi	Shambles	suembesi
Shag2	suegi	Shambolic	suembujnko
Shaganippi	suegipanpo	Shame	suemini
Shaggy	suegise	Shameless	seuminilabo
Shagreen	suegirain	Shammy	suemmo
Shah	sueha	Shamo	suema
Shahaptian	suehapnti	Shampoo	suempnti

WORD (x)	EQUIVALENT (y)	WORD (x)	EQUIVALENT (y)
Shamrock	suemroki	Sharpie	supnreni
Shamus	suemosi	Sharpish	supnreso
Shan	sueho	Shat	suetn
Shand	suegbe	Shatter	suettnra
Shandrydan	suegberaidan	Shauchie	suekhunse
Shandy	suegbesi	Shauchle	suekhunron
Shandygaff	suegbesigifan	Shave	suewn
Shanghai	suegbnho	Shaven	suewnni
Shangrila	suegbnrai	Shaver	suewnsi
Shank	suekun	Shavetail	suewntele
Shankara	suekunra	Shavie	suewnse
Shannon	suehunni	Shaving	suewngnni
Shanny	suehunse	Shaw	suewe
Shant	suehunte	Shawl	suewejo
Shantung	suehuntegan	Shawnee	suewese
Shanty1	suehunto	Shay	suesn
Shanty2	suehunto	She	sua
Shanty town	igboro (town) suehunto	Shea	suan
Shape	suepon	Sheaf	suafan
Shaped	sueponde	Sheal	suajo
Shapeless	sueponlabo	Shear	suare
Shapely	sueponlo	Shearling	suaregnni
Shard	suegbaa	Shears	suaresi
Share1	suerai	Sheat	suate
Share2	suerai	Sheath	suasin
Share-out	suerai-nita	Sheathe	suasinse
Shari	suerain	Sheathing	suasingnni
Shark1	suknra	Sheave	suawini
Shark2	suknra	Sheaves	suawinsi
Sham	sueran	Sheba	suabo
Sharon	suroin	Shebang	suabogan
Sharp	supnre	Shebeen	suaboti
Sharpen	supnresi	Shechem	suakhnmo
Sharper	supnrese	Shed1	suagban

WORD (x)	EQUIVALENT (y)	WORD (x)	EQUIVALENT (y)
Shed2	suagban	Shemite	suamuyo
Shedder	suagbasi	Shemozzle	suamosunran
Sheen	suani	Shenandoha	suahunjnkin
Sheep	suapn	Shenanigan	suahungini
Sheep berry	suapn berrai	Shensi	suasin
Sheep cote	sueapnkito	Shenstone	suasintoni
Sheepish	suapnse	Shenyang	suayngan
Sheer1	suaran	Sheol	suajin
Sheer2	suaran	Shepard	suapngba
Sheemess	suaransi	Shepherd	suaphngba
Sheet1	suate	Sheppey	suapnse
Sheet2	suate	Sherardize	suaragbase
Sheeve	suawini	Sheraton	surantin
Sheffield	suafilojnra	Sherbet	suaranmi
Sheikh	suakhi	Sherd	suarejo
Shekel	suaknra	Sheridan	suaraijn
Shekinah	suaknhun	Sherif	suaraifn
Sheldon	suagbain	Sheriff	suaraifun
Sheldrake	suagbainki	Sheriffmuir	suanraifunmora
Shelf	suafon	Sherlock	suarankin
Shelikof	sualokn	Sherman	suaranye
Shell	sualle	Sherpa	suarapan
Shellac	sualleko	Sherramoor	suarramooro
Shellack	suallekin	Sherrington	suarrogantin
Shelled	suallede	Sherry	suareai
Shalley	suallese	Sherwani	suaranwain
Shelta	sualete	Shet	suate
Shelter	sualeto	Shet	suate
Shelta	suelete	Shetland	suatnledain
Shelter	sualeto	Sheuch	suakhun
Sheltie	sualetie	Shew	suawn
Shelve	sualewn	Sheyenne	suasunhun
Shelves	sualewnsi	Shiah	sunleke
Shem	suamo	Shibboleth	sunbolelesi

WORD (x)	EQUIVALENT (y)	WORD (x)	EQUIVALENT (y)
Shibeli	sunbejn	Shine	sunene
Shicker	sunkisi	Shiner	sunenesi
Shickered	sunkiside	Shingle1	sungnron
Shidehara	sunjinhun	Shingle2	sungnron
Shield	sunjoin	Shingles	sungnronsi
Shier	sunrai	Shining	sunenegnni
Shiest	sunset	Shinkin	sunsikin
Shift	sunfia	Shinny	sunenese
Shiftless	sunfialabo	Shinplaster	sunsipanseto
Shifty	sunfiato	Shintiyan	suntnyan
Shiism	sunmosin	Shinto	suntokn
Shigella	sungnlle	Shiny	sunenese
Shiite	sunato	Ship	sunpn
Shikar	sunknra	Ship	sunpn
Shikaree	sunknrai	Shipboard	bugbasunpn
Shikoku	sunkiko	Shipload	sunpnlogbi
Shiksa	sunkisa	Shipmate	sunpnmote
Shilka	sunlako	Shipment	sunpnmutto
Shill	sunlle	Shippen	sunpnya
Shillelagh	sunlleghan	Shipper	sunpnsi
Shilling	sunllegnni	Shipping	sunpngnni
Shillong	sunlogn	Ship yard	yandan sunpn
Shilly-shally	sunllo suello	Shire	suran
Shiloh	sunllosn	Shirk	suraki
Shilpit	sunlepe	Shirley	suralese
Shim	sunmo	Shirr	sunrran
Shimmer	sunmmorai	Shirt	suratn
Shimmy	sunmmo	Shirting	suratnse
Shin	sunsi	Shish kebab	sunseknbe
Shinar	sunsirai	Shit	sutie
Shinned	sunside	Shittim	sutietemo
Shin-bone	sunsi-boin	Shive	sunwn
Shin-dig	sunsidign	Shiver1	sunwnsi
Shindy	sunjise	Shiver2	sunwnsi

WORD (x)	EQUIVALENT (y)	WORD (x)	EQUIVALENT (y)
Shivery	sunwnrai	shore1	surami
Shoal1	sujo	shore2	surami
Shoal2	sujo	shoreing	suramignni
Shoaly	sujose	shoreline	suramilehun
Shoat	suti	shoreward	suramiwegba
Shock1	suki	shom	sumo
Shock2	suki	short	sute
Shock3	suki	shorten	sutesi
Shocker	sukisi	shortage	sutegun
Shocking	sukignni	shortening	sutesignni
Shod	sujn	shortia	sutie
Shoddy	sujnse	shortly	sutelo
Shoe	suse	Shoshone	susune
Shoer	susesi	Shoshonean	susuknnihn
Shofar	sufan	Shot1	sutn
Shogun	sugunta	Shot2	sutn
Shogunate	suguntayo	Shotgun	sutngunta
Sholapur	sulepn	Shotepeening	sutnpnnignni
Shone	sune	Shotten	sutntin
Shoo	sun	Should	sujon
Shoofly	sunfolo	Shoulder	sujonsi
Shooin	suni	Shout	sutu
Shoogle	sunjiron	Shouter	sutusi
Shook	sungban	Shouther	sutinsi
Shook	sungban	Shove	suwn
Shoon	sunsi	Shovel	suwnlo
Shoot	sunta	Shoveler	suwnlosi
Shooting	suntagnni	Show	suwo
Shoot out	sunta nita	Showbiz	suwobuse
Shop	supn	Shower	suwosi
Shoplift	supnlefia	Showgirl	suwogirin
Shopper	supnsi	Showoff	suwooffan
shopping	supngnni	Shown	suwai
shoran	suran	Showy	suwose

WORD (x)	EQUIVALENT (y)	WORD (x)	EQUIVALENT (y)
Shrank	sureki	Shuffle	sunfijn
Shrapnel	surepnti	Shuffler	sunfijnsi
Shred	sureja	Shufty	sunfiase
Shrew	surewn	Shul	sunjo
Shrewd	surewnjo	Shulamite	sunjomuyo
Shrewdie	surewnjose	Shun	sunsa
Shrewish	surewnjosi	Shunt	sunsate
Shrieke	suraikn	Shush	sunsin
Shrill	suraille	Shut	sunti
Shrimp	suraipon	Shute	suntiyo
Shrine	surain	Shutter	sunttisi
Shriner	surainsi	Shuttle	sunttnbo
Shrink	suraiki	Shy1	suin
Shrinkage	suraikigun	Shy2	suin
Shrive	suraiwin	Shylock	suinlokn
Shrivel	suraiwinlo	Shyster	suinseto
Shriven	suraiwini	Si	so
Shroff	suranfn	Sial	sojn
Shroud	suranjn	Sialid	sojnjo
Shroud	suranjn	Sialkot	sojnkiti
Shrove	suranwin	Sialo	sojnmi
Shrovetide	surawintijin	Sialogog	sojnmigon
Shrub	surabe	Sialoid	sojnmijo
Shrub	surabe	Siam	somo
Shrubbery	suraberai	Siamang	somogun
Shrug	suragbi	Siamese	somosi
srdShrubbery	suraberai	Siang	sogin
Shrug	suragbi	Sib	sobe
Shrunk	suraki	Sibelius	sobejnsi
Shtick	sutikin	Siberia	soberai
Shuck	suknun	Siberian	soberaihn
Shucking	suknungnni	Sibilant	soboletn
Shucks	suknunsi	Sibling	sobejngnni
Shudder	sunjnra	Sibilate	soboleyo

WORD (x)	EQUIVALENT (y)	WORD (x)	EQUIVALENT (y)
Sbilati	soboleyo	Sidero	soojorin
Sibuyan	sobeyun	Sidero	soojoron
Sibyl	sobolo	siderolite	soojorinleyo
Sibylline	sobollohun	Siderroscope	soojorinsokpon
Sic	soka	Sidirosis	soojorinso
Sic	soka	Siderostat	soojoronsetnti
Sic	soka	Siderward	soojowegba
Siccative	sokknyowin	Sideways	soojowelosi
Sicel	soknlo	Sidewheel	soojowhinlo
Sicily	sokijin	Siding	soojognni
Sick	sokuo	Sidle	soojosi
Sickbay	sokuobosua	Sidney	soojoin
Sickbed	sokuobeje	Sidon	soojnle
Sicken	sokuose	Sidra	soojnra
Sicker	sokuosi	Sie	soo
Sickish	sokuosu	Soebengebirge	soobeginigunrai
Sickle	sokuoran	Siècle	sookuo
Sickle-cell	sokuoran knjjn	Siedice	soojnsi
Sickly	sokuolo	Siegbahun	soogbain
Sickness	sokuonisi	Siege	soogbi
Sick-pay	sokuo panyio	Siege	soogbi
Sicyon	sosnsi	Siegfried	soogbifan
Siddur	soodura	Siegttell	soogbitojjn
Side	soojo	Siemens	soominisi
Side	soojn	Siena	soorai
Sideboard	bugbasoojo	Sienna	sooran
Sideboards	bugbasoojo	Sierozem	soorasinmi
Sidelight	soojoleghe	Sierra	soorrai
Sideline	soojolehun	Sierra leone	soorrai jnknhun
Sidelong	soojologun	Sierra madre	soorrai morain
Sedereal	soojnraijo	Sierra morena	soorria morain
Sidereal day	soojnraijo dase	Sierra Nevada	soorrai hunwajn
Side road	soojo-rojin	Siesta	sooseto
Sidenite	soojorinyoo	Sieur	soora

WORD (x)	EQUIVALENT (y)	WORD (x)	EQUIVALENT (y)
Sieve	soown	Signify	sooganfe
Sieve tissue	soown tisesun	Signor	sooganran
Sieyes	sooyesi	Signora	soongarai
Sifaka	soofaka	Signorelli	sooganraille
Siffle	soofe	Sigmnorina	soognarin
Sift	soofia	signnorino	sooganroin
Sigh	sooyan	signory	sooganrai
Sight	sogbe	signrd	soogangba
Sighted	sogbede	signpost	sooganpiseto
Sightless	sogbelabo	signwriter	sooganwanto
Sightly	sogbelo	sii	soo
Sigil	sooganlo	sika	sokan
Sigismund	soogansemujn	sikang	`
Sigla	sooganle	sike	sokn
Sigma	sooganmo	sikh	sokhn
Sigmate	sooganmote	Sikhism	sokhntmosi
Sigmoid	sooganmujo	Sikhotealin	sokhntijan
Sign	soogan	Sikkm	soknmo
Signall	sooganjjo	Silage	solegun
Signal 2	sooganjo	Silane	soleni
Signal-box	sooganjo-bosi	Silas	solesi
Signalize	sooganjose	Silazane	solesehun
Signally	sooganjin	Sila	sole
Signalman	sooganjomoye	Silanceous	solesuwa
Signalment	sooganjomutto	silence	solekn
Signatory	soogantnrai	silencer	soleknsi
Signature	soogantnran	silent	soletn
Signature tune	tuhun sogantnran	silent butler	soletn butejnra
Signboard	bugbasoogan	silent majority	mojuraito soletn
Signet	soogante	silentiary	soletnrai
Signet-ring	rogan-soogante	silenus	solesi
Significance	sooganfikosi	silesia	solesia
Significant	sooganfikotn	silex	solesi
Significant figure	figira soogantfikotn	silhouette	solehuntn

WORD (x)	EQUIVALENT (y)	WORD (x)	EQUIVALENT (y)
silic	soleko	silures	soleraisi
silica	soleko	Silurian	solerain
silicane	solekohun	silurid	soleraijo
silicate	solekoyo	sylvan	solewain
siliceous	solesuwa	silvanus	solewainsi
silicic	solekiko	silver	solewa
silicide	solekiji	silver berry	solewa berrai
siliciferous	solekifirosi	silvering	solewagnni
silicife	solekife	silverly	solewalo
silicle	solekuo	silvern	solewaran
silicon	solekin	silvery	solewarai
silicon chip	khipn solekin	silvester	solewaseto
silicone	solekinnu	silvi	solewo
silicosis	solekiso	silviculture	solewokunjiaran
siliculose	solekilose	sil vous plait	sole wasi pantn
silique	solekue	sim	soma
siliquose	solekuose	sima	soma
siliquous	solekuosi	simar	somara
silistria	solesetnran	simaruba	somarabo
silk	soleke	simarubaceous	somarabosuwa
silkaline	solekelehun	simbor	somberan
silken	solekesi	simchath	somkhosin
silky	solekese	simcoe	somkise
sill	solle	simeon	somale
sillabub	sollebu	simian	somani
silliman	sollemoye	similar	somajora
sillimanite	sollemoyeyo	similarity	somajoratn
silly	sollese	similarly	somajoralo
silo	solo	simile	somajo
siloam	solomi	similia	somajosi
siloxane	solosanun	similitude	somajotujin
silt	soleto	simious	somanisi
siltation	soletoyoon	simla	somajn
silthiane	solesihun	simmer	sommorai

WORD (x)	EQUIVALENT (y)	WORD (x)	EQUIVALENT (y)
simms	somaso	sin1	sote
simnel cae	koki sominijo	sin2	sote
simoleon	somojnsi	sinai	sotejn
simon	someni	sinaibin	sotejnbin
simoniac	someniki	Sinaloa	sotelosi
simonian	somenihn	sinanthropus	sotesirapini
simonianism	somenihnmosi	sinapine	sotepohun
simonides	somenijisi	sinapism	sotepanmosi
simony	somenise	sinarquist	sotekunrasi
simoom	sommo	since	sotonsi
simp	sompo	sincere	sotoknran
simper	somporin	sincerely	sotoknranlo
simple	somporon	sincerity	sotoknraitn
simpler	somporonsi	sinciput	soteknpiti
simpleton	somporontin	sind	sotejn
simplex	somporon	sinbad	sotebaje
simplici	somporonki	sindry	sotegberai
simplicidentate	somporonkijinhateyo	sine	sotan
simplicident	somporonjinhate	sine	sotan
simplicity	somporonkitn	sinecure	sotankunrai
simplify	somporonfe	sine die	sotan dile
simplistic	somporonsuko	sine mora	sotan mora
simply	sompolo	sine prole	sotan ponjua
sims	somasi	sine qua non	sotan kun nini
simulacra	somujoknra	sinew	sotanwa
simulacrum	somujoknrama	sinful	sotefunjn
stimulant	somujotn	sing	sogan
similar	somujora	Singapore	soganporai
simulate	somujoyo	Singaradja	soganraijn
simulcast	somujokosotn	Singe	sogansu
simultaneous	somujotasi	Singer	sogansi
simultaneous equatior	ekunyoon somujotansi	Singer	sogansi
		Singhalese	soghanlese
simurg	somgbon	Single	soganron

WORD (x)	EQUIVALENT (y)	WORD (x)	EQUIVALENT (y)
single file	fijan soganron	sinophile	sotupheron
singles	soganronsi	sinophobe	sotuphobe
singlet	sogantn	sinter	sootnra
singleton	soganrontn	sinuate	soteyo
singly	soganlo	Sinuiju	soteniju
singsong	sogansongan	sinuous	soteyo
singspiel	sogansepnlo	sinuous	sotese
singular	soganjnra	sinuosity	sotesooto
singularity	soganjnraitn	sinus	sotesi
singularize	soganjnraise	sinusitis	sotesooso
sinh	sohon	sinuosotomy	sotesootemo
Sinhalese	sohonlese	sinusoid	sotesoojo
Sinicism	soknkimosi	sion	soon
Sinigrin	soginroon	siox	sooso
sinister	soteseto	siouan	sooansi
sinistrad	sotesetnrejn	sip	soonpe
sinistral	sotesetnrejo	siphon	soonpha
sinistrorse	sotesetnrase	siphonage	soonphagun
sinistrous	sotesetnrasi	siphonapterous	soonphapntiraisi
sink	sooki	siphonophore	soonphaphiran
sinker	sookisi	siphonstele	soonphasetojn
sinkhole	sookihinlu	sipper	soonpnsi
sinking fund	funjn sookignni	sippet	soonpnti
sinless	sotelabo	sir	sora
sinner	soteron	sire	soran
sinn fein	sotun feni	siren	sorain
sino-	sotu	sirenian	sorainhn
sinoatrial	sotuteraijo	siret	soraita
sinology	sotulogbon	siriasis	soranso
sinologue	soknlogbiso	sirius	soraisi
sinology	sotulogbon	sirloin	soralohn
sinologist	sotulogbonsi	sirocco	sorikki
sinological	sotulogbonkojo	sirrah	sorrai
sinon	sotuni	sirup	soraipo

WORD (x)	EQUIVALENT (y)	WORD (x)	EQUIVALENT (y)
sirvente	soraiwinto	sitotoxin	sootetoosia
sis	sose	sitotropism	sootetnrapnmosi
sisal	sosejo	sittang	sottngan
siscowet	sosekiti	sitter	sottnra
sisera	soseran	sitting	sottngnni
siserary	soseranrai	sittus	sotnse
siskin	sosekin	situate	sotnyo
sisley	soserain	situated	sotnyode
sismondi	sosemenijo	situation	sotnyoon
siss	sosue	situla	sotnjo
sissified	sosuafide	situnder	sotnjnra
sissy	sosua	sit-up	sotn pake
sister	soosira	sit-upon	sotn pakesi
sisterhood	soosirahinjo	situs	sotnse
sister-in-law	soosira ni leofin	sitzbath	sotiebosin
sisterly	sosiralo	siva	sowa
sistine	soosihun	sivaism	sowamosi
sistroid	soositnrajo	sivan	soowain
sistrum	soositnrun	sivapithecus	sowapiniknsi
sisyphean	soosophohun	sivas	sowasn
sisyphus	soosophosi	siver	sowasi
sit	sotn	siwash	sowese
sit	sotn	six	sose
sitan	sotnran	sixer	sosesi
sitar	sotnra	sixte	soseto
sitcom	sotnkia	sixteen	sosetoon
sit-down	sotn-juan	sixth	sosesi
site	sooto	sixtieth	sosetnsi
sith	sootnsi	sixtine	sosetin
sit-in	sootn-in	sixtus	sosetnsi
sitka	sootnko	sixty	sosetn
sito	soote	sizable	soosebe
sitology	sootelogbon	size1	soose
sitosterol	sootesitnora	size2	soose

WORD (x)	EQUIVALENT (y)	WORD (x)	EQUIVALENT (y)
sizeable	sooseron	skelp	seknrapn
sizy	sooson	skelton	seknrato
sizz	soosue	skep	sekngba
sizzle	soosueron	skeptic	sekngbako
sizzler	soosueronsi	skeptical	sekngbakojo
sjambok	sejamba	skepticism	sekngbakomosi
skagen	sekangin	skerry	seknrrai
skagerrak	sekangunrrai	sketch	seknte
skall	sekanjnra	sketchy	sekntesi
skaith	sekansia	skew	sekwe
skald	sekajon	skewer	sekwesi
skat	sekanya	skewgee	sekwegan
skate1	sekanyo	skewness	sekwenisi
skate2	sekanyo	ski	sukia
skateboard	bugbasekanyo	skiagraph	sukiaganpha
skater	sekanyosi	skiapodes	sukiapindiesi
skatole	sekanyajoin	skiascope	sukiasekipon
ske	sekn	skiascopy	sukiasekipe
skean	seknhn	skibob	sukibu
skeat	seknto	skid	sukijn
skedaddle	seknjnduo	skiddoo	sukijnun
skeen	seknhun	skient	sukito
skeet	seknte	skiff	sukife
skeg	sekngi	skiing	sukignni
skeigh	sekngn	skijoring	sukijnraggni
skein	seknso	skill	sukijan
skeldock	seknradeki	skilled	sukijande
skele	sekele	skillet	sukijan
skeletal	sekeletejo	skillet	sukijanse
skeleton	sekelete	skim	sukimo
skeletinize	sekeletese	skimbe	sukimbe
skeleton key	sekelete knsi	skimmer	sukimora
skellum	seknranma	skimmia	sukimua
skelly	seknranse	skimp	sukimpn

WORD (x)	EQUIVALENT (y)	WORD (x)	EQUIVALENT (y)
skimpy	sukimpn	skua	sukuo
skin	sukin	skulduggery	sukuodigbirai
skink	sukinkn	skulk	sukuoka
skink	sukinkn	skull	sukuojo
skinker	sukinknsi	skunk	sukuokn
skinned	sukinde	sky	suko
skinner	sukinran	skye	sukon
skinny	sukinse	skylight	sukolighe
skint	sukinte	skyline	sukolehun
skin-tight	sukin gigbain	skyrocket	sukoronkiti
skip	sukinpa	slab	sanbo
skipper	sukinpasi	slack1	sanko
skipping-rope	sukinpagnni ronpo	slack2	sanko
skirl	sukinro	slacken	sankose
skirmish	sukinronsi	slacker	sankosi
skirr	sukinrra	slag	sangn
skirret	sukinrrate	slain	sanku
skirt	sukinrai	slainte	sankuo
skiter	sukintisi	slake	sankin
skit	sukinti	slalom	sanlemo
skite	sukinta	slam1	sanma
skitter	sukinttasi	slam2	sanma
skittish	sukintase	slander	sanjnra
skittle	sukintoron	slanderous	sanjnrasi
skive	sukinwn	slang	sangn
skive	sukinwn	slangy	sangnse
skiver	sukinwnsi	slank	sankun
skivvies	sukinwowosi	slant	santé
skivvy	sukinwowo	slap	sangba
skoal	sukijo	slash	sansia
skoda	sukijn	slat	santin
skookum	sukikoma	slate	santé
skolly	sukille	slate	santé
skopije	sukipojn	slater	santesi

WORD (x)	EQUIVALENT (y)	WORD (x)	EQUIVALENT (y)
slating	santegnni	sleepy	sunpnse
slather	santinsi	sleet	sunte
slattern	santtnran	sleeve	sunwe
slaty	santeni	sleigh	sunghan
slaughter	sangetnra	sleight	sunghante
slav	sanwa	slendang	sudingan
slave	sanwan	slender	sudinra
slaver1	sanwansi	slenderize	sudinraise
slaver2	sanwansi	slep	sunposi
slavery	sanwanrai	sleuth	suntesi
slavey	sanwanse	slew1	sunkua
slavic	sanwiko	slew2	sunkua
slavish	sanwansi	sley	sunsn
slavism	sanwanmosi	slice	siunse
slavo	sanwn	slick	siunko
slavocracy	sanwnkansn	slicker	siunkosi
Slavonia	sanwnni	slide	siunjin
Slavonic	sanwnko	slide-rule	siunjin-rinron
Slavophile	sanwnpheron	slidell	siunjinlle
slaw	sannwe	slight	siunghi
slay	sanku	slightly	siunghilo
sleave	sunwain	sligo	siunlo
sleaze	sunsue	slim	siunmo
sleazy	sunsuese	slime	siunmi
sled	sunjn	slimline	siunmolehun
sledder	sunjnra	slimey	siunmose
sledding	sunjngnni	slimsy	siunmosn
sledge	sungbon	slimy	siunmise
slee	sunse	sling1	siungun
sleek	suknni	sling2	siungun
sleekit	suknnite	sling shot	siungun sutn
sleep	sunpn	slink	siunkn
sleeper	sunpnsi	slinky	siunknse
sleepless	sunpnlabo	slip1	siunyo

WORD (x)	EQUIVALENT (y)	WORD (x)	EQUIVALENT (y)
slip2	siunyo	slovenia	sonwinisi
slip3	siunyo	slovenly	sonwinilo
slipper	siunyosi	slow	sonwe
slippery	siunyosia	sloyd	sonsejn
slippy	siunyose	slub	suwebe
slit	siunte	sluber	suwebesi
slither	siuntesi	sludge	suwegbon
sliver	siunwa	slue	suwe
slivno	siunwakn	slue	suwe
slivovitz	siunwawose	slug1	suwelo
sloane	sonhun	slug2	suwelo
slob	sonbu	slugabed	suwelobeje
slobber	sonbusi	sluggard	suwelogbaa
slock	sonki	sluggish	suwelose
sloe	sonse	sluice	suwesi
slog	songbi	sluicegate	suwesigiyo
slogan	songin	sluit	suweta
sloganeer	songinsi	slum	suwemo
sloid	sonjo	slumber	suwembe
sloop	sonpo	slumberous	suwembesi
slop	sonpn	slumbery	suwemberai
slope	sonpon	slumgullion	suwemgunllesi
sloppy	sonponse	slumgum	suwemgun
slosh	sonsi	slump	suwempn
sloshed	sonside	slung	suwegn
slot	sonte	slunk	suwekn
sloth	sontesi	slur	suwera
slothful	sontesifunjn	slurp	suwepan
slouch	sonkuo	slurry	suwerrai
slough1	songbun	slush	suwesu
slough2	songbun	slushy	suwesun
slovak	sonwika	slut	suwete
Slovakia	sonwikia	sly	suse
sloven	sonwini	slype	sonsepn

WORD (x)	EQUIVALENT (y)	WORD (x)	EQUIVALENT (y)
smack1	semoke	smew	semuwe
smack2	semoke	smiddle	semujnduo
smack3	semoke	smidgen	semujngin
smack4	semoke	smilacaceous	semujnkosuwa
smacker	semokesi	smilacin	semujnsoon
small	semoran	smilax	semujnsi
smallage	semorangun	smile	semuerin
smalt	semojia	smirch	semuraki
smaltite	semojiayo	smirk	semurakn
smaltto	semojiato	smit	semutn
smaragd	semoragba	smite	semute
smaragdite	semoragbayo	smith	semosi
smarm	semoron	smithereens	semosirain
smarmy	semoronsi	smithery	semosirai
smart	semokia	smithsonian	semosisinhn
smarten	semokiasi	smithsonite	semosisinyo
smarty	semokia	smithy	semosise
smash	semosia	smitten	semutte
smasher	semosiasi	smock	semokio
smashing	semosiagnni	smockin	semokiognni
smatter	semotito	smog	semogbi
smattering	semotitognni	smoke	semokoi
smear	samurai	smoker	semokoisi
smeary	semurain	smoky	semokoise
smeddum	semujnma	smolder	semonajn
smeek	semukn	smolensk	semojainsi
smell	semurun	smollett	semojnrate
smeller	semurunsi	smolt	semona
smelly	semurunse	smooch	semookho
smelt1	semuyo	smoor	semoora
smelt2	semuyo	smooth	semonini
smelt3	semuyo	smoothie	semoninise
smelter	semuyosi	smorzando	semorasijin
smerrebrad	semurrebajo	smote	semotn

WORD (x)	EQUIVALENT (y)	WORD (x)	EQUIVALENT (y)
smother	semosira	snatch	siatesi
smouch	semokhuo	snath	siasi
smoulder	semoojnra	snaw	siawe
smudge	semugbon	snazzy	siasesi
smug	semugba	sneak	siakele
smuggle	semugbajn	sneaker	siakelesi
smuggler	semugbajnra	sned	siage
smuggling	semugbajngnni	sneer	siaran
smut	semudu	sneesh	siasun
smutch	semudusi	sneeze	siasin
smutty	semudutn	snell	siallo
smyrna	semunrain	snellen	siallose
smyterie	semunteran	snib	siabo
smyth	semunsn	snick	siakun
snack	siako	snicker	siakun
snack bar	boosn siako	snicker	siakunsi
snaffle	siafijn	snicket	siakunte
snafu	siafon	snide	siajin
snag	siagbi	sniff	siafin
snaggle	siagbijn	sniffer	siafinsi
snaggy	siagbisi	sniffer-dog	degbi-siafinsi
snail	sialo	sniffle	siafinjn
snake	siakoi	sniffy	siafinse
snaky	siakoin	snifter	siafinto
snap	siapn	snigger	siagbasi
snapper	siapnra	sniggle	siagbajn
snappish	siapnso	snip	siapa
snappy	siapnse	snipe	siapn
snare	siare	sniper	siapasi
snare	siare	snippet	siapnti
snarl1	siarejo	snippety	siapntise
snarl2	siarejo	snippy	siapose
snarsh	siareso	snips	siapnsi
snatch	siate	snit	siate

WORD (x)	EQUIVALENT (y)	WORD (x)	EQUIVALENT (y)
snitch	siatesi	snuggle	siagbaron
snits	siatese	snye	siayi
snivel	siawnlo	so1	soo
snob	siabe	so2	soo
snobbish	siabesi	soak	sookn
snod	siajo	soakage	sookngun
snood	siajokn	soaker	sooknra
snog	siagi	soakers	sooknrasi
snook	siakoon	soaking	sookngnni
snooker	siakoonsi	soaky	sooknse
snool	siajon	so-and-so	soo ati soo
snoop	siapon	soap	soopo
snooperscope	siaponsisokipon	soap	soopo
snoot	siatoo	soapbox	bosisoopo
snooty	siatoose	soapy	soopose
snooze	siasoon	soar	soorai
snoqualmie	siakunmijn	sob	sobe
snore	siaroo	sobat	sobeta
snorkel	siaroknra	sobeit	sobetn
snort	siarote	sober	sobes
snot	siate	sobranje	soberaijn
snotty	siatto	sobriety	soberaito
snout	sianita	sobriquet	soberaikue
snow	siawn	soc.	Soka
snowball	siawnrobo	socage	sookogn
snowy	siawnni	soccer	sokknra
snub	siabn	socery	soknrai
snuff1	siafun	sochi	sokhi
snuff2	siafun	sociable	sokibe
snuffbox	bosisiafun	social	sokijo
snuffer	siafunsi	social democracy	sokijo jumokansn
snuffle	siafunron	socialism	sokijomosi
snug	siagba	socialist	sokijosi
snuggery	siagbarai	socialistic	sokijosuko

WORD (x)	EQUIVALENT (y)	WORD (x)	EQUIVALENT (y)
socialite	sokileyo	so far	soo fan
sociality	sokileto	soffit	soofito
socialize	sokijose	sofia	soofin
social scence	sisunse sokijo	soft	soofia
society	sokiseto	softball	soofiarobo
socinian	sosinhun	soft-boilded	soofia-bolede
socio-	sokikn	soft drink	soofia gbakn
sociology	sokiknlogbon	soften	soofiasi
sociemetry	sokiknmutorai	softie	soofiase
sociopath	sokiknpanho	soft touch	tokhan soofia
sock1	sokin	software	soofiawerai
sock2	sokin	softy	soofiase
sockdolager	sokindejngunsi	soggy	soogbase
socket	sokiti	sogne	soogun
socket	sokiti	soho	soohn
sockeye	sokineyiri	soldisant	soojosite
socle	sokuo	solgne	soojogun
soc man	soko moye	soil1	soole
Socrates	soknrato	soil2	soole
socratic	soknratokn	soil pipe	sole popon
sod1	soojo	soilage	soolegun
sod2	soojo	soilure	soolerai
soda	soojon	soir	soorai
soda bread	soojon besigba	soiree	soorain
sodalite	soojonleyo	soixante-neuf	soosiunto-hunfan
sodality	soojonleto	soja	soojua
sodden	soojoin	sojourn	soojinran
sodium	soojonma	soke	sookoi
sodium nitrate	hetnreyo soojonma	sokol	sookojn
Sodom	soojnmi	sol	sinlo
Sodomite	soojnmiyo	sol	sinlo
sodomy	soojnmise	sola	sinlese
sofa	soofan	solace	sinlesi
sofa bed	beje soofan	solan	sinlehe

WORD (x)	EQUIVALENT (y)	WORD (x)	EQUIVALENT (y)
solanaceous	sinlehesuwa	solicitous	sinlekitesi
solander	sinlejnra	solicitude	sinlekitujin
solano	sinlekn	solid	sinlejo
solar	sinleran	solidago	sinlejogbain
solar battery	bottnrai sinleran	solidarity	sinlejoraito
solarimeter	sinleranmuto	solidify	sinlejofe
solarization	sinleranyoon	solidity	sinlejotn
solarize	sinleranse	solid-state	sinlejo setnyo
solarium	sinleranma	solidus	sinlejosi
solate	sinleto	solifidian	sinlefijoin
solatium	sinletoma	soliloquize	sinlelokunse
sold	sinllo	soliloquy	sinlelokun
solder	sinllosi	solimoes	sinlemosi
soldering iron	irin sinllosignni	solingen	sinlegini
soldier	sinllorai	solion	sinlesi
soldiery	sinllorain	solipsism	sinlepnsemosi
sole1	sinle	solitaire	sinletnrain
sole2	sinle	solitary	sinletnrai
sole3	sinle	solitary	kinfinimutto sinletnrai
solecism	sinlekimosi	confinement	
solely	sinlelo	soliterraneous	sinletnrrainsi
solemn	sinlemini	solitude	sinletnjin
solemnity	sinleminito	solliret	sinllerate
solemnize	sinleminise	sollicker	sinllekisi
solenoid	sinlehunjo	solmizate	sinlemaseyo
soleure	sinlerai	solmization	sinlemaseyoon
sol-fa	sinlefan	solo	sinleni
solfatara	sinlefantnra	solo	sinleni
solfeggio	sinlefngbako	soloist	solenisi
solferino	sinlefironkn	soloman	sinlenimoye
soli	sinle	Solomon	sinlenimosi
solicit	sinlekite	solon	sinlehun
solicitation	sinlekiteyoon	solonchak	sinlehunkhn
solicitor	sinlekiteran	solonet	sinlehunte

WORD (x)	EQUIVALENT (y)	WORD (x)	EQUIVALENT (y)
solor	sinleran	somber	soombesi
solpugid	sinlepngijo	somber	soomberai
solstice	sinlesitin	sombrero	soomberain
solubility	sinleberontn	some	soomo
solubilise	sinleberonse	some1	soomo
soluble	sinlebe	some2	soomo
solum	sinlemo	somebody	soomobojain
solus	sinlesi	someday	soomodase
solute	sinleyo	somehow	soomohinwo
solution	sinleyoon	someone	soomoleni
solutrean	sinletnran	someone	soomohun
solvable	sinlewnbe	somersault	soomoraisejia
solvate	sinlewinyo	somerset	soomoraise
salvation	sinlewinyoon	somes	soomosi
solve	sinlewin	somesthesis	soomosunwnso
solvency	sinlewinsn	something	soomosingn
solvent	sinlewinta	somite	soomoyo
sol vay	sinlewinse	somme	soonmmo
solvolysis	sinlewnjinso	sommelier	soonmmojnra
soma	sooma	somnambulate	soonmmbejnyo
Somali	soomale	somnambulism	soonmmbejnmosi
somalia	soomalesi	somni	soonm
somascope	soomasokipon	somnifacient	soonmfanseto
somatalgia	soomajigan	somniferous	soonmfirosi
somatic	soomako	somniloquy	soonmlokun
somatics	soomakosi	somnolence	soonmjnsi
somaticism	soomakomosi	somnolent	soonmjnto
somato	soomato	somnus	soonmsi
somatogenic	soomatoginko	son	isin/sin son
somatology	soomatologbon	sonance	sosesi
somatoplasm	soomatopanson	sonant	sosetn
somatopleure	soomatoponrai	sonar	soseran
somatotropin	soomatotnrapan	sonata	sosetin
somatotype	sinmatotnpon	sonatina	sosetiun

WORD (x)	EQUIVALENT (y)	WORD (x)	EQUIVALENT (y)
sondage	sonjingun	sophistic	soophnsetnko
sonde	sonjin	sophisticate	soophnsetnkoyo
sonder	sonjinra	sophisticated	soophnsetnkoyode
son et lumiere	son si lumuron	sophistry	soophnserai
sone	sonhun	sophocles	soophikunsi
sonei	sonsi	sophomore	soophimosii
song	songan	sophomoric	soophimosiiko
songster	songanseto	sophy	soophe
sonic	sonko	spoor	soonpn
soniferous	sonfirosi	soporiferous	soonpnfirosi
sonnet	sonhunte	soporific	soonpnfiko
sonneteer	sonhuntesi	sopping	soopngnni
sonny	sonse	soppy	soopnse
sonogram	sonkoganmo	sopranino	sonpnrainkn
sonora	sonkora	soprano	sonpnrain
sonorant	sonkorate	sopron	sonpnran
sonority	sonkoraito	sora	sinran
sonorous	sonkoraisi	sorb	sinra
sonsy	sonsn	sorbet	sinrati
soom	soonmi	sorbefacient	sinrafanseto
soon	soonsi	sorbefacious	sinrafansesi
sooner	soonse	sorbic	sinrako
soop	soonpn	sorbite	sinrayo
soor	soonrai	sorbitol	sinrayojin
soot	soosu	sorbonist	sinrainhunsi
sooth	soosn	sorbonne	sinrainhun
soothe	soosin	sorbose	sinrakose
soothsayer	soosnsanwi	sorcerer	sinraknran
sooty	soose	sorcery	sinraknrai
sop	soopn	sordellina	sinrajnllehun
Sophia	soophnsi	sordello	sinrajnllo
Sophism	soophnmosi	sordid	sinrajnjo
sophist	soophnsi	sordino	sinrajnkn
sophister	soophnseto	sordium	sinrajnma

WORD (x)	EQUIVALENT (y)	WORD (x)	EQUIVALENT (y)
sore	sinrai	sothic	sooseko
soredium	sinraijnma	sothis	soosesi
sorehead	sinraihegbi	sotol	sontejn
sorel	sinraijo	sotting	sonttegnni
sorely	sinrailo	sotto voce	wnso sontto
sorghum	sinraignmo	sou	so
sorgo	sinrailo	souari	sorai
soricine	sinraikihun	soubise	sobnse
sorites	sinraitosi	soubrette	sobetin
sorn	sinran	soubriquet	sobnkunto
soroche	sinrokhn	soucar	sokosi
sororate	sinroranyo	souchong	sokhign
sororicide	sinrorankeku	soufflé	sofijn
sorority	sinroraito	Soufriere	sofanran
sorosis	sinroso	Sough	sogbn
sorosis	sinroso	sought	sogbe
sorption	sinrapnyoon	souk	soka
sorrel1	sinrare	soul	sojn
sorrel2	sinrare	soulmate	sojnmote
sorrow	sinrarosi	sound1	sojoin
sorry	sinraro	sound2	sojoin
sort	sinrate	sound3	sojoin
sortie	sinratesi	sound4	sojoin
sortilege	sinratejogn	sounder	sojoinsi
sortition	sinrateyoon	soup	sonpo
sorus	sinraisi	soupcon	sonpokin
sos	sws	soupy	sonpose
sosnowiee	sosiawnse	sour	sonkan
soso	sonso	source	sonkansi
sostenuto	sonsotito	sourdine	sonkanjoin
sot	sonte	sourdough	sonkandeungbo
soteriology	sonterilogbon	sourgourd	sonkangongba
soth	sonse	souris	sonkanso
sothern	sooserna	sourpuss	sonkanpusin

WORD (x)	EQUIVALENT (y)	WORD (x)	EQUIVALENT (y)
soursop	sonkansopn	spaceship	sipasesunpn
sousaphone	sonsiphohun	spacious	sipasesi
souse	sonse	spackle	sipakiron
souse	sonsse	spade1	sipajin
soutache	sontekhn	spade2	sipajin
soutane	sontehun	spadework	sipajinwinsise
souter	sontnra	spadiceous	sipajnsuwa
south	sonsn	spadix	sipajnsi
south	sonsn	spae	sipaso
southerly	sonsnralo	spag	sipagun
southern	sonsnran	spaghetti	sipaguntte
southern cross	konso sonsnran	spaghetti bolog-	
southerner	sonsnransi	nesesipaguntte	
south sea	osa sonsn	bujingnse	
southward	sonsnwegba	spagyric	sipaloraiko
souvenir	sonwnran	spahi	sipahi
sovereign	soownregini	spain	sipanjn
sovereignty	soownreginito	spake	sipake
soviet	soowato	spalato	sipalatn
sow1	soown	spall	sipalla
sow2	soown	spallanzani	sipallasesi
sowens	soownnis	spalaltion	sipallayoon
Soweto	soownto	spam	sipamo
Sown	soownn	span1	sipahun
sowth	soowosi	span2	sipahun
soy	sosio	spancel	sipahunkn
soya	sosia	spandau	sipahunjn
sozin	sosijo	spandrel	sipahunjnra
sozzled	sosuronde	spanemia	sipahunmua
spa	sipan	spang	sipagan
space	sipase	spangle	sipaganron
space age	agun sipase	Spaniard	sipangba
spacecraft	sipasekanfia	spaniel	sipanlo
spaceman	sipasemoye	spanish	sipanso

WORD (x)	EQUIVALENT (y)	WORD (x)	EQUIVALENT (y)
spanish	sipanso	spat1	sipatn
spank	sipakan	spat2	sipatn
spanker	sipakansi	spat3	sipatn
spanking	sipakangnni	spat4	sipate
spanner	sipahunron	spathe	sipatesi
spans	sipahunsi	spatial	sipatejo
spa	sipan	spatio	sipateo
spar1	sipan	spatter	sipatnra
spar2	sipan	spatula	sipatele
spar3	sipan	spatulate	sipateleyo
sparable	sipanrobe	spavin	sipawohun
spare	sipanra	spavined	sipawohunde
spare part	pante sipanra	spawn	sipawn
sparge	sipanragn	spay	sipayo
sparger	sipanragnse	speak	sipnke
sparing	sipanragnni	speak	sipnke
spark	sipanko	speaker	sipnkesi
sparkle ·	sipankose	spear	sipnran
sparkle	sipankosesi	spearhead	sipnranhegbi
sparkling	sipankosegnni	spearmint	sipnranminte
sparoid	sipanrajo	spec1	sepnki
sparrow	sipanraiwe	spec2	sepnki
sparry	sipanrai	special	sepnkijo
sparse	sipanse	specialist	sepnkijosi
Sparta	sipantn	speciality	sepnkijoto
Spartacist	sipantnkosi	specialize	sepnkijose
spartacus	sipantnkose	specialty	sepnkijotn
spartan	sipantnsi	speciation	sepnkyoon
sparteine	sipantnhun	specie	sepnkin
spasm	sipasn	species	sepnkinsi
spasmodic	sipasnjiko	specific	sepnkifiko
spasmolysis	sipansnjinso	specification	sepnkifikoyoon
spasmophilia	sipasnpheran	specific gravity	sepnkifiko gnawoto
spastic	sipasnko	specify	sepnkife

WORD (x)	EQUIVALENT (y)	WORD (x)	EQUIVALENT (y)
specimen	sepnkimuye	speculum	sepnkunjnma
specious	spnkisi	sped	sipnja
speck	sepnkue	speech	sipnkho
speckle	sepnkuesi	speechify	sipnkhofe
speckled	sepnkueside	speed	sipnjin
spectacle	sepntikun	speeder	sipnjinse
spectacled	sepntikunde	speedo	sipnjinko
spectacles	sepntikunsi	speedster	sipnjinseto
spectacular	sepntikunjnra	speey	sipnyinse
spectate	sepntiwo	speel	sipnlo
spectator	sepntiwosi	speer	sipnro
spectator	sepntiworan	speering	sipnrognni
specter	sepntira	speiss	sipnson
sectra	sepntiran	spelean	sipnrahn
spectral	sepntiranjo	speleology	sipnralogbon
spectre	sepntirai	spell1	sipnllo
spectro	sepntiron	spell2	sipnllo
spectrobolometer	sepntironbujinmuto	spell3	sipnllo
spectrochemistry	sepntironkhnmusorai	spelling	sipnllognni
spectrogram	sepntironganmo	spelunk	sipnlukn
spectrograph	sepntironganpha	spelunker	sipnluknra
spectroheliogram	sepntironhejoganmo	spelt1	sipnlo
spectroheliograph	sepntironganpha	spelt2	sipnlo
spectrometer	sepntironmuto	spence	sipnyakn
spectrophotometer	sepntironphotinmuto	spencer	sipnyaknra
spectroradiometer	sepntironrangbomuto	spencerism	sipnyaknrain
spectroscope	sepntironsukipon	spend	sepnjon
spectroscopy	sepntironsukipe	spendthrift	sepnjonsinraifia
spectrum	sepntirama	spender	sepnjonsi
specula	sepnkunjn	spense	sepnsi
specular	sepnkunjnra	spenser	sepnsira
speculate	sepnkunjnyo	spenserian	sepnsirain
speculation	sepnkunjnyoon	spent	sepnti
speculator	sepnkunjnyoran	sperm	sepnron

WORD (x)	EQUIVALENT (y)	WORD (x)	EQUIVALENT (y)
spermaceti	sepnronkiti	sphene	sephini
spermary	sepnronrai	sphenic	sephiniko
spermatheca	sepnronsinki	sphenoid	sephinijo
spermatic	sepnronteko	sphenodon	sephinijoin
spermatid	sepnrontejo	spheral	sephiraijo
spermatium	sepnrontema	sphere	sephirai
spermato	sepnronto	spherical	sephiraikojo
spermatocyte	sepnrontosnyo	sphericity	sephiraikitn
spermatogenesis	sepnrontognhunso	spherics	sephiraikosi
spermatogonium	sepnrontogonma	spheroid	sephiraijo
spermatoid	sepnrontojo	spheroidicity	sephiraijokito
spermatophore	sepntrontophiran	spherometer	sephiraimuto
spermatophyte	sepnrontopheyo	spherule	sephiraile
spemrmatorrhea	sepnrontorrhain	spherulite	sephiraileyo
spermatozoid	sepnrontosinjo	sphery	sephiraise
spermatozoon	sepnrontosinsi	sphincter	sephiknra
spermic	sepnronko	sphinges	sephiginisi
spermine	sepnronhun	sphingomyelin	sephigonmojain
spermism	sepnronmos	sphingosine	sephigonsun
spermist	sepnronsi	sphinx	sephisia
spermo	sepnronko	sphragistics	sephangbisetoko
spermogonium	sepnronkogonma	sphygmic	sephegnmuko
spermophile	sepnronkopheron	sphygmo	sephegnmo
spermous	sepnronkosi	sphygmogram	sephegnmoganmo
sperm bank	bohakn sepnron	sphygmograph	sephegnmoganpha
sperm count	keleyo sepnron	sphygmoid	sephegnmojo
spermicide	sepnronkeku	sphygmomanometer	sephegnmoknmuto
sperrylite	sepnrraileyo	sphygmoscope	sephegnmosukipon
spet	sepnti	sphygmus	sephegnmosi
spew	sepnwn	spica	seposu
spezia	sepnsia	spicate	seposuyo
sphacelate	sephiknleyo	spiccato	seposuto
sphagnum	sephignma	spice	seposua
sphalerite	sephijnraiyo	spicery	seposuarai

WORD (x)	EQUIVALENT (y)	WORD (x)	EQUIVALENT (y)
spick	sepoki	spin	sepooyi
spick and span	sepoki ati sepohun	spin	sepoyi
spicule	sepokuo	spinabifida	sepoyibefijn
spicula	sepokue	spinaceous	sepoyisuwa
spiculum	sepikuoma	spinach	sepoyikho
spicy	seposuasi	spinal	sepoyijo
spider	sepojnra	spinate	sepoyiyo
spidery	sepojnrai	spindle	sepoyiduo
spiegelelsen	sepongnjnlesun	spindly	sepoyiduosi
spiel	seposo	spindrift	sepoyigbanfe
spieler	seposorai	spindry	sepoyigbe
spier	seposi	spindrier	sepoyigbesi
spif	sepofn	spine	sepohun
spiffing	sepofngnni	spinel	sepohunlo
spiffy	sepofnni	spineless	sepohunlabo
spiflicate	sepofankoyo	sponescent	sepohunsiknti
spigelia	sepognjan	spinet	sepohunto
spignel	sepognlo	spingarn	sepoyigiran
spigot	sepogbito	spini	sepoyn
spike1	sepoki	spiniferous	sepoyifirosi
spike2	sepoki	spinifex	sepoyifisi
spikenard	sepokigbain	spinnaker	sepoyiknra
spiker	sepokisi	spinner	sepoyiran
spiky	sepokise	spinneret	sepoyiranto
spile	sepojn	spinnery	sepoyirai
spile	sepojn	spinney	sepoyisi
spilikin	sepojankin	spinning	sepoyignni
spill1	sepollo	spinning wheel	sepoyignni whinlo
spill2	sepollo	spin off	sepoyi ofan
spillikin	sepollokin	spinose	sepohunse
spillway	sepollowelo	spinosity	sepoyisetn
spilosite	sepolosuyo	spinous	sepoyisi
spilt	sepoleto	spinoza	sepoyisan
spilth	sepolesi	spinozism	sepoyisanmosi

WORD (x)	EQUIVALENT (y)	WORD (x)	EQUIVALENT (y)
spinstabilisation	sepoyitebeseyoon	spirograph	seporaiganpha
spinster	sepoyitosi	spirogyra	seporailora
spinthariscope	sepoyisiraisokipon	spiroid	seporaijo
spinule	sepoyiron	spirometer	seporaimuto
spinulescent	sepoyironsiknti	spironolactone	seporainlekehun
spinulose	sepoyironse	spirula	seporaijn
spiny	sepoyilo	spiry	seporai
spiracle	seporaikuo	spit1	sepote
spiraea	seporain	spit2	sepote
spiral	seporai	spital	sepotejo
spirant	seporaite	spitch	sepotesi
spire	seporai	spite	sepoyo
spire	seporai	spittle	sepoteron
spirea	seporain	spittoon	sepotoo
spireme	seporaimo	spitz	sepotie
spiriferous	seporaifirosi	spitzenburg	sepotiebugan
spirilla	seporaille	spiv	sepown
spirillum	seporiallema	spivery	sepownrai
spirit	sepoora	splake	sepankoi
spirited	sepoorade	splanchnic	sepankhnniko
spirit gum	lema sepoora	splanchno	sepankhnkn
spiritism	sepooramosi	splanchnology	sepankhnknlogbon
spiritless	sepooralabo	splash	sepansia
spiritoso	sepooraso	splasher	sepansiasi
spirituous	sepoorasi	splashy	sepansiase
spiritual	sepoorajo	splat	sepantwn
spiritualism	sepoorajomosi	splatter	sepantwnsi
spiritualty	sepoorajotn	splay	sepansie
spirituel	sepooralo	spleen	seponsia
spirituous	sepoorasi	splendent	seponjnto
spiritus	sepoorasn	splendid	seponjnjo
spiro	seporai	splendid	seponjnjon
spirochaete	seporaikhointo	splendiferous	seponjnfirosi
spirochaetosis	seporaikhointoso	splendor	seponjnra

WORD (x)	EQUIVALENT (y)	WORD (x)	EQUIVALENT (y)
splendour	seponjnra	spondulix	sepojnlesi
splenetic	seponsiako	spondylitis	sepojnleso
splenic	seponsiko	spondylo	sepojnlo
splenitis	seponsiaso	sponge	sepogbo
splenius	seponsiasi	sponger	sepogbosi
spleno	seponsikn	spongiform	sepogbofon
splenomegaly	seponsiknmuganlo	sponging	sepogbosi
spleuchan	seponkhun	spongioblast	sepogbobansia
splice	sepankn	spongy	sepogbosia
splicer	sepanknra	sponsal	seposijo
spline	sepanhun	sponsion	seposoon
splint	sepanti	sponson	seposin
splinter	sepantisi	sponsor	seposusi
split	sepanti	spontaneity	sepoteluto
splodge	sepongbon	spontaneous	sepotelusi
splotch	sepontu	spontoon	sepotin
splosh	seponsi	spoof	sepofn
splurge	sepongan	spook	sepokn
splutter	sepontnra	spooky	sepoknsi
spode	sepojin	spool	sepojin
spodumene	sepojinmini	spoon	seposi
spoil	sepojia	spoor	seporan
spoilage	sepojiagun	sporades	seporanjnsi
spoiler	sepojiasi	sporadic	seporanjnko
spoilsport	sipojiasepinta	sporadosiderite	seporanjnsooraiyo
spoilt	sepojian	sporagiospore	seporangnseporai
spoke1	sepoke	sporangium	seporaingnma
spoke2	sepoke	spore	seporai
spoken	sepoknsi	soporiferous	seporaifirosi
Spoleto	sepojnto	sporo	seporon
spoliation	sepojiayoon	sporocarp	seporonkopan
spoliative	sepojiayown	sporocyst	seporonsnsu
spondaic	sepojnko	sporocyte	seporonsnyo
spondee	sepojnso	sporogenesis	seporongnhunso

WORD (x)	EQUIVALENT (y)	WORD (x)	EQUIVALENT (y)
sporogonium	seporongonma	spriggy	sepangnsi
sporogony	sporongonse	spright	sepangba
sporophore	seporonphiran	sprightly	sepangbalo
sporophyll	seporonphewe	spring	sepankan
sporophyte	seporonpheyo	springe	sepankn
sporotrichosis	seporontaraikhiso	springer	sepanknsi
sporous	seporonsi	springlet	sepankankn
sporozoan	seporonsinhn	springy	sepankansi
sporozoite	seporonsinyo	sprinkle	sepanknra
sporran	seporrain	sprinkler	sepanknrasi
sport	sepinta	sprinkling	sepanknragnni
sporting	sepintagnni	sprint	sepnti
sportive	sepintawin	sprit	sepanta
sportsman	sepintamoye	sprite	sepantan
sporty	sepintasi	spritzer	sepantasi
spot	sepinti	sprocket	seponknti
spotted	sepintide	sprout	seponta
spotter	sepintisi	spruce1	seporansi
spotty	sepintito	spruce2	seporansi
spousal	seposijo	sprue	sepora
spouse	seposi	sprug	seporangi
spout	sepota	sprung	seporangn
sprag	sepangbi	spry	sepnrai
Sprague	sepangan	spud	sepujn
sprain	sepanlo	spudder	sepujnra
sprang	sepankan	spulyie	sepujia
sprat	sepantie	spume	sepumi
sprawl	sepanwajn	spumescent	sepumisiknti
spray1	sepanye	spumone	sepumini
spray2	sepanye	spun	sepuyi
spray-gun	gunta-sepanye	spunk	sepukn
spread	sepesijn	spur	sepura
spree	sepesia	spurge	sepuragn
sprig	sepangn	spurious	sepuraisi

WORD (x)	EQUIVALENT (y)	WORD (x)	EQUIVALENT (y)
spurn	sepurun	squarrose	sekunrrosua
spurry	sepurrai	squash1	sekunsi
spurt	seputa	squash2	sekunsi
spurtle	seputoron	squashy	sekunsise
sputnik	seputokin	squat	sekunle
sputter	seputosi	squatter	sekunlesi
sputum	seputoma	squatty	sekuntn
spuyten	seputosi	squaw	sekunwo
spy	sopn	squawk	sekunworo
squab	sekunbe	squeak	sekunke
squabble	sekunbesi	squeaky	sekunkesi
squacco	sekunki	squeal	sekunjo
squad	sekungbi	squeamish	sekunmese
squaddie	sekungbise	squeegee	sekungba
squadron	sekungbire	squeeze	sekunwese
squalene	sekunjnni	squeeze-box	bosi-sekunwese
squali	sekunre	squelch	sekunkho
squalis	sekunresi	squelcher	sekunkhosi
squalid	sekunreje	squetegue	sekuntiegan
squall	sekunreko	squib	sekunbu
squall	sekunreko	squid	sekuijo
squally	sekunreko	squiffy	sekuife
squalor	sunkunjnra	squiggle	sekuigiron
squalus	sunkunlesi	squill	sekuillo
squama	sekunpe	squilla	sekuille
squamata	sekunpete	squinch	sekuikhn
squamation	sekunpeyoon	squinny	sekuini
squamosal	sekunpesijo	squint	sekuitn
squamous	sekunpesi	squire	sekunra
squamulose	sekunpejnse	squirearchy	sekunraknran
squander	sekunjnra	squirm	sekunron
squantum	sekuntema	squirrel	sekunrrelo
squantum	sekuntema	squirt	sekunte
square	sekunro	squish	sekunsi

WORD (x)	EQUIVALENT (y)	WORD (x)	EQUIVALENT (y)
Srinagar	seraingan	stagnate	setngantan
st.	set	stagnation	setngantansi
stab	setngon	stagy	setngunsi
stabile	setngonjn	staid	setnjo
stability	setngontn	stain	setnlu
stabilize	setngonse	stainless	setnlulabo
stabilizer	setngonlesesi	stair	setnrai
stable	setngonsi	stake1	setnro
stable-companion	setngonsi-kimpansi	stake2	setnro
stabling	setngongnni	stakhanovism	setnrhoinwnmosi
staccato	setnkikon	stakhanovite	setnrhoinwnte
stack	setnki	stalactiform	setnlekitifoonmo
stacker	setnkisi	stalactite	setnlekitiyo
stacte	setnkiti	stalag	setnlegn
staddle	setngbaduo	stalagmite	setnlegnmuyo
stadia	setngbase	stalagmometer	setnlegnmomuto
stadium	setngbasi	stale	setnra
stael	setnlo	stale	setnra
staff	setnfin	stalemate	setnramote
staffa	setnfan	stalina	setnrain
Stafford	setnfonjn	stalingrad	setnraingandi
stag	setngan	Stalinism	setnrainmosi
stage	setngun	Stalino	setnroin
stager	setngunsi	Stalinsk	setnrainsi
stagey	setngunse	stalk1	setnrako
stagflation	setngunfanyoon	stalk2	setnrako
staggerd	setngiagba	stalking-horse	setnrakognni-hiso
stagger	setngiasi	stalky	setnrakosi
staggers	setngiase	stall1	setnran
staggering	setngiasignni	stall2	setnran
staging	setngungnni	stallion	setnransi
Stagira	setngiran	stalwart	setnrawante
stagirite	setngiraiyo	stambouline	setnmbounlehun
stagnant	setngansi	stamens	setnmuyesi

WORD (x)	EQUIVALENT (y)	WORD (x)	EQUIVALENT (y)
Stamford	setnmfonjn	stannite	setnhunyo
stamina	setnmina	stannous	setnhunsi
staminal	setnminajo	stannum	setnhunma
stamnate	setnminayo	stanza	setnsan
stamini	setnmini	stapelia	setnpnjan
staminodium	setnminidima	stapes	setnpnsi
staminody	setnminidise	staphylo	setnphelo
stammel	setnmmulo	staphylococcus	setnphelokikisi
stammer	setnmuso	staphylococcal	setnphelokikijo
stamp	setnmpe	stapphyloplasty	setnphelopansuito
stampede	setnmpejin	staphylorrhaphy	setnphelorrhanphe
stamper	setnmpesi	staple1	setnpo
stance	setnsi	staple2	setnpo
stanch	setnkhn	stapler	setnposi
stanchion	setnkhnsi	stapler	setnposi
stand	setndan	star	setan
standard	setndangba	star	setan
standardize	setndangbase	starboard	setanbugba
stand-by	setndan-beo	starch	setanki
stand-in	setndan-ni	starchy	setankisi
standing	setndangnni	stardust	setanditn
standis	setndansi	stare	setansi
stand-up	setndan-pake	stark	setankn
stang	setngan	starkers	setaknra
Stanhope	setnhipon	starlet	setantn
staniel	setnnilo	starlight	setanleghe
stanine	setnnihe	starling	setangnni
stank	setnkan	starlit	setanleto
stanley	setnronsi	starred	setande
stann	setnhun	starry	setanrai
stannaries	setnhunraisi	start	setanta
stannary	setnhunrai	starter	setantasi
stannic	setnhunko	startle	setantaron
staniniferous	setnhunfirosi	starvation	setanwnyoon

WORD (x)	EQUIVALENT (y)	WORD (x)	EQUIVALENT (y)
starve	setanwn	statuesque	setntuekun
starveling	setanwngnni	statuette	setntuetn
stase	setnsi	stature	setnturai
stash	setnsn	status	setntusi
stasis	setnso	status quo	setntusi kuo
stat	setnti	statute	setntuto
state	setnyo	statute law	leewo setntuto
stateless	setnyolabo	statute mile	munjn setntuto
stately	setnyolo	statutory	setntutorai
stately home	himini setnyolo	staunch1	setnkhun
statement	setnyomutto	staunch2	setnkhun
state of the art	ete nfi sin setnyo	staurolite	setnraileyo
statesman	setnyomoye	stauroscope	setnraisukipon
static	setnyoko	Stavanger	setnwagnsi
statics	setnyokosi	stave	setnwn
station	setnyoon	stavesacre	setnwnknra
stationary	setnyoonrai	staw	setnwe
stationer	setnyoonran	stay1	setnsn
stationery	setnyoonrain	stay2	setnsn
statism	setnyomosi	stayer	setnsnsi
statist	setnyosi	staying power	powara setnsngnni
statistic	setnyosiko	ste	sitn
statistical	setnyosikojo	stead	sitngba
statistician	setnyosikohn	steadfast	sitngbafansa
statistics	setnyosikosi	steady	sitngbain
stative	setnyowin	steady state	sitngbain setnyo
stato	setnto	steak	sitnke
statocyst	setntosnsi	steal	sitnji
statolatry	setntolerain	stealage	sitnjigun
statolith	setntolesi	stealth	sitnjee
statoscope	setntosukipon	stealthy	sitnjeese
stator	setntueran	steam	sitnmi
statuary	setntuerai	steamboat	bootesitnmi
statue	setntue	steam engine	engbihun sitnmi

WORD (x)	EQUIVALENT (y)	WORD (x)	EQUIVALENT (y)
steamer	sitnmisi	steering	sitnraignni
steam iron	irin sitnmi	steery	sitnraise
steamship	sitnmisunpn	steeve	sitnwini
steam train	sitnmi tnreto	steeve	sitnwini
steamy	sitnmise	steffens	sitnfinisi
steapsin	sitnpnsan	stegomyia	sitngonmusi
stearate	sitnraiyo	stegosaur	sitngonsanra
stearic	sitnraiko	stein	sitngba
stearine	sitnrain	steenbok	sitngbako
stearoptene	sitnranpntihun	stele	sitnjn
stearrhea	sitnrrhain	stella	sitnran
steatite	sitntoyo	stellar	sitnransi
steato	sitnto	stellarator	sitnranraiyo
steatolysis	sitntojinso	stellate	sitnranyo
steatopygia	sitntopegan	stelliferous	sitnranfirosi
steatorrhoea	sitntorhoin	stelliform	sitnranfoon
stech	sitnkhn	stellify	sitnranfe
stedfast	sitnjnfansa	satellite	sitnrantn
steed	sitnjin	stellular	sitnranjnra
steek	sitnkn	stem1	sitnmo
steel	sitnle	stem2	sitnmo
steel band	bonjo sitnle	stemmer	sitnmmasi
steeling	sitnlegnni	stemson	sitnmosin
steelworks	worosesitnle	stench	sitnkan
steely	sitnlesi	stencil	sitnkun
steelyard	yandan sitnle	steno	sitnko
steen	sitnni	stenograph	sitnkoganpha
steep1	sitnpn	stenographer	sitnkoganphasi
steep2	sitnpn	stenography	sitnkoganphe
steepen	sitnpnsi	stenomorph	sitnkomophan
steeple	sitnpnron	stenopetal	sitnkopntijo
steer1	sitnrai	stenophagous	sitnkophijesi
steer2	sitnrai	stenophyllous	sitnkophewesi
steerage	sitnraigun	stenosis	sitnkoso

WORD (x)	EQUIVALENT (y)	WORD (x)	EQUIVALENT (y)
stenotropic	sitnkotnrapnko	stereophony	sitorainphohun
stenotypy	sitnkotnpe	steropsis	sitorainpnso
stent	sitnto	stereoscope	sitorainsokipon
stent	sitnto	stereoskiagraphy	sitorainsukiagunphe
stentor	sitntoran	stereotropism	sitoraintnrapnmosi
stentorian	sitntorain	stereotype	sitoraintnpon
step	sitnpi	stereotypy	sitoraintnpe
step-	sitnpi	stereovision	sitorainwosesi
stepbrother	sitnpibonsira	steric	sitnrako
Stephanie	sitnphini	sterigma	sitnragnmo
stephen	sitnphin	sterilant	sitnrajnte
stephanotis	sitnphiknso	sterile	sitnrajn
stepney	sitnpise	sterilize	sitnrajnse
steppe	sitnpin	sterilization	sitnrajnseyoon
stepson	sitnpisin	sterlet	sitnratn
ster	sito	sterling	sitnragnni
ster	sitosi	stern1	sitnran
steradian	sitorangbain	stern2	sitnran
stercoraceous	sitokiransuwa	sterne	sitnrani
stercori	sitokirai	sternum	sitnranma
stercoricoious	sitokiraikinsi	sternutation	sitnrantoyoon
sterculiaceous	sitokunjansuwa	sternutator	sitnrantoyoran
stere	sitorai	sternutatory	sitnrantoyorai
stereo	sitorain	steroid	sitnrajo
stereo-	sitorain	sterol	sitnrajin
stereobate	sitorainbeyo	stertor	sitnraran
stereochromy	sitorainkhiramo	stertorous	sitnraransi
stereognosis	sitorainginiso	stet	sitnsi
stereome	sitorainmo	stetho	sitnsisa
stereometry	sitorainmutorai	stethometer	sitnsisamuto
stereophone	sitorainphohun	stethoscope	sitnsisasekipon
stereophonic	sitorainphohunko	stetson	sitnsesin
stereophonics	sitorainphohunkosi	stettin	sitnsetin
stereophonism	sitorainphohunmosi	stevedore	sitnwnjnra

WORD (x)	EQUIVALENT (y)	WORD (x)	EQUIVALENT (y)
stevenage	sitnwinigun	stigmatize	setieguose
stevengraph	sitnwiniganpha	stilb	setielebe
stew	sitnwe	stilbene	setielebesi
steward	sitnwegba	stilbite	seielebeyo
stewardess	sitnwegbabo	stilboestrol	setieleburoinjn
stewart	sitnwete	stile	setiele
stey	sitnsia	stiletto	setieleto
sthenic	sesinko	still1	setielle
stiacciato	setiekkinto	still2	setielle
stibble	setiebe	stilly	setiello
stibbler	setiebesi	stillyon	setiellosi
stibine	setiebehun	stillson	setiellesin
stibium	setiebema	stilt	setielo
stibnite	setiebnyo	stilted	setielode
stich	setiekhi	stilton	setielosi
stichic	setiekhiko	stimulant	setiemujnte
stichometry	setiekhomutorai	stimulate	setiemujnyo
stichomythy	setiekhomusio	stimulus	setiemujnsi
stichous	setiekosi	sting	setiegan
stick1	setieki	stinger	setiegansi
stick2	setieki	stinging-nettle	setiegangnni-huntoron
sticker	setiekisi	stingray	setieganrai
stickle	setiekijn	stingy	setieganlo
stickler	setiekijnra	stink	setiekan
stick out	setieki nita	stinker	setiekansi
stick-up	setieki pake	stinking	setiekangnni
sticky	setiekisi	stint	setietn
stiff	setiefun	stipe	setiepn
stiffen	setiefunsi	stipend	setiepnjon
stifle	setiefunjn	stipendiary	setiepnjonrai
stigma	setieguo	stipes	setiepnsi
stigmaster	setieguoseto	stipitate	setiepntiyo
stigmatic	setieguoko	stipple	setiepon
stigmatism	setieguomosi	stipular	setiepnlera

WORD (x)	EQUIVALENT (y)	WORD (x)	EQUIVALENT (y)
stipulate	setiepnleyo	stoke	setokun
stipule	setiepnle	stoker	setokunsi
stir1	setierai	stole1	setojn
stir2	setierai	stole2	setojn
stirk	setieran	stolen	setojisi
stirl	setieron	stolid	setojnjo
stirp	setierapn	stolon	setojnsi
stirrup	setierraipo	stoma	setomi
stirring	setierraignni	stomach	setomikun
stitch	setiehun	stomacher	setomikunsi
stith	setiesi	stomachic	setomikunko
stive	setievn	stomachy	setomikunsn
stiver	setiewn	stomack	setomiki
stiver	setiewnra	stomata	setomite
stoa	setosi	stomatal	setomitejo
stoat	setotie	stomatic	setomiko
stob	setobe	stomatiferous	setomifirosi
stoccado	setokijoin	stomatitis	setomiso
stochastic	setokhisuko	stomato	setomisi
stock	setoki	stomatology	setomisilogbon
stockade	setokijin	stomatopod	setomisipindie
stockinet	setokihun	stomatous	setomise
stocking	setokignni	stome	setomin
stockiest	setokisi	stomodeum	setominjinma
stocky	setokise	stomous	setominsi
stodge	setogbon	stomp	setompn
stodgy	setogboin	stomy	setomisi
stogy	setogun	stone	setole
stoic	setokn	stoned	setolede
stoical	setoknjo	Stonehenge	setolehegini
stoichiology	setokhinnlogbon	stonemarten	setolemuratin
stoicheology	setoknunlogbon	stonemason	setolemollesi
stoicism	setoknmosi	stonepit	setolepoyo
stoit	setote	stonework	setolewinsise

WORD (x)	EQUIVALENT (y)	WORD (x)	EQUIVALENT (y)
stonk	setokan	stovaine	setowain
stonker	setokansi	stove1	setowina
stony	setolesi	stove2	setowina
stood	setojo	stover	setownra
stooge	setokogn	stow	setowo
stook	setokoon	stowage	setowogun
stool	setojon	stowaway	setowowelo
stoolball	robesetojon	stra	setnre
stoop1	setopon	strabismus	setnrebomosi
stoop2	setopon	strabo	setnrebo
stop	setopn	strabotomy	setnrebotemo
stoppage	setopangba	strachey	setnrekhn
stopper	setopnsi	straddle	setnrejn
stople	setopon	stradivari	setnrejowarai
storage	setorangun	stradivarius	setnrejowaraisi
storax	setoransi	strafe	setnrefe
store	setoran	Strafford	setnrefonjn
storeman	setoranmoye	straggle	setnregba
storey	setoraise	straight	setnregbe
storied	setoraide	straighten	setnregbesi
storiette	setoraitn	strain1	setnreun
stork	setoruka	strain2	setnreun
storm	setorau	strained	setnreunde
stormy	setorause	strainer	setnreunsi
story	setorai	strait	setnreta
stoss	setoson	straitened	setnretede
stot	setoti	straits	setnretasi
stotinka	setotinka	strake	setnrekn
stotious	setotisi	stramineous	setnreminisi
stotter	stottise	stramonium	setnremenima
stound	setojoin	stramony	setnremeni
stoup	setopan	strand1	setnrejn
stour	setorun	strand2	setnrejn
stout	setotan	strange	setnragbun

616

WORD (x)	EQUIVALENT (y)	WORD (x)	EQUIVALENT (y)
stranger	setnregbunsi	stratus	setnretesi
strangle	setnregbunle	straus	setnresi
strangulate	setnregbunleyo	strauss	setnresin
strangulation	setnregbunleyoon	stravaig	setnrewa
strangury	setnregbunrai	straw	setnrewa
strap	setnrepo	straw	setnrewa
strappado	setnrepode	strawberry	setnrewaberrai
strapping	setnrepognni	stray	setnrai
strappan	setnrepon	streak	sntasikn
strapper	setnreposi	streaky	sntasiknse
strapping	setnrepognni	strea	sntasimi
strass	setnresua	streamer	sntasimisi
strasse	setnresue	streamline	sntasimilehun
strata	setnreto	streek	sntasike
stratagem	setnretogba	street	sntasito
strata	setnretojn	streetcar	sntasitokosi
strategic	setnretoko	strength	sntasigbain
strategist	setnretosi	strengthen	sntasigbainsi
strategy	setnreto	strenuous	sntasilesi
stratford	setnretofonjn	strephosymbolia	sntasiphisombujnsi
strath	setnresi	strepitous	sntasipnti
strathcona	setnresikihun	strepto	sntase
strathmore	setnresimosii	streptococcus	sntasekikis
strathspey	setnresisepn	streptomycin	sntasemukin
strati	setnreti	streptothricin	sntasesinraikin
straticulate	setnratiknleyo	stress	sntasiso
stratiform	setnratifoonmo	stretch	sntasikhn
stratify	setnretife	stretcher	sntasikhnse
stratigraphy	setnretiganphe	stretto	sntasitto
stratocracy	setnretikansn	strew	sntasiwe
stratocumulus	setnrekokunmlesi	strewth	sntasiwese
stratopause	setnretopawnse	stria	sitarain
stratosphere	setnretosephirai	striate	sitaraito
stratum	setnretema	striation	sitaraitosi

WORD (x)	EQUIVALENT (y)	WORD (x)	EQUIVALENT (y)
striature	sitaraitose	strobila	setnrabela
strick	sitaraikn	strobilacious	setnrabelekisi
stricken	sitaraiknse	strobilate	setnrabeleyo
strickle	sitaraikise	strobilation	setnrabeleyoon
strict	sitaraiki	stroboscope	setnrabusokipon
stricture	sitaraikira	strobotron	setnrabutnroin
straddle	sitaraijo	strode	setnrajn
stride	sitaraijin	stroke	setnrankn
strident	sitaraijnto	stroma	setnramo
strife	sitaraifi	stroll	setnrarin
strigiform	sitaraigifoon	strong	setnran
strigil	sitaraigijo	strongyle	setnrajan
strigose	sitaraigon	strontia	setnratie
strike	sitarai	strontianite	setnratieyo
striker	sitaraise	strontium	setnratima
striking	sitaraignni	strop	setnrapn
strine	sitarain	strophanthin	setnraphintehin
string	sitaraign	strophantus	setnraphintesi
string	sitaraign	strophe	setnraphin
string	sitaraign	strophic	setnraphiko
stringed	sitaraignde	strophiole	setnraphijain
stringent	sitaraignto	strophulus	setnraphilesi
stringer	sitariese	stroppy	setnrapon
stringy	sitaraign	strousers	setnralese
strip1	sitaraipn	stroud	setnrajo
strip2	sitaraipn	strove	setnrawn
stripe	sitaraipo	strory	setnraya
striped	sitaraipode	struck	setnranki
striper	sitaraipon	struck	setnranki
stripper	sitaraiponsi	structural	setnrankojo
stripy	sitaraipose	structuralism	setnrankojomosi
strive	sitaraiwin	structure	setnrankojo
strobe	setnrabe	strudel	setnranjinjo
strobic	setnrabeko	struggle	setnrangbasi

WORD (x)	EQUIVALENT (y)	WORD (x)	EQUIVALENT (y)
strum	setnranmo	stumper	setnmpansi
struma	setnranma	stumpy	setnmpanse
strumpet	setnranmpnti	stun	setnha
strung	setnrangn	stung	setngan
strunt	setnranyo	stunk	setnkun
struthious	setnransinsi	stunner	setnhasi
strut	setnrante	stunning	setnhagnni
struth	setnransi	stunt1	setnta
struthionidae	setnransunsijoin	stunt2	setnta
strychnine	setnrakhnhun	stunt man	setnta moye
stuart	setnte	stupa	setnpan
stub	setnbe	stupe	setnpo
stubble	setnbesi	stupefacient	setnpofansiyo
stubborn	setnbegbain	stupefactive	setnpofanknwin
stubby	setnbese	stupefaction	setnpofanknyoon
stucco	setnkki	stupefy	setnpofe
stuck	setnki	stupendous	setnpojnsi
stuck-up	stnki pake	stupid	setnponu
stud1	setngbi	stupidity	setnponutn
stud2	setngbi	stupor	setnposi
student	setngbito	sturdy	setngbain
studio	setngbo	sturgeon	setngbile
studious	setngbonsi	sturgia	setngan
study	setngbon	stumer	setnmosi
stuff	setnfun	stutter	setnttiran
stuffing	setnfungnni	sty1	setn
stuffy	setnfunse	sty2	setn
stull	setnlle	stygian	setngbain
stultify	setnjiafe	style	setnron
stum	setnmi	stylet	setnronsi
stumbe	setnmbo	styliform	setnronfunmo
stumer	setnmura	stylish	setnronsua
stump	setnmpan	stylist	setnronsi
stumpage	setnmpangba	stylistic	setnronsuko

WORD (x)	EQUIVALENT (y)	WORD (x)	EQUIVALENT (y)
stylized	setnronsede	subquatic	snbeakunko
stylo	setnroin	subaqueous	snbeakunsi
stylobate	setnroinbeyo	subarea	snbearase
stylograph	setnroinganpha	subarid	snbearoda
styloid	setnraoinjo	subaudition	snbeaungboyoon
stylolite	setnroinleyo	subauricular	snbeaunraikuoran
stylus	setnronsi	subbasement	snbeboosomutto
stymie	setnmo	subclavian	snbekanwain
stypsis	setnpnso	subdue	snbedisi
styptic	setnpnko	subelaphine	snbejnphini
styr	setnra	subentry	snbeentnrai
styracaceae	setnraikoknni	subequatorial	snbeekuntorajo
styrax	setnraisi	suber	snberai
styrene	setnroin	suberic	snberaiko
Styria	setnrain	suberin	snberain
Styrofoam	setnronfoomo	suberization	snberaiseyoon
styx	setnsi	suberize	snberaise
suable	suebe	suberose	snberose
suasion	suesoon	subgenus	snbeginsi
suave	suewin	subgroup	snbegonpo
suavity	suewinto	subhead	snbehegbi
sub	snbe	subhuman	snbehunmoye
sub-	snbe	subhumid	snbehunmijo
subacetate	snbeakitiyo	subic	snbeko
subacute	snbeakunte	subincision	snbeinikisoon
subaerial	snbeariejo	subinfeudate	snbeinifindanyo
subah	snbehun	subinfeudation	snbeinifndanyoon
subahdar	snbehunjnra	subintrant	snbeinitnrate
subalpine	snbejopohun	subirrigate	snbeirraigiyo
subaltern	snbejotnran	subjacent	snbejaknti
subalternant	snbejotnrante	subject	snbejnkn
subalternate	snbejotnranyo	subjective	snbejnknwin
subapostolic	snbeapinsetojinko	subjoin	snbejosi
subaqua	snbeakun	subjoinder	snbejosijnra

WORD (x)	EQUIVALENT (y)	WORD (x)	EQUIVALENT (y)
subjudice	snbejogbosi	suborn	snbeoran
subjugate	snbejogiyo	subotica	snbetoki
subjunctive	snbejoknyowin	suboxide	snbeosinji
sublapsarian	snbelepnserain	subphylum	snbephewama
sublation	snbeleyoon	subplinth	snbepansin
sublease	snbejnsise	subpoena	snbeposehun
sublet	snbetn	subport	snbepinta
sublethal	snbejnsinjo	subpost	snbepinseto
sublimate	snbejnmiyo	subramose	snberaimosi
sublimation	snbejnmiyoon	subregion	snberegbile
sublime	snbejnmi	subreption	snberepnyoon
subliminal	snbejnminijo	subrogate	snberogiyo
sublunary	snbelujnrai	subrogation	snberogiyoon
submarine	snbemurami	subrosa	snberosin
submariner	snbemuramisi	subscribe	snbesekorai
submediant	snbemujnte	subscript	snbesekoraipn
submerge	snbemuraigba	subsection	snbesekntesi
submersible	snbemuraisnbe	subsector	snbeseknteran
submicron	snbemuknran	subsequent	snbesekunra
submine	snbemini	subserve	snbeserawn
subminiature	snbeminiyoran	subservient	snbeserawnto
submiss	snbemusin	subset	snbesetan
submission	snbemusinse	subside	snbesoojo
submissive	snbemusinwin	subsidence	snbesoojosi
submit	snbemutn	subsidiary	snbesoojorai
submontane	snbemenitelu	subsidize	snbesoojonse
submultiple	snbemujntepo	subsidy	snbesoojon
subnormal	snbeniranjo	subsist	snbesoosi
suboceanic	snbeokunko	subsistence	snbesoosinsi
suborder	snbeorojnra	subsistent	snbesoosinto
subordinary	snbeorojnhunrai	subsoil	snbesoole
subordinate	snbeorojnhunyo	subsolar	snbesoojnran
subordination	snbeorojnhunyoon	subsonic	snbesonko
subordinative	snbeorojnhunyowin	substance	snbesetnsi

WORD (x)	EQUIVALENT (y)	WORD (x)	EQUIVALENT (y)
snbstantial	snbesetntejo	subulate	snbeleyo
sustantialism	snbesetntejomosi	subumbrelle	snbembnraille
substituent	snbesetintuto	suburb	snbeuraib
substitute	snbesetintuyo	suburban	snbeuraibin
substitution	snbesetintuyoon	suburbia	snbeuraibua
substrate	snbesetnrayo	suburbicarian	snbeuraibekosia
substratum	snbesetnrama	subvene	snbewini
subsume	snbesumo	subvention	snbewintiyoon
subsumption	snbesumposi	subversion	snbewinsoon
subtangent	snbetehagnto	subvert	snbewinte
subtemperate	snbetompnrayo	subvitreous	snbewotiransi
subtenant	snbetinte	subway	snbewelo
subtend	snbetinjo	subzero	snbeserau
subtense	snbetinse	succedaneum	sukknhnhunma
subter	snbetnra	succeed	sukknjo
subtraqueous	snbetnrakunsi	succentor	sukkntiran
subterfuge	snbetnrafungba	success des time	sukknsi jnso tinmo
subternatural	snbetnrahetnraijo	success	sukknso
subterrane	snbetnrrain	successful	sukknsofunjn
subterranean	snbetnrrainhn	succession	sukknsoon
subtile	snbetinron	successive	sukknsoowin
subtility	snbetinronto	successor	sukknsoora
subtilize	snbetinronse	succinate	sukkihunyo
subtitle	snbetitoron	succinct	sukkiknto
subtle	snbetoron	succinctorium	sukkikntoraima
subtlety	snbetorontn	succinic	sukkihunko
subtonic	snbetoniko	succor	sukkiran
subtorrid	snbetorrajo	succor	sukkirai
subtotal	snbetotnjo	succotash	sukkitise
subtract	snbetnre	succor	sukkirai
subtraction	snbetnreyoon	succubus	sukkunbesi
subtractive	snbetnrewin	succulent	sukkunjnte
subtrahead	snbetnrehegbi	succumbe	sukkuobe
subtropics	snbetnrapnkosi	succursal	sukkuosejo

WORD (x)	EQUIVALENT (y)	WORD (x)	EQUIVALENT (y)
success	sukknso	suet	surete
succusion	sukkunsoon	suetonius	suretonisi
such	sukhi	suez	suresn
suck	sukn	suffer	suforo
sucker	suknra	sufferance	suforosi
suckle	suknron	suffice	sufikn
suckling	sukngnni	sufficiency	sufikunsn
sucrase	suknranse	sufficient	sufikunto
sucrate	suknranyo	suffix	sufisn
sucre	suknran	sufflate	sufanyo
sucrose	suknrase	suffocant	sufokntn
suction	suknyoon	suffocate	sufoknyo
suctoria	sukntiran	suffolk	sufonliki
suctorial	sukntiraijo	sffragan	sufangan
sudan	sujnna	suffrage	sufangba
sudanese	sujnnase	suffragette	sufagbatin
sudanic	sujnnako	suffragist	sufangbasi
sudarium	sujnraima	suffruticose	suforatokise
sudatorium	sujnyoranma	suffumigate	sufunmigiyo
sudation	sujnyoon	suffuse	sufunsi
sudatory	sujnyorai	sufi	sufia
sudbury	sujnbura	sufism	sufiamosi
sudd	sujon	sugar	sugira
sudden	sujoin	sugary	sugirase
sudermann	sujnronhun	suggest	sugnseyo
Sudeten	sujintin	suggestible	sugnseyobe
sudetes	sujintinsi	suggestion	sugnseyoon
sudoku	sujnkuo	suggestive	sugnseyowin
sudor	sujnran	sugh	sughan
sudorific	sujnraifiko	sugrue	suganse
sudra	sujnra	suicidal	suikekujo
suds	sujara	suicide	suikeku
sue	sure	sui generis	sui gnranso
suede	surejin	suint	suinto

623

WORD (x)	EQUIVALENT (y)	WORD (x)	EQUIVALENT (y)
suisse	suisoo	sulfonic	snlefohunko
suit	suito	sulfonium	snlefohunma
suitable	suitobe	sulfonyl	snlefohunlo
suite	suite	sulfur	snlefunra
suiting	suitegnni	sulfurate	snlefunraiyo
suitor	suiteran	sulfureous	snlefunransi
suiyiian	suiyaan	sulfured	snlefunrate
sukhumi	sukhnmi	sulfuric	snlefunrako
sukkoth	sukknsin	sulfurize	snlefunrase
sukkur	sukkinra	sulfurous	snlefunrasi
sula	snle	sulfury	snlefunrai
sulcate	snlekoyo	sulfuryl	snlefunralo
sulcus	snlekosi	sulk	snleki
sulfa	snlefan	sulky	snlekilo
sulfadiazine	snlefanjnsehun	sulla	snlle
sulfaguanidine	snlefangunhunjoin	sullage	snllegun
sulfaldehyde	snlefanjonhojin	sullen	snllesi
sulfanilamide	snlefanlehunmujin	Sullivan	snllewajn
sulfaprydine	snlefanperaijoin	sullivant	snllewate
sulfarsenide	snlefansehunjin	sully	snllese
sulfarsphenamine	snlefansephihunmini	sully	snllese
sulfate	snlefanyo	sulpha	snlephan
sulfathiazole	snlefansinsejain	sulphate	snlephanyo
sulfatize	snlefantnse	sulphide	snlephiji
sulfhydryl	snlefihogbnlo	sulphite	snlephiyo
sulfide	snlefiji	sulphonamide	snlephonhunmujin
sulfinyl	snlefinlo	sulphonate	snlephonhunyo
sulfite	snlefiyo	sulphoen	snlephonhun
sulfo	snlefo	sulphonic	snlephonhunko
sulfon	snlefohun	sulphur	snlephunra
sulfonal	snlefohunjo	sulphurate	snlephunraiyo
sulfonamide	snlefohunmuji	sulphureous	snlephunraisi
sulfonate	snlefohunyo	sulphuret	snlephunraite
sulfone	snlefohun	sulphuric	snlephunraiko

WORD (x)	EQUIVALENT (y)	WORD (x)	EQUIVALENT (y)
sulphurize	snlephunraise	sumptuous	sumpntisi
sulphurous	snlephunrasi	sun.	suna
sultan	snletin	sundae	sunadasi
sultana	snletinhun	sunda	sunada
sultanate	suletinhunyo	sunday	sunadase
sultry	snleterai	sunder	sunjnra
sulu	snlua	sundew	sunjnwin
sum	sumo	sundial	sunjijo
sumac	sumoki	sundog	sunadegbi
sumatra	sumotnra	sundry	sunjnrai
sumba	sumbe	sung	sungan
sumbar	sumbesi	sungari	sungirai
Sumbawa	sumbewa	sunk	sunki
sumbul	sumbejn	sunken	sunkisi
sumer	sumoran	sunlight	sunalighe
sumerian	umorain	sunlit	sunaleto
sumless	sumolabo	sunn	sunni
summa cum laude	summa kuo lefojin	sunna	sunna
summand	summajo	sunnite	sunnato
summarize	summarase	sune	sunni
summary	summara	sunne	sunahun
summate	summayo	sunny	sunase
summation	summayoon	sunotic	suntnko
summer	summuran	sunrise	sunaraiso
summit	sunmmutn	sunset	sunasetan
summitry	sunmmutnrai	suntan	sunateha
summon	sunmmeni	suojure	suknjorai
summons	sunmmenisi	suoloco	suknloki
summumbonum	sunmmombema	suomi	suknmi
somnambulism	sunmnumbejnmosi	sup1	supn
sumo	sumo	sup2	supn
sump	sumpn	super	supnra
sumpter	sumpnti	superable	supnrabe
sumptuary	sumpntirau	superadd	supnraddi

WORD (x)	EQUIVALENT (y)	WORD (x)	EQUIVALENT (y)
superannuated	supnranhunyo	supermarket	supnramurakia
superannuation	supnranhunyoon	supernal	supnrahunjo
superaqual	supnrakunjo	supernatant	supnrahetnte
superb	supnrabe	supernational	supnrahetnsejo
superacargo	supnrakosilo	supernatural	supnrhetnranjo
supercarrier	supnrakosnsnsi	supernaturalism	supnrahetnranjomosi
superciliary	supnrakunrai	supernormal	supnraniranjo
supercilious	supnrakunsi	supernumerary	supnrayunmoraisi
superego	supnraegbain	superorder	supnraorojnra
superelevation	supnraejinwinyoon	superpose	supnrapinsi
supereminent	supnraeminato	superpower	supnrapowara
supererogate	supnraraingiyo	superpressure	supnrapesisorai
supererogation	supnraraingiyoon	supersaturate	supnrasatnraiyo
superfecundation	supnrafnkunjnyoon	superscribe	supnrasekorai
superfetate	supnrafnteyo	superscript	supnrasekoraipn
superfetation	supnrafnteyoon	superscription	supnrasekoraipnyoon
superficial	supnrafisejo	supersede	supnrasejin
superficiary	supnrafiserai	supersedeas	supnrasejinso
superficies	supnrafisesi	supersensible	supnrasesnsnbe
superfine	supnrafini	supersensual	supnrasesnsnjo
superfluid	supnrafolujn	supersex	supnrasesia
superfluity	supnrfolutn	supersonic	supnrasonko
superfluous	supnrfolusi	superstan	supnrasetan
superfortress	supnrafontnbo	superstate	supnrasetnyo
superfuse	supnrafunsi	superstition	supnrasetiyoon
superimpose	supnraimpose	superstratum	supnrasetnratema
superincumbent	supnrainikunmbeto	superstruct	supnrasetnrako
superintend	supnrainitinjo	superstructure	supnrasetnrakorai
superintendent	supnrainitinjointo	supersubtle	supnrasnbetoron
superior	supnrai	supertanker	supnratekun
superiority	supnraito	supertax	supnratesan
superjacent	supnrajaknti	supertonic	supnratoniko
superlative	supnraletnwin	supervene	supnrawini
superlunar	supnralujnran	supervise	supnrawose

WORD (x)	EQUIVALENT (y)	WORD (x)	EQUIVALENT (y)
supervision	supnrawosesi	supralapsarian	supnranlepnserain
supervisor	supnrawoseran	supraliminal	supnranliminajo
supinate	supohunyo	supramundane	supnrnmujndain
supination	supohunyoon	supranational	supnranheyoonjo
supinator	supohunyoran	supernaturalism	supnranhetnranjomosi
supine	supohun	supraprotest	supnranpontnsi
suplex	suporon	suprarenal	supnranrehunjo
supper	supnje	suprarenalin	supnranrehunjan
supplant	supantn	suprasterol	supnransetnrjin
supple	suporon	supratemporal	supnrantompnranjo
supplement	suporonmutto	supremacist	supnroinsesi
supplemental	suporonmuttojo	supremacy	supnroinse
supplementary	suporonmuttorai	supreme	supnroin
suppletion	suporonyoon	supreme court	kiraito supnroin
suppletory	suporonyorai	supremo	supnronkn
suppliant	supantn	sur-1	sura
supplicate	supankoyo	sur-2	sura
supply	suponlo	sura	suran
support	supinta	Surabaya	suranbain
supporter	supintasi	surah	surahn
supportive	supintawin	surakarta	surankiti
supposable	supinsibe	sural	surajo
supposal	supinsijo	surance	suraisi
suppose	supinsi	surat	suratn
supposition	supinsiyoon	surbase	surabooso
suppository	supinsiyorai	surcease	suraknsise
suppress	supesiso	surcharge	surakhorangn
suppression	supesisoon	surcingle	surakingon
suppressive	supesisowin	surculose	surakuose
suppressor	supesisoran	surd	surajn
suppurate	supuraiyo	sure	surai
suppuration	supuraiyoon	surely	surailo
suppurative	supuraiyowin	surety	suraito
supra	supnran	surf	surafan

WORD (x)	EQUIVALENT (y)	WORD (x)	EQUIVALENT (y)
surface	surafansi	surrogate	surrogiyo
surfactant	surafankntn	surround	surrojoin
surfboard	bugbasurafan	surroundings	surrojoingnnisi
surfeit	surafnte	sursumcorda	surasumokigbain
surfing	surafangnni	surtax	suratesan
surge	surale	surtees	suratosi
surgent	suraleto	surtout	suratonita
surgeon	suraleran	surtout	suratonita
surgeoncy	suraleransn	suruga	suragan
surgery	suralerai	surveillance	suraworansi
surgical	suralekojo	surveillant	suraworantn
suricate	suraikoyo	survey	surawon
surinam	surainmo	surveyor	surawonsi
surjection	surajnknyoon	survival	surawowojo
surly	surajin	survive	surawowo
surma	surami	survivor	surawowosi
surmise	suramuse	sus	susi
surmount	suramounte	susa	suse
surname	surahemo	susanna	susewa
surpass	surapanso	susceptance	susiknpntisi
surplice	surapankn	susceptibility	susiknpntibeleto
surplus	surapolusi	susceptible	susiknpntibe
surprint	surapante	sushi	susun
surprisal	surapansejo	susian	susia
surprise	surapanse	susiana	susiahun
surra	surra	suslik	susiliki
surreal	surreinjo	suspect	susipnto
surrealism	surreinjomosi	suspend	susipnjon
surrebuttal	surrebuttnjo	suspender	susipnjonso
surrebutter	surrebuttnra	suspense	susipnya
surrein	surreini	suspension	susipnyase
surrender	surrejnra	suspensor	susipnyaran
surreptitious	surrepntitosi	suspensive	susipnyawin
surrey	surese	suspensory	susipnyarai

WORD (x)	EQUIVALENT (y)	WORD (x)	EQUIVALENT (y)
suspicion	susipnkuo	swacked	swakide
suspicious	susipnkuosi	swaddle	swadisi
suspire	susiporai	swadeshi	swajinsi
susquehanna	susikunhun	swag	swagba
suss	susin	swagbelly	swagbabejnran
sussex	susinsn	swage	swagbi
sustain	susitelu	swagger	wagbisi
sustenance	susitinsi	swahili	swahasi
sustentacular	susitintoknjnra	swain	swani
sustentation	susitintoyoon	swale	swajn
sustention	susitinyoon	swallow1	swajjnmi
susurrant	susirrain	swallow2	swajjnmi
susurrate	susirraito	swam	swama
susurrus	susirraiso	swami	swamo
suther	susnra	swamp	swamipo
sutler	sutojnra	swamper	swmiposi
sutra	sutoran	swan	swahn
suttee	suttnron	swanee	swahnse
sutter	suttnra	swannery	swahunrai
suttle	suttnron	swank	swakn
suture	sutnrai	swankie	swaknsi
suum cui que	sumo ki kun	swanky	swaknse
suva	suwa	swap	swapo
suwalk	suwaliki	sward	swagan
suwannee	suwahun	swarf	swafan
suzerain	suzerain	swarm1	swaron
suzerainity	suserainto	swarm2	swaron
suzuki	suseki	swarmer	swaronsi
svalbard	swajngba	swart	swasu
svelte	swajnte	swath	swasuo
swa	swa	swarthy	swasuosi
swab	swabo	swarve	swawo
swabber	swabosi	swash	swasun
Swabia	swabose	swastika	swaseknti

WORD (x)	EQUIVALENT (y)	WORD (x)	EQUIVALENT (y)
swat	swate	swept	swegban
swatch	swatesis	swerve	swewo
swath	swasan	sweven	swelala
swathe	swasuin	swi	sunin
swatter	swattnra	swift	swinfia
sway	swaya	swifter	swinfiasi
swazi	swaso	swig	swingba
swaziland	swasoledain	swill	swinjan
swe	sue	swim	swinwe
sweal	swejo	swim	swinwe
swear	sweran	swimmeret	swinweraite
sweat	sweyo	swimmingly	swinwegnnilo
sweated	sweyode	swindle	swinjnra
sweater	sweyosi	swindler	swinjnrasi
swede	swejin	swine	swinnu
sweden	swejinsi	swing	swinji
swedenborg	swejinsibogan	swinge	swinjin
swedenborgianism	swejinsibogainmosi	swingeing	swinjingnni
swedish	swejinso	swinger	swinjinsi
sweeny	swesise	swing-wing	swinji-winjn
sweep	swegba	swinging	swinjignni
sweeper	swegbasi	swingle	swinjinron
sweeping	swegbagnni	swinish	swinnuse
sweepy	swegbase	swink	swinkn
sweer	sweran	swinnerton	swinrantin
sweet	swedun	swipe	swinpo
sweeten	swedunse	swipple	swinporon
sweetheart	swedunhetan	swirl	swinrai
sweetie	swedunsi	swirly	swinraise
sweetish	swedunsu	swish	swinsia
sweetness	swedunnisi	swiss	swinso
swell	swewu	switch	swinte
swelling	swewugnni	switched-on	swintede ni
swelter	swewusi	switcher	swintesi

WORD (x)	EQUIVALENT (y)	WORD (x)	EQUIVALENT (y)
swith	swinsin	sycee	sosise
swither	swinsinsi	sycon	sokinu
switzer	swinsesi	syconium	sokinuma
switzerland	swinsesiledain	sycophancy	sokiphinisn
swivel	swinwalo	sycophant	sokiphinitn
swivet	swinwate	sycorax	sokiransi
swizz	swinsu	sycosis	sokiso
swizzle	swinsuron	sydney	sodain
swo	suo	syene	sosin
swobe	swobe	syenite	sosinto
swollen	swowusi	syke	sokn
swoon	swosi	syllabary	sojnranbnrai
swoop	swogba	syllabic	sojnranbnko
swop	swoop	syllabicate	sojnranbnkoyo
swoosh	swosoon	syllabify	sojnranbnfe
sword	swojoin	syllabism	sojnranbnmosi
sworder	swojoinsi	syllabist	sojnranbnsi
swore	sworan	syllabize	sojnranbnse
sworn	sworon	syllable	sojnranbn
swot	swotn	syllabub	sojnranbnbe
swoun	swoni	syllabus	sojnranbnsi
swound	swojoin	syllepsis	sojnranpnso
swum	swowe	syllogism	sojnrogbonmosi
swung	swoji	syllogistic	sojnrogbonsuko
swy	swose	syllogize	sojnrogbonse
sy	so	sylph	solephn
sybaris	soberai	sylphid	solephnjo
sybarite	soberaite	sylva	sojnwa
sybarite	soberaite	sylvan	sojnwain
sybaritic	soberaiteko	sylvanite	sojnwainte
sybo	soboo	sylvanus	sojnwainsi
sycamine	soknmini	sylvatic	sjnwako
sycamore	soknmorai	sylvester	sojnwnse
syce	sosi	sylvestral	sojnwnseraijo

WORD (x)	EQUIVALENT (y)	WORD (x)	EQUIVALENT (y)
Sylvia	sojnwan	symphonize	somphohunse
sylvian	sojnwanhn	symphony	somphohun
sylviculture	sojnwakunjiaran	symphysis	sompheso
sylvite	sojnwayo	symplectic	somporonko
symbiout	sombakosi	symplegades	somporonjesi
symbiosis	sombakoso	sympodium	sompindiema
symbol	sombajo	symposiac	sompinseko
symbolic	sombajokn	symposiarch	sompinseknra
symbolical	sombajoknsi	symposium	sompinsema
symbolics	sombajoknsi	symptom	sompnti
symbolism	sombajomosi	symptomatic	sompntiko
symbolist	sombajosi	symptomatology	sompntitologbon
symbolistic	sombajosukn	syn	sose
symbolize	sombajose	synagog	sosegonko
symbology	sombajogbon	synagogal	sosegonkojo
symmetalism	sommitojomosi	synagogue	sosegonkun
symmetrical	sommutoraikojo	synalepha	sosejnphn
symmetrist	sommutoraisi	synalgia	sosejngan
symmetrize	sommutoraise	synantherous	sosesinrasi
symmetry	sommutorai	synapse	soseposi
symonds	somkojnsi	synapsis	soseposo
symons	somenisi	synarchy	soseknran
sympathectomy	sompansiotemo	synarthrosis	sosesinrasi
sympathetic	sompansioko	synaxis	sosesiso
sympathcotonia	sompansiokitihun	sync	soseko
sympathin	sompansiosi	syncarp	sosekopan
sympathize	sompansiose	syncarpous	sosekopansi
sympathy	sompansio	syncategorematic	sosekotignranmuko
sympatric	sompanraiko	synch	sosekhi
sympatry	sompanrai	synchro	sosekhnra
sympetalous	sompntijosi	synchromesh	sosekhnramoso
symphile	sompheron	synchrone	sosekhnrain
symphonic	somphohunko	synchronic	sosekhnrako
symphonious	somphohunsi	synchronicity	sosekhnrakito

WORD (x)	EQUIVALENT (y)	WORD (x)	EQUIVALENT (y)
synchronism	sosekhnramosi	synecology	sosunknlogbon
synchronize	sosekhnrase	synectics	sosunknkosi
synchronoscope	sosekhnrasokipon	syneresis	sosunraisi
synchronous	sosekhnrasi	synergist	sosunrailosi
synchroscope	sosekhnrasokipon	synergism	sosunrailomosi
synchrotron	sosekhnratnran	synergy	sosunrailo
synclastic	sosekansuko	synesis	sosunsi
synclinal	sosekihunjo	synesthesia	sosunsunwnsia
syncline	sosekihun	syngamy	sosegimo
synclitism	sosekiuntemosi	synge	sosegn
syncom	sosekimu	syngenesis	sosegnhunso
syncopate	sosekiponyo	synizesis	sosesiso
syncopation	sosekiponyoon	synkaryon	soseknrain
syncope	sosekipon	synod	sosejo
syncrasy	soseknrasn	synod	soaejo
syncretism	soseknramosi	synodic	sosejoko
syncretize	soseknrase	synoecious	sosekisi
syncrisis	ssosekanso	synoekete	soseknto
syncsignal	soseknsooganjo	synonym	sosetumo
syncytium	sosekotoma	synonymize	sosetumose
syndactyl	sosedakntilo	synonymous	sosetumosi
syndactylism	sosedakntilomosi	synonymy	sosetumon
syndesis	sosejnso	synopsis	sosepnsi
syndesmo	sosejoma	synoptic	sosepnko
syndesmology	sosejomalogbon	synostosis	sosetosi
syndesmosis	sosejomasi	synousiacs	sosesiakosi
syndetic	sosejotnko	synovial	sosewnmi
syndeton	sosejntoni	synovitis	sosewnmisi
syndic	sosejokn	synsepalous	sosepanjosi
syndicalism	sosejoknmosi	syntactics	sosetekankosi
syndicate	sosejoknyo	syntagma	sosetegboin
syndrome	sosegbnmo	syntax	sosetosi
syne	sosun	synthesis	sosesuwn
synecdoche	sosunkndekhn	synthesize	sosesuwnse

WORD (x)	EQUIVALENT (y)	WORD (x)	EQUIVALENT (y)
synthesizer	sosesuwnsesi	systematize	sositnmuse
synthetise	sosesuwnse	systematology	sositnmulogbon
synthetism	sosesuwnmosi	systemic	sositnmko
synthetic	sosesuwnko	systematic	sositnmuko
syntonic	sosetoniko	systematism	sositnmumosi
syntony	sosetoni	systematist	sositnmusi
synura	soserami	systematize	sositnmuse
sypher	sophiran	systole	sosetoron
sypher	sophiran	syzygy	sosiselo
syphilis	sophijansi	sze	sosi
syphilitic	sophijanko	taal	tejo
syphilology	sophijanlogbon	tab1	tebe
syphiloma	sophijanmo	tab2	tebe
syphilophobia	sophijanphobua	tabacin	tebekin
syracuse	sorakunse	tabanid	tebehajo
syrette	soranto	tabard	tebejoin
syria	soraisi	tabaret	teberai
syriac	soraiki	tabasco	tebekise
syrian	sorain	tabby	tebebo
syringe	soraigbn	tabernacle	tebekinron
syringe	soraigbn	tabernacular	tebekinronsi
syringomyelia	soraigbnjnmi	tabes	tebese
syrinx	soraisi	tabescent	tebeseknti
syro	sorain	tabesdorsalis	tebesejnranjosi
syrphid	soraphojo	tablas	tebelesi
syrphus	soraphosi	tablature	tebeletnran
syrtis major	sorasi mojura	table	teberon
syrup	sorapon	tableau vivant	teberoin wowote
syssarcosis	sosoorakiso	tableland	teberonledain
systaltic	sosetajnko	tablet	tebetn
system	sositnmo	tabloid	teberonjo
systematic	sositnmuko	taboo	taboo
systematism	sositnmumosi	tabor	tebero
systematist	sositnmusi	taboret	teberotn

WORD (x)	EQUIVALENT (y)	WORD (x)	EQUIVALENT (y)
taborine	teberohun	tachysterol	techiasetnrajin
tabu	teb	tacit	tekiti
tabular	tebejnran	taciturn	tekitnran
tabularasa	tebejnrase	tacitus	tekitisi
tabularize	tebejnraise	tack1	tekun
tabulate	tebeleyo	tack2	tekun
tabulator	tebeleyoran	tack3	tekun
tacamahac	tekomuhun	tacket	tekunto
tacan	tekojn	tackies	tekunsi
tace	tesi	tackle	tekuo
tacet	tekiti	tackling	tekuognni
tache	tekhn	tacky1	tekunse
tacheo	tekhn	tacky2	tekunse
tacheometer	tekhnmuto	tacnode	teknknjin
tacheometry	tekhnmutorai	taco	teki
tachina	tekhnun	tacoma	tekimo
tachinid	tekhinjo	taconic	tekinko
tachisme	tekhnmosi	taconite	tekiyo
tachisto	tekhnseto	tact	tekan
tachistoscope	tekhnsetosokipon	tactful	tekanfunjn
tacho	tekho	tactic	tekanko
tachograph	tekhoganpha	tactical	tekankojo
tachometer	tekhomuto	tactics	tekankosi
tachometry	techomutorai	tactile	tekanron
tachy	tekhia	tactility	tekanleto
tachycardia	tekhiakogbain	taction	tekansi
tachygraph	tekhiaganpha	tactless	tekanlabo
tachygrapher	tekhiaganphasi	tactometer	tekanmuto
tachygraphy	tekhiaganphe	tactual	tekanjo
tachylyte	tekhialote	tacubaya	tekunbain
tachymeter	techiamuto	tad	tedie
tachymetry	techiamutorai		

WORD (x)	EQUIVALENT (y)
tachyon	tekhiasi
tachyphylaxis	tekhiaphelesosi

WORD (x)	EQUIVALENT (y)
tadpole	tediepinjn
tadzhik	tediekese

635

WORD (x)	EQUIVALENT (y)	WORD (x)	EQUIVALENT (y)
tadzhikistan	tediekesetan	taian	telosi
tae	tese	taig	teloga
taedium vitae	tesejnma wintnse	taiga	telogan
taedong	tesejngon	tail1	tele
tael	telo	tail2	tele
taenia	tesosi	taiback	teleboki
taenia fuge	tesosi fungba	tailboard	telebugba
taeniacide	tesosikeku	tailcoat	telekitie
taeniasis	tesosiso	tailgate	telegiyo
tafferel	tefirolo	tail-light	tele leghe
taffeta	tefinto	tailing	telegnni
taffrail	tefirailo	tailor	teleran
taffy	tefese	tailored	telerande
tafia	tefesi	tailor-made	teleran-mojain
taft	tefia	tailpiece	telepansi
tag1	tegan	tain	telu
tag2	tegan	tain	telu
tag end	tegan enjan	tainan	teluhun
tagalong	teganto	tainaron	telurain
taganrog	teganro	taine	teluse
tagger	tegansi	taino	teluko
tagliatelle	tegiunyoron	taint	telutn
tagmeme	teganmomu	taipei	telopn
tagmemics	teganmomukosi	taiping	telopngan
tagore	teganrai	taiwan	telowin
tagua	tegun	taiyiian	teloyan
tagus	tegunsi	taiz	telosi
tahina	tehihun	taj mahal	tejan moha
tahiti	tehito	take	tekn
tahitian	tehitohn	taker	teknsi
tahr	tehia	taking	tekngnni
tahsil	tehsujn	takia makan	tekinkinmi
tahsildar	tehisujoran	taku	tekun
tai	telo	talapoin	tejnpanun

WORD (x)	EQUIVALENT (y)	WORD (x)	EQUIVALENT (y)
talar	tejnra	tally	tejjnse
talaria	tejnrain	tally-bo	tejjnse-bu
talaud	tejngbun	tally man	tejjnse moye
talavera	tejnwara	talmud	tejnmujo
talbot	tejnbu	talmudist	tejnmujosi
talc	tejnki	talon	tejnso
talca	tejnko	talos	tejnso
talcose	tejnkise	taluk	tejnke
talcum	tejnkuo	talus	tejnsi
tale	tejn	tamable	temobe
talent	tejnto	tamalo	temode
taler	tejnra	tamalpuis	temojnpnsi
tales	tejnsi	tamandua	temojua
taligrade	tejangandie	tamarack	temoraiki
talion	tejain	tamarau	temorau
taliped	tejanpodie	tamarin	temorain
talipes	tejanposi	tamarind	temoraijin
talipomanus	tejanpomasi	tamarisk	temoraisia
talipot	tejanpote	tamasha	temosun
tallsman	tejjnmoose	tamatave	temotnwa
tallsmanik	tejjnmooseko	tambora	temburan
talk	tejo	tambour	temburai
talkathon	tejosesi	tambourin	temburin
talkative	tejotawin	tambourine	teburain
talkback	tejoboki	tame	temni
talker	tejosi	tamein	temnini
talkie	tejose	tamerlans	temurajain
talking	tejognni	tamil	temole
tall	tejjn	tamis	temosi
tallage	tejjngba	tammany	temmose
tallahassee	tejjnhunse	tammerfors	temmurafonsi
tallboy	tejjnboyn	tammerkoski	tammurakiso
tallina	tejjnhun	tammuz	temmusn
tallow	tejjora	tammy	temmse

WORD (x)	EQUIVALENT (y)	WORD (x)	EQUIVALENT (y)
tamoshanter	temosuntnra	tango	tegbako
tamp	tempn	tangram	teganmo
tampa	tempan	tangy	tegbasi
tampala	tempanlo	tanimbar	tekombe
tampan	tempanjn	tanis	tekoso
tamper	tempnsi	tanist	tekosi
tampere	tempnrai	tanistry	tekosirai
tampico	tempoki	tanjib	tekojan
tampion	temponse	tanjore	tekojinra
tampon	tempon	tanjungpriok	tekojoinpanko
tam-tam	tem toma	tank	tekun
tan1	teko	tanka	tekun
tan2	teko	tankage	tekungun
tana	tekon	tankard	tekungba
tanager	tekongnra	tanked up	tekunde pake
tanagra	tekonngan	tank engine	tekun engbihun
tananarove	tekonnraiwn	tanker	tekunsi
tanbark	tekoborakn	tannage	tekkogun
tancre	tekoknra	tannate	tekkoyo
tandem	tekojora	tanned	tekkode
tandjungpinang	tekogbainpon	tanenberg	tekkoinbegan
tandoor	tekodeinsi	tanner	tekkosi
taney	tekose	tannery	tekkorai
tang	tegba	tannhauser	tekkohesi
tanganyika	tegbainyika	tannic	tekkonko
tangelo	tegbanlo	tannic acid	akijo tekkonko
tangent	tegbainto	tanniferous	tekkofirosi
tangential	tegbaintojo	tannin	tekkoisi
tangerine	tegbanrain	tansy	tekoson
tangible	tegbabe	tanta	tekoto
tangier	tegbasi	tantalite	tekotoleyo
tangle	tegbaron	tantalic	tekotoleko
tangle berry	tegbaron berrai	tantalite	tekotoleyo
tangly	tegbalo	tantalize	tekotolese

WORD (x)	EQUIVALENT (y)	WORD (x)	EQUIVALENT (y)
tantalous	tekotolesi	tapis	tepnso
tantalum	tekotolema	tapesler	teposejnra
tantalus	tekotolesn	tappan zee	tepnpan se
tantamount	tekotomonunte	tapper	tepnsi
tantara	tekotoran	tappet	tepnti
tantivy	tekotowe	tapping	tepngnni
tant mieux	tekotn muwasi	tappit	tepiti
tanto	tekoton	tappoon	tepiposi
tant pis	tekotnpisi	tapsaltarie	tepnsanjyoran
tantra	tekotnra	tapster	tepnseto
tantrism	tekotnramosi	tapti	tepnta
tantrum	tekotnrama	tapuya	tepnyan
tanzania	tekosinsi	taquari	tekunra
tao	teona	tar1	tesun
taoism	teonamosi	tar2	tesun
taos	teonasi	tara	tesua
tap1	tepn	taramasalata	tesunmusanleyo
tap2	tepn	tarantass	tesuntasi
tapa	tepan	tarantella	tesuntolle
tapas	tepansi	tarantism	tesuntnmosi
tapadera	tepanjinran	taranto	tesuntn
tapajos	tepanjinsi	tarantula	tesuntnjn
tapalo	tepanlo	tarapon	tesunpon
tape	tepo	tarawa	tesunwa
taper	teposi	taraxacum	tesunsekuo
tape record	tepo rekigba	tarbell	tesunbejnro
tape recorder	tepo rekigbasi	tarboosh	tesunboose
tapestry	teposerai	tarboy	tesunboyn
tapetum	tepotima	tardenolsian	tesunjinjoinsi
tapeworm	tepoworon	tardigrade	tesunjingandie
taphephobia	tephephobua	tardo	tesundie
taphonomy	tepheknmo	tardy	tesundin
tapioca	tep-nkoin	tare1	tesue
tapir	tepnra	tare2	tesue

WORD (x)	EQUIVALENT (y)	WORD (x)	EQUIVALENT (y)
targ	tesungi	tarshish	tesusue
targe	tesungba	tarsier	tesusiasi
target	tesungbe	tarso	tesuso
targeteer	tesungbesi	tarsometatasus	tesusomutotesunsi
targum	tesungima	tarsus	tesusia
tarheel	tesunhe	tart1	tesuntn
tarifa	tesunfan	tart2	tesuntn
tariff	tesunfe	tart3	tesuntn
tarim	tesunmi	tartan	tesuntan
Tarkington	tesunknti	tartar	tesuntnra
tarlatan	tesunjntn	tartar	tesuntnra
tarmac	tesunmkn	taartare	tesuntnran
tarmacadam	tesunmknjnra	tartareous	tesuntnransi
tarn	tesuin	tartarian	tesuntnrain
tarnal	tesuinjo	tartaric	tesuntnraiko
tarnation	tesuinyoon	tartaric acid	akijo tesuntnraiko
tarnish	tesuinse	tartarous	tesuntnrasi
tarnow	tesuinwa	tartary	tesuntnrai
taro	tesuo	tartlet	tesuntnsi
tarot	tesuto	tartarate	tesuntnrayo
tarpan	tesupan	tartarize	tesuntnraise
tarpaulin	tesupnjain	tartarous	tesuntarasi
tarpela	tesupnjn	tartessus	tesuntnsin
tarpon	tesupon	tartufe	tesuntnfe
tarquin	tesukuo	tarty	tesuntnse
tarradiddle	tesunrajinduo	tarzan	tesunsia
tarragon	tesunragon	Tashkent	tesuknti
tarragona	tesunragonsi	tasimeter	tesiamuto
tarriance	tesunrasi	task	tesia
tarrier	tesunrasi	task force	tesia foonse
tarrow	tesunrase	taskmaster	tesia moseto
tarry1	tesunro	taslar	tesijan
tarry2	tesunro	tasman	tesimojn
tarsal	tesusiajo	tasmania	tesimojia

WORD (x)	EQUIVALENT (y)	WORD (x)	EQUIVALENT (y)
tase	tesi	taupe	teunpon
tass	tesoo	taurine	teunrain
tassel	tesoojo	tauris	teunraisi
tasset	tesootn	tauro	teunron
taste	tesio	taurocholic	teunronkhijnko
tasteless	tesiolabo	tauromachy	teunronmukhn
taster	tesiosi	taurus	teunronsi
tasting	tesiognni	taut	teuntn
tasty	tesiose	tauten	teuntnsi
tat1	tetn	tautang	teuntngun
tat2	tetn	tauto	teunto
tat3	tetn	tautog	teuntogon
ta-tami	tetnmo	tautologism	teuntologbonmosi
tatar	tetnran	tautologist	teuntologbonsi
tatary	tetnrai	tautologize	teuntologbonse
tatie	tetnse	tautology	teuntologbon
tatle	tetojn	tautomeric	teuntomurakn
tattler	tetojnra	tautomerism	teuntomurasi
tatouay	tetose	tautomerization	teuntomuraseyoon
tatra	tetnra	tautonym	teuntonimo
tatter	tettnra	tavern	tewnran
tatterdemallon	tettnrajinmullesi	taverner	tewnransi
tatter sail	tettnra sanlo	taw	tewo
tattered	tettnrade	taw	tewo
tatting	ettngnni	tawdry	tewojnra
tattle	tettojn	tawie	tewose
tattler	tettojnra	tawny	tewoin
tattoo1	tettoo	tawny owl	owiwi tewoin
tattoo2	tettoo	taws	tewosi
tatty	tetto	tax	tesan
tau	teun	taxable	tesanbe
taught	teunkho	taxaceous	tesansuwa
taunt	teunto	taxation	tesanyoon
taunton	teuntosi	taxco	tesanki

WORD (x)	EQUIVALENT (y)	WORD (x)	EQUIVALENT (y)
taxi	tesansi	teasel	tiesejo
taxiarch	tesansiknra	teaser	tiesesi
taxidermist	tesansijnramosi	teaset	tiesetn
taxidermy	tesansijnramo	teat	tiete
taximeter	tesansimuto	teasel	tiesujo
taxine	tesansiun	tebet	tibeyo
taxis	tesanso	tech	tokhi
taxite	tesanyo	technetium	tokhinitema
taxman	tesanmoye	technic	tokhiniko
taxon	tesankn	technical	tokhinikojo
taxonomist	tesanknmosi	technicality	tokhinikojotn
taxonomy	tesanknmo	technician	tokhinikohn
taxpayer	tesanpanyesi	technique	tokhinikun
taygeta	telegnto	techno	tokhikn
taylor	teleran	technocracy	tokhiknkansn
tayra	telerai	technocrat	tokhiknkanta
tazza	tesppe	technography	tokhiknganphe
te	ti	technolator	tokhiknletnran
te	to	technolithic	yokhiknlesiko
tea	tie	technological	tokhiknlogbonkojo
tea bag	bogba tie	technology	tokhiknlogbon
teach	tinkho	techy	tochise
teacher	tinkhosi	tect	tnto
teaching	tinkhognni	tectology	tntoknlogbon
teak	tinki	tectonic	tntoknseko
teal	tinjn	tectonics	tntosekosi
tam	tima	tectrix	tntoraisi
team-mate	tima mote	tecumsel	tokunse
teamster	timaseto	ted	togbaa
teamwork	winsisetima	tedder	togbaase
teapot	tiepote	teddy	togbain
tear1	tieran	teddy boy	togbain boyn
tear2	tieran	tedium	tojinma
tease	tiese	tedious	togbaasi

WORD (x)	EQUIVALENT (y)	WORD (x)	EQUIVALENT (y)
tedium	togbaama	Teheran	toheran
tee	tose	tehri	toherai
tee1	tose	tehuantepec	tohuntepn
tee2	tose	tehuelche	tohunlokhn
tee-hee	tose-hese	teigitur	tognteran
teem1	toomo	teil	tolo
teem2	toomo	teind	tojon
teen	toon	tejuco	tojoki
teen	toon	teknonymy	tokinknmo
teenage	toongun	tektite	tokntiyo
teenager	toongunsi	tel	tojn
teens	toonsi	tela	tojn
teensy	toonse	telaesthesia	tojnsunwnsia
teeny	tooese	telamon	tojnmeni
teeny-bopper	tooese-bopnsi	telangiectasia	tojngbainkntisia
teeny-weeny	tooese-winise	telangiectasis	tojngbainkntiso
teepee	too-pnya	telautogram	tojnauntoganmo
tees	toosi	telautograph	tojnauntoganpha
teeter	tootesi	telaviv	tojnwowo
teeth	toosi	tele-	toj n
teethe	toosia	tele-ad	tojn-adi
teething-ring	toosiagnni rogan	telecardiogram	tojnkogbakoganmo
teetotal	toototnjo	telecast	tojnkosotn
teetotaler	toototnjosi	teledu	tojndun
teetotum	toototnma	telefinalist	tojnfihunjosi
teff	tofin	telega	tojngi
teflon	tofijnsi	telegenic	tojnginko
teg	togbn	telegnosis	tojnginiso
tegmen	togbnmosi	telegonus	tojngonsi
tegner	togbnran	telegony	tojngonse
tegular	togbnjn	telegram	tojnganmo
tegular	togbnjnra	telegraph	tojnganpha
tegument	togbnmuye	telegrapher	tojnganphasi
te-hee	to hesi	telegraphic	tojnganphako

WORD (x)	EQUIVALENT (y)	WORD (x)	EQUIVALENT (y)
telegraphone	tojnganphohun	telestich	tojnsetinhun
telegraphoscope	tojnganphesekipon	teletherapy	tojnsinranpo
telegraphy	tojnganphe	telethermometer	tojnsinronmuto
telegu	tojngbun	telethon	tojnsesi
telekinesis	tojnkihunso	teletype	tojntnpon
telemachus	tojnmokhnsi	teleutospore	tojnwaseporai
telemark	tojnmurokn	teleview	tojnwowin
telemarketing	tojnmurakiagnni	televise	tojnwose
telemeter	tojnmuto	television	tojnwosesi
telemetry	tojnmutorai	telex	tojnsn
telencephalo n	teojnenknphejnsi	telfer	tojnfiro
teleology	tojnknlogbon	telford	tojnfonjn
teleost	tojnknsi	telfordize	tojnfonjnse
telepathy	tojnpansio	telharmonium	tojnhanmenima
telephone	tojnphohun	telic	tojnko
telephonic	tojnphohunkn	teliostage	tojnknsetngun
telephonist	tojnphohunsi	telium	tojnma
telephonograph	tojnphoknganpha	tell	tojjn
telephony	tojnphohunse	teller	tojjnsi
telephoto	tojnphotin	telling	tojjngnni
telephotograph	tojnphotinganpha	telltale	tojjntejn
telephotography	tojnphotinganphe	tollurate	tojjnraiyo
teleplasm	tojnpanson	telluric	tojjnraiko
teleprinter	tojnpantesi	telluride	tojjnraiji
teleprompter	tojnponmpntisi	tellurion	tojjnrain
teleradio	tojnrangbo	tellurite	tojjnraiyo
teleran	tojnran	tellurium	tojjnraima
telescope	tojnsekipon	tellurise	tojjnraise
telescopium	tojnsekiponma	tellurnickel	tojjnrankhilo
telescopy	tojnsekipe	tellurous	tojjnraisi
telescript	tojnsekoraipn	tellus	tojjnsi
teleset	tojnsetn	telly	tojjnron
telesis	tojnso	telo	tojnkn
telesthesia	tojnsunwusia	telodynamic	tojnkndainsemuko

WORD (x)	EQUIVALENT (y)	WORD (x)	EQUIVALENT (y)
telolecital	tojnknsekitijo	temptation	tompntiyoon
telphase	tojnphanse	tempting	tompntignni
telpher	tojnphiro	tempura	tompere
telson	tojnsin	ten	tin
telstar	tojnsetan	tenable	tinbe
telugu	tojngbun	tenace	tinki
temblor	tombejnra	tenacious	tinkisi
tembuland	tombejnra	tenacity	tinkitn
tembuland	tombuledain	tenaculum	tinkuoma
temerarious	tomuraraisi	tenaille	tinlelle
temerity	tomuratn	tenancy	tinungbesi
temesvar	tomsewara	tenant	tinungbe
temp	tompn	tenant farmer	fanmosi tinungbe
temper	tompnra	tenantry	tinungberai
tempera	tompnran	tenasserim	tinsoorain
temperament	tompnranmutto	tench	tinkho
temperamental	tompnranmuttojo	tend1	tinjo
temperance	tompnransi	tend2	tinjo
temperate	tompnratn	tendency	tinjoinsn
temperature	tompnratnran	tendentious	tinjointosi
tempest	tompnsia	tender1	tinjosi
tempestuous	tompnsiasi	tender2	tinjosi
tempi	tompa	tender3	tinjosi
templar	tompansi	tenderize	tinjosise
template	tompantue	tenderizer	tinjosisesi
temple1	tompejo	tendinous	tinjoinsi
temple2	tompejo	tendon	tinjoin
tempo	tompo	tendril	tinjorailo
tempolabile	tompolebajn	tenebrae	tinniborain
temporal	tomporajo	tenebrific	tinniboraifikn
temporality	tomporarontn	tenebrous	tinniboraisi
temporary	tomporarai	tenedos	tinnijnso
temporize	tomporase	tenement	tinnimutto
tempt	tompnti	tenendum	tinjnma

WORD (x)	EQUIVALENT (y)	WORD (x)	EQUIVALENT (y)
tenerif	tinraife	tent	tinto
tenesmus	tinsemosi	tentage	tintogun
tenet	tinte	tentacle	tintokun
teniacide	tinsiakeku	tintation	tintoyoon
teniasis	tinsiaso	tentative	tintoyowin
tenner	tinsi	tented	tintode
tennessee	tinsoonse	tenter	tintosi
tennessean	tinsoonsehn	tenterhook	tintosihinko
tennis	tinson	tenth	tinsi
tennyson	tinsesin	tentie	tintose
tennesonian	tinsesinhn	tenue	tinni
teno	tinko	tenuis	tinniso
tenochtitian	tinkhitito	tenuous	tinnisi
tenon	tinkosi	tenure	tinnirai
tendonitis	tinkosiso	tenuto	tinnito
tenor	tinran	teo	tosin
tenorite	tinraiyo	teocalli	tosinkolle
tenorrhaphy	tinranrhanphe	teosinte	tosinsinte
tenotomy	tinrantemo	tepee	toponse
tenosynovitis	tinransosewoso	tepefy	toponfe
tenpenny	tinpnnise	tephra	tophan
tenpin	tinposn	tephrite	tophanyo
tenrec	tinreko	tephrosin	tophonsi
tense1	tinse	tepid	toponjo
tense2	tinse	tepidarium	toponjoraima
tensible	tinsebe	tequila	tokunle
tensile	tinseron	ter	tara
tensimeter	tinsemuto	ter	tnra
tensiometer	tinsinmutto	tera-	tnran
tension	tinsesi	teral	tnranjo
tensity	tinseto	teraph	tnranphin
tensor	tinseran	terat	tnrante
tent	tinto	teratism	tnrantemosi
tent	tinto	terato	tnranto

WORD (x)	EQUIVALENT (y)	WORD (x)	EQUIVALENT (y)
teratogen	tnrantogin	terhune	tnrahun
teratogenic	tnrantoginko	teriyaki	tnraiyan
teratogenous	tnrantoginsi	term	tnron
teratogeny	tnrantoginse	termagant	tnrongunte
teratoid	tnrantojo	terman merill	tnroin muraille
teratology	tnrantologbon	termer	tnronsi
teratoma	tnratoma	terminable	tnronhunbe
terauchi	tnrankhi	terminal	tnronhunjo
terabia	tnranbua	terminate	tnronhunyo
terbium	tnrabuma	termination	tnronhunyoon
terce	tnrakn	terminational	tnronhunyoonjo
terceira	tnraknran	terminative	tnronhunyowin
tercel	tnraknjn	terminator	tnronhunyose
tercelet	tnraknte	terminer	tnronhunsi
tercentenary	tnrakntirain	termini	tnronhun
tercet	tnraknti	terminism	tnronhunmosi
terebene	tnranbehun	terminology	tnronhunlogbon
terebic	tnranbeko	terminus	tnronhunsi
terebinth	tnranbesi	termitarium	tnronteraima
terebinthine	tnranbesinun	termite	tnronte
teredo	tnrande	termless	tnronlabo
terence	tnrainsi	termor	tnronra
terensa	tnrainse	tern	tnran
terensian	tnrainsehn	tern	tnran
terensing	tnrainsegnni	ternary	tnranrai
terephthalic	tnrapisejnko	ternate	tnranyo
terete	tnrato	ternate	tnranyo
tereus	tnrasi	terne	tnranun
terfa	tnrafan	terni	tnranse
tergal	tnragan	ternion	tnransesi
tergeminate	tnragnmuyo	ternopol	tnranpinjn
tergiversate	tnragiwnseyo	terpander	tnrapanjnra
tergiversation	tnragiwnseyoon	tero	tnra
tergum	tnragun	terpene	tnrapnhun

WORD (x)	EQUIVALENT (y)	WORD (x)	EQUIVALENT (y)
terpineol	tnrapohunjin	terrify	tnrraife
terpinol	tnrapnhunjin	terrigenous	tnrraiginsi
terpsichore	tarapnsekhiran	terrine	tnrrain
terpsichorean	tarapnsekhirain	territorial	tnrraitoranjo
terra	tnrra	territorialism	tnrraitoranjomosi
terralba	tnrrajobu	territoriality	tnrraitoranjotn
terrace	tnrrase	territorialise	tnrraitoranjose
terracotta	tnrrakitto	territorian	tnrraitorain
terra firma	tnrra firoin	territory	tnrraitoran
terrain	tnrrain	terror	tnrraran
terraincognita	tnrranukiginita	terrorism	tnrraranmosi
terramycin	tnrramunkin	terrorist	tnrraransi
terrane	tnrroin	terrorize	tnrraranse
terrapin	tnrrapan	terry	tnrrai
terraaqueous	tnrrakunsi	terse	tnrase
terrarium	tnrraraima	tertenant	tnratinte
terrasigillata	tnrrasoogillete	tertial	tnratojo
terrazzo	tnrrasua	tertian	tnratosi
terre	tnrran	tertiary	tnratorai
trrebonne	tnrranbonun	tertium quid	kunjo tnratoma
terre haute	tnrran hunte	tertullian	tnratollesi
terrene	tnrranhun	teruel	tnrailo
terrene	tnrranhun	tervalent	tarawajnso
terrplein	tnrranporoin	terzarima	taraseraimo
terrestrial	tnrransetnraijo	terzetto	tarasetto
terret	tnrrato	terylene	tnralohun
terrelenant	tnrrantinte	teschen	tnsikhin
terreverte	tnrranwinti	tesla	tnsijn
terrible	tnrraibe	teslin	tnsijan
terribly	tnrraibelo	tessa	tasoo
terricolous	tnrraikijosi	tessellated	tasoojnrayode
terrier	tnrraisi	tessellation	tasoojnrayoon
terrier	tnrraisi	tessera	tnsooran
terrific	tnrraifiko	tesseract	tnsooranko

WORD (x)	EQUIVALENT (y)	WORD (x)	EQUIVALENT (y)
tessitura	tnsootnran	tete-a-tete	tnto si tnto
test1	tnsi	tete a tete	fori kori
test2	tnsi	tete beche	tnto bekhn
test	tnsi	teth	tnso
testa	tnsita	tether	tnsosi
testaceous	tnsitaknsi	tethys	tnsose
testament	tnsitamutto	teton	tntesi
testamentary	tnsitamuttorai	tetra-	tntern
testate	tnsitato	tetrabasic	tnternbooso
testator	tnsitatoran	tetrabrach	tnternbankho
test bed	beje tnsi	tetracene	tnternknsa
tester	tnsiran	tetrachord	tnternkhogba
testes	tnsitasi	tetrarch	tnternkhn
testicle	tnsitakuo	tetracid	tnternkijo
testiculate	tnsitakuoleyo	tetracycline	tnternsnkihun
testificate	tnsitafikoyo	tetrad	tnternjn
testification	tnsitafikoyoon	tetradymite	tnterndainmuyo
testify	tnsitafe	tetradynamous	tnterndainsemosi
testimonial	tnsitamenijo	tetraethyllead	tnternsiollejn
testimony	tnsitameni	tetragon	tnterngun
testis	tnsitaso	tetragonal	tnterngunjo
teston	tnsitase	tetragram	tnternganmo
testosterone	tnsitasetoroin	tetragrammaton	tnternganmmotin
testudinal	tnsitagbainjo	tetrahedral	tnternhejnrajo
testudinate	tnsitagbainto	tetrahedrite	tnternhejnrayo
testudo	tnsitadie	tetrahedron	tnternhejnran
testy	tnsito	tetralogy	tnternlogbon
titanic	tntehako	tetramerous	tnternmuraisi
tetanize	tntehase	tetrameter	tnternmuto
tetanus	tntehasi	tetramorph	tnternmophan
tetany	tnteha	tetrapetalous	tnternpntijosi
tetarto	tutesuto	tetraploid	tnternponjo
tetartohedral	tntesutohejnrajo	tetrapod	tnternpindie
tetchy	tntekho	tetrapody	tnternpindiese

WORD (x)	EQUIVALENT (y)	WORD (x)	EQUIVALENT (y)
tetrapterous	tnternpntiransi	texture	tnsoran
tetrapylon	tnternpejnsi	teyde	tnlojin
tetrarch	tnternkhnra	th	si
tetraseme	tnternsemo	thaddeous	sangbainsi
tetraspore	tnternseporai	thackeray	sanknrase
tetrastich	tnternsetinhun	thailand	sanloledain
tetrastichous	tnternsetinhun	thalomencephalon	sanlomaknphijnsi
tetrastyle	tnternsetnron	thalamic	sanlemako
tetrasyllable	tnternsojnranbe	thalamus	sanlemasi
tetravalent	tnternwajnso	thalassemia	sanlesoomua
tetrazine	tnternsun	thalassic	sanlesooko
tetrazzini	tnternsunhun	thalasso	sanlosa
tetrode	tnteronjin	thalassocracy	sanlosakansin
tetraoxyde	tnterosinji	thalassograph	sanlosaganpha
tetryl	tnterelo	thalassophobia	sanlosaphobua
tetter	tnttesi	thalazole	sanlosejoin
tetuan	tntehun	thaler	sanleran
tetzel	tnteselo	thales	sanlese
teucria	tnkunran	thalia	sanlesi
teucrian	tnkunrain	thalictrum	sanlekoraima
teugh	tnghon	thalidomide	sanlejomujin
teuton	tntoni	thalic	sanleko
teutonic	tntoniko	thallium	sanllema
teutonism	tntonimos	thaloid	sanllejo
teutonize	tntonise	thallophyte	sanllepheyo
tevere	tnwnran	thallous	sanllesi
texas	tnsinse	thallus	sanllese
texoma	tnsinmo	thalweg	sanlewinlo
text	tnso	thames	sanmisi
textile	tnsoron	than	sansi
textual	tnsojo	thanage	sansigun
textualism	tnsojomosi	thanato	sansito
textualist	tnsojosi	thanatoid	sansitojon
textuary	tnsorai	thanatophobia	sansitophobua

WORD (x)	EQUIVALENT (y)	WORD (x)	EQUIVALENT (y)
thanatopsis	sansitopnso	thedansant	sindajotie
thanatos	sansitosi	thee	sinse
thane	sansii	theek	sinseko
thanet	sansite	theelia	sinsejan
thank	sanki	theelol	sinsejin
thankless	sankilabo	theft	sinfia
thant	santn	thegither	singisira
thapsus	sanpnse	theine	sinhun
thar	sansa	their	sinrai
that	santo	theirs	sinraisi
thatch	santokn	theism	sinmosi
tahumate	sanmuto	theleme	sinlema
thaumatology	sanmutologbon	thelittis	sinleso
thaumatrope	sanmutnrapon	thelma	sinlemo
thaumaturge	sanmutorai	thelon	sinjnsi
thaw	sanwn	them	sinma
thaxter	sansieto	thematic	sinmokn
thayer	sansesi	theme	sinmo
the	sin	theme park	sinmo panka
theceous	sinsuwa	themis	sinmuse
theanthropic	sinhunsnrapnko	themistocles	sinmusetokun
theanthropism	sinhunsnrapnmosi	then	sinsi
thearchy	sinknran	thenage	sinsigun
theater	sinseto	thenar	sinsiran
theatin	sinsetin	thence	sinsun
theatre	sinsetorai	thenceforth	sinsunfonsi
theatrical	sinsetoraikojo	thenceforward	sinsunfonwegba
theatricalism	sinsetoraikojomosi	theo-	sisin
theatrics	sinsetoraikosi	theobald	sisinbojon
thebaine	sinbohun	theobroma	sisinbonmuje
thebes	sinbesi	theobromine	sisinbonmujesi
theca	sinki	theocentric	sisinkntiraiko
thecate	sinkito	theocracy	sisinkansn
thecodont	sinkideyo	theocrat	sisinkanta

WORD (x)	EQUIVALENT (y)	WORD (x)	EQUIVALENT (y)
theocritus	sisinkantosi	thera	sinran
theodicy	sisinjnse	therapeutic	sinranponko
theodolite	sisinjnleyo	therapeutics	sinranponkosi
theodore	sisinjnra	therapy	sinranpo
theodoric	sisinjnrako	there	sinran
theodosius	sisinjnsesi	thereby	sinranbeo
theogongy	sisingonse	therein	sinranni
theologian	sisinlogbonsi	theremin	sinranmini
theological	sisinlogbonkojo	thereof	sinranfan
theologize	sisinlogbonse	ttheresa	sinransua
theology	sisinlogbon	thereto	sinranto
theoma	sisinmo	theriaca	sinrankn
theomachy	sisinmokhn	therianthropism	sinrainsnrapnmosi
theomancy	sisinmoyesi	theriomorphic	sinrainmophanko
theomania	sisinmohan	therm	sinron
theomorphic	sisinmophanko	therma	sinronsi
theomorphism	sisinmophanmosi	thermal	sinronjo
theonomy	sisinknmo	thermanesthesia	sinronsunwnsia
theopathy	sisinpansio	thermea	sinronsi
theophagy	sisinphije	thermal	sinronlo
theophany	sisinphinise	thermesthesia	sinronsunwnsia
theophilus	sisinpheronsi	thermidor	sinronjnra
theophobia	sisinphobua	thermion	sinronsia
theophylline	sisinpheroin	thermionics	sinronsiakosi
theorbo	sisinrabu	thermistor	sinronsetosi
theorem	sisinrami	thermit	sinrontn
theoretic	sisinramiko	thermo-	sinronkn
theoretical	sisinramikojo	thermobarograph	sinronknboraganpha
theoretician	sisinramikohn	thermobarometer	sinronknboramuto
theorist	sisinraisi	thermocentery	sinronknkotnrai
theorize	sisinraise	thermocline	sinronknkihun
theory	sisinrai	thermocouple	sinronknkilepo
theosophy	sisinsoophn	thermodynamics	sinronkndainsemukosi
theotocopuli	sisintokiponle	thermogalvanometer	sinronkngijowajnmuto

WORD (x)	EQUIVALENT (y)	WORD (x)	EQUIVALENT (y)
thermogenesis	sinronkngnhunso	therophyte	sinraipheyo
thermogram	sinronknganmo	theropod	sinraipindie
thermograph	sinronknganpha	thersites	sinrasotnsi
thermography	sinronknganphe	tehrsitical	sinrasootnkojo
thermohaline	sinronknhajohun	thesauric	sinsanrako
thermojunction	sinronknjoknyoon	thesaurosk	sinsanrasia
thermokinematics	sinronknkihunmukpso	thesaurous	sinsanrasi
thermolabile	sinronknlebajn	thesaurus	sinsanraso
thermoluminescence	sinronknlumanaseknsi	these	sinse
thermoluminous	sinronknlumanasi	theseus	sinsesi
thermolysis	sinronknjinso	thesis	sinseso
thermometer	sinronknmuto	thespian	sinsegbain
thermopenetration	sinronknpnyatnrayoon	thespis	sinsegbaso
thermophilic	sinronknpheronko	thessaly	sinsoolo
thermophile	sinronknpheron	thessalonian	sinsoojnaihn
thermopile	sinronknpojn	thessalonica	sinsoojnsikn
thermoplastic	sinronknpansuiteko	theta	sinte
thermopylae	sinronknpelosi	thetic	sinko
thermos	sinronknsi	thetis	sinso
thermoscope	sinronknsokipon	theurgy	sinrailo
thermosetting	sinronknsettangnni	thew	sinwa
thermosphere	sinronknsephirai	thewtess	sinwalabo
thermosiphon	sinronknsoopha	they	sinyo
thermostable	sinronsetnbe	thi	sin
thermostat	sinronknsetnti	thiamine	siamini
thermostatics	sinronknsetntikosi	thiazine	siasehun
thermotank	sinronkntejnkn	thick	sinki
thermotaxis	sinrontesanso	thicken	sinkisi
thermotensile	sinronkntinsejn	thickening	sinkisignni
thermotherapy	sinronknsinranpo	thicket	sinkiti
thermotics	sinronknkosi	thickness	sinkisi
thermotropism	sinronkntnrapnmosi	thickset	sinkisetn
therrmy	sinronse	thief	sinfe
theroid	sinraijo	thiers	sinraise

WORD (x)	EQUIVALENT (y)	WORD (x)	EQUIVALENT (y)
thieve	sinfewn	thiosinamine	sinkosoomini
thievery	sinfewnrai	thiospirillum	sinkoseporaillema
thievish	sinfewnsi	thouracil	sinkouraikun
thigh	singan	thiourea	sinkourein
thigmo	singimo	thir	sinra
thigmotaxis	singimotesanso	third	sinrata
thigmotropism	singimotnrapnmosi	third degree	sinrata dagirai
thill	sinlle	third reich	sinrata rekhi
thimble	sinmbe	thirl	sinralo
thin	sinun	thirlage	sinralogba
thine	sinhun	thirst	sinrate
thing	singn	thirsty	sinratese
thingummy	singnmmo	thirteen	sinratoon
think	sinro	thirteenth	sinratoonsi
thinker	sinrosi	thirtietn	sinratnsi
thinking	sinrognni	thirty	sinratn
think-tank	tekun-sinro	this	sinyi eyi
thinner	sinunran	thistle	sinyiron
thinnish	sinunse	thistledown	sinyiron juan
thio	sinko	thistly	sinsilo
thoaldehyde	sinkojojinhoji	thither	sinyinrai
thiocyanate	sinkosnknyo	thietherward	sinyinraiwegba
thiocyanic	sinkosnknko	thixotropy	sinsantnrapo
thioether	sinkoesunra	tho	sin
thiofuran	sinkofunran	thole	sinron
thiokol	sinkoki	thole	sinron
thiol	sinkojn	thomas	sinmise
thionic	sinkokin	thomism	sinmimosi
thionine	sinkonihun	thompson	sinmpnsn
thiony	sinkoseji	thong	singan
thiopentone	sinkopintoni	thor	sinrau
thiophene	sinkophini	thoraco	sinranki
thionyl	sinkosilo	thoracoplasty	sinrankipansuito
thioscetic	sinkosekitiko	thoracotomy	sinrankitemo

WORD (x)	EQUIVALENT (y)	WORD (x)	EQUIVALENT (y)
thoracic	sinrankiko	thrawn	sinrewoin
thorax	sinransi	thread	sinranjn
thoria	sinran	thread	sinranjnse
thorianite	sinrainyo	threap	sinranpi
thorite	sinraiyo	threat	sinranta
thorium	sinraima	threaten	sinrantasi
thorn	sinrin	three	sinranta
thorny	sinrinse	thremmatology	sinranmmotelogbon
thoron	sisaron	threnody	sinraindun
thorough	sisaronghan	threonine	sinrainhun
thoroughgoing	sisaronghalognni	thresh	sinransia
thorp	sisapan	thresher	sinransiase
those	sisase	threshold	sinransijon
thoth	singbon	threw	sinranwn
thothmes	singbonmosi	thrice	sinraita
thou1	sisan	thrift	sinraifia
thou2	sisan	thriftless	sinraifialabo
though	sisanghan	thrifty	sinraifiase
thought1	sisanghan	thrill	sinraijnra
thought2	sisanghanto	thriller	sinraijnrasi
thoughtless	sisanghantolabo	thrips	sinraipnsi
thousand	sisanjn	thrive	sinraiwn
thrace	sinresi	throat	sinrato
thracian	sinresihn	throaty	sinratose
thraldom	sinrejonma	throb	sinrabe
thrall	sinrejjo	throe	sinrase
thrang	sinregan	thrombin	sinrambn
thrash	sinresia	thrombo	sinrambo
thrasher	sinresiasi	thrombocyte	sinrambosnto
thrasoniical	sinresonkojo	thrombogen	sinrambogin
Thrasybulus	sinresobujn	thromboplastin	sinrambopansetin
thrave	sinrewn	thrombosis	sinrambooso
thraw	sinrewe	throne	sinrain
thraw	sinrewe	throng	sinragan

WORD (x)	EQUIVALENT (y)	WORD (x)	EQUIVALENT (y)
thropple	sinrapopon	thunderation	sunsojnrayoon
throstle	sinrasiaron	thunderous	sunsojnrasi
throttle	sinraittoron	thundery	sunsojnrai
through	sinraigba	thunderstorm	sunsojnrasetorau
throughhither	sinraigbasesi	thur	sunra
throughout	sinraigbanita	thurber	sunrabe
throve	sinraiwn	thurible	sunraibe
throw	sinraiju	thurifer	sunraifiro
throw-in	sinraiju-nu	thuriferous	sunraifirosi
thrown	sinraiwoin	thuringia	sunrangan
throwster	sinraijuseto	thursday	sunraudase
thru	sinre	thus	sunse
thrucydides	sinrejojinsi	thwack	swaki
thrum1	sinrema	thwart	swate
thrum2	sinrema	twing	swagn
thrummy	sinremose	thy	sio
thrush1	sinreso	thyestean	siosetohn
thrush2	sinreso	thyestes	siosetosi
thrust	sinresi	thylacine	siolekin
thud	sunjan	thyme	sioma
thug	sungba	thymelaeceous	siomalekesuwa
thugery	sungbarai	thymia	siomua
thuggee	sungbase	thymic	siomako
thuja	sunja	thymine	siomuni
thule	sunle	thymol	siomajin
thulia	sunlesi	thymus	siomasi
thulium	sunlema	thyratron	siorantnra
thumb	sumbe	thyreoid	siorejo
thumbkin	sumbekin	thyro	sioran
thumbling	sumbegnni	thyrohyoid	sioranhojo
thump	sumpn	thyroid	sioranjo
thumping	sumpngnni	thyroiditis	sioranjoso
thun	sunso	thyrotoxicosis	siorantoosikiso
thunder	sunsojnra	thyrotropin	siorantnrapan

WORD (x)	EQUIVALENT (y)	WORD (x)	EQUIVALENT (y)
thyroxine	sioransesi	ticky tacky	tikise tekunse
thyrse	sioruse	ticonderoga	tikinjnragan
tyrsoid	siorusejo	tidal	tijinjo
thrsus	siorusesi	tidbit	tijinbeto
thysanuran	siosesiran	tiddledywinks	tijinrondiewokn
thyssen	siosesin	tiddle	tijnron
ti	ti	tiddler	tijnronsi
tiara	tilade	tiddly1	tijinlo
tiber	tibe	tiddly2	tijinlo
tiberias	tibesn	tide	tijin
tibertt	tibetto	tidemark	tijinmurokn
tibesti	tibetosi	tidetable	tijintebe
tibet	tibesi	tidings	tijingnsi
tibetan	tibesihn	tidy	tijinse
tibia	tibua	tie	tiso
tibiotarsus	tibetesunsi	tied	tisode
tibulle	tibujnra	tie-in	tiso-nu
tibulles	tibujnrasi	tielno	tilokn
tic	tikoi	tiemannite	tisomahunyo
tical	tikojn	tien	tinse
ticdonloureux	tikoideloraisi	tientain	tinsetelu
tick1	tiki	tie-pin	tinso-poha
tick2	tiki	tiepolo	tinsopolo
tick3	tiki	tier	tisora
tick4	tiki	tier	tisora
ticker	tikisi	tierce	tisorasi
ticker-tape	tikisi tepon	tieree	tisorase
ticket	tikiti	tierra	tisorra
ticking	tikignni	tie-up	tiso-pake
tickle	tikiron	tie-rod	tiso-ronjn
tickler	tikironsi	tiff	tifun
ticklish	tikironse	tiff	tifun
tick-tack	tiki tekun	tiff	tifun
tick-tock	tiki toki	tiffany	tifini

WORD (x)	EQUIVALENT (y)	WORD (x)	EQUIVALENT (y)
tiffin	tifije	tillotson	tijnratosin
tiger	tingba	tilly vally	tijnrase wojnrase
tigerish	tingbase	tilt	tijia
tight	tigbain	tilt	tijia
tighten	tigbainse	tilth	tijiasi
tights	tigbainsi	timagami	tinmogimi
tiglic	tigirako	timaru	tinmorai
tigon	tigisi	timbal	tinmbojn
tigre	tigiron	timbale	tinmboje
tigress	tingbabo	timber	tinmbe
tigring	tigirahun	timbered	tinmbede
tigris	tigirai	timbering	tinmbegnni
tida	tijon	timberline	tinmbelohun
tijuana	tinjuahun	timbre	tinmbero
tike	tiko	timbrel	tinmberojo
tiki	tikan	timbreled	tinmberojode
tilde	tirojin	time	tinmo
til	tinro	timeless	tinmolabo
tilapia	tinronpan	timely	tinmolo
tilbury	tinroburai	gimepiece	tinmopansi
tile	tinron	timer	tinmosi
tiler	tinronsi	time signal	tinmo soganjo
tilin	ginrongnni	time signature	tinmo sogantnran
tiliaceous	ginronsuwa	timetable	tinmoteberon
till1	tijnra	timid	tinmoji
till2	tijnra	timing	tinmognni
till3	tijnra	timocracy	tinmokansn
till4	tijnra	timorous	sinmoraisi
tillage	tijnragun	timothy	tinmosiotimothy
tilandsia	sijnradansia	timpani	tinmpanlu
tiller	tijnrasi	timpanium	tinmpanma
tiller	tijnrasi	tin	tin
tiller	tijnrasi	tinamon	tinmeni
tillot	tijnrato	tincal	tinkojo

WORD (x)	EQUIVALENT (y)	WORD (x)	EQUIVALENT (y)
tin can	tin kohun	tintinnabulum	tintehunbejnma
tinct	tinte	tintometer	tintemuto
tintorial	tintoraijo	tiny	tise
tincture	tintora	tion	yoon
tinder	tinjnra	tion	tesi
tinder-box	tinjnra bosi	tip1	tipn
tine	tin	tip2	tipn
tinea	tinun	tip3	tipn
tineid	tinunjo	tip-off	tipn fifo
ting	tign	tipper	tipnra
tingaling	tignjognni	tiperary	tipnrarai
tinge	tigini	tippet	tipnti
tingle	tigiron	tipple	tipnpo
tinhorn	tinhuran	tipple	tipnpo
tin god	tin godi	tippy	tipnse
tin hat	tin hate	tipstaff	tipnsetnfin
tink	tinko	tipster	tipnseto
tinker	tinkosi	tipsy	tipnsn
tinkle	tinkose	tiptoe	tipntose
tinlizzle	tinlesun	tiptop	tipntopn
tinned	tinnide	tip-up	tipn pake
tinner	tinniran	tirade	tiraijin
tinnitus	tinnisi	tirailleur	tiraillerun
tinny	tinse	tirana	tirain
tin-opener	tin opnyasi	tire1	tirai
tin pan	tinpanu	tire2	tirai
tin plate	tin pantue	tire3	tirai
tinpot	tinpote	tire	tirai
tinsel	tinsua	tirai	tirai
tinsmith	tinsemosi	tired	tiraide
tint	tinte	tireless	tirailabo
tint	tinte	tiresias	tiraisosi
tintinnabular	tintenhunbejnra	tiresome	tiraisoomo
tintinnabulation	tintehunbejnyoon	tiring	tiraignni

WORD (x)	EQUIVALENT (y)	WORD (x)	EQUIVALENT (y)
tirl	tiraji	titer	titnra
tirnovo	tiranknwn	tit for tat	titn for tetn
tiro	tinro	titchy	titnkho
tirolese	tinrojnse	titfer	titnfiro
tiros	tinrosi	tithable	titnsanbe
tirrivee	tinrraiwisi	tithe	titnsan
tis	ti si	tithing	titnsangnni
tisane	tisanun	tithonus	titnsasi
tishri	tisunrai	titi	tito
tisiphone	tisiaphohun	titi	tito
tissue	tisesun	titian	titohn
tissue-paper	tisesun panpnsi	titian	titohn
tizza	tisun	titicaca	titokiko
tit1	titn	titillant	titolletn
tit2	titn	titillate	titolleyo
tit3	titn	titillation	titolleyoon
tit	titn	titivate	titoweyo
titan	tinta	titlark	titoleknra
titanate	tintayo	title	titoron
titaness	tintabo	titled	titoronde
titanesque	tintakun	titman	titomoye
titanic	tintako	titmouse	titomosio
titania	tintase	tito	tito
titanic	tintako	tito	tito
titanism	tintamosi	titograd	titoganjn
titanite	tintayo	titoism	titomosi
titanite	tintayo	titrant	titnraitn
titanium	tintama	titrate	titnraiyo
titanomachy	tintamokhn	titration	titnraiyoon
titanosaur	tintasanra	titre	titnran
titanthere	tintasinran	titter	tittnrin
titanous	tintasi	tittle	tittnron
titbit	titnbe	tittle tattle	tttnron tettojn
tite	titoo	titivate	tittnweyo

WORD (x)	EQUIVALENT (y)	WORD (x)	EQUIVALENT (y)
tittup	tittupn	tocopherol	toknphirojin
titubation	tittubeyoon	tocsin	toknson
titular	tittojnra	tod	todi
titus	titosi	today	todase
tiu	tirun	toddle	todiduo
tivoli	tiwnlo	toddler	todiduosi
tizzy	tisunse	toddy	todide
tmess	timnise	to-do	too/de
tnt	taraintnratojnhun	todt	todesi
to	to, si, ni ti pelu	tody	tode
to	to	toe	tosn
to	to	toecap	tosnkopn
to	too	toed	tosnde
toad	tojn	toey	tosnlo
toady	tojnse	toff	tofin
toast	tosunse	toffee	tofinse
toast	tosunse	toffee-apple	aporon-tofinse
toaster	tosunsesi	toft	tofia
tobacco	tobuki	tofy	tofu
tobaccon	tobukin	tog1	togba
tobacconist	tobukinsi	tog2	togba
tobago	tobugan	toga	togbaa
tobias	tobuasi	together	tognsira
toboggan	toboogan	togetherness	tognsirasi
tobool	toboojin	toggery	togbarai
tobolsk	toboojinsia	toggle	togbaron
toby	tobi	togo	togan
toby jug	tobi jogba	toheroa	toheron
tocantins	tokojnkin	toil	tole
toccata	tokiti	toile	tolesi
tocharian	tokhirain	toilet	tolete
tocher	tokhisi	toilet paper	panpnsi tolete
toco	tokn	toilet roll	rollo tolete
tocology	toknlogbon	toiletry	toleterai

WORD (x)	EQUIVALENT (y)	WORD (x)	EQUIVALENT (y)
toilette	toletn	toluic	toluko
toils	tolesi	toluide	toluji
toilsome	tolesoomo	toluidine	tolujoin
toit	toote	toluol	tolujin
tokay	tokese	toluyl	tolulo
token	tokiun	toluyi	toluyi
tokened	tokiunde	tom	tomi
tokenism	tokiunmosi	tomahawk	tomahakwo
tokyo	tokiyo	tomalley	tomajnrase
tola	tojan	tom and jerry	tomi ati jnrrai
tolan	tojain	toman	tomiha
tolbutamide	tojabutemujin	tomatin	tomitin
told	tojnra	tomato	tomiti
tole	tojn	tomb	tombo
tole	tojn	tombac	tomboki
toledo	tojnde	tombigbee	tombogbnbe
tolerable	tojnraibe	tombola	tomboojn
tolerance	tojnraisi	tombolo	tomboolo
tolerant	tojnraite	tomboy	tomboyn'
tolerate	tojnraiyo	tombs	tombosi
toleration	tojnraiyoon	tombstone	tombosetole
tolidine	tojnjoin	tom, dick, and	tomu diki ati harrai
toll1	tojnra	harry	
toll2	tojnra	tome	tomni
tollage	tojnragba	tome	temni
toll-bridge	tojnra-bangbon	tomentose	tomnitose
toller	tojnrasi	tomentum	tomnitnma
toll-gate	tojnra-giyo	tomfool	tomfonjia
toll-road	tojnra-ronjn	tomfoolery	tomfonjiarai
tollie	tojnrase	tomfuller	tomfunjjnsi
toltee	tojiase	tommy	tomjin
tolu	tolu	tommy-gun	tomjin-gunta
toluate	toluyo	tomo	tomoo
toluene	toluhun	tomodromic	tomoogbnmoko

WORD (x)	EQUIVALENT (y)	WORD (x)	EQUIVALENT (y)
tomography	tomoognaphe	tonometer	toniknmuto
tomorrow	tomoorrawa	tonometry	toniknmutorai
tompion	tompnsi	tonoplast	toniknpansi
tomsk	tomsia	tonoscope	toniknsokipon
tom thumb	tomusumbe	tonsil	tonisule
tomtit	tomotitn	tonsillectome	tonisulletemni
tom-tom	tomutin	tonsillitis	tonisulleso
tomy	temo	tonisillotome	tonisullotemni
ton	toni	tonsillotomy	tonisullotemo
tonal	tohunjo	tonsorial	toniseraijo
tonalite	tohunleyo	tonsure	tonisesn
tonality	tohunleto	tontine	tonitin
to name	to hemo	ton-up	toni-pake
tonaphasia	toniphisia	tonus	tonisi
tone	tohun	tony	tonise
tonetic	tohunko	too	too
tong	togn	too	toon
tonga	togini	too	tun
tongarera	tobiniranwa	too	tu
tongs	tognsi	took	tookn
tongue	tognso	tool	toonse
tonic	toniko	tool	toonse
tonicity	tonikito	toom	tooma
tonight	tonigheu	toombs	toombe
tonite	toniyo	toon	tosin
tonk	tonikn	toot	toose
tonka	toniknsi	tooth	toosi
tonkabean	toniknsibehun	toothless	toosilabo
tonkin	tonikin	toothpick	toosiponkn
tonle	toniron	toothsome	toosisoomo
tonnage	tonigun	toothy	toosise
tonneau	tonihunle	tootle	toseron
tono	tonikn	tootsy	toosesi
tonograph	toniknganpha	toozie	toosie

WORD (x)	EQUIVALENT (y)	WORD (x)	EQUIVALENT (y)
top1	topn	topsy	topnso
top2	topn	top-up	topn-pake
topaz	topnsin	toque	tokue
topazolite	topnsinleyo	tor	tora
top brass	topn-bansoo	tor	tora
top dog	topn degbi	torah	toran
tope	topon	torbernite	toraberanyo
tope	topon	torch	toransi
tope	topon	torchlight	toransileghe
topectomy	topntemo	torchon	torankn
topee	topnse	tore	torai
topek	topnki	toreador	toraijnran
Topeka	topnkin	toric	toraiko
topepo	topnpo	torii	toraii
toper	toponsi	torino	torain
tophet	tophitn	torment	toramuta
tophus	tophisu	tormentil	toramutale
topi	topan	tormentor	toramutasi
topiary	topanrai	torn	torau
topic	topnko	tornado	toraude
topical	topnkojo	torne	toraun
topless	topnlabo	toroid	toraijo
topnotch	topnnknto	toronto	torointe
topo	topo	torose	toronse
topographer	topoganphasi	torpedo	toraipn
topography	topoganphe	torpid	toraipon
topology	topologbon	torpor	toraipi
toponym	topomo	torquate	toraikunyo
toponymy	topomosi	torque	toraikun
topotype	topotnpon	torquay	toraikn
topper	topnra	torquemada	toraikunmojn
topping	topngnni	troques	toraikunsi
topple	topnron	torr	torra
tops	topnsi	torrefy	torraife

WORD (x)	EQUIVALENT (y)	WORD (x)	EQUIVALENT (y)
torrens	torraisun	tory	torai
torrent	torraita	tosa	torai
torrential	torraitajo	tosa	tosi
torreon	torraisi	toscana	tosikini
torrey	torraise	toscanini	tosikinini
torricelli	torraiknjjn	tosh	tosie
torricellian	torraiknjjnsi	toss	tosia
torrid	torraijo	toss-up	tosia-pake
torsade	toraiwe	tot1	totn
torsibility	toraiwesnrontn	tot2	totn
torsion	toraiwesi	total	totnjo
torsk	torasia	totalisator	totnjosiran
torso	toraso	totalitarian	totnjoterain
tort	torati	totality	totnleto
torte	toratn	totalizator	totnjoseran
tortellini	toratojjnni	totalize	totnjsoe
tortfeasor	torati fnse	totalizer	totnjosesi
torticollis	toratikillesi	totally	totnjin
tortile	toratiron	totaquine	totnkunhun
tortilla	toratille	tote1	totu
tortillon	toratillesi	tote2	totu
tortious	toratisi	tote bag	totu bogbn
tortive	toratiwn	totem	totuma
tortoise	toratesun	totemism	totumamosi
tortala	toratejn	totem-pole	totuma pinjn
tortoni	toratehun	tother	totesira
tortricid	toraterai	toti	totin
tortuga	toratngan	totipalmate	totinpanjomote
tortuous	toratnwesi	totipotence	totinpotinsi
tortuousity	toratnwetn	tottenham	tottinha
torture	toratnwe	totter	tottnra
torulose	toraunlose	totting-up	tottingnni-pake
torus	toraunsi	totum	totinma
tory	torai	toucan	toknhn

WORD (x)	EQUIVALENT (y)	WORD (x)	EQUIVALENT (y)
touch	tokan	tournado	toorande
touch-and-go	tokan-si-lo	tourney	tooranse
touchdown	tokan juan	tourniquet	toorankuo
touché	tokhan	tournure	tooranrai
touché	tokhan	tours	tooraisi
touching	tokangnni	touse	toose
touch-line	tokan lehun	tousle	tooseron
touch me not	tokan mi ti	touslesmois	tooseronmosi
touch-paper	tokan panpnsi	toussaint	toosantoni
touchstone	tokansetole	tout	tonita
touchy	tokanse	toutensemble	tonitaensumbe
tough	togbain	touter	tonitasi
toughen	togbainsi	touvarisch	tooweransi
toughie	togbainse	tow1	toowa
toul	tojan	tow2	toowa
toulon	tojain	toward	toowegba
toulouse	tojanse	towardly	toowegbalo
toun	towin	towards	toowegbasi
toupee	topanun	tow-bar	toowa boosn
tour	toorai	towel	toowalo
touraco	tooraiki	toweling	toowallognni
tourcoing	tooraikigan	tower	toowaro
touraine	toorain	towered	toowarode
tourbillion	tooraibajnransi	towerhee	toowahun
tourer	tooraise	towering	toowarognni
tourette	tooraitn	town	town
tourism	tooraimosi	townee	townse
tourist	tooraisi	townie	townsi
tourist class	kansoo tooraisi	tow-path	toowa panho
touristy	tooraiseto	township	townsunpn
tourmaline	toorainmojnhun	towy	toowase
tournal	tooranjo	towzie	toowasi
tournament	tooranmutto	tox	toosia
tournedos	toorandesi	toxaemia	toosiamua

WORD (x)	EQUIVALENT (y)	WORD (x)	EQUIVALENT (y)
toxalbumin	toosiajobumini	tracheid	tnrekhnjo
toxaphene	toosiaphini	tracheitis	tnrekhnso
toxemia	toosiamua	tracheo	tnrekhnko
toxic	toosiako	tracheophyte	tnrekhnkopheyo
toxication	toosiakoyoon	tracheoscopy	tnrekhnkosekipo
toxicity	toosiakitn	tracheotomy	tnrekhnkotemo
toxico	toosiaki	trachle	tnrekhnron
toxicogenic	toosiakiginko	trachoma	tnrekhomo
toxicology	toosiakilogbon	trachy	tnrekhoi
toximania	toosiamohan	trachyte	tnrekhoiti
toxicophobia	toosiakiphobua	trachytic	tnrekhoitiko
toxicosis	toosiakiso	tracing	tnrekngnni
toxin	toosiasi	track	tnreko
toxisterol	toosiasetojin	track suit	suito tnreko
toxoid	toosiajo	trackage	tnrekogun
toxophili	toosiapheron	trackless	tnrekolabo
toxophilite	toosiapheronyo	tract1	tnreto
toxoplasmosis	toosiapansonso	tract2	tnreto
toy	tosie	tractable	tnretobe
toy boy	boyn tosie	tractarian	tnretorain
toyama	tosiemo	tractarianism	tnretorainmosi
toynbee	toynbe	tractate	tnretoyo
toyo	toyo	tractato	tnretota
toyon	toyosi	tractile	tnretojn
trabeated	tnrebeyode	traction	tnretoyoon
trabeate	tnrebeyo	tractive	tnretowin
trabeation	tnrebeyoon	tractor	tnretoran
trabecula	tnrebeknjn	trad	tnrejn
trace1	tnrekn	trade	tnrejin
trace2	tnrekn	trade-in	tnrejin ni
tracer	tnreknra	trader	tnrejinra
tracery	tnreknrai	tradescantia	tnrejinsekotie
trachea	tnrekhnsi	trading	tnrejingnni
tracheal	tnrekhnjn	tradition	tnrejinyoon

WORD (x)	EQUIVALENT (y)	WORD (x)	EQUIVALENT (y)
traditional	tnrejinyoonjo	traject	tnrejnkn
traditionalism	tnrejinyoonjomosi	trajectory	tnrejnknrai
traditive	tnrejinyowin	tralatition	tnreletoyoon
traditor	tnrejinse	tralatitious	tnreletoyosi
traduce	tnrejisi	tram	tnremo
traducianism	tnrejisihnmosi	tramlines	tnremolehun
trafalgar	tnrefanjngan	trammel	tnremmulo
traffic	tnrefunko	trammie	tnremmusk
trafficator	tnrafunkosi	tramontane	tnremenitelu
traffic island	tnrefunko isnledain	tramp	tnrempo
traffic-light	tnrefiko leghe	tramper	tnremposi
tragacanth	tnregankosi	trample	tnremporon
tragedian	tnregbauhun	tramploline	tnrempolehun
tragedy	tnregbau	tram way	tnrema welo
tragic	tnregbauko	trance	tnresun
tragicomedy	tnregbaukimwadun	trance	tnresun
tragopan	tnregonpan	trangam	tnregnmo
tragus	tnregbasi	tranny	tnrehn
tralk	tnrejnka	tranquil	tnrekunsn
tralket	tnrekato	tranquilize	tnrekunsnse
trail	tnrejn	tranquilizer	tnrekunsnsesi
trail-blazer	bansunsi tnrejn	tranquilize	tnrekunsinse
trailer	tnrejnra	tranquillizer	tnrekunsinsesi
trailing edge	ajnge tnrejngnni	trans-	tnresi
train	tnreto	transact	tnresiaknti
training	tnretognni	transactinide	tnresiakntinjin
trainasium	tnretosiama	transaction	tnresiakntiyon
trainee	tnretose	transalpine	tnresiajopohun
trainer	tnretosi	transatlantic	tnresiatelesiko
traipse	tnrepnse	transberkelian	tnresibeknjain
trait	tnretan	transcalent	tnresikojnto
traitor	tnretanse	trascaspia	tnresikosopan
traitorous	tnretansesi	transcaucasia	tnresikoinkosia
trajan	tnrejan	transceiver	tnresiknwinisi

WORD (x)	EQUIVALENT (y)	WORD (x)	EQUIVALENT (y)
transcend	tnresiknjn	tranship	tnresisunpn
transcendent	tnresiknjnto	transhumance	tnresihunmoye
transcendental	tnresiknjntojo	transience	tnresiunsi
transcendentalism	tnresiknjntojomosi	transient	tnresiunto
transcontinental	tnresikintihuntojo	trasigent	tnresiginte
transcribe	tnresikorai	transilient	tnresialeto
transcription	tnresikoraipnyoon	transilluminate	tnresillumanayo
transculturation	tnresikunjiaranyoon	transilluminator	tnresillumanayosi
transcurrent	tnresikunrraito	transistor	tnresitaran
transducer	tnresijiknra	transistorize	tnresitaraise
transect	tnresiknte	transit	tnresiyo
transept	tnresipnti	transit camp	kompn tnresiyo
transeunt	tnresileyo	transition	tnresiyoon
transfer	tnrresifiro	transitive	tnresiyowin
transferable	tnresifirobe	transitory	tnresiyorai
transferal	tnresifirojn	translate	tnresileyo
transferase	tnresifironse	translator	tnresileyoran
transferee	tnresifirose	transleithania	tnresijnsohun
transference	tnresifironsi	transliterate	tnresiletoraiyo
trainsferor	tnresifiron	translocate	tnresiloknyo
transferin	tnresifirin	translocation	tnresiloknyoon
transfiguration	tnresifigiranyoon	translucent	tnresiluknti
transfigure	tnresifigiran	translunar	tnresilujnran
transfinite	tnresifinitin	transmarine	tnresimurami
transfix	tnresifisn	transmigrant	tnresimagnraite
transform	tnresifoonmo	transmigrate	tnresimagnraiyo
transformation	tnresifoonmoyoon	transmigration	tnresimagnraiyoon
transformative	tnresifoonmoyowin	transmissible	tnresimusinbe
transformer	tnresifoonmose	transmission	tnresimusinse
transformism	tnresifoonmosi	transmit	tnresimutn
transfuse	tnresifunsi	transmittancy	tnresimuttnsn
rainsfusion	tnresifunsoon	transmitter	tnresimuttnra
transgress	tnresigiraiso	transmogrify	tnresimogiraife
transgression	tnresigiraisoon	trasmontane	tnresimenitelu

WORD (x)	EQUIVALENT (y)	WORD (x)	EQUIVALENT (y)
transmutation	tnresimuteyoon	transvalue	tnresuwajoin
transmute	tnresimuto	transverse	tnresuwinso
transnational	tnresihetnsejo	transvestite	tnresuwinsnyo
transneptunian	tnresihunpnti	transylvania	tnresolewa
transnormal	tnresiniranjo	trap1	tnrepo
transoceanic	tnresiokunko	trap2	tnrepo
transom	tnresoonmo	trapdoor	tnrepodeinsi
transonic	tnresonko	trapeze	tnrepnse
transoxiana	tnresiosinhun	trapezium	tnrepnsema
transpadane	tnresipanjain	trapezius	tnrepnsesi
transparency	tnresipanrasn	trapezohedron	tnrepnsehejnra
transparent	tnresipanrato	trapezoid	tnrepnsejo
transpicuous	tnresipokun	trappean	tnrepnhn
transpierce	tnresiporansi	trapper	tnreposi
transpire	tnresiporai	trappena	tnrepnhun
transplant	tnresipantn	trappings	tnrepognnisi
transponder	tnresiponjnra	trappist	tnrepose
transpontine	tnresipontin	traps	tnreposi
transport	tnresipinta	trapunto	tnreputo
transportable	tnresipintabe	trash	tnresia
transportation	tnresipintayoon	trash can	tnresia kojn
transport café	kofin tnresipinta	trashy	tnresiase
transporter	tnresipintase	trasimeno	tnresimini
transporter bridge	bangbon tnresipintase	trass	tnresin
transpose	tnresipose	trattoria	tnrettora
transposition	tnresiposeyoon	trauma	tnremua
transputer	tnresiputo	traumatic	tnremuako
transsexual	tnresisesiajo	traumatism	tnremuamosi
transship	tnresisunpn	traumatize	tnremuase
transubstantiation	tnresnbesetnteyoon	traumatophobia	tnremuaphobua
transudate	tnresudayo	traumatropism	tnremuatnrapnmosi
transude	tnresujn	travail	tnrewanlo
transuranic	tnresuraiko	travancore	tnrewankiran
transvaal	tnresuwajo	trave	tnrewn

WORD (x)	EQUIVALENT (y)	WORD (x)	EQUIVALENT (y)
travel	tnrewnlo	tree	tasia
travel agency	aginse tnrewnlo	tref	tesifu
travelled	tnrewnllode	trefoil	tasifonjia
travelers cheque	khnkun tnrewnllosi	trehala	tasihajn
travelog	tnrewnlogbo	trehalose	tasihalose
traverse	tnrewinso	treillage	tesillegun
travertine	tnrewintihun	treilschite	tasilesekiti
travesty	tnrewinsia	trek	tasirin
travois	tnrewosi	trellis	tasille
trawl	tnrewojn	trematode	tasimujin
trawler	tnrewojnra	tremble	tasimuji
tray	tnreya	tremendous	tasimujinse
tray mobile	tnreya mobajn	tremetol	tasimuti
treacherous	tasiakhnrasi	tremolite	tasimoliyo
treachery	tasiakhnra	tremolo	tasimoji
treacle	tasiakun	tremor	tasimira
tread	tasiajn	tremulant	tasimujite
treadle	tasiajnron	tremulous	tasimujisi
treason	tasiase	trench	tasinkho
treasonable	tasiasebe	trenchant	tasinkhote
treasonous	tasiasesi	trencher	tasinkhosi
treasure	tasiasura	trencherman	tasinkhosimoye
treasuere	tasiasuraise	trenches	tasinkhosi
treasury	tasiasurai	trend	tasijn
treat	tasiato	trendy	tasijnse
treatise	tasiatose	trengganu	tasigbain
treatment	tasiatomini	trent	tasito
treaty	tasiatnso	trenteet quarante	kunrainto tasitoton
treaty pot	tasiatnso pote	trenton	tasitin
trebbia	tasibua	trentino	tasitoni
treble	tasibe	trepan	tasipan
trebizond	tasibusejn	tepang	tasipangn
trebuchet	tasibekhnti	trephine	tasiphini
tecento	tasiknto	trepidation	tasipntiyoon

WORD (x)	EQUIVALENT (y)	WORD (x)	EQUIVALENT (y)
treponema	tasipohunma	tribadism	taraibajomosi
trespass	tasipanun	tribalism	taraibijomosi
tress	tasiso	tribasic	taraibiseko
tressed	tasisode	tribe	taraibi
tressure	tasisorai	triblast	taraibansia
trestle	tasisoron	triblet	taraibitn
tret	tasite	tribo	taraibin
trevally	tasiwajin	tribology	taraibinlogbon
treves	tasiwa	triboluminescence	taraibinlumanaseknsi
trevis	tasiwaso	triboluminocene	taraibinlumanaknun
trews	tasiwa	tribrach	taraibankho
trey	tasise	tribromethanol	taraibonmutnhunjin
tri	ta(eta)	tribrophenol	taraibonphinijin
tri	tarai	tribulation	taraibejnyoon
triable	taraibe	tribunal	taraibenijo
triacid	tarakejo	tribunate	taraibeniyo
triad	taraijo	tribune	taraibeni
triage	taraigba	tributary	taraibetorai
triagonal	taraigunjo	tribute	taraibeto
trial	teraijo	trice	taraikn
trial balance	teraijo bojosi	tricennial	taraiknhunjo
triangle	tarainigun	tricentennial	taraikntihunjo
triangular	tarainigunran	triceps	taraiknpo
triangulate	tarainigunyo	triceratops	taraiknratopn
triangulation	tarainigunyoon	trichiasis	tarairunso
triangulum	tarainigunma	trichina	tarairunhun
triarchy	taraiknran	trichinize	tarairunhunse
triassic	taraisinko	trichinopoly	tarairunhunpose
triastomic	taraisetomuko	trichinosis	tarairunhunso
triaxial	taraisojo	trichinous	tarairunhunsi
triaxis	taraisosi	trichite	tarairunyo
triazine	taraisuhun	tricho	taranrun
triazole	traisujoin	trichocyst	taranrunsnyo
tribade	taraibajo	trichogyne	taranrunloyun

WORD (x)	EQUIVALENT (y)	WORD (x)	EQUIVALENT (y)
trichoid	taranrunjo	tridentine	taraijintin
trichology	taranrunlogbon	tridentum	taraijintnma
trachoma	taranrunma	tridimension	taraidiminitosi
trichome	taranrunmo	tridiurnal	taraidiranjo
trichomonad	taranrunmenijn	triduum	taraidima
trichoniasis	taranrunhunso	triecious	taraisuwa
trichopteran	taranrunpntiran	tried	taraide
trichosis	taranrunso	triennial	taraihunjo
trichotomy	taranruntemo	triennium	taraihunma
trichroism	taraikhironmosi	trier	taraisi
trichromatic	taraikhironmuko	trierarch	taraisiknra
trichromatism	taraikhironmumosi	trirearchy	taraisikhnran
trick	taraikn	trieste	taraisetn
trickery	taraiknra	trieteric	taraitnrako
trickish	taraiknsia	trifacial	taraifansijo
trickle	taraiknron	tafid	taraifijo
tricklet	taraikntn	trifle	taraifijn
trickster	taraiknseto	trifling	taraifijngnni
tricksy	taraiknse	trifocal	taraifoonknjo
trick track	taraikn tnreko	trifold	taraifonjo
tricky	taraiknsi	trifoliate	taraifonjiayo
triclinic	taraikiunko	trifolium	taraifonjiama
triclinium	taraikiunma	triforium	taraifonraima
tricolour	taraikijoran	triformed	taraifoonmode
tricorn	taraikinra	trifurcate	taraifunrakoyo
tricostate	taraikisetnyo	trig	taraign
tricot	taraikiti	trig	taraign
tricrotic	taraiknrako	trigeminal	taraignmuhunjo
tricuspid	taraikunsopo	trigeminus	taraignmuhunsi
tricycle	taraisnkuo	trigger	taraigan
tricyclic	taraisnkuoko	trigger	taraigan
tridecane	taraijinkona	triglyph	taraigilophn
trident	taraijinto	triglyceride	taraigiloknrajin
tridentate	taraijintotn	trigon	taraigun

WORD (x)	EQUIVALENT (y)	WORD (x)	EQUIVALENT (y)
trigonal	taraigunjo	trimethadione	taraimusunjnhun
trigonometer	taraigunmuto	trimethylpentane	tarimusunlopntelu
trigonometry	taraigunmutorai	trimetric	taraimutoraiko
trigonous	taraigunsi	trimetrogon	taraimutnragun
trigraph	taraiganpha	trimmer	taraimmora
trihedral	taraihejnrajo	trimming	taraimmognni
trihedron	taraihejnrasi	grimolecle	taraimojnkun
trihydrate	taraihogbanyo	trimolecular	taaimojnkunran
trihydric	taraihogbanko	trimonthly	taraimenisilo
trijugate	taraijogiyo	trimorph	taraimophan
trike	taraikn	trimorphism	taraimophanmosi
trilateral	trailetnraijo	trimurti	taraimuraye
trilateration	trailetnraiyoon	trinal	taraihunjo
trilby	trailebe	trinary	tarihunra
trilemma	trailemma	trincomablee	taraiknmule
trilinear	trailehunran	trindle	taraijnron
trilingual	trailihagunjo	trine	tarain
triliteral	trailitoranjo	trinidad and	taraingba ati tobagon
trilithon	trailesi	Tobago	
trill	taraijnra	trinil	taranle
trillion	taraijnransi	trinitarian	taraintorain
trillium	taraijnranma	trinitrate	taraintnreyo
trilobati	trailoobeto	trinitro	taraintnra
trilobite	trailoobeyo	trinitrobenzene	taraintnrabesnhun
trilocular	trailokuoran	trinitrocrenol	taraintnraknranjin
trilodomethane	trailodemusanhun	trinitrophenol	taraintnraphinjin
trilodothyronine	trailodesioroinhun	trinitrotoluene	taraintnratoluhun
trilogy	trailogbon	trinity	tarainto
trim	taraimo	trinity	taraintn
trimaran	taraimoran	trinket	taraiknti
trimer	taraimora	trinkum	taraikuo
trimerous	taraimorasi	trino	taraikn
trimester	taraimoseto	trinocular	taraiknkuoran
trimester	taraimuto	trinodal	taraiknjinjo

WORD (x)	EQUIVALENT (y)	WORD (x)	EQUIVALENT (y)
trinomial	taraiknmujo	triplicate	taraipanknyo
trinominal	taraiknmuhunjo	triplicity	taraipankitn
trio	tarain	triplite	taraipanyo
trioca	tarainki	triploblast	taraibansia
triode	taraijoin	triploid	taraiponjo
trioecious	tarainkinsi	triploidy	taraiponjose
triolein	taraijointe	triplopia	taraiponpan
triol	taraijin	tripod	taraipindie
triolet	taraikotn	tripodal	taraipindiejo
trional	tarainsi	tripody	taraipodun
triose	tarainse	tripoli	taraipole
triosonata	tarainsoote	tripolitania	taraipoletohun
trioxide	taraiosinjn	tripos	taraipose
trip	taraipo	tripper	taraiposi
tripartite	taraipanteyo	trippet	taraipnti
tripartition	taraipanteyoon	tripping	taraipngnni
tripe	taraipn	triptane	taraipotelu
tripedal	taraipndiejo	trippterous	taraipntiransi
tripersonal	taraipnrasinjo	tripptolemus	taraipntimosi
tripersonality	taraipnrasinjotn	triptych	taraipntikho
tripetalous	taraipntijo	triptyque	taraipntikun
triphase	taraiphanse	tripudiate	taraipujiyo
triphenylmethane	taraiphinlomusunhun	tripura	taraipuran
triphibian	taraiphibehn	trip wire	taraipo worai
triphibious	taraiphibesi	triquetrous	taraikuntnrasi
triphithong	taraiphisogan	triadiate	tarairanjnnayo
triphilite	taraiphileyo	trireme	tarairemo
triphylite	taraipheleyo	trisagion	taraisegboin
tripinate	taraipohayo	trisagium	taraisegbima
tripitaka	taraipotika	trisect	taraiseknte
triplane	taraipanyun	trisectrix	taraiseknteraisi
triple	taraipon	triseme	taraisemo
triplet	taraipontn	trisepalous	taraisepnjosi
triplex	taraiponsi	triseptate	taraisepntiyo

WORD (x)	EQUIVALENT (y)	WORD (x)	EQUIVALENT (y)
triserial	taraiseraijo	triumvirate	taraigbnseto
trishaw	taraisue	triune	taranun
triskaidekaphobia	taraisekoijnkaphobua	triunitarian	taranntorain
triskelion	taraisekuejnsi	triunity	taranuntn
triscele	taraiseknjn	trivalent	taraiwajnso
trismus	taraisemosi	trivet	taraiwnti
trisoctahedron	taraisookntihejnran	trivia	taraiwn
trisomic	taraisoomuko	trivial	taraiwnjo
trispermous	taraisepnron	triviality	taraiwnjotn
trisporous	taraiseporaisi	trivialize	taraiwnjose
tristan	taraisetin	trivium	taraiwnma
triste	taraisuto	trix	taraisi
tristich	taraisetinhun	troas	tnrase
tristichous	taraisetinhunsi	troat	tnrato
tristimulus	taraisetinmujnsi	trobriand	tnrabanun
trisulphide	taraisnlephiji	trocar	tnrakosi
trisylable	taraisollebe	trocha	tnracho
tritagonist	taraitogonis	trochaic	tnrakhokn
tritanopia	taraitinpan	trochal	tnrkhojo
trite	taraite	trochanter	tnrakhotesi
tritheism	taraisinmosi	troche	tnrakho
tritiate	taraiteyo	trochee	tnrakhose
triticale	taraitekojn	trochelminth	tnrakholominisi
triticum	taraitekun	trochilus	tnrakhnlosi
tritium	taraitema	trochlea	tnrakholo
triton	taraitoha	trochlear	tnrakholoran
triton	taraitoha	trochoid	tnrakhojo
tritone	taraitoni	trochophore	tnrakhophiran
triturate	taraitnreyo	trod	tnrajn
trituration	taraitnreyoon	trodden	tnrajnsi
triumph	taraigbe	trog	tnragn
triumphal	taraigbejo	troglodyte	tnragondainte
triumphant	taraigbetn	trogon	tnragun
triumvir	taraigbnse	trojan	tnrajan

WORD (x)	EQUIVALENT (y)	WORD (x)	EQUIVALENT (y)
troika	tnrata	trophallaxis	tnrapheransosi
troilism	tnralemasi	trophic	tnraphnko
trios	tnraso	tropho	tnraphn
trojan	tnrajan	trophoblast	tnraphnbansia
troke	tnrakn	trophogenesis	tnraphngnhunso
troll	tnrallo	trophoplasm	tnraphnpanson
trolley	tnrallose	trophotherapy	tnraphnsinranpo
trolling	tnrallognni	trophotropism	tnraphntnrapnmosi
trollop	tnrallopn	trophozoite	tnraphnsinyo
trollope	tnrallopon	trophy	tnraphe
trombamarina	tnrambemurain	tropic	tnrapnko
trombetas	tnrambeto	tropical	tnrapnkojo
trombidiasisi	tnrambajinasn	tropicalize	tnrapnkojose
trombone	tnramfohun	tropine	tnrapnhun
trammel	tnrammojn	tropism	tnrapnmosi
tromomania	tnramumohan	tropist	tnrapnsi
trompe	tnrampon	tropo	tnrapo
tromso	tnramso	tropology	tnrapologbon
tron	tnrain	tropopause	tnrapopawnse
trona	tnrahun	tropophilous	tnrapopheronsi
trondhem	tnrajnhama	tropophyte	tnrapopheyo
troop	tnrapo	troposphere	tnraposephirai
trooper	tnraposi	tropous	tnraposi
troopial	tnrapojn	troppo	tnrapnpo
troopship	tnraposunpn	tropy	tnrapose
troostite	tnrainsiyo	trossachs	tnrasookhnsi
trop	tnrapn	trot	tnrate
tropacocaine	tnrapnkikoin	trot	tnrate
tropacolum	tnrapnkilema	troth	tnrasi
tropaeolin	tnrapnnijan	trotline	tnratelehun
tropaeolum	tnrapnnilema	trotsky	tnratesukn
troparion	tnrapnrain	trotskyite	tnratesuknti
trope	tnrapon	trotter	tnrattesi
tropeolin	tnraponjan	trotyl	tnratelo

WORD (x)	EQUIVALENT (y)	WORD (x)	EQUIVALENT (y)
troubadour	tnragbigboran	trudege	tnrangbon
trouble	tnragbile	trudgen	tnrangbonsi
troublous	tnragbilesi	true	tnranse
troude loup	tnrajin lopo	truffle	tnranfijn
trough	tnragbi	trug	tnrangn
trounce	tnrasi	truism	tnranmosi
troupe	tnrapon	trujillo	tnranjinllo
trouper	tnraponsi	truck	tnrakn
troupial	tnraponjo	trull	tnranlle
trouse	tnralese	truly	tnranlo
trouser	tnralese	truman	tnranmoye
trousers	tnralesesi	trump1	tnranfo
trousse	tnrasoo	trump2	tnranfo
trousseau	tnrasooan	trumpery	tnranforai
trout	tnrata	trumpet	tnranfon
trouvere	tnraworan	trumpeter	tnranfonsi
trover	tnrawnra	trumps	tnranfosi
troville	tnrawojnra	truncate	tnrankeyo
trow	tnrawo	truncated	tnrankeyode
trowel	tnrawolo	truncheon	tnrankhnsi
troy	tnrayin	trundle	tnranduo
troyes	tnrayinsi	trunk	tnrankn
truancy	tnransasi	trunk line	tnrankn lehun
truant	tnransa	trunnel	tnranhunlo
trucial	tnransinjo	trunnion	tnranhunsi
truck1	tnranko	truss	tnranso
truck2	tnranko	trusses	tnrasosi
truckage	tnrankogba	trust	tnransi
trucker	tnrankosi	trustee	tnransise
truckie	tnrankose	trusteeship	tnransisesunpn
truckle	tnrakojn	trusting	tnransignni
truculence	tnrankunsi	trusty	tnransito
truculent	tnrankunto	truth	tnransi
trudeous	tnranjnun	try	terai

WORD (x)	EQUIVALENT (y)	WORD (x)	EQUIVALENT (y)
trying	teraignni	tuberculate	tubonkunleyo
trylon	teraijnsi	tuberculin	tubonkunlesi
tryma	teraimo	tuberculo	tubonkunko
try-on	terai ni	tuberculosis	tubonkunkoso
try-out	terai nita	tuberculous	tubonkunkosi
trypanosome	teraipnsoonmnu	tuberiferous	tubonfirosi
trypanosomiasis	teraipnsoonmunso	tuberoid	tubonjo
tryparsamide	teraipansanmujin	tuberose	tubonse
trypsin	teraipnsan	tuberosity	tubonsetn
trypsinogen	teraipnsangin	tuberous	tubonsi
tryptophan	teraipntophin	tubiform	tubefoon
tryst	teraitn	tubing	tubegnni
tsade	tsejin	tubingen	tubegnnisi
tsana	tsehun	tubular	tubejnra
tsar	tserai	tubulate	tubejnyo
tsatskoe	tseraikosi	tubulation	tubejnyoon
tsetse	tsesun	tubule	tubejn
tsugaru	tsungira	tubuliflorous	tubejnfonraisi
tsunami	tsunhunmi	tubulous	tubejnsi
tstutsugamushi	tsunganmuse	tubulure	tubejnran
tu	tu	tucana	tukohun
tuan	tuni	tuck	tuki
tuareg	turailo	tuck	tuki
tuatara	tuterai	tuck	tuki
tutha	tutesin	tuckahoe	tukihinse
tub	tubuu	tucker	tukisi
tuba	tubo	tucker	tukisi
tubal	tubejo	tucket	tukiti
tubate	tubeyo	tuck-in	tuki-in
tubby	tubuuse	tucoman	tukinmo
tube	tube	tucson	tuknsin
tuber	tubon	tude	tujin
tubercle	tubonkun	tudor	tujnran
tubercular	tubonkunlera	tuesday	tundase

WORD (x)	EQUIVALENT (y)	WORD (x)	EQUIVALENT (y)
tufa	tufan	tumular	tumojnra
tuff	tufon	tumulose	tumojnse
tuffet	tufonte	tumult	tumojia
tuft	tufia	tumultuous	tumojiasi
tug	tugbe	tumulus	tumojnsi
tugela	tugbejn	tun	tuha
tuggurt	tugberai	tuna	tuhau
tuille	tusijnjo	tuna	tuhau
tuit	tusiyo	tunable	tuhaube
tuition	tusiyoon	tundra	tujnra
tula	tujn	tune	tuhun
tularemia	tujnraimua	tuneless	tuhunlabo
tule	turon	tuner	tuhunsi
tulip	turonpo	tung	tugun
tulipomania	turonpomohan	tungsten	tuguntin
tullamore	tullemosii	tungstic	tuguntinko
tulle	tulle	tungstite	tuguntinto
tulsa	turonse	tungting	tuguntignni
tum	tumo	tungus	tugunso
tumble	tumpo	tungusian	tugunsohn
tumbler	tumposi	tungusic	tugunsokn
tumbrel	tumporai	tunguska	tugunsoka
tumefacient	tumofanseyo	tunic	tuhako
tumefaction	tumofanknyoon	tunica	tuhaki
tumefy	tumofe	tunicate	tuhakiyo
tumerosity	tumoraisetn	tunicle	tuhakun
tumerscence	tumoseknsi	tunis	tuhasi
tumescent	tumoseknti	tunisia	tuhasia
tumid	tumoji	tunket	tuhakin
tumidity	tumojito	tunnel	tuhalo
tummy	tummo	tunny	tuhase
tumor	tumoru	tuolumni	tujinmini
tumour	tumorun	tup	tupn
tump	tumpon	tupelo	tupnlo

WORD (x)	EQUIVALENT (y)	WORD (x)	EQUIVALENT (y)
tupi	tupo	turgent	turaigante
tupian	tupohn	turgensce	turaigansekn
tupperware	tupnrawerai	turgescent	turaiganseknti
tuque	tukun	turgid	turaigan
tuquoque	tukuokun	turgidity	turaiganto
turacou	turaikn	turgite	turaiganyo
turanian	turaikn	turgor	turaigansi
turanian	turanrain	turgot	turagnto
turban	turaibo	turin	turon
turbary	turaibose	turk	turaikn
turbellarian	turaibejnrorain	turkey	turaiknsi
turbid	turaibn	turki	turaiki
turbidimeter	turaibnmuto	turkie	turaikiko
turbinal	turaibejo	turkish	turaiknso
turbinate	turaibeyo	turkism	turaikimosi
turbination	turaibeyoon	turmeric	turaimorako
turbine	turaibe	turmoil	turaimoje
turbit	turaiba	tum	tunrai
turbo	turaibe	tumer	tunraisi
turbofan	turaibefanye	turnery	tunrairan
turbogenerator	turaibegnhunransi	turning	tunraignni
turbojet	turaibejntu	turnip	tunraipo
turboprop	turaibeponpo	turnix	tunraisi
turbot	turaibeto	turnkey	tunraiknsi
turbulence	turaibejnsi	turn-off	tunrai fifo
turbulent	turaibejnyo	turn-on	turai ni
turco-	turaika	turnover	tunraiownra
turd	turaijo	turnpike	tunraipokn
turdine	turaijoin	turnstile	tunraisetinron
turdiform	turaijofoon	tumtable	tunraitebe
tureen	turaisi	tum-up	tunrai pake
turenne	turain	turnvercin	tunraiwnkin
turf	turaife	turpentine	turaipnti
turfan	turaifan	turpeth	turaipnsi

WORD (x)	EQUIVALENT (y)	WORD (x)	EQUIVALENT (y)
turpin	turaipoha	tutila	tutuejn
turpitude	turaipntijin	tuum	tuma
turps	turaiposi	tuva	tuwa
turquoise	turaikuosun	tux	tusan
turrel	turrai	tuxedo	tusande
turret	turraitn	tuyeres	tuyorai
turrical	turraiknjo	twa	twn
turriculate	turraiknleyo	twaddle	twnjnron
turtle	turaron	twain	twndi
tuscan	tusokin	twang	twngan
tuscany	tusoknse	twangle	twngansi
tuscarora	tusokiran	twankay	twnkanse
tush	tuse	twas	twnso
tush	tuse	twasome	twnsoomo
tusk	tusia	twat	twnto
tusker	tusiasi	twattle	twnttoron
tussah	tusooa	tway	twnse
tussis	tusoosi	tweak	tweko
tussle	tusoole	twee	twese
tussock	tusooki	tweed	twede
tut	tute	tweedle dum and	twederon duo ati de
tutankhamen	tutinkhimo	twee	
tutelage	tuntojngbon	tweedy	twedese
tutelar	tuntojnra	tweet	tweto
tutelary	tuntojnrai	tweeter	twetosi
tutenag	tuntogan	tweeted	twetode
tutocaine	tuntokoin	tweeze	twejose
tutor	tuntoran	tweezers	twejosesi
tutorage	tuntorangun	twelfth	twejisi
tutorial	tuntoraijo	twelfth night	twejisi nigheu
tutoyer	tuntosesi	twelve	twejiwn
tutii	tutte	twenty	twesetn
tutty	tuto	twentieth	twesetnsi
tutu	tutue	twenties	twesetnsii

WORD (x)	EQUIVALENT (y)	WORD (x)	EQUIVALENT (y)
twerp	twepan	two	twn
twi	twin	twofer	twofiro
twibil	twinbejn	ty1	to
twice	twinse	ty2	tn
twicer	twinsesi	tybalt	tnbejia
twickenham	twinkinhun	tyburn	tnbusun
twiddle	twinjnran	tyche	tnkhn
twig1	twingi	tycoon	tnkoon
twig2	twingi	tydeus	tndiesi
twigged	twingide	tydides	tndedisi
twiggen	twingisi	tying	tngnni
twilight	twinleghe	tyke	tnko
twilit	twinlito	tyler	tnjnra
twill	twinjnra	tylopod	tnjopindie
twin	twinhun	tylosis	tnjoso
twinned	twinhunde	tymbal	tnmbojn
twinning	twinhungnni	tymp	tnmpo
twine	twinwe	tympan	tnmpan
twinge	twingn	tympanic	tnmpanko
twinkle	twinko	tympanist	tnmpansi
twinkling	twinkognni	tympanitis	tnmpanso
twirl	twinrai	tympanites	tnmpanyosi
twirp	twinraipn	tympanum	tnmpanma
twist	twinlo	tympany	tnmpanse
twister	twinlosi	tyndale	tnjnjain
twistor	twinlora	tyndall	tnjnjjo
twit1	twinti	tyndallization	tnjnjjoseyoon
twit2	twinti	tyndareus	tnjnraisi
twitch	twintisi	tyne	tnhun
twitcher	twintisi	type	tnpon
twitter	twintito	type	tnpon
twitter	twintito	typecast	tnponkosotn
twitter	twintito	typha	tnphan
twixt	twinso	typhlitis	tnphojuso

WORD (x)	EQUIVALENT (y)	WORD (x)	EQUIVALENT (y)
typhlo	tnphoju	tyrolienne	tnrohunjo
typhlology	tnphojulogbon	tyrone	tnroin
typholsis	tnphojuso	tyrosinase	tnrosunse
typho	tnphon	tyrosine	tnrosun
typhoeus	tnphonsesi	tyrosinosis	tnrosunso
typhogenic	tnphonginko	tyrothricin	tnrosankin
typhoid	tnphonjo	tyrrhenian	tnrrhain
typhoidin	tnphonjoin	u	u e
typhomania	tnphonmayisi	uaupes	uthunpnsi
typhoon	tnphonsia	ubangi	ubegan
typhoon	tnphonji	ubermensch	uberoinse
typhus	tnphonsi	ubiety	ubeto
typical	tnponkojo	ubiquitarian	ubekuntorain
typify	tnponfe	ubiquitarianism	ubekuntorainmosi
typist	tnponsi	ubiquitous	ubekuntosi
typo	tnpo	ubiquity	ubekunto
typographer	tnpoganphasi	uchean	ukhnhun
typographic	tnpoganphako	udder	ujjomu
typographical	tnpoganphakojo	udo	ujnmi
typographically	tnpoganphakojin	udometer	ujnmimuto
typography	tnpoganphe	uele	ulele
typology	tnpologbon	uganda	ugijnna
typothetae	tnposeto	ugli	ugira
tyr	tnra	uglify	ugirafe
tyramine	tnranmini	ugly	ugirase
tyrannical	tnrankojo	ugly	burewa
tyrannicide	tnrankeku	ugrian	ugirain
tyrannize	tnranse	ugric	ugirako
tyrannosaurus	tnransanra	uigur	ungiran
tyranny	tnranse	uit	unite
tyrant	tnranta	ꞌuintahite	unitehunyo
tyre	tnrai	ukase	uknse
tyrian	tnrain	ukrain	uknrain
tyro	tnro	ukulele	ukulele

WORD (x)	EQUIVALENT (y)	WORD (x)	EQUIVALENT (y)
ulcer	ujnknra	umbelliferous	umbejnrofirosi
ulcerate	ujnknrayo	umbellulate	umbejnroleyo
ulceration	ujnknrayoon	umber	umberan
ule	ujn	umbilical	umbejnkojo
ulema	ujnmo	umbilicate	umbejnkoyo
ulent	ujnto	umbilicus	umbejnkosi
ullage	ujjngba	umbra	umbo
ullswater	ujjnwetnra	umbrage	umbogun
ulmaceous	ujnmosuwa	umbrageous	umbogunsi
ulna	ujnhun	umbrella	umbojjn
ulose	ujnse	umbria	umboran
ulster	ujnseto	umbrian	umborain
ulterior	ujntnraran	umbriferous	umboraifirosi
ultima	ujntemu	umiac	umokin
ultimate	ujntemutn	umlak	umleke
ultimately	ujntemutnlo	umlaut	umleto
ultimatum	ujntemutnma	umnak	umkin
ultimo	ujntemo	umpire	umpnran
ultimogeniture	ujntemogintnran	umpteenth	umpntoonsi
ultra	ujntnre	un-1	nu
ultra-	ujntnre	un-2	ni
ultra-high	ujntnre higha	un-3	nu
ultraist	ujntnresi	unable	nuberon
ultramarine	ujntnremurami	unabridged	nuabangbonde
ultramontane	ujntnremenitelu	unacademic	nuakojinmuka
ultraphotic	ujntnrephotinko	unanimity	nuanimiitn
ultrasonic	ujntnresonko	unanimous	nuanimiisi
ultrasonics	ujntnresonkosi	unapt	nuapnti
ultra vires	ujntnre winransi	unbar	nuboosn
ululant	ujnhute	unbound2	nubojoin
ululate	ujnhuyo	uncial	nikoijo
ulyanovski	ujainknwa	unciform	nikoifoon
ulysses	ujainsesi	uncinate	nikoihunyo
umbel	umbejn	uncle	niknra

WORD (x)	EQUIVALENT (y)	WORD (x)	EQUIVALENT (y)
unco	nikio	unionist	enisosi
uncock	nukiko	unionize	enisose
uncouth	nukinis	union jack	jako eniso
unction	nikntose	unique	enikin
unctuous	nikntosi	unisex	enisesia
uncut	nukunte	unison	enisesi
under	nijnra	unisonal	enisesijo
underpass	nijnrapanso	unit	enitn
underpay	nijnrapnyio	unitarian	enitnrain
ungula	nugunjo	unitary	enitnrai
unguent	nugunte	unite	eniton
unguentry	nugunterai	united	enitode
unguiculate	nugunlekoleyo	unitive	enitnwin
unguiform	nugunlefoon	unitize	enitnse
unguinous	nugunlesi	unity	enitn
unguis	nugunleso	universal	eniwinsejo
ungula	nugunle	universe	eniwinse
ungular	nugunleran	universon	eniwinsesi
ungulate	nugunleyo	university	eniwinseto
unguligrade	nugunlegandie	unjust	nujose
uni	eni	unkennel	nukinhunlo
uniat	enito	unless	nulabo
uniaxial	enisosijo	unlinedl	nulehun
unicameral	enikomurajo	unsex	nusesua
unicellular	eniknjjnran	unsure	nusurai
unicorn	enikiran	unto	nuto
uniform	enifoonmo	unnugun	nungun
uniformity	enifoonmutn	up-	pake
unify	enife	upholster	pakehimose
unigeniture	enigintnran	upholsterer	pakehimosesi
unijugate	enijogiyo	upholstery	pakehimoserai
unilateral	eniletnraijo	upon	pakesi
uniliteral	enilitoraijo	upper1	pakepo
union	eniso	upper2	pakepo

WORD (x)	EQUIVALENT (y)	WORD (x)	EQUIVALENT (y)
uppish	pakeposi	urethan	uresun
urachus	uraikhosi	urethra	uresirai
uraeus	uraisi	urethritis	uresiraiso
ural	urale	urethro	uresiron
uralic	uraleko	uretic	ureko
uralite	uraleyo	urge	uranle
urania	urain	urgency	uranlesn
uranism	uranmosi	urgent	uranleto
uranite	uranyo	uria	uresi
uranium	uranma	uriah	uraihun
urano	urankn	uric	ureko
uranous	uransi	urico	ureki
uranus	uransa	uriel	uraile
urban	uraigbe	uric acid	akijo ureko
urbanism	uraigbemosi	urinal	uremijo
urbanite	uraigbetn	urinary	uremirai
urbanity	uraigbetn	urinate	uremirai
urbanization	uraigbeseyoon	urinate	uremiyo
urbanize	uraigbenise	urination	uremiyoon
urbanology	uraigbelogbon	urine	uremi
urchin	uraikha	urinemia	uremimua
urdu	uraide	uriniferous	uremifirosi
ure	ure	urino	uremini
urea	urein	urinogental	ureminigintojo
urease	ureinse	urinogenous	ureminiginsi
uredinales	urejainjosi	urinoscopy	ureminisokipo
uredinium	urejainma	urinous	ureminisi
uredo	uredie	urmia	uramua
ureide	urejin	urn	uramu
uremia	uremua	uro	uroo
uret	uretn	urobilin	uroobejan
ureter	uretnra	urochord	urookhijora
ureterectomy	uretnratemo	urochordata	urookhijorate
uretero	uretnran	urodele	uroojinron

WORD (x)	EQUIVALENT (y)	WORD (x)	EQUIVALENT (y)
urogenital	uroogintojo	usherette	usinsibo
urogenous	urooginsi	usk	usia
urolith	uroolesi	usnach	lesekin
urolithiasis	uroolesiso	usquebaugh	lesekunbegan
urology	uroologbon	ustilago	usuntejngon
uropod	uroopindie	ustion	usuntesi
uropygial	uroopegbnjo	ustulate	usunteleyo
uropygium	uroopegbnma	ustulation	usunteleyoon
uroscopy	uroosokipo	usual	lesejo
uroxanthin	uroositesin	usually	lesejosi
ursa major	urusia mojuran	usufruct	lesefiraikun
ursine	urusiani	usufructuary	lesefiraikunra
urspracho	urusopankho	usurer	usuraise
ursula	urasuale	usurious	usuraisi
ursuline	urasulehun	usurp	usuraigba
urtext	urutnso	usurpation	usuraigbayoon
urticaceous	urutaknsuwa	usury	usurai
urticaria	urutaknran	ususloquendi	ususonkunjo
urticate	urutaknyo	ut	uto
urtication	urutaknyoon	ute	ute
uru	iru	utensil	utesnle
urubamba	urumbejn	uterine	uterain
uruguay	urugun	uteritis	uteraiso
urundi	urujn	utero	utera
urus	urusi	uterus	uteraisi
urushiol	urusejin	utgard	utegagbaa
us	wa	uther	usinra
usable	lesebe	utica	utiko
usage	lesegun	utile	utijn
usance	lesesi	utilitarian	utijntorain
use	lese	utilitarianism	utijntorainmosi
user	lesesi	utility	utileto
usher	usinsi	utilize	utijnse
usher	usinsi	utipossiditis	utiposoojnso

WORD (x)	EQUIVALENT (y)	WORD (x)	EQUIVALENT (y)
utmost	utemosua	vaal	wajo
utopia	utopn	vaasa	wasiso
utopian	utopnsi	vast la hogue	wasi hingan
utopianism	utopnmosi	vacancy	waknsn
utricle	utaraiko	vacant	waknte
utricular	utaraikojnra	vacatia	wakntesi
utriculitis	utaraikojnso	vacate	waknyo
utriculus	utaraikojnsi	vacation	waknyoon
utrillo	utaraillo	vacationist	waknyoonsi
utter1	utto	vaccinate	wakihunyo
utter2	utto	vaccination	wakihunyoon
utterance	uttosi	vaccinationist	wakihunyoosi
utterance	uttosi	vaccinator	wakihunsi
utterly	uttolo	vaccine	wakihun
uttermost	uttomosua	accinia	wakihan
u turn	u tunrai	vacciniaceous	wakihansuwa
uva	uwa	vaccinization	wakihunseyoon
uvarovite	uwaraiwnyo	vaccinotherapy	wakihunsinranpo
uvaursi	uwaraisi	vacherin	wakhnran
uvea	uwnni	vacillate	wakilleyo
uvea	uwnni	vacillating	wakilleyognni
uveitis	uwnniso	vacua	wakuo
uveous	uwnnisi	vacuity	wakuotn
uvula	uwujn	vacuole	wakuojn
uvular	uwujnra	vacuous	wakuosi
uvulitis	uwujnso	vacuum	wakuoma
ux	usin	vade	wajin
uxmal	usinmojn	vade-mecum	wajin-mokuo
uxor	usinran	vagabond	wagbaboun
uxorial	usinraijo	vagary	wagbarai
uxoricide	usinrankeku	vagina	wagbnhun
uxorious	usinraisi	vaginal	wagbnhunjo
uzhok	usookn	vaginate	wagbnhunyo
uzbek	usebnko	vaginectomy	wagbnhuntemo

WORD (x)	EQUIVALENT (y)	WORD (x)	EQUIVALENT (y)
vaginismus	wagbnhunmosi	valet	wajnta
vaginitis	wagbnhunso	valetudinarian	wajntugbarain
vagino	wagbnka	valgus	wajngbun
vagitus	wagbnsi	valhalla	wajnha
vagotonia	wagontinsi	valiant	wajntn
wagracy	wagirai	valid	wajngbe
vagrant	wagiraite	validate	wajngbeyo
vagrom	wagiramo	validity	wajngbetn
vague	wagbun	valine	wajnhun
vagus	wagbunsi	valise	wajnse
vail	wasua	valium	wajnma
vail	wasua	valkyrie	wajokuraini
vain	waisi	valladolid	wajnrgbile
vainglory	waisigonrai	vallation	wajnrayoon
vair	warie	valleculla	wajnrakun
valance	wajosi	valles	wajnrasi
vale	wajn	valletta	wajnratto
valediction	wajndiknyoon	valley	wajnrase
valedictorian	wajndikntorain	vallomrose	wajnramosua
valedictory	wajndikntorai	valmy	wajnmo
valence1	wajnso	valois	wajnsin
valence2	wajnso	valois	wajnsin
valencia	wajnson	valona	wajnhun
valenciennes	wajnsonhusi	valonia	wajnhunsi
valency	wajnsosi	valor	wajnran
valentine	wajnsohun	valorization	wajnraiseyoon
valentinian	wajnsohunsi	valorize	wajnraise
valera	wajnra	valorous	wajnransi
valerate	wajnraiyo	valour	wajnrai
valeria	wajnran	valparaiso	wajnpanraiso
valerian	wajnrain	valuable	wajoinbe
valerianaceous	wajnrainsuwa	valuation	wajoinyoon
valeric	wajnrako	valuator	wajoinran
valery	wajnrai	value	wajoin

WORD (x)	EQUIVALENT (y)	WORD (x)	EQUIVALENT (y)
valval	wajnwnjo	vanillin	wainjnrun
valvate	wajnwnyo	vanir	wainran
valve	wajnwin	vanish	wainsn
valvelet	wajnwnti	vanity	waitn
valvular	wajnwnran	vanity bag	waitn bogbn
valvule	wajnwnra	vanner	vainran
valvulitis	wajnwnraso	vanquish	wainkuesi
vambrace	wambanso	vantage	waintegba
vamoose	wamoosun	vansette	wainsetto
vamp1	wampe	vapid	wapnjo
vamp2	wampe	vapor	wapnra
vampire	wampera	vaporescence	wapnrasneknsi
vampirism	wamperamosi	vapori	wapnran
van1	wain	vaporific	wapnrafiko
van2	wain	vaporimeter	wapnraimuto
van	wain	vaporing	wapnraignni
vanadate	waingboyo	vaporish	wapnraisu
vanadic	waingboko	vaporization	wapnraiseyoon
vanadinite	waingbohunyo	vaporize	wapnraise
vanadium	waingboma	vaporizer	wapnraisesi
vanadous	waingbosi	vaporous	wapnraisi
vancouver	wainkiwin	vapour	wapnran
vandal	wainbaje	vaquero	wakunro
vandalism	wainbajemosi	vara	wara
vandalize	wainbajese	vara	waran
vanden	wainbasi	varanger	waraignsi
vander	wainbaran	varangian	waraigini
vandyke	wainbakn	varanian	waranrain
vane	wainsi	vardar	warajnra
vaner	wainsn	vareuse	wariese
vang	waingbi	vari	warai
vanguard	waingungba	variable	waraibe
vanilla	wainjnran	variance	waraisi
vanillic	wainjnranko	variant	waraiyo

WORD (x)	EQUIVALENT (y)	WORD (x)	EQUIVALENT (y)
variation	waraiyoon	varsity	waraseto
varicella	waraiknjjn	varuna	warunhun
varicellate	waraiknjjnyo	varus	warasi
varicelloid	waraiknjjnjo	varus	warasi
varico	waraiki	varve	warawn
varcocele	waraikiknjn	vary	warai
varicose	waraikise	varying	waraiggnni
varicosis	waraikiso	vas	wasi
varicosity	waraikisetn	vasari	wasirai
varicotomy	waraikitemo	vascular	wasikunjnran
varied	waraide	vasculum	wasikunjnma
variegated	waraingiyode	vas deferens	wasi diefiranse
variegation	waraingiyoon	vase	wasian
varietal	waraintojo	vasectomy	wasekntemo
variety	warainto	vaseline	wasianlehun
variform	waraifoon	vashti	wasuye
vario	warain	vaso	wasoo
variola	warainle	vaso dentine	wasoo jinhatn
variolate	warainleyo	vasodilator	wasoojnleyoran
variole	warainle	vassal	wasoojo
variolite	warainleyo	vassalage	wasoojogun
variolitic	warinleko	vassalize	wasoojose
varioloid	warainlejo	vast	wasua
variometer	warainmuto	vastation	wasuayoon
variorum	warainron	vasteras	wasuaranse
various	waraisi	vastity	wasuaseto
varityper	waraitnponsi	vasty	wasuase
varix	waraise	vat	watn
varlet	waratn	vatic	watnko
varletry	waratnrai	vatican	watnkohn
varmint	waramute	vaticanism	watnkohnmosi
varna	warahun	vaticide	watnkeku
varnish	warahunse	vaticinal	watnkohunjo
varro	warron	vaticinate	watnkohunyo

WORD (x)	EQUIVALENT (y)	WORD (x)	EQUIVALENT (y)
vatter	wattnra	veer	wnrai
vatutin	watutin	veer	wnrai
vau	wanu	veery	wnraise
vauban	wanubon	vega	wngi
vaucheriaceous	wanukhnransuwa	vega	wngi
vaucluse	wanukanse	vegan	wngisi
vaud	wandie	vegetable	wngitobe
vaudeville	wanudiewojnra	vegetal	wngitojo
vaudois	wanudiesi	vegetarian	wngitorain
vaudois	wanudiesi	vegetarianism	wngitorainmos
vaughan	wanughan	vegetant	wngitote
vault	wanujia	vegetate	wngitoyo
vault	wanujia	vegetation	wngitoyoon
vaulting	wanujiagnni	vegetative	wngitoyosi
vaunt	wanuto	veggie	wngise
vaunt courier	wanuto kiraisi	vehement	wnhemutto
vauntie	wanutosi	vehicle	wnhikuo
vaux	wanusi	vehmgericht	wnhungiraikho
vavasor	wawesi	veil	wnsua
vaward	wawegba	vein	wnsa
veadar	wnjnra	veined	wnsade
veal	wnwo	veining	wnsagnni
vection	wntoyoon	veinlet	wnsatn
vector	wntoran	vela	wnle
vectorial	wntoraijo	velamen	wnlemuye
vecturism	wntoraimosi	velar	wnleran
veda	wndaa	velarium	wnleraima
vedanta	wndaato	velarize	wnleraise
vedda	wndn	velarium	wnleraima
vedde	wnde	velate	wnleyo
vedder	wndaasi	velation	wnleyoon
vedette	wndetin	velcro	wnleknra
vedic	wndaako	veldt	wnlejia
vee	wnn	veleta	wnleto

WORD (x)	EQUIVALENT (y)	WORD (x)	EQUIVALENT (y)
veliger	wnlegira	vender	wnnijnsi
veligerous	wnlegirasi	vendetta	wnnijntte
veliki	wnlekun	vendome	wnnijnmo
velitation	wnletoyoon	vendor	wnnijnra
velites	wnletosi	vendue	wnnijan
velleity	wnlleseto	veneer	wnnirai
vellicate	wnllekoyo	vener	wnnisn
vellum	wnlema	venerable	wnniraibe
veloco	wnloki	venerate	wnniraiyo
velocipede	wnlokipndie	veneration	wnniraiyoon
velocity	wnlokito	venereal	wnniranjo
velodrome	wnlogbnmo	venereology	wnniranlogbon
velours	wnlowesi	venery	wnnirai
veloute	wnloseki	venesection	wnniseknteyoon
velum	wnlema	venetia	wnnitin
velure	wnloran	venetian	wnnitinhn
velutinous	wnlotinsi	venetic	wnniteko
velveret	wnlowitiran	veneto	wnnito
velvet	wnlowiti	venezia	wnisia
velveteen	wnlowitisi	venezuela	wnisunjn
velvet	y	venezuelo	wnsunlo
vena	wnhun	vengeance	wngbasi
venal	wnhunjo	vengeful	wngbafunjn
venality	wnhunrontn	venial	wnsijo
venatic	wnhunko	venice	wnsisn
venation	wnhunyoon	venire	wnsirai
vend	wnnijn	venireman	wnsiraimoye
vend	wnnijn	venison	wnsise
vendable	wnnijnbe	venite	wnsito
vendace	wnnijnse	venizelos	wnsiselo
vendee	wnnijnsn	venn diagram	wnsi jinaganmo
vendetta	wnnjnta	venom	wnmoo
vendee	wnnijnun	venomous	wnmoosi
vendemiaire	wnnijnmuran	venose	wnsoo

WORD (x)	EQUIVALENT (y)	WORD (x)	EQUIVALENT (y)
venosity	wnsooto	veracious	wnraikisi
venous	wnsoosi	veracity	wnraikito
vent1	wnti	veracruze	wnraiknra
vent2	wnti	veranda	wnraijn
ventage	wntigba	verano	wnraikn
ventail	wntite	veratric	wnratnrako
venter	wntisi	veratridine	wnratnrajoin
venter	wntisi	veratrine	wnratnrajoin
ventiduct	wntidikiti	veratrine	wnratnrain
ventilate	wntileyo	veratrize	wnratnrase
ventilation	wntileyoon	verb	wnbe
ventilator	wntileyoran	verbal	wnbejn
ventose	wntise	verbalism	wnbejnmosi
ventrad	wntnrejn	verbalist	wnbejnsi
ventral	wntnrejo	verbalize	wnbejnse
ventricle	wntnraikuo	verbatim	wnbetima
ventricose	wntnraikise	verbena	wnbehun
ventricular	wntnraikuoran	verbenaceous	wnbehunsuwa
ventriculose	wntnraikunse	verbiage	wnbegun
ventriloquial	wntnrailokunjo	verbify	wnbefe
ventriloquism	wntnrailokunmosi	verbigerate	wnbegnraiyo
ventriloqize	wntnrailokunse	verbose	wnboose
ventro	wntnra	verbosity	wnbooseto
ventspils	wntisipnjn	verboten	wnbootin
venture	wntnrai	verdant	wngbate
venturesome	wntnraisoomo	verdantique	wngbatekun
venturous	wntnraisi	verde	wngbn
venue	wnise	verderer	wngbnsesi
venule	wniron	verdi	wngbi
venulose	wnironse	verdict	wngbiko
venus	wnsuan	verdigris	wngbigirai
venusberg	wnsuanbegan	verdin	wngbisi
venza	wnisa	verditer	wngbitnra
vera	wnrai	verdure	wngbnrai

WORD (x)	EQUIVALENT (y)	WORD (x)	EQUIVALENT (y)
verdurous	wngbnraisi	vermin	wnronhun
vereeniging	wnregingnni	verminate	wnronhunyo
verein	wnrein	verminous	wnronhunsi
verge1	wngbe	vermoulu	wnronje
verge2	wngbe	vermouth	wnronloti
verger	wngbesi	vernacular	wnrankuo
vergil	wngbelo	vernacularism	wnrankuomosi
verglas	wngansi	vernal	wnranjo
veridical	wngbainkojo	vernalize	wnranjose
verification	wnraifikoyoon	vernation	wnranyoon
verify	wnraife	verner	wnransi
verily	wnrailo	vernicose	wnrankise
verisimilar	wnraisoomajora	vernier	wnransesi
verisimilitude	wnraisoomajotujin	vernissage	wnransoogun
verism	wnraimosi	vernon	wnransi
veritable	wnraito	verny	wnranse
veritas	wnraitosi	verona	wnroin
verity	wnraitn	veronal	wnroinjo
verjuice	wnraijomisi	veronese	wnroinse
verlain	wnrojain	veronica	wnroinko
vermeer	wnromaran	verrazano	wnrransekn
vermeil	wnromule	verrocchio	wnrronkun
vermi	aron	verruca	wnrronko
vermin	wnron	verrucano	wnrronkokn
vermicelli	wnronknjjn	verrucose	wnrronkise
verimicidal	wnronkekujo	versailles	wnsanllosi
vermicide	wnronkeku	versant	wnsante
vermicular	wnronkunle	versatile	wnsetinron
vermiculate	wnronkunleyo	verse	wnso
vermiculation	wnronkunleyoon	versed	wnsojn
vermiculite	wnronkunleyo	versemonger	wnsomenignra
vermiculose	wnronkunlese	versicle	wnsokuo
vermiform	wnronfoon	versicular	wnsokuoran
vermillon	wnronllesi	versiera	wnsoran

WORD (x)	EQUIVALENT (y)	WORD (x)	EQUIVALENT (y)
versify	wnsofe	vesie	wnsun
version	wnsosi	vesoul	wnsojn
verso	wnsoo	vespasian	wnsoopnse
verst	wnsun	vesper	wnsupn
versus	wnsosi	vesper	wnsupn
vert	wnte	vesperal	winsupnjo
vertebra	wnteban	vespers	wnsupnsin
vertebral	wntebanjo	vespertillonine	wnsupntiroinhun
vertebrate	wntebanyo	vespertine	wnsupntihun
vertebration	wntebanyoon	vespiary	wnsuporai
vertex	wngtesi	vespid	wnsupojo
vertical	wntekojo	vespine	wnsupohun
vertical	wntekun	vespucci	wnsupoki
verticillaster	wntekunseto	vessel	wnsujn
verticillate	wntekunleyo	vest	wnsn
verticity	wntekitn	vesta	wnsnna
vertiginous	wntepoyisi	vestal	wnsnnajo
vertigo	wntepoyi	vested	wnsnde
vertumous	wntemosi	vestee	wnsnse
vervain	wnwasia	vestiary	wnsnrai
verve	wnwan	vestibule	wnsnbejn
vervet	wnwanta	vestibular	wnsnbejnra
very	wnrai	vesteralen	wnsnrainjn
vesica	wnsuko	vestige	wnsngn
vesical	wnsukojo	vestigial	wnsngijo
vesicant	wnsukote	vestment	wnsnmutto
vesica piscis	wnsuko posekisi	vestry	wnsnrai
vesicate	wnsukoyo	vesture	wnsnran
vesicatory	wnsukorai	vesuvian	wnsunwain
vesicle	wnsukuo	vesuvianite	wnsunwainyo
vesico	wnsuki	Vesuvius	wnsunwosi
vesicula	wnsukuojn	vet1	wnti
vesicular	wnsukuojnra	vet2	wnti
vesiculate	wnsukuojnyo	vetch	wntisi

WORD (x)	EQUIVALENT (y)	WORD (x)	EQUIVALENT (y)
veteran	wntiran	vibrio	wogbanka
veterinarian	wntiranrain	vibrioid	wogbankajo
veterinary	wntiranrai	vibrissa	wogbansoo
veterinary surgeon	suralesi wntiranrai	vibroscope	wogbansokipon
vetiver	wntiwere	vibrotropism	wogbantnrapnmosi
vetluga	wntiwere	viburnum	wongbanranma
vetluga	wntilogan	vicar	woknran
veto	wntin	vicarage	woknrangun
vetter	wnttnsi	vicarial	woknraijo
vex	wnsia	vicariate	woknraihyo
vexation	wnsiayoon	vicarious	woknraisi
vexatious	wnsiayosi	vicarly	woknranlo
vexed	wnsiade	vicarship	woknransunpn
vexil	wnsiale	vice1	wokn
vexillary	wnsiallerai	vice2	wokn
vexillate	wnsialleyo	vice3	wokn
vexillum	wnsiallema	vice-chancellor	wokn-khokiknjjn
via	wosi	vice-president	wokn-pesisoojotn
viable	wosibe	vicegerency	wokngnrasn
viaduct	wosidikit	vicegerent	wokngnrato
vial	wosijo	vicenary	woknrai
viand	wosije	vicennial	woknhunjo
viatic	wosiko	vicenza	woknse
viaticum	wosikoma	viceregal	woknregijo
vibes	wogbansi	viceregent	woknregito
vibrant	wogbantn	vicereine	woknrainhun
vibraphone	wogbanphohun	viceroy	woknrase
vibrate	wogbanyo	vice versa	wokn winse
vibratile	wogbantinron	vichada	wokhojn
vibratility	wogbantinrontn	vichy	wokhun
vibration	wongbanyoon	vichyssoise	wokhunsoonse
vibrato	wogbanto	vichy water	wokhun wetnra
vibrator	wogbanran	vicinal	woknnijo
vibratory	wogbanrai	vicinage	woknnigun

WORD (x)	EQUIVALENT (y)	WORD (x)	EQUIVALENT (y)
vicinity	woknnito	viewer	wowinsi
vicinism	woknnimosi	viewpoint	wowinpintoni
vicious	woknsi	vigil	wogbile
vicissitude	woknsesitujin	vigilambulism	wogbilembejnmosi
vicissitudinary	woknsesitujinra	vigilance	wogbilesi
vicksburg	wokibegan	vigilant	wogbiletn
vicontiel	wokintilo	vigilante	wogbileto
victim	woknma	viguette	wogantn
victimize	woknmase	viguetter	wogantnsi
victor	woknran	vigo	wogon
victoria	woknrin	vigor	wogbiran
victorian	woknrain	vigoroso	wogbiranso
victorianism	woknrainmosi	vigorous	wogbiransi
victoriana	woknrainsi	vigour	wogbiran
victorius	woknraisi	viir	woora
victory	woknrai	viking	wokinga
victual	woknje	vile	wojn
victualage	woknjegun	viliaco	wojnkin
victualer	woknjeran	vilify	wojnfe
victualler	woknjjeran	vilipend	wojnpnjon
vicuna	wokunna	vill	wojnra
vide	wojin	villa	wojnran
vicdlicet	wojinlekiti	villadom	wojnrandeo
video	wojnron	village	wojnrangn
videogenic	wojnronginko	villagery	wojnrangnrai
videotex	wojnrontesn	villain	wojnrain
vie	woin	villainess	wojnrainbo
vienna	woinhe	villainous	wojnrainsi
vienne	woinhun	villainy	wojnrainse
viennese	woinhese	villnella	wojnranlle
viennois	woinknsi	villanelle	wojnranllo
vientiane	wointihun	villard	wojnragba
vietnam	wotnmini	villatic	wojnranko
view	wowin	villain	wojnrein

WORD (x)	EQUIVALENT (y)	WORD (x)	EQUIVALENT (y)
villeinage	wojnreingun	vineyardist	winhunyandansi
villiform	wojnrunfoon	vingtetun	wingntotun
villosity	wojnrunsetn	vini	winiu
villous	wojnrunsi	vinic	winiuko
villus	wojnrun	viniculture	winiukunjiaran
vilyui	wojnyun	viniferous	winiufirosi
vim	womi	vinificator	winiufikoran
vimen	womini	vinification	winiufikoyoon
viminal	wominijo	vinometer	winiumuto
vimineous	wominisi	vinosity	winiuseto
vin	win	vinous	winiusi
vina	winta	vinson	winisin
vinaceous	winsuwa	vintage	wintogbaa
vinasse	winsoo	vintage car	kosi wintogbaa
vinnigrette	winnigiraitn	vintager	wintogbaasi
vincennes	winknhunsi	vintner	wintoran
vincent	winknti	viny	winiuse
vincentian	winkntihn	vinyl	winlo
vinci	winkn	viol	wokoji
vincible	winknbe	viola1	wokole
vinculum	winkunramo	viola2	wokole
vindhya	wingbain	violate	wokoleyo
vindicate	wingbakoyo	violence	wokojnse
vindication	wingbakoyoon	violent	wokojnso
vindicative	wingbakoyosi	vilescent	wokojnseknti
vindicatory	wingbakoyorai	violet	wokojntn
vindictive	wingbaknti	violin	wokojnta
vine	winhun	violist	wokojnsi
vinegar	winhungan	violoncellist	wokoleniknllosi
vinegarette	winhungantn	violoncello	wokoleniknllo
vinegaroon	winhungansi	violone	wokoleni
vinegary	winhunganse	viosterol	wokosootojin
vinery	winhunrai	viper	wopnra
vineyard	winhunyandan	viperous	wopnrasi

WORD (x)	EQUIVALENT (y)	WORD (x)	EQUIVALENT (y)
vipersbugloss	wopnrasebugonsua	virtue	waraitn
viraginity	worangantn	virtuosity	waraitnsetn
virago	waraigon	virtuoso	waraitnso
viral	warunjo	virtuous	waraitnsi
vire	warai	virtute	waraito
virelay	waraileyn	virulence	warunjnsi
vireo	waraiko	virulent	warujnso
vireonine	waraikohun	virus	warun
viresceence	waraiseknsi	viry	warain
virescent	waraiseknti	visa	wosiun
vir et uxor	warai ati usinran	visage	wosigun
virga	waraigi	vis-à-vis	wosi-a-wosi
virgate	waraigiyo	viscacha	wosikikho
virgin	waraigan	viscera	wosiknra
virginal	waraigon	visceral	wosiknrajo
virginal	waraigon	viscid	wosikijn
virgina	waraigansi	viscidity	wosikijntn
virginisan	waraiganhn	viscose	wosikise
virginity	waraigantn	viscosimeter	wosikisemuto
virgo	waraign	viscosity	wosikiseto
virgulate	waraignleyo	viscount	wosikaleyo
virgule	waraignjn	viscountey	wosikaleyose
viridescent	waraijoseknti	viscountess	wosikaleyobo
viridian	waraijohn	viscous	wosikise
viridity	waraijotn	vise	wose
virile	waraile	visibility	wosebeleto
virilism	warailemosi	visible	wosebe
virility	waraileto	vision	wosesi
viripotent	waraipotinto	visional	wosesijo
virl	warai	visionary	wosesirai
virology	warunlogbon	visit	wosetn
virtu	waraita	visitant	wosetnsi
virtual	waraitnjo	visitation	wosetnyoon
virtually	waraitnjin	visitor	wosetnran

WORD (x)	EQUIVALENT (y)	WORD (x)	EQUIVALENT (y)
visitorial	wosetnraijo	vitreous	wintoransi
visor	woseran	vitrescence	wintoranseknsi
vista	wosetn	vitrescent	wintoranseknti
vistula	wosetujn	vitrescible	wintoransekibe
visual	wosejo	vitri	wintorai
visual aid	aajo wosejo	vitrifacture	wintoraifanknran
visuality	woserontn	vitrification	wintoraifikoyoon
visualize	wosejose	vitriform	wintoraifon
visualizer	wosejosesi	vitrify	wintoraife
visvitae	wosewintnse	vitrine	wintorain
vitaceous	wintnsuwa	vitriol	wintoraijin
vitae	wintnse	vitriolic	wintoraijinko
vital	wintnjo	vitriolize	wintoraijinse
vitality	wintnleto	vitruvius	wintoraiwe
vitalize	wintnjose	vitta	wintto
vitamer	wintnmura	vittate	winttoyo
vitamin	wintnmo	vittorio	winttorain
vitaminize	wintnmose	vituline	wintolehun
vitaminology	wintnmologbon	vituperate	wintopnrayo
vitascope	wintnsokipon	viva1	winwa
vite	winte	viva2	winwa
vitebok	wintebesia	vivace	winwakn
vitellin	wintejnran	vivacious	winwaknsi
vitelline	eintejnrain	vivacity	winwakitn
vitellus	wintejnrasi	vivandiere	winwainjnran
vitesse	wintesoon	vivarium	winwaraima
vit	winto	viva voce	winwa wnso
vitiate	wintoyo	vive	winwn
vitiated	wintoyode	viverrine	winwnrrain
viticulture	wintokunjiaran	vivers	winwnrasi
vitiligo	wintolegon	vives	winwnsi
vitim	wintomi	vivian	winwahn
vitoria	wintoran	vivid	winwajo
vitrain	wintorain	vivify	winwafe

WORD (x)	EQUIVALENT (y)	WORD (x)	EQUIVALENT (y)
viviparous	winwapansi	voice-over	wnnso-ownra
vivisect	winwaseknte	void	wnjua
vivisection	winwaseknteyoon	voidable	wnjuabe
vixen	wonsesi	voidance	wnjuasi
viz.	wose	voile	wnron
vizard	wosegba	voila	wnran
vizarded	wosegbade	voir dire	wnrai dirai
vizier	woserai	voix	wnniso
vizierate	woseraiyo	vol.	wnjn
vizor	woseran	volcanic	wnjnkin
v-neck	u-hunko	volant	wnjnte
vladimir	wanjnmora	volaplic	wnjnpanko
vltava	wantowa	volar	wnjnra
vo	wn	volar	wnjnra
vocable	wnkobe	volatile	wnjntinran
vocabulary	wnkobjnra	volatility	wnjntinrontn
vocal	wnkojn	volatilize	wnjntinranse
vocalic	wnkojnko	volanvent	wnjnwinti
vocalism	wnkojnmosi	volcanic	wnjnkonako
vocalist	wnkojnsi	volcanism	wnjnkonamosi
vocalize	wnkojnse	volcanist	wnjnkonasi
vocation	wnkoyoon	vulcanize	wnjnkonase
vocational	wnkoyoonjo	volcano	wnjnkona
vocative	wnkoyowin	volcanology	wnjnkonalogbon
voces	wnsosi	vole	wnjn
vociferant	wnsofiraitn	volery	wnjnrai
vociferate	wnsofiraiyo	volga	wnjngan
vociferous	wnsofiraisi	volhynia	wnjnhohan
vodka	wnkan	volitant	wnjntatn
vogue	wngan	volitation	wnjntayoon
vogul	wnganjn	volitient	wnjntato
voice	wnnso	volition	wnjnyoon
voice-box	wnnso-bosi	volitive	wnjnyowin
voiceless	wnnsolabo	volkhov	wnjnkhiwa

WORD (x)	EQUIVALENT (y)	WORD (x)	EQUIVALENT (y)
volkslied	wnjnkisan	volute	wnjnwe
volley	wnjnrase	volution	wnjnyoon
volleyball	robownjnrase	volva	wnjnwa
volos	wnjnsn	volvulus	wnjnwalosi
volost	wnjnsi	vomica	wnbiko
volsci	wnjnseko	vomit	wnmbi
volscian	wnjnsekoin	vomitive	wnmbise
volt	wnjia	vomito	wnmbu
volt	wnjia	vomitory	wnmburai
volta	wnjiase	vomitus	wnmbisi
volta	wnjiase	vomiturition	wnmbiraiyoon
voltage	wnjiagun	von	wnsi
voltaic	wnjiako	voodoo	wnnidein
voltaism	wnjiamosi	voodooism	wnnideinmosi
voltameter	wnjiamuto	vora	wnrun
voltammeter	wnjiamomuto	voracious	wnrunsesi
volte-face	wnjiato-fansi	vorlage	wnrajngan
volti	wnjiasi	voroneth	wnroinsi
voltigeur	wnjiasignran	vorous	wnrunsi
voltmeter	wnjiamuto	vortex	wnraiyi
voltumo	wnjiarain	vertical	wnraiyikojo
voluble	wnjnbe	vorticist	wnraiyisi
volume	wnjnmo	vorticose	wnraiyikise
volume	wnjnmo	vertiginous	wnraiyigansi
volumeter	wnjnmuto	votary	wntorai
volumetric	wnjnmutoraiko	vote	wnto
voluminasity	wnjnminaseto	voter	wntosi
voluminous	wnjnminasi	votive	wntowa
voluntarism	wnjnteraimosi	vouch	wnkhn
voluntary	wnjnterai	vouchee	wnkhnse
voluntaryism	wnjnterainmosi	voucher	wnkhnsi
volunteer	wnjnteran	voussoir	wnsoora
voluptuary	wnjnpntirai	vow	wnwi
voluptuous	wnjnpntisi	vowel	wnwilo

WORD (x)	EQUIVALENT (y)	WORD (x)	EQUIVALENT (y)
vowelize	wnwilose	wacke	wekie
vox pop	wnniso popn	wacky	wekiun
vox populi	wnniso popnlo	wad	wejo
voy	wnyun	wadding	wejognni
voyage	wnyungun	waddle	wejoron
voyageur	wnyungunran	waddy	wejoin
voyeur	wnyunran	wade	wejin
vraisemblance	wnraisembesi	wader	wejinsi
vryburg	wnraibugan	wadi	wegbani
vug	wego	wadjak	wejoja
vulcan	welekona	wadmal	wejomujn
vulcanite	welekonayo	wadna	wejina
vulcanization	welekonaseyoon	wadset	wejosetn
vulcanize	welekonase	wadsetter	wejosettnsi
vulcanology	welekonalogbon	wae	weni
vulgar	welegira	wafer	wefiro
vulgarian	welegirain	wafer-thin	sinto-wefiro
vulgarism	welegiramosi	waff	wefan
vulgarity	welegiraitn	waff	wefan
vulgarize	welegiraise	waffle1	wefanjn
vulgate	welegiyo	waffle2	wefanjn
vulgo	welegan	waffle-iron	irin-wefanjn
vulnerable	weleranbe	waft	wefia
vulnerary	weleranrai	wafter	wefiasi
vulpecula	welepnkun	waftage	wefiagun
vulpecular	welepnkunran	wafture	wefiaran
vulpicide	welepokeku	wag1	wegn
vulpine	welepohun	wag2	wegn
vulpinite	welepohunyo	wage	wegbi
vulture	weletnran	waged	wegbide
vulva	welewa	wager	wegbisi
vy	wesi	waggery	wegbirai
waal	wejn	waggish	wegbise
wabash	webesi	waggle	wegbiron

WORD (x)	EQUIVALENT (y)	WORD (x)	EQUIVALENT (y)
waggly	wegbilo	walker	werinsi
wagner	wegnran	walkie-talkie	werinse-tejose
wagnerism	wegnranmosi	walking	weringnni
wagon	wegbe	wall	wejnra
wagonage	wegbegba	wallaby	wejnrabe
wagoner	wegbesi	wallace	wajnrase
wagonette	wegbetn	wallach	wejnrakhi
wagonlit	wegbelito	wallachia	wejnrakhin
wagtail	wegntele	wallah	wejnrahun
wahoo	wehoon	wallaroo	wejnraru
wahoo	wehoon	waller	wejnrasi
waif	wefan	wallet	wejnrato
wail	wehu	walloon	wejnroin
wain	wesa	wallop	wejnrapn
wainscot	wesasokiti	wallow	wejnrai
wainscoting	wesasokitignni	wally	wejnran
waist	wesnsi	walrus	wejnrin
waistline	wesnsilehun	walter	wejiasi
wait	wetan	walton	wejiatin
waiter	wetansi	waltz	wejiase
waiting game	gimo wetangnni	waly	wejan
waiting-list	lesi wetangnni	wamble	wembe
waitress	wetanbo	wame	wemkun
waive	wewan	wampish	wempnsi
waiver	wewansi	wampum	wempan
wakanda	wekanda	wamus	wemaso
wake1	wekn	wan	weni
wake2	wekn	wand	wejn
waken	weknni	wander	wejnra
wakener	eknnisi	wanderlust	wejnralusi
wakerife	weknraifin	wane	wehun
wale	weron	waney	wehunse
wale	weron	wangle	wegnron
walk	werin	wanigan	wehungan

WORD (x)	EQUIVALENT (y)	WORD (x)	EQUIVALENT (y)
wanion	wehunsi	warpath	weranpanho
wank	wekoi	warrant	werraitn
wankel engine	engbihun eekoiran	warrantor	werraitnran
wanker	wekoisi	warranty	werraitnsi
want	wetn	warren	werrain
wanting	wetngnni	warrener	werrainsi
wanton	wetnsi	warrigal	werraigia
wap	wepn	warring	werraignni
wapiti	wepnti	warrington	werraigntin
war	weran	warrior	werrairan
warbl	weranbe	warship	weransunpn
warbler	weranbesi	wart	werate
ward	wegba	warta	werata
ward	wegba	warthog	weratehin
warden	wegbase	wartier	weratesi
warder	wegbasi	warty	weratese
wardrobe	wegbarobe	wartime	werantinmo
wards	wegbasi	wary	weranse
wardship	wegbasunpn	was	wesi
ware	werai	wase	wesin
warehouse	hinlese warai	wash	wese
warfare	waranfanrai	washboard	bugbawese
war-game	weran-gimo	washer	wesesi
warhead	weranhegbi	washer-up	wesesi-pake
warhorse	weranhiso	washerwoman	winmoyewesesi
warlike	weranlikn	wshing	wesegnni
warlock	weranlokn	washington	wesegntin
warm	weron	washstand	setndanwese
warmonger	weronmenignra	washy	wesesi
warmth	weronsi	wasp	wesipo
warn	weran	waspish	wesipose
warning	werangini	wassail	wesoonlo
warp	weraipo	wast	wesii
warpaint	weranpantoni	wast	wesii

707

WORD (x)	EQUIVALENT (y)	WORD (x)	EQUIVALENT (y)
wastage	wesiagun	waver	wewinsi
waste	wesita	waverley	wewinsiroin
waster	wesitasi	wavey	wewinlo
wasting	wesitagnni	wavy	wewinse
wastrel	wesitaran	wax1	wesun
wastry	wesitarai	wax2	wesun
wat	weti	waxen	wesunsi
wat	weti	waxy	wesunse
watap	wetipan	way	welo
watch	wetiso	way	welo
watch	wetiso	way back	welo boki
watchman	wetisomoye	wayfarer	welofansi
watchword	wetisowijo	way of life	welo lifin
wate	weto	wayward	welowegba
water	wetomi	we	awa
water table	wetomi teberon	weak	wnkoi
wateree	wetomise	weaken	wnkoisi
watery	wetomisi	weakling	wnkoignni
watson	wetisin	weakly	wnkoise
watt	wetti	weakness	wnkoisi
wattage	wettigun	weak point	wnkoi pintoni
watteau	wettiele	weal1	wnjo
watterson	wettirasin	weal2	wnjo
wattle1	wettiron	weald	wnjon
wattle2	wettiron	wealth	wnjosi
wattmeter	wettimuto	wealthy	wnjosise
wattusi	wettusi	wean	wnnu
wauk	wekin	weaner	wnnusi
waul	wejin	weaning	wnnugnni
wave	were	weapon	wnpasi
wave	wewin	weaponed	wnpaside
wavelet	wewintn	weaponeer	wnpasiran
wavell	wewinlle	weaponry	wnpasirai
wavellite	wewinlleyo	wear	wnwo

WORD (x)	EQUIVALENT (y)	WORD (x)	EQUIVALENT (y)
weariful	wnwofunjn	weeny	wnnise
wearing	wnwognni	weep	wnpo
weariless	wnwolabo	weepie	wnposi
weary	wnwose	weepy	wnpose
weasand	wnsanjn	weet	wndun
weasel	wnselo	weever	wnwosi
weasel word	wnselo wijo	weevil	wnworo
weather	wnsiaran	wee-wee	wnse-wnse
weathered	wnsiarande	weft	wnfia
weatherize	wnsiaranse	weigela	wngnjn
weatherproof	wnsiaranponfin	weigh	wngbi
weave1	wnniwe	weighbridge	wngbi bangbon
weave2	wnniwe	weigh-in	wngbi-nu
weaver	wnniwesi	weight	wngbite
web	wnbe	weighting	wngbitegnni
webbing	wnbegnni	weightless	wngbitelabo
weber	wnbesi	weightlifting	wngbitelefiagnni
webster	wnbeseto	weighty	wngbitese
wed	wngbe	weimaraner	wnmurainsi
wed	wngbe	weir	wnran
wedding	wngbegnni	weird	wnranjn
wedge	wngba	weirdo	wnranjan
wedlock	wngbelokn	weismannism	wnsmuhunmosi
wednesday	wngbedase	weka	wnka
weds	wngbesi	welch	wnjnsi
wee1	wnse	welcome	wnjnkiawa
wee2	wnse	weld	wnjopo
weed	wnkow	welfare	wnjnfini
weeds	wnkosi	welkin	wnjnkin
weedy	wnkose	well1	wnjnro
week	wnkn	well2	wnjnro
weekly	wnknlo	welsh	wnjnso
weel	wnlo	wellsite	wnjnrosootn
ween	wnni	welt	wnjia

WORD (x)	EQUIVALENT (y)	WORD (x)	EQUIVALENT (y)
welter1	wnjiasi	whang	whagan
welter2	wnjiasi	whangee	whaganse
wen	wni	wham	whamu
wench	wnikin	wharf	whafiro
wend	wnijn	wharfage	whafirogun
went	wnta	what	whate
wentle	wntoron	whaup	whapo
wept	wnpnti	wheal	whnjo
were	warai	wheat	whnte
we're	wa ran	wheatear	whnteeran
werner	waranrai	wheaten	whntesi
wernerite	waranraiyo	what stone	whnte setole
weser	wnsera	wheedle	whnjnron
wesley	wnseroin	wheel	whnlo
wesleyan	wnseroinhn	wheel	whnlo
wessex	wnsesia	wheeler	whnlosi
west	wnsi	wheelie	whnlose
westering	wnsiraignni	wheen	whnni
westerly	wnsirailo	wheeze	whnsufe
western	wnsiran	wheezy	whnsufese
westerner	wnsiransi	whelk	whnkiti
westernize	wnsiranse	whelk	whnkiti
westward	wnsiwegba	whelk	whnkiti
wet	wnmi	whelky	whnkitise
wether	wnmira	whelm	whnjnmi
wetland	wnmiledain	whelp	whnjnpn
wetter	wnmmisi	when	whnse
wex	wnsun	whence	whnsesi
whack	whakin	where	whnran
whacker	whakinsi	whereas	whnranse
whaisle	whasnron	wherefrom	whnrnfonwa
whale	whajain	wherever	whnranwasi
whaler	whajainsi	wherry	whnrrai
whaling	whajaingnni	wherve	whnraiwo

WORD (x)	EQUIVALENT (y)	WORD (x)	EQUIVALENT (y)
whet	whnsia	whipping	whoinpngnni
whether	whnsiasi/boya	whipple	whoinporon
whew	whnai	whipstall	whoinpnsetnran
whey	whnsun	whir	whoinro
which	whose	whirl	whoinrolo
whichever	whose	whirler	whoinrolosi
whichever	whosiwasi	whirligig	whoinrologan
whid	whojn	whirlybird	whoinrolobarai
whidha	whojnhun	whirry	whoinrrai
whiff	whofun	whish	whoinse
whiffet	whofunte	whish	whoinse
whiffle	whofunjn	whisht	whoinsn
whiffler	whofunjnra	whisk	whoinsia
whig	whogbi	whisker	whoinsiasi
whiggamore	whogbimosii	whiskey	whoinsian
whiggery	whogbirai	whisky	whoinsiase
whigmaleerie	whogbimujnra	whisper	whoinsnso
while	wholo	whist	whoinsu
whilst	wholosi	whistle	whoinsufe
whim	whomi	whistler	whoinsufesi
whimbrel	whomberan	whit	whointn
whimper	whompe	whitby	whointnbe
whimsical	whomsekojo	white	whointe
whimsicality	whomsekoleto	whitebirch	whointebarasi
whimsy	whomse	whiten	whointesi
whin	whoin	whiteness	whointenisi
whinchat	whoinkho	whitey	whointese
whine	whoinsi	whither	whointnra
whinge	whoingn	whiting1	whointegnni
whinger	whoingnsi	whiting2	whointegnni
whinny	whoinse	whitish	whointesi
whip	whoinpn	whitlow	whointnwu
whipper	whoinpnsi	whitney	whointnse
whippet	whoinpnti	whitsun	whointnsuna

WORD (x)	EQUIVALENT (y)	WORD (x)	EQUIVALENT (y)
whitter	whointtnra	wichita	winkhito
whittier	whointtnsi	wick	winkuo
whittle	whointtnron	wick	winkuo
whitling	whointtngnni	wick	winkuo
whiz	whoinsi	wicked	winkuode
who	who/ewo/elewo	wicker	winkuosi
whoa	whose	wickerwork	winkuowinsise
whole	whojo	wicket	winkuote
wholism	whojomosi	wickiup	winkuopake
wholly	whojose	wickliffe	winkuolefn
whom	whoma	wicopy	winkipe
whomever	whomawasi	widdle	wingbijn
whoo	whu	widdy	wingbise
whoop	whoopn	wide	winjin
whoopee	whoopnse	widely	winjinlo
whooper	whoopnra	widen	winjinsi
whooping cough	whoopngnni kigbe	widgeon	wingboin
whoops	whoopnsi	widor	winjnra
whop	whopn	widow	winjua
whopper	whopnsi	widower	winjuasi
whopping	whopngnni	width	winjinsi
whore	whorai	wield	winjon
whoredom	whoraideo	wieldy	winjonse
whoremonger	whoraimenignra	wielieska	winjnsiko
whorish	whoraise	wien	winsi
whoreson	whoraisin	wiener	winran
whorl	whoraijo	wienerschnitzel	winransekhntisi
whort	whorate	wieprz	winpnra
whortle	whoratoron	wife	wofn
whose	whose	wig	wogbi
who's who	who si who	wigan	wogbain
whosoever	whosoowasi	wigeon	wogboin
why	whase	wiggery	wogbirai
wi	win	wiggin	wogbisi

WORD (x)	EQUIVALENT (y)	WORD (x)	EQUIVALENT (y)
wigging	wogbignni	will2	winjnra
wiggle	wogbijn	willamette	winjnramitn
wiggler	wogbijnsi	willard	winjnragba
wight	wogbe	willemite	winjnmiyo
wight	wogbe	william	wnjnramo
wigner	wogbiran	willie	winjnrase
wigwag	wogbiwe	willies	winjnrasi
wigwam	wogbimo	willing	winjnragnni
wilber	winjnbe	willis	winjnraso
wilbur	winjnbua	williwaw	winjnrawo
wilco	winjnki	willkle	winjnrakuo
wild	winjia	willow	winjnran
wildcat	winjiakoti	willowy	winjnranse
wilde	winjian	willy	winjnrase
wildebeest	winjanbeseyo	will-nilly	winjnrase nirause
wilder	winjiasi	wilminton	winjnmogntin
wilder	winjiasi	wilson	winjnsin
wilderness	winjiaransi	wilt	winjnti
wilfire	winjiafinna	wilt	winjnti
wildgean	winjiagini	wilton	winjntin
wilding	winjiagnni	wily	winjnse
wildlife	winjialifin	wimble	winmbelu
wildpansy	winjiapanse	wimbledon	winmbelusi
wildparsler	winjiapanseroin	wimple	winmpo
wildparsnip	winjiapansepin	win	winla
wile	winjn	wince	winsi
wiley	winjnse	wincey	winsise
wilful	winjnfunjn	winceyette	winsisetn
wilfred	winjnfiran	winch	winsun
wilhelm	winjnhun	winchester	winsunseto
wilkes	winjnki	wind1	winfe
wilkins	winjnkin	wind2	winfe
will	winjnra	windage	winfegun
will1	winjnra	windbag	winfebogbi

WORD (x)	EQUIVALENT (y)	WORD (x)	EQUIVALENT (y)
winder	winfesi	wiper	woinpnsi
winder	winfesi	wire	woinran
windigo	winfegbon	wiring	woinrangnni
winding	winfegnni	wiry	woinranse
windlass	winrfelesun	wisdom	wogbonjn
windle	winferon	wise1	wogbon
windle	winferon	wise2	wogbon
windling	winferongn	wiseacre	wogbonaknran
window	winfewo	wisecrack	wogbonkanko
windsor	winfesin	wise man	wogbon moye
windy	winfese	wisent	wogbonto
wine	winiun	wiserite	wogbonraiyo
wine bar	boosn winiun	wish	wise
winebibber	winiunbibosi	wishbone	wiseboun
wing	wingun	wismer	winsemora
winged	wingunjo	wisp	winsepo
winger	wingunsi	wispish	winseposi
wingless	wingunlabo	wisteria	winsetoran
wink	winka	wister	winseto
winker	winkasi	wistful	winsetofunjn
winkle	winkaron	wit	winso
winner	winlasi	witan	winsohn
winning	winlagnni	witch	winsosi
winning-post	pinseto-winlagnni	witchcraft	winsosiknrafe
winnow	winlawai	witchery	winsosirai
wino	winkun	witchetty	winsositto
winsome	winsoomo	wite	winson
winsor	winsin	witenagemot	winsongunmote
winston	winsetin	with	winse pelu
winter	wintnra	withal	winsejo
winterize	wintnraise	withdraw	winsegbanwa
wintry	wintnrai	withe	winsin
winy	winnise	wither	winsira
wipe	woinpn	witherite	winsiraiyo

WORD (x)	EQUIVALENT (y)	WORD (x)	EQUIVALENT (y)
withers	winsirasi	wodge	wogbon
withershins	winsirasunsi	woe	wogba
within	winsinu	woeful	wogbafunjn
without	winsi nita	woebegone	wogbabelohun
withstand	winsisetndan	woever	wogbaawn
withy	winsise	wog	wogbi
witless	winsolabo	woggle	wogbiron
witling	winsognni	wok	wokun
witness	winsosi	wokas	wokunsi
witness-box	bosi-winsosi	woke	wokn
witney	winsose	woken	woknsi
witt	winsso	wold	wojia
witted	winssode	wolds	wojiasi
witten	winssosi	wolf	wojifa
witticism	winssokimosi	wolfe	wojifan
witting	winssognni	wolffe	wojnifun
witting	winssognni	wolfish	wojifunse
wittol	winssojin	wolfish	wojifase
witty	winssose	wolfram	wojifaran
witzchoura	winssekhiran	wolframite	wojifaraimuyo
wive	winfe	wollaston	wojnrasetin
wives	winfesi	wollastonite	wojnrasetinyo
wivern	winforan	wolseley	wojnseroin
wiz	waso	wolver	wojifarun
wizard	wasogbaa	wolverine	wojifarain
wizardery	wasogbaarai	wolves	wojifasi
wisen	wasue	woman	womoye
wisen	wasue	womanhood	womoyehinjo
wizened	wasuede	womanish	womoyesi
woad	wojaro	womanize	womoyese
woald	wojon	womanly	womoyelo
wobble	wobe	womb	wombe
wobbly	wobese	wombat	wombota
woden	wogbain	women	winmuye

WORD (x)	EQUIVALENT (y)	WORD (x)	EQUIVALENT (y)
womera	winmuran	word	woro
won	wonlu	wordage	worogun
wonder	wonjnra	wording	worognni
wonderful	wonjnrafunjn	wordy	worose
wonderland	wonjnraledain	wore	woran
wonderment	wonjnramutto	work	worose
wondrous	wonjnrasi	workable	worosebe
wonky	wonko	world	worojn
wonsan	wonsin	worldly	worojnse
wont	wonto	worm	woron
won't	wonti	wormy	woronse
wonted	wontode	worr	woran
woo	woose	worrisome	woraisoomo
woo	woose	worry	worai
wood	woogi	worse	worase
wood anemone	ahunmnni woogi	worsen	worasesi
wood hoopoe	woogi hinposi	worship	worasinpo
woodsia	woogisia	worst	wonsi
woodsy	woogisi	worsted	wonsijo
woody	woogise	wort	woole
wooer	woosesi	worth	woolo
woof	woofi	worthless	woololabo
woof	woofi	worthy	woolosi
woofer	woofiro	wot	wonso
wool	woojn	wotton	wonsotin
woolen	woojnsi	would	wonjon
woollen	woojnrasi	wound1	wonjoin
woolly	woojnrase	wound2	wonjoin
woomera	woomuran	wove	wonwe
woon	wooni	woven	wonwesi
woorali	witirai	wow1	wowo
woozy	woosia	wow2	wowo
wop	wopn	wowser	wowosesi
worcester sauce	woroknseto	wrack	wanka

WORD (x)	EQUIVALENT (y)	WORD (x)	EQUIVALENT (y)
wraith	wanto	writ1	weraite
wrangle	wangnjn	writ2	weraite
wrangle	wangnron	write	weraito
wrangler	wangnronsi	writer	weraitosi
wrap	wanpan	write-up	weraito-pake
wraparound	wanpanarojoin	writhe	weraise
wrap-over	wanpan-ownra	writhen	weraisesi
wrapper	wanpansi	writing	weraitognni
wrapping	wanpangnni	written	weraittosi
wrasse	wansoon	wrong	wongn
wrath	wansi	wrong side	wongn soojo
wreak	weraiko	wrote	wonto
wreath	weraisi	wroth	wonsi
wreathe	weraise	wrought	wongbo
wreck	weraikn	wrought iron	wongbo irin
wreckage	weraikngun	wrung	wongun
wrecker	weraiknsi	wry	weran
wren	werain	wryneck	weranhunko
wrench	werainsi	wuchereria	wukhnraian
wrest	weraisi	wud	wujia
wrestle	weraisijn	wuldenite	wujndainyo
wrestler	weraisijnra	wulfenite	wujnfiniyo
wretch	weraiti	wurm	wuron
wretched	weraitijo	wurt	wurate
wrick	weraikn	wy	wai
wriggle	weraign	wyandot	waindetn
wright	weraigbe	wyatt	waitto
wring	weraigan	wych-	waisi
wringer	weraigansi	wychelm	waisijnmo
wringing	weraigangnni	wychhazel	waisi hasujo
wrinkle	weraikuo	wylie	waijin
wrinkly	weraikuose	wyom	waimo
weist	werai	wyvern	waiwnran
wristlet	weraitn	x mispron	s si

WORD (x)	EQUIVALENT (y)	WORD (x)	EQUIVALENT (y)
x chromosome	si khironmusoomo	xero	serau
xanthate	sansinyo	xerochore	seraukhiran
xanthein	sansinnu	xeroderma	seraujnrama
xathelasma	sansinsemo	xeroform	seraufoonmo
xanthian	sansinhn	xerography	serauganphe
xanthic	sansinko	xeromorphy	seraumophanse
xanthin	sansa	xerophilous	seraupheransi
xanthine	sansahun	xerophthalmia	serauphisijnmua
xanthippe	sansapn	xerophyte	seraupheyo
xantho	sanssa	xeroprinting	seraupantegnni
xanthocarpous	sanssakopansi	xeroesere	serauserain
xanthochroid	sanssakhironjo	xerosis	serauso
xanthoma	sanssama	xerotropism	serautnrapnmosi
xanthophylls	sanssaphewe	xerox	serausi
xanthopsia	sanssapnsia	xerxes	serausin
xanthous	sanssasi	xi	si
xanthus	sansase	xingu	singun
xe	see	xion	sioon
xebec	sebnko	xiphi	siphia
xenia	sehisi	xiphisternum	siphiasutoran
xenial	sehijo	xiphoid	siphiajo
xeno	sehon	xiphosuran	siphiaseru
xenocrates	sehonknrato	xmas	simosn
xenogamy	sehongimo	xo	soo
xenogenesis	sehongnhunso	xy	sisan
xenoglossia	sehongonsia	xylan	sianlesi
xenoliths	sehonlesi	xylem	sianlomi
xenon	sehonsi	xylene	sianlohun
xenophanes	sehonphini	xylic	sianlokn
xenophobe	sehonphobe	xylidine	sianlojoin
xenophobia	sehonphobua	xylo	siangi
xenophon	sehonphohun	xylocarpous	siangikopansi
xeric	serauko	xylograph	siangiganpha
xerion	serain	xylography	siangiganphe

WORD (x)	EQUIVALENT (y)	WORD (x)	EQUIVALENT (y)
xyloid	siangijo	yald	yanjon
xylophagous	siangiphijesi	yald	yanjon
xylophone	siangiphohun	yale lock	yanjn lokn
xylose	siangise	yalta	yanjia
xylotomous	siangitemosi	yalu	yanjua
xylotomy	siangitemo	yalung	yanjuagun
xyl	sianji	yam	yanmo
xylyl	sianjilo	yamal	yanmojn
xylylene	sianjilohun	yamen	yanmuye
xyst	siansi	yamer	yanmosi
xyster	siansite	yammer	yanmmosi
y1	y	yangze	yangunse
y2	y lo	yank	yankan
y3	e, o, an, in, se	yank	yankan
yabber	yabosi	yankee	yankanse
yablonol	yaboun	yanking	yankangnni
yacht	yakho	yantra	yantnra
yacht	yakho	yap	yanpo
yachting	yakhognni	yarborough	yanbooroghan
yachtsman	yakhosimoye	yaqui	yankun
yacker	yasesi	yard1	yandan
yaff	yafi	yard2	yandan
yaffle	yafijn	yardage	yandangun
yagger	yagnsi	yard-arm	yandan-araimu
yah	yaho	yardie	yandansi
yahoo	yahoo	yare	yara
yahaweh	yahoonwa	yarn	yaran
yahwehism	yahoonwamosi	yarrow	yarraiwe
yahwehist	yahoonwasi	yashmak	yasemo
yahwehistic	yahoonwasiko	yataghan	yateghan
yaird	yangba	yaupon	yaposi
yak	yaki	yaw	yawa
Yakima	yakimo	yaw	yawa
yakut	yakitu	yawl	yawajn

WORD (x)	EQUIVALENT (y)	WORD (x)	EQUIVALENT (y)
yawn	yanwn	yeoman	ynknmoye
yawp	yanwnti	yeomanry	ynknmoyerai
yaws	yanwnsi	yeoman warder	ynknmoye wegbasi
yay	yasi	yerk	ynknra
yazoo	yasoon	yes	ynse
yel	yn	yes-man	ynse-moye
ye2	yn	yesterday	ynsetnradase
yea	ynni	yestern	ynsetnran
yeah	ynha	yesteryear	ynsetnraynrai
yeal	ynjo	yet	ynte
yealing	ynjognni	yett	ynttn
yean	ynun	yew	ynwe
yeanling	ynungnni	yid	yigbi
year	ynrai	yiddish	yigbiso
yearbook	ynraibooko	yield	yinsejo
yearling	ynraignni	yin	yinsi
yearly	ynrailo	yip	yingbo
yearn	yneran	yippee	yingbose
yearning	ynerangnni	yird	yingba
yeast	ynsia	yirr	yinro
yeasty	ynsiase	yob	yibe
yeats	yntosi	yodel	yijnro
yegg	ynge	yoga	yigan
yeid	ynduo	yoghurt	yigbnmi
yeld	ynjo	yogi	yigin
yell	ynjnro	yoicks	yikesi
yellow	ynjnron	yoke	yikn
yelp	yngbo	yokel	yiknsi
yemen	ynmuye	yoking	yikngnni
yen1	ynhun	yolk	yiliki
yen2	ynhun	yolky	yilikise
yengeese	ynhungnse	yom	yimo
yenta	ynto	yon	yinsi
yental	yntojo	yond	yinjn

WORD (x)	EQUIVALENT (y)	WORD (x)	EQUIVALENT (y)
yonder	yinjnra	yuman	yunmoye
yore	yiran	yummy	yunmmo
yorick	yirako	yunan	yunnini
york	yirakn	yup	yunpo
yorker	yiraknra	yupon	yunpon
yorkist	yiraknsi	yuppie	yunposi
yorkshire	yirakisuran	z mispronounced	s
yoruba	yoruba	zabaglione	sebogiunhun
yoruba	yirabo	zacatecas	sekitisi
yosemite	yisemuyp	zacaton	sekitin
you	yin	zachaeus	sekhitosi
young	yingbi	zachariah	sekhirain
youngster	yingbiseto	zachary	sekhirai
younker	yinknra	zadar	segbiro
your	yinran	zadok	segbiko
youth	yinsi	zaffer	sefnro
yowe	yinwe	zagreus	segbiran
yowie	yinwesi	zagros	segbiro
yowl	yinwejn	zaire	serain
yo-yo	yi-yi	zama	sema
y track	ya tnreko	zamarra	semarra
ytterbia	yittnrabua	zambezi	sembesi
ytterbium	yittnrabuma	zambia	sembua
yttria	yittnran	zamia	semini
yttrium	yittnraima	zamora	semorai
yucca	yunkki	zandwill	segnwijnra
yuchi	yunkhin	zant	setin
yuga	yungan	zanthoxylum	setinsiangima
yugostavia	yungonsewini	zany	sesue
yucon	yunkin	zanzibar	sesuebosi
yuit	yunte	zap	sepn
yule	yunjo	zapata	sepnti
yuletide	yunjotijin	zapatco	sepntiko
yuma	yunmo	zara	serin

WORD (x)	EQUIVALENT (y)	WORD (x)	EQUIVALENT (y)
zaralite	serinleyo	zenger	sehagira
zarathustra	serinsuntnra	zenith	sehansi
zareba	seraibe	zeno	sehn
zarf	serafe	zenobia	sehnbua
zarzuela	serosuejn	zeolite	seknleyo
zastruga	sesiraigan	zephaniah	sephanhun
zea	seki	zephyr	sepherai
zeal	sekiji	zephyrus	sepheraisi
zealot	sekijito	zeppelin	seponjain
zealotry	sekijitorai	zero	serau
zealous	sekijisi	zest	sesii
zeaxanthin	sesansinsi	zeta	sete
zebadiah	sebogbnhun	zethus	setesi
zebedee	sebogbnsi	zeugma	sewagunma
zebra	sebora	zeus	sewasi
zebra crossing	sebora konsognni	zeuxis	sewasusi
zebu	sebua	zibet	sibnte
zebulon	sebuajnsi	ziggurat	sigunrai
zecchino	sekkhikn	zigzag	sigesege
zechariah	sekhorain	zigzag	sigesege
zedekiah	segbikin	zigzagger	sigesegeran
zedoary	segirain	zilch	silosi
zee	seya	zillion	sijnrain
zeeman	seyamoye	zimbabwe	simowewe
zein	setio	zinc	sinki
zeit	setto	zincalism	sinkijimosi
zeitgeist	settognsi	zincate	sinkiyo
zeke	sekn	zinciferous	sinkifirosi
zeminder	semojnra	zincify	sinkife
zemun	semosn	zincite	sinkinyo
zenana	sehahun	zincograph	sinkiganpha
zen	seha	zincography	sinkiganphe
zend	sehajn	zinfandel	sinfidainjo
zendik	sehajnkn	zing	sigan

WORD (x)	EQUIVALENT (y)	WORD (x)	EQUIVALENT (y)
zingaro	siganrai	zonule	sinunron
zingiberaceous	singibesuwa	zoo	sinso
zinjanthropus	sinjnrapnsi	zoogeographic	sinsogbilephako
zinkenite	sinkunyo	zoogloea	sinsogonsi
zinnia	sihun	zooid	sinsojo
zion	sinse	zoolatry	sinsoletorai
zonism	sinsemosi	zoological	sinsologbonkojo
zionward	sinsewegba	zoology	sinsologbon
zip	sinpo	zoom	sinmo
zipper	sinposi	zoom lens	sinmo jnso
zippy	sinpose	zoometry	soonmutorai
zircon	sirankin	zoomorphism	sinsomophansi
zirconate	sirankinyo	zoon	sinsosi
zirconia	sirankinsi	zoophile	sinsopheron
zirconium	sirankinma	zoophilism	sinsopheronmosi
ziron	sirin	zoophilous	sinsopheronsi
ziska	sisia	zoophobia	sinsophobua
zither	sisnrai	zoophyte	sinsopheyo
zizith	sisose	zooplasty	sinsopansuito
zizzle	sisufe	zoosperm	sinsosepnron
zodiac	sinjnko	zoosporangium	sinsoseporaingnma
zoa	sinsi	zoospore	sinsoseporai
zian	sinhn	zootomy	sinsotemo
zodiac	sinjoki	zootoxin	sinsotoosia
zodiacal	sinjokiji	zoot	sinsotn
zoe	sinse	zori	sinrai
zoetrope	sinsetnrapon	zoril	sinrun
zoic	sinko	zoroaster	sinrosuntnra
zoisite	sinsooyo	zoroastrian	sinrosuntnrain
zombi	sinmbesi	zorostrianism	sinrosuntnrainsi
zonal	sinhunjo	zorrilla	sinrolle
zonate	sinhunyo	zoster	sisotnra
zone	sinhun	zouave	sisewn
zonked	sinhunknde	zousia	sinsesia

WORD (x)	EQUIVALENT (y)
zucchetta	sukkhntte
zucchetto	sukkhntto
zucchetto	sukkhntto
zucchini	sukkhini
zug	sugbaa
zugspitze	sugbaapnti
zulu	sulu
zurich	surakhn
zuyder	susejnra
zwieback	swinboki
zwingli	swingnlo
zwitterion	swinttnrasi
zygapophysis	sagunpopheso
zygo	sajo
zygoma	sajomu
zygomatic	sajomuko
zygomorphic	sajomophanko
zygosis	sajoso
zygote	sajota
zyme	samn
zymic	samnko
zymo	samo
zymogen	samogin
zymogenesis	samognhunso
zymogenic	samoginko
zymology	samologbon
zymolysis	samojinso
zymometer	samomuto
zymosis	samoso
zymotic	samoko
zymurgy	samogan

Printed in the United States
By Bookmasters